Contemporary Performance InterActions

Theatre's performative InterActions with the politics of sex, race and class, with questions of social and political justice, form the focus of the Contemporary Performance InterActions series. Performative InterActions are those that aspire to affect, contest or transform. International in scope, CPI publishes monographs and edited collections dedicated to the InterActions of contemporary practitioners, performances and theatres located in any world context.

More information about this series at
http://www.palgrave.com/gp/series/14918

Yana Meerzon • David Dean
Daniel McNeil
Editors

Migration and Stereotypes in Performance and Culture

palgrave
macmillan

Editors
Yana Meerzon
Department of Theatre
University of Ottawa
Ottawa, ON, Canada

David Dean
Department of History
Carleton University
Ottawa, ON, Canada

Daniel McNeil
Department of History
Carleton University
Ottawa, ON, Canada

Contemporary Performance InterActions
ISBN 978-3-030-39914-6 ISBN 978-3-030-39915-3 (eBook)
https://doi.org/10.1007/978-3-030-39915-3

This Palgrave Macmillan imprint is published by the registered company Springer Nature Switzerland AG.
The registered company address is: Gewerbestrasse 11, 6330 Cham, Switzerland

Acknowledgements

This book was first conceived at the Migration/Representation/Stereotypes conference that convened at the University of Ottawa in April 2017. This bilingual and international conference was organized by David Dean, Daniel McNeil, Yana Meerzon, Sylvain Schryburt, and Natalia Vesselova, and would not have been possible without the generous support and labour of many academics, artists, students, administrators and theatre enthusiasts. We would like to pay special tribute to Peter Kuling, Tina Goralski, John Lockhart, and Angela Hache of the Department of Theatre, University of Ottawa.

We would also like to extend special thanks to the Canadian and international artists who participated in this conference, including Chokri Ben Chikha of Action Zoo Humain (Belgium), Keira Loughran, Daniel David Moses, Henry Daniel, the UK performer Natasha Davis, who brought her one-woman *Teeth Show* to Ottawa, and the company *Voyageurs Immobiles* from Montréal, its artistic director Milena Buziak and performers Hodan Youssouf and Florence Blain Mbaye for presenting a staged-reading of the play *Traversée* by Estelle Savasta.

Without the supportive and good-humoured work of student-volunteers (Véronique Belinge, Ryan Borochovitz, Kyle Cameron, Emily Connell, Katarina Ghdaye, Brittany Johnston, Kellie MacDonald, Ludmylla Mar Dos Reis, Jonas Mclean, Patrick Michael Teed, and Agostino Delannoy from the University of Ottawa; and Sara Hollett and Phoebe Mannell from Carleton University), the successful delivery of the conference would not have been possible.

Material support from the Department of Theatre and the Department of Modern Languages and Literatures, Studies in Migration Research Group, the Vered Jewish Canadian Studies Program, Research Development Program, and Faculty of Arts at the University of Ottawa, School of Arts, Media, Performance, and Design, York University, as well as the Carleton Centre for Public History (CCPH), the Department of History, and the Migration and Diaspora Studies Initiative (MDS) at Carleton University, helped us to bring diverse voices together and imagine new directions for the study of migration and stereotypes. A stipend from the Playwrights Guild of Canada and a Connections Grant from the Social Sciences and Humanities Research Council of Canada facilitated the major revision and adaptation of conference papers. The writing of the book's introduction was supported by the Mellon Foundation's Public Humanities Scholars Program and the Jackman Humanities Institute.

Although Sylvain and Natalia were unable to continue with the project as co-editors, they remain a big part of this book. We would also like to extend our special thanks to Emily Cuggy and Elizabeth Paradis who were exemplary copy editors; Aly Murphy for helping us compile the index; Elaine Aston and Brian Singleton, who supported this project from the outset and accepted it into their innovative book series; Jack Heeney and Eileen Srebernik, who provided invaluable assistance shepherding this project into publication; and the various photographers and artists who allowed us to use their work as illustrations for the book.

We would like to pay tribute to our contributors for their collegiality, incisive analysis, and ability to push us into some fresh thinking about migration and stereotypes in performance and culture.

Finally, this book is dedicated with love to Alex Taylor-McNeil for her infectious joy, which makes everything better; to Calum Dean for his passion and commitment to social justice; and to the Meerzon family for constant support, understanding, and encouragement.

David Dean
Daniel McNeil
Yana Meerzon

Contents

Notes on Contributors

Zaheeda P. Alibhai is a PhD candidate in Religious Studies with a specialization in Canadian Studies at the University of Ottawa. Her research investigates the critical intersections between religion, law, politics, media in the study of identity, multiculturalism, and pluralism in Canadian and international contexts. She has contributed to several volumes exploring religion, public policy, and pluralism. Her research is supported by the Social Sciences and Humanities Research Council of Canada (SSHRC).

Nimo Bokore is an assistant professor at the School of Social Work at Carleton University. For over a decade, Bokore's research focused on refugee resettlement in Canada. As a resettled refugee from Africa, Bokore brings a rich perspective and profound approach to her work. Her research projects include: how Canadian-Somali women conceptualize war trauma and forced migration, and how these circumstances influence their later resettlement process; and Exploring the Unique Experiences, Opportunities, and Challenges in Accessing Postsecondary Education for Somali-Canadian Youth in Ontario.

Helin Burkay holds a PhD in Sociology from Carleton University and works on cultural politics of food, heritage, memory, and development. In 2018, she completed a post-doctoral fellowship at the Rachel Carson Center for Environment and Society at the Ludwig-Maximilians-Universität München.

Ida Casilli is a drama teacher, director, and producer of Italian descent, who has worked for leading UK participatory arts companies. In the last four years she has produced work inspired by topics of social interest, including an oral history project celebrating minorities in the UK (Brasiliance/Stonecrabs Theatre), a dance festival narrating the experience of migrants and refugees (Migration Europa Exchange Festival/*Counterpoint Dance)*, and an award-winning show portraying a refugee child's metaphoric journey to a planet of hope (The Other/*Footprint Project*). Her previous research is published in Avanguardia Theatre reviews and *Patria Letteratura*.

J. Douglas Clayton is Professor Emeritus at the University of Ottawa, Canada. He is the author of *Pierrot in Petrograd*, a study of commedia dell'arte in Russia, of numerous articles on Anton Chekhov, and of books on Alexander Pushkin's verse novel *Eugene Onegin* and his historical drama *Boris Godunov*.

Sarit Cofman-Simhon holds a PhD in Theatre Arts from the University of Minnesota, Minneapolis, USA. She is Academic Head of the Theatre Department at Emunah College in Jerusalem, and a lecturer in the School for Performing Arts at Kibbutzim College in Tel Aviv. Her main fields of research are theatre and Judaism, and multilingualism in the Israeli theatre.

David Dean is a professor in the Department of History at Carleton University in Ontario, Canada, and co-director of the Carleton Centre for Public History. He recently edited *The Companion to Public History* (2018), and has authored, edited, or co-edited several books and numerous articles in journals such as *Early Theatre*, *Re-thinking History*, *Memoria e Ricerca*, *The Public Historian*, *Museum & Society*, and the *Journal of British Studies*. Working especially on performances of the past in contemporary society, he is a member of the steering committee of the International Federation for Public History and co-editor of the new journal *International Public History*.

Michalis Georgiou holds his PhD in Theatre Studies from the Freie Universität Berlin (2014). His articles have been published in journals and newspapers considering Greek-German cultural relationships. He works as Junior Manager Royalty Processing at BMG Production Music US in Berlin.

Peter Kuling is an assistant professor in the School of English and Theatre Studies at the University of Guelph. He has edited special issues of *Canadian Theatre Review* on Digital Performance and Theatre and Sports while also contributing to new anthologies on topics like Theatre and Immigration and Digital Theatre in Canada.

Kasia Lech holds a PhD from University College Dublin, lectures at Canterbury Christ Church University. Her publications focus on verse in theatre, translation, and multilingualism. Lech trained at the Polish National Academy of Theatre Arts and has performed internationally. She co-founded Polish Theatre Ireland and is an executive director at TheTheatreTimes.com.

Daniel McNeil is an Associate Professor of History at Carleton University in Canada. He was the inaugural Public Humanities Fellow at the University of Toronto in 2019–20 and has previously held the Ida B. Wells-Barnett Professorship of African and Black Diaspora Studies at DePaul University in the United States. His award-winning book, *Sex and Race in the Black Atlantic*, maps the cultural and intellectual histories of Black and mixed-race identities that work within, across, outside, and against the nation-state.

Yana Meerzon is a Professor of Theatre Studies at the University of Ottawa. She has published on theatre of exile and migration, and cultural and interdisciplinary studies. Her books include *A Path of the Character: Michael Chekhov's Inspired Acting and Theatre Semiotics* (2005) and *Performing Exile—Performing Self: Drama, Theatre, Film* (2012). She has also co-edited several book collections and special issues of journals on these topics.

Kee-Yoon Nahm is an Assistant Professor of Theatre and Film Studies at Illinois State University. He has published articles in *Theater, Performance Research, Situations: Cultural Studies in the Asian Context*, and the *Journal of American Drama and Theatre*, among other academic journals and essay collections. His research interests include the self-conscious appropriation of cultural stereotypes, as well as performances of Korean national and diasporic identity in the twentieth and twenty-first centuries. Nahm also works as a dramaturg, translator, and critic in the United States and South Korea.

Gana Ndiaye is a PhD student of social and cultural anthropology at Boston University, USA. Ndiaye holds an MSc in Intercultural Mediation (Belgium) and Lille 3 University (France), and an MA in French Studies from the University of Illinois at Urbana-Champaign.

Laura Purcell-Gates is Reader in Drama and founder of the Arts and Social Change Research Group at Bath Spa University in the UK, and co-artistic director of UK-based puppetry company Wattle and Daub. She is a member of the AHRC Peer Review College in the UK and of the AHRC international research network Objects with Objectives: Applied Theatre and Puppetry. Her main areas of research concern intersectional approaches to hybrid bodies within puppetry, object theatre and cyborg performance, performance and medical humanities, disability and performance, arts and displacement, and theatre and puppetry for social change.

Alda Terracciano is an honorary research associate at University College London and co-leader of the Centre for Critical Heritage Studies Embracing the Archive cluster. She researched digital economy at Queen Mary University of London, directed the Black and Asian performing arts archive Future Histories, and is artistic director of Aldaterra Projects.

List of Figures

Spectacular Bodies, Unsettling Objects: Material Performance as Intervention in Stereotypes of Refugees

The Suitcase as a Neurotic Container in the Israeli Theatre: The Return of the Wandering Jew

Tasting the Nation: Food, Identity, and Belonging in Canada

Mobility and Cultural Citizenship: The Making of a Senegalese Diaspora in Multiethnic Brazil

Claiming Their Voice: Foreign Memories on the Post-Brexit Stage

Introduction

Daniel McNeil, Yana Meerzon, and David Dean

It is a truth universally acknowledged that anyone writing a novel about "the British intellectual Left in the late twentieth century, who began by looking around for some exemplary figure to link its various trends and phases, would find themselves spontaneously reinventing Stuart Hall" (Eagleton 1996). After departing Jamaica on a Rhodes scholarship, Hall encountered and survived the distilled Englishness of Oxford in the 1950s. As director of the Centre for Contemporary Cultural Studies between 1968 and 1979, he developed telling metaphors for the British public in which the people who migrated from Africa, Asia, and the Caribbean to the United Kingdom became the "sugar you stir" in the great British cup of tea (Hall 1978). As Professor and Head of the Department of Sociology at the Open University from 1979 until his retirement in 1997, he grappled with the authoritarian populism of Thatcherism, a crisis of law and order, and political rhetoric that depicted migrants as unrecognizable

D. McNeil (✉) • D. Dean
Department of History, Carleton University, Ottawa, ON, Canada
e-mail: daniel.mcneil@carleton.ca; david.dean@carleton.ca

Y. Meerzon
University of Ottawa, Ottawa, ON, Canada
e-mail: ymeerzon@uottawa.ca

Y. Meerzon et al. (eds.), *Migration and Stereotypes in Performance and Culture*, Contemporary Performance InterActions,
https://doi.org/10.1007/978-3-030-39915-3_1

aliens that threatened to pollute, undermine, or swamp British greatness. Although we still await the great British novel to feature a character modelled on Hall, posthumous collections of his essays and the Stuart Hall Library at Rivington Place in London attest to his abiding influence on British society and culture.

This interdisciplinary collection of essays pays homage to the political and critical tradition of British Cultural Studies exemplified by Hall's work and seeks to avoid the pitfalls of recent North American work that appropriates Hall as "the godfather of multiculturalism" (Yardley 2014; Martin 2014). The co-editors of the book—first and second-generation migrants to Canada from British, Caribbean, and Russian diasporas—have not only shared Hall's bewilderment with American Cultural Studies, they have also sought to consider a different possibility to political and social scientists in the West who primarily read multiculturalism as a "governmental and/or rhetorical aspiration that is primarily about group cultural rights and formal institutional inclusion" (Valluvan 2019). Our goal is not to translate and simplify the informal, messy dimensions of urban multicultures for the benefit of readers and practitioners who find it difficult to grasp the points being made (Hall 1992b; MacCabe 2008; McNeil 2015). Indeed, we have written elsewhere about "shy elitists" who, fearing that metaphor, irony, and allusions to literary fiction may not be intelligible to a broad cross-section of North Americans, end up throwing the baby of imaginative, radical work on convivial multicultures out with the bathwater of exclusionary nationalism, Eurocentrism, and racial and religious discrimination (Tator and Henry 2006, 141; Henry and Tator 2006, 235; McNeil 2020).

To transform the merely professional discussions of multiculturalism, immigration, and "race relations" into something more lively and radical, our project delves beneath the media headlines about the "migration crisis," Brexit, Trump, and similar events and spectacles that have been linked to the intensification and proliferation of stereotypes about migrants since 2015. In our initial gathering at an interdisciplinary, international, and bilingual conference on Migration/Representation/Stereotypes at the University of Ottawa in 2017, we expressed our commitment to bringing together Cultural Studies and Performance Studies, amongst other fields, to address stereotypes that (1) reduce groups to a few, simple, essential characteristics (such as irrationality, rhythm, animism, oneness with nature, and sensuality); (2) symbolically fix these characteristics as essential and natural features of people and groups; and (3) tend to occur when there are gross inequalities of power (Hall et al. 1978; Hall 1992a; Hall 1997).

Our shared interests in Hall's intellectual project and legacy encouraged us to pursue the type of collaborative writing project that is often deemed essential to conjunctural analysis that examines "the coming together of often distinct though related contradictions" in a particular historical moment (Hall 1979; Grossberg 2019). In this collection of essays on Migration and Stereotypes in Performance and Culture, we consider the multiple problematics that emerge in a historical moment in which there are more displaced persons than at any time since World War II (approximately 244 million people were defined as international migrants in 2015, a 41% increase since 2000). We examine, for example, how neoliberal and neoconservative rhetorics conjoin to express anxieties about migrants "suspected of spreading various diseases and contagions" that threaten the production of "healthy, self-regulating, and self-fashioning citizens" (Iton 2008, 133). We show how discourse about migration intersects with the desires of subaltern subjects to "push for inclusion amongst those protected by the state while at the same time acknowledging the limits of this recognition" (Iton 2008, 202). We pay attention to affective landscapes in which multicultural national citizens are accorded greater universality and legitimacy in opposition to refugees and other groups that are imagined to be "monocultural" Others or multicultural global citizens (Melamed 2006). Essays in this collection apply keywords in Cultural Studies and Performance Studies such as abjection, agnotology, neoliberalism, precarity, securitization, self-fashioning, the society of the spectacle, and surveillance to disrupt attempts to fix refugees as dangerous, violent threats, revolting subjects as well as ineffectual, passive victims (Tyler 2013; Butler 2016; Žižek 2016). Contributors also ask how artists, academics, and practitioners may intervene in a conjuncture that is dominated by the policing of borders (the gated community, the carceral state, the walls to defend the greatness of the homeland, etc. [Goldberg 2008]), and the presumption that migrants are problems to be solved by more efficient management, increased surveillance and reformist gestures of recognition, inclusion, integration, settlement, and civic participation.

Committed to a collaborative, interdisciplinary, and multinational approach that treats the nation as one frame of meaning amongst others, this collection is able to bring together a range of discourses about citizenship and settler coloniality that, when separated from each other, disarticulated, and struggled against in isolation, cannot be recognized, contested, and challenged. It arranges contributions into three research areas and fields of inquiry—Theatre and Performance Studies, Cultural and Migration Studies, and Applied Theatre and History. There are, however, revealing overlaps and connections across the three parts that invite readers to imagine new ways of belonging with time, space, and each other (Grossberg 2000, 89).

The Lives of Others: Precarious Bodies and Self-Fashioning

Recent scholarship has demonstrated the ability of theatre and performance to seize the attention of audiences that may be desensitized to statistics about the deaths of anonymous refugees and migrants. In telling stories about migration and confronting the bodies of the performers with the bodies of spectators in the immediacy of a live performance, theatre practitioners can transform nameless migrants into individual agents with personal histories, memories and identities. Moreover, they may resist the tendency to sentimentalize or simplify the condition of exile by treating migrants as always and only victims or comedic stereotypes (see, for example, Bauman 2004, 2011; Boym 2001; Hoffman 1990; Jestrovic 2013; Kristeva 1991; Lamming 1992; Meerzon 2012, 2017, 2018; Rudakoff 2017; Said 1984; Wilmer 2018; Zaroulia 2018). Recent studies of political theatre and cultural performance have considered the refugee challenge in Europe as an invitation to construct "a mythopoetics of migration" through theatre and cultural performance (Cox 2014). Theatre practitioners have used the tactics of adaptation as well as documentary, autobiographical, applied and multilingual theatre, and critical counter-mapping (Balfour 2013; Jeffers 2013; Nolette and Babayants 2017; Meerzon and Pewny 2018). They have also developed movement-based theatre (Mitra 2015), intercultural theatre work (Gilbert and Lo 2007; McIvor 2016), and performance interventions and activism (Fleishman 2015; Marschall 2018).

The chapters in "The Lives of Others: Precarious Bodies and Self-Fashioning" bring together close readings of theatre and film produced by several provocative, suggestive, and explorative artists. The interdisciplinary overlap—from traditional theatre performance to performance intervention, activism, and film—deepens our understanding of the impact migratory and intercultural performances have on the conversation about the seduction and danger of cultural stereotypes. The cultural other—recognized and felt through the materiality of a migrant or diasporic body, objects displaced people carry, and languages they speak—often serves as a token of theatrical verisimilitude and authenticity that theatrical interventions and films seek when they artistically address migration. Despite their noble goals, such representations might overuse the stereotype, and hence risk further propagating the phenomenon of danger-fetishism (Ahmed 2000) and verging on political pornography (Sontag 2003). Hence chapters in this part consider how artists and scholars may contest the exploitation precarious bodies by political and media institutions and performance activists.

In her reflections on the *The Dead are Coming* (2015), a performance intervention by the German performance company The Centre for Political Beauty that seeks to energize and mobilize crowds, Meerzon shows that despite their good intentions, such artistic provocations might fall victims of their political objectives, as unintentionally they might re-enforce the negative tropes of anti-migration discourses that envisage today's displacement as bodily overflow and human waste. In contrast, Purcell-Gates demonstrates that familiarity of objects and bodies that meet in the intimate space of a theatre performance can serve as an antidote to the dangers of over-representation and stereotyping. She reminds us that in the age of technological innovations that intersect with and hijack human bodies, domestic and natural objects as well as nuanced storytelling can significantly challenge media-driven and over-simplified representations of refugees. Thus, as this part argues, a focus on making performances with "live materials" in theatres of migration can provoke more powerful affective responses. Kee-Yoon Nahm proposes another compelling perspective on the (ab)use of ethnic and cultural stereotypes on stage, specifically when it comes to the use of a racialized body. Nahm argues that theatrical performances often employ racial stereotypes for the sole purpose of making audiences—especially those who are not racialized minorities—feel uncomfortable. He reminds us that producing and multiplying racist stereotypes is not confined to the past, and so theatre is in the privileged position to make spectators confront and wrestle with their feelings of uncertainty, guilt, and responsibility when watching stereotypes on stage. This search for truth and authenticity that marks performance works about migration or created by refugee or migrant artists often characterizes their engagement with other material elements of performance. For example, the suitcase—a necessary prop of travelling—has become a leading visual and conceptual trope in mythologizing migration on many international stages. One of the primary symbols to refer to relocation, displacement, and exile, Sarit Cofman-Simhon argues, the suitcase has emerged as a special object in Jewish cultural memory and Israeli identity more specifically. Often, in the collective psyche of Israeli audiences, belonging and homelessness are symbolically linked. However, the suitcase—both as a material object and a powerful image of exile—can also be a commanding stereotype. It can trigger collective and personal memories and serve as a reminder of the terrible pasts, but it can also act as a symbol of hope and future. In this case, a stereotype can become a welcome artistic trope and symbolic repetition.

Paradoxically, language—words themselves—can become the material signifier of migration, specifically when the traveller realizes that speaking in a new tongue and addressing new audience, he/she is inevitably caught within the impossibility of cultural translation, as suggested by Gayatri Chakravorty Spivak (2000). Although focusing on the medium of film, J. Douglas Clayton offers a compelling argument on impossibility of translating self for the other, regardless of the medium or language one must use. Focusing on Andrey Tarkovsky's film *Nostalghia* (1983), one of the most compelling and insightful films about the hardships of exile and produced by one of the iconic figures of the twentieth-century art scene, who was himself an outcast, Clayton examines how this cinematic masterpiece deploys a familiar narrative of migration as personal nostalgia and creatively subverts stereotypes produced by the state. On the one hand, Tarkovsky's film offers a recognizable representation of the Russian intellectual standing alone and above the circumstances that led to their exile; on the other, it investigates whether a migrant can take his art with him and translate it for a new cultural environment. In this example, stereotypes work both ways—a host culture recognizes a foreigner as other and a traveller holds cultural and ideological presumptions that he brought from home. Clayton insists that the impossibility of translation or self-translation for the other becomes a device of filmmaking and narrative commentary as offered by Tarkovsky's cinematic style. Using the poetry of his father that serves as an inspiration for the aesthetics of his film, Tarkovsky provocatively asks if film offers a better medium to translate the materiality of a national culture and exilic self that poetry does not. This part, "The Lives of Others: Precarious Bodies and Self-Fashioning," therefore, aims to mobilize the complexity of stereotype—on the one hand, each article condemns the overuse of stereotype that can only re-enforce the precarity of migrant experiences; on the other hand, it demonstrates that when it comes to performative representation stereotypes are unavoidable. It insists that when theatre or film employ stereotypes, its makers are responsible for understanding, acknowledging, and critically examining the potential emotional, psychological, and even legal impact these stereotypes can produce both on the subject matter of the performance and their audiences. Without such awareness, the political goals and the ethical outcomes of any performance about migration remain questionable.

Multiculturalism, Citizenship, and Belonging: Deep Equality and Diasporic Cultures

In addition to building on new research at the intersection of Migration and Performance Studies, this collection complicates and exemplifies new keywords in Cultural Studies and Migration Studies. In his much-cited *Keywords: A Vocabulary of Culture and Society*, Raymond Williams (1976) had no entries for "migration," "immigration," or "borders." *The Revised Vocabulary of Culture and Society*, edited by Tony Bennett, Lawrence Grossberg, and Meaghan Morris (2005) also omitted these contested and critical terms (although it did include the keywords "sovereignty," "diaspora," "human rights," "mobility," "post-colonialism," and "race" that relate to the study of migration and borders). To address this gap in the field of Cultural Studies, Casas-Cortes et al. (2014, 59) have proposed new keywords that specifically address migration and borders for scholars and practitioners who seek to (1) study new problem-space or problematics, following the deepening of globalization, the 2007–2008 financial crisis, and austerity politics, (2) critically support movements, such as "No One is Illegal" and "No Border," which contested the illegalization and demonization of migrants and creatively used new forms of digital and social media, and (3) "deconstruct and transform the established repertoires of both traditional and critical migration studies in productive ways."

What is this "traditional" in "traditional migration studies"? Although historians of migration have chronicled the spread of Homo erectus and Homo sapiens from the Rift Valley in Africa to Europe and other continents between 1.5 million and 5000 BCE and explained how Ancient Greek, Roman, Mesopotamian, Inca, Indus, and Zhou empires depended on migration (Koser 2007), Casas-Cortes et al. (2014) are primarily concerned with what has been framed, imagined, and invented as traditional in the relatively recent past. They associate the development of traditional migration studies with the movement of Europeans to the New World at the end of the nineteenth century and the "guest worker regime" in West Germany and other European countries in the 1950s and 1960s, which are said to inform its residual Eurocentrism, its relationship to industrialization, and its concern with the social and economic integration of the migrant (Casas-Cortes et al. 2014, 61–62).

In contradistinction to traditional migration studies, Casas-Cortes et al. associate critical migration studies with interventions that carefully engage with critical race theory, feminism, labour studies, and transnationalism to disrupt the assumption that respectable, rational, and "common sense" discussions of migration include ones that talk about a "migration crisis" threatening European sovereignty. Public intellectuals working within a tradition of critical migration studies approach, for example, may seek to smuggle discussions of a crisis of European institutions, overdevelopment, or capitalism into a liberal public sphere. Historical approaches to critical migration studies may emphasize the predominant migration event of the eighteenth and nineteenth centuries—a slave trade that forced an estimated 12 million people from mainly western Africa across the Atlantic to the Americas and across the Indian Ocean and the Mediterranean—rather than focus on movement to and from Europe. Critical migration scholars interested in space, place, and difference may demonstrate how the use of the term "climate refugees" has recycled and redeployed racist notions of environmental determinism and a natural hierarchy of development in which "primitive Others" were framed as passive objects in need of aid, expert management, and supervision (Piguet 2013). In short, critical migration studies tend to draw on intellectual traditions that express scepticism about the deployment of the term "clash of civilisations" to describe conflicts between Western civilizations and the non-Western world (Huntington 1993), and invites reflection about the dangers of a "clash of ignorance" inspiring fearful and anxious responses to anything that is deemed foreign (Said 1978, 2001; Rappaport 2018).

Building on recent developments in critical migration studies, the chapters in "Multiculturalism, Citizenship, and Belonging: Deep Equality and Diasporic Cultures" address national citizenship ceremonies, international sporting events, and diasporic communities in which the stereotypes of migrants are sustained, reproduced, negotiated, and conditioned. The authors in this part address the processes whereby migrants bridge and maintain engagements with "host countries" and "societies of origin." They consider the ethics and aesthetics of translocal, diasporic identities in unsettling national conversations on migration that primarily revolve around the surveillance and recognition of immigrants and racialized groups. As Zaheeda P. Alibhai demonstrates in her analysis of the ban against wearing the niqab and burqa at the Canadian Citizenship Ceremony between 2011 and 2015, the racialized female body becomes an object of political and ideological manipulation, a hostage not simply to mediatized and performative discourses but to the legislative practices of Canada that guarantee freedom of one's cultural, religious, and linguistic expression. In such a context, the Canadian state assumes the role of arbiter of religious praxis as well as human rights and freedom of expression. Helin Burkay and David Dean also address an oft-overlooked area of Canadian governmentality. Drawing on public debates about what constitutes Canada's national dish, as well as restaurant menus, food festivals, and a recent stamp issue celebrating Canadian desserts, they reveal the tensions underlying the elusive concept of Canadian cuisine and posit that it is more productive to speak of a culinary tradition that is dynamic, adaptive, and multidimensional.

Shifting focus from Canadian state practices to lived multicultures in Brazil, Gana Ndiaye uses migration records and ethnographic field research conducted in Rio de Janeiro and São Paulo to illustrate the long history of Senegalese settlement in Brazil, the diversity of Senegalese migrants and the networks that channel them in the country, and the strategies by which they showcase their cultural difference and claim "cultural citizenship." Peter Kuling also addresses the intersection of body, state, and performance in Brazil by studying stereotypes about refugees deployed by athletes, reporters, and the organizing Olympic Committee during the 2016 Olympics. Using promotional materials and broadcasts created by the official Brazilian and international corporate media for the 2016 Games—particularly those related to the performance of the Refugee Olympic Team—Kuling demonstrates how media outlets have sought to elicit sympathy for refugees while simultaneously commodifying and fetishizing athletic bodies for global consumption.

Dreams, Memories, and Storytelling: Applied Theatre and Communities of Praxis

We are sitting in Salar's Afghan restaurant sipping tea and chewing on pita bread. We listen as Safi, a thirty-five-year-old former literature student and refugee from Syria reminds us that those joining us have travelled across the seas and across Europe to get "to safety, to our dreams … People meet, sing, share stories of great journeys and stories of home" (Murphy and Robertson 2017, 36). We are in Zhangal, the Jungle, and we, the audience, are fully immersed in this performance of lives lived in this migrant community on the outskirts of Calais. We want to comfort Salar when he hears the news of a young man's death trying to hitch a ride on a lorry to reach Britain, shout at the French police when they attack the café, and we occasionally glare at those observing at a distance, watching what is happening before their eyes replicated on television screens in front of them. They, like us, are theatre-goers, but they sit in the balcony, beyond the cliffs of Dover; we are sitting on cushions, on benches. We are in the café. We are the café. We are migrants and refugees and volunteers. We were not assigned those roles as we entered the theatre through corridors lined with bedding and supplies for the café's kitchen. We chose them because the play has compelled us to do so, through our feelings, experiences, and imaginings. We have repositioned and reinvented ourselves in the bodies and experiences of others. We have embraced difference.

The Jungle, which ran at London's Young Vic, National, and Playhouse Theatres throughout 2017 and 2018, spoke to real issues, drew on verbatim and documented stories, and performance strategies associated with the theatre of the real and the theatre of the oppressed. Positioning the play in the traditions of applied, verbatim, documentary, and realist theatre places significance on the eight months writers Joe Murphy and Joe Robertson spent working with refugees in Calais. It appreciates the theatrical energies generated by the actors, some of whom were themselves migrants and refugees—Safi was played by Ammar Haj Ahmad, an actor trained in Damascus who ended up in Britain seeking asylum (Gill 2018). It also acknowledged that the audience, who had come for a night out, was implicit in hearing these stories rarely told and sharing experiences rarely shared. And, of course, we too had our own stories.

As the change of focus and voice in this part of our introduction suggests, we shift attention in "Dreams, Memories, and Storytelling: Applied

Theatre and Communities of Praxis" from academic explorations of stereotypes to the experiences of theatre and performance practitioners and their audiences. This final part of our book is about histories, memories, and dreams performed. It focuses on artists who use storytelling to confront xenophobia by capturing and sharing untold stories and the experiences of others. While it showcases the voices of theatre and performance activists, many who are themselves the victims of displacement or are actively engaged in working with refugee and migrant communities, the methodologies, technologies, and strategies they use are shared by public historians—academics and practitioners who create histories in the public sphere. Drawing, for example, on oral histories, the remembered stories people tell about the past, public historians, like artists engaged in documentary or verbatim theatre, re-present past stories in the contemporary present with the conviction that such work will contribute to an improved future. Recognizing their role in such history-making has led not only to more transparent and openly reflexive practices by researchers, but more importantly a sharing of authority that insists on participant engagement, influence, and control in shaping outcomes (Frisch 1990, 2003; High 2014, 2018). Each of the authors in this part speaks openly about their roles in shaping the stories of the others they re-present and represent through theatre and performance.

Having experienced the effect of war trauma first-hand, Nimo Bokore writes about her project that gives voice to Somali women's experiences of forced migration, war, displacement and marginalization. Drawing on methodological frameworks informed by autoethnography and Black Feminism, Bokore gathered the stories of twelve Somali women residing in Canada and found storytelling to be a powerful tool in the journey from trauma to healing. Enabling silenced voices to be heard is also a motive behind Kasia Lech's exploration of the work of artist-immigrants who find themselves often stereotyped, both in the media and in the theatre work they are offered to perform (as strangers or, worse, as dangerous, evil, or unwitting foreigners). Lech demonstrates how new work by migrant theatre practitioners employ many strategies, such as multilingualism, to offer new perspectives that enable a reimagining of the social, one that highlights commonalities rather than differences, and challenges stereotypes rather than reinforcing them.

Sharing Lech's interest in community-based theatre work in post-Brexit Britain, Ida Casilli offers an account of her project with the Italian community of Peterborough, UK. Drawing on oral histories and testimonies that reveal a community which embodied, and even perpetuated stereotypes attached to them from the 1920s to the 1950s, Casilli's theatrical work offered opportunities for new imagining and new storytelling. Using devised and testimonial theatre approaches, the project ended with a dramatic text and a theatre performance that reflected the personal and communal experiences of Italian migrants in the United Kingdom, but also resonated with how refugees and migrants from Africa and the Middle East are represented in contemporary Britain. Michaelis Georgiou demonstrates how the techniques of truth-telling and myth-busting privileged by documentary theatre's aesthetics can combat stereotypes when representing refugees on stage. Examining the bilingual (German-French) BAAL Novo Theater Eurodistrict theatre company's productions involving community outreach, Georgiou shows how these projects played a vital role in constructing a public space in which to discuss some of the most pressing issues in the local community while fighting stereotypes related to the political and cultural realities of today's Europe.

The book concludes with Alda Terracciano's account of her multisensory project, *Streets of… 7 Cities in 7 Minutes.* Telling the story of three routes (the Indo-European migrations, the Silk Road, the transatlantic Slave trade) as they resurface in everyday lives globally, the project included interactive memory sessions with various diasporic communities living in London. Terraciano invited participants to share memories, thoughts, and feelings about a place that signified ways of understanding identity, belonging, and home. The project aspired to rouse its audiences into some fresh thinking about the use and abuse of stereotypes and expose them to the complexity of the questions and practices of mobility in today's Europe while also engaging the voices of migrants in remapping and re-thinking the relationships between the state, the media, and the Other in post-Brexit Britain.

At the start of act five of *The Jungle*, Safi asks "When does a place become home?" (Murphy and Robertson 2017, 67). Each of the chapters in part three interrogates notions of place and home, exploring how at various times and in diverse contexts individuals and communities negotiate stereotypes that exclude and navigate difference in the desire to belong. Each of the projects discussed not only dramatizes fearful and melancholic approaches to racialized minorities and migrants, but also provides us with tools to cultivate convivial multicultural spaces in which markers of racialized ethnic difference "cease to be objects of normative supervision *in the first place*" (Valluvan 2016, 219. Emphasis original). The productions and projects discussed by Bokore, Lech, Casilli, Georgiou, and Terraciano confirm Hall's insistence that the best cultural work must destabilize categories and engage difference. Like *The Jungle*, these projects satisfy his theory of articulation, not only affirming the political nature of cultural work but being of practical value because they remain "open, partial, and incomplete" (Giroux 2000, 142; Clarke 2015).

* * *

Finding ourselves situated in a world that is framed as polarized and divisive—one in which journalists and social scientists repeatedly remind us of the perils of biases and stereotypes generating clashes and conflicts—our collection has sought to carve out the necessary theoretical and political space for informed, inspired, and interdisciplinary conversations about the myths and realities of culture, migration, performance, and stereotypes. Such spaces may cultivate reflection and praxis about what Zygmunt Bauman (2011) calls the unifying concept of dialogue—a skill which is not only the life-force of democracy and cohabitation but also something that can make the difference between us surviving together or perishing together. They may offer us opportunities to juxtapose geographies, histories, experiences, artistic practices, forms of cultural mediations, research methodologies, and academic practices as a means to resist agnotology or the cultural production of ignorance. They may even, perhaps, help us address what intellectuals such as Stuart Hall (2017a,b) and Edward Said considered a basic humanistic mission—the preservation of difference without, at the same time, sinking into the desire to dominate.

References

Ahmed, Sara. 2000. *Strange Encounters: Embodied Others in Post-Coloniality*. London: Routledge.

Balfour, Michael, ed. 2013. *Refugee Performance; Practical Encounters*. Bristol: Intellect.

Bauman, Zygmunt. 2004. *Wasted Lives: Modernity and Its Outcasts*. Cambridge: Polity Press.

———. 2011. *Collateral Damage: Social Inequalities in a Global Age*. Cambridge: Polity Press.

Bennett, Tony, Lawrence Grossberg, and Meaghan Morris, eds. 2005. *New Keywords: A Revised Vocabulary of Culture and Society*. London: Blackwell.

Boym, Svetlana. 2001. *The Future of Nostalgia*. New York: Basic Books.

Butler, Judith. 2016. *Frames of War: When Is Life Grievable?* London: Verso.

Casas-Cortes, Maribel, et al. 2014. New Keywords: Migration and Borders. *Cultural Studies* 29 (1): 55–87.

Clarke, John. 2015. Stuart Hall and the theory and practice of Articulation. *Discourse: Studies in the Cultural Politics of Education* 36 (2): 275–286.

Cox, Emma. 2014. *Theatre and Migration*. Basingstoke: Palgrave.

Eagleton, Terry. 1996. The Hippest. *Review of Stuart Hall: Critical Dialogues*, ed. David Morley and Kuan-Hsing Chen. London Review of Books 18 (5): 3–5.

Fleishman, Mark, ed. 2015. *Performing Migrancy and Mobility in Africa: Cape of Flows*. Basingstoke: Palgrave.

Frisch, Michael. 1990. *A Shared Authority: Essays on the Craft and Meaning of Oral and Public History*. Albany: State University of New York Press.

———. 2003. Sharing Authority: Oral History and Collaborative Process. *Oral History Review* 30 (1): 111–113.

Gilbert, Helen, and Jacqueline Lo. 2007. *Performance and Cosmopolitics; Cross-Cultural Transactions in Australasia*. Basingstoke: Palgrave.

Gill, Joe. 2018. From the Jungle to the West End: 'It's Not About Refugees, It's About Humans'. *Middle East Eye*, July 17. https://www.middleeasteye.net/features/jungle-west-end-its-not-about-refugees-its-about-humans.

Giroux, Henry A. 2000. Public Pedagogy as Cultural Politics: Stuart Hall and the 'Crisis' of Culture. In *Honour of Stuart Hall*, ed. Paul Gilroy, Lawrence Grossberg, Angela Mcrobbie, and Without Guarantees. London and New York: Verso.

Goldberg, David Theo. 2008. *The Threat of Race: Reflections on Racial Neoliberalism*. Oxford: Wiley-Blackwell.

Grossberg, Lawrence. 2000. The Figure of Subalternity and the Neoliberal Future. *Nepantla* 1 (1): 59–89.

———. 2019. Cultural Studies in Search of a Method, Or Looking for Conjunctural Analysis. *New Formations* 96–97: 38–68.

Hall, Stuart. 1978. Racism and Reaction. In *Five Views of Multi-Racial Britain: Talks on Race Relations Broadcast by BBC TV*, 23–35. London: Commission for Racial Equality.

———. 1979. The Great Moving Right Show. *Marxism Today* 23 (1): 14–20.

———. 1992a. What Is This 'Black' in Black Popular Culture? In *Black Popular Culture*, ed. G. Dent. Seattle: Bay Press.

———. 1992b. Cultural Studies and its Theoretical Legacies. In *Cultural Studies*, ed. Lawrence Grossberg, Cary Nelson, and Paula Treichler. New York and London: Routledge.

———, ed. 1997. *Representation: Cultural Representations and Signifying Practices*. London: Sage.

———, ed. 2017a. *Familiar Stranger: A Life Between Two Islands*. Durham, NC: Duke University Press.

———, ed. 2017b. *The Fateful Triangle: Race, Ethnicity, Nation*. Cambridge, MA: Harvard University Press.

Hall, Stuart, Chas Critcher, Tony Jefferson, John Clarke, and Brian Roberts. 1978. *Policing the Crisis: Mugging, the State and Law and Order*. London: Palgrave.

Henry, Frances, and Carol Tator. 2006. *The Colour of Democracy: Racism in Canadian Society*. Toronto: Nelson.

High, Steven. 2014. *Oral History at the Crossroads. Sharing Life Stories of Displacement and Survival*. Vancouver: UBC Press.

———. 2018. Storytelling, Bertolt Brecht, and the Illusions of Disciplinary History. In *A Companion to Public History*, ed. David Dean, 163–174. Hoboken, NJ and Chichester: Wiley.

Hoffman, Eva. 1990. *Lost in Translation: A Life in a New Language*. New York: Penguin Books.

Huntington, Samuel. 1993. The Clash of Civilizations? *Foreign Affairs* 72 (3): 22–49.

Iton, Richard. 2008. *In Search of the Black Fantastic: Politics and Popular Culture in the Post-Civil Rights Era*. Oxford: Oxford University Press.

Jeffers, Alison. 2013. *Refugees, Theatre and Crisis: Performing Global Identities*. Basingstoke: Palgrave.

Jestrovic, Silvija. 2013. *Performance, Space, Utopia. Cities of War, Cities of Exile*. Basingstoke: Palgrave.

Koser, Khalid. 2007. *International Migration: A Very Short Introduction*. Oxford: Oxford University Press.

Kristeva, Julia. 1991. *Strangers to Ourselves*. Trans. Leon Roudiez. New York: Columbia University Press.

Lamming, George. 1992. *The Pleasures of Exile*. Ann Arbor: University of Michigan Press.

MacCabe, Colin. 2008. An Interview with Stuart Hall. *Critical Quarterly* 50 (1–2): 12–42.

Marschall, Anika. 2018. What Can Theatre Do About the Refugee Crisis? Enacting Commitment and Navigating Complicity in Performative Interventions. *Research in Drama Education: The Journal of Applied Theatre and Performance* 23 (2): 148–166.

Martin, Michel. 2014. Why Stuart Hall was the 'Godfather of Multiculturalism'. *Tell Me More, NPR*, February 13.

McIvor, Charlotte. 2016. *Migration and Performance in Contemporary Ireland: Towards a New Interculturalism*. Basingstoke: Palgrave.

McNeil, Daniel. 2015. Afterword. In *Exceptional/Exceptionable Space*, ed. Lee-Michael Pronko, Luisa Ji, Thaly Crespin, Daniel McNeil, and Roger Connah. Ottawa: Vertigo Press.

———. 2020. Shy Elitism: A New Keyword in Critical Multiculturalism Studies. In *Citizenship and Belonging in France and North America*, eds. Ramona Mielusel and Simona Emilia Prutreanu. Basingstoke: Palgrave.

Meerzon, Yana. 2012. *Performing Exile—Performing Self: Drama, Theatre, Film*. Basingstoke: Palgrave.

———. 2017. A Theoretical Primer on Exile: On the Paradigms of Banishment, Displacement and Free Choice. In *Performing Exile: Foreign Bodies*, ed. Judith Rudakoff, 17–37. Bristol: Intellect.

———. 2018. Multiculturalism, (Im)Migration, Theatre: The National Arts Centre, Ottawa, A Case of Staging Canadian Nationalism. *The Journal of Contemporary Drama in English* 6 (1): 113–130.

Meerzon, Yana, and Katharina Pewny, eds. 2018. Modern Drama 61 (3).

Melamed, Jodi. 2006. The Spirit of Neoliberalism: From Racial Liberalism to Neoliberal Multiculturalism. *Social Text* 24 (4): 1–24.

Mitra, Royona. 2015. *Akram Khan; Dancing New Interculturalism*. Basingstoke: Palgrave.

Murphy, Joe, and Joe Robertson. 2017. *The Jungle*. London: Faber & Faber.

Nolette, Nicole, and Art Babayants, eds. 2017. Theatre Research in Canada/Recherche Theatrales au Canada 38 (2).

Piguet, E. 2013. From 'Primitive Migration' to 'Climate Refugees': The Curious Fate of the Natural Environment in Migration Studies. *Annals of the Association of American Geographers* 103 (1): 148–162.

Rappaport, Nolan. 2018. The Migrant Crisis is Still a Growing Burden for Europe. *The Hill*, February 26.

Rudakoff, Judith, ed. 2017. *Performing Exile: Foreign Bodies*. Bristol: Intellect.

Said, Edward. 1978. *Orientalism*. New York: Pantheon.

———. 1984. Reflections on Exile. *Granta* 13.

———. 2001. The Clash of Ignorance. *The Nation*, October 22.

Sontag, Susan. 2003. *Regarding the Pain of Others*. New York: Picador/Farrar, Straus and Giroux.

Spivak, Gayathri Chakravorty. 2000. Translation as Culture. *Parallax* 6 (1): 13–24.

Tator, Carol, and Frances Henry. 2006. *Racial Profiling in Canada: Challenging the Myth of 'A Few Bad Apples'*. Toronto: University of Toronto Press.

Tyler, Imogen. 2013. *Revolting Subjects: Social Abjection and Resistance in Neoliberal Britain*. Basingstoke: Palgrave.

Valluvan, Sivamohan. 2016. Conviviality and Multiculture: A Post-Integration Sociology of Multi-Ethnic Interaction. *Young* 24 (3).

———. 2019. *The Clamour of Nationalism: Race and Nation in Twenty-first Century Britain*. Manchester: Manchester University Press.

Williams, Raymond. 1976. *Keywords: A Vocabulary of Culture and Society*. London: Croom Helm.

Wilmer, Steve. 2018. *Performing Statelessness in Europe*. Basingstoke: Palgrave.

Yardley, William. 2014. Stuart Hall, Trailblazing British Scholar of Multicultural Influences, Is Dead at 82. *New York Times*, February 17.

Zaroulia, Marilena. 2018. Performing That Which Exceeds Us: Aesthetics of Sincerity and Obscenity during 'The Refugee Crisis'. *Research in Drama Education: The Journal of Applied Theatre and Performance* 23 (2): 179–192.

Žižek, Slavoj. 2016. *Against the Double Blackmail: Refugees, Terror and Other Troubles with the Neighbours*. London: Penguin.

PART I

The Lives of Others: Precarious Bodies and Self-Fashioning

Precarious Bodies in Performance Activism and Theatres of Migration

Yana Meerzon

In their article, "Mare Nostrum, or On Water Matters," Emma Cox and Marilena Zaroulia (2016, 141) note that as global migration is a new norm, we—artists, scholars, ordinary citizens—find ourselves "grappling with a distinct awareness of the limits of performance in the face of this most immediate and urgent of realities." This awareness emerges "alongside our understanding that forced migration is already caught within the domain of representation [...]: we classify migration, we legislate migration, we prevent or enable migration, we produce narratives and images about migration, we devise military strategies that criminalize migration" (141). At the same time, the body of a migrant remains evasive and difficult to represent without falling into blatant stereotyping, objectification, or even the further victimization of an already vulnerable subject. This difficulty with representation compels us to question the political, social, or philosophical impacts of performance activism and to consider the futility, lost opportunities, and disappointments frequently associated with them. Happenings, protests, manifestations, and organized processions

Y. Meerzon (✉)
University of Ottawa, Ottawa, ON, Canada
e-mail: ymeerzon@uottawa.ca

Y. Meerzon et al. (eds.), *Migration and Stereotypes in Performance and Culture*, Contemporary Performance InterActions,
https://doi.org/10.1007/978-3-030-39915-3_2

present what Guy Debord (2002, 1) calls "an immense accumulation of *spectacles*. Everything that was directly lived has receded into a representation." While watching political performances, therefore, we often ask: "What was it, exactly, that we were looking for a performance to do, ethically, aesthetically and politically? What did we expect?" (Cox and Zaroulia 2016, 141).

A participatory art form, performance activism often exploits the affectual power of excitement; it relies on "symbolic elements and uses of the body to communicate claims across borders and languages. [...] More and more we witness and participate in local and global acts of protest and solidarity that entail visual, aural, and behavioral figurations evaluated by demonstrators as effective ways of making claims, reclaiming spaces, and denouncing abusive conditions" (Fuentes 2015). Performance activism is also emancipatory, in Jacques Rancière's (2009) sense of the term. It desires to "dismantle the Cartesian theatrical dichotomy of actor and spectator," turning spectators into politically engaged subjects, actively performing the acts of citizenship (Lewicki 2017, 276). By aspiring to "facilitate emotional access" to social and economic indecencies (286), performance activism energizes and mobilizes crowds. In this, although somewhat paradoxically, performance activism approximates the bread and circus tradition, a popular past-time of the Roman Empire that involved "chariot races and gladiatorial games that filled the belly and distracted the mind, allowing emperors to rule as they saw fit" (Astore 2013).

Of course, I do not want to suggest a direct link between performance activism and bread and circus past-times, but they are associated: there is danger in the use of political performance as an act of misrepresentation to deliberately excite an audience. This danger is specific to performance activism aiming at representation of the migration crisis. To remind their audiences of our transience and to focus our attention on the precariousness of life, this work stages migration as bodily overflow. It also creates circumstances of voyeurism that can edge on political pornography: "all images that display the violation of an attractive body are, to a certain degree, pornographic," Sontag (2003, 6) writes. "But images of the repulsive can also allure." Although performance activism often succeeds in mobilizing people, it also appeals to our desire for spectacle. Likewise, it begs the question of what could possibly be an adequate response to a humanitarian catastrophe, be it a war, a genocide, or a migration crisis.

This question has been raised before: from Theodor Adorno to Jacques Derrida, Emmanuel Levinas to Judith Butler, many political philosophers have challenged the aesthetics of the representation of a mutilated, raped, abused, or dead body. In theatre, there is a long tradition of fascination with staging violence. Projects that aim to raise awareness about legal, political, and social controversies surrounding migration and asylum seeking repeatedly emphasize the material experiences of migration and the body of a migrant—a site of physical suffering, an object of unwanted gaze, and, by extension, the subject of an artistic experiment. Such bodies often turn into stereotypical representations of *stranger-danger* and *stranger-fetishism* (Ahmed 2000).

For Levinas (1998), the concept of *face* stands as a metonym for both a divine entity and a human being; it acts as a "condition for humanization" (Butler 2004, 141), a reminder of our ethical responsibility towards others. Through representation, we attribute a human quality to any type of Other. At the same time, representation risks producing a personification that may "evacuate the face" as well as perform "its own dehumanization" (Butler 2004, 141). By questioning the results produced by the process of personification—a stereotype—Butler (2004) interrogates the concept of good intention, which often initiates problematic representational tactics, especially if its subject matter is the victimized or the suffering. The excessiveness of representation, Butler argues, can impede the acknowledgement of life's precariousness, and lead to numbness in our reception, which can undermine the face: our humanity. The excessiveness of representation can also mobilize the onlooker's empathy—the emotion prone to manipulation—rather than their critical thinking. Butler's emphasis on the ethics of representation: one's need to recognize the ambiguity of a good intention and the tension between giving the Other a voice and the potential for his/her (de)humanization through representation, forms the theoretical focus point of this chapter. In my conclusions, I return to the discussion of *responsibility for oneself* and *for other* as an act of recognizing a face, an abstract category of humanity and a synecdoche of a human body, the body of a migrant. I demonstrate that to remind spectators of our transience and to focus our attention on the precariousness of life, many productions of performance activism create the circumstances of an artistic encounter, estrangement, and voyeurism.

Theoretical Premise and Hypothesis

Explaining why Levinas' ethical philosophy is relevant in today's critical discourse about war, oppression, and migration, Butler (2004, 141) states: "when we consider the ordinary ways that we think about humanization and dehumanization, we find the assumption that those who gain representation, especially self-representation, have a better chance of being humanized; and those who have no chance to represent themselves run a greater risk of being treated as less than human, regarded as less than human, or indeed not regarded at all." To Butler, such assumptions can be erroneous. The excessiveness of representation does not rely on the strategies of recognition; it often capitalizes on the workings of a gaze: "we see the migrant as a victim; we sympathize, we empathize" (Cox and Zaroulia 2016, 148). Moreover, we realize that such gaze can turn a migrant's body into an object of fetishism. Sontag (2003, 6) identified this process with a form of pornography, one seeking pleasure in identifying with the victim. Cox and Zaroulia (2016, 148) argue similarly that, "Confronted with such imagery, we don't understand what we see," elaborating that, "We misinterpret it. We see the image of the boy[1] and remember the image of another child playing, perhaps ourselves. The present image picks and haunts our past."

At the same time, as Sontag (2003, 97) writes, when staging the dead body, it is the photographer and the spectator's vulnerability that the image addresses. It points at our profound ignorance of what another's pain means or entails, and what unimaginable mark it leaves on the body and soul of its victim. Looking at the photographs of dead soldiers or any victims of an act of violence, we must realize: "These dead are supremely uninterested in the living: in those who took their lives; in witnesses—and in us" and "we truly can't imagine what it was like. We can't imagine how dreadful, how terrifying war is, and how normal it becomes" (Sontag 2003, 97–98). This argument echoes Adorno's dictum about the impossibility of writing poetry after the Holocaust (2003). Any representation of such atrocity, Richardson argues (2005, 1) would fall into "the tension between ethics and aesthetics inherent in an act of artistic production that reproduces the cultural values of the society that generated the Holocaust." At the centre of this issue are questions about the unspeakable, the silence, and the truth of the past and its remembrance, about fact and fiction, and the problematic aesthetics of *representation-as*—a subjective picture of the past as experienced, remembered, and interpreted by a survivor, or as a fictionalized account (Lang 2000). These areas of concern are echoed in today's political performances, specifically when the body of a migrant emerges as a guarantee of theatrical truth and of the authenticity of suffering. Mythologizing migration this way, the figure of a migrant risks to become "defaced," the consequence of representation itself (Butler 2004, 143). My example of this tendency is the 2015 intervention *The Dead are Coming*—a weeklong series of political actions or "operations" produced by the Berlin-based performance group Zentrum für Politische Schönheit/ The Center for Political Beauty (CPB).

Staging *The Dead are Coming*, CPB aimed at "transform[ing] piles of corpses into individuals who lost their lives," turning "refugees into people" (Musyal 2015). The project

> began with the transport of the bodies of Syrian refugees who had died in the Mediterranean and were brought by the [CPB] from Italy to Berlin to be given a proper funeral ceremony. The initiative inspired individuals around Germany and Austria to erect makeshift graves, which began to pop up on roadsides and green spaces, imitating in style those burial grounds assembled in front of the Parliament. Their unknown makers thereby took part in the [CPB's] ethico-political mobilization to mourn the deaths of nameless refugees and to problematize the very absence of a public sphere where such expressions of grief could take place. (von Bieberstein and Evren 2016, 454–555)

The Dead are Coming, 2015: A Brief Example

According to its website, Zentrum für Politische Schönheit/The Center for Political Beauty (CPB), established in 2010 by political theorist Philipp Ruch, is "an assault team that establishes moral beauty, political poetry and human greatness while aiming to preserve humanitarianism. The group's basic understanding is that the legacy of the Holocaust is rendered void by political apathy, the rejection of refugees and cowardice. It believes that Germany should not only learn from its History but also take action" (The Center for Political Beauty). A grass-roots organization, as also stipulated by its website, the CPB aims to fight "against human rights violations" and remind the state of its duty to "protect the most vulnerable" (Lewicki 2017, 277). Aligned with the company's previous projects, *The Dead are Coming* clearly illustrates the artists' moral and political intentions. In its artistic tactics, *The Dead are Coming* utilizes documentary and immersive performance that relies on its audiences' mobilization, disorientation, and desire for play. Using the corpse of a refugee as evidence of injustice, a performative prop and a symbolic object, it also calls our attention to the materiality, vulnerability, and mortality of our own bodies and experiences.

On June 16, 2015, the *New York Times* reported:

> A 34-year-old woman was buried in a Berlin cemetery on Tuesday, thousands of miles from her home in Syria and hundreds from the shores of Italy that eluded her while she was alive. Pallbearers carried a white coffin covered with a red shroud and flowers and laid it before rows of empty chairs, each taped with a sheet of white paper bearing the name of a German politician. The woman perished at sea on her way to the Italian coast in early March. Her name was withheld to protect her surviving husband and three children, who are in Germany and seeking asylum. [...] With her family's permission, her body was exhumed from a plot in Sicily and buried in Germany as part of a political demonstration called "The Dead are Coming," which was organized by the Center for Political Beauty, a Berlin-based art group that focuses on protest. (Eddy 2015)

Reburial was the third step in the CPB's four-tier performance event, which included conducting extensive research into the conditions of asylum seeking in Europe—CPB's planning department collected "visual evidence of a cold storage room in Augusta [Sicily], in which 17 bodies were lying wrapped in plastic bags and stacked in piles, with blood pooling underneath"[2]; publishing the results of their research story in the German newspaper in the article entitled "Was wir sehen müssen"/"What we need to see", (282); "identifying two 'unknown' deceased refugees from Syria, contact[ing] their relatives, gain[ing] their families' permission to exhume their undignified graves, and transport[ing] their bodies across Europe"; and performing the act of public burial (Lewicki 2017, 281–82). As part of the final step, "a building plan poster between the Parliament and the Chancellery, which announced that the German Interior Ministry and Frontex [...] were collaborating in the construction of a 'Memorial for the Unknown Refugee'" (284) was put up, and the CPB solicited 5000 German citizens for a procession, the March of the Determined, which ended with the digging of a dozen graves in the Square of the Republic (Lewicki 2017, 284) designated to be used for the burial of refugee bodies. The intervention revealed how the CPB was compelled to provide a public commemoration for the perished refugees in light of the European governments' denial of these people's rights to life and official burial or mourning. Lewicki (2017, 283) describes the burial, writing:

> In a third act of citizenship, the artists collective conducted a public burial to restore the deceased's dignity. The artists contacted cemeteries with the request to hold a funeral for two Syrian refugees, a man and a woman. A majority of cemeteries in Berlin declined arguing that they did not see themselves in a position to fulfil the criteria of the Islamic ritual […] However, a director of one of those cemeteries decided not to obey her orders and allowed the man's funeral to take place in Berlin-Schöneberg, whilst the woman's burial took place at the Muslim cemetery in Berlin-Gatow. A local Imam performed the religious ritual, and each individual's story was told during the ceremony.

Even though *The Dead are Coming* was carried out in cooperation with the local authorities, including imams, priests, and gravediggers, the public response varied from highly enthusiastic to half-hearted.

> In "Süddeutsche Zeitung" newspaper, Sonja Zekri commented that the campaign borders on "political pornography." She also asked: "What will come next? The Center for Political Beauty has undertaken drastic, but clever campaigns. But this action only highlights the powerlessness of the victims." In contrast, Volker Beck, speaker for the human rights policy of the party "The Greens" was ambivalent. "It is offensive and impious to use dead refugees as an object in an artistic intervention." But Beck also sees a need to improve the political situation. "The European Union must do everything to identify these people." Katja Kipping, leader of the Left Party, deemed the action to be "pushing limits, but that's exactly why it manages to directly hit those sensitive topics." Rupert Neudeck, [co-founder of the non-profit refugee assistance association Cap Anamur-Deutsche Not-Ärzte e.V. (German Emergency Doctors)], who is also on the board of trustees of the Center for Political Beauty, defended the artist's radical and shocking scenes. (Mund 2015)

Some Syrian refugees who received asylum status in Germany questioned the ethics of this artistic work as well (Dyer 2015). In these hesitant responses, one can detect concerns similar to Butler's about the power of representation when a migrant body is subjected to political and artistic framing: the danger of that body becoming a stereotype of suffering and victimhood, and of a good intention transforming into the populist past-time.

The CPB artistic manifesto explains some of these controversies. It positions the group as engaging in "action-based art" that carries a "vision of a better fight for human rights," expressed through the aesthetics of *aggressive humanism*.

> The term aggressive humanism merges two concepts that have commonly been deemed incompatible: European humanism and aggression. Occidental humanism was the epitome of human love, benevolence and friendliness. It vindicated the position of education, love and benevolentia with decidedly friendly means. [...] The term aggressive humanism argues that the fight for human rights is being fought in too friendly a fashion. The concept of aggressive humanism points to a group of highly ambitious human rights activists that offer political resistance. (The Center for Political Beauty, 2014)

Aggressive humanism links the work of the CPB to the origins of Western theatre, specifically to the myth of Antigone and her desire to pay respect to the dead, even if the price is her own life. Staging *The Dead are Coming*, the group intended to "protest the tightening of the EU's refugee policy" (Mund 2015). Calling the German government to account for its immigration policies and practices, the group planned to "exhibit their actions in the 'punishment-free' space of art" (Musyal 2015). They invited leading politicians and media to attend the ceremony, with the "Minister of Interior Thomas de Maizière and his wife, along with Chancellor Angela Merkel and her husband [...] to sit in the first row" (Mund 2015). None of the politicians joined the performance; "Followed by members of the group, representatives from the cemetery, and others, two white coffins covered in red shrouds and flowers were brought to the grave and one of them lowered into the ground after imam Abdallah Hajir, joined by other Muslims, had spoken the fatiha prayer" (von Bieberstein and Evren 2016, 457). In his eulogy, Hajir "denounced the European border regime and the depiction of refugees as greedy criminals seeking to take advantage of Europe" while attendees "approached the grave and added soil and flowers in personalized gestures of mourning amid a general atmosphere of silence" (458). In this ritual, the CPB thus engaged with the symbolic functions of, as Lefebvre (1992, 185–188) expresses it, the *body as a social construct* and the *body as an object of worship*. In the words of Verdery (2000, 20), "Reburying of anonymous dead calls for a particular type of re-evaluation of history," when "entire social categories [...] are repositioned or associated with different sets of values. Dead body politics of this sort have the important effect of inserting such re-evaluation directly into the lives of persons, families, and small groups"; such manipulation of a dead body calls for political maneuvering and the rewriting of history (26–7). It makes us speak about the unthinkable, even if it prioritizes emotions over thoughts.

In its heavy symbolism, *The Dead are Coming* generated a level of ethical discomfort that Cox and Zaroulia (2016, 146) attribute to "the way the interventions were situated uneasily between different domains of representation and social practice—or perhaps more precisely, between artistic performance, political convocation and religious event. The activist/performers were engaged in *real* burials of *real* corpses. Its choreography was religious, with prayers led by an imam, but at the same time the event was attended by members of the media, framed by political speeches, recorded for public dissemination and ultimately agitation." What is more problematic, I propose, is the way the company made this event participatory, constructing it within the aesthetics of immersive theatre.

(Dead) Body as Evidence: Truth Versus Fiction

In *The Dead are Coming*, the CPB "explicitly plays with and blurs the conventional separation between a sphere of political action privileging facts and documentary evidence and a stage of artistic expression understood as 'unreal'" (von Bieberstein and Evren 2016, 464). Claiming that "they were neither in the business of art, nor satire, nor activism," the CPB staged the burial "as the public enactment of a possibility" (465). "Neither show, nor representation," it was reality "performatively staged, thereby partaking in the work of imagination and representation" (466). In this artistic gesture, the CPB put forward a plea for authenticity, making the burial a distant cousin to Documentary Theatre. "Playfully switching between the factual and the fake," *The Dead are Coming* was produced with the "aesthetics of truth making," in which "the invocation of 'alternative realities' […] challenges conventions of intelligibility that circumscribe what counts as performance and reality, art and politics" (466). The intervention relied on the technology, text, and body triad (Martin 2006, 9) that often marks the workings of Documentary Theatre. "In documentary theatre, the performers are sometimes those whose stories are being told. But more often than not documentary theatre is where 'real people' are absent—unavailable, dead, disappeared—yet re-enacted. They are represented through various means, including stage acting, film clips, photographs, and other 'documents' that attest to the veracity of both the story and the people being enacted" (Martin 2006, 9). In *The Dead are Coming*, the coffin of a 34-year-old Syrian woman buried in a Berlin cemetery has taken on this symbolic and practical function of authenticating truth. Although the coffin was never opened during the ceremony, it came to represent the victim's body. The coffin turned into the "stage object"; it carried the idea of a truth and thus became a substitute for the body of the victim.

Often, in Documentary Theatre, actors "perform both as themselves and as the actual personages they represent. The absent, unavailable, dead, and disappeared make an appearance by means of surrogation" (Martin 2006, 10). Functioning as a kind of time-machine, the actor's body reflects the performer's own past, the historical or fictional setting a story, and the temporal context of the performance and its reception. An example of a "twice-behaved behavior," actors' bodies help turning a document into a public performance (20). A canvas onto which a new story, the story of making and performing a migrant self, is projected, it becomes a performative object displayed for the audience's consumption, such that the conflict between the autobiographical and the fictional (which a migrant body evokes) drives the drama forward. Political interventions stage the trauma of migration by bringing the materiality of human experience, the corporeality of life, to the forefront of their artistic and philosophical investigation. By bringing real people (or their substitutes, including objects or corpses) on stage, these interventions intend to deploy the appearance of truth (Martin 2006, 10) and they fight to restore the dignity and value of individual experience.

The relation between truth and fiction, between fact and editing, is a point of ethical discomfort in making Documentary Theatre, in general. By bringing real people (or their corpses) on stage, political intervention relies on the materiality of a theatrical sign (Malzacher 2010, 81), In *The Dead are Coming* the coffin with the corpse of a refugee is intended to accentuate the performance's fleeting sense of the present. It also turns the attention of its spectators/participants to their own embodied and thus highly personal senses of reality.

In its embodied or, rather, phenomenological dimensions, the body serves as the container for our histories and memories. It stores our past in our changing, aging cells, which turn the body into a site of death, offering the promise of departure. In its semiotic functions, the body acts as a canvas to write on; it turns into the site of another's gaze and becomes the

Other. Subjected to different types of looks and general scrutiny, the body of a stranger takes on even more specific functions. An uncanny manifestation of the duality of our own self, it foregrounds the sense of deep disconnection we carry within us.

Kristeva (1991, 191–192) theorizes uncanny as the problem of foreignness, a feature that each of us already carries within ourselves. Historically, Kristeva explains, a foreigner has been often identified "in negative fashion" as someone who "does not belong to the group, who is not 'one of them', [...] the other of the family, the clan, the tribe," described so either according to the law of the soil or according to the law of blood (95). With the emergence of nation-states, the foreigner turned into someone "who does not belong to the state [...], does not have the same nationality" (96), and hence falls beyond the duties and the privileges of the nation. The fascination (positive or otherwise) we associate with foreignness, Kristeva proposes, essentially stems from the one type of difference that identifies a foreigner: the difference of not belonging; the colour of one's skin and the religion one practices become the fundamental markers of foreignness that differentiate between the right of man and the right of citizen (96–97).

Expanding upon this, Sara Ahmed (2000, 51–52) adds the power of embodied encounter. The materiality of the body—one's skin colour, body type, postures, the gait and speed of one's movements, and the sounds one makes—represent an impassable elemental border between oneself and another. The body of another is a sealed phenomenological experience, unavailable both in its materiality and in its semioticity, meaning that "the stranger is produced through a dialectic of proximity and distance" (Cooke 2002, 56). When we recognize the figure of a foreigner, this unknown Other, as alien, the phenomenon of *stranger-fetishism* takes place. As Ahmed (2000, 2) writes, "The alien recuperates all that is beyond the human into the singularity of a given form. The alien hence becomes a fetish." Stanger-fetishism takes many forms and is often rooted in our prejudice. One of such forms is our obsession with the figure of the migrant, who is allegedly invading the territory to which one belongs and destroying the safety of one's community (Ahmed 2000, 5).

Staging migrant bodies as a point of truth and as a mechanism for accentuating a spectator's experience of alienation from the self, in the context of any edited, selected, or fictionalized framework in any political intervention, can bring the idea of stranger-fetishism to life; this was the effect of *The Dead are Coming*. A staged embodied encounter with a migrant induces "Brechtian distancing that asks spectators to simultaneously understand the theatrical, the real, and the simulated, each as its own form of truth" (Martin 2006, 12). It can also move Ahmed's political project forward, as she insists, building on Levinas, that the act of encounter (and performance encounter specifically) can serve as humanity's useful tool for identifying the otherness of the Other as the otherness in oneself (Ahmed 2000, 5).

Bodies of Excitement: On Audience Participation

The methodologies used by The Center for Political Beauty in *The Dead are Coming* to incite public excitement are quite unsettling. Aspiring to actively engage with the wrongdoings of society, Documentary Theatre frequently appeals to our sense of a disconnection between the truth of an experience and its representation, but it rarely involves its audiences directly in state politics. Although the CPB shares ideological goals with Documentary Theatre, as its website explains, it seeks to go beyond them, believing that art must "provoke and rise in revolt" (The Center for Political Beauty), which had prompted the CPB to cast its audience as one more technology of the real (Martin 2006, 9). The bodily encounters across the performance frame—real people standing in front of other real people as "bodies of evidence"—defines the company's "aesthetics of sincerity" (Cox and Zaroulia 2016, 147). Mobilizing their audiences physically, the CPB offered spectators a participatory experience. Based on its aptitude to play with and confuse reality and fiction, it turned participants into the makers and consumers of spectacle. This is how von Bieberstein and Evren (2016, 455–456) describe their experience as participants of *The Dead are Coming*:

> The news of the campaign reached us with short notice. Those linked up via social media to the [CPB] heard that the "dead were coming" only a day or two before the first burial was set to take place. By way of a crowdfunding platform, supporters were called upon to assist in covering the costs of the exhumations, transfers, and burials, and invited to attend the funeral of several migrants who had died while trying to cross the borders of the European Union. Within a day or two, about €34,000 was raised. Sponsors were promised rewards that included a psychiatric report on the interior minister's state of mind (in return for 10 euro), the chance to drive the excavator that would break through the fence in front of the Chancellery during the

> "March of the Determined" (in return for €2,500) and a weekend in the Greek-Turkish borderlands with a guided tour of mass graves, room and board included (in return for €5,000).

The effect such acts of participation produce, however, is two-fold. On the one hand, it does create political awareness. On the other, it prompts euphoria. Like sensationalist photography, participation through provocation is "fatally linked to the momentary" (Butler 2007, 955). Unlike Brechtian epic theatre, which uses alienation, metaphor, and story-telling to appeal intellectually to its audiences' social consciousness, the CPB employs techniques stewed in sensation and wonder. Consequently, people who are not normally prone to violence cannot resist giving in to their basic instincts, something that Sontag (2003, 77–80), building on Freud, identifies with the pleasure we receive from observing or staging a ferocious act. By engaging its audiences with such emotional and visceral experiences as excitement, physical mobilization, and a sense of righteousness, the CPB not only wishes to make them directly face the dangers of the refugees' journey, but the team relies on the affectual power of immersive theatre, its ability to confuse reality and fiction by turning the audiences into active players in the game of theatrical transformation. As the March of the Determined came to a close, "the participants themselves, rather than the artists, [...] 'got their hands dirty' to dig the memorial. They erected signs such as 'Borders kill' and 'Nobody is illegal'" (Lewicki 2017, 284). This part of the performance was "scripted only to the degree that the animated video and the instructions for pop-up graves had been circulated" (284). The CPB leaders relied on the assumption that engaging their audiences in the act of doing would appeal to their desire for pleasure through excitement. The bread and circus tradition often builds on these instincts too. It unleashes our hidden thirst for violence. When the violent act is not produced, we feel cheated because no photographic image or theatrical metaphor can provide authenticity the way the materiality of the body and the real act of violence can. The ethics of representation lies in the artist's realization of this responsibility.

The Dead are Coming indicated a troublesome tension between the subject matter and the artistic methods the group employed (Marschall 2016), as it violated "our aesthetic assumptions about proper burials and proper mourning. [...] By tapping into this 'powerful magic' of the corpse [CPB] channeled the haunting force of dead bodies to draw attention to the 'death worlds' [...] that underlie and condition contemporary Europe" (von Bieberstein and Evren 2016, 463). It is at the parameters of *The Dead are Coming*'s artistic execution that an uneasiness between this politically charged act and an ethical dilemma exists. As von Bieberstein and Evren (2016, 464) state:

> the campaign explicitly plays with and blurs the conventional separation between a sphere of political action privileging facts and documentary evidence and a stage of artistic expression understood as "unreal." This lies at the core of their "mission" more generally. In a presentation of their work, members of the group emphasized that they were neither in the business of art, nor satire, nor activism. Instead they introduced themselves as a "storm troop for the erection of moral beauty, political poetry and great humane magnanimity" and defined what they do as the creation of a parallel foreign policy.

Despite these proclamations, the burial event was staged "as the public enactment of a possibility, offering a performative example of how those whose lives are deemed not worth grieving could and should—if we lived in a world of 'political beauty'—find their final rest" (465). The group insisted, at the same time, that despite its performative aspects, the burial was "absolutely real. This was neither show, nor representation, but reality" (465). In reality, *The Dead are Coming* has turned into a social media event. Traces of its social media tactics can be found on the company's elaborate website and Facebook page. "The burial video posted by the Center for Political Beauty on their YouTube page is something of a semiotic car crash […] Certain elements of the event seem to merge European funeral and corporate/convention dress codes: the sombre pallbearers, who are older white (presumably German) men, wear black suits, black ties, white gloves and white name badges. Other male and female participants are identifiable by their dress as Islamic" (Cox and Zaroulia 2016, 147). This chapter, however, does not aim to provide a recipe for an ethically sound performative intervention, nor does it make moralizing conclusions. Simply, like the CPB itself, it tries to raise awareness of the uneasy tension between noble goals and the populist means of their realization, in which performance activism seems to be often caught.

Conclusion

Representation is the work of dramaturgical and performative construction. To discuss the power of representation in the theatre of migration is to analyze the mechanisms of narrative composition used to make the figure of a refugee. Visual representation relies on the process of framing, in the theatre of migration representation often turns into a tool for myth-making. As Hanif Kureishi (2014) puts it, "the immigrant has become a contemporary passion in Europe, the vacant point around which ideals clash. Easily available as a token, existing everywhere and nowhere, he is talked about constantly. But in the current public conversation, this figure has not only migrated from one country to another, he has migrated from reality to the collective imagination where he has been transformed into a terrible fiction." Performance activism creates a sense of discomfort as it excessively relies on the power of re-enactment and on the audience's excitement about this form of representation. It often builds upon and references the energy of the crowd. This strategy can be both effective and dangerous. By appealing to peoples' desire for spectacle, it also ignites our nostalgia for strong ruling and nationalist sentiment. An example of this uneasiness can be found in a subsequent performative intervention the CPB made.

For their 2016 project *Devouring the Refugee*, the artists engaged four tigers, in a specially erected pavilion next to the Maxim Gorki theatre in Berlin, to entertain tourists. This intervention supported an ultimatum: the company's promise to make the tigers devour a refugee if the German government did not respond to their demand to fly Syrian refugees to Germany using a special jet sponsored by German citizens. This premise fueled audiences' anticipation and arousal not only in Germany but across the world—all were eagerly wondering if and how the company would honour their promises. In their promotion video for this project, the CPB referenced the bread and circus entertainment customs of the Roman Empire as a point of correspondence between today's Germany and its government. That tourists with photo-cameras and iPhones took selfies in front of the tigers illustrates my point. The desire for violence—watching someone being devoured by a tiger, even if this someone is supposedly a volunteer refugee fed-up with their suffering, desiring to stop the injustice of asylum seeking systems once and for all—is deeply rooted in the conflicted nature of humanity, characterized by the struggle between our two major drives: Eros, associated with sexual desire, creativity, and reproduction, and Thanatos, associated with the desire for power, destruction, aggression, and death.

Positioning performance activism within Levinas' (1998) insistence on our responsibility for the other can keep our basic instincts under control, although it does require effort. Responsibility is a product of our labour and spiritual and ethical consciousness, the hard work of an educated mind. It is never moralistic, but does teach us to recognize the dangers of populist technologies and provocation, even when used for the right cause.

Notes

1. Here, the authors refer to the photograph of the Kurdish boy who drowned in the summer 2015, on his way to the Greek island of Kos from the Turkish resort town of Bodrum. This photograph made the boy "a symbol of refugee crisis" (Ensor 2016), but also exemplified the "digitalized banality of evil" (Butler 2007, 960) in the way we use mediation to construct our view of the world.
2. "The artist collective reported that most individuals whose bodies appeared on the shore in Augusta had carried documents and could have been identified; nevertheless, it was not common practice to notify family members (personal conversation). Instead, the deceased were buried as 'unknown' in local cemeteries. The long duration and conditions of storage deviate from standards across the globe, but specifically violate Islamic rituals that require a timely inhumation. Such practices further deny non-European citizens the yet to be codified right to a decent burial [...], and families are deprived of their entitlement to learn about the death of their loved ones" (Lewicki 2017, 282).

References

Adorno, Theodor W. 2003. *Can One Live After Auschwitz? A Philosophical Reader.* Edited by Rolf Tiedemann. Translated by Rodney Livingstone and others. Stanford: Stanford University Press.

Ahmed, Sara. 2000. *Strange Encounters: Embodied Others in Post-Coloniality.* London: Routledge.

Astore, William. 2013. Bread and Circuses in Rome and America. *Huffington Post*, June 10. http://www.huffingtonpost.com/william-astore/bread-and-circuses-in-rom_b_3414248.html.

von Bieberstein, Alice, and Erdem Evren. 2016. From Aggressive Humanism to Improper Mourning: Burying the Victims of Europe's Border Regime in Berlin. *Social Research* 83 (2): 453–479.

Butler, Judith. 2004. *Precarious Life. The Powers of Mourning and Violence.* London: Verso.

———. 2007. Torture and the Ethics of Photography. *Environment and Planning: Society and Space* 25: 951–966.

Cooke, Paul. 2002. Review. Review of *Strange Encounters: Embodied Others in Post-Coloniality* by Sara Ahmed. *Gender Forum* 1: 55–9.

Cox, Emma, and Marilena Zaroulia. 2016. Mare Nostrum, or On Water Matters. *Performance Research* 21 (2): 141–149.

Debord, Guy. 2002. *The Society of the Spectacle.* Detroit: Black and Red.

Dyer, John. 2015. Activists Shame German Government by Burying Corpses of Migrants in Berlin. *Vice News,* June 17. https://news.vice.com/article/activists-shame-german-government-by-burying-corpses-of-migrants-in-berlin.

Eddy, Melissa. 2015. Migrant's Funeral in Berlin Highlights Europe's Refugee Crisis. *New York Times,* June 16. http://www.nytimes.com/2015/06/17/world/europe/migrants-funeral-in-berlin-highlights-europes-refugee-crisis.html?_r=1.

Ensor, Josie. 2016. 'Photo of My Dead Son Has Changed Nothing,' says Father of Drowned Syrian Refugee Boy Alan Kurdi. *The Telegraph,* September 3. http://www.telegraph.co.uk/news/2016/09/01/photo-of-my-dead-son-has-changed-nothing-says-father-of-drowned/.

Fuentes, Marcela A. 2015. Performance, Politics, and Protest. In *What Is Performance Studies?,* ed. Diana Taylor and Marcos Steuernagel. Durham, NC: Duke University Press. http://scalar.usc.edu/nehvectors/wips/performance-politics-and-protest.

The Center for Political Beauty. http://politicalbeauty.com/.

Kristeva, Julia. 1991. *Strangers to Ourselves.* Trans. Leon Roudiez. New York: Columbia University Press.

Kureishi, Hanif. 2014. The Migrant Has No Face, Status or Story. *The Guardian,* May 30. https://www.theguardian.com/books/2014/may/30/hanif-kureishi-migrant-immigration-1.

Lang, Berel. 2000. *Holocaust Representation: Art within the Limits of History and Ethics.* Baltimore: Johns Hopkins University Press.

Lefebvre, Henri. 1992. *The Production of Space.* Trans. Donald Nicholson-Smith. Oxford: Blackwell.

Levinas, Emmanuel. 1998. *Entre Nous: On Thinking-of-the-Other.* Trans. Michael B. Smith and Barbara Harshav. New York: Columbia University Press.

Lewicki, Aleksandra. 2017. 'The Dead Are Coming': Acts of Citizenship at Europe's Borders. *Citizenship Studies* 21 (3): 275–290.

Malzacher, Florian. 2010. The Scripted Realities of Rimini Protokoll. In *Dramaturgy of the Real on the World Stage,* ed. Carol Martin, 80–87. New York: Palgrave Macmillan.

Marschall, Anika. 2016. The State at Play? Notions of State(less)ness in Contemporary Interventionist Performances. *Critical Stages*, 14 (December). http://www.critical-stages.org/14/the-state-at-play-notions-of-statelessness-in-contemporary-interventionist-performances/.

Martin, Carol. 2006. Bodies of Evidence. *The Drama Review* 50 (3): 8–15.

Mund, Heike. 2015. Provocative Artists Rebury Remains of Refugee. DW.COM, June 17. http://www.dw.com/en/provocative-artists-rebury-remains-of-refugee/a-18522573.

Musyal, Sören. 2015. Den Lebenden die Toten. *The Europea*, June 25. http://www.theeuropean.de/soeren-musyal/10316-die-toten-kommen-kunstaktion-fuer-fluechtlinge.

Rancière, Jacques. 2009. *The Emancipated Spectator*. Trans. Gregory Elliott. London: Verso.

Richardson, Anna. 2005. The Ethical Limitations of Holocaust Literary Representation. *ESharp: Borders and Boundaries* 5 (Summer): 1–19. http://www.gla.ac.uk/media/media_41171_en.pdf.

Sontag, Suzan. 2003. *Regarding the Pain of Others*. New York: Verso.

The Center for Political Beauty. 2014. Aggressive Humanism: Of Democracy's Inability to Generate Great Human Rights Activists. Trans. Barbara Juch. *Medium*, July 9. https://medium.com/@politicalbeauty/aggressive-humanism-bbff64cf4296#.igfmeaete.

Verdery, Katherine. 2000. *The Political Lives of Dead Bodies: Reburial and Postsocialist Change*. New York: Columbia University Press.

Spectacular Bodies, Unsettling Objects: Material Performance as Intervention in Stereotypes of Refugees

Laura Purcell-Gates

Husam Abed is a Palestinian refugee puppetry artist who runs Dafa Puppet Theatre, based in Prague, with his Hungarian partner, Réka Deák. The company performs and facilitates workshops in refugee camps and theatre festivals across the Middle East and Europe, often focusing on the animation of found objects within camps. They prioritize simplicity and metaphor in their work, a core rationale for their use of puppetry and object theatre within performances that often incorporate the human body. For Dafa, puppetry and object theatre allow for a distancing from literal interpretation in performance, which can reinforce stereotypes by merely replicating surface codes of meaning. Instead, Dafa looks to puppetry and object theatre as modes of displacing and thereby transforming these codes, by transferring meaning from the human body into puppets, and from objects' functional use into symbolic associations. They are interested in the ways in which puppetry and object theatre can "transform the

L. Purcell-Gates (✉)
Bath Spa University, Bath, UK
e-mail: l.purcell-gates@bathspa.ac.uk

Y. Meerzon et al. (eds.), *Migration and Stereotypes in Performance and Culture*, Contemporary Performance InterActions,
https://doi.org/10.1007/978-3-030-39915-3_3

space" by turning a dining table, for example, into a representation of the earth. Their focus on using found objects allows them to bring traces of associations and use, objects' genealogies, into the performance space to layer the objects with additional meaning (Abed and Deák 2017). *The Smooth Life* is Abed's 2016 solo show, directed by Deák, exploring his family's history migrating between refugee camps, with a focus on Abed's experiences growing up and his complex relationship with his father. The piece is performed to small audiences in intimate settings such as apartment kitchens. Abed uses objects including grains of rice, photographs, a map, a frame drum, and puppets made from cardboard, wood, and family photographs as he leads the audience through his story. In this analysis, I focus on three types of materials that Abed and Deák utilize in the piece: grains of rice, a map of the Middle East, and photographs.

When I interviewed Abed and Deák in 2017, they spoke of their shared desire to tell Abed's personal story in a simple way, a task made difficult by the platform of history on which his story and that of his family has taken place. Deák described Abed's initial work on the show as being too overtly political, which prevented him from exploring his story beyond existing and well-rehearsed political and historical narratives—narratives that courted stereotype. As they developed the piece together, they focused on returning to the theme of simplicity, using puppetry and object manipulation to delve into the layers of the story without becoming fixed within flattened and foreclosed interpretations of events. This focus on simplicity led them to choose simple materials such as rice and wood, as well as "concrete" materials coded with political and social meanings such as a map and photographs, to trace Abed's story, and that of his family, with and alongside Abed's physical presence in the performance.

The Smooth Life therefore deploys both puppetry and object theatre at the centre of its storytelling. The term object theatre derives from *théâtre d'objets* in Europe that emerged during the 1980s and involved the theatrical animation of everyday objects (Margolies 2013). Object theatre overlaps with a genre coined by Frank Proschan in 1983 of "performing objects … material images of humans, animals, or spirits that are created, displayed, or manipulated in narrative or dramatic performance" (4). Proschan's definition links the animation of objects to puppetry—for example, when a match or a ball takes on the characteristic of a human subject. Today, *théâtre d'objets*, performing objects, and puppetry are often approached by scholars and practitioners as forms of "material performance," which draw on new materialisms including object-oriented ontologies to foreground the agency of inanimate objects. In puppetry scholar Dassia Posner's (2015, 5) words, material performance is "performance that assumes that inanimate matter contains agency not simply to mimic or mirror, but also to shape and create."

In my examination of object theatre, I draw on Bill's Brown's (2001) concept of thing theory, an area within new materialisms that focuses on the meanings given to objects by human subjects and the concurrent ways in which things mediate and partially constitute social relations and the human subject. Brown draws on Heidegger's differentiation between "things" (that which exists in the world prior to human interpretation) and "objects"(that which is used or worked with)—to distinguish the ontic "thing" (that which can exist without subjects) from the ontological "object" (a specific creation of subjects). I draw on Brown's emphasis on the ways in which ontological objects mediate and constitute social relations and the human subject in my examination of puppetry and object theatre in *The Smooth Life*, and the ways in which such human/object interactions can intervene in and disrupt the stereotyping of representations of refugees in which images are fixed and depth of meaning is collapsed into foreclosed interpretation. I also turn my focus to the ontic thing in order to consider the ways in which material attributes and processes, such as decay, figure into the performance alongside the object's mediation and constitution of social relations.

I focus in particular on the notion of detritus, or that which is discarded and excluded from use-value, linking the detritus of decaying objects to the process of human abjection within the stereotype. I draw here on Imogen Tyler's (2013) analysis of social abjection of asylum seekers in *Revolting Subjects: Social Abjection and Resistance in Neoliberal Britain*, in which she examines the ways in which media, political, and social discourses around asylum seekers in twenty-first century UK have contributed to an "asylum invasion complex" marked by a "deliberate conflation of migrants into a singular national abject—the bogus asylum seeker" that limits any transformative potential of the recognition of suffering and injustice. Arguing that this relentless dehumanization is a necessary component to the maintenance of the neoliberal state, Tyler advocates a critical counter-mapping grounded in affect—or melancholic states—as a necessary response:

> The recognition of suffering and injustice has limited transformatory political potential in a context where the deliberate conflation of migrants into a singular national abject—the bogus asylum seeker—has overwhelmed public

> culture. Nevertheless, the *melancholic states* that critical processes of counter-mapping make visible are important critical responses to the ontological obliteration of personhood that is central to Britain's neoliberal immigration industry. This mapping can produce alternative ways of looking, however partial, depressed, reactive and liminal the ensuing knowledge might be. (76)

One form of such counter-mapping, I suggest, is a theatrical remapping of material detritus from an abjection model—the exclusion of detritus as part of subject formation and accepted social relations—to a model in which detritus forms a central component of subject formation and social relations through its foregrounding as site of meaning and affect. To return to Brown's (2001) formulation of the ontological object, I suggest that in theatrical contexts that invite spectators to participate in the affect produced by objects typically dismissed as "mere things"—what Brown describes as "beneath objecthood"—the processes of abjection that underpin stereotyped representations of refugee bodies can be reconfigured from an inclusion/exclusion model to a space to *linger* with these excluded objects, bodies, and feelings. This process is layered and deepened by paying attention to what is happening with materiality in the space. In *The Smooth Life*, this attention reveals materials insisting on humanity (rice) and materials (maps and photographs) whose decay matters.

Rice and Abjection

In a 2016 video of the show performed in a Swedish apartment kitchen, Abed introduces himself to the audience, then leaves his assistant to show a PowerPoint presentation that contextualizes his family's history while he begins cooking dinner for the audience in the background. Abed and Deák discussed with me their interest in sharing food with the people with whom they come into contact through their work. For them, making and eating meals together is a core component of community building, and one that they always incorporate into their puppetry work whether facilitating workshops or performing shows. Often this communal meal takes place following the theatrical event; in *The Smooth Life* it is embedded into the show itself.

In the piece, Abed makes multiple uses of grains of rice. He cites two sources for this choice: a saying from his grandfather that Palestinians are spread all over the world in diaspora like grains of rice that have been thrown, and a workshop he took with Simon Rann of the Philippe Genty

Company in which they worked with multiple materials including rice (2017). This workshop planted in Abed's imagination the idea of using rice in a theatre piece, which became the impetus for the decision while making *The Smooth Life*. For Abed and Deák, using rice on the map allowed them to play with a fluctuating metaphor anchored by a solid object. The map in this context represents solidity, both literally and figuratively, as it refers to a concrete reality even though, as discussed above, they strategically depict this concrete reality as fluctuating and contested. Abed emphasizes that using rice as a metaphor made it easier to talk about Palestine without becoming too literal. Addressing the material properties of rice and its potential for theatrical use, Deák describes rice as "so fragile, so small, so tiny, you can cook it, eat it." Abed identifies an additional layer of meaning: "If you put all these grains of rice together in [a] big sack, it has its weight, it's effective." For Abed and Deák, rice therefore serves as a potent metaphor for diaspora in exile, in which people who might feel weak separately are able to bring their abilities together in a collective. The use of rice also allows Abed and Deák to play with scale, as the human body is depicted from the small-scale grain of rice through the slightly larger-scale puppets and finally the life-size body of Abed. As each of these scales are performed on the map, they are simultaneously rendered larger-than-life in contrast to the map dimensions, providing spectators with multiple layers of perception of the scale of the human body on the stage of human-created border demarcations.

Rice makes its first appearance behind the audience as Abed boils water and begins cooking a chicken and rice casserole. As the audience watches the PowerPoint presentation, the sounds of dry rice being poured into a pot are audible in the background. When the PowerPoint presentation ends and Abed returns to the table, he introduces the audience to members of his family, represented by individual grains of rice which he carefully picks up on his finger, kisses, then lays on the map covering the table. As Abed describes his family's movement between camps, he carefully shifts the grains of rice along the surface of the map. Members of the audience peer closely at these individual rice grains, which have been given an affective resonance of loved individuals by Abed's gentle and personal interactions.

Abed traces his father's journey from Karama Refugee Camp to Baqa'a Palestinian Refugee Camp in Jordan in 1968, where Abed is born and the family begins to grow. The individual grains of rice are replaced with a mound of rice poured over the site on the map, leaving a small mountain of grains. "But it didn't happen like this," Abed states, repeating a trope within the piece that questions its own narration. "But the story—my story—didn't start here," a repeated line as he begins telling the story, questions the origins of a personal story that is connected both biologically to ancestors and additionally to multiple intertwined historical narratives. When Abed forms the rice into a mound on the map and says "But it didn't happen like this," he is referring to the previous moments in which he performed, in a gentle and humorous way, family members leaving camps by carefully placing them in different places on the map with a kiss, implying that their movements were as gentle as his physical handling of them. In fact, these moments referenced the forced Palestinian migrations of 1948, so it "didn't happen like this."

"But it didn't happen like this" marks a shift in tone for the piece from gentle and humorous to tense. Abed pushes the mound of rice to the Palestinian portion of the map. He stares at it for a moment, then smashes it with his fist, scattering grains of rice across the map. When the grains of rice cease to be singular individuals given emotional resonance through Abed's intimate interactions with them, and instead are simply poured into a mound, a doubling of perception occurs that is central to puppetry and object theatre. The grains of rice continue to represent individual humans on a larger scale, and simultaneously conjure imagery of maggots, uncomfortably resonating with discourses of filth and contagion—"swarms," "scum," "sewage"—central to Tyler's (2013) analysis of the asylum invasion complex. Abed's smashing of the pile with his fist therefore resonates not only as the representation of historical violence, but in the moment of performance the audience is invited to have a visceral response of horror (these are loved individuals) and disgust (associated with maggots).[1]

Abed continues his piece with a focus now on more conventional puppets, small wooden carved figures with Abed's family photographs for faces, though he continually returns to the animation of rice grains. Rice performances shift between people in the narrative, to food that Abed and his siblings crave, to musical instruments as it is poured into the frame drum, to water pouring over Abed, leaving rice grains stuck to his head (Fig. 1). Abed describes these moments as drawn from a childhood ritual, when his grandmother would wash him in a circular bathtub. He wished to reenact this ritual of bathing/purification using rice which carries multiple connotations in the piece: of his family members, and in this moment of seeds and thus the potential of rebirth. The moment both invests the

Fig. 1 Husam Abed with rice and drum in *The Smooth Life* (2016). Image by Dafa Puppet Theatre

grains of rice with additional layers of meaning, and enmeshes the notion of family with that of potential and rebirth.

At the end of the piece, Abed brings out his chicken casserole and serves it to the audience. The dish contains cooked rice and is thus imbued with the strands of meaning that have been woven into rice throughout the performance. The act of consuming rice in this moment holds multiple layers of significance. Margolies describes food as acting on and altering the person consuming it: "it is the material most apt to call into question the fixed division between living and lifeless matter" (2015, 330). Bennett (2010) positions food as an actant

> in an agent assemblage that includes among its members my metabolism, cognition, and moral sensibility ... Food, as a self-altering, dissipative materiality ... enters into what we become. It is one of the many agencies operative in the moods, cognitive dispositions, and moral sensibilities that we bring to bear as we engage the questions of what to eat, how to get it, and when to stop. (51)

In the moment of communal consumption of rice at the end of *The Smooth Life*, these multiple ontologies of food as a material intersect with the multiple strands of significance with which rice has been layered throughout the performance. The moment is potent and has provoked different responses from audience members. Abed and Deák describe a performance of the piece in Jordan in which some audience members reacted negatively to this moment: "You are eating the refugees now!" This was not Dafa's intention; Abed emphasizes that communal eating is associated, amongst other things, with the process of death: "When people die, you celebrate death by life [eating], we are still here, we exist—this is what I want to say" (2017). This moment, for Abed, is about celebrating life, and through the communal meal celebrating the fact that "we still exist, this is our identity, this is who we are." He also associates it with a culture of generosity and of hosting people that he connects to being Palestinian.

The communal meal at the end of *The Smooth Life* enacts these intentions and functions as a locus on which multiple meanings are played out. The audience members' reactions in Jordan point to the symbolism of ingesting the food that has been imbued with additional layers of meaning, though it is not the only possible reaction to this symbolism. One alternate response I would like to consider is that the moment of shared eating enacts abjection in reverse. The object with its array of ontological meanings—including exclusion from human subjectivity—is consumed into the bodies of everyone involved in the theatrical event. Each of these object animations retains the doubling of perception initiated by Abed's opening introductions of and affectionate interactions with his family: the grains of rice are always the loved individuals that Abed gently kissed, even as they shift representations. An affective response towards the grains of rice has been established that resonates throughout their multiple enactments, lending a sense of care and humanity to "mere things." This elevates them to the status of ontological object that retains its human-associated status even when being used as accessory to human narrative and, ultimately, as human food. If the process of abjection is about dehumanization in the service of subject formation in order to construct boundaries around the human, Abed's use of object theatre in his multiple deployments of rice is about insisting on a lingering humanization of that which would normally lie outside those boundaries. This provides a critical counter-mapping, in Tyler's (2013) terms, grounded in affect and opening space to experience differently that which is normally excluded from the human.

Mapping and Metaxis

The theme of mapping frames *The Smooth Life*. At the centre of the performance space, around which the audience sits and on which Abed and the puppets/objects perform, is a large circular wooden turntable, covered by a map of the Middle East. Dafa Puppet Theatre structure their work around the ontology of objects, and according to Deák they used the map in the piece because a map has the same type of reality as a photo in that it is a "real object" with use-value. They chose the round table for its associations with the earth on which the map sits, layering the map-object with both its functional and symbolic meanings. Early in the devising process, Abed simply opened the map on the table, emphasizing its functional use. Later, he and Deák decided to fix it to the table "because we felt it had to be fixed" (2017). Abed describes this decision to make the map a permanent part of the table as an intervention in the performance space and connects it to a feature of puppet theatre to "change the space." He and Deák wished to transform the experience of "where are we now" for the spectators by introducing the table first as a dining table, then allowing it to shift meaning through the presence of the map.

As a dramaturgical device, the map allows Abed and Deák to intertwine the multiple stories in the piece which share themes of travelling, immigration, and evacuation. The map's physical presence on the table helps Abed make visible his journey as well as those of his parents and grandparents, including which camps his grandparents entered and left, the journey of Abed's mother returning to Baqa'a camp on an airplane, the family's journey from Damascus to Iran, and Abed's father taking Abed in a car back to Jordan. For Abed and Deák, making these journeys visible was of central importance to the piece, yet they wanted to find a way to avoid being "too concrete, too political" in order to tell a story that could function on a symbolic level and not become too associated with "daily politics" (2017). The map therefore represents concrete reality in symbolic form, and the forms of puppetry and object theatre Abed uses on the map allow for a layering of metaphor and a focus on a personal story that can shift across and between the boundaries of overdetermined historical and political narratives. According to Deák, this was a key strategy, as the difficulties of freeing the story from this narrative overdetermination was not only on the spectators' side but on Abed's as well. Specifically, Abed and Deák's aim for the piece was to avoid stereotypes of Palestinian victimization that would foreclose alternate meanings for Abed's story, both in its telling and its reception. Such a foreclosure of meaning, for Abed, would prevent specificity and render invisible moments that punctured this narrative overdetermination.

On a personal scale, this approach allowed Abed to explore the specificity of his own story; on a larger scale it was linked for Abed to his officially unrecognized existence of Palestine, which contests his identity as a Palestinian refugee. Sonja Kuftinec (2009) writes:

> The contested triangle of land between the Jordan River, the Mediterranean Sea, and the Gulf of Aqaba serves not only as a stage *for* conflict, but also spatially stages the vectors *of* that conflict, particularly control over boundaries of land, identity, historical narratives, and acceptable political action. That is, conflict enters not only on the land *per se*, but on who locates and controls territorial boundaries and passage through them, and what (often depersonalized) logic sustains that control. (108)

Abed and Deák's use of a map intentionally sought to intervene in this staging of conflict through mapping Abed's story and his identity on and through a map of Palestine. As they developed the piece, they struggled to find a map that identified "Palestine," until they spotted one by chance at a shop in Prague. This is the map they continue to use in the performance, and the issue of its transformation and decay as an object—at some point it will become so faded and torn that it will be unusable—is of crucial importance due to the difficulty they will find in replacing it.

This object decay and its implications for *The Smooth Life* serve as an experiential metaphor for Abed's continual struggle for validated existence as a Palestinian refugee. His ability to tell his story as he chooses is linked to the material existence and legibility of a rare map that he will struggle to replace. The act of repeatedly telling his story using the map contributes to its decay, putting him in an impossible position: to preserve the map, he cannot tell his story, yet once the map becomes detritus without use-value, his story and identity are rendered invisible. Jane Bennett (2010) proposes a vital materialism to trouble distinctions between matter and life, drawing on Latour to argue for an agentic materiality—matter as "actant." Eleanor Margolies (2015) draws on this approach in her investigation of puppetry/object performance that uses formless materials such as food, clay, and compost. While Margolies' focus is on formless materials in performance and their potential to tell stories that "extend beyond the human in time and space, working on cosmological, geological, or evolutionary timescales" (332), I wish to consider Abed's map, and its potential to tell stories beyond the apparent narrative and its symbolic role in performance, through the lens of this vital materialistic approach to puppetry and object theatre.

This requires a brief diversion into, and slight repurposing of, Augusto Boal's (1995) concept of metaxis, the "state of belonging completely and simultaneously to two different, autonomous worlds: the image of reality and the reality of the image" (43). For Boal, metaxis is derived from Plato's use of the term to denote the middle space between humans and gods which dynamically negotiates the totality of the universe. In Boal's usage it allows for an understanding of the transformative potential of theatre and forms a central analytic for his Theatre of the Oppressed techniques, including Forum Theatre, in which the space between performer and spectator is renegotiated to construct the "spect-actor," and Image Theatre, in which participants become aware of themselves simultaneously existing in the world and witnessing themselves engaging with the world. The term is often understood in general terms as referring to simultaneously existing in the real and the imagined, facilitated by theatrical practice. Warren Linds (2006) expands on this definition to include considerations of metaxis in the natural world. This includes drawing on scholars such as Humberto Maturana and Francisco Varela to link Boal's metaxis to biological systems such as ants self-organizing into anthills, in which "the function of each component is to participate in the production or transformation of the set of relations" (Linds 2006, 116). Linds also draws on Fritjof Capra's distinction between designed and emergent systems, and his argument for thinking systematically in order to tap into the metaxic space of the web of interconnections within and between humans and the world. For Linds, considering Boal's metaxis through the lens of biological systems and systemic analysis contributes to comprehending and utilizing the liberatory potential of theatrical processes. By foregrounding the ways in which systems, of which we are always a part, change, we can harness that potential for change by embracing the "groundlessness" of being liberated from an ontological either/or perspective (Maturana and Varela quoted in Linds 2006, 115).

This linking of Boalian theatrical metaxis to the material world of humans/animals/systems resonates both with Bennett's (2010) call to reconsider nonorganic/organic boundaries and the false equating of life and agency solely to the latter, and with Margolies' (2015) framing of theatrical use of formless materials as extending human stories in time and space. By considering Abed's performance with the map as a metaxic system, Abed and the map are embedded together in the decay of the map and the stakes of this decay for Abed. They are part of one material process within which the lens of focus can be trained on, for example, the material decay of the map—accelerated by Abed's performance with it—or on the process of Abed negotiating his identity within official non-recognition. What is crucial here is that both events are material processes and systems within which the object and the human are intertwined: Abed's identity is threatened with the status of detritus alongside the map's decay into detritus. A focus on such processes as interconnected dynamic systems, as Linds suggests following Maturana and Varela, sidesteps the foreclosure of meaning and the tendency towards fixed knowledge:

> Groundlessness welcomes the unexpected. Whenever we find ourselves holding tightly to being in a certain place, or seek to control outcomes, the in-between invites us to step into "another domain where coexistence takes place" (Maturana and Varela 1992, 246), a both/and rather than an either/or space. When knowing and experiencing are located in the shifting terrain of in-between-ness, new possibilities emerge for action and knowing. (2006, 115)

Abed's performance with the map, as an ongoing process of metaxic repetition, allows for new possibilities of action and knowing. Such a process avoids the foreclosure of meaning that Abed and Deák wished to work against as they created a piece that attempts to resist stereotypes as it transverses overdetermined narrative vectors of political power, contested land, victimization framings, and national and personal identities.

Stereotyped Images and Decaying Photographs

I turn now to Abed's mobilization of photographs within the piece. As discussed above, the piece begins with a PowerPoint presentation that reads as a documentary of sorts, providing context for the forced migration of Abed's family and tracing their movements between refugee camps. This performance mode mimics familiar media framings of historical narratives, and it is easy for the audience to "read" the photographs on the slides as their positions as consumers of media are highly familiar and rehearsed. When Abed later brings out a tattered photo album with similar family pictures and presents puppets with cutouts of the faces of family members from these photographs (Fig. 2), the position of the spectator is unsettled; this is a personal use of photographs that sits outside of the circulation of images in the media. The intimacy of the setting, a kitchen, and

Fig. 2 Husam Abed with photographs in *The Smooth Life* (2016). Image by Dafa Puppet Theatre

Abed's physical proximity to the audience seated around the table blurs the lines between theatrical event and social interaction, transforming the social relations that constitute this moment of image consumption.

The puppetry furthers this unsettling, as pictures of faces that the audience initially consumed through a familiar documentary-style performance are now a material part of a human figure animated by Abed. This performatively enacts another moment of double-vision. The stereotyped image is literally combined with a performing object that resists this fixity through both its phenomenological "thereness," to use Andrew Sofer's term (quoted in Posner 2015, 5)—these are carved and painted pieces of wood sitting on the table—and through its status as a puppet, both alive (human subject) and dead (object). As mentioned above, puppetry and object theatre are fertile sites for the unsettling of flattened representation through their double status as alive/dead, human/object. When Abed presents a puppet with a photograph of a face that we have previously seen in its stereotyped form, the stereotype itself becomes unsettled, simultaneously retaining and disrupting its fixed associations. It is in this space of unsettled doubling, I suggest, that a useful critical remapping can occur.

At the end of the piece, following the story of his father's death, Abed places a painted wooden box on the table. He lifts one side of the box, places the puppet figure of his father inside, and gently closes it. He turns the box around to reveal windows, then begins turning a handle causing photographs to scroll across the windows on the inside of the box.

This is an object that Abed has been exploring in Dafa's work for several years. He describes it as a nineteenth and early twentieth-century form of Arabic storytelling with multiple names, primarily *Sandook aldonia*, literally translated as "life box." Other names include *Sandook alajab* or "wonder box," and *Sandook alfurja* or "watching box" (2017). In workshops, Dafa uses the *Sandook aldonia* to facilitate participants telling stories from their lives by placing photographs inside the box, then using the handle to scroll the images across the windows as they tell their stories. In *The Smooth Life*, Abed used the *Sandook aldonia* to wordlessly tell the story of his father in the moments of his death, visually representing the idea of one's life flashing before their eyes. By placing the puppet of his father inside the *Sandook aldonia*, the box becomes his coffin. Layered with the scrolling images of his life, the box is simultaneously a coffin and a "life box"; Abed emphasizes that "this is our [family's] life box, this is our life." The box here with its windows opening onto photographic images suggests the screen on which media images are displayed and from which they are consumed within a circulation of the stereotype. The presence of the physical box and its hand-operated scrolling mechanism opening onto a view of print photographs detaches the "screen" from its mediatized economy, inviting spectators to witness and consume the photographs in a different way. The presence of the puppet of Abed's father inside the box adds an additional layer of materiality to the photographs, providing an actual depth to the "screen" that masks a body.

In addition to these symbolic connections to death, Abed's use of physical photographs in the piece can also be linked to detritus, as the photographs are decaying. The process of converting physical photographs to digital form for media presentation freezes the process of decay, effectively removing the materiality of the object from the realm of life, aging, and death. Margolies (2015) notes the potential of material performance that foregrounds the "unseen liveliness of matter," arguing that "[r]ather than attempting to create an illusion of life in the lifeless, such performances highlight the process of humans noticing and responding to fundamental material properties, as well as the variety of possible interactions between humans and the material world" (322–323). In this case, the fundamental material properties of the photographs are again doubled: they are both material objects that are becoming faded, creased, and torn, and faces of Abed's family members who have, since the taking of the photograph, aged and/or died. They carry material and affective traces of their travels with Abed and his family. In their representation on the PowerPoint, the audience knows to consume them as historical artifacts, representations of a fixed past. As components of the puppets on the table, they are material witnesses to Abed's story that are aging and decaying in the moment of performance, occupying an ontological space outside of the fixity of media-driven representation. Having already been scanned into digital format, the photographs are detritus. They no longer have functional use; yet in this moment of performance, they are inextricably bound with Abed's personal narrative and physical presence, inseparable from his own aging body in the room.

Conclusion

In *The Smooth Life*, the potential of material performance to unsettle processes of exclusion is harnessed through processes of doubling and ontological instability. Processes of exclusion that are addressed in the piece include national and identity erasure, overdetermined narratives that foreclose multiple meanings, and the reduction of objects to "mere things," each of which enacts an abjection that produces human and material detritus. I have suggested that Abed and Deák made strategic use of the materials to subvert, interrupt, and deftly work around stereotypes grounded in and producing abjected bodies in order for Abed to trace a personal, flexible, and shifting story through a landscape of fixities of meaning. Rice functions both as a metaphor for family and abjected bodies, and as food that is ingested by Abed and the audience in a process that enacts a reversal of abjection. The physical, concrete presence of an officially unsanctioned map that asserts Abed's identity as a Palestinian refugee functions as both a material assertion of identity and as a transformative space of metaxis within which identity is continually negotiated. Abed deploys photographs in a mode of familiar, fixed media images, and subverts this mode of image consumption by placing material photographs in the performance space. This subversion is additionally layered with the material properties and processes of the photographs that carry traces of Abed's past as they age and decay.

Material performance in *The Smooth Life* has two functions in resisting and subverting stereotypes. The first function focuses on the strategic use of the material object by the human performer to produce particular affects and perceptions. The latter focuses on the material properties of both the object and the human body, on what these multiple materials *do* in the performance space as they operate together as an interconnected system of transformation and decay through which affect and perception circulate and, potentially, shift. This dual function marks Brown's (2001, 4) distinction between "objects" and "things" in which closer attention to the ways in which the object asserts itself as a thing allows for an understanding of the object as not merely an object separate from the subject, but as a particular subject–object relation. This distinction is key to the emerging deployments of thing theory and new materialisms in theatre and performance studies. In *Performing Objects and Theatrical Things*, Marlis Schweitzer and Joanne Zerdy (2014) suggest that "Where this work (possibly) departs from its historical predecessors is in the willingness of human artists and audiences to listen to and act on object lessons and to rethink their relationship with nonhuman entities" (3).

In this analysis I have sought both to focus on Abed and Deák's strategic use of materials in the performance and to consider the ways in which a focus on the "object lessons" in the piece layered these strategies with meanings enmeshed in material processes which incorporate ontologies of human and object. Both arenas of focus are ways of paying attention to the material in the space, following Brown's (2001, 1–2) metaphor drawn from A.S. Byatt's *The Biographer's Tale* of shifting one's focus from looking *through* a window, the functional use of the object, to looking instead *at* it and seeing the dirt on the glass. Practitioners of puppetry and object theatre inherently pay attention to materials as they manipulate them to create perceptions and affects. By deepening and sharpening this to include an attentiveness to materiality and the ways in which both puppetry and object theatre are modes of material performance, the human subject is brought into relation with the materials in the piece. This disrupts the process of fixing meaning central to the stereotype, in this case towards refugee bodies, both by asking audience members to linger with the affects and perceptions produced by ontologically destabilized detritus and by disrupting models of inclusion/exclusion that incorporate the full spectrum of materiality in the space.

Note

1. In my 2017 interview with Abed and Deák, I described my interpretation of this moment and asked whether the "maggot" reference had been intentional. Abed confirmed that this reading had not been their intention, but said that their use of materials and objects in the piece was meant to function on multiple metaphoric levels, and therefore he welcomed various interpretations.

References

Abed, Husam. 2016. The Smooth Life. *Vimeo*, October 23. https://vimeo.com/188585280.

Abed, Husam, and Réka Deák. 2017. Interviewed by Laura Purcell-Gates, July 4.

Bennett, Jane. 2010. *Vibrant Matter: A Political Ecology of Things*. Durham: Duke University Press.

Boal, Augusto. 1995. *The Rainbow of Desire: The Boal Method of Theatre and Therapy*. London: Routledge.

Brown, Bill. 2001. Thing Theory. *Critical Inquiry* 28 (1): 1–22.

Kuftinec, Sonja. 2009. *Theatre, Facilitation, and Nation Formation in the Balkans and Middle East*. London: Palgrave Macmillan.

Linds, Warren. 2006. Metaxis: Dancing (in) the in-between. In *A Boal Companion: Dialogues on Theatre and Cultural Politics*, ed. Jan Cohen-Cruz and Mady Schutzman, 114–124. London: Routledge.

Margolies, Eleanor. 2013. Arthur Rimbaud and the Puppets in Charlestown. *Times Literary Supplement*, September 25. https://www.the-tls.co.uk/articles/public/arthur-rimbaud-and-the-puppets-in-charlestown.

———. 2015. Return to the Mound: Animating Infinite Potential in Clay, Food, and Compost. In *The Routledge Companion to Puppetry and Material Performance*, ed. Dassia N. Possner, Claudia Orenstein, and John Bell, 322–335. London: Routledge.

Posner, Dassia N. 2015. Material Performance(s). In *The Routledge Companion to Puppetry and Material Performance*, ed. Dassia N. Possner, Claudia Orenstein, and John Bell, 5–7. London: Routledge.

Proschan, Frank. 1983. The Semiotic Study of Puppets, Masks, and Performing Objects. *Semiotica* 47 (1–4): 3–44.

Schweitzer, Marlis, and Joanne Zerdy. 2014. Introduction: Object Lessons. In *Performing Objects and Theatrical Things*, ed. Marlis Schweitzer and Joanne Zerdy, 1–20. London: Palgrave Macmillan.

Tyler, Imogen. 2013. *Revolting Subjects: Social Abjection and Resistance in Neoliberal Britain*. London: Zed Books.

Theatrical Border Crossings: Stereotypes against Realism in the Plays of Young Jean Lee

Kee-Yoon Nahm

Since her debut as a playwright-director in 2003, Young Jean Lee has attracted critical attention for her bold theatre pieces that tackle racism, feminist subjectivity, religion, and other political themes that require deft handling. Her style is difficult to pin down, as she adopts entirely different techniques and approaches for each new project, usually building her pieces out of discussions and improvisation sessions with her cast members on a pressing contemporary issue rather than preparing a completed script before rehearsals begin. Nevertheless, she has gained a reputation for creating ingenious, thought-provoking theatre; a review for one of her pieces in the *New York Times* begins: "Young Jean Lee is, hands down, the most adventurous downtown playwright of her generation" (Isherwood 2012). Before founding her own theatre company in 2003 in order to produce and fund her own work, Lee avidly followed the work of experimental theatre companies based in New York, such as the Wooster Group,

K.-Y. Nahm (✉)
Illinois State University, Normal, IL, USA
e-mail: knahm@ilstu.edu

Y. Meerzon et al. (eds.), *Migration and Stereotypes in Performance and Culture*, Contemporary Performance InterActions,
https://doi.org/10.1007/978-3-030-39915-3_4

New York City Players, and Radiohole (Clements 2017). As such, she follows in the footsteps of the American avant-garde, favouring patchy structures and sensory disorientation over the smoothness of conventional plot and character. Despite her distance from mainstream theatre and the deliberately off-putting nature of her work, Lee's career took off in the past decade. Her play *Straight White Men*, which premiered in 2014, was produced at the Hayes Theatre in 2018, making Lee the first Asian-American female playwright on Broadway.

As Lee gains mainstream recognition, this is an opportune time to take stock of her earlier career, in which she was primarily known for innovative pieces that explored representations and stereotypes of people of colour in the United States. Indeed, her success is especially noteworthy considering the ways in which her previous work purposefully deployed racist imagery to make audiences uncomfortable, a tactic that has given her the nickname "a queen of unease" (Soloski 2015). She prevents responses that treat her work as a satire of racist stereotypes as artifacts of the past, instead forcing her spectators to grapple head-on with these offensive images and the feelings of shame, guilt, and disgust that they produce.

In this chapter, I examine two works, *Songs of the Dragons Flying to Heaven* (2006) and *The Shipment* (2009), in which Lee seeks to affect the audience's perceptions of race. Her plays do not overtly perform migrant experiences and representations, although *Songs of the Dragons* engages with Orientalist stereotypes that impact Asian immigrants and their American-born children. Still, I argue that her ingenious handling of racial representation—for example, the enactment of African American stereotypes in *The Shipment*—critically intervenes in the cultural economy of the United States where images of Others (including migrants) are produced and consumed. In the first section of this chapter, I provide an overview of the ways in which racial stereotypes have been handled in theatre and performance vis-à-vis more "truthful" representations of people of colour before demonstrating the ways in which Lee's work both stages and undermines the distinction between these two categories. Moreover, I highlight the ways in which Lee politicizes theatrical form itself, asking who has had access to realist characterization—in other words, complex, individuated figures that connote psychological depth and socio-political agency. The jarring collision of explicit racist stereotypes and characters seemingly grounded in everyday reality exposes the ways in which realism has buttressed whiteness and nationalism on the American stage, often at the expense of people of colour and recent migrants. Drawing from Henry Giroux's (2005) work on border pedagogy, I argue that Lee's experimental theatre counteracts the ideological power of stereotypes by turning the audience into border crossers across theatrical forms, an intervention that can make up for limitations in approaches that advocate for "accurate" representations of stereotyped groups.

The Border Between Stereotype and Realism

At least from the perspective of aesthetics and technique, realist characterization and stereotype seem to oppose one another. We generally evaluate a fictional character as "realistic" to the extent that its creator does *not* resort to stereotypes. Narrowing the focus to the history of drama and theatre, think of how characters in Henrik Ibsen and George Bernard Shaw's plays assert their "truthfulness" (which is to say their modernity) against a background of stock characters and ethnic caricatures in nineteenth-century melodrama, vaudeville, and minstrel shows. In the early to mid-twentieth century, growing demands to abolish harmful stereotypes of women, people of colour, and other socially alienated groups were accompanied by the call to create "realistic" representations of these minorities and their experiences, ideally by writers and performers who belong to the formerly stereotyped group in question. Theatrical realism served not only as a tool for raising awareness of social issues in modern drama since Ibsen; it was also a coveted cultural apparatus that allowed minority groups to replace distorted images and prejudiced associations with respectable and empathetic characters. Thus, the 1959 Broadway production of Lorraine Hansberry's social realist play *A Raisin in the Sun* is celebrated as a landmark event in African American theatre history for opening a field of representation that was previously exclusive to the white mainstream.

In this chapter, I propose a limited definition of the term "realism" that highlights the politics of racial representation in theatre and performance. I use realism as a mode of characterization in theatre that is delineated in opposition to past stereotypes. In this context, it is less important how "authentic" the character is than the fact that they challenge histories of racist representation onstage. It is somewhat of a commonplace to invoke a relational binary of stereotypical and realist characterization in American theatre historiography that focuses on various post-Civil War movements.[1] For example, Harvey Young (2013, 7–8) defines African American theatre as "the effects of artists who challenged widely popular Jim Crow stereotypes and caricatures who more accurately resembled—in look, mannerism, and everyday concerns—the folks who resided in black neighborhoods." Theatre that engages with racial politics often becomes a struggle between modes of representation: Lena Younger in *A Raisin in the Sun* against the Mammy stereotype in earlier American popular culture.[2] Brian Herrera (2015, 138) calls the stereotype "an unyielding antagonist in a sustained battle over the discursive features of representational truth." The very act of calling out racial stereotypes implies an interventionist alternative that, I argue, entails a *discourse* of realism, even if critics and artists disagree on what this mode of representation looks like in practice. (Few of the Latina/o performances that Herrera examines conform to the tradition of American realist drama.)

The binary of realism and stereotype can be mapped onto other binaries with political ramifications, such as mainstream and fringe, domestic and foreign, Self and Other. Thus, the binary creates a border that separates characters into those who are culturally "in" and "out." My intention is not to reify this theatrical border; as I will discuss below, Lee structures her plays so that spectatorship moves across it. Before discussing Lee's work, however, it is worth considering the privilege (and thus the political repercussions) of racial representations crossing over to the realist side: namely, the privilege of being apprehended, rationally and emotionally, as human. Ntozake Shange (1992, 68) wrote in her introduction to *spell #7*, a play that stages the conflict of stereotype and authenticity in performances of blackness: "i have not ceased to be amazed when i hear members of an audience whispering to one another in the foyers of theaters /that they had never imagined they cd feel so much for characters/ even though they were black." Freedom from stereotypes was (and still is) a priority for theatre artists of colour because they clear a path for empathy. In other words, the push into realist territory counters the dehumanizing force of the stereotype, a force that in turn validates discrimination and exclusion of the stereotyped group, if not outright violence towards them. Racial struggles in the theatre also play out as unseen struggles over borders of aesthetics, form, and dramaturgy.

However, realism itself came under critical scrutiny in the latter half of the twentieth century. Roland Barthes' (1989) concept of the "reality effect" demystified the textual codes that undergird realism's stake in verisimilitude. In theatre and performance studies, feminist critics in the late-twentieth century rigorously exposed the ideological foundations of realism, reading patriarchal and heteronormative regimes of truth into what was conventionally labelled "naturalistic" or "kitchen-sink" drama by the mid-twentieth century. Elin Diamond (1997, 4–5) argues that "realism, more than any other form of theatre representation, mystifies the process of theatrical signification" so that it becomes difficult to identify and challenge the cultural biases that sustain that representation of reality. This framework reveals that American realist drama in the tradition of Eugene O'Neill, Tennessee Williams, and Arthur Miller generally assumed a normative subjectivity that was straight, white, and male.[3] Furthermore, the focus on middle-class domesticity excluded recent migrants from realism's field of representation.

In step with these critical positions, theatre artists have explored theatrical alternatives to realism that specifically address its ideological foundations as a guarantor of normative realities. For example, the lesbian feminist theatre collective Split Britches lampooned sexist and heteronormative stereotypes through strategies of masquerade and gendered role playing, rather than pursue more realistic portrayals of women in "straight" plays.[4] George C. Wolfe's *The Colored Museum* (1986) includes a scene titled the "The Last Mama on the Couch Play" that spoofed Lorraine Hansberry's *A Raisin in the Sun*, or rather, the self-congratulatory discourse surrounding Hansberry's play—what Wolfe calls "the laziness of some white producers declaring, '*A Raisin in the Sun*. This is what it means to be Negro. This is what it means to be Black. We need to look no further, the search is done'" (quoted in Rugg and Young 2012, 416). Wolfe's biting satire demonstrates that the cultural legitimacy that comes with realist representation comes at the cost of subscribing to a white normative ideal, reducing black performance to a narrow notion of domestic realism modelled on canonical white playwrights. "The Last Mama on the Couch Play" shifts gears into a cliché-ridden all-black musical before regressing into a blackface minstrelsy sequence; the struggle between stereotype and realism comes full circle. This scene suggests that the white gaze can overpower any attempt to secure cultural legitimacy through realist representation.

In response, African American artists since the end of the twentieth century (including Wolfe) have purposefully revived racist stereotypes that were excised from the public sphere, calling attention to the economies of spectatorship that confine black performance regardless of theatrical form, in a trend that Shawn Marie Garrett (2002) dubbed the "return of the repressed." Similarly working with terminology adopted from psychoanalysis, José Esteban Muñoz (1999) established the concept of disidentification, a strategy integral to queer people of colour but one that has proven versatile enough to inform a broad range of minoritarian performances. According to Muñoz: "Disidentification is a mode of performance whereby a toxic identity is remade and infiltrated by subjects who have been hailed by such identity categories but have not been able to own such a label" (185). Muñoz's ideas resonate with other scholarship on the self-reflexive return to stereotypes in theatre and performance, such as Josephine Lee's (1997) discussion on harnessing "the seductive possibilities of the stereotype" to reclaim them for Asian American political consciousness, as well as Brian Herrera's (2015) coinage "executing the stereotype" to describe the ways in which Latina/o stereotypes in American popular culture are enacted in order to be buried. Underlying all of these theories is Homi K. Bhabha's (2004, 95) influential definition of the stereotype as both the "effect of probabilistic truth and predictability"—in other words, a discursive product of colonial power-knowledge—but one that "must always be in *excess* of what can be empirically proved or logically construed." It is this excess that renders any stereotype ambivalent, thus creating space to rewrite its racial script through embodied performance.

Working in this lineage, Lee also seeks to undermine the ideological power of stereotypes by overperforming them. However, her plays draw attention to the binary of stereotype and realism itself, the binary that I argue encapsulates racial performance in modern American theatre history. *Songs of the Dragons* and *The Shipment* both contain sharp transitions in modes of representation and spectatorship. Rather than slipping from a parody of domestic realism to an all-black musical and, finally, a blackface minstrelsy as in *The Colored Museum*, Lee intends the shifts between stereotype and realist characterization to be jarring and confusing.

I propose the term "theatrical border crossing" to describe this dramaturgical feature, in part to make the case that Lee's work offers unique insight into the politics of representing migration. As a means of moving beyond the framework of simply labelling migrant figures in mainstream culture as "good" or "bad," Lee targets the audience's mode of spectatorship, as opposed to the stereotyped migrant, as that which moves across borders of theatrical form, national identity, and race. While I do not want to necessarily ascribe an instructive function to Lee's work, I find parallels between Lee's deliberate shaping of the audience's perception and Henry Giroux's (2005, 20–21) notion of border pedagogy, which seeks to "create pedagogical conditions in which students become border crossers in order to understand otherness in its own terms," while also "educating students to both read [cultural] codes historically and critically while simultaneously learning the limits of such codes, including the ones they use to construct their own narratives and histories." *Songs of the Dragons* and *The Shipment* explode stereotypes of Asian Americans and African Americans on the one hand, but they also ingeniously expose the ways in which white normativity shapes perceptions of "realistic" characters, especially among white spectators who typically do not have to navigate this border in their identity formation. The work of Jacques Rancière (1991, 2009) informs my application of pedagogical theory to Lee's theatre. Beginning with the parable of the "ignorant schoolmaster," Rancière developed a definition of aesthetics that incites politically engaged and emancipatory modes of spectatorship through what he calls the "redistribution of the sensible." By way of the linkage among aesthetics, politics, and pedagogy that Rancière proposes, it is possible to apply Giroux's border pedagogy to Lee's work: *Songs of the Dragons* and *The Shipment* purposefully manipulate the audience's perceptions of race in ways that can shake loose the implicit biases and normative frameworks that guide our decoding of dramatic characters and stereotypes onstage.

To be clear, my intention is not to turn the border into a metaphor for theatrical form, to obscure actual border politics that dehumanize migrants and invalidate their experiences. Rather, I am interested in the ways in which theatrical forms interact with political lines. Realism as a form that historically served as a vessel for white normativity in American theatre can never be politically neutral. Such borders are not negated when playwrights of colour also write characters with psychological depth and social standing. Lee's plays place that border onstage so that the audience may cross it, casting theatrical realism as an object of aesthetic and ideological reflection rather than a container for either affirmative or critical representations of race.

Enforcing Borders: *Songs of the Dragons Flying to Heaven*

On numerous occasions, Lee has described her creative process as first identifying the play that she wants to write less than anything else, and then forcing herself to write it—a method that she learned from Mac Wellman when she studied playwriting at Brooklyn College. In an interview with the *New York Times*, she explains the purpose of this unconventional writing method: "My whole aesthetic is about fighting complacency. So if I make a show that goes against my instincts of what I want to do, that creates a very tense and complicated dynamic" (Piepenburg 2007).

That was the inception of *Songs of the Dragons*, Lee's attempt to write an identity politics play about her own background as a 1.5-generation Korean immigrant—an idea that gave her severe anxiety. The play features two groups of characters who take turns presenting disjointed, skit-like scenes that do not add up to a coherent plot. The first group consists of four Asian women. Three of them wear traditional Korean garments, strikingly colourful and billowy, in stark contrast to the minimalist set and modern costumes of the other characters. The three figures are virtually indistinguishable, more so because at first they speak only in their native languages which, according to Lee's (2009, 34) published text, would ideally be a mix of Korean, Chinese, and Japanese. In later scenes, they switch to broken English with heavy "Asian" accents. These women often engage in physical comedy, giggling while playfully slapping and chasing one another around the stage. Gradually, they accumulate stereotypical associations of exoticized Asian femininity, their childlike innocence slipping into hyper-sexualized images of obedient yet promiscuous young girls. These Asian women are denied any sense of agency. All they can do is smile back when the audience gawks and chuckles at their foreignness.

These Orientalist stereotypes mark Asian bodies as perpetually alien, becoming major obstacles for Korean Americans and other Asian immigrant communities in the United States.[5] Such racist imagery, ingrained in American popular culture, has a psychological toll on the fourth Asian woman in the play: the "Korean American." Unlike the others, she dresses in a T-shirt and jeans, and speaks assertively in impeccable English. From her very first lines in the play, the Korean American distinguishes herself from the rest of the group at their expense:

> Have you ever noticed how most Asian-Americans are slightly brain-damaged from having grown up with Asian parents? It's like being raised by monkeys [...]. Asian people from Asia are even more brain-damaged, but in a different way, because they are the original monkey. (Lee 2009: 39–40)

Later, she makes racist faces and gestures at the Koreans, and mimes kung fu and eating rice with chopsticks. She hates the other women for reinforcing the worst stereotypes of her ethnicity. But Lee is not interested in portraying the Korean American as a self-hating victim. Instead, the figure puts spectators in an awkward position as she constantly covets their approval and empathy regarding her harsh treatment of the others, as in the quotation above where the Korean American directly addresses the audience. The audience is forced to constantly second-guess Lee's intentions behind this explicit racism, uncertain whether the play is making fun of Koreans, making fun of stereotypical perceptions of Koreans, or passing off racism as satire, and so on in an inescapable loop.

Rather than resolve this tension, Lee offers her audiences relief. These disturbing scenes with Asian actors are alternated with scenes of a heterosexual white couple engaged in an extended diagnosis of their romantic relationship. The couple's dialogue is so insipid that it becomes an extended joke: they express a vague desire for excitement in their lives, pamper one another with adages of self-worth, indulge in fantasies of travelling to Africa, and discuss signing up for healthcare-covered couples counselling. At one point, White Person 1 says outright, "You know what's awesome? [...] Being white," to which White Person 2 responds nonchalantly, "I guess I never thought of it. And when I do think of it I feel like an asshole" (Lee 2009, 71). In contrast to the bizarre performances of the Korean women, the white couple is easily recognizable as a satire of white privilege and social insulation. It is easier to laugh comfortably at them, perhaps even empathize with them to a degree. Karen Shimakawa (2007, 100) observes that the white characters "seem suddenly, unexpectedly, *heartfelt*—it is difficult not to be moved by their naked emotionalism in these last moments." By allowing the audience to revert to conventional modes of spectatorship predicated on character psychology and emotionality (in other words, by placing the white couple closer to realism, however ironic the portrayal may be), Lee provides relief directly after scenes of acute racial unease. But then, the play returns once again to the weird Asians. The play's structure—alternating between these two groups of characters—begs the question: why is it difficult to have the same kind of sympathy for the Asian characters, who suffer much harsher ordeals? Does it have to do with their mode of representation?

The Korean American eventually fails to separate herself from her Othered sisters. She dons the same traditional garments and participates in a climactic movement sequence in which the four women take turns miming acts of gruesome self-mutilation and suicide. For example, "*Korean 3 cuts off her breast, bites a chunk out of it, throws her breast into the audience, [and] spits the chunk at the audience*" (Lee 2009, 64). Notably, Lee dampens the horror of this grotesque scene, as the women enact their repeated deaths to the sugary tune of Mariah Carey's "All I Want for Christmas Is You." This sequence utterly dehumanizes the Asian women. Stereotypically submissive to violence and bodily infringement, these Othered bodies are devoid of pain and consequence. Overwhelmed by incongruous sensory stimuli and racially charged imagery, it is difficult for the audience to *feel* anything.

The scene ends abruptly when the white characters reconquer the stage, shooing the Koreans away by "*shaking their chairs at the Koreans like lion tamers*" (Lee 2009, 64). There is no suggestion of physical force; the white characters awkwardly wield the chairs at a safe distance as if their hearts are not in it, while the Asians scamper offstage of their own accord. In a video recording that the Young Jean Lee Theatre Company has made available online, the audience laughs vocally at this ridiculous tableau—arguably the most vigorous guffaw in the performance.[6] *Songs of the Dragons* is carefully structured to elicit this laugh, granting audiences relief at the precise moment when the grotesque suicide sequence ends. Furthermore, Lee "tricks" spectators into laughing at Asian bodies being deported from the stage because their foreignness is just too much to handle. The women make one final interruption after this scene to deliver a half-serious apology to offended audiences and the Korean people in a droning voice. After they show themselves out with a deep bow, the white couple take full control of the stage, talking about their failing relationship for almost twenty minutes—about a quarter of the production's run-time—until the play ends.

The tableau of two white people chasing away a stereotyped minority group effectively draws a border on the stage. Or rather, *Songs of the Dragons* calls attention to a theatrical border that had been operating in the background all along, influencing the ways in which audiences responded differently to the Asian stereotypes and comparatively realistic white couple. Realist characterization trumps the discomfort of explicit stereotypes, which overlaps with the white normative mainstream's exclusion of inassimilable Asian and Asian American identity formations. In a self-reflexive manner, Lee rehearses the policing of this long-standing border in American society and culture. It enacts the border politics that separate two groups of people—Asian and white—and two racialized modes of representation—stereotype and realism. Lee explains: "Because naturalism is associated with white people, there's a racial divide. Stereotypes are people of colour and women, and naturalism is straight white men and [some] women" (pers. comm. 2014). She understands that any expression of Asian American experience under this schema must grapple with this invisible border. Indeed, realist family dramas by playwrights of colour are frequently perceived as being "about" racial identity, while realist plays by and about white people are rarely classified in this way. Writing the anti-identity politics play, Lee instead shows that theatrical borders have historically barred non-white characters from the privileges of individuality and universality that realist characterization supposedly offers. By reserving realism only for the white characters, Lee demonstrates that white privilege is not only a socio-economic concept but also one that entails *aesthetic* norms.[7] Meanwhile, on the other side of the border, everything slides back into familiar stereotypes.

The structure of *Song of the Dragons* also has the potential to dismantle this theatrical border. The disorienting oscillation between the two groups generates friction within the act of spectatorship, shaking the audience out of their comfort zones. Muñoz (1999, 32) writes: "The migrant status can be characterized by its need to move back and forth, to occupy at least two spaces at once. [...] The very nature of this migrant drive eventually wears down the coherency of borders." Rather than present migrant characters onstage, Lee's innovative work turns the audience into figurative migrants, who make multiple journeys across the border between stereotype and realism. The audience also crosses over perceptual boundaries in *The Shipment*, continuing the formal experimentalism of *Songs of the Dragons.* In her later play, however, the theatrical border crossing occurs at one pivotal point in the two-part performance.

Crossing Borders: *The Shipment*

Lee structures *The Shipment* in two discrete acts: a series of short segments "structured like a minstrel show—dance, stand-up routine, sketches, and a song," followed by "a relatively straight naturalistic comedy" (2010, 5). Here, Lee explores black representation, developing the piece with a cast of five African American actors who improvised scenes in rehearsal based on stereotypes that black actors generally face in their careers. One early sequence features a stand-up comedian who jokes crudely about racial tension between white and black people. He fires the opening shot, so to speak, insulting and berating white people, which eases the audience into going along with the black stereotypes that appear in the following scene as the same kind of racial satire. This skit, an abbreviated crime drama featuring a half-baked character named Rapper Omar, quickly runs through African American typecasting and stereotypes in mainstream media, such as the street rapper, the drug dealer, and the gangster criminal. Within minutes, audiences are given Rapper Omar's (entirely predictable) life story: his early days on the dangerous streets, his prison sentence, his meteoric rise as a rap star, and his demise into decadence.

Lee wrote the second half of the play based on roles that the cast said that they would like to play. The same actors from the first part, now with fleshed-out characters, chat about office politics and emotional problems while sipping drinks at an informal cocktail party. The theatrical mode shifts abruptly from presentational to utterly *re*presentational—fourth wall and all. A dramatic conflict arises when Thomas, the host of the party, shockingly announces that he has poisoned everyone's drinks out of despair over his failures in life. But then—surprise again!—he reveals it was all a joke. To alleviate the tension and awkwardness in the room, the guests decide to play a game called "Library." In this game, everyone must make up a sentence that could plausibly belong in a book randomly chosen from Thomas' shelf. The host then chooses the best entry. After a weak practice round, the guests play in earnest using as their prompt the chapter "Negro Superstitions" from an ethnography book titled *Black Magic*. The play abruptly ends in the middle of this round:

THOMAS:	(*Bursting out laughing*) "The Negro believes that a Negro's hands and feet are white because the moon done touched 'em in Africa!" […]
OMAR:	I'm sorry. I'm sorry, but I have to say that I'm really uncomfortable with all of this. I just don't think we'd be doing this if there were a black person in the room. (*Pause.*)
DESMOND:	I guess that would depend on what kind of black person it was. (*Blackout.*) (Lee 2010: 53)

The play ends here, leaving the audience in the dark momentarily to think back on their impressions of the characters in the cocktail party scene, with the revelation that the black actors were not performing black roles. (Were the characters white, then?) Lee structures a clever twist at the end; indeed, Thomas and the other characters had said nothing about race, although the numerous references to alcohol and drugs echo the black stereotypes set up in the first part, the "kind of black person" that the American media reproduces incessantly. Once again, the audience must apprehend stereotypes and realist characterization alongside one another. Yet unlike *Songs of the Dragons*, this play explores the ways in which assumptions and biases travel across this aesthetic boundary through the bodies of the five black actors, in addition to the audience's perceptions of race.

It is worth tracing the path of racial representation in the play to understand how Lee once again conjures a theatrical border. The play's structure seems fragmented and random at first, but *The Shipment*'s dramaturgy is razor-sharp. The stand-up comedy routine highlights racial politics as a central theme, underscoring the comedian's blackness even as he trades in what he self-mockingly labels "'White people are like this, and black people are like that' jokes" (Lee 2010, 11). This underscored blackness then merges with stereotypes of crime and "inner city" culture in the Rapper Omar section. As Lee wrote in the author's note for *The Shipment*: "The performers wore stereotypes like ill-fitting paper-doll outfits held on by two tabs, which denied the audience easy responses (illicit pleasure or self-righteous indignation) to racial clichés and created a kind of uncomfortable, paranoid watchfulness in everyone" (5). As a result, the second act feels off-kilter and artificial, even though the characters in the upper middle-class cocktail party conform to the realist mode. In the Rapper Omar scene, the performers are directed to "*deliver their lines and move as flatly as possible*"—in other words, to not modulate the language with "black" dialects (16). Yet strangely, it is most apparent in the cocktail party that these actors are putting on a show. The twist ending confirms the feeling that these characters are somehow unnatural, as they had been cast across racial lines. At the same time, Lee points out the problematic assumptions that turn what is technically a naturalistic scene with a "colour-blind" cast playing non-stereotypical roles into a performance thoroughly inflected by race. These figures are stuck on the border between stereotypes and realism, subconsciously scrutinized and interrogated by the audience as they try to cross over into the field of realist representation.

Although the play is based on the African American actors' experiences of being typecast, it is a mistake to view *The Shipment* as a play about blackness. Instead, Lee focuses on building dramatic structures that strategically induce certain modes of spectatorship while inhibiting others when looking at racially marked bodies. Her goal is not to represent identity as a given truth or a locus for politics, but rather to highlight the tensions, complexities, and barriers that exist in *all* representations of race. We tend to point at explicit stereotypes as the only images that are politically charged when they are but one region in a larger map of racialized representation, performance, and spectatorship. Lee's work grants us a full view of that topography, including the unseen borders that reinforce white normativity on the American stage.

But if the structure of *Songs of the Dragons* calls attention to the border, *The Shipment* takes its audience across it. In that regard, the enigmatic title of the play could refer to the black stereotypes presented in the first half. Lee crafts the performance so that these stereotypes subliminally exert influence over the audience's perception of the realist characters in the second half, creating the lingering feeling that something is "out of bounds." *The Shipment* enacts a theatrical border crossing, situating the audience in a stereotype-filled environment, and then relocating them to a realist setting with all the cultural baggage of the former intact. It is the audience's positionality within the politics of representation that migrates through the play's two-fold structure, rather than the characters. Lee has noted that her audiences tend to be consistently "[c]ollege-educated, city-dwelling, liberal, probably not evangelical Christian" (Lee 2008). Lee is interested in impacting the ways in which such spectators with good intentions perceive race in the theatre, slyly pointing out their implicit biases. While these audiences are perhaps less threatening to migrants and people of colour compared to those who openly express racism and xenophobia, their smug, "been-there-done-that" attitude regarding race can be an equally challenging obstacle in the struggle for representational equity in American culture. From the perspective of migration politics, these white liberal audiences have never had to navigate the border—whether that is a national border, an internal border (of race, ethnicity, class, gender, sexuality, religion, ability, etc.), or the racialized theatrical border that I have described above. These audiences have always felt "at home" in mainstream culture, a structure of feeling that realism reinforces not only in its focus on middle-class domesticity but also white normativity. Lee's plays shake audiences out of that complacency by shuttling them across the border, asking them to adopt new and unfamiliar modes of spectatorship that blur the perceptual line between blatant stereotypes of Others and characters that are true to life. (*Whose* life?)

When Lee embarks on a new project, she thinks first of the intended effects of the performance on the audience. She describes her playwriting process as building a psychological trap for her audiences that can bypass the conscious assumptions and attitudes preventing deeper engagement with racial politics:

> I do kind of have a bee in my bonnet about race, and nobody wants to hear a person of color ranting about race and how unfair the world is to them. You know you don't want to hear people whine and accuse white people. All of these things are very unpopular. So to find a way to talk about the things that bother me in a way that's not going to make everybody roll their eyes and dismiss it, so that's the hardest thing for me in making theatre that is political is trying to trap the audience so they can't escape through ways of their dismissive loopholes. (Lee 2008)

This can be read as a statement on the difficulty of truly crossing borders in the theatre, of successfully applying Giroux's (2005) border pedagogy to art. The problem is not that audiences are prohibited from crossing racial, cultural, and aesthetic borders because they are walled off and policed; rather, the problem is that many audience members who profess to be liberal and culturally inclusive are unwilling to move out of familiar territory, of becoming subjects of migration themselves. In some cases, audiences fail to recognize a discriminatory border when one clearly exists—for example, those who treat unequal casting opportunities as a matter that can be simply resolved by giving the part to the "most talented" actor. Lee's innovative work with theatrical form pushes against these entrenched boundaries in a way that creates potential to redraw the map in a more inclusive way. In that regard, I understand Lee's metaphor of the trap as a compulsory border crossing that allows us to see racial representation from new perspectives and hopefully become more mobile and flexible in our readings of race in other art and cultural texts. Rancière (2009, 46) calls attention to dissensus as a form of critical spectatorship that can "crack open the given and the obviousness of the visible, in order to sketch a new topography of the possible." Lee's plays deconstruct both racist stereotypes and realist characterization, two modes of representation that are each in their own way "self-evident" and thus too easily consumed uncritically. Through her plays that stage theatrical border crossings, Lee effectively redraws the map of racial representation.

* * *

Young Jean Lee's innovative approach to theatrical form offers a more sophisticated way to address and critique racial stereotypes. As the discourse on representation and politics developed and continues to develop, we have become too eager to point at stereotypes and call for their expulsion once and for all, so that they do not "taint" good representations—good in the sense of being accurate, respectable, positive, truthful, and so on. In this view, realism becomes an antidote to stereotyping. But we should remember that stereotypes are part of a larger regime that grants representational privilege to whiteness. The critical discourse on stereotypes and the politics of representation should recognize the fact that realism itself plays a part in sustaining a perceptual border that alienates minorities and cultural Others, a fact that Lee's work illustrates in surprising ways.

Viewing her work through the concept of border crossing complicates another topographical figure of speech that is used frequently in theatre criticism and scholarship: that of the avant-garde supposedly "pushing the boundaries" of the artform. This idea implies forward movement—in other words, historical progress—in aesthetics, form, and technique, which in turn renders some artistic approaches obsolete. In theatre history, realism has been the definitive foil for the avant-garde since the late-nineteenth century; the stuffy drawing room that forward-thinking theatre artists must dismantle. The commonplace rhetoric of leaving realism behind in the push towards new frontiers (despite its stubborn refusal to go away, I should add) can limit our critical engagement with realism's ideological foundations, especially the ongoing discrimination between (white) plays about universal human experience and identity politics dramas that are narrowly tied to a racial minority. Plays such as *Songs of the Dragons Flying to Heaven* and *The Shipment* demonstrate that realism can still create politically eye-opening experiences if it is handled thoughtfully. Lee's work calls for a different understanding of an avant-garde that crosses borders and enters unfamiliar territory. Rather than posit progress into an unknown, romanticized future, her plays ask that we find and breach the various borders that divide our society in the present moment.

Notes

1. The comprehensive reference book *A Companion to Twentieth-Century American Drama*, edited by David Krasner, illustrates my argument here. Most of the chapters on various identity-based theatre movements in the

latter half of the twentieth century discuss the ways in which theatre artists sought to challenge or critically dissect extant negative stereotypes. See chapters: Mike Sell, "The Drama of the Black Arts Movement"; Daphne Lei, "Staging the Binary: Asian American Theatre in the Late Twentieth Century"; Ann Haugo, "Native American Drama"; Tiffany Ana Lopez, "Writing Beyond Borders: A Survey of US Latina/o Drama"; Julia Listengargen, "From Eccentricity to Endurance: Jewish Comedy and the Art of Affirmation"; and Jill Dolan, "Lesbian and Gay Drama."

2. Of course, these distinctions are never clear-cut. Margaret Wilkerson notes that the specter of the stereotypical Mammy conditions the ways in which white audiences would have understood Lena Younger as a character. Nevertheless, she follows the binary scheme I outline here, imagining Hansberry's struggle "to reveal the humanity, the truth, the energy, and the complexity that emerges from a stereotype" (Elam and Krasner 2001, 335).
3. For a discussion on the valorization of psychological interiority in interwar American drama and its associations with middle-class white male identity, see Joel Pfister, *Staging Depth: Eugene O'Neill and the Politics of Psychological Discourse*.
4. See Kate Davy, *Lady Dicks and Lesbian Brothers: Staging the Unimaginable at the WOW Café Theatre* (2010), especially Chapter 5, "Staging the Unimaginable."
5. For a discussion of Orientalist stereotypes in American popular culture and their effects on Asian-American communities, see Robert G. Lee, *Orientals: Asian Americans in Popular Culture* (1999); and Krystyn R. Moon, *Yellowface: Creating the Chinese in American Popular Music and Performance, 1850s–1920s* (2005).
6. The video is available online at http://youngjeanlee.org/work/songs-dragons-flying-heaven/.
7. Lee pursued this relationship between realism and whiteness further in her most recent play, *Straight White Men*. The comically unsubtle title is reminiscent of a subtitle to *Songs of the Dragons* that Lee had used in early productions: "A Show About White People in Love." *Straight White Men* is the result of Lee's attempt to write in the style she found least interesting: a three-act naturalistic family drama in the tradition of Eugene O'Neill and Arthur Miller. It is telling that Lee was only able to meet this self-imposed challenge by writing exclusively about the most privileged social group in American society, this time pushing people of color out of the representational frame altogether and into the space between scenes, where they handled the stage transitions. For a discussion on *Straight White Men* and its relationship to Lee's earlier work, see my article "Visibly White: Realism and Race in *Appropriate* and *Straight White Men*" (2015).

References

Barthes, Roland. 1989. *The Rustle of Language*. Trans. Richard Howard. Berkeley and Los Angeles: University of California Press.

Bhabha, Homi K. 2004 [1994]. *The Location of Culture*. 2nd ed. New York: Routledge.

Clements, Alexis. 2017. Young Jean Lee on Her Lear. *The L Magazine*, January 20. http://www.thelmagazine.com/2010/01/young-jean-lee-on-her-lear/. Accessed 18 Oct 2017.

Davy, Kate. 2010. *Lady Dicks and Lesbian Brothers: Staging the Unimaginable at the WOW Café Theatre*. Ann Arbor: University of Michigan Press.

Diamond, Elin. 1997. *Unmaking Mimesis*. New York: Routledge.

Elam, Harry J., and David Krasner, eds. 2001. *African American Performance and Theater History: A Critical Reader*. Oxford: Oxford University Press.

Garrett, Shawn Marie. 2002. Return of the Repressed. *Theater* 32 (2): 26–43.

Giroux, Henry. 2005. *Border Crossings: Cultural Workers and the Politics of Education*. 2nd ed. New York: Routledge.

Herrera, Brian Eugenio. 2015. *Latin Numbers: Playing Latino in Twentieth-Century U.S. Popular Performance*. Ann Arbor: University of Michigan Press.

Isherwood, Charles. 2012. Beneath Pink Parasols, Identity in Stark Form. *The New York Times*, January 16. http://www.nytimes.com/2012/01/17/theater/reviews/young-jean-lees-untitled-feminist-show-review.html?. Accessed 18 Oct 2017.

Krasner, David, ed. 2005. *A Companion to Twentieth-Century American Drama*. Malden, MA: Blackwell Publishing.

Lee, Josephine. 1997. *Performing Asian America: Race and Ethnicity on the Contemporary Stage*. Philadelphia: Temple University Press.

Lee, Robert G. 1999. *Orientals: Asian Americans in Popular Culture*. Philadelphia: Temple University Press.

Lee, Young Jean. 2008. Young Jean Lee by Richard Maxwell. Interview by Richard Maxwell. *BOMB Magazine*, November 8. https://bombmagazine.org/articles/young-jean-lee/. Accessed 18 Oct 2017.

———. 2009. *Songs of the Dragons Flying to Heaven and Other Plays*. New York: Theatre Communications Group.

———. 2010. *The Shipment and Lear*. New York: Theatre Communications Group.

Moon, Krystyn R. 2005. *Yellowface: Creating the Chinese in American Popular Music and Performance, 1850s–1920s*. London: Rutgers University Press.

Muñoz, José Esteban. 1999. *Disidentifications: Queers of Color and the Performance of Politics*. Minneapolis: University of Minnesota Press.

Nahm, Kee-Yoon. 2015. Visibly White: Realism and Race in *Appropriate* and *Straight White Men*. *Journal of American Drama and Theatre* 27 (2).

Pfister, Joel. 1995. *Staging Depth: Eugene O'Neill and the Politics of Psychological Discourse*. Chapel Hill: University of North Carolina Press.

Piepenburg, Erik. 2007. Faith Confronted, and Defended, Downtown. *The New York Times*, May 6. http://www.nytimes.com/2007/05/06/theater/06piep.html?_r=0?. Accessed 18 Oct 2017.

Rancière, Jacques. 1991. *The Ignorant Schoolmaster: Five Lessons in Intellectual Emancipation*. Trans. Kristin Ross. Stanford: Stanford University Press.

———. 2009. *The Emancipated Spectator*. Trans. Gregory Elliott. New York: Verso.

Rugg, Rebecca Ann, and Harvey Young, eds. 2012. *Reimagining A Raisin in the Sun: Four New Plays*. Evanston, IL: Northwestern University Press.

Shange, Ntozake. 1992. *Plays: 1*. London: Methuen Drama.

Shimakawa, Karen. 2007. Young Jean Lee's Ugly Feelings About Race and Gender. *Women & Performance: A Journal of Feminist Theory* 17 (1): 89–102.

Soloski, Alexis. 2015. Scorching Dragons. *The Village Voice*, September 26. http://www.villagevoice.com/arts/scorching-dragons-7157968. Accessed 21 May 2015.

Young, Harvey, ed. 2013. *The Cambridge Companion to African American Theatre*. Cambridge: Cambridge University Press.

The Suitcase as a Neurotic Container in the Israeli Theatre: The Return of the Wandering Jew

Sarit Cofman-Simhon

Suitcases abound on Israeli stages. One finds them in mainstream as well as fringe theatres. Israeli theatre thus is responding to the geographical ephemerality that is part of the consciousness of almost all of its spectators: nearly everyone in Israel has experienced either migration or exile—if not they themselves, at least their parents. These are not the fashionable, functional suitcases of travelers and tourists, but containers of suffering and anxiety that encapsulate the identity of their owners. On Israeli stages they are emblematic and constitute an icon of the Wandering Jew. By focusing on the suitcase as a symbolic prop, I would like to propose a brief typology of how Israeli theatre represents Jewish migration and explore four Israeli productions that tackle deterritorialization. These productions intrinsically engage with the central myths of Israeli identity—the Bible, Diaspora, the Holocaust, and Israel's wars.

Be'Amharit Ze Nishma Yoter Tov (It Sounds Better in Amharic) (2001) by Yossi Vassa presents the Jewish immigrant's suitcase; *Orzey Ha'mizvadot*

S. Cofman-Simhon (✉)
Kibbutzim College, Tel-Aviv, Israel

Y. Meerzon et al. (eds.), *Migration and Stereotypes in Performance and Culture*, Contemporary Performance InterActions,
https://doi.org/10.1007/978-3-030-39915-3_5

(*Suitcase Packers*) (1983), a canonic Israeli play by Hanoch Levin, deals with the Israeli Jew's emigrant suitcase; *Mechakim Le'Godot* (*Waiting for Godot*) by Samuel Beckett staged by Joshua Sobol (2015) relates to the Jewish refugee's suitcase; finally, Rina Yerushalmi's 1995 production *Va Yomer, Va Yelech* (*And He Said, And He Walked*), part of her *Bible Project*, concludes by tracing a connection between the paradigmatic case of Jewish wandering, the biblical Exodus, and contemporary Israel's wars. All productions centre on the suitcase as a stage prop, and as a cypher for human mobility: in each play the suitcase instantiates a different metaphor, according to the characters' various epistemological and ontological positions (immigrant, emigrant, exiled, refugee). I will be looking into these myths of identity and belonging as narratives of perpetual homelessness.

The Wandering Jew has been a central stereotype applied to Jews in Western culture, an essentialist view, making unrootedness integral to Jewish identity. Yet for Jews, Diaspora has been complemented by the belief in redemption and in returning to a utopian homeland. Paradoxically, the establishment of the State of Israel and the end of Jewish displacements has not terminated the sense of geographical ephemerality for Jews living in Israel. Suitcases in the Israeli theatre portray the tension of a story of a neurosis: the homecoming of the Wandering Jew.

Jewish Utopia and Dystopia: Wandering in Space and Time

In a book dealing with contemporary Hebrew drama, *Fields and Luggage* (2014), Avraham Oz points to the main themes of Israeli theatre as being land (or lack of it) and migration. The front cover illustrates people inside a crooked wagon seated near a table, as if in an itinerant living room. Their grim expressions and the luggage piled on the wagon roof tell of their stories as landless wandering Jews. Two thousand years of migration colour the depths of Israeli consciousness and drama, even when and where the wandering is supposed to have come to an end. In a similar vein, Shimon Levy (2016, 63–64) remarks that:

> The suitcase is a frequent stage-prop in the canonic Israeli theatre, and as a theatrical prop it is more a Jewish object than Israeli in its character ... In the depth of Israeli experience are traces of Jewish anxieties, remains of the fear of expulsion, of enforced wanderings ... These suitcases allude to the Jew within the Israeli, people who depend on suitcases, those who in fact have

> not yet put down roots, who are still not completely at home, are always on the road to somewhere, on the road from somewhere ... The suitcase reveals the Israeli collective subconscious.

Indeed, in Jewish memory, migrations and returns to homeland are markers of national consciousness. The trope of migration or exile is foundational to Jewish nationhood and religion, and the Israeli ethos is founded on the grand narrative of repeated exile from and return to Zion.[1] This trope of cyclical return has been the formative force in Jews' self-identification as wanderers for whom the only topos with the status of home is the Promised Land.

The stereotype of the Wandering Jew appears in works of non-Jewish artists, as well as in Jewish writings. In premodern Europe, an itinerant life of permanent migration was perceived as a punishment and a plague. According to the Christian legend, the Wandering Jew (also known as Ahasver) was doomed to roam the world until the end of days. As a derogatory image, it meant that God had cursed the Jews for their unbelief in Jesus. This trope of the eternal Jew, with its anti-Jewish connotation, evolved over centuries alongside the actual process of Jews moving from one place to another, itself not an insignificant influence on the literary shaping of Ahasver. Such migrations were usually, but not only, a result of frequent expulsions and harassments that included collective murder. Concomitantly, Jews were perceived as rootless, cosmopolitan people, in the worst sense of the word. The legend claims that the Jew will never pass away, nor settle down. Rejected by all nations, the eternal Jew wanders and disrupts the purity of nations and the geography of borders. Moreover, he is immortal because he is not human: "In many ways the Wandering Jew was like a vampire: he could not die and therefore he could not really live," indicates Shelly Zer-Zion (2008, 135).

Intriguingly, Judaism itself has also considered exile a divine punishment, albeit for different reasons. Starting with the biblical punishment for Cain's fratricide, "You shall become a ceaseless wanderer on earth" (Genesis 4:12), wandering was contrasted with settling down in peace: "Each will sit under their own vine and under their own fig tree, and no one will make them afraid" (Micah 4:4). Thus, historical exiles have been viewed by Jews as having theological explanations, and most compellingly, as belonging to a narrative ultimately including redemption and return to the Land of Israel. This teleological pattern of an ahistorical narrative, of recurring homecoming, finds expression in the Israeli theatre.

Formative Jewish migrations that framed later experience include the Egyptian, the Babylonian, and the Roman exiles, each of them constituting a realm of memory for Jews. As Jan Assman (2015, 3) observes, "The biblical Exodus from Egypt launched a narrative version of the revolutionary birth of both a people and a religion," including a political patrimony in the Promised Land. Dated to the fourteenth century BCE, the Exodus story constitutes the mythical migration to the Promised Land that has marked Jewish consciousness and been an emotional wellspring for the ethos of Israeli Jews. As such, it is celebrated each year during the Passover holiday. Yet Jonathan Boyarin (1992, 523) remarks that "the politics of Exodus constitute an exemplary case of the link between history and interpretive reading," pointing to the fact that whereas archaeological facts are ambiguous, in Jewish tradition the story of Exodus is firmly linked to national homecoming. Canonic Jewish texts address the descent to Egypt and the slavery there not as historical events, but rather as punishment for sinning against God and as a story of redemption.[2]

Another massive migration was the Babylonian exile: the ancestors of the modern Jews were deported from Judah[3] to Babylon by King Nebuchadnezzar, around 580 BCE. After the overthrow of Babylonia by the Persians, King Cyrus gave the Jews permission to return to their native land in 537 BCE. In the Hebrew Bible, the captivity in Babylon is presented as a punishment for idolatry and disobedience to God and followed by deliverance.

Yet the ultimate formative exile, the Roman exile, which eventually became the Jewish Diaspora of two millennia, occurred in 70 CE. The rabbis of the era attributed the destruction of the Temple and of Jerusalem to a punishment from God for the "baseless hatred" that pervaded Jewish society at the time. Most Jews who became dispersed adhered to their Judaism throughout a long and far-flung Diaspora, remembering the lost homeland in their daily prayers, and reiterating year after year on Passover night the mantra of the eternal return: "Next year in Jerusalem." They have also observed an annual fast day, regarded as the saddest day in the Jewish calendar, commemorating the destruction of the First and Second Temples of Jerusalem, and the exile from the Holy Land. These ritual practices function as a vital conduit, transmitting memory and a sense of belonging through reiteration. The theological aspect of exile as punishment has always been complemented by the Jewish faith in national redemption—the belief that the Jews would ultimately return to the homeland from which they had been uprooted. Migration is therefore viewed in Jewish thought as a spatial yet atemporal move, occurring again and again, with Zion at its centre, and as final destination. Prior to the establishment of the State of Israel, Jews identified themselves as living in spatial and temporal in-betweenness: "The Wandering Jew turned into a *realm of memory*, which constructed the Jewish exile as a dystopia of no-place, and the Diaspora Jew as a no-body entity," writes Zer-Zion (2008, 133). The exile thus played a central role in conserving memory and consolidating Jewish identity: living in dystopia and believing in a utopian return to the Promised Land implied that exile was temporary, that spatial homelessness would come to an end. "The *epic* of return is the implicit paradigm of the Jewish journey," explains Sidra DeKoven Ezrahi (2000, 8). This belief was decisive in preserving a distinct, essentialist Jewish identity over time and space. Yet as Galit Hasan-Rokem (2018) indicates:

> Artists and thinkers secularized the Christian motifs of the legend and transformed the Wandering Jew into an icon of modern Jewish revolution ... Various ideologies of the early 20th century foresaw an end for the journey of the Wandering Jew in the near future: Communists suggested that he would disappear with the dissolution of nations, Zionists believed that he would return home and no longer be a wanderer. The Wandering Jew has not disappeared from contemporary literature, among Jews and others. The most surprising may be the presence of this figure in a number of Israeli novels from the seventies to the recent years.

Arguably, most paradoxical is his updated presence in secular Israel, in plays in which the Wandering Jew makes an entry, holding his shabby suitcase.

The Poetics of Suitcases

Andrew Sofer (2006, 164) remarks that a stage prop's mobility and portability "between here and there, between now and then, has undeniable consequences for the ontological status of its carrier." Indeed, the suitcase as a stage prop strives to demonstrate nomadic agency and the loss of control. It always risks congealing into a symbol of human helplessness and victimization. As a trope, the suitcase "remains subject to the directions of those playwrights who seek to arrest, frame, and emblematize it. But as a dynamic prop, it orchestrates the gaze of the spectators towards its trajectory onstage" (Sofer 2006, 164). Moreover, suitcases point at the ephemerality of the present by marking an impending journey. Thus, as Sofer would have it (2006, 164), they instill a sense of unease and instability into what is occurring on stage, and "continually disrupt the human economies they traverse."

The suitcase acquires a mysterious dimension. We hardly ever know what the characters have chosen to carry with them, what is important for them. Which items have they kept from their former lives? The opacity of the suitcase hides the relationship between the characters' past and future homes.

Moreover, the suitcase represents an assault on stage time, by pointing at the temporality through which the would-be traveler passes. It is a liminal object, representing the act of moving, of crossing not only borders but also limits and boundaries. Frequently, this liminal experience of spatial and temporal freedom, as if promising a better future, is equally a mourning for the past. People holding suitcases frequently linger in no-man's land, in in-betweenness, detached from the immediate reality which does not accept them or which they want to escape, and heading towards the unknown.

The Jewish-Israeli Immigrant Suitcase: Biblical Homeland as Utopia

Ezrahi (2000, 7) points out that an idealized, utopian image of a remote homeland is by definition associated with an episteme of homelessness: "The yearning for ultimate homecoming is compatible with the most radical form of homelessness and the most protean notion of home." Furthermore, she indicates:

> The modern, not unlike the romantic, discourse on home, exile, and return, captures the intensified longing for a place of origin as ultimate reference or antecedent—the presumption of a paradise whose loss or absence preserves it in a kind of negative space. (9)

The lost paradise and the Zionist ethos of return to a concrete homeland was a common theme on Israeli stages in the early days of local theatre; characters arriving from the Diaspora holding suitcases were a symbol of hope and triumph over two thousand years of exile. In contemporary Israeli theatre, though, the suitcase of the Jewish newcomer is very rarely encountered. Intriguingly enough, the trope of yearning for the Holy

Land is currently found in shows staged by Israelis of Ethiopian origin. In *The Jerusalem Dream* (2016), a documentary film directed by Meni Elias, Ethiopian Israelis tell of their dream of Jerusalem during their childhood in Ethiopia:

> Growing up in Ethiopia, when we heard "Jerusalem," we thought it was gold from top to bottom.
> Whenever I saw a flock of birds in a V-formation, lots and lots of birds, I'd ask: "What's that Dad? What are all those birds?" He'd say: "They came from Jerusalem."
> Take us to Jerusalem, so that we may see Jerusalem. Don't let us die before we see Jerusalem.

The Black Jewish community of Ethiopia—the *Beta Israel* (House of Israel)—has existed for at least fifteen centuries, in isolation from other Jewish communities around the world, and developed a unique set of religious practices—in some ways quite different from what is typically considered "Jewish." In 2019 almost 150,000 Ethiopians live in Israel, barely two percent of Israel's Jewish population. Local theatre companies presenting plays in both Amharic (the language of Ethiopia) and Hebrew have been warmly received by Israeli theatregoers. In these performances, actors of Ethiopian origin tell the story of their excruciating odyssey on foot from Ethiopia. The memory of the journey and of the dream of Jerusalem is negotiated and reconfigured. The narrative of the Ethiopian community emphasizes the sacrifice endured by those who immigrated in their effort to reach Jerusalem: many walked on foot to Sudan and suffered famine, and even those who were airlifted made difficult journeys on foot to get to the assembly point. They view the journey to Israel as an act of will and determination, motivated by the dream of the Promised Land. By contrast, other Israelis experienced the event primarily as an accomplishment of the State of Israel than that of the newcomers, as the *New York Times* reported:

> Israel fell into joyous celebration tonight as the Government announced the successful conclusion of an emergency airlift of 14,500 Ethiopian Jews, nearly the entire Jewish population, in just under 36 hours. "We've stood up to our obligation and completed the operation bringing all the Jews," Prime Minister Yitzhak Shamir declared tonight. (Brinkley 1991)

This declaration displays both a patronizing approach erasing the sacrifice and heroism of the newcomers and, at the same time, the fact that the State of Israel views itself obliged to offer them a safe home.

The productions *It Sounds Better in Amharic* (2001) and its counterpart *Yahid B'meeno* (*One of a Kind*) (2006), both directed by Shai Ben-Atar and co-written with Yossi Vassa, present the narrative of heroic journey, and concomitantly, a most naïve version of the ancient Jewish meta-narrative. Produced by the Nephesh (Soul) Theatre, a small theatre whose productions "reflect a plurality of beliefs, depicting different communities within Israeli society that must develop a common language and achieve mutual respect," (Nephesh Theatre n.d.) both productions were warmly received.[4] In *It Sounds Better in Amharic*, Vassa tells the story of his family's wandering on foot from Ethiopia to Sudan and, from there, to Israel. He was ten years old when he and his parents, two little brothers, and grandmother left their village on foot in the dead of night and embarked on the dangerous journey. Vassa tells of his childhood, starting with how he used to count sheep on the mountain, and ending with how this skill helped him during math classes in Israel. When the teacher talked about counting, digits, and numbers, he found the explanations too abstract and not helpful. At one point it occurred to him that instead of digits and numbers he should think of counting sheep, and instantly became the best pupil in his arithmetic class.

Vassa operates in the African storyteller tradition: holding a simple, old-fashioned blue suitcase, he tells the story of those months in Sudan, in both Amharic and Hebrew, comparing his family's experience with the biblical Exodus from Egypt. In a comic number he explains that rather than travelling on foot, he would have much preferred to have had a Ferrari and drive all the way from Ethiopia to Sudan:

> If I just had a Ferrari, I would turn on the air conditioner at 7 o'clock in the morning, and make it to Sudan by 2 o'clock in the afternoon. Relax, catch a plane to Israel, and by 7 o'clock in the evening get my passport, start learning Hebrew, and already complaining about discrimination.

The Vassas were not ordinary refugees. As opposed to the worldwide African diaspora caused by slavery, for them Africa was Diaspora. In their own eyes, they were a particular type of immigrants who finally, yet paradoxically, were starting their journey back home, to a place that they had never encountered before but had always dreamed of. Home is in this case is not the place they were familiar with, but the place they were dreaming about, the location of wishes, in fact, the parallel of the lost paradise. Using the suitcase as a container of memories and as a mini-museum of the Diaspora, Vassa relates his family belief that one day they will reach Jerusalem and be delivered. He cancels the suitcase's opacity: opens and closes it, empties its contents and puts them back, hides behind it, transforms it into a detective's suitcase, hugs it. The suitcase encapsulates his past life, and Vassa exposes it with gestures of unsuspecting dedication, with a sense of belonging, trusting the spectators as partners and brothers in his ancient new home.

Yet in the second part of the show Vassa tells about the bold encounter with reality: Jerusalem is not solid gold, his family was sent to live in an unattractive town, skin colour became an issue, the encounter between the family's rural past and the high-tech economy of Israel was painful. Local stereotypes surfaced, raising new anti-anti-essentialist categories, as Paul Gilroy (1993) would have it: Diaspora was essential for defining Jewish identity, and in this respect, the Vassas could claim their belonging to the ancient homeland. Yet black Jews were a novelty in Israel, and ethnic absolutism, with the ambivalent experience of Ethiopian Jews being inside and outside the modern and postmodern West, set them apart in Israeli terms. As the production demonstrates, homecoming was not sheer salvation, and home was not utterly utopian.

The other play, *One of a Kind*, a production for children, shows the story of Vassa's family's journey on foot to Israel. It won first prize at the Haifa[5] International Children's Theatre Festival, it toured the United States in 2008 and received there warm responses:

> Told through the eyes of AndArgay, a charming and creative child, *One of a Kind* incorporates music, dance and video. But what is most fascinating is the way it melds Jewish and African traditions of family, song, dance and storytelling. And it does all this in a way that is always accessible to children. (Simmons n.d.)

In the play, the grandmother is ill and she dies in a Sudanese camp. Vassa dreams that in the night she comes to him and says: "I am only a dream, but you will fulfill the dream of getting to Jerusalem."

As we can see, back in Ethiopia the image of the Holy Land, the imagined homeland, was compelling and had nothing to do with reality; the imagined home was purely utopian, as it used to be for centuries, for most

Jews in Diaspora. These plays thus invite the spectators to unsettle stereotypes and suggest that, corollary to their homecoming, these newcomers faced an unexpected Jewish essentialism. The seeds of disillusion were embedded in the very utopian image of homeland, such an image possibly leading to a sense of eternal homelessness: as the dream of return to Zion became reality, what was once a romantic discourse could easily be transformed into a dystopian space.

The Jewish-Israeli Emigrant's Suitcase: Homeland as Dystopia

The Jewish poetics of exile and return was metamorphosed in the twentieth century by homecoming to the ancient homeland, which triggered a critical engagement with the only place that had the status of the real.

The play *Suitcase Packers* (1983), by the critically well-received playwright Hanoch Levin, subtitled "Comedy with Eight Funerals," tells of Jewish characters who want to leave Israel where, paradoxically enough, they find there is no room for their personal dreams, which have nothing to do with Jerusalem. This production demonstrates how paradigms of utopian thinking about homecoming may fail when confronted with the absence of an ideal reality and displays the profoundly neurotic sense of being eternally unhoused. Originally directed by Michael Alfreds, it premiered in 1983 at the Cameri Theatre in Tel-Aviv, one of the major stages of Israel.

Hanoch Levin was one of the most prolific and at the same time controversial Israeli playwrights. The plot of *Suitcase Packers* is quite simple: in a certain neighbourhood, people pack suitcases, give speeches about the need to leave for another country, and then unpack. They complain about each other being provincial, bemoan their narrow lives, but do nothing about it. In between, some of them die and funerals pass by. What all these characters are articulating is the aspiration to go far away from their everyday reality, to escape their own life, like Irina in Chekhov's *Three Sisters* who wants to escape to Moscow. Yet Irina dreams of a different, more meaningful future, while Levin's characters are eager to flee not just a location, but also themselves. They have very few expectations:

Zigi: It's a small place here, you understand. The size of a dice. Abroad nobody is looking inside your pants …

Bella: I have no illusions. London isn't waiting for me. I'll be lonely there as I am here, and maybe it will be like that for the rest of my life. But in London there are more movies, good music … people are more polite … The despair becomes more comfortable there. (Levin 1983)

Most characters dream of getting far away, basically, as a gesture of deserting their prosaic life, not of getting rich or living a different life. The supposed travel abroad is a gesture of pessimism, not any kind of affirmation. All of them are aware that they may have to return. Bella summarizes aloud what everybody around her thinks tacitly: "One day you go to Europe, smiling, and one day you return to Asia, in tears." Europe is much more elegant, but is not waiting for them, and they are condemned to a Diaspora in the Levant. It sounds like a contradiction in terms, but the Promised Land does not look attractive enough. It is of major significance that the dream driving them is not only of moving to a more cosmopolitan city but about escaping their country altogether. These characters, whose parents emigrated from Europe to Israel, long for the old continent. At the same time, they know that Europe is not their home, and the desire to move stems from an existential sense of rootlessness. The suitcase thus functions as the prop of their epistemological position as eternal Wandering Jews. It forms the container of their identity: an ontological homelessness. In the play, the suitcases point at a dichotomous here/there. What they are running away from remains behind in Asia; the little they plan to take on their one-way journey is compactly packed: a negation of the present, without hope for the future. With its restricted capacity, the suitcase forces the one-way packers to classify and categorize not just their belongings but their entire history too. Evidently, they are not going anywhere, yet each act of packing marks anew the renunciation of their parents' coming "home" from the Diaspora. "Home" must remain virtual, for when it becomes real, it loses its utopian dimension. These suitcases display nomadic agency and loss of control. It is their ancestors' wanderings that they are unconsciously, and pathetically, attempting to reconstruct. There is a sense of restlessness in these characters, a feeling that they are not connected to a place, that instability is a defining aspect of their existence.

Suitcase Packers has been translated into a number of languages and staged in New York (2003), Warsaw (2006), Budapest (2012), Moscow (2011), and elsewhere. Unsurprisingly, these interpretations have stressed the play's existential and universal dimension, not the neurotic Jewish sense of homelessness:

> The name of the play highlights the fact that in this world ultimately all of us seemingly travel and tote heavy bags with our memories and illusions until we reach our final stop destination … In front of our very own eyes the grey days of a small community, many generations of several families–parents, grandparents, children and grandchildren all come to life, funny and at the same time beautiful people who yearn for love, to love and be loved. Most of the characters however also dream of a fuller life, one that might be possibly lived out in somebody else's shoes, or at least in somebody else's costume, especially somewhere else, in another city, another country, or another time. ("The Suitcase Packers." *Slovak National Theatre Bratislava*)

A Hungarian critic writes:

> *Suitcase Packers* catches, as do most Levin plays, the essential pathos of our lives as well as their ridiculousness so that we get both laughter (lots of it), and some tears. If death is there to remind us of our lives and their meaning, then the theatre, a kind of reconstruction of life, is a reminder squared. A performance is momentary and transient, more so than the life it imitates. ("Hanoch Levin: suitcase packers 2013/advisor, assistant." *Kotka Gudmon*)

Finally, the Russian production at Moscow Academic Mayakovsky Theatre announces that:

> The dramatis personae of the comedy *Suitcase Packers* is a whole page of endless Zils and Zvis, who are tied with the bonds that one cannot make head nor tail of. One sketch follows the other … What's more, there are deaths and funerals, and tears, and visions of the deceased. Laughter by Levin is an insight in the comical yet at the same time absurd and desperate order of human life. ("Suitcase Packers." *Moscow Academic Theatre of Vladimir Mayakovsky*)

It is no surprise that international productions did not grasp the sense of eternal homelessness that resonates in the play: it is profoundly Jewish. The theme of existential wandering corresponds with Jewish Israeli audiences' experience of interminable exile and Diaspora, of being eternal Wandering Jews. Levin's play illustrates how these characters are living in "no-place," in aporia. Their existential feeling and experience is, in Martin

Heidegger's terms, that of being eternally unhoused in Being. Heidegger employs "thrownness" to characterize the state of unhoused Being that falls into non-place. This is what I view as neurotic in the Jewish Israeli suitcase: the impossibility of feeling at home anywhere, even in the long-dreamed-of homeland.

Holocaust and the Jewish Refugee's Suitcase: A Spiritual Homeland

The philosopher George Steiner (1970, 4) advocates Jewish homelessness and staying in the Diaspora as a cosmopolitan act defining Judaism: "I absolutely believe that such uprootedness is a decisive part of Judaism, and because, in a very small, personal way, such a mode of life holds trust with that central European humanism and Judaism which Hitler and Stalin made to ruin."

Steiner advocates a virtual, spiritual homeland, as Amnon Rubinstein (2004) explains:

> The homeland of the Jews is the book, not the soil, and they should remain eternal wanderers. This is the reason for Steiner's objection to Zionism, which exchanged the book as homeland with "the Golan Heights and Gaza." He considers the state of wandering, the absence of roots, as the telltale mark of high culture. In his words: "Trees have roots, people have legs"; and "people should collect passports like stamps."

In Steiner's view, Jewish alterity and the lack of a political entity explain Jews' part in human progress.

The problem with Steiner's view of existential uprootedness is evident when Jews become haunted refugees, or in Steiner's words, when they become victims of "negative ontology." In that case, even he admits that they may need a more-than-spiritual homeland. The next production I will discuss, the Yiddish Israeli staging of Samuel Beckett's *Waiting for Godot* (1949) directed by Yehoshua Sobol (2015), tackles this issue. Even though the text does not indicate any suitcase for the two main characters, it is basically a play about homelessness. Sobol did add two shabby suitcases as a symbol of helplessness and victimization, and altered the ending, transforming it into a play about Jewish refugees during World War II.

The most common interpretation of *Waiting for Godot* is that waiting is an eternal existential state, and thus Vladimir and Estragon are going nowhere. They remain where they are and wait for eternity. Sobol's interpretation of the play was rather subversive: he based his staging on a book published in 2008 by Pierre Temkine, who offered the interpretation that Vladimir and Estragon are Jews waiting to be smuggled over the Spanish border in 1943. They are carrying suitcases and waiting for someone called Godot to help them cross the border clandestinely. Analysing the play, Temkine argues that Beckett must have sought and found a certain distance, so that the readers or spectators who lived through the events would not recognize them on any conscious level but would rather live them from within, so to speak. The Yiddish[6] Israeli production directed by Yehoshua Sobol, altered the ending, transforming it into a play about Jewish refugees during World War II eventually deciding to flee Europe by themselves.

Yiddishpiel is the name of the Israeli Yiddish theatre. Established in 1987 in response to a vital need to reestablish the lost honour of Yiddish language and culture and to revive them, the theatre has mostly staged plays written in Yiddish in Eastern Europe, along with some translations of worldwide drama. To produce Beckett's play was a daring artistic decision, since most of the Yiddishpiel's audience are senior citizens, who expect some Jewish nostalgia: stories about their diasporic past, beloved Yiddish songs, Jewish humour. The abstract plot of *Waiting for Godot* was unexpected, and at the same time, challenging. The majority of the spectators came from Eastern Europe, their parents having lived there during World War II, and many were Holocaust survivors. For them, Sobol's interpretation was compelling. Thus, Sobol changed the play's ending: Vladimir and Estragon decide to leave, take their suitcases and step off the stage into the auditorium, breaking the "fourth wall" convention. They pass through the audience and go out. Having the two characters leave and not wait for Godot was an optimistic statement regarding the possibility of salvation of sorts, and of Jewish independence. According to Sobol, they left for Israel, thus reinforcing the Zionist narrative of a safe place for Jewish refugees (Fig. 1).

George Steiner, like the Jewish philosophers Hermann Cohen and Franz Rosenzweig before him, views exile as "a necessary condition for the advancement of Judaism's moral and cultural message" (quoted in Sagiv 2012, 201). Refraining from the positions of power that determine historical and political events, the Jews would maintain a superior sense of morality and contribute to a cosmopolitan civilization: "By submitting themselves to the laws of history and the corrupting influence of power

Fig. 1 Dori Engel as Vladimir and Yuval Rappaport as Estragon in *Waiting for Godot*, by Samuel Beckett. Directed by Yehoshua Sobol. July 2015. Yiddishpiel Theatre, Tel-Aviv. Photo by Gérard Alon

politics, the Jews would betray their noble destiny" (quoted in Sagiv 2012, 201). As Rosenzweig put it:

> To the eternal people, home never is home in the sense of land, as it is to the peoples of the world who plow the land and live and thrive on it, until they have all but forgotten that being a people means something besides being rooted in a land. The eternal people has not been permitted to while away time in any home. It never loses the untrammeled freedom of a wanderer, who is more faithful a knight to his country when he roams abroad. (quoted in Sagiv 2012, 201)

The Jewish refugee's suitcase is, in Israeli terms, the most loaded sign: it encapsulates the image of the displaced, the victim, the refugee; the eternal Wandering Jew. Sobol's interpretation neither touches on Jewish utopian homecoming, nor the noble cosmopolitan role and spiritual homeland which Steiner and Rosenzweig attribute to the eternal people, but conveys the existential need for a safe home, the need to live "housed in being." In Sobol's *Waiting for Godot* it is the trope of "ontological unwantedness" that is very much at work.

From Biblical to Palestinian Suitcases: Homecoming and Israel's Wars

In 1936 David Ben-Gurion, head of the de facto Zionist government, and eventually the first prime minister of Israel, was asked to identify the basis of the Jewish claim to the Land of Israel. He replied: "The Bible is our mandate." Ben-Gurion viewed the establishment of the State of Israel as a utopian fulfillment of the biblical narrative. Yet the Israeli-Palestinian political conflict that ensued has kept this question alive and it has been examined by many theatre makers and artists, director Rina Yerushalmi among them. Along with the Itim Ensemble, a special, innovative group, Yerushalmi launched the creation of the spectacular *Bible Project*, an eight-hour-long performance consisting of two independent but interrelated productions: *Va Yomer, Va Yelech* (*And He Said, And He Walked*), staged in 1995, and *Va Yishtachu, Va Yara* (*And They Bowed, And He Saw*), staged in 1998. The much-acclaimed project was performed in Israel, Hamburg, Berlin, London, Australia, and New York. It was based on excerpts from the Hebrew Bible, delivered verbatim by twelve actors and actresses, all dressed in black. Staging biblical themes is a major challenge in Israel, as Sharon Aronson-Lehavi and Freddie Rokem (2010, 227) imply:

> Israeli theatre history is marked by numerous dramatic adaptations of biblical stories and theatrical "confrontations" with the Bible itself, precisely because of its linguistic, historical, and mythical status and its powerful presence in the collective Israeli consciousness.

Indeed, "confrontation" with the biblical text has been a pillar of the Jewish national movement since its inception, and new interventions enter a space of contested readings. In Israel the Hebrew Bible, with its mythical status, acquired more than a religious meaning, as pointed out by one of the German theatre critics (quoted in Aronson-Lehavi and Rokem 2010, 227), referring to Yerushalmi's project:

> The director and the ensemble set off on a journey after the collective soul of the State of Israel. The actors live within the tension between the brutal

duty to maintain the ancient myth, and the modern aspiration for personal happiness.

Yerushalmi staged the biblical texts in ways that comment on the social and political present of Israeli society. The second part of the performance *Va Yelech* (*And He Walked*) depicts the recent history of Israel and the Jews: "Yerushalmi theatrically suggests that the Exodus from Egypt and the biblical conquering of the Land of Israel have been repeating in modern times," say Aronson-Lehavi and Rokem (Fig. 2):

Fig. 2 *Va Yomer. Va Yelech (And He said. And He Walked)*. Based on the Hebrew Bible. Directed by Rina Yerushalmi. Itim Ensemble. January 1996. Photo by Gadi Dagon. Rina Yerushalmi Collection, The Israeli Center for the Documentation of the Performing Arts, Tel Aviv University

> Especially topical was the second part of the first production, *Va Yelech* which draws parallels between the biblical story of the Exodus from Egypt and the conquest of the Land of Israel and the twentieth-century ordeals of the Jewish people. The twelve actors open this part holding brown suitcases that in Israeli culture have become icons of the Holocaust and thus signify Holocaust survivors. Gradually, however, the actors become transformed from a group of victimized wanderers into a solid, martial group ready to conquer the Land of Israel, fight in devastating wars, and even sacrifice their children. (227)

The biblical Exodus, via exile and sufferings, is linked to scenes of war, displaying the circumstances of Israel's present:

> Following the scenes that depict the Holocaust and the wandering in the desert, the group fronts the next stage that is a necessary part of building the state—the wars. Here Yerushalmi demonstrates the painful price of the wars as the performance platform slowly becomes a graveyard, geometrically covered with cards on which biblical verbs are printed. (Aronson-Lehavi and Gal 2008, 162)

The semiotic instability of the suitcases the actors hold enables the metamorphosis from Wandering Jews into Israeli soldiers. Through this mutation, we witness the painful price of recurring wars.

The juxtaposition of victims with victimizers, of Jewish refugees during World War II and the Palestinians who became refugees after the war to establish the State of Israel, constitutes a central motif of homecoming and homelessness within contemporary Israeli discourses. The tension between these apparently opposed extremes, where the homecoming of one person becomes the homelessness of another, is for many Jewish Israelis unacceptable. One of the Israeli productions of the *Suitcase Packers* did reveal its political subjectivity, and the unavoidable analogy between the Jewish suitcase and the Palestinian suitcase: in 2004 the Department of Theatre Arts at Haifa University staged the play with a dual cast: one Hebrew-speaking, the other Arabic-speaking. The Palestinian students acted the translated play at the Al-Midan Theatre in Haifa. The outcome was unexpected:

> [W]hen it was performed in Arabic, for a mixed Jewish and Arab audience and became a huge success, it eventually caused the closure of the theatre. Apparently we … broke some rules by achieving, or even pursuing, successful, communicative political theatre. (Itzhaki 2009, 104)

The play in Arabic (staged by the same director, Amit Gazit) unsettled the status-quo. Widely acclaimed when it was acted in Hebrew, it caused controversy when acted in Arabic. Obviously, it was not the linguistic matter per se; it was the sound of painful symmetry and tension between the epistemological condition of the Hebrew-speaking audience in Israel, and its Arabic-speaking counterpart. The political reality haunted the production: clearly, the Palestinian audience identified with the characters onstage and appropriated their experience of rootlessness as an expression of their own sense of inner exile, even of those spectators who were born in Haifa and had never moved away from their natal neighbourhood. The Palestinian Israeli spectators redefined the Diaspora, locating it inside Israel. The subjective aspects of political and ethical circumstances, as well as the existential aspects of the play, turned the suitcases into political props: whereas for the Jewish Israeliss the suitcase was a mark of homeless wanderers, for the Arab Israelis it constituted a sign of displacement from home, of deterritorialization.

Some years earlier, a similar sensitivity sparked a notorious incident in the Israeli theatre. The play *Ephraim Returns to the Army* by Yitzhak Laor, written in 1985 but first produced in 1989, was banned due to a scene centering on a schoolbag: an Arab boy uses it to camouflage the family's jewels. The play deals with an Israeli military governor in the West Bank:

> Ephraim: Eighteen years ago I had an officer ... a quiet man ... with an East-European accent ... We conquered Quneitra [in Syria]. Suddenly a Syrian boy crossed the street with a schoolbag on his back ... The officer told me to stop the boy and check his schoolbag, because he's got jewels in it, and then give him back the jewels. I stopped the boy ... He had jewels in the schoolbag. We gave them back to him and let him go. We asked the officer how he knew. He said: that's how I hid my family's jewels, when the Germans came.

Although the Haifa Theatre acquired the rights to the play, it was banned by the state censor. Eventually, following a legal process, the Supreme Court overturned the censor's decision (1987), and as a consequence, censorship of theatre was abolished a year later. Laor ended up victorious, yet outside the world of theatre was deemed "too extreme for us." Avraham Oz (2014, 22) explains:

> [This] dramatic moment ... had drawn a defamatory analogy between the conduct of the IDF [Israel Defence Forces] and that of Nazi soldiers. Apart

> from the damaging implications of banning an image that belongs to the integral meaning of the play … the censor's judgement tellingly marks the full-range trajectory of the ideological bias informing the censorship.

This déjà vu was more than painful: the image of a boy who became a refugee after a war with the State of Israel and is now carrying a schoolbag as an accessory that represents the migrant or nomad's political and ethical circumstances is something that reaches beyond the Jewish experience of homecoming.

Conclusion

The stereotype of the Wandering Jew became an essentialist trait of Jews as, effectively, dependent on suitcases. Yet in Jewish eyes, this trope has always been complemented by "the *epic* of return" as "the implicit paradigm of the Jewish journey" (Ezrahi 2000, 8). This belief was decisive in preserving a distinct, essentialist Jewish identity over time and space. The dependence on suitcases has been internalized by Israelis and, as a neurotic container, the suitcase reveals the Israeli collective subconscious: in the productions discussed here, eternal displacement and migration is a trope associated with Jewish culture, and has religious and cultural connotations.

In embracing the figure of the Wandering Jew, these productions express ambivalence towards anti-essentialist positions: on the one hand, as we have seen in the case of Ethiopian Jews, the plays contest the idea that there is a necessary and fixed ethnic essence, an organic phenomenon, unique or intrinsic to Jews (wandering included). On the other hand, the productions invite conversation in order to unsettle stereotypes. The plays adopt an ambivalent position: while wandering was formative for the Jewish nation, homecoming does not put an end to the sense of being "unhoused in Being," and in making this assertion, the productions amount to a call for dialogue.

An affinity with the nation's founding narratives inevitably colours the Israeli theatre's struggle with issues of immigration, uprooting, and exile. As a stage prop, suitcases enact both epistemological and ontological predicaments in these productions. In *It Sounds Better in Amharic*, the epistemological condition is of homecoming. In *Suitcase Packers*, it is the longing for the Diaspora following the ontological switch caused by the establishment of a homeland; in *Waiting for Godot*, suitcases indicate the hope for salvation, thanks to the existence of a concrete homeland. Rina Yerushalmi took these ideas a step further in her *Bible Project*, drawing a line between the biblical Exodus, the Jewish refugee's suitcase during World War II, and Israel's wars.

Deep in the Israeli consciousness, spatial and temporal uncertainty is the backdrop against which every story is related. Each character entering the stage holding a suitcase arouses anxieties and memories of severance, for "those who in fact have not yet put down roots, who are still not completely at home, are always on the road to somewhere, on the road from somewhere" (Levy 2016, 63–64). On Israeli stages, these are not the fashionable, functional suitcases of travelers and tourists. They are an icon of the Wandering Jew.

Notes

1. Zion is a place name often used as a synonym for Jerusalem as well as for the biblical Land of Israel as a whole. The word is first found in 2 Samuel 5:7 which dates from c. 630–540 BCE according to modern scholarship. It originally referred to a specific hill in Jerusalem (Mount Zion).
2. There are two main explanations: (1) the sins of the Patriarch Abraham, for which his grandchildren were enslaved, and (2) slavery was a divine educational process for the Hebrews prior to their becoming a nation.
3. Judah is the Hebrew name for Judea.
4. See Paulenne Simmons in the references list and Aryeh Dean Cohen, "Israel's Eddie Murphy," *The Jerusalem Post Magazine*, May 2, 2002, pp. 25–27, Accessed September 29, 2019, http://www.nepheshtheatre.co.il/amharic/am_reviews_and_articles_8.html.
5. Haifa is a city in north Israel.
6. Yiddish is the language spoken by East European Jews.

References

Aronson-Lehavi, Sharon, and Nissim Gal. 2008. Wholly Unholy: Religious Iconography in Israeli art and Performance. *Performance Research: A Journal of the Performing Arts* 13 (3): 154–162.

Aronson-Lehavi, Sharon, and Freddie Rokem. 2010. Word and Action in Israeli Performance. In *Contesting Performance: Global Sites of Research*, ed. Jon McKenzie, Roms Heike, and C.J. Wan-ling Wee, 222–235. London: Palgrave Macmillan.

Assman, Jan. 2015. Exodus and Memory. In *The Afterlife of Events. Perspectives on Mnemohistory*, ed. Tamm Marek, 115–133. Basingstoke: Palgrave Macmillan. https://archiv.ub.uni-heidelberg.de/propylaeumdok/3746/1/Assmann_Exodus_2015.pdf. Accessed 13 May 2019.

Boyarin, Jonathan. 1992. Reading Exodus into History. *New Literary History* 23 (3): 523–554.

Brinkley, Joel. 1991. "Ethiopian Jews and Israelis Exult as Airlift Is Completed." *New York Times*, May 26. https://www.nytimes.com/1991/05/26/world/ethiopian-jews-and-israelis-exult-as-airlift-is-completed.html.

Ezrahi, Sidra DeKoven. 2000. *Booking Passage: Exile and Homecoming in the Jewish Modern Imagination*. Berkeley: University of California Press.

Gilroy, Paul. 1993. *The Black Atlantic: Modernity and Double Consciousness*. Cambridge, MA: Harvard University Press.

Hasan-Rokem, Galit. 2018. Is the Wandering Jew in Contemporary Israeli Literature a Paradox? UCLA presentation, May 10. Accessed May 12, 2019. https://www.cjs.ucla.edu/galit-hasan-rokem-is-the-wandering-jew-in-contemporary-israeli-literature-a-paradox/.

Itzhaki, Tal. 2009. Ways of Unseeing: Glass Wall on the Main Stage. In *Political Performances: Theory and Practice*, ed. Susan C. Haedicke et al., 97–109. New York: Rodopi.

Kotka Gudmon. n.d. Hanoch Levin: Suitcase Packers 2013/Advisor, Assistant. Vígszínház Commedy Theater Budapest. http://kotkagudmon.com/suitcase-packers/. Accessed 12 May 2019.

Hanoch Levin: suitcase packers 2013/advisor, assistant. *Kotka Gudmon*, n.d. kotkagudmon.com/suitcase-packers/. Accessed 12 May 2019.

Levin, Hanoch. 1983. *The Suitcase Packers*. Theatre script. http://www.hanochlevin.com/plays2-5/p295. Accessed 11 Feb 2016.

Levy, Shimon. 2016. *Israeli Theatre: Times, Spaces, Plots*. Tel Aviv: Resling.

Moscow Academic Theatre of Vladimir Mayakovsky Website. n.d. Suitcase Packers. http://en.mayakovsky.ru/performance/na-chemodanakh/ Accessed 6 May 2019.

National Theatre Bratislava Website. n.d. The Suitcase Packers. http://snd.sk/en/inscenation/2612/the-suitcase-packers. Accessed 6 May 2019.

Nephesh Theatre Website. n.d. About Nepesh Theatre. http://www.nepheshtheatre.co.il/innerpages_en/about/about_en.html. Accessed 3 June 2020.

Oz, Avraham. 2014. *Fields and Luggage*. Tel Aviv: Resling.

Rubinstein, Amnon. 2004. George Steiner's Zionist Heresies. *Haaretz*, January 27. https://www.haaretz.com/1.4682513.

Sagiv, Assaf. 2012. George Steiner's Jewish Problem. In *The Wounds of Possibility: Essays on George Steiner*, ed. Ricardo Gil Soeiro, 194–212. Newcastle upon Tyne: Cambridge Scholar Publishing.

Simmons, Paulenne. n.d. A *CurtainUp* Review. One of a Kind. www.curtainup.com/oneofakind.html.Slovak. Accessed 28 Sep 2019.

Sofer, Andrew. 2006. *The Stage Life of Props*. Ann Arbor: University of Michigan Press.

Steiner, George. 1970. *Commentary* 49, no. 5.

Suitcase Packers. n.d. *Moscow Academic Theatre of Vladimir Mayakovsky*. http://en.mayakovsky.ru/performance/na-chemodanakh/. Accessed 6 May 2019.

The Suitcase Packers. n.d. *Slovak National Theatre Bratislava*. snd.sk/en/inscenation/2612/the-suitcase-packers. Accessed 6 May 2019.

Zer-Zion, Shelly. 2008. The Cobbler's Penalty: The Wandering Jew in Search of Salvation. In *Jews and Shoes*, ed. Edna Nahshon, 133–148. Oxford: Berg Publishers.

Keeping the Candle Aflame: Andrey Tarkovsky's Search for Spirituality in a Foreign Land

J. Douglas Clayton

"The entire history of Russian emigration bears out the Western view that 'Russians are bad emigrants'; everyone knows their tragic incapacity to be assimilated" (Tarkovsky 1987, 202). With this statement from his book *Sculpting in Time*, Andrey Tarkovsky sets the tone for the chapter on his film *Nostalghia* (1983). Despite the etymological similarity of the term to the English "nostalgia"—that is, a longing for the past, as presented in the American scholar Svetlana Boym's (2001) study of the fascination of Russians of the 1990s for the pre-revolutionary Russian past—Tarkovsky instead had in mind what we call "homesickness," the sense of loss of values and rejection of the "heathen" dominant culture he finds in Italy. Tarkovsky's choice in spelling the title of the film (the "h" after the "g" mimics the Russian pronunciation rather than the Italian or English) is intended to stress the difference in meaning. His film investigates on a deep philosophical and religious level the nature and reasons for this

J. D. Clayton (✉)
University of Ottawa, Ottawa, ON, Canada
e-mail: jdclayt@uottawa.ca

Y. Meerzon et al. (eds.), *Migration and Stereotypes in Performance and Culture*, Contemporary Performance InterActions,
https://doi.org/10.1007/978-3-030-39915-3_6

malaise, which he clearly felt very deeply. In his work, Tarkovsky stresses the difference between his reaction to the cultural treasures of the West—in this case, Italy—and the stereotypical response of Russians who idealize western European culture and bow down before the icons of Italian painting, sculpture, and architecture. Such culture-seeking Russian tourists are seen everywhere, not only in Florence, Venice, and Rome, but also in London, Paris, and other famous cultural sites. In *Nostalghia*, Tarkovsky uses the image of the protagonist Gorchakov, a Russian poet who has come to Italy to research the life of an eighteenth-century Russian serf musician, to act out the filmmaker's own feelings towards his Italian exile. To be sure, it can be argued that the representation of Italians in the film is stereotypical (for example, the lack of religious feeling of the Italian intelligentsia, exhibited by the Italian interpreter Eugenia, or the love of consumer goods, such as shoes, about which Gorchakov complains); but there is much in the character of Gorchakov that can also be called stereotypical, such as his love of vodka or his extreme intellectual positions regarding such matters as translation. The stereotypical nature of the characters of both Gorchakov and Domenico, his Italian counterpart in the latter part of the film, is, however, tinged with considerable irony (which, in the case of Gorchakov, is self-directed). That is to say, there is a playfulness that mitigates their apparent stereotypical intent.

The critical analysis of *Nostalghia* has largely focused on certain cinematic aspects, especially the combined final image of Gorchakov's house within the ruins of an Italian cathedral, or the interspersed black-and-white dream-like shots, suggesting Gorchakov's longing for Russia, of a house resembling the Tarkovsky's dacha in Russia, of Gorchakov's apartment in Moscow, and of a Russia-like landscape with Gorchakov's wife, son, and dog. For Naficy (2001, 178) these are the signs of a "quest for a lost harmony"—what Dempsey (1981, 15) calls "a deep longing for a state of Eden-before-the-Fall innocence and bliss." Ultimately, the film's closing image is clearly an unsatisfactory attempt to create artificial harmony; in fact, it could be argued that Tarkovsky intended to suggest that "never the twain shall meet"—that the two worlds of Italy and Russia are too far apart for any reconciliation, so that the final shot is as ironic as it is lyrical. As Martin (2011, 162) writes of the film: "It is Tarkovsky's most eloquent depiction of alienation."

Although the film was shot in Italy and only the main protagonist is Russian, the work is deeply embedded in Russian poetry and visual culture and there are important elements in the film that link it back to the fundamental themes of Tarkovsky's work. To do the film justice, it is necessary to go back in time and examine certain contexts that are reflected in the film and contribute to the complex meanings that it generates. One theme in particular that has not received sufficient attention is that of poetry—specifically the poetry of Andrey Tarkovsky's father, Arseny. The film has as its background the tragic division between the Russian homeland and Russians abroad that marked the history of twentieth-century Russian art. Throughout the Soviet era, the Soviet authorities viewed Russian emigrants as non-persons, "enemies of the people." There is a long tradition of Russian exiles beginning as early as the time of Ivan the Terrible. Nothing, however, could compare to the hundreds of thousands who fled Soviet Russia during and after the civil war of 1918–1921. Among those hordes were poets, writers, and creative artists of all kinds. They scattered all over the world: Europe (Germany, Yugoslavia, France), China, the United States, and Latin America. Some took root in their new environments, while others fell victim to *nostalghia*. One of the most tragic figures was the poet Marina Tsvetayeva. She lived in extreme poverty in Paris and was ostracized by other Russian exiles when her husband, Sergey Efron, became a Soviet agent. In 1937, the Tsvetayevs' daughter Ariadna decided to return to the USSR. She was followed by Sergey and, in 1939, Marina, who found work as a translator in Moscow. Shortly after Marina's return, Ariadna and Sergey were arrested. Marina committed suicide in 1941 and her husband was executed shortly after. Marina Tsvetayeva's fate illustrates the hopeless choice that presented itself to Russian poets: they could leave Russia and be cut off from their readers, language, and culture; or they could remain in or return to the USSR with little chance of continuing their work as poets (or at least, publishing it), and risking arrest at any moment. Tsvetayeva's fate, incidentally, parallels that of Pavel Sosnovsky, the composer whose stay in Italy is the subject of Gorchakov's research in the film: we learn that after returning to Russia, Sosnovsky committed suicide. The question of whether or not to leave Russia was indeed a life-or-death problem for Russian artists, and a problem that, as Le Fanu (1987, 110) points out, had no solution. Upon her return to Russia, Tsvetayeva found herself sharing the fate of numerous poets, such as Boris Pasternak and Anna Akhmatova, who found themselves in "internal exile"—unable to leave the USSR, and unable to practice their art. This concept of "internal exile" appears to be a typically Russian phenomenon, the result of the persecution of creative figures by the authorities and the deep reluctance of Russian artists to be separated from their homeland. The artists were not physically displaced, but the inability to publish forced them to recede into their private spaces and create without publication. In some cases, they lived long enough to see their works published; in others, their work only appeared posthumously.

One of the few members of the Soviet cultural elite to befriend Tsvetayeva on her return to her homeland was Andrey Tarkovsky's father, the poet Arseny Tarkovsky (1907–1988). After Tsvetayeva's death, Arseny Tarkovsky dedicated a cycle of poems to her, which were written over many years. In 1946, although he had been wounded and decorated in the war, he came under attack from party officials, along with Anna Akhmatova, who had made the deliberate decision not to emigrate in the 1920s, preferring not to be separated from her Russian homeland. As part of the effort to impose the party's grip over intellectual life in post-war Soviet society, Akhmatova, along with the prose writer Mikhail Zoshchenko, was expelled from the Union of Writers and publicly criticized in front of the politburo by Andrey Zhdanov, the party official in charge of cultural matters. This made life extremely difficult: she lost all sources of income and could not publish her work. As part of the same campaign, the publication of Arseny Tarkovsky's first book of poetry, which was already in production, was halted, ostensibly because it did not contain any poems about Stalin. This was a severe blow to the poet. Essentially, he found himself in the same "internal emigration" as Akhmatova, although, like her, he continued to write poetry (which remained unpublished) in addition to translating into Russian the work of poets written in other languages of the USSR. It was only in 1962—sixteen years after he had fallen from grace—that his first volume of poetry appeared.

That year coincided with the appearance of *Ivanovo detstvo*, or *Ivan's Childhood* (1962), the first feature film by Arseny's son Andrey. After he had shot four more feature films in the USSR, which have become classics of world cinema, the obstacles placed in Andrey's way by the authorities obliged him to leave for Italy. Here, he made a documentary film about Italy, followed by the feature film *Nostalghia*, which turned out to be his penultimate work.[1] Thus Andrey Tarkovsky, unlike his father or Akhmatova, left the USSR in order to practice his art. In the post-Stalin era, those who were forced to leave the country—including such eminent artists as the poet Joseph Brodsky and the cellist Mstislav Rostropovich—lost their citizenship and were unable to return to their homeland. Tarkovsky's case was special: when he left the USSR, his citizenship was never revoked, nor did he lose the title of People's Artist of the Soviet Union. He was in a curious no-man's land—neither exile nor emigrant, but unwilling to return to a situation in the USSR in which he would be unable to work.

It had always been difficult for Tarkovsky to pursue his career, given that his deeply poetic and spiritual work was antithetical to the atheist values of the Communist Party and contradicted the officially promulgated style of socialist realism. He struggled to obtain funding for his film projects, and his works were subjected to cuts and even withheld from circulation. In a letter to his father, who tried to persuade his son to return to the USSR, Tarkovsky wrote that "of the twenty or so years that I was employed in Soviet cinema, about seventeen I spent idle and without hope. Goskino [the Soviet agency that controlled the film industry] did not want me to do my work" (Filippov 2012, 353). Finally, unable to continue his career in the Soviet Union, he obtained permission to leave the USSR and work in Italy. He first made a documentary film about the country titled *Tempo di viaggio* (1983), but then the possibility appeared of a contract for a feature film, which Tarkovsky titled *Nostalghia*, supported financially by the Italian television chain RAI and co-sponsored by Goskino. Shooting began in October 1982, and the film was completed in time to be shown at the Cannes Film Festival in 1983, where it received several awards. At the same time, the political situation inside the USSR had changed with the demise of leader Leonid Brezhnev on November 10, 1982. His replacement was Yury Andropov, who had been chairman of the KGB and was an ideological hard-liner. It became clear to Tarkovsky that he would be unable to continue his career in the USSR, and he resisted attempts to persuade him to return, even though he failed to get permission for his son Andriusha to join him.

Tarkovsky (1987, 202) writes about *Nostalghia*: "I wanted to make a film about Russian nostalgia—about that state of mind peculiar to our nation which affects Russians who are far from their native land." The protagonist Andrey Gorchakov is a Russian poet who is collecting material about Pavel Sosnovsky, an eighteenth-century Russian composer who was exiled to Italy. In the film we hear his interpreter Eugenia read to Gorchakov the text of a letter sent by Sosnovsky, a serf, describing his brutal treatment at the hands of his master. In the letter, Sosnovsky states: "I could try to ensure that I never return to Russia, but the very thought is like death. It surely cannot be that for as long as I live I shall never again see the land where I was born: the birches and sky of my childhood" (Tarkovsky 1987, 211). Sharing Sosnovsky's letter with Eugenia is Gorchakov's way of letting her know that a relationship between them will not work. It expresses the pain of separation—stronger than simply homesickness, but rather a deeper spiritual link with the motherland—which Russians have traditionally called ***nostalghia***. In an interview with the Swedish journalist Gideon Bachmann (1984), Tarkovsky defines the term: "[it] signifies the yearning for what is far away, for those worlds that cannot be united, but it is also yearning for one's native home, one's spiritual identity."

In an interview with Tarkovsky by the German journalist and documentary filmmaker Ebbo Demant (1989, 348; my translation), Tarkovsky defines his task in *Nostalghia* in the following way:

> I tried to ensure that the scenario of *Nostalghia* contained nothing superfluous and secondary that might stop me from achieving my main objective, which was to convey the state of someone who has entered into a deep contradiction with the world and himself, who cannot find the balance between reality and the sought-after harmony, and who therefore is experiencing a nostalgia arising not only from his geographical distance from his native soil, but also an overall sadness regarding the wholeness of existence. I was dissatisfied with the scenario until finally a certain metaphysical unity emerged in it.

Thus, Tarkovsky sees the true purpose of the film as an investigation of the state of disconnectedness and incompleteness that is the human condition, brought to the surface and dramatized by the displacement of exile. He became disoriented in Italy and was repulsed by the excess of artistic beauty. In *Nostalghia* there is no dwelling on the beauty of Italy: most of the film is shot indoors, and most of the landscapes, shot in sepia, are chosen for their similarity to Russia and represent Gorchakov's longing for his homeland.

In Tarkovsky's films, sequences of images are interrelated, so that resonances of meaning are created. Rather than the "doubles" seen by Johnson and Petrie (1994, 164), we find layered characters that combine several different images. This is true of the characters in *Nostalghia*. It is not a coincidence that Oleg Yankovsky, the actor chosen by Tarkovsky for the role of Gorchakov, was visually similar to photographs of the young Arseny Tarkovsky, Andrey's father. At the same time, it is evident that in the character of Gorchakov, whose first name is also Andrey, Tarkovsky is describing the feelings he himself experienced in Italy. Gorchakov is thus a composite figure with elements of both Andrey and his father. Andrey's father, Arseny, is elsewhere deeply present in the film: extracts from two of his poems are read over the course of the film and the female protagonist, the Italian translator and interpreter Eugenia, has been reading a book of his translated poetry.[2] To extend the "chain of associations," we should note that in one of Arseny's poems read in the film he references his own father, Aleksandr. There is thus a paradigmatic chain of references: Aleksandr, Arseny, Andrey, Gorchakov. To this we can even add Sosnovsky, whose experience in Italy is recalled in the letter; and even Andrey Tarkovsky's son Andriusha, who is symbolized in the film by Domenico's son. This chain of association reflects the deep interconnectedness with family and homeland that forms the broad cultural context of the film: Gorchakov's pain is the pain of separation from his wife, children, Moscow apartment, country cottage, and even dog,[3] all of which haunt the dream-like sequences.

Notwithstanding these layers of meaning, it should be recognized that Gorchakov is a sort of self-portrait, a "performance" by the filmmaker of his own predicament. There are, however, some superficial differences. For example, Gorchakov pines for his wife, whereas Tarkovsky's wife was present and assisted during the filming; unlike the failed romance between Gorchakov and Eugenia, there is no evidence of Tarkovsky's attraction to any female interpreter; Gorchakov is a poet, whereas Tarkovsky is a film-maker; and there is no evidence that Gorchakov has political difficulties with the Soviet authorities that might have driven him to undertake a research trip to Italy (indeed, at the end of the film he is about to return to his homeland when he suddenly hears of Domenico's impending demonstration of faith and decides to take up the Italian's challenge). These differences between Tarkovsky and Gorchakov, however, only serve to underline the deeper resemblances between them. These encompass their shared values: spiritual life, a belief in the uniqueness of Russian culture, views on the impossibility of translating poetry, and religious beliefs. To some extent, Gorchakov and Tarkovsky's shared traits are stereotypically Russian: for example, Gorchakov's rejection of materialism (he wonders why Italians need so many shoes) is clearly shared by the filmmaker. Gorchakov's vices, too, are stereotypically Russian, such as his bingeing on vodka and (to some extent) his attachment to cigarettes.

Gorchakov's shared values with Tarkovsky are expressed in the fate of Arseny's book of poems, translated into Italian, that the translator and interpreter Eugenia is reading. Gorchakov tells Eugenia that poetry cannot be translated into another language. When she gives him the book he angrily throws it into a corner. Some of the anger no doubt comes from Tarkovsky's realization of the cultural differences between Russians and Italians that render difficult the task of making a film in this environment, just as they make impossible any romantic relationship between Gorchakov and Eugenia, however much she tries. Later, we see the book burning as Gorchakov lies drinking vodka. In an interview, Tarkovsky talked about the impossibility of importing or exporting culture, of "appropriating another people's culture." He continues: "The reproduction and distribution of culture is harmful to its essence and spreads only a superficial impression. It is not possible to teach one person the culture of another" (Mitchell 1982, 54). Such a radical position seems to undercut the very project of the film and clearly expresses Tarkovsky's anger at being unable to make films in his own country.[4] To Gorchakov's outburst, Eugenia responds: "And music?" raising the question of the translatability of an artwork from one form to another. The unstated question is: "And images?" That is to say, if poetry cannot be translated from one language to another, is it possible to translate a poem into a film? Essentially, then, the film asks how a work of art can be performed in another country in another genre; how can a migrant take his art with him and make it work in a new cultural environment? Tarkovsky in fact takes the issue even further, turning his father's poetry into film and injecting it into a foreign environment—a sort of double transposition. The film itself is its own reply to Eugenia's question, since the last part of the film, in which Gorchakov carries a flickering candle across the empty Roman Baths of Saint Catherine and back, can be seen as a transformation into images, a realization of a symbol in a poem by Arseny Tarkovsky, an extract from which is read aloud during the film:

> I am a candle, I at the feast burned out,
> Gather my wax in the morning's light
> And this page will hint to you about
> How to cry and when to be proud is right,
> And how you should easily let go and die,
> Divvying up to others the banquet's last third,
> And in the shelter of a chance refuge lie
> And after death flare up like the word. (Arseny Tarkovsky 1993, 335; my translation)

This poem develops an image from Arseny's very first published poem:

> Flickering like a little yellow tongue
> The candle melts down more and more.
> That's how you and I live
> The soul burns and the body melts. (Arseny Tarkovsky 1993, 15)

Prime among the meanings contained in both poems is the notion of the sacred, of the spirituality of human life, symbolized by the candle: the human being is like a candle, composed of the wax—the body, which is burnt out by life—and the soul, the spirit that transcends the flesh. Gorchakov's act of faith is also a self-reflective metaphor for the trials Tarkovsky experienced in filmmaking, which for him was both a creative and sacred duty, one that would wear him down and eventually cost him his life.

Religion is another deep value shared between Gorchakov and his creator. One of the first shots in the film concerns the visit to the church in Monterchi where Piero della Francesca's painting *Madonna del Parto* was located. When Gorchakov and Eugenia stop their car near the church, she comments that the fog-shrouded view resembles Russia in the fall; this is the first of a number of instances where images of Russia and Italy are "montaged" in an attempt to seek parallels between the two countries. It is as if she is trying to persuade Gorchakov to accept Italy, but he rejects this argument. Although they have driven a long way to view the painting, he refuses to go and look at it. Eugenia goes to the church alone and, while viewing the painting, she has a conversation with the sacristan who tells her that in order for the Holy Mother to grant her a wish—whatever it might be—she must first kneel. Eugenia finds she cannot, and asks the sacristan why the women praying in the church are able to kneel. He tells her it is because they have faith (*fede*); the fact that she cannot kneel signals that she does not. The final shot of the sequence in the church focuses on the mass of candles placed there by women supplicants, establishing a link between the candle and the notion of faith. This link will be present until the death of both Gorchakov and the other protagonist, Domenico.

Regarding Gorchakov's refusal to see the painting, Nariman Skakov (2012, 168–169) writes: "His irritation, stemming from a feeling of alienation, is overpowering, and it prevents him from enjoying the aesthetic pleasures the foreign country has to offer." The meaning of the scene, however, lies not in Tarkovsky's avoidance of any aesthetic experience (although he professed that he had become saturated by the excesses of artistic beauty that he experienced in Italy), but rather in the fact that he rejects aesthetic experience that is not grounded in faith. Here, Gorchakov is clearly expressing Tarkovsky's own deeply held views. The reason for Gorchakov's refusal to see the Madonna can be found in Tarkovsky's diary. He writes about a visit to Loreto on May 3, 1980: "I felt it was wrong that I can't pray in a Catholic cathedral; not that I cannot, but that I don't want to." Then, to his delight, in the cathedral in the town of Porto Nuovo, he discovers an Orthodox icon of the Vladimir Mother of God: "I couldn't believe it: suddenly to see an Orthodox ikon [*sic*] in a Catholic country, when I had just been thinking about not being able to pray at Loreto. It was wonderful" (Andrey Tarkovsky, 245). Later, in the entry for March 22, 1982, he writes: "Went [...] to Porto Nuovo with Pepe to pray to my Vladimir Mother of God. It made me feel so much easier" (307). Here we see the expatriate Russian looking in an alien land for a familiar spiritual sign with which he can connect. Gorchakov, a projection of Tarkovsky, shares his distaste for Catholic religious art.

The meaning of the candle, already present in the poetry of Arseny Tarkovsky, is clearly associated in this early scene with faith. Later, Gorchakov asks Eugenia the meaning of the Italian word, which she translates into Russian for him. It is the quality of *fede* that Gorchakov recognizes in Domenico, and which arouses his interest in the idealistic mathematics teacher who had confined his family to their house for seven years. Perhaps Gorchakov recognizes in Domenico a kindred spirit.[5] His encounter with Domenico marks the end of Gorchakov's potential romance with Eugenia. An imagined, composite figure, Domenico can be seen as Gorchakov's Italian counterpart. The link between *fede*, which had been the subject of Eugenia's conversation with the sacristan, and the candle reemerges when Domenico passes Gorchakov a candle. Domenico feels driven to perform the action of crossing the Baths of Saint Catherine with a lighted candle, but the bathers, who consider him insane, have prevented him from doing so, fearing he will drown. He therefore entrusts the task—an act of faith—to Gorchakov, who performs it at the end of the film and then dies. The Roman bath, with its sulfurous fumes, is a realized metaphor for a devastated, hellish pagan world. Those who bathe in it and reject Domenico as a madman are the denizens of this living hell.[6] Gorchakov's feat echoes the life of Arseny, whose poetry had been a flickering candle of spirituality borne through the dark times of persecution and internal exile, and brought to a triumphant end. Again, the candle is a realization of a metaphor: the body has melted and only the flame of the soul is left, flaring up like the word.

Gorchakov's alienation stems from his initial failure to recognize the moral equivalent of Russian spirituality in Italy. The images of Italy presented in the film are almost post-apocalyptic—or perhaps more accurately post-diluvian—visually represented by the drained Baths of Saint Catherine with their mud-caked bicycles, bottles, and other detritus. Churches are roofless and flooded with water. Instead of candles there are cigarettes. Eugenia, whose long-haired beauty recalls the classical paintings of the Madonna (a close-up of her is juxtaposed with one of Piero della Francesca's painting), is childless, going from man to man, and finally ending up with a comical figure of an Italian Lothario named Vittorio. The sacristan, who believes that the purpose of a woman should be to bear and raise children, pronounces a verdict on her: "You want to be happy. There are more important things." She cannot attract Gorchakov, who in his dreams and reveries sees his wife and children either in Moscow or in the Russian countryside. In Gorchakov's dream, Eugenia and Maria caress each other in a mirror image: they both personify womanhood and are both beautiful; however, the purpose of this "doubling" is not to emphasize their external similarity, but the difference in their values.[7] Similarly, the later doubling of Andrey and Domenico serves to differentiate the nature of their spiritual beliefs. Immediately after there is a shot of Maria pregnant, incarnating the woman's role Eugenia rejects. When Domenico asks Gorchakov about his wife, whether she is like della Francesca's Madonna, Gorchakov replies that his wife is indeed like her, only black. This enigmatic remark becomes understandable when we recall Tarkovsky's joy when he discovered a copy of the Russian icon Vladimir Mother of God at Porto Nuovo. That icon, which is indeed much darker than della Francesca's Madonna, is in fact an "unspoken presence" in the film: something clearly on the filmmaker's mind (we recall the role of the icon in *Andrey Rublyov*). Suggestively, Tarkovsky dedicated the film to his mother, Maria, which is also the name of Gorchakov's wife in Moscow, linking them both directly to the notion of the Madonna as the ideal woman. Moreover, in Gorchakov's vision of his wife, she, like della Francesca's Madonna, is pregnant. Gorchakov's wife has a spirituality that the Italian intellectual Eugenia has lost: the latter recalls having wept the first time she saw della Francesca's painting, but now she tells the sacristan she is "just looking." Although Gorchakov tells Eugenia he finds her pretty in a certain light, she is only the visual incarnation of the Madonna, not the essence. Instead of bearing candles, she is associated with cigarettes (whose whiteness and burning end is a sort of parody of a candle). She gives

Domenico a cigarette, and indeed her last words are "I am going to buy cigarettes."[8]

In addition to the question of faith, the other important theme in *Nostalghia* is that of the apocalypse. The theme is linked with the image of Domenico who, as Johnson and Petrie (1994, 161) point out, is a version of the Russian *yurodivy* (religious visionary). He is, however, more than that. According to Tarkovsky, the idea for Domenico was suggested by Tarkovsky's Italian scenarist Tonino Guerra and was based on a real-life fanatic who had locked himself and his family up in expectation of the end of the world. However, he also contains features reminiscent of Savonarola, who preached to the multitudes and attempted to demonstrate the truth of his words through a trial by fire (which ended farcically when it started to rain).[9] Savonarola was later condemned by a tribunal and burned to death. In the film, Domenico also locks up his family in anticipation of the apocalypse. When they are finally released by the carabinieri, his son asks, "Papa, is this the end of the world?" The utopianism and apocalypticism in Domenico's speech before he sets himself aflame is adumbrated in Gorchakov's outburst concerning the impossibility of translation: he claims that the only solution is the elimination of frontiers. But that would hardly end the problem of different languages; language barriers are more secure than any border. It is Domenico who eventually seeks the unity of all of humanity in his final, utopian declaration: "we must build pyramids" and "it is the so-called sane people who have led the world to the brink of catastrophe." Domenico has faith, and his death is an ironic *auto da fe*, but he has very few listeners, and in the end he literally "flares up like the word," dousing himself awkwardly with gasoline and, after fumbling with the lighter, finally setting himself on fire "like a candle," thus realizing the metaphorical image at the end of Arseny Tarkovsky's poem cited above. At the same time, there is a great deal of irony in the portrayal of Domenico. His attempt at a sermon on the Capitoline Hill ends farcically: the recording of Beethoven's Ninth Symphony is garbled, and he has practically no audience. By resorting to the grandiose gesture of setting himself on fire, Domenico is a stereotypical depiction of the Italian tendency towards the theatrical; thus, it is not the migrant observer, but the native Italian who is the stereotype.

Domenico's grandiose gesture stands in contrast to Gorchakov's action. When the Russian poet visits Domenico, the latter asks him to take upon himself the feat of carrying the candle across the Baths of Saint Catherine because "we have something big planned in Rome." At first, Gorchakov avers, asking "Why me?" Then, even after he has accepted the candle, he puts it on the shelf before finally taking it.[10] His hesitation is evident in his intended departure, which he only puts off when Domenico reminds him, through a telephone call from Eugenia, of his commitment. His feat of carrying the candle across the drained Baths of Saint Catherine is humble and understated, unlike Domenico's self-immolation, which is clumsily executed to the point of being comic. It is the difference between the music of Bach, associated with Gorchakov, and Domenico's love of Beethoven's Ninth Symphony, which is first broken off when they meet in Domenico's house, and then again during the immolation scene. The humility, intimacy, and sincerity of Gorchakov's action seem to express a deeper faith than Domenico's bombast and "maximalism," as Tarkovsky calls it (1987, 206). In Rome, Gorchakov is planning to return to Russia, but hears from Eugenia what Domenico is planning. Taking a taxi to the Bagno Vignoni, he carries the candle Domenico has given him across the empty Baths of Saint Catherine, dying as he reaches his goal, while Domenico makes a grandiose speech and then sets himself aflame while standing on the horse of the statue of Marcus Aurelius on the Capitoline Hill. Each chooses a different way to die for his vision. Each "triumphs" in a certain measure over the Roman paganism of a fallen world. There is, however, a deep irony in the two actions: as Domenico declares, *urbi et orbi*, "Great things end, small ones last forever." The difference in style between Gorchakov and Domenico suggests, as in the case of Maria and Eugenia, that there is a "border" between the Russian and the Italian worlds, so that Domenico's magnificent gesture is doomed to be forgotten, while Gorchakov's modest feat will be forever meaningful. The difference is surely a confirmation that the dream of a world without borders is truly impossible. Nariman Skakov (2009, 330) writes: "The impossibility of the structural unity of the Tower of Babel serves as an extremely potent trope for dealing with the discourses of *Nostalgia*." In a metapoetic sense this is true, since we see Tarkovsky struggling to combine the two visual idioms of Russia and Italy in the fabric of the film. At the same time, for Tarkovsky the divisions of the world are part of a deeper spiritual malaise that all of his films seek to overcome, something that requires faith in miracles. Gorchakov's act of faith can be read as a metaphor for Tarkovsky's belief in the power of his art to bring about spiritual salvation. Domenico's final declaration and self-immolation are presented ironically as a stereotypically exaggerated and ultimately empty example of Italian bombast. Gorchakov's feat, by contrast, is presented absolutely without irony.

If the image of Gorchakov is a cinematic "self-portrait," it contains an extremely poignant element, namely the death of the poet, who suffers a heart attack and passes away at the very moment that he carries the lighted candle to the far side of the Bath of Saint Catherine. Given the high degree of autobiographical similarity between the protagonist of the film and the filmmaker himself, we are justified in reading Gorchakov's death as an example of autothanatology—that is to say, the character Gorchakov's symbolic enactment of his author's own impending death. Only three years later, in December 1986, having completed what turned out to be his final film *The Sacrifice*, Andrey Tarkovsky himself died of lung cancer. Since we know that Tarkovsky was a heavy smoker, we are obliged to re-examine, in contemplating the meanings contained within the film, the parallel noted above between the candle and the cigarette: Gorchakov dies clutching the candle, whereas his author, so to speak, dies clutching a cigarette. Here, at least, we can trace a hint of self-irony on Tarkovsky's part.

The final image with which the viewer is left returns us to Tarkovsky's plight in Italy. Samardzija (2004, 304) sees it as a utopian, unifying image: "The use of black and white in the shot links it to the nostalgic images that haunt Gorchakov. It suggests that the unification of the contrary spaces has occurred belatedly. […] And yet, the fact that Italy and Russia occupy the same space in the shot […] imparts a utopian element to the image." Surely, a simpler and more convincing reading of the scene is that Gorchakov/Tarkovsky, with his spiritual values intact and expressed in the warmth of family life experienced in the dacha, is imprisoned in Italy, surrounded inescapably by the ruins of a lost, dead spirituality. The film as a whole, and this final image in particular, expresses the author's rejection of the spiritually empty country in which he finds himself, a country whose ruined churches epitomize the loss of faith that has overcome the people. There can be no harmony in the final image, only an expression of the author's humble but genuine faith encapsulated in the image of his home and family. Tarkovsky's response to Italy is the inverse of the usual situation of the migrant, stereotyped and even rejected by the receiving society.

Nostalghia is a perfect example of the transposition of the Russian poetry of Arseny Tarkovsky into the images of his son Andrey. The filmmaker transcends the cultural boundary inhibiting translation by switching genres, although he was vocal in rejecting the very notion of interlingual translation which, ironically, had been a large part of Arseny's activity. Arseny was deeply troubled by his son's departure from Russia. For him, it was unthinkable to be a poet outside the confines of the homeland:

perhaps for this reason he tried his utmost to persuade his son to return to Russia. But exile for a poet, who works with words in the isolation of his study, is not the same as exile for a filmmaker, whose materials are physical images and sound. The filmmaker needs money and resources to produce films, as well as a distribution circuit. He also needs to be free of political interference. *Nostalghia* was Tarkovsky's answer to the political masters in Goskino, for whom a film demonstrating the spiritual superiority of Russia was an unacceptable response to the political atheism that was the ideology of the Soviet Union, and at the same time a magnificent *auto da fe*, the gesture of a man who undoubtedly knew that he had little time left to live. It is a sad irony that, as he lay dying in Paris, Tarkovsky's homeland was changing in profound ways that could have made possible his eventual triumphant return.

Notes

1. His final film, *The Sacrifice*, was made in Sweden in 1986. Andrey Tarkovsky died on December 29, 1986, in Paris.
2. We should note that the Russian *perevodchik* means both "translator" *and* "interpreter." Eugenia seems to be present in the latter role. This does not mean that she escapes Gorchakov/Tarkovsky's ire at the entire notion of translating and explaining one culture to another. His hostility echoes Nabokov's famous refusal to produce anything but a brutally literal translation of Pushkin's *Eugene Onegin*.
3. As Zoran Samardzija (2004, 202) points out, the fact that Domenico has a dog establishes a "spiritual bond" between him and Gorchakov.
4. It may also reflect a certain anger at the fate of many Soviet poets—Akhmatova, Pasternak, and Arseny Tarkovsky—who instead of pursuing poetry were condemned to translate. Ultimately, Andrey Tarkovsky's comment seems to be about his father, who had been condemned by the Soviet regime to pursue what the son sees as a meaningless task.
5. Domenico's bizarre action provokes the question: is the suffering of his family a parallel to the suffering of Andrey Tarkovsky's own family, destined to be separated for years, especially Andrey and his son, Andriusha, because of the father's pursuit of his work? The shots of Domenico and his son, and the son's question when they are released by the police from captivity—"Papa, is this the end of the world?"—seem to have a deeply personal meaning for the filmmaker. Although Andrey's wife and collaborator, Larissa, was able to join him abroad, the Soviet authorities refused to allow Andriusha to join them, essentially using him as hostage to control his father's activities.

6. The fact that the bathers call Domenico mad and stop him from carrying out his feat is perhaps an echo of the imprisonment in psychiatric hospitals of dissenters in the Soviet Union.
7. As Johnson and Petrie (1994, 162) write, Eugenia is "inescapably linked with the materialism and corruption of modern society."
8. As lines of motifs in the film, cigarettes and candles are closely related to the line of the cigarette-lighter (see Turovskaya 1989, 132).
9. I am grateful to Jakub Sadowski for pointing out the clear resemblance of the image of Domenico to Savonarola.
10. One recalls Jesus's prayer: "Father, if thou art willing, remove this cup from me; nevertheless, not my will, but thine, be done" (Luke 22.42). Tarkovsky (1987, 206) references this Biblical passage speaking about Domenico: "Gorchakov is not able to save Domenico from the role he has implacably assigned himself—without asking life to let the cup pass him by."

References

Bachmann, Gideon. 1984. O prirode nostal'gii. Interv'iu s Andreem Tarkovskim vel Gideon Bachmann. *Chaplin*. The Andrey Tarkovsky Media Archive. http://tarkovskiy.su/texty/Tarkovskiy/Bachmann.html.

Boym, Svetlana. 2001. *The Future of Nostalgia*. New York: Basic Books.

Demant, Ebbo. 1989. V poiskakh utrachennogo vremeni. In *O Tarkovskom*, ed. M. Tarkovskaya, 342–389. Moscow: Progress.

Dempsey, Michael. 1981. Lost Harmony: Tarkovsky's *The Mirror* and *The Stalker*. *Film Quarterly* 35 (1): 12–17.

Filippov, Viktor. 2012. *Andrey Tarkovsky: sny i yav' o dome*. Moscow: Molodaya gvardiya.

Johnson, Vida T., and Graham Petrie. 1994. *The Films of Andrei Tarkovsky: A Visual Fugue*. Bloomington: University of Indiana Press.

Le Fanu, Mark. 1987. *The Cinema of Andrei Tarkovsky*. London: BFI Publishing.

Martin, Sean. 2011. *Andrei Tarkovsky*. Harpenden: Kamera Books.

Mitchell, Tony. 1982. Tarkovsky in Italy. *Sight and Sound* 50 (1): 54–56.

Naficy, Hamid. 2001. *An Accented Cinema: Exilic and Diasporic Film-Making*. Princeton: Princeton University Press.

Samardzija, Zoran. 2004. 1+1=1: Impossible Translations in Andrey Tarkovsky's 'Nostalghia'. *Literature/Film Quarterly* 32 (4): 300–304.

Skakov, Nariman. 2009. The (Im)possible Translation of *Nostalgia*. *Studies in Russian and Soviet Cinema* 3 (3): 309–333.

———. 2012. *The Cinema of Tarkovsky: Labyrinths of Space and Time*. New York: I.B. Tauris.

Tarkovsky, Andrey, dir. 1983. *Nostalghia*. RAI 2 and Sovinfilm. DVD. Grange Communications Inc., 1984.

———. 1987. *Sculpting in Time*. Trans. Kitty Hunter-Blair. New York: Alfred A. Knopf.

———. 1993. *Time within Time: The Diaries 1970–1986*. Trans. Kitty Hunter-Blair. New York: Verso.

Tarkovsky, Arseny. 1993. *Blagoslovennyi svet*. Ed. M. Tarkovskaya. St. Petersburg: Severo-Zapad.

Turovskaya, Maya. 1989. *Tarkovsky: Cinema as Poetry*. Trans. Natasha Ward and Ed. Ian Christie. London: Faber and Faber.

PART II

Multiculturalism, Citizenship, and Belonging: Deep Equality and Diasporic Cultures

Read Her Lips: The Ban on Wearing the Niqab and Burqa at the Canadian Citizenship Ceremony 2011–2015

Zaheeda P. Alibhai

Any contemporary study that focuses on Muslim women carries with it a history and discourse that influences not only the author, before a single word has been written, but also the reader before a single word has been read. In other words, the history of the study of Muslim women and Islam is contentiously intertwined and shaped by colonial and imperial history. In the twenty-first century, nowhere do Orientalist notions and governmentality intersect more fully than in policy debates concerning Muslim women and citizenship. This chapter critically analyses the global, national, and religious dimensions that formed the basis for the 2011–2015 Canadian Conservative government's ban on the wearing of face coverings, specifically the niqab (face covering with the eyes showing) and burqa (full-body covering with netting in front of the eyes) during the Oath of Citizenship at Canadian citizenship ceremonies. The ban against wearing the niqab and burqa is analysed as a public act that provides the

Z. P. Alibhai (✉)
University of Ottawa, Ottawa, ON, Canada
e-mail: zalib020@uottawa.ca

Y. Meerzon et al. (eds.), *Migration and Stereotypes in Performance and Culture*, Contemporary Performance InterActions,
https://doi.org/10.1007/978-3-030-39915-3_7

foundation for the development of political agendas. My argument highlights the reproduction of historical narratives in contemporary ones, illustrating how colonial history invades the present (Lister 2003) and the resilience of certain notions of Islam and women that travel across centuries and contexts (Karim 2000).

However, the purpose of this chapter is not to provide a full analysis of this history or determine whether wearing the niqab and burqa is a religious obligation or cultural practice. Rather, I am concerned with the representation of the burqa and niqab in light of the misrepresentations of the religion of Islam, misrepresentations that formed the basis for prohibiting face coverings during the Oath of Citizenship at Canadian citizenship ceremonies. Such misrepresentations overlook the religious and cultural significance of the niqab and burqa from within different interpretations of Islam itself. In framing the ban not as a religious issue but a cultural one, the state assumes the role of arbiter of religious praxis by entering into a historically theological debate within different interpretations of Islam.

The debates over the niqab and burqa play into larger security discourses and speak to a broader issue that has been active globally since September 11, 2001, when the surveillance and control of those perceived as Muslim became justified under the guise of national security. This chapter focuses on the national dimensions that formed the basis for the Canadian Conservative government's joint prohibition of the niqab and burqa and argues that the ban emphasized both legal and social norms of inclusion and exclusion of Canadian citizenship. I conclude by highlighting the ways in which reflective voices shifted the divisive discourse from "horizontal inequality" (Stewart 2017) towards "deep equality" (Beaman 2017) between citizens.

Contemporary Context

On December 12, 2011, Jason Kenney, the Canadian Minister for Immigration, Citizenship, and Multiculturalism between 2008 and 2013, announced that the Conservative government was placing a ban on all face coverings, specifically the niqab and burqa, during the Oath at Canadian citizenship ceremonies. The government's rationale was that the Oath of Citizenship is a public act of devotion and loyalty to Canada in front of one's fellow citizens and thus cannot be sworn when one's face was hidden. Minister Kenney stated that the citizenship oath is a public declaration of one's desire to join "the Canadian family, which an individual makes in front of their fellow citizens and representatives of the state" (Herhalt 2014). He further commented that the Canadian family is undergirded by liberal democratic values including respect for the freedom of religion, equality between men and women, as well as equality of all citizens before the law. Kenney argued that covering one's face undermined those basic liberal values, calling the practice a "cultural" and "tribal" custom and "not a religious obligation." He asserted that it is not a coincidence that tribal societies, which force women to cover their faces, tend to treat women as property. Having established these parameters and defined covering as "tribal," Minister Kenney then stated that a covered face is disrespectful when an individual interacts with the state and fellow citizens in a public environment such as the citizenship ceremony, and that the Canadian government would not lend the legitimacy of the Canadian state to such practices. It could well be argued that liberal conceptions of freedom and equality are both political and prescriptive projects that have contemporary implications for different modes of being in the world. In her study of the urban women's mosque movement in Egypt, Saba Mahmood (2005) has demonstrated that the desire for freedom from or subversion of norms is not an innate desire that motivates human beings at all times, but that it is profoundly mediated by cultural and historical conditions. Mahmood argues that we must start to look at the ways in which operations of power construct different kinds of bodies, knowledge, and subjectivities, and whose trajectories do not rely on normative assumptions of liberatory politics.

When knowledge is shaped within a matrix of power relations, its contemporary manifestation retains that same shape. The rhetoric that informs former minister Kenney's statements can be situated within the same discourses that sustain the colonial logic identified in this chapter. These similarities have serious implications for contemporary definitions of religion and its role in Canadian public life. To begin, we must first consider the complex background of the veil from the colonial period to today, before exploring the ramifications of this history that is at play in the Canadian ban against wearing the niqab and burqa during the oath allegiance at the Canadian citizenship ceremony.

The Historical Context: Egypt

The notion that face covering is oppressive was born from the impulse to dominate (Bullock 2010). Throughout the colonial age, Western colonial powers encountered what they termed the "veil," and thus the constructed image of veiling as a "backward" and "oppressive" practice entered the Western colonial imagination. The veil became a divisive symbol that combined all three strands of colonial and imperial rhetoric of cultural, religious, and gender-based superiority. Colonialists saw veiling as an overarching symbol of the perceived degradation of women they believed to be inherent to Islam, and as evidence of the supposed backwardness of the religion/people/civilization monolith. The veil as a symbol thus reflected the power dynamic at the heart of this aggressive conflation, and was regularly associated with the rhetoric of "holding women back" and "keeping women under men's thumbs" (Valenta 2006, 457). Consequently, it was only through "lifting" or "casting off" the veil that Muslim women and Islamic societies could progress towards civilization and participate mentally, morally, and socially in modern life (449).

During the nineteenth century in Egypt, British Consul-General Lord Cromer championed the cause of "unveiling" Muslim women, claiming the veil was a hazard to their moral and mental development. Cromer denounced the veil as being fundamentally oppressive, a way of subordinating Muslim women under the irrational rule of Muslim men. In this way, for much of the nineteenth and twentieth centuries, the veil provided a potent visual marker of what colonial and imperial powers constructed as Islamic inferiority, a symbol of backwardness whose intrinsic nature colonialists claimed was oppressive to women, in contrast to the freedoms allowed to women by colonial Christianity (Valenta 2006, 449). It must be noted that Lord Cromer's emphatic demands for the emancipation of women did not extend beyond the colonies. He was a founding member and president of the Men's League for Opposing Woman Suffrage in Britain (449).

Religion(s) in Context: Communities of Interpretations

Unfortunately, modern debates surrounding the burqa and niqab continue to be shaped by the gendered colonial discourse on the veil. Contemporary views often reproduce colonial rhetoric that perceives the burqa and niqab as symbols of oppression and subordination. In March 2015, former Prime Minister Stephen Harper resurrected this argument in the Canadian House of Commons, when he asked Parliament, "Why would Canadians, contrary to our own values, embrace a practice at that time that is not transparent, that is not open and frankly is rooted in a culture that is anti-women" (Chase 2015). Harper was responding to the Federal Court of Appeal's ruling that the Conservative government's ban on face coverings during the Oath of Citizenship was unlawful.[1] He proceeded to argue that the ban on face coverings was not an issue of religious freedom, but one of defending Canadian identity since "Muslim women are not obligated, not required to cover their faces in public," and at any rate, "most moderate Muslims support the ban" ("Will Stephen Harper regret remark on niqab?" 2015).

Multiple aspects of the former Prime Minister's statements are problematic. For one, the significance and the role of covering in Islam is not so clear. Islam is a global faith with over one billion followers. Muslims encompass a multiplicity of cultural, ethnic, regional, linguistic, and racial pluralities coupled by interpretive heterogeneity. From this reality, Muslims are considered a "community of communities" (Karim 2000, 1) of heterogeneous interpretations, cultures, social organizations, traditions, and societies marked by "intra-communal difference and religious plurality" (Hirji 2010, 8). Notwithstanding this enormous diversity, some Muslims claim cultural "Muslimness" rather than religious "Muslimness" (Abu-Lughod 1995; Göle 1996; Selby 2016). Debates over covering are complex and filled with tensions, ambiguities, and contradictions that have existed since Muslim state formation and the beginnings of early Muslim communities. Muslim women who cover do so for a variety of reasons, including as a tool of empowerment or modesty, or a public expression of religious, ethnic, and cultural identity. For some, veiling is a religious obligation; these women interpret specific verses in the Qur'an (24:30–31; 33:59) as divine commands to cover as an embodiment of modesty and an integral step on their road to piety. These verses have been interpreted, debated, and argued amongst varying communities both inside and outside of Islam. Scholars, historians, and communities differ over this historically complex issue. However, women who cover believe that in order to cultivate the necessary attributes of self, the Islamic virtue of modesty must be lived and embodied in order to be realized. These women believe that covering expresses "true modesty" and is the means through which modesty as a virtue is attained. For them, modesty is the norm that they seek to cultivate, and the veil is the bodily form of that norm. Therefore, the veiled body becomes the essential means through which modesty is both created and expressed (Mahmood 2005, 23).

Katherine Bullock (2010) questions the discourse that "pushes" Canadian Muslim women who cover out of the nation. Her research demonstrates that Muslim women in Canada who cover assert their pride in being Canadian, being Muslim, and covering—there is no conflict between their religious and national identities nor is there a loyalty test from one or the other. Atasoy (2003) found that young, highly educated, and professional Canadian Muslim women choose to cover as a medium to represent their "Canadianness." Historically and contemporarily, covering has never been a fixed practice and reflects the complexity of how religious belief and social reality are shaped and constituted by one another.

The Deeper Principle: Read Her Lips

The former Prime Minister Stephen Harper stated that the citizenship oath is the moment when prospective citizen joins the Canadian family and that it is offensive that someone would hide their identity during that moment ("Niqab-citizenship ceremony ruling will be appealed, PM says" 2015). On the Canadian Broadcasting Corporation's television programme, *Power & Politics*, former minister Kenney implied that citizenship ceremony regulations provided a dual function. First, that the face of the individual must be uncovered in order to visually verify that they are indeed reciting the Oath of Citizenship—that her lips are *seen* moving. Second, the "deeper principle" frames the oath as a public act of loyalty to Canada which must therefore be recited "uncovered" to express devotion to Canada and its democratic values ("Face veils banned for citizenship oath" 2011).[2] The implicit message is that a woman who wears the burqa or niqab cannot recite the Oath of Citizenship authentically and thus cannot be loyal to Canada. This rhetoric casts the woman who chooses to wear a burqa or niqab as duplicitous, whose loyalty remains with those "tribal societies" and in opposition to the Canadian state. The subtext creates a prosthetic citizenship (cited in Perera 2009, 228) for Muslim women who cover, such that they are deemed suspicious or disloyal even if they are born in Canada or immigrate to Canada and abide by the ban. The state demands the removal of the burqa or the niqab *only* at the specific moment the oath is recited, which symbolically identifies the burqa and niqab as threats. The rhetoric implies that the state is under constant and absolute threat and, therefore, women who wear the burqa or niqab can undermine the legitimacy of the state. Furthermore, it suggests that citizens should be on guard against the perceived threat of Muslim women. Whenever statements are made that uphold loyalty as a Canadian value, the loyalty and devotion of Muslim women are implicitly called into question as a transgression against the state. Moreover, the state adds a physical precondition for Canadian citizenship: an uncovered face (Razack 2018, 176). According to Joseph Pugliese (Perera 2009, 228), this is when citizenship acts as a prosthesis, a foreign part whose addition allows a subject to function but remains visibly adjunct to the body. It is a citizenship that cannot be corporeally owned or nativized. It is precisely this notion of citizenship that isolates and stigmatizes individuals by representing them as illegible to the nation (Melamed 2011, 39).

The public proclamations made by Prime Minister Harper and Minister Kenney brought particular identities into being and asserted authority over all of them. When the former Prime Minister stated that the citizenship oath must be recited "openly" and "freely," he inferred that women who wear the niqab or burqa are hiding something or being deceptive. His statement cast doubt as to the internal motives of a woman who chooses to recite the oath while wearing her niqab. Therefore, in everyday interactions, the state influences how women who wear the burqa and niqab are perceived and treated within the nation. Moreover, public space becomes the place where national identity and proper religious identity are actualized through the prism of visibility—after all, a good citizen/believer has nothing to hide (Amiraux 2016, 42).

It must be noted that in certain situations, Canadian Muslim women who wear the burqa or niqab do not object to publicly uncovering or showing their faces. Currently, women who wear the burqa or niqab show their faces during airport security checks, for identification cards, and when accessing hospital services. Similarly, the recitation of the oath at the Canadian citizenship ceremony is often approached in the same cooperative spirit (Clarke 2013).

Canadian Politics and Geopolitical Narratives: Egypt, Again?

In its attempt to justify the ban on face coverings during the Oath of Citizenship, the Canadian Conservative government used as "evidence" a religious decree made by the late Egyptian Sheikh Mohammad Sayyed Tantawi's[3] dismissing the burqa and niqab as secondary cultural practices not founded in Islam. In 2009, Sheikh Tantawi issued a fatwa (religious decree) and instigated a public campaign to ban female students from wearing the niqab at Egyptian universities. In this way, the current context in Egypt had a direct bearing on the contemporary Canadian ban. Moreover, what remains absent from Tantawi's decree—and thus the Canadian government's authoritative "evidence"—is the specific religious and political context, and the diversity of interpretations and tensions from which policies, decrees, and theological arguments arise that characterize the niqab and burqa as cultural practices not founded in Islam.[4]

The decree made by the late Sheikh Tantawi must be seen within the wider historical debate and contentious contemporary political struggle that had been going on in Egypt during this time. The ban against wearing the niqab in Egypt has been at the centre of the power struggle between the Egyptian state and Salafist Muslims.[5] Al-Azhar Mosque is considered an institution of the Egyptian state and plays a role in state policy formation. The decree was used to curb increasing Salafist public presence and political organizing in order to curtail Salafist influence in Egypt.[6] More importantly, sectarian Salafist Muslim women believe that wearing the burqa and niqab is a religious obligation and part of their religious practice (Al-Fartousi and Mogadime 2012, 171).

During the Canadian debates surrounding the ban, the niqab became an entity in and of itself: as the material site where geopolitical discourses, national narratives, and religious scripts combined and conflicted. In this respect, Egyptian government, politics, religion, and culture were intertwined in ways that blurred history, divisive parties, competing religious organizations, and boundaries into a social and political matrix that ultimately bled into the Canadian landscape. The Canadian government policy buttressed by certain Canadian Muslim organizations lays bare the complex historical arguments that have been used for centuries by Muslims and non-Muslims alike to argue for and against wearing the niqab and burqa. Supporting Tantawi's decree and lauding the Canadian government's ban was the Canadian Muslim Congress (MCC), a self-proclaimed "moderate Muslim" organization that argued that covering is rooted in Middle Eastern culture and not in Islam. Tariq Ramadan (2010) argues that "moderate Muslim" is a political construction that serves the political needs of the time. The MCC not only supported the Canadian Conservative government's "courageous decision" but also pressured the government to expand the ban to other areas of public life. In October 2009, the MCC demanded that the federal government introduce legislation that would ban the wearing of niqabs, burkas, and other face coverings in public. Crucially, the MCC condemned the burqa and niqab using the rhetoric that we have seen above, which has its origins in the colonial exercise of power. The MCC calls veiling a practice that "reflects a mode of male control over women" and is a "vestige of medieval culture that has no place in Canada where our modern sensibilities have come to recognize the equality of men and women as an inalienable right for all" (Downie 2013, 30). Similarly, former minister Kenney echoed the MCC when he stated that the niqab "reflects a misogynistic culture—a treatment of women as property rather than people, which is anchored in medieval tribal customs as opposed to any religious obligation" (Solomon 2015). The Muslim Canadian Congress must be seen in a wider context that has emerged post-9/11 and that has framed most debates regarding Muslim cultural politics (Zine 2012, 14). These debates evoke concerns about how immigrants are integrating within the nation and whether immigrants are adopting "Canadian values" (6).

Citizenship debates play into these discourses and speak to a broader issue that has been reactivated globally since September 11, 2001. The surveillance and control of Muslims and those perceived as Muslims become justified under the guise of national security and the stiffening of national narratives. This is most clearly seen by statements that position religious belief as a transgression of national identity and values. Former Canadian Prime Minister Stephen Harper argued that the ban against face coverings was not an issue of religion but one of defending Canadian identity and the broader values of "an equal and open society" (Chase 2015). Indeed, concealed by discourses of conflicting values, this reveals an effective political tactic of shaping citizens through self-discipline that emphasizes both social and legal norms of inclusion and exclusion of citizenship.[7] In this way, nations and national identities are continuously being shaped, reshaped, contested, and recontested not only within a continuum of renewal but also in relation to difference (Yuval-Davis 1997).

According to Oliver Roy (2009), when a religious tradition claims to be the "true" religion, it is one that at any given moment explicitly posits culture as otherness. The centrality of the concept of "culture" as an explanatory tool made in the arguments by the Canadian government and the Muslim Canadian Congress not only redefines religion as culture but, as Joan Wallach Scott (2009, 7) implies, culture becomes an entity of objectively discernable values and traditions that come to be seen as homogeneous, immutable, and stagnant. Complexity, politics, and history are absent and become the effect of a very particular, historically specific political discourse that enacts a particular version of reality.

When the power of the state, dominant interpretations of a single religion and powerful organizations collude; they control the boundaries of what is accepted as "real" religion and who is considered a "real" citizen in the nation. In this way, a specific idea of religion emerges at the expense of religious diversity, religious freedom, and the protection of citizen rights guaranteed in the Canadian Charter of Rights and Freedoms. In Canada, multiculturalism not only reflects a demographic reality but a constitutional commitment to preserve and enhance the multicultural heritage of Canadians. According to Lori Beaman (2012), the separation of church and state is more of a Canadian cultural belief than it is a constitutional truth. For example, the preamble to the Charter of Rights and Freedoms explicitly states that Canada is founded upon principles that recognize the supremacy of God and the rule of law, guaranteeing "religious freedom." Bruce Ryder (2005, 174–175) argues that freedom of religion and state neutrality require that governments avoid laws or policies that seek to enforce the practices of a particular religion or indoctrinate citizens in particular beliefs. However, the ideal of religious freedom and state neutrality crumble when a singular form of believer is legitimized and tolerated in political spaces and is thereby made worthy of the protection and benefits of religious freedom, while other forms of religiosity are deemed illegitimate and unworthy of protection (Amiraux 2016, 41).

In this way, the steady stream of characterizations made by the "native voice" (MCC) and echoed by the Canadian government designate women who wear the niqab or burqa as prosthetic believers. A new layer of meaning is attached to the burqa and niqab, one that should be understood as constituting new forms of power (Beaman 2014, 54). The net effect of this becomes the marginalization or othering of a group's religious beliefs and embodied practices. These beliefs and practices become "defined out" as no longer religious (McGuire 2008, 74) and no longer worthy of the protection of one's right to religious freedom under the constitution (Beaman 2014, 54).

Therefore, the constitutional guarantee of religious freedom and the cultural belief in the separation of state and religion dissolves, and instead emerges as a tool of governmentality: what Michel Foucault (1978) refers to as the conduct of conduct, or a form of activity aimed to shape, guide, or affect the conduct of individuals or, rather, citizens and believers. In the case of the ban on the niqab and burqa, the Canadian government redefines a religious obligation as a cultural product, or a strategy for religious and cultural assimilation to form new, tolerable, and more comfortable (i.e. state-approved) identities. The dominant, state-sanctioned interpretation of religion and religious tradition becomes invisible in the public sphere and renders the minority and less dominant claims to public space even more visible (Amiraux 2016, 8) and more of a clash of national values and legitimate religious beliefs. It is here where the prosthetic citizen and believer is mutually and legally defined, shaped, and disciplined by the Canadian government. Varying textual interpretations, different authority figures, complex political arrangements (e.g. between the Egyptian state and religious institutions), cultural factors, and social concerns slip into Canadian public life where they are reproduced and codified in policy. Moreover, the Canadian government participates in theology shopping[8] by selectively choosing and discarding which religious beliefs and practices are legitimate (real) and adjudicating based on this preference. This creates a false sense of a singular theological interpretation within Islam.

In this way, the semantic linking of modern governance and historical narratives effaces the power relations between different interpretations of the same religion, as well as the modality of power relations that operate according to a specific idea of how religion and religious practice should or should not be expressed and organized in the public sphere. These strands of biopower, what Foucault (1978) terms the modality of power that operates through the orchestration and regulation of daily life, became more visible when the public statements made by the Canadian government and the Muslim Canadian Congress laid bare *islamophobic* and *islamophilic* discourses (Shirock 2010). In part, a particular model of Muslim womanhood becomes constructed and assumed as normative. Muslim women who do not wear the burqa and niqab assume a normative mantle of a monolithic Muslim Woman as the standard by which other Muslim women must conform in order to be accepted by the nation. At the heart of these discourses is a simplistic bifurcation between static identities that are based on fixed normative qualities of "good" Muslims and "real" Islam versus "bad" Muslims and "false" Islam. Thus, while the heterogeneity of "Islam" remains undisturbed in this instance, the narrative of a monolithic construction of women who wear the burqa or niqab as "oppressed" and victims of "tribal societies that treat women as property" ("Face veils banned for citizenship oath" 2011) is sustained. More importantly, the key assumption made by the Canadian government and the Muslim Canadian Congress are that women wearing the niqab or burqa are coerced into wearing them. While there may be some women who are forced into covering, a survey conducted by the Canadian Council of Muslim Women (CCMW) found that the majority of respondents surveyed had chosen to wear the niqab and burqa of their own free will. In some cases, this choice was made despite the protests of their families, male members included (Herhalt 2014).

At the state level, intracommunal difference as represented to the state and by the state itself "may well undermine whole groups of Muslims who do not conform to the 'Islam' defined by those who have been seen by the state as having the authority to define Islam, and concurrently have power and influence over the state" (Hirji 2010, 20). This creates a type of interlegality where the state participates in the intermingling of norms, meanings, values, and legal (religious decree by one interpretation) elements into the practice and rule of the national legal order (Hoekema 2008, 4). Talal Asad (2006, 498) argues that the state itself can assume the role of religious authority because it embodies a single absolute power and purports to represent transcendental neutrality. The critical point here, as Stuart Hall (1996) argues, is that citizenship and national culture are not simply imbricated webs of allegiance, bonding, or symbolic identification of the "social imaginary" but, rather, they are structures of power. As such, the state can face the political task of shaping the beliefs of believers, good/real Muslims versus bad/false Muslims (Mamdani 2002, 767) in ways that are most conducive to the secular complexion of the state. Lori Beaman (2014, 46) argues that these are the remnants of a Christian hegemony embedded in Canadian social and political institutions. Beaman cautions that when the intertwining of the state and particular religions becomes indistinguishable and they become embedded in the social structure, institutions, and policy, it may become impossible to untangle them from one another. Therefore, the relationship between the Canadian state and religious institutions must be watched very carefully. This is most clearly seen in the way that culture, religion, and religious freedom have been imagined, shaped, and redefined in the ban on face coverings during the Oath of Citizenship. Islam as a global faith is objectified within a singular authority figure structure (an ambiguous mix of Egyptian authorities and "moderate Muslim" organizations) that works to maintain and sustain the Canadian Conservative government's position that "most moderate Muslims agree with the public aspect of the citizenship ceremony" ("Will Stephen Harper regret remark on niqab?" 2015). In fact, Abou El-Fadl (2005) contends that the "moderate Muslim" designation is political and coercive and is used to confirm and uphold the religious legitimacy of the idea of a one true and authentic Islam. Moreover, public statements disguised as theological decrees not only serve as a mode to render religious judgments and precedents, but the state representative acts as a religious textual exegete and becomes the interpreter, mediator, and authority figure in doctrinal debates vis-à-vis Muslims and non-Muslims alike.

The residual effects of the language used by Conservative Government officials, as well as the public shaming techniques and the epistemic violence embedded in their public statements, directly affected and continues to shape the daily lives of Canadian Muslim women who wear the niqab, burqa, or hijab, or are perceived to wear them. These spatial politics add to the colonial narrative by creating the niqab as *the* iconography of fear, which in turn influences some Muslim women's experience in the nation state (Gökarıksel 2012). The National Council of Canadian Muslims confirmed that it received several reports of Muslim women being verbally or physically assaulted. Various media outlets reported a series of violent acts against women who wear or are perceived as wearing the niqab, burqa, or hijab.[9] The reported incidents had a common thread, namely that the victims' niqab, hijab, or perceived hijab were pulled off their head (MacCharles and Spurr 2015). However, it was also in the public *in between* spaces that more reflective voices shifted the focus from horizontal inequality towards deep equality between citizens.

From Horizontal Inequality to Deep Equality

In her article, "Horizontal Inequalities: Barriers to Pluralism,"[10] Frances Stewart (2017) states that horizontal inequalities (HIs)—inequalities among groups of people—are multidimensional and are seen across various economic, social, political, class, and cultural dimensions and racial, ethnic, religious, and gender identities (Stewart 2). Large HIs in nations can create justice gaps between citizens and are "clear drivers of exclusion" that include "a lack of respect for other cultures" (5). Most often, HIs are place based, meaning that they are shaped by the particular political, social, and cultural history of societies and produce specific sets of national narratives, identities, ideologies, and practices. Yet, as Stewart argues, some horizontal inequalities based on categories of identity utilize socially constructed markers of difference such as religion and make visible the close linkage between horizontal inequalities and colonial history. As we have seen, the linkage between horizontal inequality and colonial history leads to contemporary tensional positions that constitute divisive lines that reinforce exclusionary boundaries amongst citizens (Alibhai 2019). Talal Asad (2006) argues that the implications of this tensional character is a distinctive feature of modern liberal governance that uses self-discipline, participation, and law as elements of exclusive citizen (identity) formation. Stewart cautions that while it becomes crucial to reduce HIs for social stability and justice in pluralist societies—it is insufficient by itself and requires a combination of approaches (5). Lori Beaman (2017) argues for moving away from "master narratives" of clashes and conflicts of differences between citizens and shifting towards approaches of negotiation, generosity, agonistic respect, similarities, and narratives of equality, in other words, *deep equality* amongst citizens. Deep equality centres on the collection of empirical evidence that explores, understands, and maps micro-level "everyday" instances where difference is negotiated within the values of caring, neighbourliness, and shared humanity (3) to make way for similarities between people. Deep equality is not about "differences" and the plurality of identities receding in the background but rather, a reconstituted and engaged equality that pushes past the ideals of simply "living together" as citizens and towards the continuous process of living *well* together (Elver 2012, 200) as neighbours.

It is also in the public *in between* spaces that more reflective voices can shift the focus from horizontal inequality towards deep equality between citizens. For instance, Canada's first Muslim senator, Mobeena Jaffer (2015), wrote an opinion piece in the *Vancouver Sun* titled, "Zunera Ishaq is a Canadian Hero," in which she characterized Zunera Ishaq, who challenged the ban on face coverings during the citizenship ceremony, as a hero for standing up for Canadian values. In another example, future Prime Minister Justin Trudeau argued that women who wear the niqab strengthened the Canadian family. During the 2015 Canadian federal election debates, Canadians watched and listened as a sitting Prime

Minister and his officials laid bare an exclusive ideal of what kind of citizen had the "right" values (i.e. an uncovered face). Harper and his government implied that women who wore the niqab were offensive, and that their values, although guaranteed in the constitution, conflicted with so-called Canadian values. Some Canadians expressed their disdain at such exclusionary notions of who, according to the Conservative government, could belong to the "Canadian family," by creating Twitter hashtags (#DressCodePM) and Tumblr sites (Niqabs of/du Canada). Canadians shared pictures of themselves with their faces covered by hockey masks, surgeon masks, and ski masks, and questioned if Harper would consider them offensive or disloyal to Canada; whether they were still part of the Canadian family. Others voted with their faces covered during Canada's 2015 general election to show their solidarity with women who wear the niqab and to protest against the divisive rhetoric of what a Canadian citizen should look like, be spoken about, or treated. In this way, op-eds to twitter hashtags transform the colonial-influenced narrative of Muslim women who wear the niqab to provide a powerful space for deep equality to flourish and relationships of negotiation and engagement become possible.

Conclusion: Read Her Editorial

The title of this chapter, "Read Her Lips," reflects and emphasizes the harm that occurs when stereotypes and representations slip into government policy. Indeed, while many Canadians expressed apprehension over the idea of the niqab, they were more apprehensive of a sitting Prime Minister publicly shaming Zunera Ishaq, a prospective Canadian citizen, and marginalizing the small minority of Muslim women who wear the niqab from the Canadian family. Ishaq, the woman at the centre of the debate, published an editorial in Canada's highest circulated newspaper, the *Toronto Star*, titled "Why I intend to wear a niqab at my citizenship ceremony." Ishaq recognized that, while wearing the niqab during the Oath of Citizenship might prevent Canadians from reading her *lips*, they could instead read her *words* that expressed her love, devotion, and active citizenship to Canada.

On October 19, 2015, Canadians along with new citizen Zunera Ishaq took to the polls in Canada's forty-second federal election and elected a new Liberal government. In her first act as attorney general and Minister of Justice, the Honourable Jody Wilson-Raybould formally and legally retracted the 2011–2015 niqab ban, declaring that the retraction was a symbol of the values that make us Canadian—those of diversity and inclusion (Crawford 2015).

Notes

1. The case began when Zunera Ishaq immigrated to Canada from Pakistan in 2008. Zunera legally challenged the Conservative government's ban on wearing the niqab during the citizenship ceremony. For case overview, see Zaheeda Alibhai (2018) Case Study: Zunera Ishaq v. Minister of Citizenship and Immigration. *EUREL: Sociological and Religious Data on Religions in Europe and Beyond*. See http://www.eurel.info/spip.php?article3035.
2. It is important to note that prior to the recitation of the oath, prospective citizens must sign the legally binding written version of the oath.
3. Sheikh Tantawi was a leading spiritual leader in Sunni Islam. He served as the Grand Mufti of Egypt from 1986 to 1996, when former Egyptian president Hosni Mubarak appointed him Grand Imam of Al-Azhar. Tantawi served in this position until his death in 2010.
4. In Egypt, Islam has come to embody a variegated process of movements, ideas, and practices. For some Egyptian Muslims, Islam is the cultural topography from which the Egyptian nation was built, a doctrinal system with political and juridical connotations of the proper ordering of state and society, and/or a system of beliefs harmonized to daily life. Whether women should cover their faces is a long-standing debate among scholars.
5. Salafism is a distinct interpretation of Sunni Islam.
6. We see these same politics playing out in France where the niqab has become linked to Salafist extremists.
7. Colleen Bell (2011, 106) has argued that, in security discourses, conflict situations are "dramatized and presented as supreme priorities." In this way, conflict situations are fashioned as more authentic if they are perceived as urgent and requiring immediate action.
8. Hoekema (2008) uses the concept of "discourse shopping" to describe "actors" switching from one style of doing justice and normative repertoire to another.
9. In Toronto, for example, a woman was wearing a scarf over her hair to protect it from the rain when someone ripped it off her and told her to go back to where she came from.
10. For a detailed analysis, see the Global Center for Pluralism publication series *Accounting for Change in Diverse Societies* that focuses on six international cases that examine specific moments when a country amended its approach to diversity by either expanding or eroding the foundations of inclusive citizenship. See Global Centre for Pluralism https://www.pluralism.ca.

References

Abou El-Fadl, Khaled. 2005. *The Great Theft: Wrestling Islam from the Extremists*. New York: Harper San Francisco.

Abu-Lughod, Lila. 1995. Movie Stars and Islamic Moralism in Egypt. *Social Text* 42: 53–67.

Al-Fartousi, May, and Dolana Mogadime. 2012. Media Representations of Muslim Women Wearing the Burka: Criticism and Implications. In *Politics, Participation & Power Relations*, ed. Richard C. Mitchell and Shannon A. Moore, 169–182. Rotterdam: Sense Publishers.

Alibhai, Zaheeda P. 2018. Case Study: Zunera Ishaq v. Minister of Citizenship and Immigration. *EUREL: Sociological and Religious Data on Religions in Europe and Beyond*, February 15. http://www.eurel.info/spip.php?article3035.

———. 2019. The Boundaries of Religious Pluralism. In *Emergent Religious Pluralisms*, ed. Jan-Jonathan Bock, John Fahy, and Samuel Everett, 49–71. London: Palgrave Macmillan.

Amiraux, Valerie. 2016. Visibility, Transparency and Gossip: How Did the Religion of Some (Muslims) Become the Public Concern of Others? *Critical Research on Religion* 4 (1): 37–56.

Asad, Talal. 2006. Trying to Understand French Secularism. In *Political Theologies: Public Religions in a Post-Secular World*, ed. Hent de Vries and Lawrence E. Sullivan, 494–526. New York: Fordham University Press.

Atasoy, Yildiz. 2003. Muslim Organizations in Canada: Gender Ideology and Women's Veiling. *Sociological Focus* 36 (2): 143–158.

Beaman, Lori G. 2012. Beyond Establishment. *The Immanent Frame*. April 27. https://tif.ssrc.org/2012/04/27/beyond-establishment/.

———. 2014. Between the Public and the Private: Governing Religious Expression. In *Religion in the Public Sphere: Canadian Case Studies*, ed. Solange Lefebvre and Lori G. Beaman, 44–65. Toronto: University of Toronto Press.

———. 2017. *Deep Equality in an Era of Religious Diversity*. Oxford: Oxford University Press.

Bell, Colleen. 2011. *The Freedom of Security: Governing Canada in the Age of Counter-Terrorism*. Vancouver: UBC Press.

Bullock, Katherine. 2010. Hijab and Belonging: Canadian Muslim Women. In *Islam and the Veil: Theoretical and Regional Contexts*, ed. Theodore Gabriel and Rabiha Hannan, 161–180. London: Continuum International Publishing Group.

CBC News. 2011. Face Veils Banned for Citizenship Oath. *Canadian Broadcasting Corporation,* December 12. www.cbc.ca/news/politics/story/2011/12/12/pol-kenney-citizenship-rules.html.

———. 2015. Will Stephen Harper Regret Remarks on Niqab. *Canadian Broadcasting Corporation,* March 12. https://www.cbc.ca/news/canada/manitoba/will-stephen-harper-regret-remark-on-niqabs-1.2993130.

Chase, Steven. 2015. Niqabs 'Rooted in a Culture That is Anti-Women,' Harper Says. *The Globe and Mail,* March 10. https://www.theglobeandmail.com/news/politics/niqabs-rooted-in-a-culture-that-is-anti-women-harper-says/article23395242/.

Clarke, Linda. 2013. Women in Niqab Speak: A Study of the Niqab in Canada. *Canadian Council of Muslim Women.* http://ccmw.com/women-in-niqab-speak-a-study-of-the-niqab-in-canada/.

Crawford, Alison. 2015. Justin Trudeau's Government Drops Controversial Niqab Appeal. *Canadian Broadcasting Corporation,* November 16. https://www.cbc.ca/news/politics/niqab-appeal-appeal-citizenship-ceremonies-canada-jody-wilson-raybould-1.3321264.

Downie, Caitlin. 2013. Constructing Islamophilia Within the Muslim Community: The Case of the Muslim Canadian Congress. *Amsterdam Social Science* 5 (1): 25–46.

Elver, Hilal. 2012. *The Headscarf Controversy.* Oxford: Oxford University Press.

Foucault, Michel. 1978. *The History of Sexuality.* Vol. 1, The Will to Knowledge. New York: Pantheon Books.

Gökarıksel, Banu. 2012. The Intimate Politics of Secularism and the Headscarf: The Mall, the Neighborhood, and the Public Square in Istanbul. *Gender, Place & Culture* 19 (1): 1–20.

Göle, Nilüfer. 1996. *The Forbidden Modern: Civilization and Veiling.* Ann Arbour: University of Michigan Press.

Hall, Stuart. 1996. *Modernity: An Introduction to Modern Societies.* Cambridge, MA: Blackwell.

Herhalt, Chris. 2014. Study Dispels Stereotypes About Ontario Women Who Wear Niqabs. *Canadian Council of Muslim Women.* January 30. http://ccmw.com/ccmw-national/study-dispels-stereotypes-about-ontario-women-who-wear-niqabs/.

Hirji, Zulfikar. 2010. Debating Islam from Within: Muslim Constructions of the Internal Other. In *Diversity and Pluralism in Islam: Historical and Contemporary Discourses amongst Muslims,* ed. Zulfikar Hirji, 1–30. London: I.B. Tauris.

Hoekema, Andre J. 2008. Multicultural Conflicts and National Judges: A General Approach. *Law, Social Justice & Global Development Journal* 12 (2): 1–14.

Global Centre for Pluralism. https://www.pluralism.ca/.

Jaffer, Mobeena. 2015. Opinion: Zunera Ishaq is a Canadian Hero. *Vancouver Sun*, March 30. www.vancouversun.com/life/Opinion+Zunera+Ishaq+Canadian+hero/10928395/story.html.

Karim, H. 2000. *Islamic Peril: Media and Global Violence.* Montreal: Black Rose Books.

Lister, Ruth. 2003. *Citizenship: Feminist Perspectives.* New York: New York University Press.

MacCharles, Tonda, and Ben Spurr. 2015. Harper Pitting Country Against Muslims, Some Niqab Wearers Say. *Toronto Star.* October 7. https://www.thestar.com/news/federal-election/2015/10/07/harper-pitting-country-against-muslims-some-niqab-wearers-say.html.

Mahmood, Saba. 2005. *The Politics of Piety: The Islamic Revival and The Feminist Subject.* Princeton: Princeton University Press.

Mamdani, Mahmood. 2002. Good Muslim, Bad Muslim: A Political Perspective on Culture and Terrorism. *American Anthropologist* 104 (3): 766–775.

McGuire, Meredith. 2008. *Lived Religion: Faith and Practice in Everyday Life.* New York: Oxford University Press.

Melamed, Jodi. 2011. *Rationalizing Violence in the New Racial Capitalism.* Minneapolis: University of Minnesota Press.

Muslim Canadian Congress. The Muslim Canadian Congress. Muslim Canadian Congress. http://www.muslimcanadiancongress.org.

Perera, Suvendrini. 2009. Invested with Violence: Culturalism, Coloniality and "Denaturalised" Citizenships. In *Beyond the Hijab Debates*, ed. Tanja Dreher and Christina Ho, 222–234. New Castle: Cambridge Scholars Publishing.

Ramadan, Tariq. 2010. Good Muslim, Bad Muslim. *New Statesman America*, February 12. https://www.newstatesman.com/religion/2010/02/muslim-religious-moderation.

Razack, Sherene H. 2018. A Site/Sight We Cannot Bear: The Racial/Spatial Politics of Banning the Muslim Woman's Niqab. *Canadian Journal of Women and Law* 30 (1): 169–189.

Roy, Olivier. 2009. *Holy Ignorance: When Religion and Culture Part Ways.* New York: Columbia University Press.

Ryder, Bruce. 2005. State Neutrality and Freedom of Conscience and Religion. *Supreme Court Law Review* 28 (1): 169–199.

Scott, Joan Wallach. 2009. *Politics of the Veil.* Princeton: Princeton University Press.

Selby, Jennifer A. 2016. 'Muslimness' and Multiplicity in Qualitative Research and in Government Reports in Canada. *Critical Research on Religion* 4 (1): 72–89.

Shirock, Andrew. 2010. *Islamophilia/Islamophobia: Beyond the Politics of Enemy and Friend.* Bloomington: Indiana University Press.

Solomon, Evan. 2015. Jason Kenney on the Niqab, the Oath and #PeopleLikeNenshi. *Macleans.ca*, October 2. http://www.macleans.ca/politics/ottawa/for-the-record-jason-kenney-on-the-niqab-the-oath-and-peoplelikenenshi/2015/10/06.

Stewart, Francis. 2017. Horizontal Inequalities and Pluralism. *Accounting for Change in Diverse Societies*. Global Center for Pluralism. www.pluralism.ca.

Valenta, Marka G. 2006. How to Recognize a Muslim When You See One. In *Political Theologies: Public Religions in a Post-Secular World*, ed. Hent de Vries and Lawrence E. Sullivan, 444–474. New York: Fordham University Press.

Yuval-Davis, Nira. 1997. *Gender and Nation*. London: SAGE Publications.

Zine, Jasmine. 2012. *Islam in The Hinterlands Muslim Cultural Politics in Canada*. Vancouver: University of British Columbia Press.

Tasting the Nation: Food, Identity, and Belonging in Canada

Helin Burkay and David Dean

"Sweet Canada" is the name of a new series of five stamps recently issued by Canada Post each featuring an iconic Canadian dessert: the Nanaimo bar, the sugar pie, the blueberry grunt, the Saskatoon berry pie, and the butter tart. Reflecting Canadians' fondness for these desserts, Canada Post argued that "[o]ur country's traditional desserts offer more than just a scrumptious way to end a meal—their origins are a tasty part of our history" (Canada Post 2019, 6). As Michael Maloney has recently argued, even in the new electronic age stamps continue to "play an active role in building national identity" (Maloney 2013). These dessert stamps can certainly be seen as an endeavour by the Canadian state to insist on another sweet narrative, namely that through their shared love of these desserts Canadians can celebrate a sense of belonging to the nation (see Fig. 1).

H. Burkay
Department of Sociology, Carleton University, Ottawa, ON, Canada

D. Dean (✉)
Carleton University, Ottawa, ON, Canada
e-mail: david.dean@carleton.ca

Y. Meerzon et al. (eds.), *Migration and Stereotypes in Performance and Culture*, Contemporary Performance InterActions,
https://doi.org/10.1007/978-3-030-39915-3_8

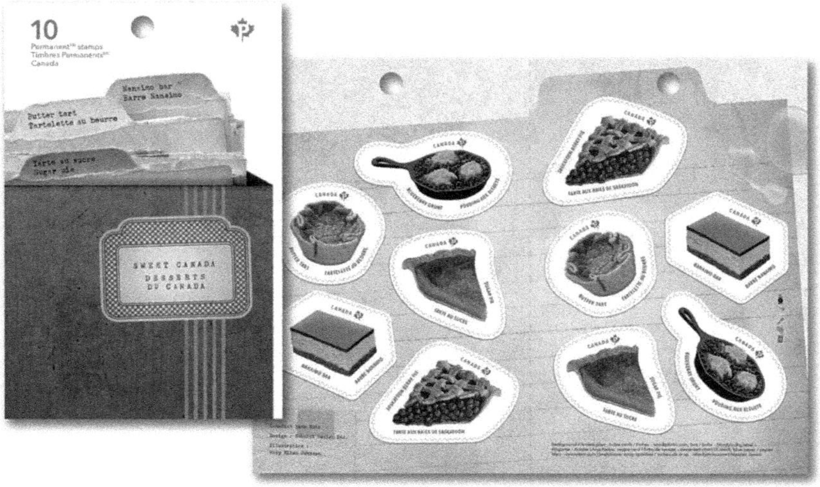

Fig. 1 Canada Post, Sweet Canada: Permanent™ Domestic stamps – Booklet of 10. Screenshot taken 31 May 2019. Source: https://www.canadapost.ca/shop/collectors/stamps-by-theme/people-and-places/p-404113144.jsf?icid=Estore%7CMaywesuggest%7CProd%7CSlot_2

How might we reflect on the variety of claims of what constitutes Canadian cuisine? How might we imagine culinary narratives of Canadian food in menus, cookbooks, and recipes as practices of representation and enactment of difference at particular historical conjunctures? What are the tensions underlying the elusive concept of Canadian cuisine and what is at stake politically in attempts to fix its definition? What is the role and agency of migrant communities in defining Canadian food? We argue that part of the answer to these questions lies in troubling and complicating Canadian cuisine as a monolithic category and as a single culinary tradition confined to the borders of the nation. Building on a closer look at various moments in Canadian culinary history, we draw attention to the particular historical and contemporary tensions between attempts to fix the definition of a national culinary tradition in Canada and the continuous interpretations, adaptations, changes, and innovations of culinary practices by different communities.

There are two clearly identifiable scholarly approaches to culinary nationalism. The first, associated particularly with tourism and hospitality studies, takes national cuisine as a category that can be technically identified based on ingredients, techniques, and culinary literature, with a view to both differentiate and brand a culinary identity of authentic national cuisine (Jacobs 2009; Ferguson 2004). The second is the more critically engaged discussion around national cuisine as a political construction and culinary practices as embedded in a myriad of colonial and transnational networks of commodities and agro-food relations (Appadurai 1988; Mintz 1996). Our approach is informed especially by the latter and posits that both the technical and narrative components of Canadian cuisine should be seen as a series of continuous adaptations that reflect the political, cultural, and economic dynamics of nation-building in Canada, starting with the arrival of European settlers to our own contemporary, environmentally sensitive, and multicultural culinary orientations. We develop this approach by loosely following the lead of Hersch Jacobs (2009) in his attempt to define Canadian cuisine by examining geographically specific ingredients and public knowledge generated through menus, cookbooks, encyclopedias, recipes, and official discourse. In taking these two components and turning them upside down, we show that the search for an authentic and uniquely Canadian cuisine is a politically powerful tool used to make claims about ownership, belonging, and nationhood.

Food as an Analytical Lens

There is nothing as mundane and as contested as food when it comes to the cultural politics of representation with respect to migrant identities, past and present colonial relations, and a changing national imaginary. Even in its most everyday state, food is much more than its ingredients. It is an edible curation of relations, representations, rituals, and symbols. Food, however, is so ordinary that it is easy to overlook the connections it reveals, as well as the contestations it brings forward in terms of belonging, representation, authenticity, and ownership. These contestations around recipes, ingredients, and techniques, as well as etiquettes of consumption, are fruitful places for identifying the dynamic politics of representation and stereotypes. Storytelling, memory work, constructing identity, and feelings of belonging revolve around making, serving, and eating food. As such, food encapsulates myriad social, political, cultural, economic, technological, and ecological connections in an edible form.

Social performances and the public presence of food also go beyond edibility. Images, techniques, processes, menus, recipes, and stories of food circulate and evoke sensory experiences, moral judgments, or aesthetic claims that contest belonging, authenticity, and ownership. National, regional, and local narratives around food and culinary culture are full of claims about whose knowledge deserves recognition, who belongs and who does not. Contrary to the relatively depoliticized site of sensory experience and aesthetic appeal of food in public discourse, menus, recipes, and cookbooks are not just repositories of knowledge on food. They are also interventions of belonging and politicized commentaries on identity. Food hides the cruelty of forced connections of global commodity chains, colonial histories, and agricultural labour that generates profit in return for making edible ingredients abundantly available in the mass markets, especially for middle-class consumers. Although everyone eats, food deserts and unequal access to food cut across class and racial lines, making food a politically charged divider as much as a unifier.

The tensions between the practices and narratives around Canadian food demonstrate that food is a political conversation, a performative statement, an economic negotiation of resources, and a mundane daily act of sustenance. Critical engagement with some of the narratives and relations around food in Canada provides a uniquely powerful lens to understand the temporal and spatial contradictions that make up Canadian national discourse and imaginary.

Using food as an analytical lens enables us to reflect on the ways that Canadian cuisine is formed and transformed beyond national borders, and by transnational culinary histories embedded in the global circulation of ideas, ingredients, and peoples. In that sense, food is one of the most productive ways of imagining difference, plurality, and its contestations. As an omnipresent and yet highly contested and complex entity, the narratives around the value and meaning of food are condensed forms of nodes at a conjuncture of contradictions. As such, there is a good argument to be made in favour of using food as an analytical category rather than simply a thematic variation in approaches to issues of multiculturalism, citizenship, and belonging.

In the following pages, we focus on three culinary moments in Canada. First is the colonial-settler moment, where Canada's culinary identity reflected the troubles of the colonial-settler political project and was situated within international culinary narratives. In the second section, we draw attention to multicultural nation-building by focusing on hyphenated restaurants, menus, and how migrant communities negotiate their belonging by redefining Canadian culinary identity in distinct ways. In the last section, we reflect on the current moment in the changing conversation of national culinary identity by focusing on debates around local sustainable cuisine and the environmental sensitivities that define the identity of Canadian cuisine.

Pies, Tarts, and Poutine

Readers of Canada Post's *Details* magazine learn that the origins of the sugar pie can be traced back to France (colonists were forced to adapt the homeland recipe by using maple syrup instead of brown sugar), that the earliest butter tart recipe dates from 1900, and that the blueberry grunt was a version of traditional English steamed pudding. Yet these confident statements mask competing origin stories, at least for the butter tart. This small pastry traditionally filled with butter, sugar, and egg, with a soft gooey-liquid centre and crusty top, could simply be an English-Canadian version of the much earlier French-Canadian sugar pie. Another possibility is that it was an adaptation of the English treacle tart; the first treacle tart recipe was published in England only one year before the Women's Auxiliary of the Royal Victoria Hospital of Barrie, Ontario (1900) published the first butter tart recipe in their cookbook (Jewry 1899, 578). Given, however, that the recipe's author was Mary Ethel Macleod, whose maiden name Cowie suggests that her ancestors came from the Scottish Borders, it seems at least plausible that the pie's origins lay in that region's well-known sugar pies filled with fruit and sometimes nuts.

These are foods then that reference not only a shared yearning for sweets but a shared colonial past which is not untroubled by discussions of origins and authenticity. If their Canadian-ness lies in the colonial settler homelands, what makes them distinctive from the sugar pies and butter tarts of England, Scotland, France, and Belgium? This does not seem to be a problem for the Saskatoon berry pie. It claims to be an "original Canadian recipe" because, as Canada Post is equally keen to point out, the berry was a "staple for Indigenous peoples and early settlers" and its name (like that of the city) "is derived from a Cree word misâskatômina". (Canada Post 2019, 6). Again, however, like the adoption of maple syrup as a substitute for brown sugar, colonial-settler desserts may use ingredients cultivated, prepared, and consumed by Indigenous peoples, but they are made apparently more delectable through their repositioning within European culinary traditions. These are not only stories of colonial-settler adaptation and adoption, they are tales of appropriation that mask histories of cultural genocide. The national imaginary of the "tasty" origins "of our history" involving the butter tart, the sugar pie, and other desserts from the beginning of twentieth century coincides with the brutal intervention of European settlers into Indigenous food resources, cultivation, and production (Murton 2012, 227; Daschuk 2019, 34–36, 115–119). Canada's culinary narrative project is embedded in a national colonial-settler imaginary and in a political economy of "whitening" Canadian culinary identity and history.

Butter tarts, sugar pie, and Saskatoon berry pie frequently appear in lists compiled by journalists and foodies seeking to identify a single food or dish that represents all Canadians. It is, however, poutine that regularly comes out on top. Consisting of fries covered by a layer of cheese, curds, and smothered in gravy, poutine is associated with francophone communities across Canada, especially in the province of Québec. Culture Trip's Hayley Simpson (2017) defines poutine as the number one uniquely Canadian dish followed by the Nanaimo bar and the butter tart and then, in ninth place, the Saskatoon berry pie. The Toronto-based site Chopsticks + Forks also has poutine as the front-runner, as did the crowdsourced survey run by the national *Globe and Mail* newspaper (Allemang 2010) and Manitoba's Live & Learn, a website dedicated to introducing Canada to new Manitobans. Indeed, poutine so often tops the list in discussions seeking to determine Canada's national dish that *Maclean's* magazine (2012) ran a feature on "12 foods Canada has given the world (besides poutine)."

If there is apparent consensus that poutine is *the* national Canadian dish, it is also striking that such contests have many overlapping foods—tourtière, BeaverTails pastries, peameal bacon, Montréal bagels, Québec's split pea soup, Newfoundland's fish and brewis (cod with hard bread), and Atlantic Canada's figgy duff (scone with raisins), as well as Nanaimo bars, butter tarts, and Saskatoon berry pies. This last dish is the only frequent member of the select club with decidedly Indigenous roots. Indeed, Live & Learn is the only list to include the standby of caterers offering definitively native cuisine: bannock. Before Europeans arrived, Indigenous peoples made breads from corn, various plant roots, sap, and berries. How this related to Scottish bannock—unleavened bread baked on a griddle over an open fire— is unclear; however, the name was claimed by Indigenous peoples for what was, and has become, a cherished and determinedly Indigenous locally-based food (Cyr and Slater 2016).

The Halifax Donair and the Japadog

Adaptation has always been a two-way street. Chopsticks + Forks, drawing inspiration from Toronto's Kensington Market, listed Hawaiian pizza as a top Canadian food because it was invented in Chatham, Ontario. They also noted sushi pizza (a deep-fried rice patty topped with sushi), presumably a Japanese-Canadian take on an Italian-Canadian original (Sim n.d.). Hayley Simpson (2017) included the donair in her list of uniquely Canadian dishes. This traditional Turkish dish of bread-wrapped meat (similar to the Lebanese shawarma and Greek gyro) was adapted to local tastes in the 1970s by Peter Gamoulakos, a Greek Canadian based in Halifax who substituted lamb for beef and developed a sweet sauce to accompany the dish. On the other side of the country, in Vancouver, Japanese Canadian Noriki Tamura created the Japadog in 2005 incorporating nori, radish, and Japanese sauces into a new version of the traditional North American fast food. Such adaptations are performances of belonging speaking back to a Canadian society structured by a policy of multiculturalism that requires inclusivity while celebrating difference (Jackson 2016; Japadog n.d.).

From a cultural-political perspective, rituals, symbols, and narratives around food make these adaptations a performative act that hinges on the politics of belonging. As Sarah Daynes (2004, 159) argues, "food and music are the easiest tools to transport memories." Food is the *madeleine* of the migrant identity, an involuntary memory that enacts the affect of a particular memory from a distant past and a distant place (Proust 1981). Making, serving, and tasting certain foods create a sensory teleportation to the perceived original moment. Food, however, rarely remains the same when it is transported. Each time a recipe is made, the enactment of the memory it represents is recreated differently.

Preserving recipes, adhering to a particular way of preparing and serving food, has as much to do with repetition of the taste as it has to do with staging and performing a social ritual. Understanding the performance element in the process of replicating recipes is informed by Richard Schechner's (1985, 38) concept of performance as "twice behaved behavior." Seeking to replicate, for example, a grandmother's pierogi recipe, is an act of what Schechner calls "rebecoming" in the sense that the cook seeks to "rebecome what they never were but wish to have been or wish to become." Yet in the context of food—growing, purchasing, assembling, preparing, cooking, sharing, eating—this act of rebecoming also becomes embodied memory work, imagining how, in this case, the grandmother performed the same actions within different spatial and temporal contexts. For the migrant grandchild, seeking to capture the texture, taste, colour, and smell of the treasured handed-down recipe for "baba's pierogis" is an act of remembering as well as replication, and of homage as well as recreation. It can be seen as an embodied practice of representing the migrant self and a celebration of diaspora.

Yet in this performance there are inevitably questions about "getting it right." How to find the "right" ingredients, how to ensure that contemporary tools and technologies do not disturb the "rightness" of the dish, and how to evaluate the authenticity of the final product with a view to the next performance. These are questions shared in many restagings of the past, from historical reenactments to historical feature films, novels, and plays. Freddie Rokem (2001) suggests that, in their performances of past events, actors draw on theatrical energies and become "hyper-historians." While they cannot fully experience the past that was, they nevertheless are "'redoing' or 'reappearing' as something/somebody that has actually existed in the past" (13). The present-day cook performs similarly as they seek to replicate a dish based on historical recipes, whether found in cookbooks or passed down through generations of families, households, and communities. The cook's sense of getting the dish right ("Just like the original") is not based on academic historical verisimilitude, but on sensory self-assessment ("Oh, this tastes right") and ideally the confirmation of others ("Yes, it tastes just like I remember").

The matter of origins, then, becomes an important topic for consideration when using food as an analytical tool. Like Rokem's (2001) actors, the cooks of today cannot experience the dish that was, they can only seek to faithfully reproduce it to the best of their abilities and circumstances. Inevitably, this is a matter of negotiation: alternatives must be sought, substitutes accepted, and compromises made. Therefore, in this edible act of rebecoming, claims about representation based on notions of originality and authenticity, of primary-ness or first-ness, are rendered rather meaningless. As such, food and culinary identity for migrant communities are both claims to the memory of homeland as well as an adjustment, hybridization, borrowing, and finding of a version of hyphenated identity within the hegemonic culture. This is especially true with regards to food because, as we argue here, dishes and recipes are troubled by competing origin stories and complicated by transnational and diasporic influences.

Like the Halifax donair and Japadog, the adjustments of recipes, cookbooks, and migrant food identities do not only happen in domestic spaces within the confines of migrant groups. Through cookbooks and restaurant menus, the culinary narratives and sensory experiences of migrant identities become part of public discourse. In the Canadian case, the hyphenated restaurant fulfills this role. They are not only places that promise *madeleine* moments. The visibility of semantic interventions in menus, either hyphenating the culinary tradition by calling themselves Chinese-Canadian or Italian-Canadian or through putting the Canadian food in a separate section of the menu, acts as an intervention to what constitutes Canadian identity as well as a marketing ploy to cater to a larger consumer palate beyond the migrant community.

Take for example the Free Times Café in Toronto, which specializes in "Authentic Homemade Jewish, Middle Eastern & Canadian Food." Their "Canadian, Eh?" section features a range of burgers (Ontario beef) and sandwiches (chicken club), salads and snacks (fries, chicken fingers, nachos and guacamole—decidedly not Canadian in origin), and poutine. Searching online for menus turned up the Happy Palace in Peterborough, Ontario, which serves "Chinese & Canadian Food." On their menu, Canadian food consists of various types of burgers (plain, cheese, banquet, chicken) and sandwiches (club, toasted Western, grilled cheese, BLT), fries, and poutine. Coniston, Ontario's ManWah House, offers similar burgers, pogos (battered sausages on a stick), fries, onion rings, and poutine in the Canadian section of their menu.[1] With the exception of poutine, what seems to pass as Canadian food for these owners, chefs, and customers are American-style fast food dishes.

Hyphenated restaurants and their menus are situated at the intersection of a dynamic public discourse on belonging in the present and collective memory of the past, making food an active part of social and cultural politics of social inclusion. Thus, the visibility of a hyphen is not just a matter of remembering and reenacting taste from home; it also secures a part in the mainstream society, negotiating visibility by claiming inclusion, and thus actively making and transforming home in Canada by adopting and adjusting to the ingredients, techniques, and technologies available.

The hyphenated restaurants and visibility of diverse culinary traditions can also be situated within a particular colonial context, where the knowledge of and interest in the "other" (and its culinary ways) was a cultural asset within the middle-class vernacular and its claims to whiteness. In Canadian national imaginary, imagining inclusivity through food appeared as a safer and less political way of creating a national narrative. As Donna Gabaccia points out, however, this depoliticized narrative of "culinary pluralism" is founded on the political tension of its period (1998, 86). It has been made available by global migration from the South, which is itself a product of deep-seated inequalities that trouble the benign, depoliticized narratives of culinary multiculturalism domestically.

The Canuck Burger, the Canadian Pizza, and the Springtime Canadian Dosa

Pluralistic imaginaries and inclusive food narratives have been very much part of Canada's official discourse especially since the Second World War and have been woven into the country's mainstream middle-class identity. However, celebration of diversity in the aftermath of the Cold War looked very different from the vibrant cosmopolitanism of later periods. For example, in 1968, the International Institute of Metropolitan Toronto published a cookbook consisting of mostly European and Eastern European dishes to acknowledge and publicize the culinary pluralism of its day (Iacovetta 2012, 371).

Before hyphenated restaurants and the adoption of culinary multiculturalism became fashionable even in its embryonic forms, Canadian cuisine first struggled to define its culinary homeland as distinct from British colonial identity. For example, the Royal Banquet of 1939 was a direct commentary on Canadian identity through culinary curation. In that period, culinary inclusiveness meant claims of lineage to European culinary traditions based on provincial cultural demographics in Canada while at the same time acknowledging British influence (Ungar 2012, 353). Inclusivity in national culinary discourse did not include the different immigrant communities that live in metropolitan areas, such as Vancouver's South Asian community, whose food cultures were simply dismissed as "smelly" with "strange modes of dress and habits" (Mehta 2012, 156).

In its current incarnation, debates around what constitutes Canadian cuisine takes a different turn in the face of an established official narrative of multiculturalism and the local food movement. In an effort to capture what constituted Canadian national cuisine, Jacobs applied a traditional approach to identifying boundaries of an elusive and ever-changing Canadian culinary identity (2009). Like most national projects, the parameters of what constituted a national cuisine drew on the example of the

French gastronomical school. Following the methodology that was developed in the process of constructing French cuisine, Jacobs compiled the ingredients, techniques, and combinations considered to be predominantly Canadian and came to the conclusion that it is impossible to define Canadian cuisine in the same way as French, Chinese, or Italian cuisine. He offers a number of reasons for this including the geographical vastness of Canada, the influence of successive waves of immigrants, and the sheer diversity of ingredients and techniques that are mixed and matched in ways that transform even the most basic recipes. For Jacobs, what makes a cuisine distinctly Canadian is the use of ingredients and techniques native to Canada, in other words, those that have their roots in Indigenous culinary traditions, which of course is a culinary tradition and method of sustenance that the state systematically sought to destroy (Jacobs 2009).

In 2018, organizers of the Canada on a Plate festival invited locals and visitors to Ottawa, the nation's capital, to "[e]xplore our national cuisine" in order to "[s]avour inspired dishes that capture the Canadian experience through our taste buds."[2] Local restaurants offered a variety of appetizers, entrees, and desserts. Scrolling through the sample menus, some foods surprise with their claims to be distinctively Canadian. The "Canuck Burger" (Canuck being slang for Canadian) insists on its Canadian-ness by granting citizenship to cattle ("100% Canadian ground beef patty"). Granting the same to pigs presumably makes the "Canadian Pizza" Canadian as well, with its "signature home-made pizza sauce, topped with pepperoni, fresh mushroom, and chopped bacon." The same is seen with "The Roaster," a Montréal-style bagel filled with "Fresh Canadian Alberta Angus AAA Beef" and "locally sourced Swiss Cheese." Setting aside the Swiss cheese, many of the dishes on offer were Canadianized versions of international cuisines: dosas "with a Canadian springtime twist" filled with fiddleheads and local cheese; English muffins with "peameal-style [Canadian] bacon"; and a butter cauliflower curry with wild rice (a staple Indigenous food). Canadian-ness seems to be found less in the dishes themselves than in the geo-identity of animals, plants, and grains. Maple syrup made an appearance as an ingredient in savoury entrees (infusing onions, brushing salmon, flavouring whipped cream), and of course desserts ("Canadian Maple Ice Cream... sweet, creamy, delicious and so Canadian"). Two of the philatelic desserts are present: Nanaimo bars and butter tarts, the latter said to be a "true representation of a Pioneer Canada dessert!"[3]

The special foods prepared by restaurants for the Canada on a Plate festival clearly indicate that what makes Canadian food Canadian is the use of ingredients found in Canada. The Ottawa restaurant Social declares its focus to be "on progressive Canadian cuisine," inviting clients to indulge "in our Canadian free-style cuisine." Most of the menu items incorporate, translate, and transform locally, regionally, and nationally sourced ingredients into a range of dishes, such as seafood linguini, beef stroganoff, and lamb tagine. Italian, Russian, and Moroccan influences sit alongside only one clearly identifiable Canadian menu item: sockeye salmon from British Columbia. "Progressive" and "free-style" are arguably code words for eclectic and fusion. They support our contention that we need to trouble rather than sustain claims for a fixed national culinary tradition.

As much as it seems like a rupture from previous narratives of culinary nationalism, focusing on ingredients and their origins resonates with the changing scene in haute-cuisine urban restaurants like Social in Ottawa. At this specific conjuncture, what constitutes "Canadian" in menus and cookbooks of new gastronomical culture emphasizes locally sourced, sustainable, Canadian-produced ingredients. In this context, the narrative of national cuisine depends much less on imagining the country as a vast land with a unified culinary tradition. The new culinary interventions into Canadian identity in these restaurant menus imagine a culinary identity that values micro-local resourcing of ingredients, community connections to farmers and producers, as well as unprecedented levels of amalgamation and experimentation with culinary diversity in current Canadian society. The menus and cookbooks reflect the celebration of the local as an ecological parameter beyond administrative borders of cities and regions, combining it with the richness of variety of combinations inspired by diverse ethnic culinary traditions. The need to hyphenate seems to have disappeared and what once would have been considered "ethnic" has become mainstream within new definitions of Canadian cuisine.

Conclusion

We have argued that attempts to define a distinctive Canadian culinary tradition in a singular and fixed way reveals the impossibility of capturing what is a complex, dynamic, adaptive, and multi-dimensional affair. Food as a social practice and cultural ritual resists these attempts, as does the political landscape, both Canada's colonial origins and successive waves of immigration. This makes it difficult for the search for a culinary national identity to rise above the banality of stereotypes and what Svetlana Boym has called "the dictatorship of nostalgia" (2001, 154). Public debate about what constitutes distinctively Canadian dishes and the changing foodscapes in Canadian cities reveal the high stakes of the politics of representation.

The elusiveness of defining a national culinary identity is a political possibility of inclusion and creativity. Shifting the focus from finding a fixed definition, the vastness, diversity, and multi-layeredness of political contestations around food makes it possible to think of Canadian food as a performative and creative practice beyond the stereotypical representation of the migrant communities that rely on recreating and negotiating their belonging. It allows for the adaptation, mixing, changing, and remaking of belonging. Thinking about food beyond the confines of national cuisine and foregrounding its production also forces us to reckon not only with the representation of migrant communities, but also with the politics of the land and the sustainability of food as a resource within the context of the current ecological crisis and colonial-settler legacy.

Notes

1. Similar items feature on the menu of the Antler Poutine and Burger self-styled Canadian restaurant in Kracow, Poland (see https://www.facebook.com/antlerkrakow/). Many thanks to Natalia Vesselova for this reference.
2. See http://canadianeats.ca/.
3. A dispute has emerged over the accuracy of Canada Post's visual representation of the Nanaimo bar (Mooney 2019).

References

Allemang, John. 2010. We Like Our National Symbols Rooted in the Past, and in Quebec. *Globe & Mail*, July 3. Updated May 2, 2018.https://www.theglobeandmail.com/life/we-like-our-symbols-rooted-in-the-past-and-in-quebec/article1379403/.

Appadurai, Arjun. 1988. How to Make a National Cuisine: Cookbooks in Contemporary India. *Comparative Studies in Society and History* 30 (1): 3–24.

Blog of Lists. 2012. 12Foods Canada Has Given the World (Besides Poutine). *Maclean's*, August 3. https://www.macleans.ca/society/life/12-foods-canada-has-given-the-world-besides-poutine/.

Boym, Svetlana. 2001. *The Future of Nostalgia*. New York: Basic Books.

Canada Post. 2019. Sweet Canada. *Details* 4 (April–June): 6–7.

Cyr, Monica, and Joyce Slater. 2016. 'Got Bannock?' Traditional Indigenous Bread in Winnipeg's North End. In *Indigenous Perspectives in Education for Well-Being in Canada*, ed. Frank Deer and Thomas Falkonberg, 59–73. Winnipeg: Education for Sustainable Well-Being Press.

Daschuk, James. 2019. *Clearing the Plains: Disease, Politics of Starvation, and the Loss of Indigenous Life*. Regina: University of Regina Press.

Daynes, Sarah. 2004. The Musical Construction of the Diaspora: The Case of Reggae and Rastafari. In *Music, Space and Place: Popular Music and Cultural Identity*, ed. Sheila Whiteley, Andy Bennett, and Stan Hawkins, 25–41. London: Ashgate.

Ferguson, Priscilla Parkhurst. 2004. *Accounting for Taste: The Triumph of French Cuisine*. Chicago: University of Chicago Press.

Gabbaccia, Donna. 1998. *We Are What We Eat: Ethnic Food and the Making of American Culinary Identity*. Cambridge: Harvard University Press.

Iacovetta, Franca. 2012. Food Acts and Cultural Politics: Women and the Gendered Dialectics ofCulinary Pluralism at the International Institute of Toronto, 1950s-1960s. In *Edible Histories, Cultural Politics: Towards a Canadian Food History*, ed. Franca Iacovetta, Valerie J. Korinek, and Marlene Epp, 359–386. Toronto: University of Toronto Press.

Jackson, Lisa. 2016. The Delicious History of the Halifax Donair. *Food Network Canada*. October 31. https://www.foodnetwork.ca/shows/great-canadian-cookbook/blog/the-delicious-history-of-the-halifax-donair/.

Jacobs, Hersch. 2009. Structural Elements in Canadian Cuisine.*Cuizine* 2 (1).

Japadog. n.d. History. Japadog. http://www.japadog.com/.

Jewry, Mary. 1899. *Warne's Model Cookery: With Complete Instructions in Household Management and Receipts*. London: F. Warne.

Maloney, Michael. 2013. 'One of the Best Advertising Mediums the Country Can Have': Postage Stamps and National Identity in Canada, New Zealand and Australia. *Material Culture Review/Revue de la culture matérielle*77 (January 2013).

Mehta, Julie. 2012. Toronto's Multicultural Tongues: Stories of South Asian Cuisines. In *Edible Histories, Cultural Politics: Towards a Canadian Food History*, ed. Franca Iacovetta, Valerie J. Korinek, and Marlene Epp, 156–169. Toronto: University of Toronto Press.

Mintz, Sidney W. 1996. *High, Low and Not At All: Tasting Food, Tasting Freedom: Excursions into Eating, Culture, and the Past*. Boston: Beacon Press.

Mooney, Harrison. 2019. No-Bake, No Rules: Canada Post Says Everyone Makes Nanaimo Bars 'A Little Differently'. *Vancouver Sun*, April 19. https://vancouversun.com/news/local-news/no-bake-no-rules-canada-post-says-everyone-makes-nanaimo-bars-a-little-differently.

Murton, James. 2012. John Bull and Sons: The Empire Marketing Board and the Creation of a British Imperial System. In *Edible Histories, Cultural Politics:*

Towards a Canadian Food History, ed. Franca Iacovetta, Valerie J. Korinek, and Marlene Epp, 225–248. Toronto: University of Toronto Press.

Proust, Marcel. 1981. *Remembrance of Things Past*. New York: Vintage.

Rokem, Freddie. 2001. *Performing History: Theatrical Representations of the Past in Contemporary Theatre*. Iowa City: Iowa University Press.

Schechner, Richard. 1985. *Between Theatre and Anthropology*. Philadelphia: University of Pennsylvania Press.

Sim, Jusep. n.d. 10 Foods 'Born and Made in Canada.' Chopsticks + Forks. https://www.chopsticksandforks.com/10-foods-made-in-canada/.

Simpson, Hayley. 2017. 10 Signature Canadian Dishes and Where to Try Them. *Culture Trip*. March 8. https://theculturetrip.com/north-america/canada/articles/10-signature-canadian-dishes-and-where-to-try-them/.

Ungar, Molly Pulver. 2012. Nationalism on the Menu: Three Banquets in the 1939 Royal Tour. In *Edible Histories, Cultural Politics: Towards a Canadian Food History*, ed. Franca Iacovetta, Valerie J. Korinek, and Marlene Epp, 351–358. Toronto: University of Toronto Press.

Women's Auxiliary to the Royal Victoria Hospital. 1900. *Royal Victoria Cook Book*. Barrie: S. Wesley. Noted excerpt: https://www.simcoe.ca/Archives/Pages/Mrs-MacLeods-Butter-Tarts.aspx.

Mobility and Cultural Citizenship: The Making of a Senegalese Diaspora in Multiethnic Brazil

Gana Ndiaye

In major metropolitan areas of Brazil, such as Rio de Janeiro, São Paulo, and Porto Alegre, the Senegalese community attracts public attention through many sociocultural and religious practices. In addition to the public celebrations of Senegalese national holidays and of victories of the national soccer team by the Senegalese community as a whole, the Muslim migrants called Murids (followers of the Muridiyya, a Sufi order found in Senegal and some West African countries) organize marches during Muslim religious holidays. The *Baay-faal*, a sub-group of the Murids, who can be recognized by their unique, colourful patchwork outfits, perform devotional music in public spaces around socio-religious organizations called *dahira*.

Studies of Senegalese migrations to Brazil have focused on the networks that channel the undocumented Senegalese migrants to Brazil and on the challenges the Senegalese at large face in the Brazilian job market

G. Ndiaye (✉)
Boston University, Boston, MA, USA
e-mail: gndiaye@bu.edu

Y. Meerzon et al. (eds.), *Migration and Stereotypes in Performance and Culture*, Contemporary Performance InterActions,
https://doi.org/10.1007/978-3-030-39915-3_9

(Tedesco and Grzybovski 2013; Tedesco and Kleidermacher 2017; Baeninger et al. 2018). When they do not focus solely on economic processes, those studies have examined private religious practices and solidarity among Senegalese Murid migrants (Baggioet al. 2017). Thus, they overlook the way Senegalese Muslim migrants signal their religious and ethnic identity in the Brazilian public sphere and speak against stereotypes about Islam, Africanness, and clichés of the Senegalese migrant as a *camelô* (street vendor) in mere search of economic gains. This chapter examines how discrete profiles of Senegalese migrants embody and project notions of Muslim and African identities in Brazil, and how the meanings of the repetitive public actions of the Senegalese affect their host communities.

For that purpose, I first situate the recent waves of Senegalese migrants to Brazil in a long history of their settlement in the country and in a broader context of the crisis in their traditional European destinations in order to examine the challenges that their presence poses for both local authorities and researchers. I start by showing current popular and media images of Senegalese immigrants, often reproduced in social scientific literature, and how they fail to illustrate not only the long history of Senegalese settlement in Brazil but also the diversity of profiles of Senegalese migrants and networks that channel them into the country as well as broader migration patterns to Brazil.[1]

Then, I argue that a distinguishing feature of Senegalese immigrants in Brazil is their involvement in economic and cultural activities, in which they showcase their cultural difference and claim "cultural citizenship." As Renato Rosaldo (1994, 57) defines it, "cultural citizenship refers to the right to be different (in terms of race, ethnicity, or native language) with respect to the norms of the dominant national community, without compromising one's right to belong, in the sense of participating in the nation state's democratic processes." Therefore, an ethnic group claims cultural citizenship when its members emphasize their right to be different without alienating themselves from the majority culture and without neglecting their political participation. In a context of increased ethno-racial protests and Afro-Brazilian activism (Johnson III 2006, 170; Paschel and Sawyer 2008, 198; Osuji 2013, 1491), the fact that the Senegalese put forward their cultural difference makes them highly visible and triggers various responses from both the state and local populations. I show that unskilled workers, the most salient category in terms of media coverage and social scientific inquiry, use the ethnic performance of religious identity to create venues for intercultural dialogue, and have led to many cases of conversion to Islam by Brazilians and marriages between Brazilians and Senegalese.

I argue that the strategies the Murids use to counter stereotypical representations tied to their Muslim and African identities entail bodily work (through dress and self-presentation, for example), claiming public visibility and recognition through regular marches and marking of space and time, all of those actions contributing to the cultivation of a positive image of the migrant community. I examine how different categories of Brazilians react to the Senegalese presence, and how Senegalese immigrants make sense of the fact that non-white Brazilians can choose to identify with several intermediate colours that separate them from blacks (Twine 1998, 87; Schwarcz 2003, 27–30). I add to existing literature that demonstrates how racial boundaries are still sharp even though most Brazilians celebrate racial mixture (Silva and Reis 2012, 383–4). In the same vein, I show that the way the Brazilian government is dealing with new waves of unskilled Senegalese migrants is consistent with Brazil's historical attempts to bring in the "desirable immigrant" (Lesser 2013, 4): a white one.

Images and Profiles of Senegalese Migrants in Brazil

There are three major phases in the arrivals of Senegalese to Brazil, each corresponding with a shift in the country's foreign policies with sub-Saharan Africa or with a change in its economy. Each of these phases has produced discrete profiles of migrants.

Senegal and Brazil started their diplomatic relations in 1961, with an emphasis on the cultural connections between the two countries, which President Leopold Senghor stressed on his presidential visit to Brazil in 1964 (Kaly 2001). Throughout the 1970s and 1980s, Brazil maintained complex relationships with Senegal, especially when Senegalese diplomats supported Angolan exiles in Brazil, working for the independence of their country from Portugal (Davila 2010, 172). These ties brought the first Senegalese exchange students, trainees, and artists to Brazil in the 1990s (Kaly 2001, 463). The boom of the Brazilian economy after 2000 intensified the diplomatic and economic relations between Senegal and Brazil under President Lula (Rizzi et al. 2011, 65).[2] That coincided with the arrival of the first significant flows of unskilled Senegalese migrants (Tedesco and Grzybovski 2013, 323). The Brazilian government was also seeking to attract international students to its higher education institutions (Feijó 2013, 37) while branding the country as a rising diplomatic and economic power and a sanctuary for refugees of various countries.[3]

The data on Senegalese migrants in Brazil is scarce and highly problematic. The Brazil government provided no data for the Senegalese in the UN Population Division 2017 report on migrations; although it did for Lusophone African countries (United Nations). However, the Brazilian Commission for Refugees reports that there have been 7206 Senegalese asylum seekers in Brazil between 2010 and 2015 (Comitê Nacional para os Refugiados 2016, 8), while the UN Refugee Agency representative in Brazil notes that "the majority of those applicants are migrants who left their country for economic reasons" (UNHCR/ACNUR 2014, 1–2). Those migrants have particularly attracted public and media attention. A November 11, 2014 news report by *R7*, a private radio and television network, illustrates the popular image of the Senegalese (often associated with Haitians) as migrants who entered Brazil without authorization via the Amazonian forest (Fala Brazil 2014). The video shows a group of migrants, referred to as "Senegalese and Haitians," in a camp where aid workers help them to process applications for *protocolos* (temporary residence permits) and work permits. Besides the inability to quantify these flows—"*eles são milhares*," or, "they are many," says the report—there is a manifest oversimplification of the composition of the group of migrants discussed and the dynamics that brought them to Brazil. To avoid that shortcoming, one should consider two important things. First, sophisticated networks of smugglers exist between Brazil and Senegal, which is a major transit zone for West African migrations. These smugglers can even obtain Senegalese passports for other West African migrants who they then channel into the destination countries (Goldberg 2004). Not only is Senegal a transit zone but West African migrants also develop survival mechanisms against the "bunkerization" of developed countries. These mechanisms include trafficking official documents,[4] applying from an African country where a given embassy is said to deliver more visas, or getting the passport of a country whose citizens have fewer visa requirements for a given destination, to name a few. One Senegalese migrant in Brazil confided to me: "I had to go to Ivory Coast in order to apply for a Brazilian visa. Someone told me it was easier to get one there. When my attempt failed, I had to pay for the road trip via Ecuador."

The smugglers are, to a large extent, the ones who inform prospective migrants of the possibility of "asylum shopping"[5] (Siegfried 2015) in

Brazil, as many of my informants have maintained. When I asked how he managed to enter Brazil without a visa, thirty-six-year-old I.S. replied: "If someone can travel to Brazil via Ecuador without a visa, it is because he has highly-placed accomplices somewhere. If they want to prevent us from coming, they know how to do it." For all these reasons, it is safe to say that the notion of "Senegalese" undocumented immigrants in Brazil is very slippery.

It is also problematic to assume that all "Senegalese" migrants "took the road"—that is to say, they came to Brazil via the Amazonian forest.[6] That is even more true given that after having entered a country without authorization, as Juan Thomas Ordóñez (2015, 100) says of the Guatemalans in the San Francisco Bay Area, economic migrants "discover" the possibility of asylum. Not being able to migrate to find work legally, many migrants who arrive in Brazil via the Amazon are helped by NGOs to file applications for refugee status. The availability of these possibilities, which are absent in Europe (Fassin 2001), produce discrete subsets of migrants who play with state regulations and attract special media attention.[7]

At times, misconceptions about Senegalese migrants may not be explained only by ignorance of key aspects of the phenomenon. Media outlets that seem to have political or nationalist agendas spread images of Senegalese in Brazil as taking opportunities away from nationals. The following anecdote is an illustration. In April 2014, the *Prefeitura* (Chief Administration) of Campos, Rio de Janeiro, announced that its employment program called *Balcão de Empregos* (job fair) helped 26,000 people—among them two Senegalese—find jobs. The title of the notice that featured the two young Senegalese, whom I met in person, says: "*Balcão de empregos insere senegaleses no mercado de trabalho*" ("Career development program helps Senegalese find jobs") (Prefeitura de Campos 2015). A day later, *Globo*, a media group known for its positions against welfare and migration policies under Lula and Dilma, took the information and published it under the title: "*Balcão de empregos em Campos, RJ, já inseriu 26 mil senegaleses*" ("Career development program in Campos, Rio de Janeiro, has already helped 26,000 Senegalese find jobs").[8]

Interestingly, the same images of Brazil being "swamped"[9] by African migrants are salient in the works of many social scientists. Using push-and-pull theories[10] (Massey et al. 1993, 440), the tendency has been to lump African immigrants together and argue that from the 1990s, Brazil started receiving Africans "who see [Brazil] as an Eldorado" (Rangel 2013, 129).

Such approaches tend to focus more on the job market experiences of less educated migrants and the challenges related to their mobility across borders (Tedesco and Grzybovski 2013; Herédia 2015). They say little about the socio-cultural processes related to the Senegalese presence in Brazil. One observes similar academic treatment of the Senegalese in Latin America at large, where everyday lives are reduced to "refugee, study and work experiences" (Malomalo et al. 2015, 1).[11]

Also, as the media and social scientists focus on Senegalese migrant workers, they seem to ignore broader migration patterns in Brazil.[12] Looking at immigration in terms of countries of origin gives little insight into broader social and historical structures of immigration from Africa, the continent which "has almost negligible representation among immigrants in the Americas" (SICREMI 2012, 13). In terms of sheer numbers, European immigrants make up "fully one fourth to one-third of all immigrants in Brazil" (SICREMI 2012, 13). Similarly, the argument that richer countries attract people from poor ones seems too simplistic to account for current migration trends in Brazil. In the city of São Paulo, for example, the major migrant communities come from developed countries. Five European countries—Portugal (100,855), Italy (33,388), Spain (26,496), Germany (9751), and France (6749)—and the United States (8475) are in the top fifteen. Interestingly, the list has no African countries (Observatorio do Turismo, n.d.).

In the advertisement below (Fig. 1), Paul, a twenty-seven-year-old French national, offers not only French classes but also English services ("*Eu posso ajudar para INGLES tambem*," or, "I can help with English as well"). His Portuguese suggests that he has newly arrived in Rio de Janeiro, and his description of himself frames him as an economic migrant:

> Bonjour!
> Eu sou de Françia, aqui no Rio para trabalhar.
> Preparaçao para os teste e os exames, proponho-me mudar de casa ou a fora em outro lugares para cursos de Francês em diferentes níveis.
> [Good morning!
> I am from France. I am here for work.
> Help with tests and exam… I offer French classes, all levels, at home or elsewhere.]

Cases like Paul's abound in Rio, and the fact that they go almost unnoticed illustrates how Brazil has historically favoured European and, to a

Fig. 1 A language tutoring advertisement at the Philosophy and Social Sciences Institute (IFCS), Federal University of Rio de Janeiro, May 2016 (Credit: Photo by Gana Ndiaye)

lesser extent, Asian immigration (Lesser 2013, 4; Karam 2007, 166), and how Brazilian society has accepted those categories. At the same time, even though the focus seems to be on African economic migrants, little attention is paid to the cultural processes at play and the heterogeneity of the migrant population. Because of the diversity of their profiles and the variety of their occupations in Brazil, the Senegalese offer a compelling case to examine in this respect.

A significant number of Senegalese students came to Brazil to pursue university studies. Surprisingly, and until very recently, they constituted the majority of the migrant population from Senegal. In the city of Rio de Janeiro alone, I met five Senegalese university professors, three graduates of the naval school, and two agricultural engineers. They are former students of the PEC-G program, a scheme that gives students from some developing countries the opportunity to pursue undergraduate studies in

Brazil. For some of them, Brazil was supposed to be a transit zone. E.D., a freelance journalist, is a good example. He told me:

> I came here to continue my studies after I got a BA from the University of Dakar. I have been here for ten years now. I never thought I would stay in Brazil this long. I planned to go to the USA after a few years, after the MA.

Others have embraced their transnational status and claim their belonging to both Senegal and Brazil. Mamour, a PhD in electrical engineering and a professor at a public university, said:

> I am, and I remain Senegalese, even though my daughters were born here. I am not going to return Senegal to work there. I invest there, nevertheless. I try to be useful to Brazil as well. I am one of the coordinators of a project that seeks to provide Favelas with solar energy.

Brazil is also attracting Senegalese who studied in developed countries. The majority of Senegalese migrants who arrived after completing their education in developed countries live in the ZonaSul, Rio's wealthiest and safest neighbourhood, if we consider its low homicide rate (thirty-two percent), according to Rio's Public Safety Institute, compared to the northern parts and suburbs of the city (Instituto de Segurança Pública n.d.). The Zona Sul neighbourhood of Barra da Tijuca is the home of Lans, a university professor. He visited Brazil for one year in the early 2000s and returned to work there upon completing a doctorate in economics from Paris 3 University in France. He told me, "I came back to work in Brazil because I feel at home here. This country gave me a lot, and I go to Senegal very often because I have relatives there, but I live here."

Other Senegalese graduated from universities and invested in commerce or farming near Rio city. For example, Mamour, a university professor of electrical engineering, and his wife, Sokhna, started Africa Arte and the Espaço Savanna shopping centre in the Catete neighbourhood.[13] The business specializes in Senegalese/African fashion and cuisine, but also organizes events that Mamour and Sokhna hope will bring Africans and Brazilians together. Mamour said, "I represent Senegal and Africa. I employ people here and there [in Senegal]. By setting up this business, we hope to be useful to both countries economically and culturally." This understanding of belonging ties into Iris Young's (1986, 5) critique of radical activists and theorists' proposition of an ideal of community that "exhibits a totalizing impulse and denies difference ... within and between subjects." By foregrounding their African/Africa identity while claiming to belong to Brazil, Lans, Mamour, and Sokhna exemplify what Young advocates for and calls the "politics of difference," a conception of "social relations that embody openness to unassimilated otherness with justice and appreciation" (23).

The stories of entrepreneurs like Mamour and Sokhna serve to debunk the stereotypical image of the Senegalese as *camelôs* (street vendors). On the contrary, while they seek to find niches in the Brazilian economy, they are developing what political philosophers and anthropologists like Rosaldo (1994) have called cultural citizenship. The concept offered a lens for scholars who attempted to capture broader conceptions of citizenship that emerged out of the globalization and multiculturalism debates. As Rosaldo (1994), among other scholars, theorized it, cultural citizenship points to the cultural politics of minorities and uncouples civil and political rights with social and cultural rights. In other words, cultural citizenship calls for the recognition and respect of the cultural rights of minority groups, their "right to be different," while not alienating themselves from the dominant culture or forsaking their political participation. In addition, the concept "includes and goes beyond the dichotomous categories of legal documents, which one either has or does not have, to encompass a range of gradations in the qualities of citizen" (Rosaldo 1994, 57). This conception of citizenship is useful for understanding the ways in which immigrants who have not obtained political citizenship manage to claim social and cultural rights without laying claim to voting rights, for instance, or access to certain privileges that social welfare provides. The concept of cultural citizenship is also a useful analytical lens for capturing the various ways in which minorities, in general, and migrant communities, in particular, challenge dominant expectations about appropriate modes of belonging by simultaneously claiming cultural differences and collective rights using the language of human rights.

In the following section, I show that even *camelôs* do not limit themselves to earning a living on the sidewalks, for they engage in cultural citizenship claims. I will examine how the Murids, the group of Senegalese I chose because they were the first to have *dahiras* in Brazil and for their social activism and heterogeneity in terms of legal documents and profiles, attempt to make themselves at home in Brazil through the performance of ethnic and religious identity.

Contesting Spaces, Shaping Places and Identities

The district of Niteroi, a suburb of Rio, is home to a large portion of *baol-baols*, particularly of Murids, followers of Muridiyya. The Muridiyya is one of the Sufi brotherhoods found in Senegal. Its founder was a Senegalese man named Cheikh Ahmadou Bamba (1853–1927), also known as *Khadimou Rassoul* (the servant of the Prophet) or *Serigne Touba* (in Wolof, the marabout of Touba, the holy city for the Murids in central Senegal).[14] As for *baol-baol*, the term initially refers to anybody who comes from the Baol region in Central Senegal. However, within the Senegalese diaspora in general, *baol-baol* is a synonym for less educated migrants, that is to say, those who work in the primary and secondary sectors of the informal economy (Hart 1973, 69): construction workers, meat factory workers, and *camelôs*. Many of the so-called *camelôs* see Brazil as a transit zone, as this extract from my interview with E.N. illustrates:

> When I left Senegal, I never thought I would be a construction worker here. It is a difficult job. I was hoping it would be easy to get a visa to go to the USA. I know many people who left and have gone to Mexico and who will try to cross the border. Others have gone to Argentina.

Within *baol-baols* appears a category of itinerant traders. Having state authorizations for travelling across continents, they connect different migratory spaces—Brazil, Argentina, Europe—with Senegal, and supply the informal traders, especially the undocumented ones who cannot enjoy free movement across borders, with all sorts of goods during each of their trips. These transmigrants (Glick Schiller 1999, 94) specialize in the trade of art objects and sustain the business of small street vendors across national boundaries (Diouf 2000, 679; Grillo 2007, 199). They constitute what I would call an Art'spora. I use the term in reference to the word "Diam'spora" that Sylvie Bredeloup (2007) coined to refer to the sort of diaspora created by the traders from the Senegal River Valley that specialized in the trade/smuggling of diamonds between West and South Africa in the early 1970s. A typical itinerant trader who I interviewed said:

> I went to France in 1968. I would go from flea market to flea market from Belgium to Spain. Life became hard in Europe, that is why I left. I arrived in Brazil on December 1, 2004. In the beginning, I would bring craft objects and give it to the boys [the street vendors] and go back to Senegal

> or France. Now I do not do that [travel a lot]. I do most of the carving here. I am getting old, you know.

Despite the heterogeneity of their origins, they mainly depend on the religious networks that the *dahiras* create, like their counterparts in the United States, who have been studied by Babou (2002), Kane (2011), and Diouf (2000). A *dahira* refers to an organization of the Murid Sufi order.[15] It also refers to an actual gathering of Murids, during which they recite the Koran and the Sufi poetry written by Serigne Touba. Depending on the places and the circumstances, a *dahira* can have various functions, even if the salient one in Brazil is the creation of survival mechanisms.

Miller (2007, 36) distinguishes "three zones of citizenship, with partially overlapping but also distinct historicities." These zones of citizenship are the political, the economic, and the cultural. As immigrants in Brazil, the Murids stress the economic and cultural dimensions of their global citizenship. Even though there are instances in which they claim part of the political rights as global citizens, the Murids mainly emphasize their cultural right in order to ensure their economic survival. I construe this commodification of culture as a survival mechanism in which the *dahira* plays a vital role. Like the *dahiras* described by Cheikh Anta Babou (2002) in the case of Murid migrants in New York City in the late 1990s, the *dahiras* are a powerful network of solidarity that is critical to the survival of newcomers. As Larissa de Lomnitz (1981) showed:

> The survival mechanisms of the marginalized comprise the whole of their system of social relations … social networks of mutual assistance … represent part of an informal economic system, parallel to the market economy, which is characterized by the use of social resources and operates on the basis of reciprocal exchange between equals. (11–12)

By "marginalized," de Lomnitz meant those who lack a well-defined role in the industrial production system (17). In that respect, the role of a Murid *dahira* is a religious, economic, and cultural nexus that serves various ends.

Murid migrants attempt to mark the space and make themselves culturally visible in the host country, which they quickly turn into a continuation of the holy city of Touba.[16] That occurs through (re)naming. Murids hyphenate any Brazilian city in which they find themselves. Thus, we have Touba-Rio and Touba-São-Paulo, among others. With the (re)naming comes the creation of a *siège social*[17] or *Keur Serigne Touba* (the house of Serigne Touba in Wolof language). The *Keur Serigne Touba* operates as a religious centre and, most importantly, as a solidarity hub. Depending on the size of the migrant community and their financial resources, the *Keur Serigne Touba* is typically an apartment or house that is rented or purchased by the migrant community. Newcomers are hosted in the centre until they can find housing. Migrants who lose their jobs or whose personal business is in crisis (for instance, if the police have seized a *camelô*'s belongings) may also live in the *Keur Serigne Touba* until they regain financial stability. During a *dahira* (the meeting), members regularly contribute a sum to fund various projects and help people in need. Causes may include expensive medical bills, an initial budget for a new migrant trying to work as a street vendor, a return ticket for someone whose migratory project has failed and who wishes to return home, and repatriation of the body and belongings of a deceased migrant. For all these reasons, and to paraphrase Oscar Lewis' (1952) notion of "urbanization without breakdown," one can talk of transnationalism without breakdown in the sense that moving to Brazil does not seem to constitute an obstacle to religious and cultural practices for these Murids.

Another important performative strategy for the Murids to remain in the public eye is to mark the calendar with a yearly celebration called Bamba Day. It commemorates the day Cheikh Ahmadou Bamba was exiled to Gabon by the French colonizers for his peaceful opposition to colonialism. Organizing Bamba Day requires an advanced level of integration in the host country. Permission from city officials is required to authorize the traditional march, which is accompanied by Sufi poetry and Koran recitation, along a street or around the town. Through Bamba Day, the Murids aim to spread the message of the Muridiyya, which is centred around two pillars: worship and hard work. In Brazil, as *dahiras* become more active in combatting stereotypes, the marches have also become a platform for debunking negative portrayals of Africans and Islam. During Bamba Day, various flyers that reject global terrorism are displayed by marchers as shown in this picture taken during Bamba Day celebrations in Porto Alegre on December 2, 2015 (Fig. 2).

Self-fashioning, particularly through clothing, is also a powerful performative strategy for projecting an attractive image of the Senegalese community while meeting economic goals. A.D. is a *camelô* who sells Senegalese outfits and crafts in Copacabana. When I asked if he wears the colourful patchwork outfits of a sub-group of the Murid called *Baay-faal* to work,

Fig. 2 Murids carrying a banner that says "Islam is a Religion of Peace" during a march. In Porto Alegre, RS. On December 2, 2015 (Photo by ASDPA)

he replied, "Of course! Almost every day! That is what attracts people. Some even want to take photos with me." I find useful Michel Foucault's (1988, 19) concept of technologies of the self, or "how an individual acts upon himself"; the operation an individual effects on their body, soul, thoughts, conduct, and way of being in understanding the effect of Murid politics of difference within Brazilian hierarchized societies.

Brazilian anthropologist Roberto DaMatta (1987) highlighted the way Brazilians seek to maintain hierarchies in the public sphere through bodily work. In Brazil, he argued, the *casa* (home) is the site of personal relations and hierarchies, and the *rua* (street) is that of impersonal ones. In order to maintain those hierarchies, Brazilians mark the passage from the private to the public sphere by a self-fashioning so that everyone knows who is who. The *Baal-faal* function in this sense as a significant marker of African/ black pride in the Brazilian public sphere. Similarly, African migrants, particularly Senegalese, have encouraged many Afro-Brazilians to engage in public displays of their African roots. One illustration of that is the recent surge of *moda Africana*, or African fashion in Brazil.[18] In short, the cultural artefacts, besides providing economic capital, are means through which migrants forge enduring relationships with the local community. Some of those cultural encounters result in locals embracing Islam/

Muridiyya and often result in marriage. However, the Senegalese presence is raising important issues, both for policymakers and within the Brazilian society.

Local Responses and Policy Implications

Stressing the relative success of Murid migrants and their cultural activism should not overshadow the diverse local responses tied to media coverage of the flow of African migrants to Brazil in recent years. Reactions vary from one place to another and from one ethnic group to another. Many of my informants described more hostile interactions in southern Brazil than in Rio de Janeiro, for example. As S.M.N. told me: "There is much racism in the South. I lived in Caxias for some time, and it is nothing compared to Rio. Here, there are more blacks and whites [who] are more welcoming. I think, as Senegalese, they are sort of curious about us."

Thus, the Senegalese (and by extension, the West Africans) in Brazil, especially students, found themselves compared continuously to black Brazilians. As Mauricio, a Bissau Guinean graduate student in literature at the Federal University of Rio de Janeiro complained: "it is disconcerting for me when some whites tell me 'you are better than our Blacks.' How can black Brazilians like us [Africans] if whites always compare us to them or Afro-Brazilians are made to believe that we take their jobs or benefit from their quotas in university programs." What Mauricio is referring to here is the difficult relationship that Africans have with some Brazilians whom one could identify as black but who do not identify as such themselves. In a country where one is neither black or white but rather can be one of the 136 human hues (Schwarcz 2003, 27–30) in the Brazilian colour spectrum (Twine 1998, 87), many of my informants expressed surprise at people they would consider "black brothers" who completely shun and avoid them. That explains what S.M.N., a young *camelô* in Copacabana, meant when he boldly said: "the most racist are the light-skinned blacks." What he soon found out was the meaning of blackness in Brazil as discussed by Schwarcz.

The so-called racist light-skinned blacks are in sharp contrast with other black Brazilians, those who defend Afrocentric views. Aida, one of my interviewees, jokingly maintained that they "think that because you come from the 'Motherland,' you must be a Candomblé priest." These kinds of reactions demonstrate the ongoing racial boundary-making in Brazil, even though the negation of racism and claims of racial democracy are widespread.

Finally, there are the black Brazilians who, like interviewee O.S., think that "you are not African enough because you are not a practitioner of Umbanda, Candomblé or Christianity."Such a view that even some black activists hold is problematic in many ways. A question that one could raise here is why Brazilians in general and Afro-Brazilians in particular find it normal if a West African is Christian, but problematic if they are Muslim. Even though Portuguese started "planting" (Groves 1958) Christianity in West and Central Africa as early as the sixteenth century, it was two centuries later that European missionaries had a real impact in West Africa. On the contrary, Islam arrived in Senegal between 1040 and 1044—long enough for it to become Senegalese. Therefore, assuming migrants are not Muslim is even more problematic, given that ninety-four percent of the Senegalese population is Muslim. By this logic, only a few non-Muslim Senegalese would make it to Brazil.

Restrictive Brazilian immigration policies are also consistent with the fear certain media outlets distil through claims that undocumented Senegalese are coming in large numbers and passing as refugees. Diplomatic pressures from Brazil caused Ecuador to reinforce control at its borders, and decree N. 000088 of the *Ministerio de Relaciones Exteriores y Movilidad Humana* (Ministry of Foreign Affairs and Human Mobility) established the visa requirement for Senegalese citizens starting from November 16, 2015 (República del Ecuador 2015).

One of the ten passengers with whom I flew from Madrid to Dakar on June 30, 2014, was arrested for undocumented immigration as soon as we landed. While we were on board, he told me how his attempt failed because of tighter border controls in Ecuador during the FIFA World Cup hosted by Brazil. The Brazilian government went further. A decision from its Ministry of Justice required an entrance visa for holders of *protocolos* (residence permits). That meant that asylum seekers who had not yet received a decision on their application and who had temporarily left Brazil could no longer re-enter without a visa. On October 3, 2016, around thirty migrants, including Senegalese, were held at Guarulhos International Airport for days due to that decision.[19]

Negative media images of Senegalese, and African migrants more broadly, indicate that the question of first- and second-generation Senegalese in Brazil will soon become a critical issue. The case of Makeda Foluke is a telling example of this concern. In June 2016, the São

João de Meriti municipality in the state of Rio de Janeiro refused to register the daughter of a black couple because of her African name. According to the parents, who have been interviewed by many media outlets, the officials argued that Makeda Foluke, the Yoruba name for the Queen of Sheba, could cause prejudice to the daughter when she grows up. Thus, they suggested that the parents use a "Portuguese" first name (Cruz 2016). A court decision finally allowed the parents to get Makeda Foluke in the *Registro Civil de Pessoas Naturais* (Civil Registry of Natural Persons).[20] This story points to Brazil's double standards in dealing with what is foreign. While privileging a Portuguese one, the *Registro Civil* rejects the African name.

Conclusion

This chapter has highlighted the long history of Senegalese immigrants' presence in Brazil, and the wide range of their profiles and activities, in contrast with their stereotypical representations as *camelôs* and factory workers by the Brazilian media and many social scientists. It offered an analysis that is not limited to economic factors—which have been the focus of the literature on the topic—and shows differing treatment and attitudes toward Senegalese migrants due to religion and, most importantly, ethnicity. Through cultural citizenship claims, cultural brokerage, and performance of ethnoreligious identity, the Senegalese and other African migrants are helping challenge stereotypes about Africa and Islam, while forging alliances with black Brazilians. Further research could address the experiences of second-generation African immigrants in Brazil, and the conditions under which the possibility of a hyphenated Senegalese-Brazilian identity exists, especially with regard to a much-discussed Brazilian contradiction: the belief in the myth of racial democracy coupled with a widespread devaluation of blackness (Twine 1998). While unskilled workers and undocumented migrants, on the one hand, and refugees, on the other hand, continue to be the salient categories in terms of media coverage and social scientific inquiry, further research should continue to examine how the focus on the economic side of human mobilities simultaneously obscures and produces categories of subjects whose lived experiences do not fit neatly into the refugee versus migrant dichotomy.

Notes

1. I draw from three ethnographic field trips (thirteen months) to Rio de Janeiro, São Paulo, and Porto Alegre between 2014 and 2018.
2. President Wade and President Lula had five official meetings between 2005 and 2009, either through state visits or during the UN General Assembly. Interviews I conducted in Rio de Janeiro and São Paulo in the summer of 2016 indicated that the first Senegalese immigrants arrived around 2008.
3. In January 2015, the Ministry of Justice announced that Brazil "broke its record" of the number of foreigners granted refugee status.
4. A smuggler was recorded by his Senegalese client explaining how he can obtain an entry visa and a *Protocolo* for someone who is in Senegal if they are willing to mail their passport and pay CFA 2,000,000 (around $3500). If agreement is reached, the migrant will be entering Brazil for the first time, whereas the "legal" papers they will carry indicate that they are returning after a visit to Senegal (see http://www.sen360.fr/video/xalass-ndoye-bane-parle-des-traffic-de-visas-au-bresil-avec-mamadou-mohamed-ndiaye-tfm-40086.html, accessed September 15, 2016).
5. The expression has been used to refer to how asylum seekers choose between countries that are likely to grant them refugee status.
6. I interviewed seven people who arrived in Brazil via this route. They would pay someone in Dakar who was in charge of arranging with his partner in Ecuador proof of a hotel reservation, which was the only document necessary to pass border control, since Senegalese did not need a visa to travel to the country. From Ecuador, the migrants were transported—"if needed [they would] get in the trunks," one interviewee told me—via Peru to Brazil. Once in Brazil, the smugglers often "advise [them] to declare refugee status so as to get food and assistance and hope for papers." Ecuador started requiring visas for Senegalese on November 16, 2015.
7. In theorizing super-diversity, Steve Vertovec (2007, 1025) stresses this diversification of migrant populations.
8. I visited Campos, where there was only a family of four Senegalese and had the chance to know the people mentioned in the story. See Globo (2015).
9. This is the term Michael Fallon, British Secretary of Defense, used in October 2014 to talk about migrants in British East Coastal cities.
10. These theories maintain that people from poor countries are driven by employment, war, crime, and other "push factors" to developed countries.
11. See also Tedesco et al. (2013).
12. A Google search for "senegaleses no brasil" yields hundreds of items that have the phrase "haitianos e senegalese" in their titles, the Haitians being the ones associated with Senegal.

13. Africa Arte has a strong social media presence: https://www.facebook.com/africaarte/.
14. See Cheikh Babou (2007) for a thorough discussion of the genesis and the philosophy of Muridiyya.
15. Other Sufi brotheroods also have *dahiras*, but it is generally accepted that the practice was started by Murids, particularly by a guide called CheikhMbackéGaindéFatma.
16. Interestingly, as shown by Babou (2005), the creation of the city of Touba and the genesis of Muridiyya during colonial time followed a process somewhat like the one I am describing here. I adapted the title of this section from that paper.
17. One can even add that the *Keur Serigne Touba* also serves as a "*siège culturel et cultuel*": beyond its regular function as the venues for Koran recitations and the reading of Sufi poetry in Arabic, in places where there is no mosque, the headquarters of the *dahira* (*siège culturel*) becomes the site for Friday and Muslim holidays, prayers thus becoming a *siège cultuel*, where worship takes place.
18. For a report on Senegalese designers in São Paulo, see Romàrio de Oliviera, "Moda Afro: calças, saias, vestidos, sapatos, acessórios," *iG São Paulo*, July 7, 2017, https://ultimosegundo.ig.com.br/colunas/afro-igualdade/2017-07-07/moda-afro.html (accessed July 20, 2018).
19. A mediation from the National Council for Refugees led the Brazilian government to postpone the application of the new law until December 31, 2016.
20. The Madeka case led many Senegalese I interviewed to ponder over the future of their own children in Brazil.

References

Babou, Cheikh Anta. 2002. Brotherhood Solidarity, Education and Migration: The Role of the *Dahiras* among the Murid Muslim Community of New York. *African Affairs* 101 (2002): 151–170.

———. 2005. Contesting Space, Shaping Places: Making Room for the Muridiyya in Colonial Senegal, 1912–1945. *Journal of African History* 46 (2005): 405–426.

———. 2007. *Fighting the Greater Jihad: Ahmadu Bamba and the Founding of the Muridiyya of Senegal, 1853–1913.* Athens, OH: Ohio University Press.

Baeninger, Rosana, et al., eds. 2018. *Migrações Sul-Sul.* São Paulo: NEPO-UNICAMP.

Baggio, Fábio, Paolo Parise, and Wagner Lopes Sanchez, eds. 2017. *Diásporas Africanas e Processos Sociorreligiosos.* São Paulo: Paulus.

Bredeloup, Sylvie. 2007. *La Diam'spora du Fleuve Sénégal.* Toulouse and Paris: Presses Universitaires du Mirail; IRD Editions.

Comitê Nacional para os Refugiados. 2016. *Sistema de Refúgio Brasileiro: Desafios e Perspectivas*. Brasilia: Ministerio da Justicia.

Cruz, Cintia. 2016. Pais Obtêm na Justiça o Direito de Registrar a Filha com Nome Africano. *Globo*, June 6. https://extra.globo.com/noticias/rio/pais-obtem-na-justica-direito-de-registrar-filha-com-nome-africano-19474082.html#ixzz4QD4rxxEC.

DaMatta, Roberto. 1987. *A Casa e a Rua: Espaço, Cidadania, Mulher e Morte No Brasil*. Rio de Janeiro: Editora Guanabara.

Davila, Jerry. 2010. *Hotel Trópico: Brazil and the Challenge of African Decolonization, 1950–1980*. Durham: Duke University Press.

de Lomnitz, Larissa Adler. 1981. *Como Sobreviven los Marginados*. 5th ed. Buenos Aires: Siglo XXI Editores.

Diouf, Mamadou. 2000. The Senegalese Murid Trade Diaspora and the Making of a Vernacular Cosmopolitanism. *Public Culture* 12 (3): 679–702.

Fala Brazil. 2014. Conheça Histórias de Haitianos e Senegaleses que Chegam ao Brasil pela Floresta. *R7*, November 22. https://recordtv.r7.com/fala-brasil/videos/conheca-historias-de-haitianos-e-senegaleses-que-chegam-ao-brasil-pela-floresta-06102018.

Fassin, Didier. 2001. Quand le Corps Fait loi. La Raison Humanitaire dans les Procédures de Régularisation des Étrangers. *Sciences Sociales et Santé* 19 (14): 5–34.

Feijó, Rosemeri Nunes. 2013. A Internacionalização da Educação Superior no Brasil: Um Estudo de Caso de Alunos Estrangeiros do Programa de Pós-Graduação em Antropologia Social/UFRGS. Tese de Mestrado, Universidade Federal do Rio Grande do Sul.

Foucault, Michel. 1988. In *Technologies of the Self: A Seminar with Michel Foucault*, ed. Luther H. Martin, Huck Gutman, and Patrick H. Hutton. Amherst: University of Massachusetts Press.

Glick Schiller, Nina. 1999. Transmigrants and Nation-States: Something Old and Something New in the U.S. Immigrant Experience. In *The Handbook of International Migration: The American Experience*, ed. Charles Hirshman, Philip Kasinitz, and Josh De Wind, 94–119. New York: Russell Sage Foundation.

Globo. 2015. Balcão de Empregos em Campos, RJ, Já Inseriu 26 mil Senegaleses, *Globo,* April 13. http://g1.globo.com/rj/norte-fluminense/noticia/2015/04/balcao-de-empregos-em-campos-rj-ja-inseriu-26-mil-senegaleses.html.

Goldberg, A. 2004. *Ser Inmigrante no es una Enfermedad. Inmigración, Condiciones de Vida y de Trabajo. El Proceso de Salud/Enfermedad/Atención de los Migrantes Senegaleses en Barcelona*. Tesis Doctoral, Universitat Rovirai Virgili.

Grillo, Ralph. 2007. Betwixt and Between: Trajectories and Projects of Transmigration. *Journal of Ethnic and Migration Studies* 33 (2): 199–217.

Groves, Charles Pelham. 1958. *The Planting of Christianity in Africa, Volume 4: 1914–1954*. London: Lutterworth.

Hart, Keith. 1973. Informal Income Opportunities and Urban Employment in Ghana. *The Journal of Modern African Studies* 11 (1): 61–89.

Herédia, Vania Beatriz Merlotti, ed. 2015. *Migrações Internacionais. O Caso dos Senegaleses no Sul do Brasil*. Caxias do Sul: Editora Belas-Letras.

Instituto de Segurança Pública. n.d. Consulta Interativa sobre Letalidade Violenta. Governo do Estado de Rio de Janeiro. http://www.ispvisualizacao.rj.gov.br/Letalidade.html. Accessed 20 Jan 2019.

Johnson, Ollie, III. 2006. Locating Blacks in Brazilian Politics: Afro-Brazilian Activism, New Political Parties, and Pro-Black Public Policies. *International Journal of Africana Studies* 12 (2): 170–193.

Kaly, Alain Pascal. 2001. Os Estudantes Africanos no Brasil e o Preconceito Racial. In *Migrações Internacionais: Contribuição para Políticas*, ed. Mary Garcia Castro, 463–478. Brasília: Comissão Nacional de População e Desenvolvimento.

Kane, Ousmane Oumar. 2011. *The Homeland Is the Arena. Religion, Transnationalism and the Integration of Senegalese Immigrants in America*. Oxford: Oxford University Press.

Karam, John Tofik. 2007. *Another Arabesque.Syrian-Lebanese Ethnicity in Neoliberal Brazil*. Philadelphia: Temple University Press.

Lesser, Jeffrey. 2013. *Immigration, Ethnicity, and National Identity in Brazil, 1808 to the Present*. Cambridge: Cambridge University Press.

Lewis, Oscar. 1952. Urbanization Without Breakdown: A Case Study. *The Scientific Monthly* 75 (1): 31–41.

Malomalo, Bas´Ilele, et al. 2015. *Diáspora Africana e Migraçãona Era da Globalização: Experiências de Refúgio, Estudo, Trabalho*. Curitiba, Brasil: Editora CRV.

Massey, Douglas S., et al. 1993. Theories of International Migration: A Review and Appraisal. *Population and Development Review* 19 (3): 431–466.

Miller, Toby. 2007. *Cultural Citizenship: Cosmopolitanism, Consumerism, and Television in a Neoliberal Age*. Philadelphia: Temple University Press.

Observatorio do Turismo, Cidade de São Paulo. n.d. Communidades Estrangeiras Vivendo em São Paolo. http://www.observatoriodoturismo.com.br/pdf/COMUNIDADES_ESTRANGEIRAS.pdf. Accessed 20 July 2015.

Ordóñez, Juan Thomas. 2015. Some Sort of Help for the Poor: Blurred Perspectives on Asylum. *International Migration* 53 (3): 100–110.

Osuji, Chinyere. 2013. Confronting Whitening in an Era of Black Consciousness: Racial Ideology and Black-White Interracial Marriages in Rio de Janeiro. *Ethnic and Racial Studies* 36 (10): 1490–1506.

Paschel, Tianna S., and Mark Q. Sawyer. 2008. Contesting Politics as Usual: Black Social Movements, Globalization and Race Policy in Latin America. *Souls* 10 (3): 197–214.

Prefeitura de Campos. 2015. Balcão de Empregos Insere Senegaleses no Mercado de Trabalho. *Prefeitura Municipal de Campos dos Goytacazes– RJ*. https://www.campos.rj.gov.br/exibirNoticia.php?id_noticia=30588. Accessed 14 April 2015.

Rangel, Larissa. 2013. Destino Surpresa. In *Cadernos do Estrangeiro: Destinos Migratórios, Desejos Individuais, Projetos Comunitários*, ed. Mohammed El Hajji and Luana Balthazar, 129–139. Rio de Janeiro: UFRJ, ECO, PETECO.

República del Ecuador. 2015. Ciudadanos de 11 Países Requieren de Visa para Ingresar a Ecuador. *Ministerio de Relaciones Exteriores y Movilidad Humana*. https://www.ministeriointerior.gob.ec/ciudadanos-de-11-paises-requieren-de-visa-para-ingresar-a-ecuador. Accessed 20 July 2015.

Rizzi, Kamila Raquel, et al. 2011. O Brasil na África (2003–2010): Política, Desenvolvimento e Comércio. *Revista Conjuntura Austral* 2 (5): 61–81.

Rosaldo, Renato. 1994. Cultural Citizenship in San Jose, California. *PoLAR* 17 (2): 57–63.

Schwarcz, Lilia Moritz. 2003. *Not black, not White: Just the Opposite. Culture, Race and National Identity in Brazil.* Working Paper Number CBS-47-03, Oxford: University of Oxford Centre for Brazilian Studies.

SICREMI. 2012. *International Migration in the Americas.Second Report of the Continuous Reporting System on International Migration in the Americas (SICREMI)*. Washington: Organization of American States.

Siegfried, Kristy. 2015. Refugee Versus Migrant: Time for a New Label? *IRN*, June 16. http://www.irinnews.org/analysis/2015/06/15/refugee-versus-migrant-time-new-label. Accessed 20 July 2015.

Silva, Graziella M.D., and Elisa P. Reis. 2012. The Multiple Dimensions of Racial Mixture in Rio de Janeiro, Brazil: From Whitening to Brazilian Negritude. *Ethnic and Racial Studies* 35 (3): 382–399.

Tedesco, João Carlos, and Denize Grzybovski. 2013. Dinâmica Migratória dos Senegaleses no Norte do Rio Grande do Sul. *Revista Brasileira de Estudos de População* 30 (1): 317–324.

Tedesco, João Carlos, and Gisele Kleidermacher, eds. 2017. *A Imigração Senegalesa No Brasil e na Argentina: Múltiplos Olhares.* Porto Alegre: EST Edicoões.

Twine, France W. 1998. *Racism in a Racial Democracy.* New Brunswick, NJ: Rutgers University Press.

UNHCR/ACNUR. 2014. *Refúgio no Brasil: Uma Análise Estatística (Janeiro de 2010 a Outubro de 2014). Factsheet.* Brasil: UNHCR/ ACNUR.

Vertovec, Steve. 2007. Super-diversity and Its Implications. *Ethnic and Racial Studies* 30 (6): 1024–1054.

Young, Iris Marion. 1986. The Ideal of Community and the Politics of Difference. *Social Theory and Practice* 12 (1): 1–26.

Performance Patterns and Athletic Migration During the Rio 2016 Summer Olympic Games

Peter Kuling

Competing under the flag of the Olympic Movement, refugee athletes walked together as an imagined nation for the first time during the Parade of Nations at Maracanã Stadium during the Rio de Janeiro Summer Games in 2016. Ten athletes hailing from countries such as Syria, the Democratic Republic of Congo, South Sudan, and Ethiopia joined the procession while being announced as simply the "Refugee Olympic Team." Standing ovations followed as they walked in and waved, allowing International Olympic Committee (IOC) President Thomas Bach to reiterate: "This [Refugee Team] will be a symbol of hope for all the refugees in our world, and will make the world better aware of the magnitude of this crisis" (olympic.org). These athletes—migrants living between nations—were referred to by sportscasters as citizens from the nation of their birth who found a kind of athletic salvation at all-new training facilities in surrogate host countries. Not unlike other Olympic competitors who hail from

---

P. Kuling (✉)
University of Guelph, Guelph, Canada
e-mail: pkuling@uoguelph.ca

Y. Meerzon et al. (eds.), *Migration and Stereotypes in Performance and Culture*, Contemporary Performance InterActions,
https://doi.org/10.1007/978-3-030-39915-3_10

across the globe yet train in G8 countries, such as the USA, Germany, and France, this refugee team became emblematic of the IOC's political position as a safe non-national place for refugees to temporarily have citizenship in the eyes of the world. None of the refugee athletes won any medals during competition, leaving many to wonder what flag and anthem would have been hoisted and played if any of them had medalled in Rio.

Moments of public performance at the Rio Summer Games—in competition, during ceremonies, and within media coverage—provide useful entry points to clearly understand how diverse refugee, international, and multicultural political identities are actively enacted, performed, and stereotyped through sport. Since the IOC evoked the idea of Brazil hosting the first "refugee" games, active themes and images of migration and refugees emerged—consciously as well as unconsciously—from different athletes, reporters, and even the organizing committee in Brazil. For example, the IOC developed a video playlist on their YouTube channel to showcase videos about the new Refugee Olympic Team, which corresponded to a heavy social media campaign—#TeamRefugees—used throughout Rio 2016. Great public empathy for the struggles faced by refugees occurred through these produced media, yet problems resulted for the athletes themselves as their self-narratives of migration branded them as outsiders, in coverage but also in competition. These are athletes who fled persecution in their homelands to compete as non-nationals—sometimes against people from their previous country—only to be reintroduced as "others" by competing as citizens of a non-nation composed of only refugees. None of them are discussed without mentioning their original national contexts, which further reintegrates them into the homelands they fled from in order to avoid persecution or worse; their identities are now reimagined through their appearance as survivors and via the stereotypes attached to them by media broadcasters, global audiences, and even the IOC.

Sports, as a performance experience, illustrate Richard Schechner's (1998) vision of the concepts of both play and ritual: systems of performance within dedicated communities with performance procedures and, although unknown, systematic outcomes and results from the play engaged in by competitors. Sports consistently erupt with performance moments used by audiences to engage with vast and complex systems of difference; athletes and fans all negotiate and decode—correctly and incorrectly—perceived encounters with bodies, rules, and feelings, all erupting on the field of play. According to Schechner, "An eruption is like a theatrical event because it is not the accident itself that gathers and keeps an audience. They are held by the reconstruction and reenactment of the event" (176–77). Whether a goal has been scored or someone wins, everyone—media, players, officials, and audiences—all react immediately to this eruptive potential in sport performances, often letting their own response persist long after these events are complete. In these moments, audiences "make" these eruptions matter and proceed to move through ritual behaviour in an effort to negotiate their feelings, which is how everyone at a sporting event "plays" throughout and after the experience.

My work will use four major questions to analyze sports and Olympic performance elements present during the Rio Games, with clear and often unexpected "refugee" connections. In doing so, I will demonstrate how different performance moments—on the field, in ceremonies, during media coverage—collectively contributed to privileged ways of falsely engaging with the global refugee crisis through stereotypes and assumptions during these Olympics. These four questions are all addressed and answered throughout the various examples featured here. First, I show how aspects of Brazil's work to prepare their nation to receive international migrants, refugee athletes, and global visitors became complicit in further stereotyping, rebuking, or celebrating intercultural differences. Second, how do performance elements focused on individuals' origin points—nationally or culturally—always evoke places of origin and thereby enforce a kind of reverse migration on refugees, or others performing refugeeism? Third, how do audiences respond to identity parameters used to generate play and stereotype individual athletes and their national origins in our contemporary world? Can different levels of performance at the Olympics alter audience reactions to these cultural experiences? Finally, I look at global politics: what political messages are infused into thematic refugee and migration performances, which often include the words, bodies, images, and more of victimized people? Do athletic competitions further displace refugees by oversimplifying their trauma?

Various examples from Rio 2016 will showcase how mixed media experiences—television, artistic performances, athletics, and social media platforms—transformed a variety of performance moments. Some points will focus on the environmental and class-based policies concerning venue development prior to the Games. The opening ceremonies at Maracanã Stadium focused artistically on imagery related to refugee and migration experiences through specific use of costume and make-up design, dance, and ceremonial choreography. For example, recurring imagery characterized Brazil as the happy final arrival point for global refugees, which historically includes many Japanese migrants. Other odd performance moments of reverse migration—the returning "home" of notable celebrities of Brazilian origin such as Gisele Bündchen—are key moments intended to reiterate Brazilian pride and identity to international audiences. Sadly, most live television broadcasts spent more time talking about Gisele's husband, Tom Brady, as she walked across the stadium pitch. Other ill-fated appropriations of refugee narrative sympathies—and subsequent appeals for clemency followed by forced apology—appears in interviews and social media posts by U.S. swimmer Ryan Lochte after he pretended to be held up at gunpoint in Rio. Lochte's use of refugee stereotypes such as feeling lost in a foreign land, being seduced into turning over money and documents, and being unfamiliar with local laws all fuelled global empathy for the fake robbery. Ryan Lochte's false victimization demonstrates how quickly one can harness misguided sympathies amongst global Olympic audiences. Despite all this, pre-existing familiarity with refugee stereotypes developed and promoted by the IOC appears to have served Lochte's conceptual development of his social media hoax gone wrong. All of these curious examples demonstrate a peculiar synthesis between ritual and play throughout the Olympics as the political decision to synthesize the plight of refugees with the national and positive aims of contemporary sports fails miserably.

The history of the Olympic Games itself structures its evolution as a migration of the human spirit and potential towards "global" competition. We can break down the countless images, performances, and symbols that champion the story of overcoming obstacles in a new environment—usually a foreign land—within the company of the greatest atheletes of all-time. These days, popular sports often seem to have less to do with unexpected athletes achieving success as they do with maintaining power relationships amongst larger nations with invested interest in continued global influence. We rarely see stories of atypical national triumph and pride in the face of remarkable odds like the Jamaican bobsled team competing at the Calgary 1988 Winter Olympics. Instead we experience the narratives of migrants, nationless athletes, and controversial socio-cultural messaging through misappropriated and stereotypical modes of simplified identity consumption circulating throughout these competitions.

National Preparations

Prior to ever setting foot on the ground in Brazil, athletes and media agencies were subject to the communication and newsworthy storm of how Rio would be a challenging experience for many due to issues of poverty, infrastructure, health, and security. While the IOC does send committees to review the host nation's progress with building venues and the Olympic Village—itself a temporary migratory "shanty town" with sponsored amenities for athletes—the story emerging from Brazil was one of lack of funding and problems with standards or acceptable codes for created spaces. In relation to the forthcoming refugee focus by the IOC for these Games, media outlets ran story after story about the concerns for safe drinking and activity water in Brazil. For athletes and attendees, fears were generated about what could be drunk to not cause serious illness and how safe it would be to row, swim, or compete in various external venues with poor levels of sanitation. Following past presentations to the IOC to win their initial hosting bid, Brazil painted Rio with the same "brush" to allay humanitarian hazards or oversights, similar to the 2008 Games in Beijing. Media reporting focused on these health hazards to alarm athletes and fans alike that they could encounter training and competition situations unlike those in their home nations; conditions akin to those often faced by refugees displaced or in holding environments. The Olympics Movement hopes audiences and reporters will focus on how host nations celebrate sports, culture, and experience, yet much of the critical discourse over Games emerges as planning committees fall short of athletic standards or displace events from genuine communities truly representative of the host nation's population.

Olga Khazan (2016), writing for *The Atlantic*, uses a powerful opening phrase: "Raw sewage flows into many of Rio's Olympic venues every day. As the prospect of a full clean-up before the Games dims, the world is left wondering, who will get sick, and how?" What began as a focus on the Games and the world soon transferred into a local story about communities ignored by the IOC and Rio organizers; problems were present before and remain ignored even as the Games began. These narratives in the wider media transformed parts of Rio proper into slums and spaces of internal populations facing conditions akin to nationless or refugee encampments. Khazan remarks how "Beijing battled suffocating air pollution. Sochi had too much sun, then too few hotel rooms." Stereotypes of non-Western nations persist from the Beijing Olympics onwards in an effort to lace performance elements of assumed stereotypes into the concerns of athletes and host nations. If a swimmer faces challenges due to the water used at the venue, then ultimately the problem remains with a nation unable to solve its own internal issues with infrastructure and population. These images of sewage-filled water venues and of homelessness beside ornate stadiums, which were started during the Brazilian 2014 World Cup, take further shape here as they are revisited and extrapolated upon. Rachel Glickhouse (2015) succinctly problematized the scatological possibilities of migrating to Brazil for the Games in her article for *Project Earth* titled "Why Brazil's Summer Games could be the shittiest Olympics ever."

Ben Carrington (2010) describes the synthesis of sports and nationalistic narratives when discussing London receiving the 2012 Olympic Games and immediately experiencing terrorist attacks on the Tube the next morning in July 2005. While these explosions did not directly result from sports backgrounds, the global focus on London was an opportune time for the terrorist plot to derail the United Kingdom. British citizens immediately underwent a collective conjuncture of their national qualities; all bonded as British and became resolute in the face of attacks on the nation. Carrington describes how many years later the London Games functioned as a means to continue addressing unity and survival: "it [sport] is accorded great powers by its boosters to produce both 'social cohesion' and 'community integration' in moments of national crisis" (141). While sports are supposedly divorced from political positions and global issues, the IOC's decision to give refugee athletes a "nation" for competition demonstrates a drastic contrary position. Sports as a competition are supposedly completely removed from external issues or concerns, but Carrington and others remind us how diverse elements of multiculturalism, nationalism, and identity become immediately implicated in their very making and structure as competitive enterprises. In fact, the IOC has attempted to withdraw any focus on specific nations or ideological movements. Even something as simple as acknowledging the unfortunate death of Georgian luge racer Nodar Kumaritashvili was only offered a brief moment of silence and lowering of the Canadian and Olympic flags during the opening ceremonies of the Vancouver 2010 Winter Games. All decisions on what to say, how to celebrate culture, and the visual representations of the Games are thoroughly tied to global political positioning.

Origin Points

Each member of the Refugee Nation took time to promote their migration experience in a promotional video for the IOC and the Brazil Olympic Committee. What emerged from these interviews are stylized mini-documentaries about immigration and the challenges faced by refugees, coupled with narrative resolutions about hope for Olympic success in order to complete the successful migration from difficult politics and national climates. Like sports stars in Major League Baseball or the FIFA World Cup, these refugees are shown training in their new host nations, far from their original homelands. Younger, single refugees in these videos focus on feeling better since undergoing the refugee process. Those with family left behind—a common trope in most narratives of refugees and immigration—hope Olympic success will amount to easy access to their new "host nation" for family members left behind.

Refugee team member Popole Misengo speaks via YouTube about the ways he hopes success in sports will alter his fate as a refugee from the Democratic Republic of the Congo. He fled Congo for Brazil to begin training to compete in Judo at the Olympics. While being showcased in this promotional video, what resonates as the most odd yet understandable idea is Popole's desire to succeed at the Summer Games solely to return to the Congo to help his family leave as refugees. His vision of personal success has everything to do with sport, but Olympic Gold translates into an ability to "afford" him return passage to help other refugees escape the Congo he left. He does not expect a welcome return or victory parade should he medal at the Olympic Games. Popole structures his entire vision of athletic and refugee success as dedicated to ideas of total departure; even being hosted by Brazil does not lead him to state he would want to stay in the host nation. None of his story focuses on images from his past, instead showcasing images of his pre-Olympic competition. The visual messaging emphasizes his lower-class housing and training neighbourhood, which is narratively compelling as an underdog image in sports, yet all too often the financial reality of genuine refugees. Often, he discusses the improved quality of his life in new nations or places, but his eyes and body illustrate that he lives in limbo between two nations. For Popole, winning would mean a gold medal for him as well as new citizenship for his entire family.

Rami Anis from Syria, a swimmer from the Refugee Olympic Team, clearly says that his life has improved in Belgium due largely to the training facilities and mutual respect he gets from fellow swimmers. Like a misguided relief effort commercial or nationalistic political campaign, Rami and Popole appear as refugees already representative of the "successful" global acceptance of refugee migration, despite their yet to be determined status as athletes. These IOC YouTube videos focus on the end points of the refugee experience by oversimplifying the "ease" of reconfiguring the refugee's public utility in their new nation as athletes. All these refugee athletes appear happy; sport appears to be able to heal their personal trauma. While this certainly was not the first instance of refugee athletic competition at the Olympics—Kuwait athletes competed as nationless during the 2004 Olympics in Athens—it was the first IOC campaign that allowed athletes to discuss connections between their original nation, their new nation, and their training nation. These multinational migrants move through a series of national spaces all the while being labelled, perhaps most importantly for political reasons, with the stigma of their home countries' human rights atrocities. The continued association of these individuals with countries they have fled as refugees ultimately links any personal success they achieve back to the place of trauma, further stereotyped as a kind of resurrection aimed to arouse sympathies from distant global audiences unfamiliar with migrant contexts.

Perhaps winning is not a component of the IOC's vision of successful migration; simply training temporarily in a host country appears to show that the Olympics have achieved a kind of immigration that Europe and the rest of the world struggles with daily. The refugees in these promotional videos have already won faux gold medals just for leaving their home countries; their national qualifier for the Olympics appears to be simply the physical anguish and emotional effect of literally fleeing national conflict as refugees. While none would step onto the podium in Rio, their appearance as a cultural capital allows the IOC to formally recognize political discord and strife through sport, a form of national booster (Carrington 2010, 141).

Audiences

The Olympics have recently offered host nations such as South Korea, Russia, Brazil, and Canada the unique opportunity, as Helene Vosters (2016, 189) puts it, to "capitalize on extended airtime to promote place and nation through notions of ethnic and cultural particularity." While athletic sports remain the ultimate focus of the Olympic Games, all organizing committees are required to include some form of cultural programming for their opening and closing ceremonies in their bids to the IOC. Beatrice Garcia (2012, xv) explains, "The cultural dimensions, and the Games cultural programme as their implementation vehicle, are the main mechanism through which the Olympic Movement can fulfill its ideological aspirations." The IOC has mandated that all Olympic opening ceremonies must include "a parade of Games participants, speeches and declarations by local and international Olympic officials and the head of state of the host nation, the raising of the Olympic flag to the accompaniment of the Olympic anthem, a performance of the host nation's national anthem, the torch relay and the lighting of the Olympic cauldron, and oaths taken on behalf of participating athletes and judges" (Hogan 2003, 106). Most Olympic Games' opening ceremonies in the modern era of the competition take the opportunity to use theatre and performance—in accordance with traditional and contemporary cultural styles—of the host nation in order to share their self-vision with the world. These artistic parts of the Olympic experience are used to colour the pervasive feelings of audience members and participants alike by infusing clear motifs and ideas into the host nation's self-identity through theatre and performance.

As Chris Arning (2013, 525) explains: "Opening Ceremony organizers have deployed an arsenal of semiotic and rhetorical tools in an attempt to impress and to mollify the various constituencies, to perform various ideological tasks." For example, the 2002 Salt Lake City Games raised a torn and damaged American flag recovered from the World Trade Center as their official flag during the opening ceremonies in a moment of national empathy and performance to the global viewership. Most Games use the arrival of the Olympic Flame as a culmination of the journey or procession of the Games into the host city. Despite assuming the procession has concluded with the Flame, other aspects of the overall performance and introduction of competitors likewise take over the procession and journeying theme as they enter the main stadium to be welcomed by crowds of fans. This moment of athletic entry and welcoming, as well as many travel and journeying performance themes visible in the Brazil ceremony, function as a means to discuss the Rio Games as using an overall tone of migration throughout its opening ceremonies. Themes of migration to Brazil—whether by external migrants arriving to settle in Brazil or current Brazilians returning home—played a central thematic role in the 2016 Rio Summer Games. Recurring immigrant stereotypes were actively layered throughout performance and artistic material, which effectively traversed into the larger narrative of the entire Games over the following two weeks of competition. Many of the ideas introduced through both aesthetic and athletic performance permeated the media coverage of the Games, athletes' embodiment of the Olympic spirit throughout the two weeks, and problematize concepts of successful versus unsanctioned immigration semiotics appearing throughout the remnant performance experiences of the Rio 2016 Games.

Olympic opening ceremonies have their greatest impact on audiences of the Games both within the venues and via the constant media attention throughout the two weeks of the Olympics. While past host nations have included some partial stories of migration in their opening celebrations, Brazil in 2016 focused heavily on the aesthetics and politics of being a new world migratory landing point. Brazil chose to actively return to the motif of "arrival" in their dance, movement, blocking, and lighting effects in the design of their artistic program. In fact, all athletes arrived and planted actual seeds, literally embedding their bodies' actions as future greenery and foliage resulting from Brazil's hosting of the Games. Throughout Maracanã Stadium in Rio de Janeiro, audiences had a chance to see Brazil as a lush and environmental haven prior to the arrival of both indigenous peoples and colonizers that transformed into the nation it represents today via the arrival of different non-Brazilian identities. Much was made of the significant number of Japanese migrants to Brazil in the 1800s that form the largest diasporic Japanese community outside of Japan. Likewise, the Portuguese arrivals as well as interactions with indigenous communities form many narrative components of the dancing and large-scale choreography, making up a huge portion of the theatrical opening of the Games.

Global Politics

Olympic Games also provide chances to offer alternative global histories to audiences watching in the stadium and throughout the world. Notably, Alberto Santos-Dumont—a Brazilian with a reasonable claim to first achieving flight—was embodied by an actor on a flying machine and allowed to fulfill his take-off and flight all around the stadium; he literally brought flight to the Americas through Maracanã Stadium on his short voyage around the arena. American broadcasters—all countries share the same visual image feed but commentate on the performance and sports in their own languages—were inclined to mention the "true" origins of flight with the Wright brothers; however, the performance and commentary function as stereotypical crisis amongst each other. An NBC reporter even mentions the constant battle between Dayton, Ohio and Kitty Hawk, North Carolina as the true birthplace of the Wright brothers' achievement. Despite this, Brazil uses an unfettered visual of the achievements of Santos-Dumont, seen as the first to use "powered" flight, to literally empower and celebrate his achievement flying above a field of athletic competition. It is worth noting the Maracanã Stadium has held many major historical football matches but was most recently featured in the 2014 World Cup final between Argentina and Germany. This building and its pitch embody many different semiotic layers as both a landscape and field of fair play for global audiences, literally a stadium most recently containing the victors of the globe's supposedly most universal sport at the end of the FIFA World Cup. In this moment, Santos-Dumont—as a character and national icon of innovation—literally flies higher than any football player and covers more ground faster than the best footballers on the planet.

Most notable to many observers of the opening ceremony was the arrival of living celebrities who encapsulate global success and during the ceremonies return home to share their successful migration with their country of origin. Not unlike refugees who leave their homelands to improve their lives, these celebrities also return home to improve the lives of friends, family, and other citizens. The appearance of supermodel Giselle Bündchen quantifies how stereotypical and problematic elements of immigration narratives would be performed and manipulated throughout these Games by people beyond the organizing committee. She may be famous for her work in front of the camera; however, general audiences and the North American media simply know her as the wife of New England Patriots quarterback Tom Brady. Like someone marrying for immigration or green card privileges, her achievements prior to marrying Brady are subsumed by her marriage and her relocation to Massachusetts with her husband.

Bündchen arrives on the pitch of Maracanã and walks the entire distance of the field to a live performance of the famous song "Girl from Ipanema." This is the first of all the forthcoming walking entrances subsequently performed by Olympic teams from around the world. She enters at a brisk pace and, in high heels, and walks what commentators called "the longest catwalk of her career." Oddly, many sportscasters who spoke on English coverage of the event defaulted to comments on her sheer athletic qualities—speed, grace, and balance—effectively transforming a homecoming walk by a "successful" migrant to America into an aesthetically-scored competitive moment like gymnastics. Using a popular Brazilian song to stereotype Bündchen as the girl from Ipanema—she is in fact from Rio Grande do Sul, Brazil's most southern state—audiences confront a moment of layered stereotyping that resounds with generalizations about misplaced experience. Her walk in the opposite direction of Santos-Dumont's flight forces us to think about both journeys together.

Following the opening ceremony, there was no larger story concerning scandal, misappropriated empathy, and legal battles at the Rio Olympics than the confusing narrative of American swimmer Ryan Lochte. While recounting some of the narrative he developed and the outcomes of his lying and performance of empathy, this research overlooks the legal ramifications of his actions in place of the ensuing performance and cultural resonance from his use of migrant themes and motifs to elicit public sympathy. "Its [sic] traumatic to be out late with your friends in a foreign country—with a language barrier—and have a stranger point a gun at you and demand money to let you leave," Lochte wrote in an Instagram post from August 19, 2016. Lochte's claims concerning the gas station robbery he experienced with his teammates demonstrates a conscious attempt at appropriation of the migration narrative for global and media sympathies. His story focuses on the ideals of being out of place in terms of national and linguistic contexts and therefore being taken advantage of by police or security forces capable of hindering his successful migration "home" to the Olympic Village. While out in the city away from the safety and security of the athletes' village, Lochte claims to have been held up at gunpoint by a Brazilian official. This would later be largely refuted by video footage and witness testimony. Notably, Lochte's own unaffected appearance returning to the Olympic Village would hurt his claims to have been so unexpectedly fearful for his life. Several broadcasters saw this evolving narrative as the common trope of an American out of place in a new nation and being taken advantage of by opportunistic Brazilians. We should see it as the opposite: new refugees being abused or appealing for clemency in the face of unjust immigrant tactics, working on sympathies to garner support for their powerless plight. Lochte clearly did not realize how hyperbole and his casual development of a false narrative—one akin to many new immigrants' first experiences with border guards and police—would serve to undo him as other evidence piled up to demonstrate the falsity of his tale.

More curious than the lie circulated by Lochte and his teammates was the surrounding media campaign with interviews and persistent mistakes. Lochte's appearance on American networks and his apology on Twitter offered the chance to perform his own fears around the robbery, which gave a privileged face to common stories of misuse of authority in the wake of migration. The most intriguing part of his apology might just be the description of how he was "out with his friends" in a foreign country. Seeking empathy for the barriers he faced as a displaced American in Brazil, he cannot help but describe the larger situation as one of leisure and privilege. Lochte's lie became the focus for much of the way Americans—themselves migrant athletes over the course of the competition in Brazil—were viewed collectively for their self-involved national character. This idea was further reinforced by the ways Giselle Bündchen is frequently stereotyped by Americans as merely Mrs. Brady rather than a successful model and career woman herself. There is no world but the American world, which Lochte's lie ultimately helped demonstrate due to his contempt for anyone claiming he was in the wrong for feeling afraid and worried, common emotions for migrants and refugees. While the USA limits migration into its own nation, Lochte's "reverse" migration performance aimed to shift sympathies towards Americans' reliance on the overall refugee narrative of these Games in tandem with Lochte's celebrity. Unlike Giselle Bündchen, whose body and presence reinforced her Brazilian return home, Lochte used social media narration to perform shock and fear from a privileged position of capturing the attention of global audiences. Lochte's story—told by any member of the IOC Refugee Nation—would have similarly used trauma and violence to drive empathy. Lochte's attempt at sympathy for an encounter with a government official and the assumed abuses he faced remains suspect for its exact truth. In the pattern of past apologies, he does little to explain why things happened and only appealed to the IOC and the United States Olympic Committee to not detract from the initiatives of the Rio Games themselves. Lochte's outburst of false experience and storytelling functioned like the eruptive performance experience already designated by Schechner (1998), which Lochte's Twitter apology claimed when he wrote: "There has already been too much said and too many valuable resources dedicated to what happened last weekend." Hoping for global ignorance of his misguided attempt to lie about his "immigrant" experiences in Brazil, Lochte's shining moment of subterfuge remains one of the most prevalent post-Rio experiences still talked about today.

Conclusion

After the Rio de Janeiro Olympic Summer Games concluded, the world turned its attention to PyeongChang, South Korea. The 2018 Winter Olympics happened at a time when unprecedented tension between neighbouring North Korea and the United States circulated from social media to missile testing in the Sea of Japan. While everything proceeded as usual, the rhetoric of politics and the stereotypes of world nations, leaders, and athletes persisted through the competition at many levels. In fact, the North and South decided to compete together as a unified Korea, resulting in the divisions between athletes often impeding their capabilities as unique national teams. The Games move through Asia for the next two installments—Tokyo, Japan, and Beijing, China—before returning to countries where the politics of refugees and immigration are likely to reappear. Paris will host the Summer Games in 2024 and Los Angeles in 2028. While neither city internally has direct issues with these competitors, issues of athletic migration to Europe or America and the pursuant claim of asylum or refugee status may occur. These are not omens of fear, but rather urban venues rife for issues of immigration experience and forthcoming stereotypes. Gone will be some of the concerns with infrastructure and coming to the fore will be thoughtlessness of the political environments or repressive politics towards outsiders that have been known to happen in each of these future host countries.

The Refugee Olympic Team did not recruit athletes for the 2018 Winter Games in South Korea. It remains to be seen if this instance of nationalizing refugees into one group during Rio 2016 will recur. Refugees have certainly not disappeared, but the relative use of them as a mode of performance and empathy at the Games may shift. They are no longer part of an ensuing ritual being used by the IOC, but this does not mean they will not play. Asian host nations' opening ceremonies have often focused on the history and unity of Korea, Japan, and China in their respective artistic presentations. Likewise, France and the United States may offer a different set of theatrical performance modes for showcasing unity, history, and responding to pressing international issues of their time. While the USA is certainly a country of global migrants, they may perform other aspects of their national history, or at least focus on different histories within California, when the world arrives in Los Angeles in 2028.

References

Arning, Chris. 2013. Soft Power, Ideology and Symbolic Manipulation in Summer Olympic Games Opening Ceremonies: A Semiotic Analysis. *Social Semiotics* 23 (4): 523–544.

Carrington, Ben. 2010. *Race, Sport and Politics: The Sporting Black Diaspora.* London: SAGE Publications.

Garcia, Beatrice. 2012. *The Olympic Games and Cultural Policy.* London: Routledge.

Glickhouse, Rachel. 2015. Why Brazil's Summer Games Could Be the Shittiest Olympics Ever. *Project Earth*, https://fusion.tv/story/40671/why-brazils-summer-games-could-be-the-shittiest-olympics-ever/?hootPostID=c0040243a1d491611d0b51ef8ea132e9. Accessed 14 April 2020.

Hogan, Jackie. 2003. Staging the Nation: Gendered and Ethnicized Discourses of National Identity in Olympic Opening Ceremonies. *Journal of Sport & Social Issues* 27 (2): 100–123.

Khazan, Olga. 2016. What Happens When There's Sewage in the Water. *The Atlantic*. March 31. theatlantic.com/health/archive/2016/03/what-happens-when-theres-sewage-in-the-water. Accessed 3 Jan 2019.

Rio 2016 Refugee Olympic Team. The Olympic Games, olympic.org/ioc-refugee-olympic-team-rio-2016. Accessed 13 Jan 2020.

Schechner, Richard. 1998. *Performance Theory.* 2nd ed. London: Routledge.

Vosters, Helene. 2016. Sochi Olympics 2014, Canadian Truth and Reconciliation, and the Haunting Ghouls of Canadian Nationalism. In *Performance Studies in Canada*, ed. Laura Levin and Marlis Schweitzer, 184–210. Toronto: Playwrights Canada Press.

PART III

Dreams, Memories, and Storytelling: Applied Theatre and Communities of Praxis

Forced Migration, Memory, and Testimony

Nimo Bokore

I often struggle with the knowledge that past and current traumas are present in my community. As a Somali living in Canada, I have seen first-hand the effects of war trauma—during the war and for years to come. I also acknowledge the differences within my community regarding memories and the presentation of history. Depending on educational background, social status, and support systems, some Somali war survivors develop helpful individualized resettlement skills that include adaptation through education, development of ethnic businesses, and involvement in community work. But others who have moved to Canada from refugee camps continue to struggle with trauma. This chapter is based on a project I completed in 2016 called "Somali-Canadian Women: Historical Past of Survival and Facing Everyday Challenges of Resettlement," which captured the life histories of twelve Somali women using oral history, storytelling, and life history methodology. Before exploring those stories, I will first situate the project within Canada's history of multiculturalism and diversity and discuss my methodology.

According to the most recent United Nations High Commissioner for Refugees (UNHCR) report, the number of global refugees has now

N. Bokore (✉)
Carleton University, Ottawa, ON, Canada
e-mail: nimo.bokore@carleton.ca

Y. Meerzon et al. (eds.), *Migration and Stereotypes in Performance and Culture*, Contemporary Performance InterActions,
https://doi.org/10.1007/978-3-030-39915-3_11

exceeded 70 million. This number of forced migrants and displaced people connotes that there is a story to be told about the human cost of war and displacement, which includes memories that are changing the lives of individuals and communities. This is a story of how twelve refugee women's struggle for identity and belonging is still connected to their past and the possibility of belonging or carving out an identity is impeded by their political, ethnic, as well as religious affiliations.

For African-born scholars like myself, this is a topic we cannot ignore as more and more of our families and people live in limbo in long-term refugee camps such as Dadaab in Kenya and Dolo Ado in Ethiopia. It is important to undertake studies that address the political and social histories of regions, the policies, and actions of humanitarian regimes, and political and religious shifts in home countries, especially in light of their gendered impacts—all are critically relevant to a comprehensive analysis of the true cost of displacement and the refugee's traumatic experiences.

My interest is in refugee and resettlement issues particularly affecting those coming from the Global South. Through personal and professional experiences, I have come to understand that war affects women more profoundly than men because gender-based violence is often used as a tool of war. For example, Ager (1999) explains that during World War II, more than 200,000 Southeast Asian women, 80 percent of whom were Korean, were abducted for use as "comfort women" to provide sexual services for Japanese soldiers. In the early 1970s, at the time of Bangladesh's independence, soldiers in the Pakistani army who were sent to suppress the rebellion raped Bengali women. According to Ager (1999, 114), "in Iran, detained teenagers executed for political reasons have first been raped, denying them the automatic entry to heaven granted to virgins." This is also true of Somalia, leading Abdi (2007, 183), a sociologist at the University of Minnesota and a scholar of Somali Studies, to declare in 2007 that the Horn of Africa, and specifically Somalia, was one of the worst places for women to live. Dr. Cawo Abdi's 2007 study shows the gendered consequence of the war in Somalia as this patriarchal society culture disintegrated and women paid the price of increased rates of emotional and physical violence. Losing the traditional male or the leader of the household protection during war increased women's vulnerability to gender-based violence.

Documenting Memories of War

I turn my attention now to the life experiences of twelve Somali women living in Canada to try to understand the impact that war has on women's lives and the lives of their children and others in their communities. I chose a life history research methodology and a black feminist framework to gather stories from these women, to explore their experiences of forced migration and their memories of war as testimonies, and to bring forth women's voices that are often culturally silenced. These women entrusted their stories to me for the purpose of recording them as testimony to what happens to women during the prolonged tribal or civil war. I gathered their stories with cultural understanding, respect, and transparency, while adhering to ethical standards and cultural guidelines. This is important to me—first as a Somali community member and a survivor of war and second because I wanted to protect the women who spoke with me.

I reviewed the available literature on civilian survivors of wars, which included a limited number of studies focusing on specific areas and used them to inform my study. Kinzie (2005), Levy and Sidel (2013), and Simich (2008) found that survivors who had experienced extreme trauma, including gender-based violence such as rape, often showed signs of persistent psychological distress. Other scholars found that civilian survivors of war struggle with mental health issues, including post-traumatic stress disorder (PTSD) and anxiety disorders, during the resettlement stage (Bhui et al. 2006; Rees and Pease 2007; van der Kolk 2014; Warfa et al. 2006). Several studies on developmental trauma argued that such experiences can trigger an ongoing autonomic activation, forming patterns of neural connection that often lead to physiological and psychological developmental deficits (Cozolino 2010; LeDoux 1996; McCormick et al. 2011; Meaney 2001; Siegel 2011). This existing wealth of knowledge in social neuroscience helped me to frame my questions, providing me with new insight that directed my own research. It also helped me to understand or be attuned to certain aspects of my participant's experience and hear their narratives differently.

Methodology

In my research, I focused on exploring women's stories and sharing their memories of survival, resilience, and hope for the future. From the individuals who responded to my call, I selected women who had arrived in

Canada between the late 1980s and early 2000s,[1] when most Somalis came to Canada. They were between the ages of 39 and 69, were born in different Somali regions in East Africa and lived in either Toronto or Ottawa.[2] I selected a life history research method because of its cultural congruence with the Somali method of sharing information and skills.[3] This method allowed me to note the humanizing aspects of the participants' stories: their emotions, views on memories of historical trauma, and their experiences of displacement and marginalization (Dhunpath and Samuel 2009; Goodson and Sikes 2001). Linde (1993, 20) describes life history research as a method used to present stories that say: "see what events have made me what I am" or, more precisely, "what you must know about me is know me." As Freire, quoted in Chin and Rudelious-Palmer (2010, 268) says: "Storytelling in a human rights context allows those who have been marginalized to tell their stories in authentic and meaningful dialogue and with the reflection that identifies causes." The life history method gave me the opportunity to connect the participants' stories of survival with their current responses to their resettlement challenges.

Adding a critical gender lens also allowed me to explore the distinctive means each participant used to navigate both the dynamics within the Somali community and the external, systemic, oppressive systems (Collins 2000) they encountered. Employing a Black feminist life history research approach meant highlighting the women's narratives and their meaning-making processes while also responding to the epistemological and ontological questions of what Collins (2000, vi) calls Black women's "self-defined viewpoints" in their journeys—an important point for documenting gendered testimonies of survival.

This methodological process allowed me to explore the impact of each stage of forced migration: (1) pre-migration, fear, and anticipation, (2) escape and survival, (3) transit and dealing with prolonged fear, gender-based violence, and emotional stress, and (4) resettlement, often in a Western country, such as Canada (Ager 1999; Papadopoulos 2002).

Relying on these analytical frameworks, I began to understand through my discussions with the women about trauma and its effects on some refugee women. "I began to understand the impact that persistent trauma and a lack of understanding of cultural norms in a new country have on refugee women's resettlement in the fourth, post-settlement stage of migration.

Prolonged War and the Process of Trauma

Some of my research participants witnessed the war between Ethiopia and Somalia in 1977–1978 and lived through the collapse of the Somali central government in 1991, as well as the prolonged ethnic war that led to the destruction of the country and the dislocation of millions of Somalis. My participants' stories about war and narratives of displacement are filled with trauma, but also, survival and resilience. I saw how some of them remain frozen by fear, overwhelmed by the impact of acute experiences of trauma, reliving it every day. As van der Kolk (2014) notes, prolonged trauma becomes the scar from an old wound, impairing the functioning of the present-day body and mind. It bridges the gap between past and present experiences, enabling the trauma to become part of the everyday lives of those who experienced it.

Trauma resides in the brain's nervous system, frequently setting off the naturally ingrained human response for survival (LeDoux 1996). It is the antithesis of empowerment and leaves women vulnerable to adversities. With this knowledge, I focused on the everyday lives of my participants to understand how both past and present social and structural issues affect their resettlement. Through this process, I also wanted to add to the historical documentation of Somali women's survival and resiliency in the past three decades that goes beyond a focus on their pain and suffering, with the hope that others will continue this research. Ultimately, studying adult's experiences of war gave me the chance to capture rich and in-depth details of survival stories. I came to understand how women from different socioeconomic, educational, and tribal backgrounds dealt with xenophobia, ethnic othering,[4] discrimination, inequality, poverty, and racialization during resettlement.

Oral Testimony and Somalis

For Somalis, storytelling is a form of remembering, testimony, and oral historical documentation. Somalis used this system of oral record keeping for centuries due to their lack of a written language until the mid-1970s, when the Somali government introduced the alphabet through a mass literacy program. Prior to that, Somalis depended on their considerable storytelling abilities and poetry recitation practices for communication and historical record keeping; these skills are fundamental cultural practices for Somalis. It is common for Somalis to include a question regarding current events in their daily greeting, saying in the Somali language, "*Maxa la sheegay*" (What is in the news? or What have been told?) It allows the individual to talk about not only one's life but also about what is happening in the larger tribal community.

Oral communication practices are also developed along gender lines. During both war and peace, boys are taught the arts of storytelling and debating, which are seen as necessary to men's social skill set, including the settling of family and tribal disputes. This oral tradition is passed from generation to generation, while poetry continues to preserve history, teaching important survival skills and instilling life lessons, values, and morals to shape the worldviews of younger generations.

Two Western-born Somali historians, B.W. Andrzejeski and I.M. Lewis (1964, 27), were fascinated by this Somali behavior and researched and described how Somalis shared their history and knowledge for centuries through oral recitation:

> Somali oral poetry of the public forum was memorized verbatim. Poetry reciters were under the strict obligation to memorize, and then reproduce as faithfully as they could, the oral texts of the poems, which they learned from poets or other poetry-reciters. Any form of willful change of the text by the reciter, such as improvised additions, deletions or substitutions, was prohibited. The reciter, who was seldom a creative poet himself, was regarded merely as a channel of communication and a memory storage device and was in no way a co-author of the version he recited.

This description shows how this ethnic group of men freely shared poetry through memorization and oral recitation. Historically, Somali nomads traveled to defend tribal territories and in search of water holes and pastural grazing lands. Along the way, they shared poetry with thousands of fellow reciters. Women have been culturally and religiously restricted from participating in this tradition, which has often limited their skills, voices, and memories.

The Challenge of Documenting Tribal and Gendered Memories of War

Somali tribal hierarchies were reinforced by the colonial powers in 1884, during the partition of Africa, and have been used to divide, disempower, and rule people along clan and sub-clan lines. Certain tribes, like the

Midgaan and Gabooye, are looked down on just as the Dalits are in India. These two minority groups, indistinguishable from other Somalis in skin color, culture, and religion, are isolated and subjected to discrimination, humiliation, and dehumanization at the hands of their fellow Somalis. The irony is that these tribes play an important economic role during both peacetime and wartime. They are skilled and resourceful groups that have historically been responsible for creating businesses, passing down cultural medical knowledge, and providing technical expertise in the creation of household and personal use items such as dishes, yet their contributions go unacknowledged and the men of these tribes are denied political participation, just like all Somali women.

For Somali women, the physical and emotional aspects of war, forced migration, and resettlement are reinforced by cultural rules and practices. For example, women have historically been denied power and silenced through the cultural practice of *hisaut,* which requires all women, regardless of age, socioeconomic status, or education, to exude modesty and display shame for going against men in political conversation or for discussing sex-related topics, whether they concern reproductive health, sexuality, or the impact of rape.

The participants in my study agreed that the culture of *hisaut or modesty* fostered a sense of humiliation and disgrace among female survivors of sexual aggression. During the war and even after resettlement, violated women, especially young girls, are often encouraged to hide their experience from members of the community, including close family. For example, a mother who becomes aware of her daughter's rape will encourage infibulation or female genital mutilation. The Somali women I spoke to struggled with war-related experiences and had the added stress of culture-based gendered silencing. They denied what they felt and had experienced, having been deliberately silenced by powerful community leaders and interest groups who do not want these types of stories on record.

Gendered political silencing is not unique to Somalis. Research shows that narratives of war are not often an accurate representation of events, but are the expression of an experience as it is remembered or presented. Pointing to these challenges, Linde (1993, 4) writes that a story is "a discontinuous unit told in separate pieces over a long period of time, since it is a long-term unit, it is necessarily subject to revision and change as the speaker drops some old meanings and adds new meanings to portions of the life story."

Understanding gendered stories of war and violence require one to pay attention to cultural limitations on what is allowed to be expressed and how it can be communicated, which affects mental and physical health as well as the documentation of memories and testimonials of survivors of wars. In my study, participants shared their experiences, thoughts, and adaptive behaviors within the context of Somali culture. Looking back into their meaning-making processes and actions, I noticed how after two decades of resettlement, cultural restrictions continued to undermine my participants' healing. Therefore, I began to focus on particular stories in their narratives of war as well as nonverbal cues that were visible in their emotional responses to painful hidden experiences.

Establishing a strong relationship and sharing my own horrible gendered experiences with my participants opened the doors for collective remembering and sharing—producing a gendered testimonial of war that allowed us to remember the painful struggle we went through and the violence we desperately want to hide. Life history researchers describe how women's experiences are shaped and modified by cultural restrictions, leading them to compartmentalize when narrating events that happened during the war. In the Somali community, narratives of survival that are shared are gendered, but also told as if it had not happened to the teller. Documenting past traumatic events necessarily requires the teller to ignore, omit, or forget certain aspects, either as a form of self-protection or because of cultural and traditional silencing. Feminist researcher Sherryl Kleinman (2007) described life histories as a method of investigating how each woman's feelings and actions are revealed in their individual voices and actions, and at each defining moment in their lives. Engaging in a life history helped me to more deeply explore the meaning-making processes in narratives of survival, allowing me to participate in the collecting of women's stories of war and the preservation of their memories and experiences. Sharing and including my own stories as a survivor also contributed to my study and the documentation of women's voices.

For me, documenting memories grows out of living through war and displacement, myself, and hearing the stories of fellow Somalis, which change over the years to fit personal comfort zones or to accommodate political and religious restrictions (the views of the storyteller inherently include his/her affiliation with powerful interest groups). Norquay (1993, 245) describes this modification of a narrative as a purposeful act of "forgetting" produced through systemic gaps, silences, and omissions within stories told by groups or survivors. For the particular women I studied, storytelling became an act or a system that is reinforced by political, cultural, or religious demarcations, where dominant narratives took over, silencing the voices of survivors and diminishing knowledge of the human cost of war. When I began collecting stories of female survivors of war as a form of historical documentation, I was confronted by the challenge this storytelling behaviour posed. Cole and Knowles (2001, 5) say that human stories are the "central epistemological construct illuminating the interion of human experience and social context." In light of this, how does the act of forgetting function when gendered memories of war are discredited and justice claims are ignored or denied? What is the emotional impact of such denial? Decades after their resettlement in Canada, Somali women still live with the silence that is continuously promoted within their culture and religion that values female modesty.

Telling My Own Story of Displacement and Migration

My history is filled with narratives of colonization, liberation, deportation, and displacement in a region that has been in the news for many decades. My own story of torture and displacement begins in 1974, with the overthrow of Ethiopian Emperor Haile Selassie by the military dictator Mengistu Haile Mariam. After securing his power, Mengistu began to selectively imprison or execute those who opposed his leadership and others assumed to be guilty by tribal or ethnic association. Unfortunately, in 1975, I was accused of opposing Mengistu. At the same time, I was lucky enough to escape his random imprisonment and death sentences with only minor physical injury. The unforgettable physical and mental torture I endured is still etched in my brain. But the roots of my story go back further.

My father was a respected religious and academic leader in the region now known as Somaliland (a former British colony). Before 1960, suspected Somali leaders like my father were often deported from one region under colonial rule to another. It was a practice carried out by all colonial powers who ruled Somali regions in the Horn of Africa, including the Italians, the French, and the British. Since my father's tribe resides in both Ethiopia and British Somaliland, he was first relocated to Ethiopia and then back to Somaliland. This created multiple forced displacements for him and his family and left me without a father in Ethiopia.

After a few years of resettlement struggles, including rebuilding my career, which was denied under the hidden systemic barriers I encountered as a non-European newcomer—an act that was justified by my "not having Canadian education or experience"—I began to accumulate a Canadian education and working with immigrants and refugees in the employment/resettlement sector. Here, I realized that service disparities exist for certain refugees, especially Muslims, particularly since 9/11. This specific barrier has had an impact on Somalis who arrived in Canada, as I did, in the late 1980s, from refugee camps scattered throughout Africa, the Middle East, and Europe.

In my professional work, I have encountered resettled refugees who are overwhelmed by the existing stressors that some authors describe as Canada's "economic apartheid." It is an economic marginalization often experienced by those seen as Others in Canada (Folson 2004; Galabuzi 2006). I remember a conversation I had with a resettled refugee who described her experiences:

> When I arrived, I was so busy taking care of my three children who were under five years old. When they became school age I began thinking about my other resettlement goals. including learning the English language to secure employment. I then found out that I did not qualify for the language programs I applied for. Feeling useless and depressed, all my nightmares [about the war] also began to get stronger. I am now having a hard time taking care of myself and my family.

I personally went through this struggle during my early years in Canada and I heard similar stories from the research participants. Resettled refugees not only deal with flashbacks of their refugee/war experiences and PTSD but also grieve the loss of their home country, which sometimes alienates them as the unwanted Other, giving them no option of ever going back. Living in a new country where they do not speak the language and sometimes have to deal with unfamiliar cultural and social landscapes, refugee women's stress also increases or persists. I worked with families who, as I did, arrived and resettled in lower-income, crime-ridden, racialized neighbourhoods. Due to the absence of affordable housing and a lack of language skills and basic education, some them continue to live in these neighbourhoods for decades after their arrival (Danso 2002). They report their struggles with urban youth violence, higher school dropout rates, disproportionate levels of poverty, homelessness, inadequate housing for large families, and racial and religious discrimination, especially following 9/11 (Bokore 2009; Bokore 2012; Somali Youth Conference). While doing my research I found there is abundant literature about immigrants and their integration, however there is an absence of literature documenting refugee experiences or the prolonged economic, social, and health impacts of trauma on these communities.

Documenting My Participants' Stories of Displacement and Migration

Throughout my data collection, analysis, and many conversations with the women in my community, I have noticed among women a commonality of certain experiences of war and ways of remembering them. One of the events frozen in time and remembered by all is the initial stage of forced migration when the realization of losing everything hits. All women, including me, remember the feeling of dread and fear. Refugee researchers such as Ager explain this feeling as the fear of the unknown and the anticipation of grief from losing one's home, land, or even country. It is disorientation that happens when people realize the magnitude of what is about to happen (Ager 1999). For some Somalis it is an experience that is repeated multiple times in different regions as internally displaced refugees seek safety or survival.

My personal memory of renewed grief was supported by two research participants with whom I shared a similar migration history. One of them described her journey when I met her for a follow-up interview. Gacalo[5] was born in eastern Ethiopia and left her birthplace for the first time during the Ethiopian Somali war in 1977–78. Over the next fifteen years, she was a refugee in Africa before her arrival in Canada in 1992. During that time, she lost her temporary home a total of five times. "I feel like I have been running most of my adult life," she said. "The worst one being in 1988 when I gave birth to my first child while running from Ethiopia to Somalia." She called it "unfortunate luck" or "coincidence" that she gave birth a second time while running from Siyad Barre's attack on Somaliland. What amazed me about this participant was her resilience, her ability to take care of her family in foreign lands, where she did not speak the language. Her resiliency helped her not only to care for her family but also to land a job here, in Canada, at which she has been working for the past two decades. Her story is one of trauma, but I was amazed by her strength and calm, even as she was sharing her story with me, talking about the positive things in her current life, including her children's achievements in higher education.

Hoodo, another participant of my study, left Ethiopia as a child during the Ethiopian-Somali war. She was a university student in Mogadishu when the longest civil war erupted and the government of Siyad Barre collapsed. She shared stories of multiple forced migrations lasting fourteen years before her arrival in Canada in 2001. Hoodo particularly remembers what happened to her when she realized, as a young adult, that she was about to lose the home where she had spent her childhood years:

> One day a family member told me to get her sugar from the store. Some military men who I think were related to Siyaad Barre were standing in front of our door and as soon as I came out they [asked] me to identify myself by my tribe. I could not tell them about my tribe because of my accent. I was afraid they will not believe me because at the time they were killing tribes from the north who spoke as I did. I was afraid when one of them pulled a gun and demanded that I identify myself again. Fortunately, my family heard my screams and came out to rescue me and explained my tribal connection to eastern Ethiopian Somalis, not Somaliland tribes. That was the defining moment for me living with fear for myself and my family. That is when my family decided it was time to leave Mogadishu and run to the unknown. As a family,[6] we rented a car and we headed toward Kismaayo, which was the safest option for us. I was afraid of what would happen to my other family from my father's side, which I could not reach because they were living in another part of the city. I met some of them a decade later and others are still living all over the world.

For Hoodo, those traumatizing memories remain with her, defining her behavioural responses to adversities or what she sees as a threat. In one of the follow-up interviews, I went to see Hoodo at her home in Toronto. When I arrived, she asked me if we could first go to a nearby Tim Horton's coffee shop to get a coffee. Since I knew the coffee shop was located in a plaza less than two blocks away from her home, I suggested that we could walk there to get fresh air and some exercise. I was surprised by her reaction to my suggestion: she quickly turned to me with an anxious face and said, "it is not safe to walk." She then went on to tell me about how one summer evening when she was walking in her neighbourhood, some teenagers driving a big car had thrown empty bottles at her, calling her a terrorist. She said: "I drive everywhere, which is not helping for my high blood pressure and weight problem. I need to exercise. I can't afford female only gyms and I can't walk on the street or park because of fear."

As refugee mothers, we all experienced significant fear brought on by the possibility of being forcibly removed from our temporary shelters or made to return to our original homes to once again face war and/or persecution. Such conditioned fear makes it difficult, if not impossible, to disassociate the past from the present. Researchers argue that these kinds of memories function outside consciousness (LeDoux 1996; Siegel 2011; van der Kolk 2014).

For survivors of warlike Hoodo, traumatic memories are triggered and resurface without any warning. For Somali Canadians, there are multiple triggers, including the stress of poverty, inadequate housing, racial/systemic oppression, and living without any external support systems or buffers. In recent decades, the Somali community has seen disproportionate levels of youth violence and increased school dropout rates, which is adding to the fears of those of us who are mothers. Two of my participants, Asli and Dalmar, talked about their experiences as community service providers helping youth with drug addiction, dropping out of school, and conflicts arising from biculturalism (Canadian and Somali) and a lack of parental understanding. Another participant of my study, Bishaaro, talked about the experience of one of her family members who was struggling with her older son's drug addiction: "This mother even tried to send her son back to Kenya to live with other family members to learn about culture and family respect, or *dhaqan celine* [returning to culture] in Somali." Many Somali Canadian mothers take their children back to their tribal homelands to learn history and ritual, including the art of storytelling and religion. Unfortunately, this young relative returned to Canada with an addiction to *khat*. Although *dhaqan celine* is designed to bring back Diaspora-born children who have lost their culture, religion, and way of life, it can create additional problems, including exposure to religious extremists, renewed tribal hate, and *khat* addiction. *Khat* is an amphetamine-like stimulant used culturally by Somali men as a form of entertainment or to pass time. The drug, when chewed, initially causes excitement and language eloquence, which is useful for political or tribal debates among men. Unfortunately, as with any drug, it also has side effects, including exhaustion, loss of appetite, sexual dysfunction, and insomnia. I grew up watching families destroyed by this addiction as users spend their time looking for a fix or being in a high called *mirqaan*. One of the participants, Dalmar, attributed the failure of her marriage to *khat*.

Asli, Dalmar, and Bishaaro talked about the impact of *khat* on the community and other participants, Ladan and Mandeeq, connected this plant to community responses to trauma. They described how men are overwhelmed by what happened in the past and by what is happing to them now in the resettlement country and begin to self-medicate with *khat*. Somali men are also burdened by the guilt and shame of losing their culturally based patriarchal power and their roles as protectors of and breadwinners for the family. These roles are now often unattainable for them due to the systemic barriers they encounter that prolong their unemployment or underemployment and lead them to withdraw from family responsibilities and seek other avenues to forget the past. Sadly, for the women and the children in Somali refugee families, *khat* usage and other behaviors, such as controlling women by imposing religious family morality and excessive religious practice, are all introduced or used by men to numb their own pain and past trauma and the stressors of living in Canada.

Conclusion

When Somali youth issues come up in Canadian news media and internet postings, the focus is usually on Somali involvement with violence and drugs, on parents sending their children to fight overseas for Islamic causes, including al-Shabaab and ISIL (Aulakh 2010; Brown 2006; The Canadian Press 2010; Said 1993). Dalmar, Landan, and Mandeeq described how frequent media representations of the Somali community's involvement with terrorist groups are adding to the negative public perception of Somalis and, hence, to the systemic barriers they face. These negative stereotypes contribute to the stress and fear of the women I interviewed for this study.

In my work with the Somali community for this study, I focused on documenting stories and memories to uncover a time in history (forced migration and resettlement) through the feelings and memories of those who experienced it. While doing so, I kept in mind my commitment to confidentiality and my desire to treat those who trusted me with their life stories with utmost respect. Even though I shared many of the women's experiences, I kept in mind my own privilege as an educated woman. I was also mindful of how stories are told and retold in contexts that are constantly changing and affecting the meaning of the story.

The participants of my study shared traumatic and powerful stories to explain their life experiences, as a testimonial of what happened to them individually and collectively as members of a tribe that has often been punished by opposing tribes. In their narratives of war, the participants highlighted what makes them vulnerable to the emotional traumas of their past and present realities.

Notes

1. This time frame coincides with mass Somali population displacement due to the 1977–78 Ethiopian Somali War, the Somali government's attack on the Somaliland people, and the subsequent collapse of the Somali central government.
2. These are the two major Canadian cities that hosted Somali refugees at the time of their initial arrival.
3. Somalis have a passion for storytelling and poetry. They have been called a "Nation of Bards" by early explorers, researchers, and novelists, such as the Canadian novelist Margaret Laurence.
4. Somalis adhere to a tribal hierarchy and discriminate against other tribes. This means that about half the population in my home region is identified as *Gaboya*, which is similar to the Untouchable caste in India.
5. All names used are pseudonyms.
6. Hoodo is referring to family members on her mother's side.

References

Abdi, Cawo Mohamed. 2007. Convergence of Civil War and the Religious Right: Reimagining Somali Women. *Signs: Journal of Women in Culture and Society* 33 (1): 183–207.

Ager, Alastair, ed. 1999. *Refugee Perspectives on the Experience of Forced Migration*. London: Cassell.

Andrzejewski, Bogumil Witalis, and Ioan Myrddin Lewis. 1964. *Somali Poetry. An Introduction*. Oxford: Clarendon Press.

Aulakh, Raveena. 2010. Somali-Canadians Caught in Alberta's Deadly Drug Trade. *The Toronto Star*, March 22. www.thestar.com/news/investigations/2010/03/22/somalicanadians_caught_in_albertas_deadly_drug_trade.html.

Bhui, Kamaldeep, et al. 2006. Mental Disorders Among Somali Refugees. *Social Psychiatry and Psychiatric Epidemiology* 41 (5): 400–408.

Bokore, Nimo. 2009. Female Survivors of African Wars Dealing with the Past and Present. *Journal of Sociological Research* 1 (1): E5.

———. 2012. Suffering in Silence: A Canadian-Somali Case Study. *Journal of Social Work Practice* 27 (1): 95–113.

Brown, Louise. 2006. Dropout, Failure Rates Linked to Language. *The Toronto Star*, June 23. http://www.yorku.ca/goldring/clippings/dropout__rates_link_language.pdf.

The Canadian Press. 2010. Canadian Somalis Fear Militant Group Targeting Youths. *CTV News*, March 18. http://toronto.ctv.ca/servlet/an/local/CTVNews/20100318/cdn_somalia_100318/20100318?hub=Toronto.

Chin, Kevin, and Kristi Rudelius-Palmer. 2010. Storytelling as a Relational and Instrumental Tool for Addressing Racial Justice. *Race/Ethnicity: Multidisciplinary Global Contexts* 3: 265–281.

Cole, Ardra L., and Gary J. Knowles. 2001. *Lives in Context: The Art of Life History Research. Kindle edition*. Lanham: Altamira Press.

Collins, Patricia Hill. 2000. *Black Feminist Thought: Knowledge, Consciousness and the Politics of Empowerment*. London: Routledge.

Cozolino, Louis. 2010. *The Neuroscience of Psychotherapy: Healing the Social Brain*. New York: W.W. Norton & Company.

Danso, Ransford. 2002. From 'There' to 'Here': An Investigation of the Initial Settlement Experiences of Ethiopian and Somali Refugees in Toronto. *GeoJournal* 56 (1): 3–14.

Dhunpath, Rubby, and Michael Samuel. 2009. *Life History Research: Epistemology, Mythology, and Representation*. Boston: Sense Publishers.

Folson, Rose Baaba. 2004. *Calculated Kindness: Global Restructuring, Immigration, and Settlement in Canada*. Halifax: Fernwood Publishing.

Galabuzi, Grace-Edward. 2006. *Canada's Economic Apartheid: The Social Exclusion of Racialized Groups in the New Century*. Toronto: Canadian Scholars' Press.

Goodson, Ivor, and Patricia J. Sikes. 2001. Developing Life Histories. In *Life History Research in Educational Settings: Learning from Lives*, ed. Ivor Goodson and Patricia J. Sikes. Maidenhead: Open University Press.

Kinzie, David J. 2005. Some of the Effects of Terrorism on Refugees. *Journal of Aggression, Maltreatment & Trauma* 9 (3–4): 411–420.

Kleinman, Sherryl. 2007. *Qualitative Research Methods: Feminist Fieldwork Analysis*. Thousand Oaks, CA: SAGE Publications.

LeDoux, Joseph. 1996. *The Emotional Brain: The Mysterious Underpinnings of Emotional Life*. New York: Touchstone.

Levy, Barry S., and Victor W. Sidel. 2013. *Social Injustice and Public Health*. Oxford: Oxford University Press.

Linde, Charlotte. 1993. *Life Stories: The Creation of Coherence*. Oxford: Oxford University Press.

McCormick, Cheryl M., et al. 2011. Social Instability Stress in Adolescent Male Rats Alters Hippocampal Neurogenesis and Produces Deficits in Spatial Location Memory in Adulthood. *Hippocampus* 22 (6): 1300–1312.

Meaney, Michael J. 2001. Maternal Care, Gene Expression, and the Transmission of Individual Differences in Stress Reactivity Across Generations. *Annual Review of Neuroscience* 24: 1161–1192.

Norquay, Naomi. 1993. The Other Side of Difference: Memory-work in the Mainstream. *International Journal of Qualitative Studies in Education* 6 (3): 241–245.

Papadopoulos, Renos. 2002. *Therapeutic Care for Refugees: No Place Like Home.* London: Karnac Books.

Rees, Susan, and Bob Pease. 2007. Domestic Violence in Refugee Families in Australia. *Journal of Immigrant & Refugee Studies* 5 (2): 1–19.

Said, Edward W. 1993. *Culture and Imperialism.* New York: Vintage Books.

Siegel, Daniel J. 2011. *Mindsight: The New Science of Personal Transformation.* New York: Bantam Books.

Simich, Laura. 2008. *Mental Health Issues Among Forced Migrants: Perspectives on Research Among Latin Americans, Somalis, Sudanese and Tamils.* Paper presented at Refugees, Forced Migration & Mental Health: Recovery from Trauma and the Destigmatization of Mental Illness, Toronto, Ontario, Friday October 31, 2008.

Van der Kolk, Bessel. 2014. *The Body Keeps the Score: Brain, Mind, and Body in the Healing of Trauma.* New York: Penguin Books.

Warfa, Nasir, Kamaldeep Bhui, Tom Craige, Sarah Curtis, Salaad Mohamud, Stephen Stansfield, Paul McCrone, and Graham Thornicroft. 2006. Post-Migration Geographical Mobility, Mental Health and Health Service Utilisation Among Somali Refugees in the UK: A Qualitative Study. *Health & Place* 12 (4): 503–515.

Claiming Their Voice: Foreign Memories on the Post-Brexit Stage

Kasia Lech

In 2017, the National Theatre premiered *My Country: A Work in Progress*, a story about Brexit (the withdrawal of the United Kingdom from the European Union) "in the words of people across the UK and Carol Ann Duffy." The play featured only British voices. Later that year, a collaboration between *The Guardian* and Headlong Theatre produced nine short movie monologues on Brexit. Only one, *Shattered*, by English actress and writer Maxine Peake, offered a migrant perspective, but its portrayal raised a question about migrant, race, gender, and cultural representations: whose perspective shapes them? The film featured an immigration lawyer, played by Nasser Memarzia, speaking with an unidentified foreign accent. The lawyer's generalized "foreignness" and profession functioned to mark his credibility to tell a story of a Pakistani woman raped by her husband and to say that "EU nationals are frightened to death they are going to be thrown out of this country." A few months earlier, the *Journal of Democracy*, one of the most influential journals in political science,

K. Lech (✉)
Canterbury Christ Church University, Canterbury, UK
e-mail: kasia.lech@canterbury.ac.uk

Y. Meerzon et al. (eds.), *Migration and Stereotypes in Performance and Culture*, Contemporary Performance InterActions,
https://doi.org/10.1007/978-3-030-39915-3_12

published articles under the heading "Britain After Brexit." The essays explored Brexit in various contexts, including the 2016 American Presidential election (Ford and Goodwin 2017). However, the perspective of migrants, whose future in the UK was decided without them, was left unexplored and its absence unnoticed by the editors (Plattner and Diamond 2017).

While the immigrants' voices have been "peripheral," their foreignness was "symbolically central" in the Brexit debate (Stallybrass and White1986, 5). The referendum became "a proxy for a debate about who should or should not be in the UK" (Burnett 2017, 88). In other words, who is a "foreigner"? The discussion has been framed by (Home Secretary, later Prime Minister) Theresa May's "hostile environment" policy to lower the number of immigrants. The pre- and post-referendum divisive rhetoric of "us" and "them" created a politically motivated, demonized, and hyper-visible image of a foreigner as a threat to British society either through claiming benefits, stealing jobs, or terrorism.[1] Following Claire Alexander's (2000) arguments, this obscured the actual absence of migrants in the debate and served to legitimize xenophobia and forms of control like the Leave campaign's slogan "Take back control." "We voted you out," said one of the abusers (Burnett 2017, 86), as if the referendum was the reality television show Big Brother. The context outlined here relates neither exclusively to the European Union migrants nor solely to migrants at all. The increased post-Brexit racism seemed to define "foreigners" as all that did not fit the past model of a "perfect Brit": white, monolinguistic, and Christian, which says more about shifts within British identity than its immigration.[2]

This chapter takes the debate on Brexit and "foreignness" to UK-based migrants. It responds to the questions about migrant identity posed in this volume's introduction by exploring how the articulation of transnational identities, foreignness, and engagement with stereotypes by UK-based EU and non-EU theatre practitioners underline their immediate responses to Brexit. The article insists that the migrant perspective is not only crucial for the debate on Brexit but, most importantly, for future directions for the UK and Europe. The essay considers the "divided Britain" and Brexit not as isolated issues, but as part of a broader European Union crisis relating to the decreased sense of commonality and solidarity amongst its member countries towards member and non-member states and citizens (Gielen 2015, 10).

The essay argues for migrants' agency over their representation, offering a platform for a new social imagination that can facilitate multicultural democratic spaces, sense of commonality, and solidarity. Rosi Braidotti (1994, 2015), who insists on the political potential of imagination, has repeatedly marked these as major challenges in the European context. This new imagination must have a translocal perspective, moving the gaze from national to a "multiplicity of spatialities within a common space marked not by firm boundaries but by the intensity and concentration of interactions" (Dirlik 2005, 397, 407). By mobilizing "translocal imagination" (Brickell and Datta 2011), this new imagination can cultivate a sense of solidarity through differences. I also insist that migrants' agency over their representation is a primary form of agency to study migrant experience and to reshape broader political discourses.

Theatre has a vital role to play here due to its potential to expand the political and social value of imagination. As Helen Nicholson (2009, 47–51) explains, in the theatre the encounter between imaginations of artists and audiences fills the gap between reality and fiction. Because of that, she says, theatre can facilitate imagining "that which was previously unimagined or unimaginable," which, in turn, challenges existing ideas and values and may evoke social change. Nicholson's point also holds in a theatre that cuts itself off from any political engagement. Just because theatre might not have a political agenda or intentions, it does not mean that it has no political roots or consequences.

My focus is on collective, cultural, and personal memories and their power to re-imagine relationships, which is enhanced by theatre (van Dijck 2004; Carlson 2003). Firstly, I look at links between politics and culture to argue for the importance of migrants' agency over their representation. The following two sections focus on theatre practitioners whose experiences spread across Spain, Argentina, Nigeria, Ireland, Poland, and the UK. I examine how they perform their agency and their transnational, translocal, and transtemporal experiences, and offer "imaginative insights into another world which, once seen, cannot be unseen" (Nicholson 2009, 58).[3]

Migrants' Agency Over Their Representation

Pascal Gielen (2015) insists that the European Union's failure to support culture is behind the decreased sense of commonality and solidarity amongst its members and current economic and political crises. Together with Thijs Lijster, Gielen argues for culture as "a reservoir of signs." These signs denote both "a formal game of similarity and differentiation" and the process of "assigning meaning as sense that gives directions and reason for existence to both people and societies" (Gielen and Lijster 2015, 20). The European project must facilitate culture that "allows its citizens to really assign meaning to it" and to connect it with what they "value in life" and how they "view the world" (20–21).

This is not a matter of creating an idealistic and homogenous idea of European culture and community; it is about offering people who live in Europe various points of engagement with and opportunities to shape a multifaceted, multifocal, and pluralistic culture that reflects the diversity of individuals that live in today's Europe. Lijster and Gielen (2015, 52–53) stress the importance of culture being "a shared practice." In the same collection of essays, Rosi Braidotti (2015, 98, 108) argues that construction of a European identity as a "multicultural democratic space" requires "adequate, positive representations of the new trans-European condition" that escapes European geopolitical boundaries, of Europe "becoming nomadic." So far, she says, Europe has collectively failed to create a shared culture. Braidotti asks how to "develop such a new European social imaginary" that can facilitate transnational, hybrid identities, symbols, and cultures (108–111). The arguments put forth by Braidotti and by Lijster and Gielen apply to the UK, its relationship with Europe, and a global context, as these are interconnected. There is an urgent need for cultural spaces that offer opportunities to contribute to, interact with, and find points of identification with hybrid identities and cultures. This brings me to the issue of migrants' visibility, representation, and agency.

Marcel Paret and Shannon Gleeson (2016, 277, 282) explain that there are "four primary forms of agency" attached to the migrant experience that are crucial for understanding the precarity-migration-agency nexus and, through that, "key dynamics around inequality and social change" amongst migrants and native communities. These forms of agency are the decision to move, the individual agency relating to working rights, collective agency of organized movements, and agency to organize "other arenas of social life." I propose that there is a fifth form of agency: the agency over representation within a public space. This agency is imperative as it works to counter the politically motivated paradox of the migrants' presence being overemphasized within the public space, while their perspective is absent (Alexander 2000, 133; Stallybrass and White 1986, 5). Moreover, examining migrants' representation within and agency over public space is an essential lens for studying the precarity-migration-agency nexus.

This type of agency relates to the right to vote in the country of residence and therefore to migrant experiences being reflected and their presence legitimized within democratic life and political discourse. It also recognizes the necessity of matching their input to the life of the country with democratic rights. Equally important is the influence over migrants' representation within socio-cultural spaces to overcome their identity as a "migrant" and frame immigrants as vital to the social fabric of modern society. This legitimizes their presence in everyday contexts, deconstructs dichotomies of native and foreign, challenges ethnocentric perspectives that native cultures have nothing to learn from foreign cultures (Pennycook 2001, 82), and facilitates a translocal gaze. This point relates not only to the stories of individuals, but also to translocal experiences of history and culture through histories and culture of migrants' native lands and, importantly, their perspective on history and culture of the country where they reside.

The form of agency I propose includes representation of languages spoken by migrant communities, as language impacts social interactions and the "distribution of power" and opportunities within society (Pennycook 2001, 84). I refer both to migrants' native languages and to the "new languages" created through interactions between migrants' mother tongues and their experiences of languages spoken in their country of residence (in different geographical contexts and various modes of learning) and their mother tongues (Kachru and Nelson 2001, 18). In the UK, it would be "new Englishes"; their diversity also arises from English being a global language (Pennycook 2001, 78) that various native and non-native communities have co-ownership of which must be recognized.

My argument links with Hannah Arendt's (1998) view on politics as a platform where everyone can be "seen or heard" (50), and as an action, understood as the ways in which people disclose to others "their unique and distinct identity of the agent" (175–176, 179–180). Arendt argues that this type of action is necessary for society to exist; without it, newcomers cannot contribute to the society, and lose a sense of solidarity and commonality (179–180, 183–184). The upcoming analysis looks at theatre as a critical platform for facilitating migrants' agency and reconstructed visibility and, through that, as a means to re-imagine communities.

The discussion focuses on three productions that present different aspects of migrant experience and exercise agency over migrant representation in new writing, translation, adaptation, and autobiography. *Bubble Revolution* is a translation of *Rewolucja Balonowa* by Polish playwright Julia Holewińska directed by John Currivan, an Irish writer, actor, and director, and co-created and performed by myself, a Polish scholar, actor, and storyteller. The current article looks at the version developed during summer 2016 in the UK in rehearsals involving myself, Currivan, and British voice coach Janet Morgan for the 2016 Edinburgh Fringe Festival. The second production, *Rosaura,* is a devised adaptation of *Life is a Dream* by Pedro Calderón de la Barca created by actors Paula Rodríguez (UK-based Spanish artist) and Sandra Arpa (Argentinean-trained Spanish actor). Rodríguez and Arpa performed it in London just after the Brexit referendum. Finally, *An Evening with an Immigrant*, an autobiographical work written and performed by British-based Nigerian Inua Ellams, premiered in July 2016 at the Soho Theatre in London.

Transnational identities and actors' creative ownership connect to my larger point about migrants' agency, hybrid identities, and translocal perspectives. I am interested in how these three productions use memories rooted in their native and non-native cultures as a platform for the audience to engage with transnational conditions in today's Europe and the UK, and explore these and spectators' own experiences through a translocal gaze. By doing so, these productions engage their audiences with foreignness, challenge the dichotomy of native and foreign, and broaden European geopolitical boundaries. The memories offer spectators various points of engagement with the productions' performance of "foreignness" as difference, not through a process of isolation, but rather through a process of connection that, following Bhabha (1994, 2), is "a complex, on-going negotiation that seeks to authorize cultural hybridities." By doing so, the actors also challenge their existing representations within socio-political and cultural spaces and take co-ownership thereof.

My perspective is not an unambiguous one. I experienced *Rosaura* and *An Evening* as an audience member (of both live and recorded performances), but I have been working on and performing *Bubble Revolution* since 2013. And, while as a scholar I am interested in how these productions use memories, as a theatre practitioner, I look for similarities in our performances of difference. "Intercultural actors"—whose "cultural reality is no longer the one prescribed by a perfect juxtaposition of national and ethnic boundaries"—often experience double-foreignness; the actor is "seen as foreigner by her social and professional environments" and spectators and, at the same time, the actor perceives "these environments and her audiences as unfamiliar" (Nascimento 2009, 9). By establishing points of tangency, I explore my connections with different performances of "foreignness," which adds another layer to these productions as platforms for engagement with trans-European conditions. It is with the issue of connection that I open my analysis.

Creating and Sustaining "Welcoming Environments"

From the start, the actors in the three productions confront spectators with the presence of their foreignness and their ownership of the event and of the space they are in; but they also establish a "welcoming environment" (as opposed to a "hostile environment") as a frame for interactions between them and the audience. In addition, they work towards extending these collaborative and welcoming frames beyond the timeframe of the performance. All actors use their native accents and *Rosaura* and *Bubble Revolution* are bilingual. The jumps between Spanish and English in *Rosaura* are emphasized by different modes of language: verse in Spanish and prose in English. In *Bubble Revolution*, I highlight various geographical roots of my English. I mix English and American vocabulary and use North-Dublin-English influences in my accent, trying to correct them with a failed attempt at the standard form of British-English pronunciation. This is to play with mono- and ethnolinguistic perspectives that associate English-speaking with the Anglo-Saxon tradition as a norm that other Englishes "abuse" (Kachru and Nelson 2001, 14–21).

Arpa and Rodríguez start *Rosaura* by establishing the right of the audience to feel lost and offering their help which they sustain throughout the play. The performance opens in darkness broken by two torch lights that examine the black box space. When the torches reveal Arpa and Rodríguez, they smile and say, "Good evening." They explain that they will tell the story of Rosaura, "the female character from *Life is a dream* by Calderón de la Barca…Do you know the play?" They wait for the answer: "Well if you get lost along the way just raise your hands." Throughout the play they check if the spectators are following, and enact sequences in Spanish translating them into or explaining them in English without patronizing the audience. "Paula, they got it," says Arpa, when Rodríguez engages in a lengthy explanation. The importance of performers also arises as the production relies on text delivery and their bodies as the main carriers of

Fig. 1 Paula Rodríguez and Sandra Arpa in *Rosaura*. Copyright Teatro Inverso

meaning (Fig. 1). In this sense, the audience's experience is similar to Segismundo's in Calderón's play guided by Rosaura as he figures out his identity in relation to the world around him. Thus, the audience may encounter the full play often divided into Rosaura's and Segismundo's plots (Sloman 1965): they hear Rosaura's story, but they may experience Segismundo's.

In the opening scene of *An Evening with an Immigrant*, Inua Ellams establishes his identity as hybrid and in flux. He frames it as playful, inviting the audience to join the fun. He dances onto the stage, accompanied by DJ Sid Mercutio's music selection, and encourages the audience to clap along. He wears traditional Nigerian attire, including a white Agbada, a zana buka, and a horse tail whip. When he takes it off, he reveals his clothes, jeans with a t-shirt, stating politely: "Never Forget to Say Thank You" (Fig. 2). Before that, however, he turns his back to the audience and moves his hips in a way that reminds one of twerking; the audience laughs. "I can't take myself seriously," Ellams responds.

By physically referencing and joking about twerking at the start of the show, Ellams immediately acknowledges and engages with existing

Fig. 2 Inua Ellams in *An Evening with an Immigrant*. Copyright Inua Ellams

stereotypes, announces his ownership of how his blackness is performed, and activates a subversive potential of laughter. Manoucheka Celeste (2016, 149) argues that twerking, culturally appropriated and made viral by an infamous performance by Miley Cyrus in 2013, is an example of limitation and "appropriation of blackness for profit in popular culture." It is a representation of black culture that builds "on essentialist and stereotypic notions, the oldest tropes of blackness." Ellams' performance plays on this but also establishes what Eric Weitz (2009, 71) calls a "comic distance" (from the stereotypes), which is a "detachment from emotion, particularly necessary for adopting a playful attitude toward any given subject." It is not "a stepping back," but rather "a leaning sideways, momentarily out of the reach of serious mode's high beams," says Weitz. Ellams continues to subvert the existing stereotypes throughout the show. For example, he explains how the presence of religious conflict and the similarities in colours of Irish (green-white-orange) and Nigerian (green—white—green) flags allowed him to find his inner Irishness. "We are just a shade away," he jokes, referring to the orange that differentiates the two flags, but also playing on the stereotypes of Irish and Nigerian bodies, and the idea of colour as a point of both differences and similarities.

Ellams introduces himself as a poet, a playwright, a performer, and an immigrant. As his memories move between Nigeria, the UK, and Ireland, the list of his identities grows. Each anecdote is accompanied by a poem that was inspired by the story told. Such a pattern of poems and memories helps the audience to avoid ethnocentric readings and to experience his poems without worrying they do not know the context. The playful opening and the informal way in which Ellams addresses the audience is also a significant factor in creating this safe environment. For example, during the live performance I attended, some spectators arrived late. Ellams acknowledged each of them either by a hand wave, a short "hey man," or "nice shoes." The manner of those comments was warm and welcoming.

"Welcoming" offers a point of departure for *Bubble Revolution*. In my performance, I ask spectators to queue before they enter as "part of the experience." The joke references communist queues, but the queue is an opportunity to create a bond between myself and each spectator and play with familiar and unfamiliar cultural contexts before the show. I welcome each spectator and ask them to draw an envelope. Each envelope has a memory about growing up in Poland in the 1980s and 1990s, collected from different Polish people[4]; space for the spectator to leave their own memory; and either a ration card or a communist dollar. A ration card entitles the spectator to one candy, and a communist dollar wins a whole box or bag of sweets. The space smells like bubble gum. These sensory elements contextualize the play's references to dreaming about sweets (rationed in 1980s Poland), but also reinforce the frame of childhood, and potentially stimulate the audience's memories (van Campen 2014) as a point of engagement with the play. During performances, I help the audience navigate the story by translating sections in Polish and explaining certain references. As a case in point, a reference to Stanisław Tymiński, a Canadian businessman of Polish origin and the strongest competitor of Lech Wałęsa in the 1990s presidential campaign, appears in the play as: "I sat next to Stan Tymiński." In the performance, I add a "footnote" (inspired by Simon Kuper's article): "a Polish Donald Trump."[5]

The immersive elements also encourage the spectator to submerge in the memories told as an experience, in a similar way to the audience in *Rosaura* and *An Evening* experience Segismundo's quest and Ellams' poems, respectively. By creating opportunities for experiencing "foreignness" more fully, the three productions increase the possibilities for the individual spectators to discover their points of connections with stories told (Machon 2013, 26). They also work to stretch this experience beyond the timeframe of performances by boosting their memorability. I ask the audience to share their memories with me (online or by writing a note) and visit *Bubble Revolution*'s website with more memories. Arpa and Rodríguez encourage the audience to read Calderón's play. After Ellams' performances, spectators can buy his poetry and collect the National Council for Civil Liberties booklets on the Human Rights Act, its British legacy (rather than something "imposed" by the EU), and its importance for everyone in the UK. These activities may continue to shape spectators' memories of the productions, increasing chances for discovering their points of connections with "foreignness" in their lives (van Dijck 2006; Cohen 2014).

The last point has double significance for *An Evening*, *Bubble Revolution*, and *Rosaura* as they are also enactments of memories. Van Dijck (2004, 262) argues that by sharing acts of remembering with others, people can "make sense of their lives in relation to the lives of others and to their cultural context." Memories "filtered through the prism of culture," as in theatre, acknowledge the "creative tension" between individual and collective histories and become an act of mediation between "individuality and collectivity as well as between past and present" (270). The upcoming analysis takes this point further, arguing that memories in the three productions are a platform for tensions and interactions between multiple collectives, cultures, places, and histories mediated through the individual actors rooted in these contexts. Spectators, by participating in these multifaceted acts of remembering, can connect their lives to transnational experiences that cross "cultural, ideological, linguistic, and geopolitical borders and boundaries of all types but especially those of nation-states" (Duff 2015, 57). They may even shift their perspective beyond the idea of nations. To paraphrase van Dijck (2004, 262), they may "make sense of their lives" in relation to translocal experiences and hybrid identities.

Such connectedness is particularly possible as the three productions mark points of tangency between different memories and the UK audiences. The actors achieve this by using what Marvin Carlson (2003, 51) describes as "ghosting": a unique quality of theatre experience to facilitate "a simultaneous awareness of something previously experienced and of something being offered in the present that is both the same and different." Carlson's explanation relates to memories rooted in specific cultural contexts. *An Evening*, *Bubble Revolution*, and *Rosaura* show that ghosting, when applied in transnational and translocal contexts, facilitates the creation of pluralistic, multifaceted, and multifocal cultural spaces that have the potential to stimulate solidarity and to reimagine one's relationship with "foreignness."

"Foreign" Memories as a Springboard for Encounters

Many stories shared in *An Evening* and *Bubble Revolution* are about coming of age and are easily relatable; the audience laughs often, signalling their emotional connections (Weitz 2009, 65). These moments feature a foreign actor and audience laughing together and breaking the convention of a foreign speaker as a "figure of ridicule, or at least condescension" (Carlson 2006, 10). As one of the social consequences of laughter is the creation of community (May 2006, 191), the communities that these moments can establish are inclusive and based on shared understandings.

It is through this frame of familiarity and emotional connection that *Bubble Revolution* and *An Evening* invite the spectators to engage with their differences. On Ellams' first day of school in London, a school bully calls him a "nigger," a "bad" word Ellams has never heard before, and it is up to a new friend to explain to him the connotations. When Ellams tells a story of Royal Mail losing his documents in the post, there are probably spectators that can relate; however, for Ellams and his family, the Royal Mail's losing their passports, birth certificates, and documentation for their application to remain in the UK meant they had to relocate to Dublin. Ellams does not explain it, but one can presume that due to the Common Travel Area's agreement, Ellams' family could cross the border between the UK and Ireland—getting out of the Home Office's jurisdiction and removing the threat of deportation—without passports.

Holewińska wrote *Bubble Revolution* as a manifesto of Poles born in the 1980s: the generation whose childhood fell during late communism, whose teenage years overlapped with the crawling capitalism of the 1990s, and who became adults as Poland was entering the EU in 2004. This collective experience is mediated through the story of thirty-year-old Vica. When performed in the UK, the play gains another layer: it contextualizes the exodus of Poles born in the 1980s after Poland joined the EU. This is the biggest group that emigrated from Poland, mainly to the UK and Ireland (Okólski and Salt 2014; Krings et al. 2016). The group forms a large part of the approximately one million Polish-born people currently living in the UK (White 2016). *Bubble Revolution* confronts the audience with the stereotypes those migrants experience as Poles living in the West: "car-thieves, drunks, trouble-makers" (Holewińska 2013, 24). To make it resonate more strongly with the UK experience, I added one more stereotype: benefit-taker. "Car-thieves, drunks, trouble-makers, benefit-takers"; the only rhyme in the text marks this single Brexit reference.[6]

The context of *Bubble Revolution* as collective experience is emphasized in the production's publicity as it helps to confront existing stereotypes. It highlights that if a spectator recognizes their own experiences in Vica's story, they also connect to many Polish people whose identity goes beyond that of a Polish plumber or benefit-taker. To take that further, the production uses memories collected from various Polish people. They form an online exhibition (Lech 2016) and spectators are given selected memories before the performances. One individual, Piotr, recalls his parents bribing a doctor in Poland for his father's life-saving surgery. The memory relates to Vica describing the death of her grandmother: "The waiting list for a hospital bed was hopelessly long," and her parents' bribe came too late to "save grandma" (Holewińska 2013, 18). Piotr's memory ghosts Vica's story, which highlights the collective experience within the play. It also strengthens the audience's connection with Vica's narration as they would have already experienced a similar story through reading Piotr's or another's memories. By sharing their memories, spectators stretch this ghosting activity beyond the time frame of the performance and beyond geopolitical boundaries of Poland, the UK, or Europe and, potentially, move beyond the idea of the nation. Examples include the second-generation Pole witnessing the fall of communism from Scotland; a visit of a Hungarian youth choir to Finland in the 1980s; and someone from Montana confessing they miss their deceased father's tricks on April Fool's Day. These memories form a transnational and translocal reservoir and the act of evoking and sharing them becomes a transnational and translocal experience.

Ellams' memories move between Nigeria, the UK, and Ireland, but they start before Ellams was born. His introduction is followed by *Ash Skinned,* a poem that links Ellams to his ancestors: "a long line of trouble makers" with "a natural thirst for battle, only quenched by / breast milk." The poem paints an easily recognizable image of a child and brings it together with a contrasting image of a warrior. This near-oxymoron establishes Ellams' identity as split and conflicted from the root; he later confirms it with stories about his ancestors and his Christian mother and Muslim father. Ellams highlights here that his story did not start when he arrived in the UK and became "a migrant"; his story has been shaped by different communities that preceded and surrounded him. This echoes van Dijck's (2004) points about memories, society, and identity; however, what van Dijck does not say and what Ellams' work shows, is how, in doing so, Ellams mediates fragmented identities of the individuals and communities he experienced. This pushes *An Evening* towards a transtemporal and transcultural encounter, which is demonstrated in the final minutes of his performance when Ellams says that the stories of the UK migrants are rooted in British soil:

> Britain invaded, pillaged, murdered, plundered 80% of earth. I think citizens of every country ever colonized have some right to come here and stick a small flag and say this part of the country is mine…Those are the wars we started. We turned these people into immigrants.

It is important that Ellams uses "we," taking responsibility for the history of the country where he now lives. He follows ghosting myths with facts: the idea of migrants as a burden is accompanied by numbers that relate to the economic contribution of migrants; the claim that there is no more space in Britain (Farage's "Breaking Point" poster is the most infamous example) is followed by the point that only 2.2 percent of the UK has been built upon.[7] Ellams also marks multicultural elements like language that are part of British culture. These final moments of *An Evening* are a call for solidarity and responsibility that goes beyond nationality, culture, religion, and so on. The power of this call arises from Ellams' ghosting that creates a transcultural web of connections, and places Ellams and spectators within it.

Rosaura engages its audience with a cultural memory of *La vida es sueño* [*Life is a Dream*] by Pedro Calderón de la Barca. The play is an integral part of Spanish and European heritage; however, says Jonathan Thacker (2007, 15), it "has made little impression on British audiences and readers" who often have Shakespeare as their point of reference (Boyle and Johnston 2007; Thacker 2007). Or, as Rodríguez and Arpa put it, the audience may not know Calderón, as the Spanish did not do such a good job popularizing his work as the English and British have with Shakespeare. There is no sarcasm in it, but one cannot help but hear the echoes of the two countries' colonial past in the phrase "good job," especially given a well-discussed connection between Shakespeare's popularity and colonization (Bates 2008; Druin 2014).

In Rodríguez and Arpa's adaptation, Rosaura's native Moscow is replaced with "Hispania" and Poland with "the Court of Europe," pushing it beyond a national context. Astolfo "dumps" Rosaura (by text) because, of course, she wasn't good enough for his aspirations to rule Europe, "a kingdom without hope." Rosaura follows Astolfo to the Court of Europe where he competes with Segismundo for votes to become the future of Europe. The reality show-style election is run by Davina McCall (presenter of the UK version of *Big Brother*) and Oprah Winfrey, who doubt whether a foreigner like Astolfo can win. In the performance, the only precisely described feature of Astolfo was his light blond mop of hair. The line was accompanied by a physical gesture visualizing the hairstyle; the spectators laughed in recognition of Boris Johnson who, as a leading figure in the 'Vote Leave' movement (and now, of course, as Prime Minister) played a lead role in another "reality show": Brexit. The connotation also echoes the post-Brexit sentiment that the "foreigners" were "voted out" (Burnett 2017, 86). As in *Bubble Revolution* and *An Evening*, laughter is shared in recognition of common experience, but also (in contrast to the other productions) in recognition of the joke's "butt." Following F.H. Buckley's (2003, 186–187) arguments, this laughter is the expression of spectators' sense of superiority over someone who does not belong to the community: the unfaithful and fickle politician.

The line about Boris Johnson does not feature in the actual script, and it seems it was added to the performance to make that specific reference at that specific time to mark the hypocrisy of people like Johnson (a descendant of migrants) or leader of the Brexit Party Nigel Farage (a descendant of migrants, married to a German citizen) calling to stop immigration. The reference to Johnson helps the story resonate with the Brexit experience, but it also works against any simplistic decoding of both the story and Brexit in a purely British context. With Johnson being positioned (through the association with Astolfo) as a foreigner wanting to take over Europe, the story escapes national boundaries and encourages the audience to read it (and their Brexit experience by extension) in a broader translocal context of corrupted politics, far-right discourses, and failed solidarity. Towards the end of the performance, Arpa and Rodríguez paraphrase in English Rosaura's lines from the beginning of Calderón's play and stretch the context of *Rosaura* beyond Europe's geopolitical boundaries: "Badly Europe, you receive a foreigner, if with blood you scrawl its entrance in your sand and they barely make it, when they make it in despair" (Rodríguez and Arpa 2016, 24–25). After, the two performers talk about a collective dream in which people welcome a stranger with the line: "Don't worry, there's space for everyone" (Rodríguez and Arpa 2016, 27).

This final dream in *Rosaura*, additionally highlighted as connected with the only appearance of English verse, evokes images of refugees seeking shelter known from the contemporary refugee crisis and the history of humanity. It also plays on an often-repeated claim that the lack of jobs, houses, spaces in UK hospitals, and so on is due to immigration. In *Rosaura*, however, like in *An Evening*, there is space. This change is reminiscent of Bert O. States' (1993, 119–120) arguments from *Dreaming and Storytelling*. He says that dreams, fiction, and memories are all based on repetition and, "If something is to be remembered at all, it must be remembered not as what happened but as what has happened again in a different way and will surely happen again in the future in still another way." Each "different" provides a platform for change of emotional relationship with past experiences. Carlson (2003, 2–3) quotes States in *The Haunted Stage* to discuss a link between a dream, theatre, and memory, and argues that theatre has the particular power to do that as this change in theatre can be reimagined, which echoes my earlier reference to Helen Nicholson (2009).

One can see such efforts in *Rosaura, Bubble Revolution*, and *An Evening with an Immigrant*. All three productions attempt to ghost the memories created in multiple contexts with the audience's memories and experiences, while at the same time embracing the differences. By doing so, Arpa and Rodríguez, Ellams, and myself not only work to reimagine our audiences' relationship with these experiences (following States' point), but also with ourselves, and our foreignness. And perhaps, at least for some spectators, this leads to a realization that, in the words of Nascimento (2009, 137), "on- and off-stage, the foreign and the foreigner are in us, inherent parts of our cultural, political, and psychological histories."

As the stories from the past overlap with present interactions in live performances and, potentially, beyond them, together with our audiences, we may start imagining a future society. It is multifaceted, multifocal, and pluralistic with diverse individuals cultivating translocal imaginations (Brickell and Datta 2011, 18) and, through that, a sense of solidarity through differences. This world "once seen, cannot be unseen" (Nicholson 2009, 58). I am under no illusion that these three productions can change the world. However, together they form a small translocal theatrical web that, if connected to other similar (and yet different) webs, can only grow, multiplying their transformative potential. It is our responsibility as scholars, artists, journalists, institutions, funders, and governments to facilitate the growth of such interconnected webs within and across different disciplines. The UK, Europe, and the world cannot pass on such an opportunity.

Notes

1. For example, see Steve Doughty and James Slack, "Record number of jobless EU migrants in Britain," *Daily Mail*, May 26, 2016, http://www.dailymail.co.uk/news/article-3611697/Record-number-jobless-EU-migrants-Britain-Hammer-blow-PM-270-000-EU-nationals-came-year.html#ixzz4pL40MmJW; Amber Rudd, "Speech," Conservative Party Conference, October 4, 2016, Birmingham, http://www.telegraph.co.uk/news/2016/10/04/jeremy-hunt-nhs-doctors-theresa-may-conservative-conference-live/; Nigel Farage, interviewed by Maya Oppenheim, *Independent*, March 23, 2017, http://www.independent.co.uk/news/uk/home-news/nigel-farage-london-terror-attack-multiculturalism-blame-immigration-lbc-radio-ukip-mep-leader-a7645586.html.
2. Linda Woodhead (2016) argues that "'no religion' has risen to rival 'Christian' as the preferred self-designation of British people," especially those under forty. However, people over sixty tend to identify as Christian and Christianity still "remains the norm," creating tensions within the society (245–247, 259–260). A similar generational split was visible in the Brexit referendum (Moore 2016), which links with Woodhead's point that an increased cultural diversity in the UK was a factor in the rise of British "nones" who in majority voted to remain in the EU.
3. I use translocal and transnational as two separate terms with the former building on "the longer-established research tradition of transnationalism" but overcoming the former's "limited focus on the nation state," directing attention to alternative discourses (Greiner and Sakdapolrak 2013, 380–381).
4. All memories are authentic; however, some names were changed.
5. See Kasia Lech, "Acting as the Act of Translation: Domesticating and Foreignizing Strategies as Part of the Actor's Performance in the Irish-Polish Production of *Bubble Revolution*," in *Dramaturgy of Migration: Staging Multicultural Encounters in Contemporary Theatre*, edited by Yana Meerzon and Katharina Pewny (London: Routledge, 2020).

6. For example, see Rebecca Perring, "How to get 'GENEROUS' British benefits: Shocking guide handed out to Polish migrants," *Express*, March 10, 2016, https://www.express.co.uk/news/uk/651386/Polish-migrant-guide-British-benefits-system-welfare-hand-outs-unemployed.
7. This is in accordance with Mark Easton's (2012) reading of the 2011 UK National Ecosystem Assessment.

References

Alexander, Claire. 2000. (Dis)entangling the 'Asian Gang': Ethnicity, Identity, Masculinity. In *Un/settled Multiculturalisms: Diasporas, Entanglements, "transruptions,"*, ed. Barnor Hesse, 123–147. Winnipeg: Zed Books.

Arendt, Hannah. 1998. *The Human Condition*. 2nd ed. Chicago: University of Chicago Press.

Bates, Robin. 2008. *Shakespeare and the Cultural Colonization of Ireland*. London: Routledge.

Bhabha, Homi K. 1994. *The Location of Culture*. London: Routledge.

Boyle, Catherine, and David Johnston. 2007. Introduction. In *The Spanish Golden Age in English: Perspectives on Performance*, ed. Catherine Boyle and David Johnston, 11–14. London: Oberon Books.

Braidotti, Rosi. 1994. *Nomadic Subjects: Embodiment and Sexual Difference in Contemporary Feminist Theory*. New York: Columbia University Press.

———. 2015. Nomadic European Identity. In *No Culture, No Europe: On the Foundations of Politics*, ed. Pascal Gielen, 97–113. Amsterdam: Valiz.

Brickell, Katherine, and Ayona Datta. 2011. Introduction: Translocal Geographies. In *Translocal Geographies: Spaces, Places, Connections*, ed. Katherine Brickell and Ayona Datta, 3–22. London: Routledge.

Buckley, F.H. 2003. *The Morality of Laughter*. Ann Arbor: University of Michigan Press.

Burnett, Jon. 2017. Racial Violence and the Brexit State. *Race & Class* 58 (4): 85–97.

van Campen, Cretien. 2014. *The Proust Effect: The Senses as Doorways to Lost Memories*. Oxford: Oxford University Press.

Carlson, Marvin. 2003. *The Haunted Stage: The Theatre as Memory Machine*. Ann Arbor: University of Michigan Press.

———. 2006. *Speaking in Tongues*. Ann Arbor: University of Michigan Press.

Celeste, Manoucheka. 2016. *Race, Gender, and Citizenship in the African Diaspora: Travelling Blackness*. London: Routledge.

Cohen, Sara. 2014. 'The Gigs I've Gone To': Mapping Memories and Places of Live Music. In *Coughing and Clapping: Investigating Audience Experience*, ed. Karen Burland and Stephanie Pitts, 131–146. Farnham: Ashgate.

van Dijck, José. 2004. Mediated Memories: Personal Cultural Memory as Object of Cultural Analysis. *Continuum* 18 (2): 261–277.

———. 2006. Record and Hold: Popular Music between Personal and Collective Memory. *Critical Studies in Media Communication* 23 (5): 357–374.

Dirlik, Arif. 2005. Performing the World: Reality and Representation in the Making of World Histor(ies). *Journal of World History* 16 (4): 391–410.

Druin, Jennifer. 2014. *Shakespeare in Quebec: Nation, Gender, and Adaptation.* Toronto: University of Toronto Press.

Duff, Patricia A. 2015. Transnationalism, Multilingualism, and Identity. *Annual Review of Applied Linguistics* 35 (2015): 57–80.

Easton, Mark. 2012. The Great Myth of Urban Britain. *BBC*, June28, http://www.bbc.co.uk/news/uk-18623096.

Ellams, Inua. 2016. *An Evening with an Immigrant.* Theatre script.

Ford, Robert, and Matthew Goodwin. 2017. A Nation Divided. *Journal of Democracy* 28 (1): 17–30.

Gielen, Pascal. 2015. Introduction: There Is a Solution to the Crisis. In *No Culture, No Europe: On the Foundations of Politics*, ed. Pascal Gielen, 9–15. Amsterdam: Valiz.

Gielen, Pascal, and Thijs Lijster. 2015. Culture: The Substructure of a European Common. In *No Culture, No Europe: On the Foundations of Politics*, ed. Pascal Gielen, 19–64. Amsterdam: Valiz.

Greiner, Clemens, and Patrick Sakdapolrak. 2013. Translocality: Concepts, Applications and Emerging Research Perspectives. *Geography Compass* 7 (5): 373–384.

Holewińska, Julia. 2013. *Bubble Revolution.* Translated by Artur Zapałowski with edits and changes by Kasia Lech and John Currivan. Theatre script.

Kachru, Braj B., and Cecil L. Nelson. 2001. World Englishes. In *Analysing English in a Global Context: A Reader*, ed. Anne Burns and Caroline Coffin, 9–25. London: Routledge.

Krings, Torben, et al. 2016. *New Mobilities in Europe: Polish Migration to Ireland Post-2004.* Manchester: Manchester University Press.

Kuper, Simon. 2016. The Rise and Fall of a Prototype Trump. *Financial Times*, June 3. https://www.ft.com/content/e37f5fd0-2848-11e6-8b18-91555f2f4fde.

Lech, Kasia. 2016. Bubble Revolution. June 2016. www.bubblerevolution.com.

Machon, Josephine. 2013. *Immersive Theatres: Intimacy and Immediacy in Contemporary Performance.* London: Palgrave Macmillan.

May, Regine. 2006. *Apuleius and Drama: The Ass on Stage.* Oxford: Oxford University Press.

Moore, Peter. 2016. How Britain Voted? *YouGov*, June 27. https://yougov.co.uk/topics/politics/articles-reports/2016/06/27/how-britain-voted.

Nascimento, Cláudia Tatinge. 2009. *Crossing Cultural Borders Through the Actor's Work: Foreign Bodies of Knowledge*. London: Routledge.

National Theatre. 2017. My Country: A Work in Progress. National Theatre. https://www.nationaltheatre.org.uk/shows/my-country.

Nicholson, Helen. 2009. *Theatre & Education*. London: Palgrave Macmillan.

Okólski, Marek, and John Salt. 2014. Polish Emigration to the UK After 2004, Why Did So Many Come? *Central and Eastern European Migration Review* 3 (2): 11–37.

Paret, Marcel, and Shannon Gleeson. 2016. Precarity and Agency Through a Migration Lens. *Citizenship Studies* 20 (3–4): 277–294.

Plattner, Marc F., and Larry Diamond. 2017. Britain After Brexit. *Journal of Democracy* 28 (1): 16.

Pennycook, Alistair. 2001. English in the World/The World in English. In *Analysing English in a Global Context: A Reader*, ed. Anne Burns and Caroline Coffin, 78–89. London: Routledge.

Rodríguez, Paula, and Sandra Arpa. 2016. *Rosaura*.Trans. Paula Rodríguez and Sandra Arpa. Theatre script.

Sloman, Albert E. 1965. The Structure of Calderón's *La vida es sueño*. In *Essays on Theatre of Calderón*, ed. Bruce W. Wardropper, 90–100. New York: New York University Press.

Stallybrass, Peter, and Allon White. 1986. *The Politics and Poetics of Transgressions*. Ithaca: Cornell University Press.

States, Bert O. 1993. *Dreaming and Storytelling*. Ithaca: Cornell University Press.

Thacker, Jonathan. 2007. History of Performance in English. In *The Spanish Golden Age in English: Perspectives on Performance*, ed. Catherine Boyle and David Johnston, 15–30. London: Oberon Books.

Watson, Robert, and Steve Albon. 2011. UK National Ecosystem Assessment. http://news.bbc.co.uk/1/shared/bsp/hi/pdfs/28_06_12_uk_national_ecosystem.pdf.

Weitz, Eric. 2009. *The Cambridge Introduction to Comedy*. Cambridge: Cambridge University Press.

White, Nicola. 2016. Population of the UK by Country of Birth and Nationality: 2015. Office for National Statistics.www.ons.gov.uk/peoplepopulationandcommunity/populationandmigration/internationalmigration/bulletins/ukpopulationbycountryofbirthandnationality/august2016.

Woodhead, Linda. 2016. The Rise of 'No Religion' in Britain: The Emergence of a New Cultural Majority. *Journal of the British Academy* 4 (2016): 245–261.

Challenging Stereotypes: *Moving Dreams* and the Italian Community of Peterborough, UK

Ida Casilli

This chapter analyses the results of the applied theatre project *Moving Dreams*, an intergenerational multimedia heritage initiative hosted by the Italian community of Peterborough, United Kingdom.[1] The project, which I designed, directed, and produced, featured first and second-generation migrant facilitators, filmmakers, and performers. *Moving Dreams* was the first part of a larger, ongoing research project exploring how applied theatre interventions can challenge negative stereotypes of migrants and refugees, by celebrating the achievements of historically marginalized communities and highlighting the power dynamics behind those stereotypes. The work aimed to compare perceptions of modern and old patterns of migration, analysing concepts of belonging, multiple cultural identities, transformative journeys, and legacies for future generations. Of the many projects taking place in a contemporary Europe, *Moving Dreams* addressed the urge of "reforging a concept of identity in a newly diverse and pluralised society" (Jeffers 2012, 11).

I. Casilli (✉)
Edinburgh, UK

Y. Meerzon et al. (eds.), *Migration and Stereotypes in Performance and Culture*, Contemporary Performance InterActions,
https://doi.org/10.1007/978-3-030-39915-3_13

Moving Dreams analysed the patterns of Italian migration between 1920 and 1950, and how the stereotypes attached to the Italian community had been embodied and/or unwillingly perpetrated by the community itself. With the project, I also wanted to investigate the similarity between these stereotypes and those currently used to define the new influx of refugees and asylum seekers hailing from Africa and the Middle East, as well as some specific European migrant minorities. *Moving Dreams* was composed of an interview stage, a workshop-based devising process, and a final performance. It included participants that contributed in different capacities, including a large representation of first, second, and third-generation Italians, but also Spanish, Albanian, Moroccan, French, Pakistani, and Polish contributors.

The project was developed and delivered in the fertile "diaspora space" of the UK, seeing "multiple subject positions juxtaposed, contested, proclaimed and disavowed" (Brah 1996, 208), in a politically heated landscape of a United Kingdom tormented by the uncertainty of the post-Brexit referendum discourse. It was set in Peterborough, a town that has grown exponentially in the last decade and benefitted from the contribution of its multicultural dwellers to the local economy. As such, the project gained a relevance within the local community, served the purpose of creating awareness, and facilitated encounters between new and old migrants, bridging the gaps between migrant communities.

Below I will discuss the background research for *Moving Dreams* and provide more information about the project itself, analysing it from a sociological and applied theatre perspective. The study includes a personal reflection on the project outcomes to date, as well as future development plans for the initiative.

Cultural Identities and Communities: Applied Theatre in Global, Regional, and Social Contexts

"Applied theatre" is an umbrella term used to describe theatre practices that are used outside the mainstream theatre context to apply and reinforce research from other fields. Applied theatre research originated between the late 1970s and the early 1980s from an increased interest in the results of participatory theatre practices created by socially and politically involved artists, including the work of Augusto Boal, leading Brazilian theatre maker and founder of Theatre of The Oppressed (TO). The principles behind TO, and its satellite theatre methods including "Forum Theatre" and "Rainbow of Desire," are based on the idea that theatre should be universally accessible. According to Boal (2006, 36), basic theatre techniques taught in the TO method could help individuals "to produce a new form of understanding, helping the subject to *feel* and, through the senses and not just intelligence, to understand social reality." Throughout my training, first as a theatre scholar and later as a director and producer, I was particularly fascinated by the power of TO. Italy had been fully exposed to Augusto Boal's work as curated by Giorgio Ursini, and organizations such as Giolli and MCE, whose founders had received formal training in TO, were running workshops for social workers and artists working within different communities.

A fledgling applied theatre practitioner, I was running storytelling workshops to facilitate cultural mediation in some suburban schools in Rome. Many stories shared by the students had an eerie resonance with the migration stories I had heard as a child from family members who had migrated abroad for work. Before moving to the UK to qualify as an applied theatre practitioner, I focused my practice and studies on the topic of cultural memory embodiment, and the inclusion of minorities in mainstream representation in Italy. I wrote a dissertation on the inclusion and representation of minorities and marginalized communities in contemporary Italian theatre, which gave me the opportunity to research some of the first Italian applied theatre experiments, including Teatro dell Albe's bilingual *A Midsummer Night's Dream*[2] and the Kenya-based theatre for development project *Pinocchio Nero* (2005) run by Marco Baliani with children living on the streets of Nairobi. Both productions were conceived and produced by established theatre directors in Italy and had roots in applied theatre projects. Both had a clear intent to represent and empower communities, enabling them to perform in a culturally vibrant environment. Nevertheless, the presence of these communities on stage embodied the political urge to take concrete action to promote inclusion and celebrate diversity. Furthermore, the community empowerment approach used by both directors, combined with a professionally-led, workshop-based devising process, succeeded in instigating a deeper level of what Augusto Boal (2008) postulates as the *change* "that spectators enact being SPECT-ACTORS. As such, spectators have the ability to change the story they are observing on stage, and therefore being inspired to change their own lives."

So, there I was, ready to bring my practice abroad and learn more skills in an international environment. I could not have predicted the challenges I would face as an international practitioner, or how my practice would develop. According to Helen Nicholson (2014, 6), "Applied Theatre practitioners and participants perform as citizens in different global, regional and social contexts, despite their cultural and identity affiliations." As an applied theatre practitioner working with many different communities, I was in close contact with participants and leaders who often had limited or basic knowledge of applied theatre research. Negotiations on technique, focus, and intent behind the creation of a more practice-based or performance-based work were often mixed with assumptions of what my contribution should have been in relation to my presumed cultural identity.

I quickly realized how the stereotypes I was labelled with because of my cultural, gender, and social identity (whether intentional or not), largely affected my freedom to fully tap into the resources of the creative industry, and disrupted the sustainability of the work I intended to do in the country. Meanwhile, the global refugee crisis was not holistically represented in the media, which fuelled the confusion and fear of the political consequences of such a crisis. Despite these obstacles, I was able to connect with and work alongside many companies and communities, challenging the status quo whenever possible. I specialized in the delivery of workshops and courses for intergenerational groups, theatre for older people, reminiscence activities for dementia patients, and youth arts.

As a European citizen, I was (and am) working in UK under the uncertain circumstances generated by the Brexit referendum. These circumstances fuelled my creativity and motivated me to pursue applied theatre research on the embodiment of stereotypes, using the Italian community in Peterborough as a starting point. My interest was in understanding how the new arrivals had embodied, coped with, or challenged prejudice, and what relevance those stereotypes would have for later generations. In short, my favourite quote from Boal I read and endlessly repeated as a student was soon going to become the motivator for my research "Nothing is going to remain the same. Let us, in the present, study the past, so as to invent the future" (Boal 2008).

Italian Diaspora: A Brief Overview from 1861 to Present

Between 1861 and 1977, a staggering 29,036,000 Italians migrated to other countries in waves following a series of different international agreements. Studies from the Multicultural History Society of Ontario (Pozzetta 1980; Pozzetta et al. 1992) have identified three main waves within the Italian diaspora. The first wave took place between 1861 and 1900, during the period of the unification of Italy. The second wave occurred between 1900 and 1914 at the beginning of World War I, with a number of migrants being associated with the fascist intelligentsia and segregated in camps alongside members of the Italian army captured in Northern Africa, the United Kingdom, and Germany. The third wave began after World War II and lasted until 1977, fuelled by the demand for unskilled labour in the growing European, American and Australian cities (Pozzetta 1992).

From the nineteenth century onwards, emigration was driven by high rates of unemployment, lack of cultivable land, poverty, overpopulation, and the absence of social welfare systems in Italy. Other factors, mostly political and economic, included the desire to escape organized crime and political corruption, lack of appropriate sanitation or food supplies, as well as overpopulation and the untameable social sprawl of the southern region (Sori 1987). Early patterns of migration to northern Europe (including Great Britain) began to shift towards the rest of the world as industrialization and the growth of world capitalism created millions of jobs for Italians searching for "work and bread." After 1945, the Italian government encouraged migration through agreements with foreign employers using earlier migrants as intermediaries (Hatton and Williamson 1994, 533).

Inevitably, Italian citizens developed a form of mutual support, with a strong community core, facilitating the employment of reliable co-citizens, and creating dedicated unions to support fellow unemployed people from their hometowns. Some former prisoners of war were assigned to recruit new workers from their towns of origin, and to facilitate the administration of "paid passage schemes" which would grant the new employees a free transfer to England. This was certainly the case for Peterborough, where the integration of new migrants was also facilitated by the church and other family-based community support initiatives (Cereste 2001). Peterborough's Italian community dates back to the post-war reconstruction period, when economic conditions in both Italy and the UK triggered migration from impoverished villages in Southern Italy and

Emilia-Romagna to England. The post-war building boom created a shortage of workers in the brickworks industry. Manual labour was demanding and not well rewarded in the eyes of British citizens. Struggling to meet the demand, the brick companies began to look overseas for workers, after having employed ex-prisoners of war and being impressed by their resilience and willingness to perform heavy duty tasks. The London and Marston Valley Brick Companies set up offices in Naples and hired labourers for the brick factories they had established in Peterborough and Bedford (Cereste 2001).

The First Development of *Moving Dreams*

Participatory theatre company Spare Tyre selected my proposal for *Moving Dreams* in a call for contributions to celebrate the company's fortieth anniversary (the celebration was officially called Spare Tyre's 40th Birthday). The project was selected under a call for entries "working with many people in many different ways." At that time, I had not yet identified a specific community to work with. Arti Prashar, the company's artistic director at that stage, encouraged me to select a community of people that shared my native language, so that the work could be developed in the community's mother tongue without marginalizing any participants who might have a language barrier. The project's subject, then, was the Italian diaspora hailing from the region where I was born[3] and who had settled in the UK mostly around the brick factories. Immediately after, I received further funding from Peterborough Presents, a consortium promoting arts activities in Peterborough and the surrounding area. The consortium had an interest in working with minority groups through the arts.

The project was called *Moving Dreams* because we wanted to collect memories and testimonies of migration in order to compare them with the present using a dream-like framework. The intent was to include pleasant (dreams) and unsettling (nightmares) content in the performance. Having worked on a similar project with the Brazilian community in London, I devised new workshop material inspired by previously tested work. As such, the *Moving Dreams* team collected memories and testimonies of migration from workshop participants and other, non-performing contributors. The material was then workshopped and devised into a play performed by the participants. The project outreach was done with the help of regional and national websites, creative networking events, and word of mouth. It was imperative that the project be intergenerational, and so it included participants aged fifty or older, aged twenty to fifty, as well as third-generation Italian teenagers. The project's intergenerational format appealed to a diverse and broad audience, including members of the Italian community who settled in Peterborough during the 1950s; their second generation; the second generation of Italian prisoners during World War II; and the newer influx of Italian migrants who arrived in Peterborough after 1980. New migrants from other backgrounds were also drawn to the work for its topical relevance and its representation of issues similar to those that they (or their relatives) were experiencing. *Moving Dreams* was hosted by Peterborough's Italian community, and as such it was also an instrument to celebrate the efforts and achievements of this specific group. The project was not restricted to Italian migrants, though, and included testimonies from people of other minority groups that either live, work, or frequently visit Peterborough, including Polish, Albanian, Spanish, French, Moroccan, and British contributors.

The location of the project was symbolic, as the Fleet Community Centre—currently run by the Italian Community Association (ICA)—is built on the premises of the London Brick Factories of Fletton, where many migrants worked upon arrival in the UK. The project consisted of two main parts, the first consisting of image selection, conducting interviews, topic development through tailored TO drama games, and performance text-building. The second part consisted of devising, rehearsals, and performance, including a filming session with a professional filmmaker. The first part of the project was attended by participants affiliated with the Italian community of Peterborough, but was also popular amongst migrants of other nationalities, especially within the younger participants' group. The second part was mostly attended by Italians, though it was strongly supported by migrants, charities, and small local businesses of other nationalities.

How We Analysed the Stereotypes Transfer: Who Are the Modern WOPs?

Gardner et al. (1970) define ethnic stereotypes in terms of trait-descriptive adjectives associated with an ethnic group label. *Moving Dreams* traded modern Italian stereotypes for those associated with their specific ethnic group during the first wave of the diaspora. Stella's research (2003) identified *WOPs, mafiosos and scrimas,* as the three main stereotypes for Italian migrants worldwide in that specific historical period.

An anglicized version of the Neapolitan word *guappo,* (dude, stud), or more credibly an acronym (Without Ordinary Passport) reflecting the lack of official papers held by Italian migrants waiting to acquire their freeman status, WOP was a derogatory slur to identify Italian migrants initially just in the United States. The stereotypical power of this term is directly and strongly interlinked to a number of not completely legal practices that many Italian migrants chose to do or were forced to do as less advantaged people of their community. These included underage labour and illegal busking, but also attempts to find work which violated the UK requirement to register with the police under the 1920 Alien Order. The term WOP arrived with North American films and literature, and was mostly used as a descriptor signalling a harsh and eccentric personality.

The word *scrima* (an inflection of the word "ice cream" pronounced with an Italian accent) was invented as a derogatory term to define loud and illiterate vendors of Italian origin. Although initially used to define ice cream vendors, the word was soon associated with the Italian loud tone of voice, allegedly due to a general lack of manners and education. Interestingly enough, the etymology of this word reflects the connection between the growth of the ice scream vending industry and the contribution of the Italian workforce to this success. Ice cream vending was, in fact, the most popular and profitable industry pursued by Italian migrants in the UK and beyond, together with carpentry and housebuilding.

Positive memories of successful and lucky migrants tend to prevail in collective memory (Stella 2003). However, many less successful individuals were recorded for their involvement in small criminal acts, including thefts, commissioned crimes, and participation in the black market. Last but not least, they were also recorded for playing intermediary roles in local criminal organizations affiliated with the mafia. Although a larger number of organized criminal acts associated with mafia was occurring in the USA, the stereotype of *mafioso* was soon acquired to imply a general untrustworthiness for Italian immigrants in Europe. Italian migrant communities were particularly closely-knit, self-sufficient, and self-reliant. These social characteristics ensured that unfair acts were punished by and within the community, as it would happen in smaller gangs or more organized criminal organizations like the mafia. The Italian *mafioso* stereotype simplified this extremely complex socio-political structure in a poignant expression of chauvinist misperception.

The Social Cycle of These Stereotypes: Staggering Similarities

Despite the inevitable changes in the historical and sociological landscape, there was a staggering similarity between the stereotypes forged to define Italian migrants and those used to address illegal migrants and asylum seekers. Furthermore, I noticed how the communities once stereotyped were using the same derogatory definitions to address the latest influx of migrants, feeding off the confusion regarding migration patterns generated or reinforced during the Brexit referendum campaigns. For this reason, the conditions of younger migrants, including Europeans (as well as Italians), were often associated with refugees. Consequently, they were deemed to hinder employment opportunities for British citizens. In addition, statistics confirmed that a conspicuous number of older Italian citizens living in Peterborough supported the Leave campaign in the Brexit referendum. Those supporters also agreed to be interviewed by the media to explain their reasoning, where they used derogatory terms and stereotypes to define new migrants.

Sociological studies would allow me to frame this occurrence as a phenomenon perfectly fitting within the social cycles' theory, the cyclical repetition of sociological phenomena, especially in the microcosm of small towns (Turchin 2005). Was there an opportunity to rehearse a Boalian "revolution" using theatre to change people's perspectives? (Boal 2008). I was convinced of the possibility to challenge that tendency, and applied theatre was the best instrument to negotiate power struggles and facilitate mutual understanding. The focus of my project narrowed to the perpetuation of stereotypes allocated to Italian migrants to the UK, and how those stereotypes were transferred to the new influx of migrants.

I decided to deliver workshops using a selection of stereotypes that addressed matters of legal status, stereotyping, and criminality. *WOP*, *Scrima*, and *mafioso* were specifically chosen for their potential to trigger the process of comparison between older and new migrants.

Both interviewees and workshop participants found it very difficult to explore creatively the *mafioso* stereotype: interviews and data collected during conversations demonstrated how there was no desire to be implicated with criminality, past or present. The Italian community of Peterborough was involved in a great deal of negotiation to integrate within the British culture. These included a strong affiliation to the local Catholic Church, and a willingness to strive for excellence in their work and behaviours. Employees of the brick factory had to demonstrate exemplary behaviour in order to maintain their workmen rights. We also worked extensively on the *scrima* stereotype: one of our participants moved to Peterborough to work as an ice- cream vendor. His first-person experience was used as a starting point. We chose to gear our research on resilience, rather than response to the offense, as suggested by this specific participant.

Moving Dreams workshop participants acknowledged the potential of working with the WOP stereotype: the concept allowed them to explore feelings related to freedom of movement. Just as the older member of the Italian community worked hard—and at times struggled—to achieve their *freeman status*, so the current migrants and asylum seekers had to face uncertainty and instability. Participants were particularly concerned with the inability of refugees to reconnect to their families, as families seem to be conceived as a safe haven by all workshop participants.

Project Participants and Their Contributions to the Play Text

During the first part of the project I collected a large number of interviews from two groups: the older people participating to the regular weekly activities run by the ICA, as well as a group of younger people at the Green Backyard, a public green space animated by volunteer-led activities. Only some of the interviewees chose to participate in the second part of the project that was meant to include a set of performative activities. At the beginning of the second part of the project, workshop participants were presented with recorded testimonies from those interviews, as well as archival photos from the Italian Community Association archive, private photos collections, the Peterborough Library. The intergenerational group of participants was creative and diverse. It included a younger group aged twenty to thirty; two young people aged ten and twelve; and an older group aged fifty-five and over. Participants had different reasons to join the project but were all brought together by the desire to talk about migration. Younger participants were fascinated by the topics, and keen to take advice, while the older participants reminisced on the Italian community's achievements and were driven to serve as an example to the younger participants:

> Fabio is holding two photos in his hands. He looks at them very thoroughly and then says: 'I can't see any difference. Two mothers and their children, that's all I can see. It could be my wife, it could be me, it could be my neighbour.' Fabio arrived in Peterborough in 2014, a male nurse looking for full time employment and a dream to perform—as a hobby, he swears. Giuseppe is looking at the same two photos, he recognises some landmarks of the old town that have now been replaced by other structures. 'My boss lived not far away, it wasn't too far from the location where this photo was taken.' Giuseppe arrived in the U.K. in 1952. A young boy then, he became an apprentice carpenter, and worked overtime to fulfil his dream: buying a motorbike. Sicili-ana's mother is a local artist of Italian descent. Sicili-ana feels as much Italian as English, and hopes to spend more time in Italy to learn about Italian cuisine, and nail the perfect touch to any pasta recipe. She is sure there is more to the Italian culture than cooking, but she thinks that cuisine is what Italians are famous for in Peterborough. (Casilli 2017b)

The nature of the group was crucial to the selection of topics for the play. The participants chose to develop the topics of work and better opportunities as the main threads of the play. These topics were relatable to both Italian participants and those of other nationalities.

The stories selected were poignant examples of resilience, compassion, and positivity, serving both as a testimony for the community, and as a comparison between past and more modern reasons for migration. The lack of work or suitable job opportunities provided common ground for both groups, including the teenagers, whose focus was geared more towards the ability to access resources necessary for their integration. Occasional mentions of food were made, but mostly as a metaphor for nourishment and appreciation. Despite my keenness to include some testimonies gathered from the children of prisoners of war, those pieces were discarded, as captivity carried a harsh reality that the group was not prepared to explore.

Storytelling with visual interaction (video clips) was chosen as the most suitable method for the performances. A few dialogues were created, featuring the onstage interaction of younger participants and older members to facilitate the performing process for those less confident with their theatrical skills.

The play's main character was Angela, a fictional third-generation Italian who grew up with a fascination for her grandparents' traditions. The character was named Angela after one of the project's most prolific interviewees; the name's qualities of protection and supernatural transformation were well suited for the character's main function. Angela's quest to learn about her Italian roots is triggered by the loss of her beloved Auntie Anna, a migrant to the UK in the 1950s, who was very well known in the community. Auntie Anna was affected by dementia; her memories were "gradually fading away" (Casilli 2017a), according to the attentive ears of young Angela. So, Angelia decides to embark on a journey of discovery to unveil the untold stories of the Italian community of Peterborough.

The topics chosen were: collection of testimonies to celebrate the legacy of people's efforts and successes; separation from families in search for a better future; fear of criminality; ice-cream vending tradition; juggling life and work; income expectations; young apprentices working hard to fulfil their dreams; overworked mothers and integrated children; freeman status and illegal migration; language barriers that transform into an unexpected asset; comparison between new and old migration patterns; and analysis of the past to create an impact on the future.

Intergenerational Practice and Breaking Stereotypes

One of the greatest strengths and challenges of this project was its intergenerational core. The project aimed to create a conversation amongst the two generations of migrants, so that each of them could share their experiences and reach a common understanding of one another's achievements.

The younger participants showed appreciation and curiosity for the experiences of the older participants. The older group was very pleased with that and, once they overcame their fear of judgement, stories and memories flowed freely, enriching the pool of archival material we had started with. We decided to include testimonies from the participants in the play text, as they had an incredible relevance to the whole discourse. Despite our interpersonal and language skills that allowed us to collect many stories with minimal effort, only a small number of interviewees agreed to perform in the play. However, hearing stories directly from the subject added to the credibility of the work and made it easier for the participants to write their own stories.

What became evident throughout the work is that the stories we were analysing were not just disembodied discourses, but were deeply embedded in the lives of the second-generation Italians born in Peterborough. They were deeply ingrained in the practices of everyday life and held intense relevance to the whole process of identification as British Italians.

As such, the stories stirred up pride and content, but also recalled a series of unpleasant memories. Second-generation interviewees remembered the uncomfortable need to refute stereotypes used to define their parents, and subsequently themselves. They chose, instead, to talk about the achievements of their families, as well as the Italian community as a whole, to gain general trust and respect. According to their recollections, their families had to work harder within their occupations: their success would not only be recognized as marker of excellence, but would also serve as a trust building tool. Their parents' ability to show good manners and respect would also help the entire community be respected and appreciated. Their parents' ability to abide the law and act formally and legally would have made the entire community trustworthy. Their childhood was profoundly affected by these experiences, not always in a pleasant manner. It became evident to me that, before comparing stereotypes, I had to celebrate the achievements of the community throughout the years, and then open a discourse.

A second major challenge was the use of language itself. As verbal language and symbolization are core structures in the development of a sense of community (Brinck et al. 2017, 141), practitioners had to deal with a multiple crossover of languages. In the interview collection stage, I had to translate interviews from a number of Southern Italian dialects into contemporary Italian to render them accessible to other Italian speakers. As a second stage, I had to translate them into English. It was clear to me how the process of translation was cutting off layers of cultural expression that gave colour and depth to the stories collected. Most of the second-generation Italian contributors and workshop participants reported how, growing up within a community they could not identify with on a cultural level, they chose to speak English amongst themselves as they could not fully understand the myriad of dialects used among the Italian settlers. When choosing the language to use for the play's script, we gave participants the freedom to use some words or sentences in different dialects. They were positioned strategically in the text so that even non-Italian speakers could understand their meaning. The physical interaction was also supporting the use of such vocabulary, amalgamating it perfectly into the text.

Non-Italian contributors and audiences responded to the activity with a lot of enthusiasm, having as an only concern that of whether their contribution could hinder their identification of Italians with a play featuring their contribution. It was noted however, in many cases, that the experience of the migrant itself had some similarity across cultures. For that reason, sentences and impressions of the non-Italian contributors featured seamlessly in the play. Similarly, non-Italian audiences were inspired by the final performance as well, and did not feel excluded or confused by the content of the play.

Performance-devising Process: Subcultures, Identification, Community Consensus, and the Power of Conveying Positive Memories

Analysing the sample of archival material and live interviews with the older members of the Italian community of Peterborough, we found a number of people reported a gradual and mostly positive integration process at the beginning of the interview process. However, a sense of nostalgia would envelop their words when reminiscing about home. We identified many representations of the notion of *home* in our interviews: most of them were concerned with the nostalgia of childhood memories of the *homeland*. Many had a more geographic connotation and a longing for long-gone community bonds, while others were concerned with the cultural values including family, decorum, and celebration that they had to leave behind when settling in the UK. All representations had a connecting thread of *diasporic intimacy* (Boym 2001, 254), where the "uprootedness and defamiliarization" of the interviewees produced a colourful carousel of memories where intimacy corresponded to a freedom of expression in its own language. The idea of home is, in fact, an imaginary place where the individual can enact a wholeness generated by a freedom of expression.

The first-generation interviewees had replaced that sense of connection with the homeland with a newly forged idea of "home away from home." This shift in focus was probably due to the lack of limitation in terms of travelling in a global era, especially within Europe. However, as the project served to celebrate the efforts of this migrant community and the positive contribution of migrants to the country's welfare, we chose to shift the focus from the tender memories of home to the creation of a diasporic identity.

Another recurring feature was the sense of split identity (Comellini 2015), in which interviewees would state their inability to fully identify as English or as Italians, after having lived in the UK for such a long time. This sense of split identity was passed to the next generation, who were either very adamant about identifying with Italian culture or looking for a dual heritage or second-generation migrant's cultural balance. Both Angela's and Concetta's monologues address this topic:

> ANGELA: Our stories are part of your story, you must keep them alive!
> I shared this dream with many people: all of them think I am longing to learn more about my culture. But what is my culture? When I am with my friends, I always feel too Italian to be English and too English to be fully Italian. When I am in Italy, I really feel like I belong there. The wind, the sun, the sea, my summertime friends. But then when I am here, I love my town, my people, my family in England. My mother suggested I should look out for the people visiting my dream to learn about my origins. Their stories won't just be hidden in old dusty books, so I should look out for them. She thinks I should start by asking all of my Auntie Anna's friends, as they will know the Italians that came to Peterborough in 1950s. Auntie Anna always had so much to say about all the miles walked in search of hope, adventure and a better future. Until the moment memories started fading away, and our curiosity couldn't be satiated anymore. (Casilli 2017a)

Whereas Angela's quest for her own heritage is completely motivated by her need to heal that sense of double identity, Concetta's monologue focuses on her ability to use her dual identity to support newcomers and maintain her heritage language.

> CONCETTA: When I was a child, I used to dream I would become a teacher. I was curious to learn the right way, if there was one. I wanted all of my friends and colleagues to be able to stand up and speak for themselves. Why? Well, why not? Why shouldn't I be a teacher? Because I was a foreigner and I couldn't speak or write properly? So… I was cleaning in the morning, and studying in the evening. And soon I became a teacher —I did it!—(cleaners whooping and cheering). Later I realized, I needed to teach Italian to my children, rather than teach English to other children. So, I am here now to be your teacher. It's never too late to learn! (Casilli 2017a)

In many interviews, speakers recollected their stories of being young people separated from their parents or families, and later reunited, often in a traumatic way. We chose to dedicate a large portion of the workshops to developing a truthful yet poetic way of narrating the stories of these people. Where no evidence of trauma was shared, stories were easier to reproduce. Some were very personal and quite unsettling. We choose two stories, both of whom performed in the play, and included some childhood memories in a wider monologue:

1. When I arrived in England, I was only 15. I came all the way up with my mother to join my dad. He came with a contract to work for the London Brick Company, with many other people from our home town. The train ride was long and I was so impatient to get off. I had not seen my father for a long time, and I had forgotten what he looked like. Especially how strict he was! He was so serious! The family needed help: my father had found me a job and I started working right away. (Casilli 2017a)
2. Once mamma showed me the route along Westfield Road over Baker Perkins Bridge and round the back behind the rugby and football pitches, all the way to our allotment. I, the eldest, was chosen to push the pram as we tried to evade even the most persistent busy bodies who largely anticipated a view of the bonnie baby in the pram. Oh, the look on their faces! What a bunch of gypsy refugees we must have seemed, dressed in old allotment clothes and cut off wellies. No wonder we stood out. We felt like round pegs in square holes. (Casilli 2017a)

The second monologue clearly displays the precarious conditions of some Italian migrants. Children were given the duty to care for their younger siblings, depriving them of the ability to enjoy their own childhood. Some children were forced to work to contribute to insufficient family incomes, as also seen in the first monologue. Parents were keen for them to behave appropriately, however their appearance could not conceal the harshness of their resettling process. The nightmare section, interpreted by two younger participants, was a precise account of an interviewee's children, shouting their disappointment for not being able to spend time with their parents, who were working almost eighteen hours a day "on physically exhausting, undesirable and often dangerous work" (Iacovetta 1992, 64).

> FEDERICO: Is Babbo Natale coming tonight, mamma? Am I going to have new clothes this year? I don't like going out with these baggy trousers, mum. Uncle Nino says this jacket used to be his son's. Why am I wearing my cousins' clothes? Can I also have a dog, and a train ticket to see my nonno in Naples?

> BEATRICE: And me, am I going to have a new doll? This one has a headache so piercing, there's a hole in her head. Look, boom! Dolly's mum works very hard, on double shifts. She is never at home with her, and when she hugs her, she always has a headache, because too much work gave her a headache. I think I need a new dolly. (Casilli 2017a)

Some interviewees requested to remain anonymous, and while they were happy to share their positive memories, they were reluctant to reveal their trying pasts. For that reason, I treasured all accounts of challenging experiences, and highlighted the endurance that the interviewees demonstrated.

Another challenging account we chose to celebrate was that of another interviewee, who was forced to choose between returning to Italy to attend to his mother at her death bed, or remaining in the UK to fulfil the five years' bond requirement on his employment contract. His inability to return to his country made the interviewee feel particularly fragile, and being unable to see his mother one last time caused him to feel displaced and uneasy.

While the younger participants identified with a myriad of subcultures, which played a crucial role in encouraging non-Italian audience members to attend the show, the older participants identified solely with the Italian community of Peterborough. Such diversity implied that some of the older participants were looking for the approval of the *older Italian community*—in other words, the other Italian people they shared their leisure time with both at the community centre and in their own communities.

Despite the incredibly rich theatrical and cinematographic Italian tradition, the older community of Italians in Peterborough was concerned that they lacked the theatrical skills necessary to take part in a community theatre project. This may be partly attributed to the fact that they were frequently exposed to folkloristic practices and/or highly skilled artistic practices in the form of regular events taking place at the community centre. The community centre functioned as a role model for artistic practice, setting a standard which seemed out of their reach. If we consider how the older Italian community had to prove their worth in the workplace by achieving excellence, some of the older community members were therefore very concerned about their perceived lack of theatrical skills. Apparently, these concerns surfaced during everyday conversations, and participants struggled to gather consensus for their decision to take part in the project because their "perceived" lack of skills might result in a poor-quality show. The concern was handled well by the group, with the younger participants reassuring the older participants of their ability to perform, and the importance of their contribution.

The Performance: Synopsis and Provocations

The final draft of Moving Dreams was staged three times in two Fletton-based community centres: ICA—The Fleet and the Green Backyard. The audience included Italian migrants, second and third-generation Italians, younger and older migrants of other backgrounds, and a large number of local people interested in the project. The play is inspired by different pieces of interviews collected throughout the project, both before and throughout the workshop process. All characters were fictitious and inspired by different interviews, in order to celebrate multiple stories without unwanted exposure. Some performers agreed to share personal material under their name, because of its relevance and resonance to the rest of the community.

In the play, protagonist Angela, a student of Italian origin, is told by her friends/fellow students that she should spend more time finding more out about her heritage and *her people*. Wondering what the expression *her people* exactly means, Angela starts questioning her idea of community as a place of belonging. So, she starts a research to unveil the stories of Peterborough Italian community. Angela starts her research collecting old photos and letters of her beloved aunt Anna, who was suffering from Alzheimer's and had recently passed away. In a quest that often takes the shape of a dream or hallucination, past, present, and future interlace. A gallery of real or invented people from the Italian Community, with stereotypical traits, appears on stage. Each character's story develops, articulates, and defies a specific stereotype:

1. An unmarried woman leaves her country to work in Peterborough as a cleaner. Ultimately, she trains to become a successful nurse.
2. A mysterious shaman-like man who runs eco-sustainable activities for its community recounts the story of his childhood under the care of his grandmother in a post war impoverished Italy, whilst his father moved to England to become a brick worker.
3. A poor child is a young carer to his six siblings. Hanging out in rags, he fills his little brother's pram with vegetables he collects in a *secret* allotment.

4. A young man tries to leave the country to assist his mother on her deathbed, but he is not allowed to board his train.
5. A young migrant misses his connection train, can't speak the new country's language and can't find his brother in law. His ability to adapt and be grateful will make him a great ice-cream vendor.
6. A mechanic saves money to buy a motorbike in secret. His hard work allows for an easier inclusion process within the local community.
7. Two children complain about not having appropriate clothing and toys. They accuse their parents of caring more about working multiple shifts than spending time with them.
8. An unskilled worker with a poor command of the English language at the time of landing, studies and qualifies as English teacher. She also opens her own language school and promotes continuous education to the entire audience.

Each story brings the audience into a historical journey that contains a clear provocation related to Italian migrant experiences from 1950–1970: situation of unsettlement, fear of their political conditions, shame about their status, and derogatory language, all of which resonated with the experiences of modern migrants and asylum seekers. The play incorporates video footage to promote a sense of dreamlike reality, where present, past, and future interlace and influence each other. The participatory sections allow for a direct interaction with the audience, creating a classroom style dialogue with some of the characters. The play ends with Angela's monologue: a call for reflection and action, where footage of old archive photos alternates with modern photos of refugees and asylum seekers landing in Lampedusa.

Endings, Evaluation, and Potential Evolutions of *Moving Dreams*

The methodology used to assess our project included live interviews, feedback forms, question and answer session and a post-show feedback session with the workshop participants. The feedback was very positive and highlighted the fact that little or no knowledge of the endeavours of the older generation Italian migrants was available to non-Italian people in Peterborough. The exemplary nature of the stories prompted reflections on the current political situation regarding the migration crisis. Just as we hoped, many audience members realized how easy it is to underestimate the difficulty of the whole migration process.

Angela's final monologue, as seen below, clearly proclaimed our wish to compare the stories narrated with those of stigmatized refugees in the present times in order to invite our audiences to have respect and understanding for their stories.

> Memories are what we are made of
> Cell by cell, feelings running deep.
> We tend to forget who we are, who we were
> what brought us to where we are
> and what made us the people we are.
>
> Our ancestors carved a path
> we are still walking.
> Different faces, different eyes wide opened
> different cultures but same concerns, same worries, same longings
> [...]
> We must keep their lessons alive,
> we must keep telling their stories
> we must fuel our journey with their wisdom.
> Lest we forget, and dreamers must not forget.
> Dreams are what keep us moving. (Casilli 2017a)

Many audience members understood and appreciated the significance of the comparison; others preferred to dismiss it. Some were clearly very moved by the testimonies, commenting that the show helped them understand what it took to change their lives completely, leaving a country where they felt they had no future and starting again in a place that was unfamiliar and sometimes unwelcoming. They had to negotiate feelings of not belonging and uprootedness and face the challenge of an uncertain future, and the performance made them proud of their family's resilience and strength. Audiences clearly felt that these were important stories to tell, that would help everyone learn to imagine what lay behind a migrant's story before judging them.

Most of the audience expressed keenness to see the show again and contribute to the project's development in the future. This project was the first of its genre to happen in Peterborough. As more funding for similar projects is invested by local consortiums and national funders, I recognize the relevance that the project had by reaching out to an isolated community, celebrating its achievements and involving community members in a professional capacity.

In addition to this, some members of Peterborough's BAME (Black, Asian, and Minority Ethnic) creative community attended the performance and were inspired to develop similar projects to celebrate their own communities' contributions to the town. Participants, interviewees, and audiences shared the value of reliving their memories or creating an empathic relationship with the stories narrated. They acquired a new meaning under the light of the current Brexit discourse and its evident connection with the global refugee crisis: participants, to some extent, were able to offer their voices to instigate resistance.

Aware of the complex relationship between communities' agendas and the politics of intention that contribute to the shaping of applied discourse (Taylor 2003, 1), I am not able to provide evidence of a transformation in the audience's perception. However, with our collection of positive responses, insights, and the inevitable learning curve of such a delicate project, I remain faithful to the small relentless changes that applied theatre can instigate.

Whilst I continue to express my gratitude to mentors and funders that made this project possible, I hope to be able to repeat the show in different towns to spread the discourse further. I have embarked on new creative endeavours, with the goal to soon develop new work on the topic. I hope that this project continues to generate a better understanding of migration patterns, serving as a starting point for new artistic discourses on migration, identity, and community.[4]

Notes

1. The project was funded by Spare Tyre, Peterborough Presents, and Forterra UK.
2. Teatro delle Albe specializes in intercultural theatre and new writing through adaptation of existing literature. See http://www.teatrodellealbe.com/eng/curriculum.php?id=1.
3. I was born in Molise with part of my family having migrated from Apulia, and part belonging to the old arbëreshë settlement of Campomarino (Molise).
4. Readers interested in more information, including images and video clips, can browse our website at https://movingdreamerstheatrecompany.com.

References

Boal, Augusto. 2006. *The Aesthetic of the Oppressed*. London: Routledge.

———. 2008. *Theater of the Oppressed*. New York: Theater Communication Group.

Boym, Svetlana. 2001. *The Future of Nostalgia*. New York: Basic Books.

Brah, Avtar. 1996. *Cartographies of Diaspora: Contesting Identities*. London: Routledge.

Brinck, Ingar, Vasudevi Reddy, and Dan Zahavi. 2017. The Primacy of the 'We'? In *Embodiment, Enaction and Culture: Investigating the Constitution of the Shared World*, ed. Christoph Durt, Thomas Fuchs, and Christian Tewes, 131–147. Cambridge, MA: MIT Press.

Casilli, Ida. 2017a. *Moving Dreams*. Play text. Unpublished.

———. 2017b. *Moving Dreams*. Project Journal. Unpublished.

Cereste, Marco. 2001. *Aliens Order: A Photographic History of the Italian Community in Peterborough from 1951 to 2001*. Peterborough: Premier Communications.

Comellini, Carla. 2015. Italian-Canadian Female Voices: Nostalgia and Split Identity. *International Journal of Language and Linguistics* 2 (5): 151–155.

Gardner, R.C., R.L. Rodensky, and D.M. Kirby. 1970. *Ethnic Stereotypes: A Critical Review. Research Bulletin No. 157*. London: University of Western Ontario.

Hatton, Timothy J., and Jeffrey G. Williamson. 1994. What Drove the Mass Migrations from Europe in the Late Nineteenth Century? *Population and Development Review* 20 (3): 533–559.

Iacovetta, Franca. 1992. *Such Hardworking People: Italian Immigrants in Post-war Toronto*. Montreal and Kingston: McGill-Queen's University Press.

Jeffers, Allison. 2012. Refugees, *Theatre and Crisis Performing Global Identities*. London: Palgrave Macmillan UK.

Nicholson, Helen. 2014. *Applied Drama: The Gift of Theatre*. 2nd ed. New York: Palgrave Macmillan.

Pozzetta, George E. 1980. *Pane e Lavoro: The Italian American Working Class*. Toronto: Multicultural History Society of Ontario.

Pozzetta, George E., Bruno Ramirez, and Robert F. Harney. 1992. *The Italian Diaspora: Migration Across the Globe*. Toronto: Multicultural History Society of Ontario.

Sori, Ercole. 1987. *L'emigrazione italiana dall' Unità alla Seconda Guerra Mondiale*. Bologna: Il Mulino.

Stella, Gian Antonio. 2003. *L'Orda: Quando gli albanesi eravamo noi*. Bologna: Rizzoli.

Turchin, Peter. 2005. Dynamical Feedbacks Between Population Growth and Sociopolitical Instability in Agrarian States. *Structure and Dynamics* 1(1).

Breaking Stereotypes: *Afrika!* and *In the Waiting Room of the Dreams*: Two Theatrical Projects with Refugees in German Border Cities Close to France

Michalis Georgiou

Since the summer of 2015, Germany has accepted approximately 1,500,000 refugees and migrants into the country. Coverage of this influx dominated the media in the first few months and the so-called "refugee crisis" remains an ongoing political and social debate (Georgiou and Zaborowski 2017). Between 2015 and 2017, the German Federal Office for Migration and Refugees received more than 800,000 asylum applications.[1] During this period, municipalities began building numerous refugee camps and the government announced plans for assimilation measures, such as language classes, lessons in German law, and work experience

I would like to thank Brendan Storch (INIT Creative) for his proof reading and editing of my text.

M. Georgiou (✉)
Berlin, Germany

Y. Meerzon et al. (eds.), *Migration and Stereotypes in Performance and Culture*, Contemporary Performance InterActions,
https://doi.org/10.1007/978-3-030-39915-3_14

opportunities to encourage refugees to integrate into German society in return for being allowed to live and work in the country. This political and cultural orientation towards integration was further advanced as the German government, alongside private companies, provided financial support for hundreds of theatres to stage performances that directly engaged with issues related to the refugee crisis.

My personal connection with this topic started in the city of Offenburg in western Germany, where I worked as an office manager, an artistic director, and a dramaturge at the local theatre, BAAL Novo Theater Eurodistrict, from 2015 to 2016. Located in the state of Baden-Württemberg, fifteen kilometres east of the river Rhine, Offenburg is the capital city of the Ortenau district. Across the river, lies the French city of Strasbourg. The BAAL Novo Theater Eurodistrict is a bilingual German-French theatre that engages in artistic and sociocultural projects, with the aim of allowing people to participate in artistic processes, while providing a voice to socially marginalized groups. When I moved to Offenburg from Berlin in September 2015, I remember being surprised by the number of refugees arriving there—something that sparked my interest in working with them, which I had the opportunity to do when the director of the theatre, Edzard Schoppmann, asked me to work as a dramaturge in applied theatre projects involving refugees from different cultural backgrounds.

I wanted to combine applied theatre theory with praxis in my work with refugees. Though a literature review helped me to prepare my methodology, I soon realized that not only does new work continuously express different views about what the concept of applied theatre means, but scholars are beginning to question its meaning and value. For example, in her PhD thesis, Karen Dainty (2018) explores how empathy and sympathy emerge in applied theatre. According to her personal experience, it is hard to determine what kind of theatre and performances bring about social change, and it is even more difficult to study applied theatre without taking into account its broader sociopolitical dimensions.[2] Applied theatre is a general term for non-mainstream theatrical activities that explore issues related to individuals, communities, or societies. My work, in general, concerns a theatre practice that seeks "outcomes beyond the artistic experience" (Baldwin 2009, 134) by first providing a space where refugees can share their personal narratives, then by creating a community between the actors and the audience (Nicholson 2005). It is in this community that a transformational process takes place: the audience is confronted with situations that encourage them to reflect upon and revise their perceptions

(Taylor 2003). In addressing issues of social justice, applied theatre has social and even political dimensions, particularly when participants experience discrimination or are economically, socially, or culturally marginalized. As James Thompson (2009, 5) mentions, however, there is a difference in its effect when a performance occurs in a specific site, such as a prison, camp, or school, or, in this case, when immigrants or refugees are the subject matter. Despite its sociopolitical dimensions, applied theatre offers no immediate resolution to social justices. In the case of applied theatre about refugees and migrants, the issue is more about how these social groups can be integrated within the host country and to what degree diversity is considered acceptable within German society. This chapter is inspired by my personal experiences, interactions, and professional engagement in applied theatre with refugees.

One third of Offenburg's citizens can trace their lineage to other countries, as they have migrant backgrounds, while around 10% of them have foreign passports representing more than one hundred different nationalities. The main group is Turks, followed by French and Italians. Nevertheless, the mass arrival of refugees which began in 2015 came as a shock to the inhabitants of this relatively small community unaccustomed to such extensive change. Sociologists William Thompson and Joseph Hickey (1999) have shown that stereotypes emerge out of cultural and socialization patterns and the mass media. In Offenburg, public debate ensuing from this wave of immigration often centred on the deplorable living conditions of the refugee camps or concerns, founded on stereotypes, that the refugee population posed a threat to the social and cultural life of the city. This intense focus on refugees was exacerbated by an attack on civilians in Paris in January 2015, resulting in the deaths of twelve people in the offices of the French satirical magazine *Charlie Hebdo* at the hands of two gunmen affiliated with an Islamist terrorist group.[3] The brutality of the attack influenced the critical response that ensued. Citizens and intellectuals around the world discussed a range of potential interpretations of the shooting, from a clash of civilizations to a reprisal operation countering the imperialistic policies of Western countries against Eastern ones (Zagato, ed. 2015).

It was against the backdrop of this worsening social situation that the director of the BAAL Novo theatre, Edzard Schoppmann, inspired by his own interactions with the refugee community, had the idea of creating a project that would bring together refugees and German citizens in an integrated performance that would tackle, head-on, the issues arising from the refugee crisis. The project's title was *Afrika!* and its main intent was to reverse public understandings of the current situation by presenting a world where the West is economically deprived and politically unstable, and the African continent offers the promise of stability, privilege, and hope. In this cultural reframing, Europeans are forced to migrate because of war, poverty, and fear of persecution based on race, ethnicity, or religious or political ideologies. They flee because they are desperate to find safety and will use any means necessary to escape. We hoped that, in addition to challenging current perceptions regarding the refugee situation, the project would actively help refugees integrate into their adopted homeland through their participation in this cultural project.

The project was divided into two parts. During the first part, our team visited the refugee camps in Offenburg and met with both social workers and refugees. The social workers provided valuable background information regarding the variety of different situations the refugees had been forced to flee, as well as the conditions in which they had arrived. After a few weeks visiting the refugee camps, our team had amassed a large network of contacts and had spent a significant amount of time socializing with the refugees. Those who had an interest in joining the project included a Gambian man, three Syrian men, a Tunisian man, a Tibetan man, an Iraqi man, and an Iranian woman. Three German men, a German woman, a girl of Italian descent, a Polish woman, and a Romanian woman—all Offenburg citizens with differing immigrant backgrounds, who had already attended different performances staged by BAAL Novo—also took part in rehearsals.

Rehearsals for *Afrika!* became the primary space where we could examine and elaborate the reasons and circumstances related to refugees' fleeing their homelands, the conditions in refugee camps, as well as issues related to integration in Germany. While narrating their personal stories, the refugee members of the cast brought a richness and eloquence to their performative expressions. It was fascinating to watch how everyone learned to relate to each other during this extensive and intense process. The script evolved throughout these rehearsals, depending on what the participants were willing to do, and provided an opportunity to create a new piece of theatre that could become part of Offenburg's experimental arts and culture history.

Whilst in the process of scheduling the premiere of *Afrika!* Paris was targeted again. On November 13, 2015, gunmen and suicide bombers carried out simultaneous attacks at the Bataclan concert hall, the Stade de

France (during a football match between France and Germany), and various restaurants and bars. These were the deadliest Islamic terrorist attacks in French History, leaving 130 people dead and around 340 wounded. President Francois Hollande described the attacks as an "act of war" organized by the Islamic State (Kühnhardt 2017, 50). Refugee participants in our project worried that their religious views might make them a target in Offenburg. Among the local citizen participants of *Afrika!* however, it raised a strong feeling of sympathy and concern about how it must feel to be a survivor in a foreign, crowded country that is uninformed about the circumstances of your escape and your present needs; they encouraged the refugees to carry on with the project. The local participants wondered how they themselves would react if exposed to the same tragic conditions and insecurity faced by refugees. This reflection prompted our decision that the woman of Polish descent and the girl of Italian descent would present parts of their personal stories, as well as the Iranian refugee woman's overall experiences. The aim was not only to present the history of the Iranian refugee woman but also to present the opportunities, the experiences, the memories, and feelings of the Polish woman when she left her country after the collapse of socialism, and the Italian girl when she left southern Italy in the 1980s in order for her parents to find a work in Germany. Sympathy and a search for empathy became the occasion for the middle-aged German man of the production to present parts of the refugees' experiences by making indirect references to the 1930s and 1940s, when some European countries were controlled through dictatorships and the states became totalitarian. We thought these approaches, which seek to reframe the current refugee situation in a way that makes them more comprehensible, relatable, and immediate for the local German audience, would more effectively raise awareness, consideration, and understanding of the issues related to war, destruction, death, insecurity, and the violation of freedom and human rights faced by refugees.

Against this background of sadness and tension, *Afrika!* premiered on December 8, 2015, in the Reithalle Cultural Center in Offenburg. Despite the negative effects of recent terrorist attacks, the audience attended, undeterred, from nearby German and French cities.

The set was minimal, consisting merely of a net on which the refugees' backpacks were hung. The middle of the stage was strewn with rags and backpacks. The backpacks were used as the main focal point of the set, being, as they are, the most important item refugees take with them on their journey. They travel light, as their trek is dangerous and arduous, discarding along the way anything that is no longer of use to them. The performance begins with the refugee participants sitting on either side of the stage, while the local performers sit in the centre singing the poem *Commit Your Way Unto the Lord* (*Befiehl du deine Wege*), written by the seventeenth-century German poet Paul Gerhardt, a piece relevant to their own sociocultural background.

After the song, the woman of Polish descent emerges from amid the rags on stage and proceeds to describe the war currently raging in the area where she used to live. She explains to the audience that she lost her husband in the conflict and is now alone with her two children. Desperate to provide a peaceful and stable life for her children, she has decided to emigrate to Africa. It's too late to receive any kind of external protection, everyone is alone now! she expresses. Following her, the girl of Italian descent, who has lived in Offenburg since childhood, enters center stage and details how the war began when she was finishing her studies. She lost her family in the ensuing violence and now believes that Africa is only safe place left for her to go, saying: "The long way to Africa is my only chance." Next, the middle-aged German man appears, explaining to the audience that he is married and an inhabitant of Offenburg. Two months ago, he decided to emigrate due to the persecution he is suffering for his evangelical Christian beliefs. He elaborates that two years ago, a military coup took place in Germany, and ever since, the state has been run by the army. There is no longer any freedom, the place is ruled by fear, persecution, and unemployment; people are oppressed, they disappear, mass executions occur, and religious freedom is banned. He explains that he has to reach a peaceful continent, and that is Africa.

This narrative material is drawn directly from personal stories told by the refugees, but is presented on stage by the citizens of Offenburg, recast into the role of victims; this reverses the contemporary situation in Germany, providing the audience with an unexpected personal, emotional link to the crisis. This approach creates an environment in which the public can come face to face with the refugee situation and reflect and revise their perceptions of it.

Gradually, the narrative is taken up by the refugee cast members, who highlight the fact that they left their homes and their countries because they had no other choice. The first issue they explore is the brutalization of women. The Iranian girl comes to the centre of the stage and stands in silence for a few seconds. Then a group on stage starts to stone her. She kneels, crying and wounded. This story is based on the "state of rejection" that happens when certain fanatical groups abuse and torture a person who has allegedly committed sacrilege. Stoning became part of the Iranian penal code in 1979, when the Islamic government established a new judiciary system. The first cases of stoning were reported in 1980, when two women were sentenced to death by stoning in the city of Kerman. Ever since, many activists have unsuccessfully struggled to abolish legal stoning (Mouri and Batmanghelidj 2016, 348).

The second issue explored is that refugees leave their homes because they fear for their lives or those of their families, usually because one or more of their basic human rights are under attack. A central right is the freedom of opinion and expression. In the performance, the Iranian girl returns to the centre of the stage and sings a traditional song. At the end, she is gagged by someone, who puts a black bag on her head. By the mid-1990s, in Iran, the government resorted to drastic measures to restrict citizen's freedom of expression and the freedom of the press. Although Iran's current Supreme Leader, Ali Khamenei, has declared the notion of human rights to be fundamental in Islamic teaching and has publicly attacked the human rights record of the United States (which has criticized the Islamic Republic for hypocrisy in return), little has been done to advance human rights in Iran (Hovsepian-Bearce 2017, 191–210; 281–95). In fact, many additional restrictions have been placed on speech, religion, and gender equality, with often brutal and extreme punishment for perceived violations (Afshari 2001, 185–200). The same is true of countries like Syria, where, according to human rights organizations, human rights violations such as the killing of civilians and violence against women have been committed by both Assad's government and the various anti-regime organizations (see, e.g., Ahmed 2017). Research by the International Organization for Migration in Iraq ("Migration Flows from Iraq to Europe: Reasons behind Migration") contends that Iraqi people express the opinion that "there are no human rights in Iraq" and, instead, a system that actively works to deny freedom of speech and expression is in operation, while people are threatened or arrested and tortured because of their political beliefs (International Organization for Migration 2016).

The third main issue explored in *Afrika!* is the desire and anxiety of refugees to find work. Our theatre's participants hoped to show to the audience that refugees do not want to beg or be dependent on the state, but, rather, productive community members with much to offer. To this effect, in one scene, all the participants address the audience, shouting repeatedly: "I want to work! I want to work!" Now that many recently arrived refugees have awaited a sufficient amount of time and have fulfilled the initial requirements to be granted asylum and search for jobs, Germany faces the challenge of incorporating them into the labour market. Generally speaking, the longer an asylum seeker has lived in Germany, the more employment or educational opportunities they will have, but it can still take months or years to secure work ("Erfolgreiche Integration. Flüchtlinge und sonstige Schutzbedürftige") (Organisation for Economic Co-operation and Development 2016). Although they are often nostalgic about their native countries and the families they left behind, most refugees still hope to create a new life in Germany. In the performance, this is imparted when the refugees address each other by shouting: "A new beginning! A new beginning!" The problems that drove many refugees in Germany to flee their home countries show no sign of ending, so they cannot go back. Most Syrians, Iranians, and Iraqis, who have fled since 2011, initially believed that war and political instability in their countries would soon be over, but in the last few years, they have realized that this is not going to happen and they must seek permanent sanctuary elsewhere. For this reason, at the end of the performance, they whisper together: "I would like to call 'the foreign' my home. I want to freely express this opinion. Here I found recognition and happiness—No, No I don't want to go back!"

The reviews of *Afrika!* in local newspapers were positive. An unknown journalist from the magazine *Galerie: Ortenau* commented that: "The experiences were used here in order for the performance to provide authenticity" (Pahn 2016). We believe that authenticity was achieved because the past experiences we staged were recreated by performers who had, themselves, lived them. What added to this sense of honesty in the emotional expressions of the cast was that individual performers revealed themselves from within the crowd as well, presenting their own personalities, spirits, characteristics, and views about their experiences, sincerely and authentically, with no pretensions.

Bettina Kühne (2015), from the journal *baden online,* stated that: "In fact, it's not just the story of the foreign participants in the theatre project. The Germans have also experienced what it's like to make a new beginning somewhere, or to integrate themselves or even to be excluded." The performance triggered memories among the local Offenburg citizens audience, as almost one third of them had migrant backgrounds, for example, at least one parent that did not acquire German citizenship by birth. They probably had also experienced migration in the past, as well as rejection by a host society, discrimination, and rights violations. *Afrika!* represented and humanized the reality refugees face by presenting a world in which Europeans are forced to emigrate because of war, poverty, and fear of persecution. On stage, they experience some of the physical and emotional discomforts that actual refugees do on their route to safety. This role reversal makes it easier for the audience to 'Put themselves in the shoes of the refugee' and to consider the experiences of those who have been forced to leave their homes to seek asylum. Empathy thus emerged as a meaningful link between the host society and the refugees. A journalist for the German-French newspaper *Eurojournalist* expressed a similar view, writing: "This is once again a great project by BAAL Novo "Africa!", it changes the roles, overturns stereotypes and expectations, and leads the audience to a new consideration about dealing with refugees" ("Afrika! Was wäre, wenn wir die Flüchtlinge wären?").

The performance raised provocative questions about identity and belonging. By "changing the roles" it was able to challenge stereotypical representations of "new arrivals" and asylum seekers and attack the idea of "us/them" thinking. It reconceptualized theatre about refugees as a debate about nationality and citizenship and turned it into a tool to foster positive, creative intercultural dialogue between refugees and their adopted society, and communicating ideas as well as experiences on the stage. Furthermore, presenting the topic of human rights, *Afrika!* generated a genuine human connection between the newly arrived refugees and the local population through its sensory intensity, social intimacy, and the co-existence of physical bodies on and offstage.[4] As a result, the project helped to stimulate social cohesion, addressing diversity, and fostering mutual understanding and appreciation between the asylum seekers and the local population—most of whom had had no contact with refugees before the refugee crisis.

The success of *Afrika!* provided us with a springboard for a second project, which began in March 2016. We had observed during the first project that from the moment refugees arrive in Germany, they are in a permanent "standby state." They wait to be granted asylum; they wait for a work permit, an apartment, to be admitted to a German language course, or in the worst cases, for deportation. It takes months or even years until they start living life at anything resembling a regular pace. During this period of waiting, they spend a lot of time thinking about their homeland and families, whilst also dreaming of the future and hoping that better days will come. We decided that the second project should put these issues on the table. We also decided to contact the refugee camp in the city of

Lahr, near Offenburg, as it is the second largest city in Ortenau and an economic hub for the surrounding area.

This project was also divided into two parts. The director, Horst Kiss, and I visited the refugee camp in March 2016 and organized a meeting to inform the refugees about the project. During the first month, we conducted in-depth oral histories with more than thirty refugees and far more informal interviews and group dialogues. Studying the cases of people seeking asylum reinforced our belief that the "standby state" experienced by refugees has negative psychological effects. Their economic hardship combines with a perceived lack of freedom, and most refugees characterized the camp as a "prison." Our research was the starting point for *In the Waiting Room of the Dreams*, a theatre piece that blends together scenes from the documented life stories of refugees in Lahr.

On July 14, 2016, a nineteen-tonne cargo truck driven by Mohamed Lahauaiaj-Bouhlel, a Tunisian resident of France, was deliberately driven into crowds celebrating Bastille Day in Nice.[5] President Hollande's reaction was to declare a state of emergency, and he announced an intensification of French airstrikes on ISIL in Syria and Iraq (Bauman 2016, 16–18). Four days later, a teenage Afghan asylum seeker attacked five passengers with an axe on a train near Würzburg in Germany. In German cities close to the border with France, a real sense of unrest was experienced and far-right-leaning parties felt vindicated in their anti-Islamic views. The terrorist attacks had a negative impact on the preparations for our project: the refugees in the Lahr camp closed themselves off from the rest of the world. They believed that people in Germany would now take a more sceptical, prejudicial view of them, and that their participation in our project might trigger a backlash against them. They also worried it could further delay their asylum applications and jeopardize their chances of staying in Germany.

We decided to carry on visiting the camp, however, and after a few weeks, two Syrian men, an Iranian man and woman, and an Iraqi man finally decided to take part in the project. The interactive nature of the rehearsals, including a range of theatre games and exercises, provided a safe space for the refugees to express themselves freely in English and to practice their German language skills. Overcoming the language barrier was among the greatest challenges we faced. Each storyteller had a desire to share their own life experiences and during rehearsals, the refugees had adequate time to narrate their personal stories and explain their feelings. Most of the time, the focus was on a traumatic experience that they wanted to make public. We noted that because they had previously been denied a platform to express themselves, these experiences had effectively been silenced, which was often felt by the refugees to be yet another injustice. Other times, it appeared that the refugees wanted their stories to act as cautionary tales. These accounts often revolved around the horrors of war and the personal losses they had suffered. The feeling of being stuck in limbo in Germany had provided enough thinking space for such memories to resurface, and these complex life stories and traumatic experiences became the "material" we used to improvise a series of dramatized skits, all of which were continually revised and transformed until the last rehearsal. The performers wrote their own dialogues, but the underlying thread running through the text was the feeling of waiting after their arrival in Germany, overlaid with the refugees' thoughts, memories, everyday life experiences, and expectations for the future.

Their psyches took another blow on December 19, 2016, when Anis Amri, a Tunisian failed asylum seeker, deliberately drove a stolen truck through a Christmas market next to the Kaiser Wilhelm Memorial Church at Breitscheidplatz in Berlin, killing twelve people and injuring fifty-six. The perpetrator was supported by the Islamic State of Iraq and the Levant, who had given him instructions. It was one of the deadliest terrorist attacks that had ever taken place in Germany (Wassermann 2017, 72–4). Tourism to the country was affected. The far-right Alternative for Germany party lost no time pointing fingers at the German government for inefficiency in confronting terrorism. Besides, stereotypical perceptions about the other and the foreign, which are static and oversimplified ideas, are based on ethnocentrism. The local public debate in Ortenau emphasized the fact that Germany hosts more refugees than it should and that the hosting of refugees would have a negative impact on the German economy and culture. After the attack, some of our participants were afraid to leave their accommodations in case of physical attacks from far-right organizations. Their thoughts and worries became part of the rehearsal process, which encouraged a relaxed and cooperative atmosphere into which improvisations and devised scenes were developed, resulting in changing the production to a continual work-in-progress throughout the following months.

The premiere of *In the Waiting Room of the Dreams* took place on January 10, 2017 in zeit.areal cultural center in Lahr and the audience came, once again, from different German and French cities. The set consists of the waiting room of an office for Migration and Refugees, with chairs and cushions on which the cast were already positioned, waiting, while the spectators arrive. They watch the audience and then start to ask questions about waiting and feelings of boredom and stagnation. After this, they began to recount their own stories, really personalizing them. The cast uses their proper names to introduce themselves to the audience. They talk about the depression that comes from the sensation of being stuck, of having to wait to be granted asylum, to be admitted to a German course, to receive a work permit, or to find an apartment. At the same time, they talked about their pasts, trying to explain the socio-political situations in their countries and the reasons for their own subsequent escapes. A Syrian refugee recounts that he had to leave his homeland after completing his university studies because otherwise he would have had to serve in the military and take part in the war. It was his father who persuaded him to flee. Although it meant leaving his relatives, friends, and familiar life behind, it was the right decision, he decided, to have taken his younger brother and made the difficult journey to Germany. Another Syrian man then explains that he left his country not only because of the war, but because his government deemed him to be a terrorist after he fought for freedom. Next, an Iranian refugee explains that his life was threatened because he adopted the Christian faith. They all explain that they travelled from Turkey to Greece, then to Macedonia, Serbia, Hungary, and Vienna, before arriving at the German border. They explain that the most difficult part of the journey, the part that still returns in their nightmares, was the crossing from Turkey to the Greek island of Lesbos. These men had spent most of their money to risk their lives crammed into a rubber boat with thirty other people. Thousands have drowned in the last few years attempting this same sea trip. An Iraqi man describes a nightmare that he often has: a king has risen up through the military hierarchy and now governs as an authoritarian dictator. His country is rich in oil and natural gas and for these reasons other countries have been trying to exploit it. Poverty and instability prevail. Many people protest against the king, who responds by using his armed forces. Terrorist organizations also participate in this conflict, fighting against the king. They use terror and religious fanaticism as a means of warfare. Other countries from the west and north now bomb his country. There is famine and poverty. Millions of children do not go to school either because the schools were destroyed or getting to school is too dangerous. War, terror, disasters—the number of refugees fleeing the country has now risen to thousands.

After this scene, a middle-aged Iranian woman comes to the centre of the stage. She explains that she used to work as a theatre director and writer for the Ministry of Culture in Iran. Her plays dealt with discrimination against women, but the Iranian government considered this too provocative. She was accused of offending Islamic values, suffered humiliating attacks, and finally lost her job. After suffering a breakdown, she decided to migrate to Europe.

In the end, although the refugees feel tired of waiting in the same room, where things remain static and they are submerged in their thoughts, they still want to express their goals and desires for the future, including their wishes to learn the German language well so that they are understood by other people, can study a profession or a science at the university, and can find a job.

As with *Afrika!* the newspaper reviews of this performance of *In the Waiting Room of the Dreams* were positive. The journalist Andreas Buchta (2017) from the *Offenburger Tageblatt* wrote: "The most painful thing is that the stories presented arise from the immediate, personal experiences of the participants. The correspondence of the audience is to react with great surprise." Again, this approach calls for imagination and empathy. The asylum seekers are the medium for autobiographical monologues, making the performance authentic and bringing the theatre community and the participants together. The journalist Jürgen Haberer (2017) from the *Lahrer Zeitung* mentioned that:

> The performance also tells about the rulers who ruin their country, about global conflicts of interest and Arab sheikhs, who buy everything with their oil-dollars. It focuses on the dream of a self-determined life and the hunger for freedom, which threatens to stifle at the end of the journey in the standby state, in the mills of the bureaucratic system.

This comment draws attention to the political dimension of the performance, which is about the current unstable and fluid situation in the Middle East, where many countries have absolutist monarchies or family-run autocracies; where there is a high risk of political and religious violence; and where terrorist groups mobilize support for their escalating campaign of violence. Western countries have also turned civil wars into international contests for regional influence, drawing diplomatic and military support from various foreign sponsors because countries with oil-dependent economies are very strategically important to them. The refugee-immigration issue has taken on explosive dimensions, due to the continued war in Syria, as well as the escalation of the economic interests of global monopolies in the geopolitically critical region ranging from the Ukraine and the Balkans to the Middle East, the Eastern Mediterranean, and Africa. It is a serious and complex political issue, with national and international economic, social, and ideological aspects. The war, the conflicts, and the ongoing violence in the Middle East are leading people to look for new lives elsewhere. The refugees who arrived in Germany now have to deal with bureaucracy, while economic analyses and forecasts show that Germany will face great difficulties in implementing integration measures and, as a result, many of the refugees will still be unemployed in a year's time.

The art of applied theatre operated democratically in *In the Waiting Room of the Dreams*, as the participants had an equal say in what was to be presented, while their own texts had been included in the final performance. This was encouraged through improvisation, as well as through adapting the process to the interests and needs of the refugee cast, enabling them to express their personal truths and draw on their personal skills. In this way I think it became clearer for the audience that the performers have something to say that's worth listening to.[6]

The performance raised awareness among both German and French audiences, educating them about the situations that have compelled refugees to flee their homelands and about the hostile conditions they face in places of sanctuary in Germany. *In the Waiting Room of the Dream*'s political dimension provided a vital space for discussions about the most pressing issues in the local community and because it showed the audience that refugees are not terrorists, or fanatics, or uncivilized, it battled cultural and political stereotypes. The performance presented refugee immigration as a response to war and crisis, international conflicts, poverty, and social, political, or religious persecution. While avoiding a discursive demarcation between good and evil, *In the Waiting Room of the Dreams* nonetheless helps to dispel myths, taboos, and misunderstandings about asylum seekers. Thus, we enter into a process of reflection on the sociopolitical and aesthetic relationship. As Herbert Marcuse (1978, 32–33) has said: "Art cannot change the world, but it can contribute to changing the consciousness and drives of the men and women who could change the world."

Notes

1. For data on topics concerning asylum, see "Aktuelle Zahlen zu Asyl," *Bundesamt für Migration und Flüchtlinge* (2017), July 2017.

2. In his book *Humanitarian Performance: From Disaster Tragedies to Spectacles of War*, James Thomson (2014) uses the term "performance" even more broadly, as an "analytical concept" that can describe practices and representations of humanitarian action in war or natural disaster zones.
3. On January 7, 2015, Saïd and Chérif Kouachi, forced their way into the offices of the French satirical magazine *Charlie Hebdo* in Paris, killing twelve people and injuring eleven others. The Kouachi brothers claimed affiliation with the Islamist terrorist group Al-Qaeda's branch in Yemen, which took responsibility for the attack. For more in detail, see *The Event of Charlie Hebdo. Imaginaries of Freedom and Control* (Zagato, ed. 2015).
4. About this capacity of the theatre see Becker et al. 2013.
5. It caused the deaths of eighty-six people and injured around 450 others. The attack was followed by an exchange of gunfire, during which the driver was shot and killed by police, see Bauman 2016, 16–18.
6. Besides, in my opinion, the successful outcome of these theatre projects was dependent largely on the non-theatrical, more social and practical factors. During the process, I realized that the more support we give to refugees' daily lives and the safer the environment we create, providing a family-feeling, the better ground is created for rehearsals. Being part of this family, I felt, was an important step in the refugee's host country. In October 2019, as I review this chapter, although I am a resident of Berlin, which is about 750 km away from Offenburg, I still maintain links with some of the refugee participants. Some of them study at Universities, others found jobs in technical professions, while some of them continue to take place in BAAL Novo's projects.

References

"Afrika! Was wäre, wenn wir die Flüchtlinge wären?" *Eurojournalist*. March 12, 2015. *http://eurojournalist.eu/afrika-was-waere-wenn-wir-die-fluechtlinge-waeren/*.

Afshari, Reza. 2001. *Human Rights in Iran. The Abuse of Cultural Relativism*. Philadelphia: University of Pennsylvania Press.

Ahmed, Habiballa. 2017. *Islamic Terrorism & Syrian Civil War*. Habiballa Ahmed. eBook.

Baldwin, Andrea. 2009. Applied Theatre: Performing the Future. *Australasian Psychiatry* 17 (2009): 133–136.

Bauman, Sygmund. 2016. *Strangers at Our Door*. Cambridge: Polity Press.

Becker, Florian N., S. Paola Hernandez, and Brenda Werth. 2013. Introduction: Imagining Human Rights in Twenty-First Century Theater. In *Imagining Human Rights in Twenty-First Century Theater: Global Perspectives*, ed. Florian N. Becker, S. Paola Hernandez, and Brenda Werth, 1–23. New York: Palgrave.

Buchta, Andreas. 2017. Flüchtlinge spielen ergreifendes drama. *Offenburger Tageblatt*. June 26.

Bundesamt für Migration und Flüchtlinge. 2017. Aktuelle Zahlen zu Asyl. Bundesamt für Migration und Flüchtlinge, July 2017.

Dainty, Karen. 2018. Empathy and Sympathy in Applied Theatre: A Qualitative Study. PhD diss., University of Leicester.

Georgiou, Myria, and Rafal Zaborowski. 2017. Media Coverage of the Refugee Crisis: A Cross-European Perspective. *Council of Europe Report, DG1*, vol. 3.

Haberer, Jürgen. 2017. Projekt als ein Stück gelebte Integration. *Lahrer Zeitung*. January 23.

Hovsepian-Bearce, Yvette. 2017. *The Political Ideology of Ayatollah Khamenei: Out of the Mouth of the Supreme Leader of Iran*. London: Routledge.

International Organization for Migration. 2016. Migration Flows from Iraq to Europe: Reasons Behind Migration. International Organization for Migration. July 2016.

Kühne, Bettina. 2015. Im Stück "Afrika"! sind die Deutschen auf der Flucht. *Baden Online*. December 3. https://www.bo.de/kultur/kultur-regional/im-stueck-afrika-sind-die-deutschen-auf-der-flucht.

Kühnhardt, Ludger. 2017. *The Global Society and Its Enemies: Liberal Order Beyond the Third World War*. Cham, Switzerland: Springer.

Marcuse, Herbert. 1978. *The Aesthetic Dimension: Toward a Critique of Marxist Aesthetic*. Boston: Beacon Press.

Mouri, Leila, and Kristin Soraya Batmanghelidj. 2016. Can the Secular Iranian Women's Activist Speak?: Caught between Political Power and the 'Islamic Feminist.'. In *Gender and Sexuality in Muslim Cultures*, ed. Gul Ozyegin, 331–353. London: Routledge.

Nicholson, Helen. 2005. *Applied Drama: The Gift of Theatre*. London: Palgrave Macmillan.

Organisation for Economic Co-operation and Development. 2016. *Erfolgreiche Integration: Flüchtlinge und sonstige Schutzbedürftige*. Paris: OECD Publishing.

Pahn, Thomas. 2016. Baal novos 'Afrika!' in Lahr. Galerie: Ortenau. April 21. https://galerie-ortenau.de/html/aktuell/aktuell_u.html?&m=6277&artikel=6244&cataktuell=859&volltextstichwortsuche=Baal+novos.+Afrika%21%E2%80%9D.

Taylor, Philip. 2003. *Applied Theatre: Creating Transformative Encounters in the Community*. Portsmouth: Heinemann Publishing.

Thompson, James. 2009. *Performance Affects: Applied Theatre and the End of Effect*. London: Palgrave Macmillan.

———. 2014. *Humanitarian Performance: From Disaster Tragedies to Spectacles of War*. Chicago: University of Chicago Press.

Thompson, William E., and Joseph V. Hickey. 1999. *Society in Focus: Introduction to Sociology*. New York: Longman.

Wassermann, Felix. 2017. Das Verwischen von Staatenkrieg, Bürgerkrieg und Frieden. In *Krieg im 21. Jahrhundert, Konzepte, Akteure, Herausforderungen*, ed. Hans-Georg Ehrhart, 71–86. Baden-Baden: Nomos.

Zagato, Alessandro, ed. 2015. *The Event of Charlie Hebdo: Imaginaries of Freedom and Control*. New York: Berghahn.

Mapping Memory Routes: A Multisensory Digital Approach to Art, Migration, and Critical Heritage Studies

Alda Terracciano

The Beginnings

Mapping Memory Routes of Moroccan Communities was produced between April 2016 and March 2017 by Aldaterra Projects, an arts and heritage organization based in London, UK which I established in 2010 to deliver socially engaged artistic practice within the field of visual arts and new media, fostering international exchange and collaborations, and developing intergenerational and creative educational programs. The project was supported by the Heritage Lottery Fund, with contributions from the Centre for Critical Heritage Studies (a collaboration between Gothenburg University and University College London), and Queen Mary University of London. It was built on a model I developed in 2012 for the Living Archaeology of the Place, a community engagement program running parallel to *Streets of…7 Cities in 7 Minutes*, a multisensory art installation

A. Terracciano (✉)
University College London, London, UK
e-mail: a.terracciano@ucl.ac.uk

Y. Meerzon et al. (eds.), *Migration and Stereotypes in Performance and Culture*, Contemporary Performance InterActions,
https://doi.org/10.1007/978-3-030-39915-3_15

that opened in London during the Olympic Games. The installation represented the culmination of eight years of artistic research focusing on uncovering the ancestral memories of three migration journeys (the Indo-European migrations, the Silk Road, and the Transatlantic Slave Trade) as they unconsciously resurface in people's everyday lives, sounds, movements, and rituals across the globe. It explored the everyday lives of people historically connected by migration journeys in Naples, Shanghai, Mumbai, Tangier, Salvador de Bahia, Lisbon, and London, configuring the concept of sensorial urbanism as a "navigation mode," a safe strategy to explore the cities.[1] Far from reproducing an objective image of them, my experience of bodily interaction with place was conveyed in seven multisensory environments in which the visual featured alongside other senses, as I described in a later article:

> The artwork that emerged from the creative process asks the audience to reconsider heavily stereotyped visual and symbolic representations of the 'other', and position oneself within the 'new epistemological project' of feminist analysis (Braidotti 2011, 73). Moving from the art space to engage with other fields of knowledge production, the artwork asks to rethink issues of vision, power, and the Western gaze, and engage with a more socially inclusive understanding of urban cultures and public spaces in our pluri-cultural cities. (Terracciano 2017a, 3)

By taking audiences beyond the regime of the visual, the installation aimed to awake a critical approach to cultural stereotypes and current geopolitical divisions, exposing the complexities of mobility in relation to the formation of cross-cultural identities in Europe. As remarked by an audience member who took part in the project evaluation: "It makes people feel normal on being different, on being themselves…so they do not need to fit into a set of stereotypes"(Ardakani 2013, 21).

In order to gauge a more in-depth understanding of the impact of the installation on London's culturally diverse audiences, I devised a series of interactive Memory Sessions with people of Brazilian, Chinese, Indian, Italian, Moroccan, and Portuguese cultural backgrounds living in London. I asked participants to share their feelings, thoughts, and memories of the cities represented in the artwork. The conversations focused on old traditions, everyday rituals, and contemporary urban life, as well as personal notions of home and cultural identity. This collective act of reminiscence, which unearthed the body language, sounds, gestures, and ceremonies unique to each city, contributed to mapping out the trajectories of ancient and contemporary migration journeys, while linking together far away continents and cultures through the participants' ancestral memories of the place.[2] The result was a unique tapestry of London's cross-cultural heritage of migration via thematic areas and geographical routes.[3] The program also highlighted the importance of co-design and the application of participatory methodologies in the production of digital art projects, as some participants' feedback revealed a wish to see their personal stories included in the artwork.[4]

Radical Empathy in the Digital Archive

Mapping Memory Routes of Moroccan Communities was a response to that call. It took shape at a personal and historical conjuncture: I was researching digital economy at Queen Mary University of London when the impact of migration from war-torn Syria and the 2017 terror incidents in London and Manchester sparked severe backlash against Muslim communities in Britain (Travis 2017). At a time when European external borders were increasingly sealed off as a way of protecting local interests against unwanted waves of immigration, I decided to design a project that would use a microscopic observation of the everyday life of Muslim communities in London to uncover the interconnectedness of our histories on both sides of the Mediterranean. The employment of immersive technologies aimed to establish an intimate connection amongst otherwise divided subjectivities, counteracting the clash of ignorance and increasing resentment against Muslim people in Western countries. Drawing from relationships established by Aldaterra Projects in 2012, I invited members of the Moroccan community in West London to co-design the new activity. In particular, I worked with Al-Hasaniya Moroccan Women's Project and Making Communities Work and Grow (MCWG) to explore the use of dynamic digital tools that would facilitate access to the underlying sociocultural values and practices shaping the tangible and intangible heritage of the Moroccan community in and around Golborne Road, including both practicing Muslims and not. As described in the funding application, the aim was:

> To explore the living heritage of members of the Moroccan communities in West London through a series of memory sessions focusing on the cultural memes of their everyday life. Extracts of their personal narratives and cultural

> memories will be then shared through a digital interactive sensorial map showing Golborne Road neighbourhood, an area in North Kensington with the highest concentration of Moroccans living in London …We will collect and share Moroccan cultural memories to facilitate an understanding of the relation between people, history, movement and geographies, and offer a response to violence and fear by positioning co-curated work in relation to the richness of experiences embedded within the community. (Aldaterra Projects 2016)

The ethical stance at the core of this process stemmed from the "affective responsibility"[5] I felt towards the intangible heritage of the place. As described by Caswell and Cifor (2016, 34) in their seminal essay on archival empathy:

> By stewarding a collection, the archivist enters into a relationship of care with the record creator in which the archivist must do her best not only to empathize with the record creator, but also to allow that empathy to inform the archival decision-making processes.

Creating an oral history archive of Moroccan memories in West London required a new participant model of co-creation that would facilitate community control of the production of the records and their future display. On this basis, I designed and delivered a new series of Memory Sessions with members of the local community, affectively recreating lived, bodily experiences across time and space for the participants. The sessions facilitated a process of collective sharing of feelings, thoughts, and memories of Morocco and Golborne Road, stimulating participants' deep engagement with cultural objects to connect the past to the present through individual memory routes. A number of research questions emerged from the process, forming the basis of what would become a wider enquiry into the role of interaction design in migration studies, critical heritage, and immersive technologies. How can we build a new awareness of urban spaces that takes into account the presence of our bodies as sensors of meaning and archives of unconscious collective memories? How can migrant communities contribute to the creation of a globally connected sensorial archive and a broader, more socially inclusive understanding of heritage? In what ways can the design of an interactive, multisensory art installation engage with cultural memories, and how can we use this to critically address heavily stereotyped visual and symbolic representations of "others"?

Using this research focus, collaboration with the HCI designer Mariza Dima led to the creation of *Zelige Door on Golborne Road*, an interactive multisensory digital installation populated by artifacts, smells, tastes, and narratives of Moroccan British citizens living, working, or visiting the area. The installation, which also functioned as a digital archive of Moroccan culture in the area, aimed at creating an experience able to craft deeper connections between people, everyday life, and ancestral memories of the place. It followed the inspiration nurtured by the previous artwork *Streets of…7 Cities in 7 Minutes*, and benefited from a new collaboration with designers and olfactory technologists at Politecnico di Milano to augment the embodied experience and "negotiate notions of identity, time, presence and transmission of cultural memories through a digital interactive interface" (Terracciano et al. 2017, 354). From the point of view of its wider social engagement, the installation was designed to explore the process of gentrification in West London and its impact on the sustainability of culturally diverse intangible heritages. As pointed out by David Hill (2016) in an article published by *The Guardian* newspaper:

> Gentrification happens when the demand for living and working space outstrips its supply in cities that people want to live in…At a city-wide level, it is vital that change processes do still allow for enough diversity of income and diversity of different types of people.

This was a critical point raised by participants in the Memory Sessions, alarmed by the speed of regeneration programs in the area and the negative impact on their lives, while planners seemed unresponsive to their needs for social housing and communal spaces. As pointed out by a participant who contributed his memories of Golborne Road:

> This is the only genuine street left, because even Portobello Road is more and more commercial. The situation is that more and more local people are leaving the area because it's becoming too expensive and they build terrible things around. The corporations are trying to make profit and this is a shame. Actually they should increase this side of community, not kill it. ("Memory of Golborne Road" 2017)

In this contested space, which lacked real political thinking and action "co-produced and co-owned through dialogue across differences in experience, values, and knowledge" (Linde and Seravalli 2018, 70), community participants became living archives of a tacit, intangible heritage rashly brushed off to make space for the shining facades of the new builds in the neoliberal city. In response to this trend, the project strived to showcase unique cultural resources and facilitate the flow of information and data amongst individuals from different social and cultural backgrounds, both within and outside the local Moroccan community, so that new meanings could surface beyond social and class boundaries, as well as stereotyped notions of cultural identity. This is in line with Ketelaar's understanding of People's Archives (2003, 8):

> Being Digital entails for archives more than preserving and providing digital documents: it presents a techno-cultural challenge to connect archives with people. Archives will be redesigned as a public sphere where individual, organisational and collective memories and stories are experienced, exchanged, and enriched.

Community Participation and Socially Engaged Artistic Practice

My engagement with the Moroccan community in Golborne Road was a reaction to the Islamophobic discourse promoted by the media, often depicting Muslim people as fundamentalist warmongers with rigid interpretations of the Holy Quran's teachings; a stereotype that had managed to polarize Western public opinion in the face of increasing global conflicts, terrorism, and widespread nationalist agendas. The installation that was produced through the project responded to such a reductionist view of the Muslim "other" by creating a playful, rich, and culturally engaging virtual experience. It included testimonies from the directors of the Al-Hasaniya Moroccan Women's Project, a community centre actively involved since the late 1980s with issues of social justice and cultural emancipation against die-hard stereotypes, promoting equal opportunities amongst Arabic-speaking migrants, refugees, and asylum-seekers. The organization, which played an important role in planning, facilitated the involvement of another local organization, Making Communities Work and Grow (MCWG), a youth centre well known to people in the area, in order to succeed in the intergenerational and cross-gender ambitions of the project.

To develop new knowledge and understandings of what makes intangible heritage, participants in the sessions were invited to discuss their culture in a context that responded to their needs and interests. Between 3rd and 5th November 2016, I delivered five Memory Sessions at MCWG, as well as an open session for local residents at Goldfinger Factory, a social enterprise providing skills and training in bespoke furniture and interiors, which was also involved in the project for the production of the physical map used in the installation. An extra session was delivered to adult men on 21 November to discuss issues related to Moroccan settlement in the area and the impact of gentrification on their lives. Participants at MCWG were split into four separate groups. Eleven young women, seven young men, thirteen women, and thirteen men were eventually involved in the activities with a total of forty-four members of the local community engaged in the sessions. Of these, twenty-four participants provided written feedback and twenty-five contributed with personal narratives, which were used in the digital installation. This high level of community engagement was achieved despite the change of staff at Al-Hasaniya a week before the planned delivery of the Memory Sessions, which limited the involvement of the women visiting this centre.

As mentioned earlier, the Al-Hasaniya centre manager had suggested diversifying the social and gender composition of the project participants by involving MCWG, the local youth centre, in the activities. Although its contribution to the project initially raised some perplexities in those advocating for a more secular approach to community life, the outcomes of the project were eventually enriched by the variety of opinions that emerged from the engagement process. The complex nature of cultural and social identities that surfaced during the project development served as a critical signpost against the risk of stereotyping the community, reflecting a wider cross section of the local Moroccan cultural heritage, and contributing to a more nuanced representation in relation to class, gender, and cultural composition. This is evidenced by the participants' feedback to the Memory Sessions, which included questions on their background, personal connections to Golborne Road, links to Moroccan culture, how they experienced it in their everyday lives, whether there was a particular object that reminded them of Moroccan culture, and how they rated the event on a scale of one to ten, including what they had enjoyed most about the session. The appointed project evaluator provided a detailed quantitative and qualitative analysis of the responses in a report produced at the end of the project, which, amongst other things, highlighted how the creative activities managed to reflect and, to some degree, shift attitudes within the community (Knapp 2017c). According to the evaluator, this is a particularly valuable achievement in consideration of the way Moroccan culture organizes itself into broad gender groups, each with its own cultural prescriptions. This is in line with Fatima Sadiqi's (2008, 165) feminist analysis, suggesting that:

> Moroccan culture is of a type that strongly constrains the behaviour of men and women. The strength of this control comes from the fact that it is channelled through powerful cultural components that closely regulate the lives of Moroccan men and women.

Sadiqi's description of Moroccan social structure as a landscape of traditional values (however much they may be contested as valid or extant in contemporary society) provides a useful backdrop to illustrate the variations in each group's feedback and the patterns emerging from the answers. The first of these is that the older women, who are more likely to be married and occupying a prominent domestic role in the family unit, were almost uniform in stating that it was food, or shopping for food, that provided a means of interacting with Moroccan culture in everyday life. Although young women too provided several answers relating to food they also talked about interior design, tea, and language—answers that suggest a liberty to think about aesthetic concerns, communicating with peers, and socializing with others, considering the role of making and offering tea in Moroccan culture. Similarly, it is interesting that young women's answers to the question of what they enjoyed most about the sessions, mentioned both memory and the senses, whilst the older women only mentioned memory. The first speculative conclusion is that older women were grateful for the chance to talk about their memories, directing the conversation around what was important to them, something that may be uncommon in their everyday life. The second speculation is that the connections to Moroccan culture that the Memory Sessions focused on provided a means of transporting participants somewhere into their past. Considering the likelihood of the older women being first-generation immigrants to the UK, it appears that the sessions were successful in transporting them not just back in time to previous experiences, but also across space to Morocco, where they first experienced the smells, sounds, tastes, and textures that were discussed in the Memory Sessions. In the case of the younger women, who are more likely to be the second generation of their families to live outside of Morocco, the first time they experienced those smells, tastes, and textures may well have been in Golborne Road. This was specifically stated in one woman's memory exhibited in the installation:

> It's very interesting because my mother died when I was younger. I was like six, seven years old, and I don't remember much about it. I didn't know how to connect to Morocco because you get this through your parents, don't you? So, I didn't get that much of a connection, and on top of it I didn't go to Morocco that often. So, for me, even though I didn't go, it's like Morocco came to London. All that dried fruit hanging on the wall, the smell of cinnamon and this sort of spices made me feel very Moroccan at the same time. ("Memory of Moroccan Market in Golborne Road" 2017)

This woman's testimony shows the crucial importance of retaining culturally-specific areas in the urban landscape, as they can facilitate cultural connections for second-generation migrants and restore a sense of unity with their intangible cultural heritage.

The responses from the men who took part in the project activities also provided a counterpoint that reinforced the gender differences perpetuated in Moroccan society. When asked about how they experienced Moroccan culture in everyday life, food was mentioned, but not as much as language and cultural values, both of which are the preserve of public rather than domestic life. Language provides the basis for the economic and juridical structure for any society, which, in a patriarchal system is largely the preserve of men. Similarly, whilst it may be the role of the mother to pass on cultural traditions through the food they provide and the home they make, it is the role of the father to uphold the cultural values of the society of which any particular family unit is but one constituent part. The implicit patriarchy and sense of ownership that this entails is evident in the way men's connections to Golborne Road were explicitly concerned with "place," both in their filmed testimonies and written feedback. Their answers indicated, almost explicitly, that the attention of the camera, and the project as a whole, empowered them to express themselves about their culture, suggesting that such opportunities are rare in the public space. In this respect, it is all the more valuable that the testimonies given by the directors of the Al-Hasaniya Moroccan Women's Project also expressed strong views with regards to "place" and cultural change in the area.[6] They fall in line with a struggle against a patriarchal system these women had opposed and hoped to change for decades, clearly positioning their views against wider societal expectations.

Although these remarks were drawn from a small sample size, they offer an interesting insight into the way projects like this can empower communities and provide a public arena for cultural reflection and discourse on cultural stereotypes, which is often hard to find.[7] It also reflects the importance of taking on board "pre-existing responsibilities," including relationships, rights, and obligations bonding community participants when designing participatory projects, as discussed by Linde and Seravalli (2018, 72) in their essay on participatory design ethics:

> These preexisting responsibilities tend to end up outside the scope and aim of co-design projects, yet they play a key role in determining if and how participation can be developed within the specific project.

Participants' involvement in project activities and their positive feedback pointed to the successful creation of a critical, dialogical space that fully embraced these responsibilities. They actively contributed to the production of new knowledge, not only in the form of digital records, but of a methodology based on an ethical approach to co-design focused on mutual learning for participants, researchers, and audiences alike.

Intangible Multisensory Heritage and Augmented Reality

While the consultation process with the local Moroccan community was taking place, the project team began to work on a new design mechanism that focused on and computationally extended the haptic, olfactory, and gustatory senses to manifest the tacit intangible heritage of the involved community. The design process of the multisensory interface was first discussed in the published extended paper abstract "Mapping Memory Routes: A Multisensory Interface for Sensorial Urbanism and Critical Heritage Studies" supporting the demo presention at CHI'17 conference, and included contributions by Mariza Dima, Marina Carulli and Monica Bordegoni. See Terracciano, et al. 2017. The idea was to accustom people interacting with the digital interface with the practice of evoking ancestral memories through bodily experiences and sensory stimulation (Chang and Ishii 2006, 50–59). This led to the creation of the multisensory interactive installation *Zelige Door on Golborne Road,* co-curated with the project participants and consisting of a physical map of Golborne Road, printed on Perspex panels and populated by physical objects relating to various aspects of Moroccan intangible heritage, which I selected during the consultation process. The map worked in conjunction with a mobile device running an Augmented Reality (AR) application, enabling the playback of video memories upon tracking a marker connected to the physical object. The memories filmed at the end of the Memory Sessions were rendered in transparency in order to retain sight of the map's background. As a result, the audience interaction with people's memories, which operates through the digital interface running the AR application, allowed for manual interaction with the culturally-specific objects contained in small, traditional Moroccan pots positioned along the two sides of the map. Moreover, in addition to the haptic, sound, and gustatory stimulations, the engineers at Politecnico di Milano developed an integrated olfactory system, which was originally positioned within the frame encasing the mobile device and later in four small cylinders positioned on the two sides of the map.[8] The olfactory device was similarly activated upon tracking a small selection of markers, augmenting the interaction with the physical objects and video memories through the use of smells.

More generally, the interactive design allowed the audience to move from the objects of the installation to the space, time, and cultural significance they reflected, allowing the street to be represented as a living archive of cultural memes expressed in the form of artifacts, behaviours, smells, tastes, and narratives of citizens making up the area. Each cultural meme required a different sense to be experienced. For example, sticks of cinnamon embodied the smell of spices used in traditional Moroccan cuisine. Prayer beads invited audiences to engage with the haptic sense to explore the meaning of this traditional cultural object. Hidden memes embodied in the objects then surfaced through gestural manipulation, for example the movement of the thumb passing through prayer beads to count religious recitations, which is common to other cultures and religions. By engaging with this multisensory interface, audiences were invited to explore the geographical location more deeply, picking up the objects and experiencing their personal ancestral memories through the activation of their senses, eventually taking them beyond the time/space coordinates of the installation.

This point is evidenced by the subsequent feedback received from visitors to the installation. *Zelige Door on Golborne Road* was launched in March 2017 at Rich Mix in London, and later exhibited at the CHI

(Conference on Human Factors in Computing Systems) 2017 conference in Denver, Colorado, at the ACM Symposium on Virtual Reality Software and Technology (VRST) 2017 conference in Gothenburg, Sweden, and the Kulturhuset Blå Stället art centre located on the outskirts of the Nordic city. In February 2018, thanks to research funding granted by University College London, it was presented at the Curve Community Centre in West London to engage survivors of the Grenfell Tower fire[9] in conversations relating to their cultural belongings, settlement in the UK, and sensorial memories of the area. In May that year, it was exhibited at Tate Modern as part of the Tate Exchange program *Producing Memory: Maps, Materials, Belongings*, curated by Queen Mary University of London to explore the role of art in supporting communities facing challenges of producing and conserving home and identity in circumstances of displacement. During the week-long residency, the installation was successful in attracting a substantial number of visitors, as well as functioning as an elicitation tool to engage visitors in a new series of Memory Sessions, with the view of creating a new artwork based on London's collective memories.[10]

Feedback provided by audiences at Rich Mix and CHI 2017 supported several of the sentiments expressed in the participants' feedback forms, lending weight to the contention that feedback data provided an accurate representation of the audience as a whole. In addition to this, the interviewees at Rich Mix were asked about the relationship that digital technology created with the sensory elements of the installation. The feedback was entirely positive, with specific mention made to how the installation had managed to bring together members of the audience who did not know each other previously, facilitating conversations and cultural exchange. Others testified to the successful achievement of the project in surfacing, negotiating, and reframing assumptions about Moroccan culture. As noted by one member of the audience at Rich Mix:

> For me, it's like I've been living through two cultures all my life and I'm always asked what would define, or what object would define my culture, and that's really difficult. So to see this kind of project where they put all of them together, all the elements, and these are objects that represent all of Morocco—that's a difficult thing I think, because there is a big difference between North, East, South and West in Morocco and it's really impressive to see that all of these are common objects and really make sense. (Knapp 2017c, Appendix II, 2)

As previously discussed, this aesthetic choice reflected an attempt to defuse stereotypes within and outside the Muslim community, reflecting the complexity of cultures coalesced within the group of participants—a plurality which was conveyed by emphasizing subtleties in regional and intercontinental differences. The close, intimate cultural encounter between participants and audience via the interactive installation also allowed for a wider reflection on the geo-political role played by Morocco as an entry point to other North African cultures. As noted by an audience member:

> Immediately I wanted to delve in. I wanted to interact, I wanted to touch, I wanted to watch the video. It has a dramatic feel but also an intimate feel to it and it felt very comfortable for people to go and pick things up. So I was impressed with it as an artwork but also as a piece of engagement that was very welcoming. (Knapp 2017c, Appendix II, 3)

The comment supports an artistic attempt at using immersive technologies as a warm medium able to promote a critical exploration of the cultural heritage of everyday life. This was also confirmed by the Al-Hasaniya centre manager, who noted:

> It was interesting to see the younger people excited about how the project came to life and the technology helped with that, and it's really important in terms of preserving heritage. (Knapp 2017b)

The MCWG manager also agreed that the integration of technology helped the project appeal to younger members of the Golborne Road community and that this should become a priority in creating sustainable intercultural dialogues: "For me it's all about the young people, we need to do more for them in order for them to talk about their lives, their memories, their experiences" (Knapp 2017a). Finally, whilst audience members appreciated the novelty of the multisensory artwork, they also revealed an appetite for projects on a grander scale with several suggesting the use of more immersive technologies in future artworks.

Conclusion

To conclude, the integration and computational extension of the tactile, gustatory, and olfactory senses in the installation, together with sound and vision, underpinned a design space aimed at facilitating a deeper understanding of the cultural patterns and everyday rituals of the community involved in this project. A collective curatorial approach that led the Moroccan community to select and describe the cultural artifacts populating *Zelige Door Golborne Road* created a direct connection and extension of the curator's space to that of the participants and the wider audiences, opening up new scenarios in critical heritage and urban studies. Touch, smell, and taste were introduced to act as relays of ancestral memories, fostering intercultural dialogue, enabling a deeper sense of identity and belonging, and facilitating the envisaging of utopian urban futures.

From the point of view of its contribution to a wider discourse on curatorial activism, *Mapping Memory Routes of Moroccan Communities* is symptomatic of a turn in contemporary art towards social practice, a trend that was institutionalized in 2005 with the creation of the Social Practice MFA at the California College of the Arts and has since dynamically increased globally. As noted in the project evaluation, amongst the most renowned artists associated with socially engaged practice are the Chicago-based artist Theaster Gates, winner of the Artes Mundi prize in 2013, and the London-based collective Assemble, winners of the 2015 Turner prize. While these artists were primarily concerned with urban renewal and revitalizing economies in disaffected communities, projects aimed specifically at developing a deep and nuanced understanding of the intangible urban heritage in the context of regeneration plans are still making their way into the mainstream public consciousness of contemporary art.

Another comparable trend is the turn towards archival practices in the digital art space. Artists such as Akram Zaatari, co-founder of the Arab Image Foundation, and Yto Barrada, founder of the Cinémateque de Tangier, have significantly contributed to a critical discourse on the use of archival material in artists' moving image practice. However, most of the projects that derive from these practices are generally aimed at recovering cultural figures or activities from the past often ignored by historians, or at examining constructions of "the self" by using personal and interpersonal archives, often set against the socio-political contradictions in contemporary society. The artwork produced through *Mapping Memory Routes* is distinct in that it created an archive which sat firmly within the dialogues that produced the oral history and socially engaged practice, engaging participants in the role of co-designers of an immersive, interactive artwork aimed at promoting social change. More generally, the project demonstrated the potential for a democratic, collective process of knowledge production in heritage and urban studies, advocating the need for researching, preserving, curating, and exhibiting stories that risk otherwise being lost or going unheard in the contemporary public debate on urban regeneration.[11] It was a pilot for wider artistic practice research to collect and creatively share the voices of London's citizens, and create a public history archive open to wider uses in education and research. The collective co-creation of the installation showed that feelings, imaginaries, and sensorial memories are part of the "archival multiverse" (McKemmish et al. 2016), and that the body itself can be considered an archive of collective cultural memories and practices. At the same time, the production of new Memory Sessions at Tate Modern reflected the cumulative nature of the process, as the interactive installation functioned as an elicitation tool for the production of new archival records, an "active agent and co-creator" of potential new work.

Finally, the project represented an attempt to set up a new space for socially engaged artistic practice in the neoliberal city, by positioning migrant communities at the centre of the critical dialogue on urban geography, architecture, heritage studies, and contemporary art. The effectiveness of the attempt was manifested in an episode that took place at the launch of the installation at Rich Mix. Having been invited to co-host the evening with members of the project team, some of the Moroccan women who had participated in the Memory Sessions prepared Moroccan mint tea and cakes for the audience. The MCWG centre manager had rented a small bus to bring the women to the event, which was attended by an audience including other first and second-generation Moroccans living in the UK, artists, academics, and members of the general public. When the evening light began to fade into the darkness of the night, the women collected their belongings, said goodbye to the project team, and walked unobserved towards the exit door. It was at that moment that the sound of their voices rose above the buzzing noise of the room; it was an ululation, a long, wavering, high-pitched vocal sound traditionally performed by women in the Middle East and North Africa at weddings and funerals. As silence fell upon the room, everybody turned towards the women gathered in a circle at the exit door, unexpectedly transported to another space and time through the spontaneous performance of this traditional ritual.

Having co-owned the artwork and the space of the exhibition, they felt comfortable sharing their lived experience with strangers, in the same way they would have done in a more familiar setting. This marked an important moment in the project, as it showed how mutual learning and collective critical thinking can support professionals, participants, and audiences in addressing complex issues beyond stereotyped representations of cultural identities, and create the space for a "heritage common" where power can be equally shared and new collective knowledge democratically produced.

Notes

1. On the issue of how sensorial urbanism theory is reflected in the artistic research practice that led to the creation of the installation, see Terracciano 2017a.
2. For a more detailed description of the Memory Sessions, see Terracciano 2017b.
3. Extracts of the Memory Sessions are available online at Living Archaeology of the Place, www.aldaterra.com.
4. In her recommendations about future developments, the evaluator pointed out that those engaged in the Memory Sessions would have liked their video recordings to become a more integral part of the exhibition. She suggested: "The exhibition can become more interactive on a community level by allowing more opportunities for creative community workshops and engagement events such as the Artists Salon and memory sessions. These events would further strengthen the link between the community members, provide more opportunities for intercultural exchange, critical thinking about the various socio political and social change aspects of the programme and build stronger relationships with members of the intercultural community" (Ardakani 2013, 31).
5. I was alerted to this feminist approach in the archiving practice by Astrid von Rosen, co-leader of the Centre for Critical Heritage Studies at Gothenburg University.
6. Amongst these memories, see "Memory of Coriander" at www.aldaterra.com.
7. On issues concerning the production of data in community projects, see Taylor et al. 2015.
8. This second option was developed by the Politecnico di Milano engineers for the presentation of the installation at Tate Modern in May 2018.
9. In the early hours of Wednesday, 14 June 2017, a fridge freezer caught fire in a flat on the 4th floor of a 24-storey residential tower block in the afflu-

ent area of North Kensington. The fire caused severe damage to the 1970s building and killed 72 people, spurring an enquiry by the government into "the circumstances surrounding the fire," including its causes, and why it spread so quickly through the largely combustible cladding system that had been installed during the building's renovation in 2016. Grenfell United, the group representing the survivors and bereaved, has since then advocated for the investigation to uncover the responsibilities of the owner of the building, the Royal Borough of Kensington and Chelsea, the landlord, the architects, and the suppliers to find out whether or not Grenfell Tower met building regulations, something residents had been disputing well before this deadly fire. See https://www.grenfelltowerinquiry.org.uk.

10. For a discussion on the creation of digital collective memories, see Steels and Tisselli 2008.
11. For a discussion on critical approaches in community research practice, see Harding et al. 2015; and Rishbeth and Powell 2013.

References

Aldaterra Projects. 2016. HLF Application Form: Mapping Memory Routes of Moroccan Communities in London.

Ardakani, Azadeh. 2013. *Aldaterra Projects Evaluation Report*. Aldaterra Projects.

Braidotti, Rosy. 2011. *Nomadic theory: the portable Rosy Braidotti*. New York: Columbia University Press.

Caswell, Michelle, and Marika Cifor. 2016. From Human Rights to Feminist Ethics: Radical Empathy in the Archives. *Archivaria* 81 (Spring): 23–43.

Chang, Angela, and Hiroshi Ishii. 2006. *"Sensorial Interfaces". Proceedings of the 6th Conference on Designing Interactive Systems*, 50–59. New York: ACM.

Harding, Mike, et al. 2015. *"Civic Engagement & Trust." Proceedings of the 33rd Annual ACM Conference on Human Factors in Computing Systems*, 2833–2842. New York: ACM.

Hill, Dave. 2016. London Gentrification: Clichés and Conundrums (and Hipsters). *The Guardian*. December18. www.theguardian.com/uk-news/davehill-blog/2016/dec/18/london-gentrification-cliches-and-conundrums-and-hipsters. Accessed 4 Feb 2019.

Ketelaar, Eric. 2003. Being Digital in People's Archives. *Archives & Manuscripts* 31 (2): 8–22.

Knapp, Ivan. 2017a. *Interview with Abderrahman Elguerbouzi*. Aldaterra Projects. March 28.

———. 2017b. *Interview with Asma Dukali*. Aldaterra Projects. March 29.

———. 2017c. *Mapping Memory Routes Evaluation Report*. Aldaterra Projects.

Linde, Per, and Anna Seravalli. 2018. Between Empowerment and Exploitation: PD Ethics in the Era of Participation. *IX Interaction* XXV (6): 70–73.

McKemmish, Sue, et al. 2016. *Research in the Archival Multiverse*. Clayton, Australia: Monash University Publishing.

"Memory of Golborne Road." 2017. Aldaterra. www.aldaterra.com/items/golborne-road. Accessed 4 Feb 2019.

"Memory of Moroccan Market in Golborne Road." 2017. Aldaterra. www.aldaterra.com/items/market. Accessed 4 Feb 2019.

Rishbeth, Clare, and Mark Powell. 2013. Place Attachment and Memory: Landscapes of Belonging as Experienced Post-migration. *Landscape Research* 38 (2): 160–178.

Sadiqi, Fatima. 2008. Gender Perception in Moroccan Culture: Cultural and Civilizational Realities. In *Cultural and Civilisational Realities*, ed. Abdelhak Azzouzi, 165–189. Paris: L'Harmattan.

Steels, Luc, and Eugenio Tisselli. 2008. Social Tagging in Community Memories. *Papers from the 2008 AAAI Spring Symposium, Conference: Social Information Processing, Technical Report SS-08-06*, 98-103. www.aaai.org/Papers/Symposia/Spring/2008/SS-08-06/SS08-06-019.pdf.

Taylor, Alex S., et al. 2015. *"Data-in-Place: Thinking through the Relations Between Data and Community." Proceedings of the 33rd Annual ACM Conference on Human Factors in Computing Systems*, 2863–2872. New York: ACM.

Terracciano, Alda. 2017a. 7 Cities in 7 Minutes: A Feminine Paradigm of Sensory Art. *Body, Space & Technology Journal*16(2).

———. 2017b. Streets of…: A Multi-sensory Experience of 7 Cities in 7 Minutes. In *Memories of a City*, ed. Jonathan Westin and Ingrid Martins Holmberg, 17–35. Gothenburg: University of Gothenburg.

Terracciano, Alda, et al. 2017. Mapping Memory Routes: A Multisensory Interface for Sensorial Urbanism and Critical Heritage Studies. In *CHI'17 Extended Abstracts*, 353–356. New York: ACM.

Travis, Alan. 2017. Anti-Muslim Hate Crime Surges After Manchester and London Bridge Attacks. *The Guardian*. June 20. www.theguardian.com/society/2017/jun/20/anti-muslim-hate-surges-after-manchester-and-london-bridge-attacks. Accessed 4 Feb 2019.

Index[1]

[1] Note: Page numbers followed by 'n' refer to notes.

Y. Meerzon et al. (eds.), *Migration and Stereotypes in Performance and Culture*, Contemporary Performance InterActions,
https://doi.org/10.1007/978-3-030-39915-3

CPI Antony Rowe
Chippenham, UK
2020-12-22 12:42

CONFETTIREGEN

SPLINTER
CHABOT

CONFETTI REGEN

Spectrum

Uitgeverij Unieboek | Het Spectrum bv

Spectrum maakt deel uit van Uitgeverij Unieboek | Het Spectrum bv,
Amstelplein 32
1096 BC Amsterdam

Eerste druk 3 maart 2020
Tweede druk maart 2020
Derde druk maart 2020
Vierde druk maart 2020

Omslagontwerp: Anton Corbijn
Uitvoering: Yaël Temminck © Antonymous BV
Auteursfoto: Anton Corbijn

Redactie: Jelte Nieuwenhuis
Afwerking omslag: DPS Design & Prepress Studio, Amsterdam
Ontwerp schutbladen: Schilderij Splinter Chabot
Fotograaf schutbladen: Ali Mousavi
Opmaak: Elgraphic

Dit boek is een gefictionaliseerde weergave van een leven vol fantasie, verbeelding en confettiregen.

ISBN 978 90 00 37063 4
ISBN 978 90 00 37064 1 (e-book)
NUR 320

www.spectrumnonfictie.nl

Zekerheid: 'Waarom draag je geen horloge?'
Worsteling: 'Omdat ik tijdloos ben.'

Rebel rebel, you've torn your dress
Rebel rebel, your face is a mess
Rebel rebel, how could they know?
Hot tramp, I love you so!

David Bowie

I just can't believe all the things people say
Controversy
Am I black or white, am I straight or gay?
Controversy
~
Some people want to die so they can be free

Prince

INHOUD

WOORD VOORAF

Een politiek pamflet schrijven: dat had ik me voorgenomen. Klimaat, duurzaamheid, internationalisering, digitalisering, technologie – bezien vanuit een jeugdig gezichtspunt. Een stem van een nieuwe generatie. Maar dat is dit verhaal niet geworden.

Er kwam iets anders naar voren. Als ik ging tikken kon ik maar over één ding schrijven. Zoals de schilderijen van William Turner een gloeiend licht laten zien, alsof hij de zon heeft kunnen vangen, zo krachtig gloeide dit verhaal in mij. Waardoor ik uiteindelijk niks anders uit mijn beringde vingers kon krijgen dan dit boek. Dit is een portret van Wobie. Van zijn worsteling, van zijn kwetsbaarheid, van zijn twijfels. Het is het portret van een innerlijke reis die hij af heeft gelegd. Een innerlijke reis die hem kilometers ver voerde zonder dat hij ook maar een stap hoefde te zetten. Een reis die ikzelf ook aflegde.

Het is een verhaal geworden over anders zijn. Over het verschil tussen *gekozen* anders zijn en *gedwongen* anders zijn. Daar ligt de essentie. Zelfs als iedereen in je omgeving het prima vindt wat je doet of hoe je bent, dat je anders bent, tóch zul je enorm worstelen. Omdat je er niet zelf voor hebt gekozen.

Dit is het dagboek van die worsteling. Voor hen die zelf ook worstelen, maar misschien bovenal voor de jongeren die aan de zoektocht moeten beginnen of er nog middenin zitten en het fijn vinden om er – al dan niet stiekem – vast over te lezen. Ik vind dat twijfels, kwetsbaarheid en worstelingen misschien een groter podium verdienen dan ze vandaag de dag krijgen.

Zij die anders zijn brengen een samenleving vooruit, geven haar kleur. Zij die anders zijn, zij die tegen de stroom in durven gaan, moeten we omarmen. Omdat ze een samenleving vleugels geven. Omdat ze in staat zijn de onzichtbare regels, kettingen en wetten ervan te doorbreken.

Misschien is het dan toch een politiek verhaal, met als onderwerp datgene wat een samenleving nodig heeft om ook echt te kunnen samenleven – vrijheid. Vrijheid om te zijn wie je diep vanbinnen écht bent. In alle kleuren, facetten en diversiteit.

Ik ben Wobie. In mijn wereld regent het glitter en confetti. Vaak knetteren er kerstlichtjes in mijn hoofd, maar soms vindt er ook kortsluiting plaats. Als kind vond ik de wereld wonderlijk, als volwassene nog steeds. Ik huppel, ik spring, ik hou van vrolijkheid en kleur. Maar ik heb ook lang gezocht en geworsteld. Ondanks de steun van mijn omgeving. Maar voordat ik aan mijn ontdekkingsreis begon, mocht ik eerst genieten van mijn jeugd. Mijn wereld was klein, ik kende de wereld buiten mijn directe omgeving niet, zoals de wereld ook mij nog niet kende.

DEEL 1
DAVID

1.

Ik was een jongetje met bruine krullige haren en groeide op in een gezin met drie andere broers en een hond. Het huis waarin we woonden was een kruising tussen dat van Pippi Langkous en Pipo de Clown. Maar dan chiquer. Deftiger. En met een vleugje Alice in Wonderland. Muren waren geschilderd in opvallende kleuren: geel, oranje, lichtroze, donkerder roze. Overal stonden meubelen met tierelantijnen. Elke stoel, elke deur, elke spiegel, elke tafel: alles moest ornamenten bevatten – dat leek de eis voor dit huis te zijn geweest. Had een meubel versieringen, vreemde kronkels en gekke draaiingen – zag het er kunstig maar in een bepaalde setting hartstikke kitscherig uit? Dan vond het een plek in het huis. Bijna vanzelf. Meubels werden niet aangeschaft omdat ze nodig waren of op een bepaalde plek dienden te staan, nee, ze werden gekocht omdat ze hier hun thuis zouden vinden. Alsof het dieren uit een asiel waren die gered moesten worden.

Daardoor was het bij ons altijd een beetje kerst. Anderen zouden het misschien een grote rommel noemen en een inbreker zou denken dat een collega hem vóór was geweest, maar voor ons was het bovenal een gezellige, veilige hemel. Elk jaar beloofden we aan elkaar dat we zouden opruimen, maar gelukkig gebeurde dat nooit. Al die spullen herbergden herinneringen of dienden als attributen voor de rijke fantasieën van mij en mijn broers. Had niet elk ding een eigen verhaal en verleden? Als een ontdekkingsreiziger kon je thuis op onderzoek uitgaan. Want wat was een houten engel voor een kind? Dat was een magisch wezen waar je hele verhalen omheen kon verzinnen. Je hoopte dat je het moment zou meemaken dat de engel tot leven zou komen. Dat opeens, vanuit het niets, langzaam de vleugels zouden gaan klapperen en de engel het tafelblad los zou laten, je een kus op je neus zou geven en via de balkondeuren naar buiten zou vliegen.

Ik was zo'n kind dat eindeloos naar die engel kon kijken. Zo'n kind dat zeker wist dat de knuffels 's nachts tot leven kwamen en me beschermden tegen het kwaad van het donkere buiten. Ik geloofde dat ik een verbond met de zon had. En met de wind. Dat ik met ze kon praten. Ook al gaven ze geen antwoord. Onderweg naar paardrijles of vioolles sprak ik de wind maar al te vaak toe. Eerst vermanend omdat hij te hard blies en ik maar langzaam vooruitkwam. Als hij dan braaf was gaan liggen, beloonde ik hem met lieve woorden. Vaak was hij dan maar heel even rustig, zodat ik hem opnieuw woest moest toespreken. Dit kat-en-muisspel ging vaak door totdat ik bezweet bij mijn bestemming aankwam.

Mijn drie broers en ik hadden allemaal eigen hobby's, een eigen lievelingsdier en een eigen lievelingskleur. Hoewel we van de buitenkant op elkaar leken was ons innerlijk verschillend. Dat was fijn, die verschillen. Alle vier mochten we ons uitleven en onze kamers inrichten zoals we wilden, waardoor elke kamer ieders eigen persoonlijkheid weerspiegelde. Als zielen verbonden in een huis. In de slaapkamer op de tweede verdieping hadden de knuffels als een tsunami de bedden overgenomen. Op de derde etage sliepen de twee oudste broers. Beide kamers waren netjes. In de ene was het zo netjes dat het binnenvallende licht vrij spel had en in de andere stond een voetbaltafel en was de hoek van de vloer bezaaid met legerpoppetjes. Klaar in een houding om te vechten, maar vechten deden ze daar nooit. Daar sliep de oudste broer van het gezin. Mijn oudste broer. Omdat hij de oudste was keken wij automatisch tegen hem op. Ik was dol op hem.

Mijn jongste broertje en ik deelden de kamer op de tweede verdieping. Daar heerste een speelgoedregime. Zo'n kamer zou ik ieder kind toewensen. Het was een kamer waarin mijn kant helemaal roze mocht zijn.

Mijn jongste broertje en ik werden in het gezin steevast 'de kleintjes' genoemd. Iets wat we niet zo fijn vonden, want als je klein bent wil je groot zijn. We scheelden nog geen jaar en sliepen sinds zijn geboorte bij elkaar op de kamer.

Eigenlijk was er nóg een broer. Een heel veel oudere broer. Dat was onze vader. Die was vrijwel altijd thuis. Aan het werk, aan het schrijven in zijn schrijfkamer. Een piepklein kamertje waar de gordijnen nooit open waren. Zo kon hij zich afsluiten van de buitenwereld. Dan kon hij eindeloos ronddwalen in zijn hoofd, in de fantasiewereld waar hij verhalen vond en naar het hier en nu bracht met pen en papier. Tikkend achter z'n laptop alsof het altijd regende. Schrijversregen. Als je dat hoorde wist je dat het goed ging, dat die nieuwe fantasiewereld in rap tempo vorm kreeg. Om zo op een ander moment weer anderen te betoveren. Al op jonge leeftijd leerde ik dat het maken van kunst in eenzaamheid plaatsvindt. Dat werd altijd extra goed zichtbaar als een van ons 's avonds zijn kamer verliet. Onze slaapkamer grensde aan de gang met de schrijfkamer. Als we stilletjes naar de gang slopen konden we papa zien werken. We zagen hem gebogen over zijn toetsenbord, alsof de fantasie een last voor hem was. Zoals Atlas de werkelijke wereld droeg, zo droeg papa de wereld van de magie. Door de gesloten gordijnen leek hij meer schaduw dan mens.

De gang naar de schrijfkamer was extra smal geworden doordat er een stuk of vijftien verhuisdozen stonden opgestapeld. In de jaren waarin we opgroeiden bleven de dozen onuitgepakt. Ze staan daar inmiddels zo lang dat zelfs mijn ouders niet meer weten wat erin verborgen zit. En eigenlijk kunnen we ze maar beter ook niet meer uitpakken, dat kan alleen maar teleurstellen. Onuitgepakte verrassingen zijn misschien wel de mooiste, omdat ze nog alles kunnen zijn, nog alles kunnen worden.

Op de vloer van de schrijfkamer lagen ladingen interviews, krantenartikelen en tijdschriften. Vaak stukken waarin mijn vader zelf stond. Een papieren tapijt van dat wat hij gezegd had in het verleden. Zo werd dat verleden langzaam verscheurd, want telkens als hij zijn schrijfkamer binnenstapte of een van ons hem een kus kwam geven, werd het beschadigd. Net als herinneringen werd zo ook wat gezegd was steeds vager en vager.

Als mijn broertje en ik niet op school waren, bij andere kinderen speelden of boven zaten te kijken naar onze broer die bezig was met een computerspel, brachten we tijd door in onze kamer. Het voordeel van samen een kamer delen was dat er altijd iemand was om mee te spelen. En als een van de twee speelgoed kreeg gingen we er allebei op vooruit. We deelden ons speelgoed altijd, zo vaak en zo veel dat we op den duur vergaten van wie nou precies wat was.

Mijn jongste broertje en ik hadden allebei een lievelingsknuffel, die altijd op ons bed stond. Als ik een nachtmerrie had kroop ik dichter tegen mijn knuffel aan. Gooide ik een deken over hem heen, zodat we samen konden schuilen. Mijn knuffel was een tijger. Een liggende tijger met z'n hoofd fier en krachtig omhoog. De tijger had een naam: Tijger. Ik was dol op Tijger. Ik wist zeker dat hij wakker werd als ik 's avonds ging slapen, stiekem over me heen sloop en alles in het huis in de gaten hield. Ik verdacht hem er zelfs van dat hij stiekem op het balkon kwam. Verboden terrein voor mijn broertje en mij. Maar dat zou ik mijn ouders niet vertellen, want Tijger kwam daar alleen om het gezin te beschermen. Als ik naar school ging liep Tijger mee. In mijn gedachten zag ik dat hij mee de straat overstak, vast vooruit rende over de stoep en langs de raamkozijnen sprong. Tijger ging overal mee naartoe. Dat voelde veilig en fijn.

Ook mijn broertje had een lievelingsdier. Dat was Leeuw. Overdag zat hij gevangen in een soortgelijke houding als Tijger. Tijger en Leeuw waren een soort broertjes. In de weekenden, als mijn broertje en ik in de ochtend te vroeg wakker waren geworden, konden we zomaar opeens bedenken dat Tijger of Leeuw jarig was. Tijger kon zo zes of negen keer per jaar jarig zijn, net als Leeuw. We hadden toen nog geen idee waar een verjaardag eigenlijk voor diende. We dachten dat het gewoon een leuk feestje was, waarbij je aandacht kreeg en alles mocht kiezen. Keizer voor een dag. Waarom je niet vaker per jaar jarig kon zijn, dat wilden we niet begrijpen. Maar dat konden we wel regelen voor Tijger en Leeuw. Vaak genoeg sprongen we 's ochtends uit bed, zochten we tussen ons speelgoed naar cadeautjes, wikkelden die in wit papier en legden die op bed. Als Tijger jarig was, werd hij uitgenodigd in het bed van Leeuw; als Leeuw jarig was, was hij welkom in Tijgers bed. Samen zaten we dan op de dekens, zetten alle andere knuffels in een kring, versierden de hele kamer met slingers en kleurtjes en lieten de jarige knuffel dan het feest betreden. Vervolgens pakten we de cadeaus uit, en wat er ook in zat, Tijger en Leeuw waren altijd blij.

Mijn broertje en ik hadden ook weleens ruzie. Op een ochtend liep een ruzie hoog op. Mijn broertje greep zijn luier vast, trok die uit, zwaaide hem drie keer boven zijn hoofd en wierp hem toen met een enorme vaart naar de andere kant van de kamer. De luier knalde tegen het stalen frame van de roze klamboe en plofte uit elkaar. Het sneeuwde beplaste luierstukjes. Overal waar je keek kwamen kleine stukjes naar beneden gedwarreld. Een luierlawine. Het glinsterde gelig in het zonlicht. Sommige stukken waren groot, sommige piepklein. We keken elkaar aan, waren even muisstil en barstten daarna in lachen uit. Het enige wat ik ondertussen deed was Tijger in veiligheid brengen. Die kon er per slot van rekening niks aan doen en verdiende het niet om onder eindeloos veel kleine ministukjes pisluier te worden bedolven.

Er woonde ook 'een zusje' bij ons. Het zusje hield van roze. Het zusje had een roze klamboe, een roze dekbed, een zee van knuffels, een roze poef: een suikerspin om in te kunnen leven. Roze rees boven alle andere kleuren uit.

Ik was het zusje. Ik was het zusje niet maar werd dat soms wel. Hij heel even een zij. Tot zusje gemaakt door de opmerkingen of de vragen van een ander, door de buitenwereld, terwijl de binnenwereld nog nietsvermoedend zat te spelen. De buitenwereld legde bloot wat nog niet blootgelegd hoefde te worden.

'Hebben jullie een zusje?' De eerste keer dat iemand dat vroeg was er niet veel aan de hand. Ik sprong achter mijn bureau vandaan en gaf aan dat het mijn bed was, met mijn spullen. De verwarring in de ogen heb ik altijd onthouden. Ik begreep de blik niet maar voelde hem wel. Die blik bleef kauwgombalachtig plakken. Telkens als er sindsdien iemand kort langskwam en onze kamer in moest, dreunde die zin naar binnen. Voor de buitenwereld was er altijd een paar seconden een zusje. Terwijl ik helemaal geen zusje wilde zijn.

2.

In groep drie moest ik een spreekbeurt geven. Iets waar ik meestal goed in was, want praten vond ik leuk. Tot ergernis van de juffen en meesters deed ik dat aan een stuk door. Met als gevolg dat ik tijdens mijn basisschooltijd meer op de gang stond dan in de klas zat. Als ik terugdenk aan die tijd zie ik die stille gangen zo weer voor me. De gangen waar stilte kon echoën. De gangen waar je perfect tikkertje zou kunnen spelen, maar helaas werd alleen ik er altijd alleen uitgestuurd. Ik moest wachten totdat klasgenootjes naar de wc gingen en dan stiekem wat langer met mij zouden blijven praten. Soms had ik het idee dat ze expres deden alsof ze veel en vaak naar de wc moesten, zodat ik daar niet zo lang in mijn eentje stond. Ik vond het lief van mijn klas. Het was een klein en stil protest, een kinderrebellie tegen de macht van de juf of meester. Ik was het type leerling van wie docenten het vooral áchteraf leuk vonden dat ik bij ze in de klas had gezeten. Als ik een spreekbeurt gaf had ik het gevoel dat ik het een beetje goed kon maken. Dan kon ik doen wat ik toch al de hele dag deed: tegen de klas babbelen. Maar dan zonder dat het me straf opleverde.

Deze keer koos ik een onderwerp waarbij ik zou merken dat niet iedereen altijd maar mee kan huppelen met de fantasie die jij in je hoofd hebt. Mijn spreekbeurt ging over Tijger. Die ging al jarenlang overal mee naartoe, dus er viel meer dan genoeg over te vertellen. Op de ochtend zelf had ik zijn haren geknipt, zodat hij er perfect uit zou zien. Tijger mocht die dag namelijk écht mee naar de school, niet alleen in mijn gedachten, maar ook in mijn armen. Onderweg naar school kwamen we een grote Deense dog tegen die hard begon te blaffen. Zie je wel, dacht ik, ik wist het wel, die hond herkent Tijger natuurlijk van de nacht, dan komen ze elkaar vast tegen. Maar Tijger vertrok geen spier. Dat vond ik een beetje flauw van hem, maar aan de andere kant begreep ik het ook weer wel; mijn broertje en mijn vader waren erbij en die mochten niet weten wat Tijger en ik geheimhielden voor de rest van de grotemensenwereld.

Met Tijger op de stoel naast me begon ik aan mijn verhaal. 'Dit is een tijger, dit is mijn tijger en deze tijger heet Tijger.' Ik keek naar de klas en vervolgens naar Tijger. Maar die bewoog niet. Sprong niet op. Deed geen kunstje. Waarom niet? Waarom deed Tijger niks? Ik begreep er niks van. In de hoop hem in beweging te kunnen brengen pakte ik zijn stoffen halsband. 'Dit is de halsband van Tijger. Liever laat ik hem vrij rondrennen, maar voor de zekerheid doe ik hem nu even om, kijk maar.' Eigenlijk was het een hoofdwarmer voor tijdens de winter, maar dat wist ik niet. Aan de halsband had ik een miniradio hangen, zo eentje die je bij je Happy Meal kreeg. Als je op het knopje drukte kwam er muziek uit. Tijger reageerde niet op de halsband, dus in een uiterste poging drukte ik op die knop. Uit het plastic speelgoed schalde muziek. Maar waar het thuis heel hard klonk, klonk het in het lokaal juist leeg en stil.

Ik keek weer de klas in, zag afwachtende blikken. Ik wist dat ik ze zou moeten teleurstellen. Ik had alles geprobeerd, maar Tijger was niet in beweging gekomen. Ik begon langzaam te snikken.

Gelukkig greep de juffrouw in. Ik mocht bij haar op schoot. En we begonnen opnieuw. Ze stelde vragen over Tijger. Wat voor dier het was, wat hij at, waar hij vandaan kwam. Ik kon het haar allemaal vertellen. Het was een knuffeldier. Hij at stiekem in de avond, ik vermoedde uit de ijskast, maar voor de zekerheid legde ik stiekem in een servet altijd een beetje van mijn avondeten in de prullenbak, zodat Tijger het daar kon vinden. Als het zuurkool was, kreeg hij heel veel. Waren het sperziebonen met rijst en pindasaus, dan kreeg hij een stuk minder. Maar ik had hem nooit horen klagen, dus dat vond hij vast niet erg. Ook op de vraag waar hij vandaan kwam, kon ik antwoord geven. Hij kwam bij papa en mama vandaan. Die hadden hem gegeven. Of ze hem *gemaakt* hadden? Nee. Tijger was er, realiseerde ik me. Gewoon opeens. Ik bedacht me dat hij gewoon op een avond ons huis binnen moest zijn geslopen en dat mijn ouders hem vonden en aan mij gaven.

De juf keek me een beetje vreemd aan, maar vond het toch wel een mooi verhaal, geloof ik. De blikken in de klas fonkelden. Ik wist het zeker, ze wilden allemaal zo'n Tijger hebben en zouden die vroeg of laat vast en zeker ook krijgen. Hoewel Tijger mij een beetje in de steek had gelaten, was ik niet boos en vergaf ik het hem direct.

3.

Ik was jarig, ik werd zes. Het huis sliep, maar ik was klaarwakker. Aan zijn ogen zag ik dat Tijger me feliciteerde. Ik bleef liggen wachten totdat het licht op de gang aanging. Vervolgens zou dan het licht in de badkamer aangaan en papa's of mama's hoofd om het hoekje verschijnen – en dan was ook voor de rest van de wereld mijn verjaardag begonnen. Of op z'n minst voor de rest van dit huis. Ik kon niet wachten. Als iemand jarig was, mochten er ballonnen en slingers worden opgehangen. Mocht er worden gezongen en kaarsjes worden uitgeblazen. Kon confetti door de lucht zweven. Ik wilde dat er elke dag iemand jarig was in huis, zodat elke dag bijzonder zou zijn en elke dag versierd mocht worden.

Het eerste licht ging aan. Het tweede licht ging aan. De deur werd geopend. Papa's hoofd kwam het hoekje om. Iets moeilijker te herkennen dan normaal, want zijn bril ontbrak. 'Er is iemand jarig!' Ook papa had zin in deze dag, dat was duidelijk. Klaarwakker sprong ik op en ging mee. Op je verjaardag werd je opgehaald en mocht je bij mama en papa komen. De grote slaapkamer met in het midden het grote zachte bed waar zij samen in sliepen. Je mocht nooit het bed in. Óf je mocht op de rand gaan zitten, óf je bleef staan, maar ín bed – dat behoorde niet tot de mogelijkheden. Behalve als je jarig was, dan was alles anders. Dan mocht je als feestvarken het bed in kruipen, naar het midden. Rechts zat mama, links zat papa en jij als jarige zat daar veilig tussenin. Ik genoot van het klauteren over de dekens, het dekbed, de kussens. Het leek wel een eindeloze slaapwolk.

Mijn jongste broertje was direct meegegaan. Al even blij. Stiekem hoopte hij vast op veel speelgoed, zodat we na school samen konden spelen. De andere broers waren inmiddels ook opgestaan en namen plaats rondom het bed. Aan het voeteneinde lagen de cadeaus. Zoals altijd prachtig ingepakt – mijn moeder maakte daar serieus werk van. Alsof de pakjes onderling ook een feestje te vieren hadden. Sommige zaten in een glitterverpakking, op andere waren vlinders geplakt, of bloemen. Weer andere waren versierd met grote strikken. Een cadeautjesbal. Een deel van de verpakking en versiersels herkende ik – mama had de gewoonte om inpakpapier en linten die ze mooi vond opnieuw te gebruiken.

Voordat ik de pakjes mocht uitpakken, werd er gezongen. Met volle overtuiging, al kon niemand echt zingen. Toch glom ik. Ik keek naar papa, naar mama, ik was jarig. Vandaag mocht ik verzinnen en bedenken wat ik wilde. Vandaag was alles leuk en vrolijk. Vandaag zou de zon schijnen in huis en daarbuiten, ook als de zon zou besluiten om niet te schijnen.

Tussen al die pakjes, in allerlei soorten en maten, lag een klein, rechthoekig cadeautje. Mama had het extra mooi versierd. Er zaten glitters en steentjes op, een lint én een vlinder. Meestal had ze zich beperkt tot één versiersel, maar dit cadeau had het allemaal. Alsof het extra bijzonder was. Een extra belangrijk cadeau. Een primus inter pares.

Ik pakte het uit, gespannen, maar bovenal ontzettend nieuwsgierig. Wat zouden mama en papa in deze verpakking verstopt hebben? Mijn kleine vingers scheurden het papier voorzichtig open. Ik kon niet wachten, maar versnelde toch niet, omdat ik de nieuwsgierigheid heerlijk vond. Langzaam kwam een kartonnen velletje tevoorschijn. Toen ik het omdraaide, zag ik wat ik gekregen had. Ik bleef kijken, zonder iets te zeggen. Het cadeau was prachtig.

Het was een rechthoekig kartonnetje met daarop allemaal verschillende plastic plakoorbellen en plastic ringen. Zilver, roze, met glitter en glinster. Sommige hadden de vorm van een dier, zoals een zeepaardje of een zeester. Andere waren rond of rechthoekig. Ik was dolblij, hield het in de lucht en keek naar mijn broers. Kijk!

Na het uitpakken van de cadeautjes kleedde ik me zo snel als ik kon aan, ik wilde terug naar mijn cadeau. Frisgewassen en in mijn verjaardagskleren pakte ik het kartonnetje en liep naar de spiegel in de badkamer. Het voelde alsof ik eindeloos naar dit moment had uitgekeken! Ik nam het eerste setje en plakte die op mijn oren. Daar zaten ze. In de spiegel zag ik mijn versierde zelf. Die twee zilveren plastic plakoorbellen, alsof ze daar altijd al hadden gehoord. Nu was ik zowel vanbinnen als vanbuiten écht jarig.

Ik liep de trap af naar de eerste verdieping, klaar voor het feestontbijt. De eettafel was een grote pingpongwedstrijdtafel. Hoe onze ouders eraan waren gekomen, wisten we niet, maar we aten er al jaren aan. Hij was gigantisch, we konden er makkelijk met z'n zessen aan eten. In het midden stond een kaarsencircus. Ik nam plaats op mijn verjaardagstroon.

Na het ontbijt werden mijn broertje en ik aan de hand van onze vader naar school gebracht. Mijn vaders hand was een lieve hand, eentje waarin mijn vingers veilig gevangen waren. Het was een hand die me op dit soort dagen veilig naar school bracht. Bij het schoolplein liet hij ons los. In de klas mocht ik op de stoel gaan staan, vuurtorenhoog, en werd er voor me gezongen. Na het zingen mocht ik trakteren, mama had een grote rieten mand met linten versierd en gevuld met chocolaatjes.

De mand werd langzaamaan steeds leger. Met de overgebleven chocolaatjes en een grote kaart met dieren erop mocht ik langs de andere juffen en meesters. In ruil voor mijn traktatie zouden ze dan wat liefs op de achterkant van de kaart zetten. Een landkaart bestaande uit lieve woorden, stickers en kleurrijke tekeningen. Ik voelde me jarig, écht jarig.

In de pauze gingen we verstoppertje spelen. Het viel me op dat de jongens uit de hogere klassen aan het lachen waren. Hard aan het lachen. Sommigen klapten zelfs naar voren. Waarom moesten ze zo lachen? vroeg ik me af. Zo vreemd was het niet dat wij op onze leeftijd verstoppertje speelden, iets waarvoor zij zichzelf duidelijk te stoer vonden.

Toen ik ze beter bekeek, zag ik dat ze wezen. Ze wezen naar ons, naar onze groep, naar de kinderen die al uit hun verstopplek waren gehaald. Maar toen ik nog beter keek, zag ik dat ze naar mij keken. Konden ze misschien zien dat ik jarig was? Ik begreep het niet en keek naar mijn schoenen. Was ik misschien vergeten mijn veters te strikken en dachten ze dat ik mijn strikdiploma niet had gehaald? Nee, ze zaten in een prachtige lus, een lus als een schoenkus. Ik probeerde te achterhalen wat er dan zo grappig kon zijn en keek naar hun vingers. Ze wezen naar mij. Ik volgde de vingers. Ik had het goed gezien, de vingers wezen naar mij, maar niet zomaar naar mij, ze wezen naar mijn gezicht. Ze wezen naar mijn oren. Alsof daar iets bizars te zien was, iets abnormaals, iets ongehoords.

Met mijn vingers ging ik naar mijn oren. Daar voelde ik wat ze zagen en direct wist ik waarom ze moesten lachen. Die zilveren plastic plakoorbellen. Mijn zilveren plastic plakoorbellen. Ik haalde ze meteen weg en stopte ze in mijn zak.

Toen we na school met papa naar huis waren gelopen en ik thuis aankwam, liep ik de twee trappen naar mijn kamer op. Tussen de andere cadeaus zocht ik naar het kartonnetje op mijn bed. Vervolgens knipte ik met een schaar de verschillende paren los, stopte ze een voor een in andere enveloppes en plakte die dicht.

De volgende dag nam ik de enveloppes mee naar school en deelde ze uit aan de meisjes uit de hogere klassen.

Er kwamen steeds meer zaken bij die niet de bedoeling bleken te zijn. Tijdens verkleedpartijen bij klasgenootjes of op school was het niet de bedoeling dat ik koos voor een prinsessenjurk, ook al was een prinsenpak maar saai; veel verder dan een cape en een houten zwaard kwam het niet. Een jurk had tenminste glitters en verschillende stofjes, of kant en kleurrijke versiersels. Dát was pas mooi. Maar hoe ouder ik werd, des te meer mensen vreemd opkeken als ik zoiets aandeed.

Jarenlang had mijn vader me in de meest bonte outfits naar school gebracht. In prinsessenjurken, in een apenpak, in een outfit waarbij ik kleurrijke en glinsterende kroontjes en hoeden op mijn hoofd droeg. Nooit was het een probleem geweest, maar langzaam maar zeker werd het iets waarvoor je je moest schamen. Er waren onzichtbare wetten die voorschreven wat hoorde en wat niet. Mijn ouders hadden mij er lang tegen kunnen beschermen, maar nu kon dat niet meer. Ik was net als mijn klasgenootjes, misschien net wat vaker bezig met vrolijke dingen, maar voor de rest hetzelfde. En toch verdwenen de prinsessenjurken langzaam uit mijn leven.

Ondertussen bleef ik op de basisschool een onhandelbare stuiterbal. Toen ik jaren later op de fiets mijn juf uit groep drie tegenkwam, juf Anneke, vertelde ze dat ik druk was geweest, vrolijk, maar druk. En dat ze een manier had ontwikkeld om dat onder controle te krijgen. Ze had in een winkel bij de knutselspullen gekeken en er tassen vol glitters, steentjes en plastic diamantjes gekocht. Die had ze vervolgens allemaal mee naar school genomen en een deel ervan in haar lade gestopt. 'Je zat vooraan in de klas, met je tafel tegen mijn bureau. Als je dan te druk of te onrustig werd, keek ik je eerst altijd aan. Soms werkte dat, werd je even rustig.'

Ik wist wel waarom. Ik was zo verliefd op haar. Had haar liefdesbrieven geschreven. Cadeautjes gegeven. Met Valentijnsdag had ik zelfs chocolaatjes meegenomen. Ik deed erg mijn best voor haar. Ze had uitgelegd dat het niet kon. Dat ik nog heel veel moest ontdekken en dat ze al een man had, met kinderen, en dat ze veel te oud voor me was, maar dat ze wel mijn juf kon zijn. 'Mijn lievelingsjuf?' had ik gevraagd. 'Ja!' was haar antwoord geweest. Ik wist nog dat ik de laatste dag van dat schooljaar huilend op het plein stond. Ik hield haar been vast. 'Maak je geen zorgen, de hele klas is overgegaan, dus na de zomervakantie zie je iedereen weer terug.' Maar ze begreep niet dat dat niet de reden was dat ik huilde. Ik was ontroostbaar omdat zij niet mee zou gaan naar groep 4.

'Maar het werkte niet altijd,' ging juf Anneke verder, 'en daarom moest ik andere manieren bedenken. Zo had ik met je ouders afgesproken dat we een boekje bij zouden houden. Een schriftje dat elke dag van huis mee naar school ging, en vice versa. Daarin schreef ik op hoe het in de klas was gegaan, en vervolgens beschreven jouw ouders hoe het thuis was.' Ik weet nog dat ik soms aan het einde van de dag naast haar bureau stond en meekeek met wat ze opschreef. Als ik te druk was geweest, kwam het erin te staan. Ik voelde dan het plezier uit mijn lichaam weglekken, want als mijn papa het zou lezen, zou ik op m'n kop krijgen. Geen twee koekjes bij de limonade als we thuiskwamen. Geen televisie in de avond. Direct naar mijn kamer. Mijn hele dag zou regenachtig en donker zijn als Juf Anneke opschreef dat ik te druk was geweest. Of als ik ruzie had gemaakt op het schoolplein. Dan wist ik al voordat de schooldag was afgelopen dat ik een probleem had. Ik deed gedurende de rest van de dag dan nog wel een poging het goed te maken, maar dat werkte nooit echt. Ik kon iets wat viel in de categorie *heel erg, heel erg stout en fout* misschien ombuigen naar *heel erg stout en fout*, maar dat maakte de straf thuis niet veel beter.

Ik wilde me alsnog verontschuldigen tegenover mijn juf. ‘Sorry,’ floepte ik eruit. Juf Anneke keek me aan. Ik zag hoe ze probeerde te bedenken waarom ik dat zei. ‘Sorry voor al die onrust, ik moet een ramp zijn geweest in de klas.’

Ze begon te lachen. Zoals alleen zij dat kon, haar tanden aan de wereld tonend. Ik vond die lach mooi. Nog steeds. ‘Nee joh, doe niet zo mal jochie!’ Die twee woorden zorgden ervoor dat ik me in één klap weer dat ondeugende jochie voelde. Juf Anneke kon me met twee woorden terugtoveren naar groep drie, naar het moment waarop ik dacht dat ik alles wist, maar zo ontzettend weinig bleek te weten. Het moment waarop ik van haar nog moest leren schrijven, moest leren lezen, moest leren stilzitten. En ik vond het heerlijk. Om weer even dat kleine kind te zijn. Los van zichtbare en onzichtbare regels, los van alles wat me later geleerd was. Ik had opeens weer zin om in de schoolbank te zitten, met haar voor de klas, en dat ze me dan alles opnieuw ging uitleggen. Ik werd weer een beetje verliefd op haar.

‘Nee joh! Je was inderdaad druk, maar ik vond het heerlijk. Echt waar! Want je was druk uit vrolijkheid, niet omdat je vervelend was. In het belang van de klas moest ik manieren bedenken om je een beetje onder controle te houden, maar ik kon er ook van genieten. Ben daarna nooit meer zoveel vrolijkheid in één lichaam tegengekomen!’ Toen ze dat zei moest ik blozen. ‘Als je dan toch te onrustig werd, niet wilde luisteren of niet wilde wachten totdat ook de andere kinderen in de klas hun som gemaakt hadden, dan moest je je tafeltje naar voren schuiven. Voorbij mijn bureau, tegen de muur aan, onder het schoolbord.’ Dat wist ik nog wel. Dat was altijd vervreemdend. Dat je loskwam van de klas en verder schoof dan de grens van de juf of de meester. Je kwam dan áchter ze terecht. Zonder uitzicht, kijkend tegen de witte muur. Ik weet nog dat ik mezelf af en toe expres naar voren liet verplaatsen, dat ik dan tegen de muur zat, terwijl de juf dan iets aan het uitleggen was. Heel langzaam draaide ik me vervolgens om. Heel langzaam draaide ik mijn stoel weg van de muur, richting alle ogen uit de klas. Ik wist dat alleen die handeling zelf al voor gelach en onrust kon zorgen. Maar de klas wist ook dat het feestje alleen maar groter werd als ze rustig zouden blijven, niet direct te hard zouden lachen. Als ik dan eenmaal was omgedraaid, begon ik gekke bekken te trekken. Of ik ging overdreven mee knikken met de juf die iets uitlegde. Ik wist dat het zou werken; de klas zou lachen. Uiteindelijk moest ik dat dan wel bekopen met een teleurgestelde blik van de juf, maar soms had ik dat ervoor over.

'Maar als je daar dan zat, tegen de muur aan, was zelfs dat niet altijd voldoende,' ging juf Anneke verder. 'Op een dag kwam ik erachter. Als je daar zat gaf ik je af en toe een plastic diamant, die je op de muur voor je kon plakken. Of ik gaf je een glinsterende ster. Of een roze sticker. Allemaal zaken die je op de muur kon plakken, van geen uitzicht toch een uitzicht maken en dan werd je rustig. En hoe langer je rustig bleef, hoe meer steentjes, diamantjes, stickers en glitters je van me kreeg. Dat werkte geweldig. Ik kon je alles geven wat glom en blonk, dan leek je drukte weg te vloeien en je focus te liggen op alles wat op de muur geplakt was.' Ik herinnerde me nog dat ik het geweldig vond, de dingen die ze me gaf. Vond ze bijzonder en prachtig. Wilde ze stiekem mee naar huis nemen. In mijn slaapkamer hangen. Op Tijger plakken. Ik had ze zelfs op mijn huid willen plakken. Omdat die glitters en die glinsters alles vrolijk en kleurrijk konden maken.

4.

Los van het lezen en schrijven moest ik ook nog een hoop leren over ongeschreven regels die langzaam binnendruppelden. Zo kwam ik erachter dat je jezelf als jongen niet mooier mag toveren in de spiegel.

Op de basisschool was het opeens een discussiepunt geweest vanaf welke leeftijd je make-up mocht dragen. Vrijwel vanuit het niets leek onze juffrouw dat onderwerp aan te snijden. Het was in groep zeven of groep acht, maar het werd alleen met de meisjes besproken. Wij werden de gang opgestuurd, de jongens, wij moesten buiten wachten. Alsof er binnen in de klas een geheim plan werd gesmeed. Het leek eeuwig te duren. Wat bespraken ze? Waar hadden ze het over? Welk geheim werd er in hun oren gefluisterd? We drukten allemaal onze oren tegen de muur, in de hoop toch iets te kunnen opvangen van wat er in de klas werd gezegd.

Toen we weer naar binnen mochten keken we vol verwachting naar de meisjes. Alsof we collectief verliefd waren, maar dan op de spanning van het geheim. Wie zou het ons vertellen? In de grote pauze op het schoolplein kwam Esther naar ons toe, een van onze stoerste klasgenoten. Zij wilde het ons wel vertellen. Ze was een meisje dat prachtig kon zingen, wat haar geliefd maakte bij de muzieklerares. Maar ze had ook een hang naar dat wat niet mocht, ze vond het spannend om de randjes op te zoeken, om de door de schoolleiding gecreeerde orde in de war te schoppen. Ze was zo'n meisje dat op het schoolplein aan de jongens liet zien wat nou het échte verschil was tussen een meisjes- en een jongenslichaam. Met een kring van mannelijke klasgenootjes om haar heen, alsof ze op het punt stond een gigantische mand met traktaties uit te gaan delen, had ze ooit zó haar broek opengemaakt en gezegd: 'Bij ons is er niet zoveel te zien hoor, bij jullie is het een stuk spannender.' Op de een of andere manier had ik het ook spannend gevonden, om te kijken. Vervolgens had Esther gezegd: 'En nu een van jullie.' Dat was het moment geweest waarop we met z'n allen een beetje onhandig hadden staan draaien, waarna twee jongens langzaam hun broek openknoopten, hun broek iets lieten zakken en hun onderbroeken naar voren trokken. Daar was te zien wat Esther voorspelde: veel meer dan bij een meisje. Hoewel alle jongens wisten hoe het eruitzag, keken we toch met z'n allen mee die twee onderbroeken in. Ik vond het spannend. Niet zenuwachtig spannend. Een ander soort spannend.

Ik herkende het een beetje. Het leek op het gevoel dat ik had als we doktertje gingen spelen en de patiënt een jongen was. Of als we na het gymmen met elkaar moesten omkleden. Ik kon het niet plaatsen, dat gevoel, maar ik vond het niet onprettig, dus ik liet het voor wat het was. Wel leek het alsof ik de enige was die die spanning ervoer. De andere jongens zag ik niet op dezelfde manier doktertje spelen, omkleden, of, zoals toen, die onderbroek in kijken. Het was alsof een tovenaar heel even wat magie mijn lichaam in liet gaan.

Nadat de twee klasgenootjes zo een tijdje hun onderbroek open hadden gehouden en ze er zeker van waren dat iedereen had kunnen kijken, kleedden ze zich weer aan.

Toen de juffen en meesters te horen kregen wat er in de

pauze gebeurd was, waren ze in alle staten. Ze moesten alleen nog de namen achterhalen van het meisje en de jongens die het gedaan hadden. Maar dat bleek lastiger dan ze op voorhand misschien hadden verwacht. Iedereen hield zijn mond. Er waren gummetjes in ons hoofd aan het werk geweest.

En dat Esther nu wist dat haar geheimen veilig waren bij ons, dat wierp nu zijn vruchten af. Esther vertelde dat de juffrouw had gesproken over het feit dat het lichaam van meisjes verandert als ze ouder worden. Het lichaam zou meer vorm en meer hobbels krijgen, en er was zelfs speciale kleding om die hobbels te begeleiden. De juf had verteld dat meisjes zelf in die fase ook iets willen aanpassen. Dat ze hun wimpers langer en hun lippen roder maken en de blos op hun wangen accentueren. Eén leerling had dat al gedaan, die had die ochtend thuis mascara opgedaan en dat was de aanleiding geweest om het daar klassikaal over te hebben. De juffrouw wilde het bespreken met de meisjes, want make-up, dat ging alleen meisjes wat aan. Esther deelde ook de conclusie met ons. Voorlopig mochten de meisjes geen getekende versiering in het gezicht aanbrengen, want dat zou voor te veel onrust zorgen. Zo leerde ik dat make-up alleen voor meisjes was en niet voor jongens. Een nieuwe wet werd toegevoegd aan het onzichtbare wetboek.

5.

Ik groeide op in wereldvrede. Ik groeide op met het idee dat overal in de wereld mensen lief en mooi met elkaar omgingen. Ik groeide op met het idee dat mijn stoep de hele wereld was. Natuurlijk wist ik dat mijn stoep niet de hele wereld was, maar ik wist wel zeker dat de hele wereld er zo uitzag als mijn stoep. De stoep waar mijn broertje en ik leerden fietsen.

Soms ging ik voor het raam staan en dan keek ik naar die stoep. Naar de bomen, de straat en de mensen die voorbijhuppelden. De wereld trok aan mij voorbij en dan keek ik nog één keer goed en knipperde ik met mijn ogen. Niet zo'n automatische knipper maar een bewuste, eentje waarbij mijn ogen lang dicht bleven. En dan, na drie seconden, deed ik ze open om te zien wat ik daarvoor niet zag en verloor ik mezelf in de illusie. Bladeren van de bomen veranderden in confetti, de straten veranderden van kleur. Wolken werden verfstrepen op een blauw doek, stoeptegels lichtten op als een discovloer. Heerlijk om de werkelijkheid naar eigen inzicht te vervormen. De stoep was de hele wereld.

Dat kwam omdat mijn broertje en ik, de kleintjes, niet naar *Het Journaal* mochten kijken. Als we tv keken was dat *Sesamstraat*. Heel soms werd ook *Het Klokhuis* toegestaan, maar als dat bijna was afgelopen, kwam papa of mama erbij zitten.

Voordat *Het Jeugdjournaal* kon beginnen, ging de tv uit. Geen nieuws. Toen vonden we dat stom, maar later zouden we onze ouders er dankbaar voor zijn. Ze hadden ons het gevoel gegeven dat de wereld een vreedzame plek was.

Langzaam begonnen er barstjes te komen in dat beeld van die veilige wereld. Vlak na de eeuwwisseling – ik wist niet wat dat inhield, maar had van mijn ouders begrepen dat het een bijzonder moment was – zag ik hoe mijn vader in de voorkamer de telefoon opnam. De lichten waren uit, het begon te schemeren, en ik had het idee dat ik verstopt zat in de schaduw van mijn vader. Alsof papa het niet door zou hebben dat ik daar stond te kijken. Ik zag hoe hij de telefoon opnam. Normaal deed hij dat nooit, wachtte hij eerst het antwoordapparaat af voordat hij opnam. Maar dit keer handelde hij meteen. Alsof hij al wist dat dit een donker telefoontje zou worden. Geen vrolijke mededelingen, alleen verdrietige woorden. Papa ging niet zitten, maar bleef staan. Meestal begon hij een telefoongesprek zittend, om dan gaandeweg op te staan. Even de benen strekken. Maar echt lopen kon hij niet, want de hoorn zat nog met een draadje vast aan de haak.

Dit keer was het anders. Papa ging niet zitten, hij bleef volledig stilstaan.

Ik zag hem daar, in de voorkamer. Buiten was het lichter dan binnen, waardoor alleen zijn silhouet te zien was. Hij nam op met een beangstigende rust in zijn stem. Zo had ik hem nog nooit horen praten. 'Ja,' zei mijn vader. Aan de andere kant van de lijn werd gesproken. Ik kon niet horen wat er gezegd werd, maar papa reageerde niet meer. Eerst dat lange verhaal van degene die had gebeld, toen de stilte. Een enorme stilte. Papa zou moeten antwoorden, iets moeten zeggen om de stilte te verbreken. Maar dat deed hij niet. Hij stond daar maar met de telefoon aan z'n oor. Hij was iets van z'n oor naar beneden gezakt, alsof zijn armspieren niet meer goed werkten door dat wat er gezegd was. Ik zag papa staan, op zijn benen, maar hoe meer ik naar hem keek, des te beter ik zag dat hij niet écht op zijn benen stond. Het was eerder alsof hij léúnde op die benen, alsof die benen hem overéínd hielden, twee krukken die een hoopje mens in de lucht probeerden te houden.

Het was stil. Zelfs de auto's leken niet meer te rijden op straat, de vogels leken niet meer te fluiten, het leven leek even in pauzestand te zijn gezet. Alsof alles even moest zoeken naar krukken, naar steun om niet in te storten. En: alsof de hele wereld even niet meer wist wat er gezegd moest worden.

Na een lang aarzelen hoorde ik papa 'oké' zeggen. Het klonk eerder als een zucht, als een ademstoot die hij met al zijn overgebleven kracht naar buiten had geperst. Alsof het zijn laatste uitademing was. Met dat geluid kwam het telefoongesprek tot een einde. Ik zag hoe papa heel erg langzaam de hoorn naar de haak bracht, alsof de wereld in slow motion was gezet. Alsof hij met het neerleggen van de telefoon de mededeling definitief zou maken en hij dat nog zo lang mogelijk probeerde uit te stellen. Vlak voordat hij dat deed vluchtte ik weg, de gang in, de trap op, naar onze slaapkamer. Ik wilde papa het idee geven dat hij alleen was geweest en niemand hem had gezien.

Later kregen we te horen wat er gebeurd was. Wat papa te horen had gekregen. Een vriend was gesprongen.

Het was een van de eerste barsten die ik had zien ontstaan in het beeld dat onze stoep de wereld was. Een paar weken na het telefoongesprek zette mama muziek aan in diezelfde voorkamer. Papa zat aan tafel, ik tegenover hem. De rest, mama en de andere broers, waren er ook. Voorzichtig klonken de eerste pianotonen van 'My Way', gevolgd door een krakende, doorleefde, bijzondere stem. In de ogen van mijn papa zag ik regen verschijnen. Tranen. Ik had papa nog nooit zien huilen. Daar had ik nooit bij stilgestaan, maar opeens wist ik dat. Ik keek in zijn ogen en wist niet hoe ik moest reageren. Papa keek terug, maar ik zag dat hij iets anders zag. Hij keek door me heen. Naar de toekomst? Naar dat wat zijn kinderen nog moesten leren? Naar de wereld? Naar het verleden? Naar alles wat hij meegemaakt had? Ik kon het niet weten, ik kon het niet raden.

Ik zag hoe mijn lieve papa een paraplu opstak maar de regen uiteindelijk niet uit zijn ogen kon houden.

Niet veel later dat jaar gebeurde er weer iets dat onze stoep als wereldtoneel op zijn grondvesten deed schudden. Er was iets gebeurd. Ver weg van ons huis. Ver weg van ons land. Torens die brandden. Mijn broers en mijn vader keken naar de televisie toen mijn broertje en ik de voorkamer in kwamen. Heel even zagen we iets. Het leek wel vuurwerk uit een grote toren. Wolken van vlammen. We wilden vragen wat het was, wijzend naar de tv, maar papa sprong op voordat we iets hadden kunnen zeggen, nam ons in zijn armen en bracht ons naar boven. 'Ga maar spelen, lieverds.' Hij zette ons op de grond in onze kamer en keek ons aangeslagen aan. 'Geen gewelddadige spelletjes vandaag, geen soldaten of legerpoppetjes, pak maar een kleurplaat. Vandaag is er geen ruimte voor geweld.' Hij liet de deur op een kier.

Als kind voelde het alsof het allemaal in een en dezelfde periode gebeurde. Een tijdje daarna zaten we opnieuw voor de tv. Er lag een wit laken op straat, over de contouren van wat een mens moest zijn geweest. Politiemensen en ambulance eromheen. Het was duidelijk iets zeer ernstigs. Het had iets met de politiek te maken. Maar wat er precies was gebeurd, dat konden we als kleintjes niet begrijpen. 'Wat is dat?' vroegen we. Ook nu was het niet de bedoeling dat we de beelden hadden gezien. Hoezeer mama en papa ook hun best deden om de boze buitenwereld buiten onze kinderhoofden te houden, in die jaren lekten de eerste druppels van buiten naar binnen. Kleine lekkages die snel afgeplakt werden. Zo bleef de stoep toch voorlopig ons wereldbeeld bepalen.

Naast *Het Klokhuis*, *Villa Achterwerk* en *Sesamstraat* was er nog een televisieprogramma dat zich onttrok aan het strenge regime van mijn ouders. Het was een traditie geworden om dat op zaterdagavond te kijken. Na het avondeten gingen wij, de kleintjes, douchen, tandenpoetsen, pyjama's aandoen. Ondertussen keken de anderen dan naar het *NOS Journaal*. Eenmaal weer beneden werden we verwelkomd door de geur van popcorn – dan wisten we dat het extra feest was. Als we alleen onze pyjama aanhadden moesten we terug naar boven, pantoffels aan, kimono aan, pas dan mochten we komen zitten. Op kaboutergrote stoeltjes namen we plaats voor de tv. En dan was het wachten op *Mooi! Weer De Leeuw*. Het was heerlijk om te kijken, en soms kregen we naast popcorn van mama ook nog eens zelfgemaakte chocolademelk – mits we beloofden onze tanden nog een keer te poetsen.

6.

David woonde in een groot huis, een villa, met bomen en bos eromheen. Een huis waarvan je droomt. Hij had ook ouders waar je als kind soms van droomt; ouders die je niet echt in de gaten hielden. David deed alsof hij een brave jongen was, maar dat was hij niet. Hij was enig kind en als hij iets aan z'n moeder vroeg, geld voor snoep of frisdrank, een nieuwe trampoline of een op afstand bestuurbare sportauto, kreeg hij het altijd. Ik ging er daarom graag spelen. Sowieso vond ik het een gave jongen. Hij was stoer. Hij was grappig. En hij was nóg drukker dan ik. Ergens had ik medelijden met de docenten die ons samen in de klas kregen. We waren losgeslagen stuiterballen die werden aangedreven met turbo-energie. Als we een goede dag hadden waren we zowel de flipper als de kast, en dat zorgde voor een eindeloze reeks aan grappen, kattenkwaad en propjes gooien.

Ik was graag bij hem. Zat naast hem in de klas, dat hadden de juffen bedacht; misschien dat als we ze niet úít elkaar zetten, maar juist náást elkaar, dat ze dan wel rustig zouden zijn. De bedachte wonderoplossing, bleek van korte duur, maar toch, wij genoten ervan. Soms tikten onze knieën tegen elkaar aan, zoals de secondewegtikker in de klok. We waren grote wijzer en kleine wijzer. Waar de wijzers de tijd aangaven, gaven wij samen het energieniveau aan.

David had zwart, dik, vol haar. Grote zwarte wenkbrauwen. Wimpers alsof hij mascara droeg. Langer en donkerder dan de langste en donkerste winternachten. En hij had knalgroene ogen. Om zijn nek hing een gouden sterretje. Dat even mooi glinsterde in het zonlicht als zijn ogen van ondeugendheid leken te branden. Groen vuur in zijn ogen dat je aanstak als je hem in zijn ogen keek. Altijd op zoek naar kattenkwaad. Hij was een rebel, een regelbreker. Veel ouders wilden niet dat hun kinderen met hem speelden. Maar tegelijkertijd wilde ieder kind juist niets liever. Zijn zwarte, golvende haar, woeste wenkbrauwen, groene ogen en zijn Elvis-glimlach mét kuiltjes zorgden ervoor dat alle meisjes uit de klas verliefd op hem waren. Niemand zei het, iedereen wist het. Maar een vriendinnetje had hij nooit.

Samen met David haalde ik op school kattenkwaad uit. We gingen kijken hoe de juffen en meesters aan de achterkant van het schoolgebouw stiekem stonden te roken. Dat kon alleen als je via een smalle doorgang tussen muurtjes via de fietsenstalling naar de achterkant van de school sloop. Daar was een bijna verstopt en vergeten binnenplaatsje waar de juffen en meesters handig gebruik van maakten. In de fietsenstalling mocht je niet komen, dus als je de leraren op het binnenplaatsje bespiedde was je al in overtreding. Ik vond dat al heel wat, maar David vond het na een paar minuten niet spannend meer. David was het type jongen dat altijd nóg een stapje verder wilde gaan. Als een feestje ballonnen, slingers en confetti was, wilde hij de champagne zijn. Als we daar lagen, op de grond, achter het metalen hek, de juffen en meesters bespionerend, bedacht David dat het spannend was als we bijna betrapt zouden worden. Eerst begon hij takjes te breken. Takjes die je tijdens het sluipen juist probeerde te ontwijken. Meteen merkten de leraren het geluid op. We drukten onszelf tegen de grond. Hoewel we het doodeng vonden, moesten we met onze handen voor onze mond ons lachen inhouden. Ik keek David aan en zag het groene vuur in zijn ogen. Hij had een nieuw idee.

Hij begon te fluiten. Een hoge toon. Fiet-fieuw. Hij wachtte een seconde en deed het toen nog eens. Olie op het vuur. Fiet-fieuw. De juffen en meesters kwamen in beweging, alsof je met een stok in een mierenhol had zitten prikken. Soms moesten we dan snel wegkruipen, terug naar het schoolplein. Soms konden we blijven zitten, achter een muurtje.

Maar soms maakte hij het helemaal bont. Drukte hij het gaspedaal van het kattenkwaad nog verder in. Zoals nu. 'Jooeeehoooeee!!!' riep hij. Keihard. Zijn stem knalde tegen de bakstenen van de binnenplaats en bleef daar echoën. De juffen en meesters sprongen op en wilden ons pakken. David zag ze rennen en lachte. Hard. Zijn hikkende, gierende lach. Onmiskenbaar zijn lach. Die zouden ze meteen herkennen. En dat vond hij het mooist, dat de juffen en meesters wísten dat hij de regels had overtreden, maar hem er niet op konden pakken. Want we zouden rennen, heel hard rennen, en wegkomen – voordat David zijn streken uithaalde blokkeerde hij altijd de poort in het hek, een kleine tak tussen de scharnieren. En dan keek hij naar mij, als om aan te geven dat ik in positie moest staan. Ik deed dan alsof ik klaar ging staan in een startblok op de atletiekbaan. En wachtte. Totdat het startschot zou klinken. Dat was zijn lach.

Als we na de pauze de klas in kwamen of tijdens het resterende deel van de pauze de juffen en meesters tegenkwamen die eerst samen op de binnenplaats hadden gezeten, dan lachte hij zijn tanden bloot. Alleen hij kon zo glimlachen. Zijn rebellie won. Bijna altijd.

We waren bij hem thuis geweest. Zijn moeder maakte altijd een extra speciale lunch voor ons. Tosti's. Soms zelfs pannenkoeken. We zaten in de keuken, ingericht als een Amerikaans wegrestaurant waar vrachtwagenchauffeurs eten. Zo'n tafel in het midden met daaromheen een leren bank. Met op het tafelblad alleen een tube mosterd en een tube ketchup. Verder helemaal leeg. Een tafel zonder zichtbare geschiedenis. Toch werden juist aan die tafel de eerste, misschien wel kleurrijkste stiftstrepen van dat schooljaar gezet.

De moeder van David zette twee grote bekers met ijs en limonade op tafel en liep toen terug naar het aanrecht, waar ze iets aan het klaarmaken was. David en ik keken elkaar aan. Opeens zag ik zijn mondhoeken omhoogkomen. Een klein beetje, genoeg om te weten dat hij moest lachen. En toen voelde ik het. Heel langzaam, heel voorzichtig. Zijn voet. Hij had warme voeten. Zijn besokte voet raakte mijn eerste paar tenen aan. Voorzichtig. Zijn voet kwam verder over mijn voet heen. Hij ging omhoog langs mijn scheen, en weer terug naar beneden. En liet mijn voet toen weer los. Zijn mama draaide zich om, kwam teruglopen met twee tosti's met tomaat, pesto en mozzarella. Zette die voor ons neer en ging weer terug naar het aanrecht.

Nu was het aan mij. Bedacht ik me. Hij had een nieuw soort kattenkwaad uitgehaald. Een kattenkwaad dat me een gevoel gaf dat ik niet goed kon plaatsen. Het was een soort spanning die ik niet snapte. Maar ik vond het geen onprettige spanning. Ik wilde meer van dit kattenkwaad, en schoof mijn voet naar die van hem. Hij bracht zijn voet omhoog. Ik bracht mijn voet omhoog. Terwijl we allebei onze hiel op de grond hielden. Onze voeten stoeiden. Ze stoeiden. En ze stoeiden. We vonden het allebei leuk, dat stoeien. Zo leuk dat we ook onze andere voet mee lieten doen. Ondertussen aten we in stilte onze tosti op. Zo stil waren we nog nooit geweest, niet in de klas, niet tijdens het bespioneren van de juffen en meesters, nooit niet. We waren stiller dan als we zouden slapen. Soms stopte het stoeien even, als zijn moeder zich omdraaide, iets op tafel kwam zetten of juist iets kwam weghalen. Zonder dat we daar afspraken over hadden gemaakt, maar we deden het, automatisch. Dit kattenkwaad moest niet betrapt worden.

'Dat was voetjevrijen,' zei David toen we zijn kamer in kwamen. De gordijnen waren dicht, overal lag speelgoed en zijn matras was dekenloos, hij had daar duidelijk onrustig geslapen vannacht. 'Ik heb dat opgezocht, voetjevrijen,' zei hij. De kuiltjes in zijn wangen leken bij deze glimlach dieper dan normaal, als je over zijn wangen zou wandelen, viel je erin, een valkuil waarin je eeuwig gevangen zou zitten. 'Geinig toch?' zei hij. 'Zeker,' zei ik, terwijl ik die spanning weer voelde. Alsof ik dit soort kattenkwaad de hele dag zou willen uithalen. En 's nachts. 'Er is meer van dit soort kattenkwaad,' zei David, alsof hij mijn gedachten kon lezen. Hij trok één wenkbrauw op, waarmee hij leek te vragen of ik er meer van wilde weten. 'Wat dan?' vroeg ik. 'Ga maar zitten', en hij wees naar de stoel die achter zijn bureau stond. De bureaustoel was het enige dat wel opgeruimd was. Alsof hij deze ochtend alleen zijn bureaustoel vrij had gemaakt, alsof hij wist dat hij die nodig zou hebben.

Ik ging zitten en David kwam achter me staan. Wat voor kattenkwaad had hij nu weer bedacht? Hoewel ik niet wist wat ik moest verwachten, had ik er wel zin in. Vaak was het bij kattenkwaad de bedoeling dat je probeerde niet betrapt te worden door degene bij wie je het uithaalde. Maar dit was anders. We deden dit kattenkwaad nu bij elkaar, samen. Ik vond David vrij geniaal, dat hij dit had bedacht.

'Blijf zitten.' Hij kwam achter me staan. Hij legde zijn linkerhand op mijn linkerschouder. Hield de hand daar. Kneep zachtjes en liet weer los. Kneep weer zachtjes en liet weer los. Kneep nog een keer zachtjes, maar hield toen vast. Met zijn duim op mijn spier op mijn rug begon hij langzaam rondjes te maken. Ondertussen gebruikte hij zijn vier andere vingers om piano te spelen op mijn schouder. Het voelde alsof hij met een hand heel voorzichtig het brooddeeg aan het kneden was. Ik genoot ervan. Soms deed het een beetje pijn, prettig pijn. Ik voelde de spanning in mijn lichaam komen. Weer die onverklaarbare spanning. Maar ik vond het geweldig. Ik wist niet dat kattenkwaad zoveel plezier kon geven. Zijn andere hand legde hij in mijn hals en liet hem daar een tijdje liggen. Hij zette een stap dichterbij en stond met zijn onderlichaam tegen mijn rug. Ik voelde zijn telefoon een beetje prikken. Eigenlijk wist ik helemaal niet dat hij die had, hij had hem nooit laten zien. Na een tijdje hield hij ermee op. 'Goed hè?' Aandachtig luisterde hij of zijn moeder niet naar boven kwam. Hij had de deur op een kier gelaten, om zo extra goed te kunnen horen of ze de trap opklom. 'Dat was goed hè?' zei hij nog een keer. 'Ja,' zei ik. Daarna liet hij me los.

'Oké, wat laat je nooit zien aan anderen?' vroeg David. Ik was opgestaan, vond het ergens jammer dat zijn hand niet op mijn schouder was gebleven. 'Hoe bedoel je?' vroeg ik. 'Nou,' – hij leek even na te denken – 'is er iets wat eigenlijk niemand van je mag zien? Iets wat je niet op straat de hele tijd aan voorbijgangers zou tonen?'

Ik keek hem aan. Wist niet zo goed welke richting hij op wilde. 'Ik denk mijn buik?' 'Nee joh, niet je buik, kijk, je buik kun je altijd overal laten zien!' En hij trok zijn T-shirt omhoog en liet zijn buik zien. Her en der zag ik moedervlekken. Alsof er na een douchebeurt wat modder was blijven zitten. 'Zie je!' riep hij nog een keer, terwijl hij de kamer rondsprong alsof hij op een stoep of op straat liep. 'Nee, je buik is niet het goede antwoord.' 'Dan weet ik het niet zo goed, denk ik?' zei ik. Of ik wist het eigenlijk wel, maar durfde het niet goed te zeggen. De spanning in mijn buik werd groter en groter, alsof een magische soep stond te koken die nu zo heet werd dat de dampen en de stoom ervan af kwamen.

'Ik heb denk ik wel iets waarmee ik niet de hele tijd op straat zou willen lopen,' zei hij. 'Wat dan?' vroeg ik. 'Nou, dit.' Hij wees naar zijn kruis. 'Dit, daarmee zou ik niet de hele tijd op straat gaan rondlopen. Ik durf het wel te laten zien hoor, maar ik vind niet dat iedereen het hoeft te zien.' Hij begon snel zijn knopen en zijn rits los te maken, alsof hij iets tegenover mij moest bewijzen. Zijn onderbroek werd zichtbaar. Hij stopte zijn hand erin waardoor er een grote bobbel ontstond en pakte toen met zijn andere hand de rand vast. Met zijn benen wiebelde hij heen en weer waardoor zijn spijkerbroek zakte tot op zijn knieën. 'Kijk!' Hij trok zijn onderbroek naar beneden, en hield zijn andere hand nog voor zijn kruis. Ik wist niet waar ik moest kijken, maar kon alleen maar kijken naar de hand die zijn kruis vasthield. 'Kijk, dít zou ik nou niet aan iedereen op straat laten zien, denk ik!' En toen haalde hij zijn hand weg, terwijl hij lachte zoals hij altijd deed. Zoals Elvis Presley lachte, maar dan stouter. En ook trotser. Hij wiebelde met zijn heupen, waardoor zijn kruis even heen en weer vloog. 'Dit is omdat ik joods ben,' – David wees op zijn kruis – 'mijn piemel is besneden, die van jou niet.' Nu begreep ik ook die kandelaar en dat sterretje. 'O,' zei ik. Hij deed zijn onderbroek weer aan, ritste zijn broek dicht en luisterde toen heel even aan de deur of zijn moeder op dezelfde verdieping was gekomen. Dat was ze. Maar dat maakte in principe voor David niet uit, zolang ze de kamer maar niet in kwam.

'Nu ben jij!' zei David, 'nu moet jij laten zien wat je op straat niet zou tonen aan voorbijgangers.' Ik herhaalde zijn actie. Knoopte mijn broek los en liet mijn broek een beetje zakken, minder ver dan hij had gedaan. Ik durfde beduidend minder dan hij. En vervolgens deed ik mijn onderbroek naar beneden. Kort. Heel kort, maar lang genoeg voor hem om hem even aan te tikken. 'Zie je wel, jij hebt hier wel huid.' Alsof hij een sterretje aanstak, zo'n tinteling voelde ik door mijn lichaam schieten.

Toen ik thuis werd gebracht vroeg papa, die aan de grote pingpongwedstrijdtafel sperziebonen zat af te halen, hoe het was geweest. 'Het was echt heel erg leuk! Morgen gaan we misschien weer spelen, als dat van jou mag, maar van Davids mama mag het in ieder geval.' 'Fijn om te horen dat het zo leuk was, jong. Wat hebben jullie gedaan? Wat was er zo leuk?' 'Gewoon!' In mijn enthousiasme klonk door dat het geen gewone speeldag was geweest. Maar papa vroeg niet door en ik ging de trap op naar mijn slaapkamer. 'Hou van jou pap!' riep ik toen ik bijna boven was. 'Gaat vanzelf weer over,' hoorde ik hem nog net zeggen.

We zouden nog heel vaak en heel veel spelen, tot dat ene moment kwam. David en ik waren weer eens onrustig geweest in de klas en dit keer was het zijn beurt om de gang op te worden gestuurd. We maakten er sinds kort een wedstrijdje van om zo theatraal mogelijk de gang op te gaan. David won meestal. Ook deze keer. Onderweg naar de gang liep hij tussen de tafels door alsof hij én dronken was én moest leren lopen én net een tik van een molen had gehad. Je zou ook kunnen zeggen dat hij een ongekend talent had voor hypermoderne dans, maar de juf vond het maar niks. Als een onrustkatalysator bracht hij de klas in beweging. Iedereen moest lachen. 'Opschieten, David,' klonk het met een vermoeide zucht. De juf had niet eens zin meer om er echt een punt van te maken. Ze leek in gedachten al ergens anders te zijn. Bij een volgende stap. Alsof ze zich deze slag gewonnen gaf, omdat ze zich concentreerde op een volgende. Toen kon ik nog niet weten dat David tijdens het uitvoeren van zijn moderne dans regelrecht de val in liep.

In de pauze kwamen we erachter wat er was gebeurd. David was van de gang gehaald en naar de andere klas gebracht. Naar groep 7A. Daarmee hadden de juffen en meesters een grens overschreden. Iedereen wist dat er altijd rivaliteit was tussen de A- en B-klassen. Niet dat die ergens op gestoeld was, nee, het was gewoon zo.

Door David in groep A te zetten hadden ze hem in vijandelijk gebied geplaatst. De leerlingen van groep A wilden hem niet hebben, maar wij vonden het al helemaal niets dat hij daar was. 'We moeten iets doen,' werd er gezegd op het schoolplein.

Toen we na de pauze werden opgehaald en naar de klas werden gebracht, kregen we te horen dat David de komende tijd in groep 7A zou blijven. Het leidde tot gejoel, geschreeuw, gedoe. Aan de andere kant van de muur hoorden we hetzelfde geluid. Waarschijnlijk had de juf daar het verhaal precies op hetzelfde moment verteld. Als in twee apenkooien ging het rumoer verder. Dit lieten we niet zomaar gebeuren.

Toen we een paar uur later het schoolgebouw uitliepen, wisten we wat ons te doen stond. De volgende dag zouden we massaal in protest gaan. En dat deden we. Nadat papa mijn broertje en mij los had gelaten op het schoolplein, snelde ik naar de afgesproken plek toe. Daar stonden al een aantal andere klasgenootjes klaar. Ook David was er. Dirck, de zoon van een van de juffen, had een groot spandoek bij zich. 'Ik krijg enorme problemen thuis als ik dit vasthoud, dus een van jullie moet het dragen.' Dat deden we. LAAT DAVID VRIJ! stond er in dikke zwarte koeienletters op. We wachtten nog even tot bijna iedereen er was en begonnen toen over het schoolplein te marcheren.

'LAAT DAVID VRIJ! LAAT DAVID VRIJ! LAAT DAVID VRIJ! ' scandeerden we. Het spandoek stak hoog boven ons uit, de dragers stonden op hun tenen om ervoor te zorgen dat iedereen het kon zien. Vanaf het bordes bij de hoofdingang kwamen twee juffen aangerend. Ze pakten de spandoeken af, ze waren woest, dat was duidelijk. Maar ze zagen ook dat er nog ouders op het schoolplein stonden te kijken. Het zou niet handig zijn om de kinderen nu de volle laag te geven.

Toen we twee aan twee in de rij stonden om te worden opgehaald, was het doodstil. De juf kwam bij ons staan, vroeg of iedereen klaar was om naar binnen te gaan, maar haar vraag werd beantwoord met een totale stilte. Vlak bij ons lokaal werd de stilte verbroken met een gigantisch kabaal. We renden naar groep 7A. Daar probeerde de juf de deur van de klas dicht te trekken, maar ze was net te laat. Kinderhanden en kinderarmen grepen de klasdeur en trokken die open. David wist wat hem te doen stond en deed een poging om het klaslokaal uit te rennen. De juf dook voor de deuropening en greep David vast. We probeerden hem uit alle macht los te trekken. Achter ons leek een vulkaan te ontploffen. Of eigenlijk twee. We hoorden de stem van onze juf de lucht ingaan, ondersteund door iets dat klonk als onweer. De directeur was erbij gehaald. Alleen David leek nog even een poging te wagen om zich uit de greep van de juf te ontworstelen, maar verder gaf iedereen zich gewonnen.

In de klas begonnen we aan deel drie van ons protest. Misschien wel het heftigste gedeelte. We zeiden niks meer. Niemand zei meer wat. Niemand deed meer wat. Niemand pakte iets. Al die jaren hadden we geluisterd naar juffen en meesters, maar nu bleek dat we als klas, als collectief, veel machtiger waren dan zij. Zolang we bleven samenwerken waren we onverslaanbaar.

Het duurde de hele ochtend. Wat de juf ook zei of deed, beweging kwam er niet. Totdat ze leek te breken. Ze zette een hoge kruk in het midden voor de klas, ging erop zitten als een treurwilg en zei dat het zo niet kon. Opeens sloeg de collectieve staking om in collectief medelijden. Dit was nou ook weer niet de bedoeling.

‘Zo gaat het niet, jongens,’ zei ze nog een keer. ‘We proberen jullie op school iets te leren, en daarvoor is het belangrijk dat er rust is. Dat er rust is om jullie zaken uit te leggen, en soms moeten we dan dingen beslissen die misschien niet leuk zijn, maar die wel even nodig zijn.’ Het bleef stil in de klas, maar het negeren was omgeslagen in luisteren. ‘En als jullie zo doorgaan moeten we als schoolleiding misschien beslissen dat David voor altijd in groep 7A blijft,’ zei ze. Dat was geen handige zet. Als een koe die met z’n snuit tegen het schrikdraad tikt, zo verkrampte de sfeer bijna weer in de richting van hakken in het zand. Maar net op tijd zette ze haar diplomatieke pet op. ‘Maar dat wil ik helemaal niet. Ik wil alleen even wat rust. Dat het even ietsjes rustiger is. En dan mag David misschien vanmiddag en anders morgen gewoon weer terugkomen.’ Iedereen leek hierna weer een beetje in beweging te komen. Sommigen gingen weer onderuitgezakt zitten, anderen legden hun ellebogen op tafel. Het was alsof de klas als een spier uit de kramp schoot. We hadden onze zin gekregen. Dolblij waren we. Maar dat zouden we niet direct laten merken. We begrepen dat dat onze positie zou ondermijnen.

Een paar uur later zat David weer bij ons in de klas. Maar van naast elkaar zitten zou het niet meer komen.

Later dat jaar kregen we te horen dat David ons zou gaan verlaten. Zijn ouders hadden besloten dat ze naar Israël zouden gaan. We wisten niet echt wat of waar dat was, behalve een gelig plekje op de wereldkaart in onze klas. Toen hij wegging voelde ik een leegte. Een leegte die niemand leek te kunnen vullen. Als ik voor paardrijles langs zijn huis fietste keek ik de andere kant op om het bordje TE KOOP niet te hoeven zien.

7.

'We gaan straks loten,' zei de juf.

Ik wist wat er ging gebeuren, ik hoopte dat ik geluk zou hebben. Ik zat inmiddels in groep acht en zes leerlingen zouden straks worden uitgekozen om de Bourdonklok op de Waalsdorpervlakte te luiden tijdens de dodenherdenking. Drie uit onze klas, drie uit de parallelklas. De Waalsdorpervlakte lag tegenover ons huis. Via het park aan de andere kant van de straat kon je er zo heen lopen. In die duinen waren tijdens de oorlog meer dan tweehonderdvijftig mensen door de Duitsers omgebracht. In de meest vredige en mooie omgeving, een golvend duinlandschap waar herten, vossen en vogels vrij konden spelen, waar duingras, dennen en bomen het landschap bepaalden – dat was de plek geweest waar de Duitsers een fusilladeplaats hadden ingesteld. Verzetsstrijders vonden daar de dood. Een groter contrast was niet denkbaar.

De juf had de loten in een mandje gedaan en schudde ze heen en weer. Het eerste briefje kwam tevoorschijn. 'Sophie,' klonk het. Opnieuw ging de hand in het mandje. Ze roerde alsof ze net wat extra peper en zout in de soep had gegooid. Ik zag de klok langzaam tikken, het soep roeren leek eindeloos te duren. 'Opletten,' zei ze, bijna streng. Tussen haar wijsvinger en duim had ze een nieuwe naam. Ze hield het papiertje rustig vast. Ik wist meteen dat ik het niet was.

'Wolf!' zei ze. Wolf was blij, slaakte een kreet. Waarna hij snel de handen voor zijn mond sloeg, uit angst dat de juf zijn getrokken lootje ongedaan zou maken omdat hij de rust in de klas verstoorde. Zo'n type was het wel, deze juf. Het type dat stiekem genoot van het straffen van kinderen. Niet dat het er dik bovenop lag, maar op de een of andere manier maakte ze ruzies altijd erger.

Ik had het zelf een keer meegemaakt. Vanuit de schoolbankjes achter me hadden twee klasgenootjes briefjes zitten schrijven. Op heel kleine stukjes papier gingen snippers informatie over en weer. Het was stil geweest in de klas, maar niet zo stil dat het geschuif van briefjes verplaatsende handen zou opvallen. Ik hoorde het wel en was nieuwsgierig. Ik scheurde een klein stukje papier van mijn schrift af en schreef met mijn lekkende vulpen of ik mocht weten waar het over ging. Ik gooide het briefje voorzichtig naar achter. Maar antwoord kwam er niet. Als bij een onbeantwoorde liefdesbrief bleef het eindeloos stil. Hoewel het gegiebel en handengeschuif steeds luider werden. Ik keek naar achteren, in de hoop op een antwoord. Dat gaven ze, maar het was anders dan ik had verwacht. Mijn twee klasgenootjes keken me aan met een blik alsof hun ouders net hadden verteld dat er spruitjes op het menu stonden. Spruitjes. Het grootste verraad dat je ouders je aan konden doen. Ze keken me aan alsof ík een spruitje was. Maar ik ben geen spruitje! wilde ik bijna uitroepen. Toen begreep ik waar ze over schreven. Ze hadden het over mij.

Zoals je een antwoord op je liefdesbrief niet moet afdwingen, zo had ik niet moeten willen weten wat er op het briefje stond. Als een kat die eindeloos vanuit een hoek naar een muis had zitten loeren, greep ik het stukje papier van tafel. Mijn hand kwam hard neer op hun schoolbank. Alsof ik een vlieg doodsloeg. Direct sloegen ze alarm, ondernamen een poging om me tegen te houden. Ik draaide me om, dook in elkaar en onder mijn schoolbank vouwde ik het briefje open op mijn schoot. *Waarom zijn wij achter Wobie gezet – hij is altijd zo druk – ik vind hem zo vermoeiend – hij heeft ook hele vreemde ouders – sws is ie vreemd*, en toen was het briefje vol geweest. Ik kwam met mijn hoofd omhoog en zag, minder verbaasd dan ik zou moeten zijn, de juf bij mijn tafeltje staan. Ze had haar armen in haar zij. Woest was ze. Helemaal klaar met de onrust die ik nu had veroorzaakt in de rekenende en sommen makende klas.

'Wat is dit nou weer voor een ongein!' Ik vermoedde dat ze eigenlijk niet écht geïnteresseerd was in mijn antwoord. Je zou kunnen zeggen dat dit niet het type juf was dat fan van me was, zoals destijds juf Anneke. Nee, dit was er eentje van het andere soort.

'Nou...' begon ik. Ik wist eigenlijk niet wat ik moest zeggen, wat ik als verdediging moest opvoeren. Zeggen dat er briefjes geschreven werden, dat zou klikken zijn, en dat wilde ik niet. 'Nou...' stamelde ik nog een keer.

'Ben je weer bezig? Ben je weer bezig?! Kun je geen moment stil zijn? Kijk! De hele klas was rustig, en nu is iedereen weer afgeleid. Door jou!'

Ze wees naar mij als een dokter die een ontsteking aanwijst. Je mag niet wijzen, hoorde ik mijn moeder zeggen – ook dat leek me niet handig om nu naar voren te brengen. Maar wat moest ik wel zeggen? Ja. Ik was voor een groot gedeelte aanstichter van de ontstane onrust. Als we met een groep fikkie zouden steken, was ik zeker een van de houthalers geweest, of misschien zelfs een van de mensen die een lucifer in z'n handen had gehad. Maar ik was niet de enige. Het was niet alleen maar mijn schuld, terwijl de juf dat nu wel suggereerde. Ik zei nog maar even niks.

'Het is ook altijd hetzelfde met jou hè? Altijd!' Ze keek me nog bozer aan en plantte een vuist op mijn bureau. Die vuist was het laatste duwtje dat nodig was om niet langer mijn mond te houden.

'Nou juf, om eerlijk te zijn, ik maakte zoveel lawaai omdat er briefjes werden geschreven, briefjes over mij, onaardige briefjes.' Ik had meteen spijt. Ik moest sorry zeggen, tegen mijn klasgenootjes, bedacht ik me, straks, in de pauze. Sorry dat ik geklikt had.

De juf kwam overeind, draaide zich om, wilde weglopen. Dat verbaasde me. Geen straf voor de briefjes? Gelukkig maar, dacht ik. In haar beweging zat een kleine aarzeling. De eerste stap was gezet, de tweede stap volgde. Ze was nu weg bij mijn schoolbank en stond in het gangpad tussen de andere leerlingen. Maar ze bleef staan. Zag ik daar een kleine aarzeling? Nee. Toch niet. Ze draaide zich om met een ruk, haalde diep adem, keek me net zo lang aan totdat ze zeker wist dat ik haar goed zou zien en horen en sprak: 'Als ik zo oud was als jij en ik achter jou zou zitten, zou ik ook dat soort briefjes over jou schrijven!' En toen liep ze weg.

In mijn hoofd ontstond onbeheersbaar onweer. Ik wist niet waar ik de bliksem heen moest laten glijden. Een bliksemafleider was er niet. Eerst pakte ik mijn kleurpotloden vast, probeerde ze samen te knijpen, om mijn woede weg te halen. Of was het geen woede? Was het verdriet? Het had in ieder geval pijn gedaan. Dat wist ik, het had veel pijn gedaan. Dit gevoel kende ik niet echt. Het klasgenootje naast me, Eveline, pakte mijn arm vast. 'Laat het gaan.' Ik keek haar aan, ze wist dat het geen zin had, maar lief was het wel. Even schoot door m'n hoofd dat ik mijn pennendoos naar die kop van die klotejuf kon gooien. Maar dat deed ik niet. In plaats daarvan keek ik haar aan. Een seconde. Dat zeg je toch niet tegen een kind? Was ik nou zo slim of was zij pedagogisch gewoon totaal incapabel? In die ene seconde klapperden die vragen en gedachten door mijn hoofd, het onweer nog steeds onverminderd onstuimig.

'Hoe kunt u zoiets zeggen?' stamelde ik. Een tweede seconde volgde. En toen kwam de derde seconde. Alsof ze een knopje in haar gezicht had ingedrukt, zo veranderde haar blik. Haar mondhoeken kwamen omhoog. Langzaam, niet heel ver, maar duidelijk genoeg. Ze lachte. Dat was haar antwoord op mijn woede.

Ik hield het niet meer en opeens herinnerde ik me wat mijn moeder had gezegd. 'Als er nog een keer iets gebeurt waarmee je het niet eens bent, bel ons dan maar op,' zei ze. Dat was waar ook. Het was niet de eerste keer dat de juf iets vreemds deed. Ik stond eindeloos vaak op de gang. Moest volgens haar getest worden, kon niet goed leren en zou eigenlijk maar beter alvast van school gehaald kunnen worden, om een nieuwe school te vinden, met speciaal onderwijs. Daar waren m'n ouders niet in meegegaan. Ik was getest, ik bleek me dood te vervelen in de klas. Was te slim. Dat had tot grote irritatie geleid bij deze juf. Toen glimlachte ze niet.

Ik stond op, liep achter mijn schoolbankje vandaan, het gangpad in.

'Ga zitten!' krijste ze opeens.

Ik dacht het niet. En ik voelde een collectieve angst ontstaan in de klas. Ik dacht aan de naam die we als klasgenootjes in de pauze ooit voor haar hadden bedacht: juf Trol.

'Ga NU zitten!' krijste ze nog een keer.

In mijn hoofd beukte de bliksem. Mijn hartslag ging omhoog. Trol. Trol Trol. Trol. Trol Trol. Trol. Trol Trol. Zo bonkte het in mijn hoofd. Maar ik zei het niet. Ik zei wat anders. 'Ik ga de gang op. Dat lijkt me beter voor u en voor mij.'

Toen ik haar bureau voorbijliep, langs het schoolbord, voor de klas, sprong ze op. 'NU! ZITTEN! JIJ! KRENG!' schreeuwde ze. Hysterisch, schoot er door m'n hoofd, wat een hysterisch wijf. Ik piekerde er niet over en zonder om te kijken liep ik door, pakte de deurklink vast, duwde de deur de eerste drie millimeter open en kon toen één bliksemschicht niet meer in bedwang houden. 'Ik ga m'n ouders bellen, Trol!' Het woord 'Trol' knetterde door de klas, alsof ik het eerste steentje van een lange dominorij om had getikt. Ik voelde een glimlach in de klas. Ik had onze bijnaam voor de juf hardop uitgesproken.

Op de gang wilde ik naar huis bellen met de openbare telefoon die daar stond. Mama's telefoonnummer hadden we lang geleden uit ons hoofd moeten leren. Ik toetste het in, maar halverwege voelde ik opeens een hand in mijn nek, een andere hand rondom mijn arm. Er werd kracht gezet, ik voelde hoe een lichaam zich op me stortte. Ik kromp uit bescherming ineen. Het was de juf, juf Trol die van achter op me was gedoken en nu uit alle macht de telefoon uit mijn handen probeerde te wurmen.

'Laat me los!' schreeuwde ik, 'blijf met je poten van me af.'

'Geef hier die telefoon! Geef nu hier die telefoon!'

Ik haalde uit, met mijn elleboog, ik haalde uit, ik gaf haar een stoot in haar maag. Toen liet ze me los. Ze keek me aan.

'Ik bel mijn ouders, dat heb ik met ze afgesproken als u weer debiel zou doen, en dat ga ik doen ook, niemand kan tussen mijn afspraken met mijn ouders komen en u al helemaal niet,' zei ik met trillende stem. Ik vocht tegen de tranen en drukte het groene hoorntje in. De telefoon ging over.

Mijn klasgenootjes hadden allemaal gezien wat er gebeurd was. Het waren op dat moment meer mijn klasgenootjes dan haar leerlingen. Ze snelde terug het lokaal in en riep dat iedereen onmiddellijk moest gaan zitten.

Nadat ik mijn moeders voicemail had ingesproken – ze was

dokter en had een spreekuur – ging ik op de grond in de gang zitten. Ik snikte. Ik wilde niet huilen, deed m'n best de tranen binnen te houden, maar af en toe ontsnapte er eentje. Ik had opeens geleerd hoe het was om beledigd te worden, echt beledigd. En ik voelde me machteloos. Want ik wist dat ik uiteindelijk de leerling bleef, en zij de juf zou blijven. Ik dacht aan m'n moeder, wist dat ze terug zou bellen en bereidde het verhaal voor dat ik zou houden. Ik keek naar de telefoon die ik terug had gestopt in de houder, tien meter bij me vandaan. Als ze me nu maar snel zou bellen...

Een paar minuten later zwaaide de deur open. De juf kwam de gang op, zonder naar mij te kijken, liep naar de schooltelefoon en haalde hem uit de houder. Ik wilde iets zeggen, maar wist dat het geen zin had. Ze liep terug naar de klas en smeet de deur achter zich dicht. Een paar minuten later hoorde ik de telefoon overgaan. Niemand die opnam.

'Als je je weer normaal kunt gedragen, mag je binnenkomen,' beet ze me toe. Ik keek haar aan. Er was een halfuur verstreken sinds ik de klas uit was gelopen. Minstens. Ik had daar al die tijd gezeten, voor me uit kijkend. Had gedacht aan mama die me niet kon bereiken en nu vast bezorgd was. Zou ze naar school komen? Zou ze papa bellen of was die vandaag aan het optreden? Ik wist het niet meer.

Ik keek mijn juf aan en riep: 'Jij moet je normaal gaan gedragen, ik blijf hier!' En ik bleef zitten.

Toen een paar minuten later de deur weer openging, was het een vriendinnetje uit de klas. Ze moest naar de wc. 'Ik mag eigenlijk niks tegen je zeggen,' zei ze, 'ik moet alleen wel naar de directeur van de school en melden dat hij z'n mail moet checken.' Ze keek me schuldbewust aan. 'Jij kunt er niks aan doen, ik red me wel bij de directeur,' zei ik minder krachtig en geloofwaardig dan ik had gehoopt. De directeur. Ik vond het doodeng. Niet dat ik bang voor hem was, maar alleen de allerstoutsten, degenen die een baksteen door het raam hadden gegooid, het brandalarm hadden laten afgaan of tijdens de pauze het schoolplein hadden verlaten, moesten zich melden bij de directeur. Nu was ik aan de beurt. Er ging een deur van een klaslokaal open. Het was de deur van groep zeven, die grensde aan de klassen van groep acht. Juf Nicole kwam de gang op. Een lieve juf, ik was dol op haar geweest toen ik vorig jaar bij haar in de klas had gezeten. Het was na juf Anneke de tweede juf op wie ik verliefd was geweest. Ze kwam de gang op, keek eerst naar rechts, toen naar links en zag wat ze zocht: mij. Met de vingers voor haar mond wenkte ze me.

‘Ze heeft het naar iedereen gemaild, de lerarenmail,’ zei juf Nicole. Ik keek haar aan. In haar ogen lag een laagje afkeuring, maar dat had niks te maken met mij, maar met de mail. ‘Kom maar even gezellig bij ons.’ Ik moest huilen. Kreeg een knuffel. Vervolgens pakte ze de koektrommel. ‘Een knuffel en een koekje, dat moet je sterk maken, denk ik,’ zei ze. De koektrommel was een bijzonder item in haar klas. Dat wist ik. Van vorig jaar nog. Als we de hele dag lief waren geweest, kon het zomaar zijn dat juf Nicole opstond en met de trommel de klas rondging. Altijd ergens anders beginnend zodat elke keer iemand anders het lekkerste koekje kon uitzoeken. Geweldig was dat. Het kon zomaar zo zijn dat de hele klas ’s ochtends aan de dag begon met het voornemen: vandaag doen we ons best voor het koekje. En iedereen deed dan keurig mee. Ik keek haar aan. ‘Neem er maar eentje,’ zei ze. Er was één koekje dat anders was dan de rest. Dat was namelijk geen koekje. Het was een chocolaatje. Een Bounty. Bounty’s waren mijn lievelingschocolaatjes. Terwijl ik hem opat, stelde ik me voor dat dit misschien een laatste overgebleven chocolaatje was van mijn traktatie van vorig jaar. Ik vond het een leuke gedachte dat die reep misschien al die tijd op mij had liggen wachten en alle keren de grijpgrage handen van de klas had weerstaan.

‘Dank u wel, lieve juf Nicole,’ zei ik zachtjes. Ze gaf me nog een glas water en begeleidde me toen naar buiten. Net op tijd, want toen ik weer achter het tafeltje op de gang zat, zag ik de deur aan het einde van de gang opengaan. Het was de directeur. Hij kwam me ophalen.

‘Hoe is het?’ vroeg de directeur. We liepen alle gangen en alle verdiepingen af en kwamen langs alle lokalen.

‘Ik weet dat ze het heeft rondgestuurd, hoor. Ze roddelt, dat moet ze zelf weten,’ antwoordde ik. Een tikje brutaal, dat wist ik, maar net niet brutaal genoeg om in de problemen te komen.

‘Maar wat is er gebeurd?’ zei hij nu wat ernstiger.

Ik vertelde het verhaal, merkte dat mijn stem bibberde en oversloeg. Toen we bij zijn kantoor aankwamen had ik alles verteld.

‘Je juf wil dat je je excuses aanbiedt,’ zei hij tegen me terwijl hij de deur van zijn kantoor achter zich dichttrok. ‘Excuses voor je gedrag en voor wat je gedaan hebt.’

In mijn hoofd ontstond lichte kortsluiting. De kerstlichtjes die er normaal mochten flikkeren, vielen uit. Voor de zoveelste keer die dag. ‘Sorry hoor, maar als we het over excuses hebben, is zij degene die ze zou moeten aanbieden.’

‘Dat ziet zij anders.’

‘Dat is dan vervelend voor haar.’

‘Toch zal je het moeten doen.’

‘Ik móét alleen dingen die van mijn ouders moeten, voor de rest moet ik niks. Ik heb u verteld wat er gebeurd is, ik zal daar geen excuses voor eisen, maar ga zeker geen sorry zeggen.’ Ik merkte dat het er bozer en brutaler uitkwam dan bedoeld. Maar ik kon mijn stem en gevoel niet helemaal beteugelen. Ik had even niks aan mijn paardrijlessen. De directeur keek me aan. Het was een aardige man, ik mocht hem graag en ik wilde dit gedoe helemaal niet. En hij volgens mij ook niet. Hij was meer het type directeur dat van mooi weer hield, niet van regen en lekkages. En toch moest hij hier een lekkend dak repareren. Alleen de vraag was: wie was het dak?

'Gaan jullie op z'n minst aan het eind van de dag even met elkaar praten. Kijk maar wat er dan uitkomt,' besloot hij uiteindelijk. Er werd geen knoop doorgehakt. Het verbaasde me ergens, maar aan de andere kant realiseerde ik me dat ik dit ook had kunnen verwachten. 'Snoepje?' zei hij, terwijl hij zich in zijn bureaustoel omdraaide richting een glazen snoeppot.

Een uur later zat ik in het lokaal. Bijna alle stoelen stonden op tafel, zoals dat altijd moest aan het einde van de dag. Eén tafel vooraan was stoelloos gebleven. Daar zat ik op, mijn voeten zweefden vlak boven de grond. We keken elkaar aan, zonder elkaar echt aan te kijken, juf Trol en ik. We hadden allebei onze versie van het verhaal verteld en nu was zij aan het wachten totdat ik mijn excuses zou aanbieden, terwijl ik aan het wachten was totdat bij haar het kwartje zou vallen dat ik dat niet zou gaan doen. De stilte duurde inmiddels ongemakkelijk lang. Het kwartje was duidelijk nog niet gevallen.

'Blijf van hem af! Waar zijn jullie? Weg bij hem! Hij gaat zijn excuses niet aanbieden! Sterker nog, hij gaat nu met mij mee naar huis!' Zo kwam mijn broertje de klas binnen. Hij was boos, mijn broertje. 'Alleen ik mag ruzie met hem maken, u heeft daar geen recht op!' zei hij. Ik voelde me gesterkt, sprong van de schoolbank af en kwam overeind. Juf Trol had dat duidelijk ook willen doen, maar een onzichtbare hand leek haar terug in haar stoel te duwen. Alsof ze wist dat deze wedstrijd niet in haar voordeel beslecht zou worden. 'Hij gaat met mij mee! En als u niet oppast hoort u nog van onze ouders! U heeft onze moeder eindeloos laten bellen zonder op te nemen, en nu heeft ze de directeur gesproken! Dat was niet zo slim van u! En dat is zacht uitgedrukt! Hoe durft u!' slingerde hij er nog achteraan terwijl hij mijn hand pakte. 'Laat die excuses van u maar zitten, ze zijn toch niks waard,' floepte ik er nog uit. En we liepen samen de klas uit.

De volgende dag deden we allebei alsof er niets gebeurd was. Maar er was wel iets veranderd. Ik wist nu hoe het voelde om op te staan tegen een macht, een autoriteit. Dat voelde goed. En mijn juf wist het ook. Ik had ontdekt hoe het voelde om op te staan en ze wist dat ik onvoorwaardelijke steun van mijn ouders zou krijgen. Ze wist ook dat de directeur uiteindelijk niet tegen hen in zou gaan.

Maar nu was de loting gaande, de loting waarmee werd bepaald wie tijdens de dodenherdenking op de Waalsdorpervlakte de Bourdonklok mocht luiden. Juf Trol trok een nieuw lootje uit de hoed. 'Andrea,' klonk het met een lichte aarzeling. Ik keek teleurgesteld naar het rekenboek dat voor me lag. Ergens had ik gehoopt dat mijn naam zou klinken, maar dat was niet het geval. Andrea klonk niet eens als mijn naam. 'O,' hoorde ik de juf zeggen. 'Andrea kan helemaal niet.' Andrea ging met haar moeder naar Australië. Het derde lootje zou opnieuw getrokken worden.

De juf graaide door het mandje. Ze pakte twee briefjes. Hield er eentje in haar linker- en eentje in haar rechterhand en liet Sophie, die vooraan zat, kiezen. 'Links,' zei Sophie. De juf vouwde het briefje open en las na enige aarzeling de naam op.

Mijn naam. Ik was dolgelukkig en voelde me vereerd.

Op 4 mei verzamelden we bij een vriendinnetje thuis, waarna we met z'n allen in een auto naar de Waalsdorpervlakte reden. Bij de parkeerplaats was het druk. Heel erg druk. Mannen in soldatenpakken liepen heen en weer, legerjeeps reden rond en mannen in blauwe overalls waren druk bezig. Iedereen was zich klaar aan het maken voor het belangrijke moment van stilte en de herdenking die zou volgen.

Het monument zag er prachtig uit. Alsof het zich klaar had gemaakt voor een belangrijk diner, een belangrijke plechtigheid. De baljurk was aangetrokken. Maar geen baljurk met eindeloos veel tierelantijnen. Nee het was een stemmige baljurk, eentje waarmee je bij de koningin op een verdrietige dag op bezoek kon gaan. Een plechtigheid zonder opsmuk; vandaag lag de schoonheid niet in de sieraden, maar in de herinnering. De vier bronzen kruisen stonden er mooi bij. Alsof ze net een douche hadden genomen en ze hun haren met shampoo gewassen hadden. Nu zaten die haren gekamd en nog een beetje nat keurig naar achter. Ouders zouden trots op ze zijn geweest. De vier kruisen waren klaar voor deze bijzondere avond, en zouden fier en krachtig iedere voorbijganger begroeten. Alsof ze soldaten waren die met hun hand aan hun voorhoofd een militaire groet brachten. Voor het monument lagen honderden geverfde dennenappels. Op kleur gesorteerd. Rood. Wit. Blauw. Aan de zijkant van het monument stonden fakkels. Het vuur brandde al. Zenuwachtig vuur, waarschijnlijk net zo zenuwachtig als wij.

We wachtten aan de duinrand totdat we werden geroepen. De ceremonie begon. Voor het monument stonden ontelbaar veel verdrietige hoofden. Een zee van zwart en donkerblauw. De trompet klonk. Stilte. Diepe stilte, waarin alleen de vogels ons lieten horen hoe vrijheid klonk.

We konden nog niet echt begrijpen hoe belangrijk vrijheid is, maar we konden het wel al voelen.

Met elke ruk die we gaven aan het dikke touw, waarmee we de klok in beweging brachten, voelde het alsof we het verleden lieten klinken. Het voelde alsof we de doden uit de duingrond naar boven lieten komen. Elke keer dat we de klok luidden was het alsof de stem van een van de mensen die voor onze vrijheid was opgestaan nog een keer klonk. Een bulderende, niet te stoppen stem, een schreeuw, van vrijheid. We trokken zo hard als we konden aan het touw. Ik keek naar de klok, wist wat we probeerden. We wilden de klok nóg hoger trekken, nóg hoger, zodat hij nog harder tegen de klepel aan zou knallen. We probeerden de klok helemaal rond te laten draaien, zoals je dat ook altijd probeert tijdens het schommelen in de speeltuin.

8.

We stonden op het schoolplein. Hoewel we inmiddels de oudsten van de school waren, speelden we nog steeds op de schommel en de wipwap. Maar deze keer bleven we naast de glijbaan staan, in plaats van dat we ervan afgleden. Er was onrust. In de positieve zin van het woord.

‘Doe het nou maar gewoon,’ zei een van mijn klasgenootjes.

‘Ja, ga ervoor,’ zei een ander. Ik durfde niet goed, maar wilde het ergens ook weer heel graag wel. ‘Maar hoe moet ik dat doen dan?’ vroeg ik. ‘Je moet haar gewoon roepen en dan zeggen wat je wilt. Kijk, ze staan net als wij ook bij elkaar in een groepje, ze kijken ook hierheen, ze hebben het vast over hetzelfde.’

Ik keek naar een groepje meisjes verderop op het plein. Achter hen waren jongens aan het voetballen, ik deed nooit mee. Tussen de meisjes stond Rose. Elk jaar had ik iemand op wie ik verliefd was, zodat ik altijd iemand kon aanbidden op Valentijnsdag. Eerst was ik verliefd geweest op de juffen. Na groep drie werd ik verliefd op een meisje uit mijn klas: Dora. Voor haar maakte ik tekeningen. Tekeningen van een boerderij met heel veel dieren. Zo zag ik onze toekomst voor me. We zouden samen trouwen, een boerderij kopen en voor heel veel dieren gaan zorgen. In mijn plezier maakte ik thuis eindeloos tekeningen die ik zo nu en dan mee naar school nam en aan haar gaf. Ze moest dan altijd lief lachen. Toen de boerderijdroom voorbij was, was ik verliefd geworden op een onbereikbaar meisje uit de hogere klassen. Ze heette Iris. Ze had lang bruin haar dat golfde over haar rug en kwam tot op haar billen. Ze was een van de stoersten. Hoe ik het ook probeerde, ik kon onmogelijk bij haar in de buurt komen. Tijdens de grote pauzes, als ook zij op het schoolplein te vinden was, deed ik m'n uiterste best om door haar gezien te worden. Soms ging ik haar zelfs zoeken met een van mijn klasgenootjes. Dan bekeken we haar vanachter een boom of een muurtje. David had daar altijd goede manieren voor bedacht, hoe we haar aandacht konden vangen of hoe we naar haar toe konden kruipen, verscholen achter bosjes of muurtjes. Ze zag ons vermoedelijk altijd maar speelde het spel mee. Wapperde nog een keer met haar haren, keek gedachteloos om en liep weer verder. In de klas fantaseerde ik dat het schoolgebouw in brand zou vliegen, dat iedereen op tijd buiten was en dat ik dan door zou hebben dat alleen Iris nog ontbrak. Terwijl de vlammen al uit het gebouw zouden slaan, de brandweer stopte met blussen en mij tegen probeerde te houden, zou ik de vlammen inrennen. In de rook, al hoestend, bijna niets meer ziend, zou ik haar zoeken. En ik zou haar vinden. Liggend op de vloer. Ik zou haar optillen, in mijn armen houden en langs de rook, langs de vlammen die aan mijn lichaam likten en klappen uitdeelden, doorlopen, naar buiten. Zoals ik Maria Jezus had zien vasthouden. Bij de hoofdingang zou ik met Iris in mijn armen naar buiten komen. Ik weet niet waarom, maar als ik me in de klas verveelde vond ik het een fantastische fantasie om op die manier aan haar te laten zien wat ik voor haar overhad. Maar hoe hard ik ook fantaseerde... het vuur kwam niet. Letterlijk noch figuurlijk. Ook die liefde werd nooit beantwoord. En toen ze in groep acht zat en het eindspel speelde moest ik hard huilen, wetende dat ze onze school ging verlaten en ik haar alleen nog in mijn droomwereld als prinses tegen het lijf zou lopen.

Maar elk jaar als Valentijnsdag naderde wilde ik per se weer verliefd zijn. Nu op Rose. Ze had blonde, golvende haren. Alsof iemand steentjes op haar kruin liet vallen, zodat haar krullen konden dansen en golven. Ik vond haar bijzonder. Heel bijzonder. Ik vond haar knap. Heel knap. En ik dacht dat ik verliefd was. Ze zou mijn eerste vriendinnetje worden. En mijn laatste.

'Weet je wat?' zei een ander, 'ik roep haar wel, dan moet je.' Voor ik er erg in had galmde hij haar naam over het schoolplein. Ze stonden aan de andere kant van een hek waar we net niet met onze hoofden overheen konden kijken. Het horen van haar naam had haar doen lachen en ik zag spanning door het meisjesgroepje schieten. Eenzelfde soort spanning was in mijn jongensgroepje te merken, maar dan net anders. Ze kwam los van de groep en alleen en eenzaam liep ze naar me toe. Ik kreeg een duwtje, ook ik was nu los en liep naar haar toe. Met het hek tussen ons in keken we elkaar aan. Tussen de stalen spijlen van het hek zat net genoeg ruimte om elkaar goed te kunnen zien. Ik was nerveus, maar wist dat er na het roepen van haar naam een mechanisme in gang was gezet dat ik niet meer kon stoppen. Als ik dat al wilde.

'Wat is er?' vroeg ze. Ik herinnerde me opeens dat ik over haar had gedroomd die nacht. Als een fotoflits schoot de herinnering door mijn hoofd, haar stem had hem aangezet. 'Nou,' zei ik, 'ik, ja, hoe zal ik het zeggen.' Met mijn handen hield ik de spijlen vast, in een poging mezelf een houding te geven. 'Nou, ik vind je eigenlijk heel erg mooi, zeg maar, en je bent altijd zo lief, en ja, je haren.' Ik keek haar aan, baalde van de onduidelijke zinnen die ik maakte, ze moest lachen. Gelukkig, dacht ik. Heel snel keek ik over mijn schouder, ik zag de jongens staan. Ze waren aan het wachten. Straks zou ik verslag moeten uitbrengen. Ik wilde een afgang voorkomen, dus verzamelde ik alle energie en moed die ik in me had, haalde diep adem en keek haar opnieuw aan. 'Zou je verkering willen?' vroeg ik. Ze moest lachen, maar niet op de verkeerde manier, nee, op de goede manier.

'En?' vroegen de jongens in koor toen ik terug in de groep was. 'Ja! We hebben verkering.' Gejuich steeg op.

De dagen die volgden verliepen onhandig. Moesten we elkaar een kus geven? Hoe moesten we elkaar gedag zeggen? Hoe dienden we ons te gedragen, moesten we hand in hand lopen? Zowel haar klas als de mijne wist ervan en het leek wel alsof ze allemaal onderdeel waren van onze verkering. Iedereen had het erover. Tijdens de pauzes wilde iedereen weten of we elkaar gedag zouden zeggen. Ik wist niet wat ik leuker vond, met haar samen verliefd zijn, of dat iedereen het ophemelde. Ik nam haar mee uit. Door haar ouders werd ze bij mij thuis afgeleverd. Ze ging mee naar een optreden van mijn vader. Na afloop vielen we op de achterbank op elkaars schouders in slaap. Of eigenlijk: Rose viel in slaap, ik deed alsof. Ik genoot van het beeld, het idee van de verkering, het idee van verliefd zijn, maar wist niet zeker of ik het ook echt was.

Aan het einde van het schooljaar eindigde ook de verkering met Rose. Dat ging zonder drama. Alsof we allebei een afspraak hadden gemaakt op het moment dat het aanging, dat het een verkering was voor een bepaalde periode. En dat die periode nu logischerwijs voorbij was.

9.

Op de laatste schooldag keken we de hele dag films en speelden we in de gymzaal, waar we gigantische hutten mochten bouwen. De gymleraar had een grote parachute, in de kleuren van de regenboog. Enorm was hij. We hielden allemaal een stukje van de parachute vast. We stonden zij aan zij, vrijwel de hele gymzaal gevuld.

'Oké,' zei de gymleraar, en dan wisten we wat de bedoeling was: iedereen deed zijn handen omhoog, het doek bewoog de lucht in en bolde naar boven, vervolgens deden we met z'n allen snel een stap naar binnen en trokken we, terwijl we gingen zitten, het doek naar beneden achter onze rug. Nu was de hele klas gevangen in de regenboogbol. Het voelde als een enorme hut, een veilige kleurrijke regenboogbubbel waarin we konden schuilen. Het leek alsof de buitenwereld niet meer bestond, maar alleen wij, met elkaar.

'Kijk,' zei de gymleraar, 'hier zijn jullie veilig. Zie de kleuren, zie elkaar, geniet van dit moment. Straks gaan jullie de school verlaten en dan is er een andere wereld waar jullie binnen zullen wandelen. Probeer de veiligheid en de kleuren van deze regenboogbol bij je te houden.' We keken elkaar aan. We wilden de school niet verlaten, maar het moest. Nog één keer zaten we met z'n allen in die bol, waarna de gymleraar het teken gaf, we opstonden en we uit alle macht de parachute omhoogtrokken en loslieten. De parachute vloog naar boven en leek daar even te zweven. En daarmee was het speelmoment over.

Toen we wegliepen van het schoolplein, mijn broertje, mijn vader en ik, voor een laatste keer hand in hand, had ik tranen in mijn ogen, en omdat ik niks kon zien was ik meer nog dan anders afhankelijk van papa's warme hand. In het park namen we even pauze. Papa ging zitten, mijn broertje en ik dronken het drankje op dat hij voor ons had gekocht bij de winkel op de hoek.

'Jongen,' zei mijn vader, terwijl hij me een aai gaf, 'je gaat straks het leven instappen. Blijf doen wat je leuk vindt, blijf dat kind dat je was op deze school, want er zijn te veel mensen die het leven van een ander leiden, of helemaal geen leven beleven. Blijf fantaseren en geloof niet te veel van wat grote mensen je straks wijs willen maken. Blijf ondeugend en kattenkwaad uithalen, kattenkwaad brengt je een stuk verder en maakt je een stuk vrijer dan het volgen van de regels.'

'Zoals David dat deed?' vroeg ik door mijn tranen heen.

'Ja,' zei mijn vader zachtjes.

In mijn lichaam voelde het alsof de wereld na vandaag een klein beetje onveiliger zou worden. Of in ieder geval mijn wereld.

10.

‘Wat vind jij?’ vroeg de vader aan de moeder. Ze zaten samen in de keuken, boven sliepen de kinderen.

‘Ik weet het niet,’ zei de moeder. ‘We moeten vooral zorgen dat hij zichzelf kan blijven, dat hij een omgeving heeft waarin hij zich veilig voelt. We doen er hier thuis al alles aan, maar ik zie dat hij steeds verder afdrijft.’

‘Ik zie het ook. Op vakantie, of tijdens het wandelen, hij loopt sinds kort liever alleen.’

‘Dat had hij ook nadat David vertrok uit Nederland.’

‘Ja, weet ik. Ik weet alleen niet hoe we hem kunnen bereiken.’

‘Misschien moeten we, als we met z’n drieën zijn, zonder z’n broers, het een keer voorzichtig aansnijden? Of juist een keer tijdens een diner benoemen hoe leuk ik het zou vinden als ik niet alleen schoondochters heb.’

‘Dat kunnen we doen, dan weet hij het in ieder geval. We moeten het denk ik niet te duidelijk zeggen, dat kan hij ook onprettig vinden misschien.’

‘Maar mijn grootste zorg ligt nu bij de nieuwe school. We hebben daar minder zicht op hem en het is een school waar groepjes, status en stoer gedrag als belangrijk worden gezien,’ zei de moeder, waarna er een stilte viel.

‘We moeten er gewoon op letten dat hij zichzelf kan blijven,’ doorbrak de vader de stilte, ‘en dat hij niet gepest gaat worden.’

‘Ik maak me zorgen dat hij alles wat hij leuk vindt, van toneel tot paardrijden tot vioolspelen, dat hij daarmee stopt.’

‘Die kans is er, dat hij net als de anderen wil zijn.’

‘Dat is hij alleen niet, daar maak ik me zorgen over.’

‘Laten we het goed in de gaten houden. Hij is emotioneler en kwetsbaarder dan zijn broers. We kunnen altijd nog vragen of een van zijn broers een oogje in het zeil wil houden, of zelf met de schoolleiding gaan zitten, mocht het niet goed gaan.’

DEEL 2
DANIËL

11.

In het weekend voor mijn eerste dag op de nieuwe school oefende papa drie keer met mij de fietsroute. Mijn wereld, die tot dan toe had bestaan uit de straat, de stoep en het park, werd opeens drastisch vergroot. Toen we aankwamen zagen we dat het schoolplein was afgesloten met een groot zwaar groen hek. Fietsloze fietsenrekken stonden te wachten op de hereniging met fietswielen. 'Dat zal je zonder mij moeten doen,' zei mijn vader, wijzend naar de ingang. Geen veilige hand meer die me bracht, geen school meer waar ik iedereen van tevoren al kende, nee, een volledig onbeschreven pagina lag voor me.

Toen ik voor het eerst naar school fietste, nu zonder papa, was ik misselijk. Mijn maag deed er alles aan om me te vertellen dat ik om moest keren. Alsof er haken in mijn lichaam waren gezet en er een touw aan die haken zat die verbonden was met ons huis. Elke trap leek de aantrekkingskracht van thuis nog sterker te maken. Ik was moe, ik had de avond ervoor vrijwel niet geslapen.

Alle brugpiepers moesten zich op de gang verzamelen, om vervolgens onder luid applaus de aula in te wandelen. Daar zat ook de rest van de school. Op het podium stond de rector. Wit haar, gouden brilletje, een donkerblauw double-breasted pak. We moesten helemaal naar voren lopen en konden bij het podium op de grond gaan zitten. We hoorden de oudere scholieren lachen en smoezen.

‘Nog even,’ begon de rector, ‘en dan zijn jullie écht VCL’ers.’ Een luid gejuich klonk op uit de zaal. ‘De eerste paar weken zullen misschien ingewikkeld zijn.’ Hij keek op ons neer, al die brugpiepers die met hun te grote tassen te weinig ruimte hadden, daar op de grond. ‘Jullie zullen vast verdwalen in het gebouw, niet alle namen weten van de docenten, jullie zullen niet iedereen kennen, maar uiteindelijk zullen jullie je weg vinden. En zullen jullie onderdeel zijn van onze prachtige school.’ Weer luid gejuich.

Met achthonderd leerlingen was het VCL (Vrijzinnig-Christelijk Lyceum) een relatief kleine school, waar iedereen elkaar kende. Heel veel mensen liepen erbij als een reclamebord voor merken. Er stonden meer Vespa’s op het schoolplein dan fietsen. Ik wist dat ik 3-0 achterstond. Merkkleding kregen we thuis niet, en een Vespa of andere scooter zat er al helemaal niet in. ‘Je kunt prima fietsen, dat is nog gezond ook.’

Toen we na het welkomstwoord de aula uit mochten, leek het wel of we in een Londense metro waren beland. Iedereen drukte elkaar opzij alsof er een enorme haast was. Met een paar klasgenoten keek ik naar ons rooster. Een getal en een letter, dat was de locatie van onze eerste mentorles. We hadden geen idee waar dat was, maar het vragen aan de ouderejaars, dat liet je wel uit je hoofd. Voor je het wist belandde je in een prullenbak. Als je daar vroeg op de dag in was gegooid, had je eigenlijk nog geluk. Want dan waren de bakken nog leeg. Belandde je er later, dan had je een probleem; dan zouden er bananenschillen of, als je echt pech had, yoghurtresten op je jas, je tas en je broek komen. Die eerste dag bleef een prullenbakbezoek me gelukkig bespaard, al zou het me later wel overkomen.

Iedereen had een eigen locker. Waar andere leerlingen hun kluisje mooi hielden, als een poppenkast of een kijkdoos die je vroeger bij handvaardigheid mocht maken, was die van mij een grote rommel. Ongeordend. Net als mijn hoofd en gevoel. Er viel nog zoveel te ontdekken op deze nieuwe school, dat ik het gevoel had alsof er duizend stuiterballen door mijn hoofd denderden. Die energie nam ik ook de klas in en al snel leerde ik ook op deze school de stilte en de leegte van de gangen kennen.

De ruimte met de lockers was helemaal beneden in het gebouw. Alle brugpiepers bleven daar vrijwel de gehele pauze hangen, alsof het een kooi in een dierentuin was. Daar was je enigszins veilig. In de kantine was je vogelvrij. De kans dat je in een prullenbak zou belanden, werd een stuk groter en je was niet langer beschermd tegen de blikken van ouderejaars. Vooral dat laatste was voor mij een ding. Ik merkte dat er iets was. Droeg ik de verkeerde kleren? Misschien, maar ik was zeker niet de enige die geen merkkleding aanhad. Nee, het leek alsof er iets anders was. Ik begreep niet wát, maar ik voelde het wel. Soms hoorde ik jongens lachen. Of riepen ze 'heeeeheeee', begeleid door een knipoog, een verkeerd soort knipoog, waarna ze vervolgens hard moesten lachen. Ik begreep niet wat de aanleiding was en voelde me niet prettig bij de extra aandacht. Daarom bleef ik in de pauze ook maar in de lockerruimte.

Vanuit daar kon ik wel naar buiten kijken, het schoolplein op. Het bleek het heiligste terrein dat je als scholier kon bereiken. Of eigenlijk de kleine betonnen piramide die op het schoolplein stond. In de gangen werd het de apenrots genoemd. De allerstoersten, de allergaafsten, de allermooisten; die mochten daar plaatsnemen. Daar werd gerookt en gelachen. Roken was alleen toegestaan als je in de bovenbouw zat en werd gezien als het ultieme doel. Wie rookte moest tijdens de pauzes immers naar buiten, wat betekende dat je behoorde tot de beste en belangrijkste groepjes van school. Want zo was het VCL ingericht, de sociale structuur bestond uit eilandjes. Met daartussenin eindeloos veel water. Hoorde je bij de ene vriendengroep, dan zat je op dít eiland. Hoorde je bij een ander groepje, dan zat je vast op dát eiland. Overvaren was eigenlijk onmogelijk. De eilanden die buiten lagen, dat waren de eilanden waar iedereen van droomde. De eilanden met zacht zand en palmbomen. Daar wilde je uiteindelijk naartoe. En zelfs buiten was er nog een hiërarchie. Waar je stond, waar je zat, met wie je rookte en met wie je sprak; alles betekende iets. En de mensen die al zittend, hangend en soms zelfs liggend op de apenrots hun sigaret opstaken en met elkaar de laatste roddels doornamen, dat waren de stoersten van de school.

'Kom Wobie, je moet mee, dit vind je sowieso hartstikke leuk,' zei Babette. Babette was iemand uit de derde. Ik kende haar van paardrijden. Toen we elkaar voor het eerst zagen in de gangen van het VCL, was ik geschrokken. Ik hield het liever geheim dat ik op paardrijden zat. In een strakke broek met leren laarzen op een paard – dat werd nou niet echt als 'cool' gezien. Maar ermee stoppen wilde ik absoluut niet. Gelukkig had ze de blik in mijn ogen begrepen en niks gezegd. Ik was haar daar dankbaar voor.

'Kom.' Ze pakte mijn hand. Leunend tegen de lockers vertelde ze over het Sinterklaascabaret. Ik had geen idee wat dat was, maar ze vertelde er zo enthousiast over. 'Op of rond 5 december vindt het Sinterklaascabaret plaats. Op het podium voert een groepje leerlingen acts en scènes uit waarbij ze de docenten nadoen,' vertelde ze. Toneelspelen, het podium, dat wilde ik dolgraag. Op de basisschool had ik op theaterschool Rabarber gezeten, daar genoot ik enorm van. En omdat ik vioolspeelde had ik ook al af en toe opgetreden. Ik wist niet wat de bedoeling precies was, maar het klonk veelbelovend. 'Geloof me maar.' Ze greep mijn arm en liet die niet meer los terwijl we drie trappen opliepen, op naar het lokaal waar de eerste meeting zou zijn.

'*Hello hellooo helloooo!*' schalde de docent die het cabaret de komende maanden zou begeleiden. Meneer Schooll, ook docent Engels. Hij leek wel wat op Sinterklaas. En op de Kerstman. Hij had een grijs, wittig baardje en was het type docent dat je middelbareschoolperiode kleur geeft. Eentje die je onthoudt.

Ik nam wat verder achterin plaats in de banken. Babette ging op de tafel zitten, naast mij, blijkbaar golden de dagelijkse schoolregels tijdens deze sessie niet.

'*Alright*,' begon meneer Schooll, '*let's start*.' We waren met een groep van ongeveer tien mensen. Ik was de enige brugpieper, verder was Babette de enige uit de onderbouw en waren er bijna geen meisjes. Ik vond het bijzonder dat de ouderejaars zomaar met mij in één ruimte konden zitten. Alsof het een diersoort was waar je niet te dicht bij in de buurt moest komen. Maar blijkbaar golden de eiland-, rook- en roddelregels die de dagelijkse gang van zaken op school bepaalden niet in dit lokaal. Hier draaide het om creativiteit en om fantasie.

De jongens uit de bovenbouw begonnen met een reeks van ideeën. Ze hadden al een paar sketches bedacht en begonnen die uit te leggen. Ik luisterde vol bewondering. Zoveel ideeën, zoveel verzinsels. Ik had er de laatste tijd last van dat ik nog maar moeilijk mijn fantasie in kon duiken. Mijn fantasiewereld wás er wel, maar het voelde alsof ik langzaam een donkere leegte in werd gezogen. Het was fijn om anderen nu eens te horen fantaseren. Fantasieën die ontsproten uit de werkelijkheid.

De bel klonk. De grote pauze was voorbij en iedereen moest weer door naar zijn klas. Ook ik. Maar meneer Schooll hield me tegen. 'Wie ben jij dan, jongeman?' vroeg hij. Ik had tijdens de sessie nog niks gezegd. 'Nou...' begon ik. Wat moest ik antwoorden? 'Hij was met mij mee. Ik denk dat hij een goede toevoeging kan zijn,' zei Babette, die in de deuropening was blijven staan.

Ik keek meneer Schooll aan en hoopte dat hij dezelfde mening had als Babette.

'*Well, well, well*. Volgens mij ben jij *just perfect* voor het spelen van mevrouw Vlieger,' zei hij. Ik keek hem aan. Mijn ogen werden groter en met mijn hand haalde ik een niet-bestaande krul weg voor mijn gezicht. Ik had geen idee wie mevrouw Vlieger was.

'Lijkt je dat wat?' vroeg hij.

In mijn hoofd vormde zich een beeld van hoe iemand met de naam 'mevrouw Vlieger' eruit zou zien.

'Ik ken haar niet, dus ik denk dat ik haar wel kan spelen,' zei ik.

'Top,' zei hij. 'Dan schrijven we die rol in het script.' Ik keek Babette aan, was haar dankbaar.

In de weken die volgden kwamen we niet alleen in de pauzes bij elkaar in het klaslokaal, we bleven ook na schooltijd in het gebouw. Tussen het oefenen en het bedenken door konden we door het gebouw lopen. Lege, stille gangen. Alleen wat leraren die de docentenkamer in- en uitliepen. Ik leerde ze daardoor snel kennen, ook omdat we van meneer Schooll drinken mochten halen in de docentenkamer.

Op den duur ging ik zelfs met de jongens uit de bovenbouw mee naar buiten. Zij rookten. Gingen op de apenrots zitten en bliezen zelfgemaakte wolkjes de lucht in. Ze vroegen of ik ook wilde. Dat wilde ik niet. Ik vond het zo vies ruiken. En daarbij, ik vond het al spannend en bijzonder genoeg dat ik met hen op het schoolplein mocht staan – als ik ook nog eens zou gaan roken, dan wist ik niet of ik alle spanning en sensatie nog aankon.

Ik was steeds meer bezig met het Sinterklaascabaret. Meer dan met de lessen die ik moest volgen en het huiswerk dat ik hoorde te maken. Afgeraffeld of niet-gemaakt huiswerk en een drukke aanwezigheid in de klas: dat was een gevaarlijke combinatie. Voor de orde in de klas maar vooral ook voor mezelf. Toch kwam ik bij een hoop docenten met veel weg, wonderbaarlijk genoeg. Nadat de bel was gegaan en iedereen naar huis mocht, zagen ze me steeds vaker door de gangen van het schoolgebouw huppelen. Het zou nog best lang duren voordat ik écht de klas uit zou worden gestuurd met een rode kaart. Dat betekende dat je je moest melden bij de rector of de conrector, met nablijven en strafregels als gevolg.

Het werd 5 december en ik zat bloednerveus aan de ontbijttafel. Voor me lag een boterham met kaas, ik had er drie kleine happen van genomen, maar als ik slikte was ik bang dat er meer naar buiten zou komen dan er naar binnen was gegaan. Alles in mijn lijf was overprikkeld. Ik had geen zin om te praten maar wílde wel praten. Ik had geen zin om te eten maar wílde wel eten. Ik had geen zin om iets te drinken maar wílde wel drinken. De zenuwen namen mijn lichaam over. Ik keek nog een keer naar mijn bord met kaas en moest kokhalzen. En nog een keer. En nog een keer. Ik rende naar boven, naar de wc, en gaf over. Er kwam weinig want er was weinig. Ik wilde de stress uitkotsen, maar dat lukte niet. De kleine hapjes en de kleine slokjes kwamen er wel uit, maar hoe ik ook mijn best deed, de zenuwen kreeg ik niet uit mijn lijf.

Mama bracht me naar school in haar auto. Als we begonnen met rijden ging de radio automatisch aan. Klassieke muziek klonk uit de boxen. Violen, een harp, piano's en op de achtergrond een triangel. Alles was belangrijk om het stuk compleet te maken, zelfs de kleinste schakel. Ik keek naar mama. Ze was thuis de stoerste van ons allemaal. Ik voelde me veilig naast haar in de auto, wilde eigenlijk dat ze een andere kant op zou rijden, weg van school. Dat ze een verkeerde afslag nam maar we allebei niks zouden zeggen. Nee, dat ze gewoon nog harder het gaspedaal zou indrukken. Ik hoorde de violen. Vanaf mijn zesde zat ik op vioolles. Op tv had ik een orkest gezien en toen er een mevrouw of een meneer met een viool in beeld kwam, had ik geroepen dat ik dat ook wilde. Ik vermoedde dat mama daar dolgelukkig mee was geweest. Papa was van de rock, mama van het klassieke. Zij speelde vroeger harp, dromen gevangen in snaren, totdat je ze bespeelde, dan kwamen ze vrij. Een prachtig instrument. Dat vond ik ook van de viool. Met de krullende vormen, de sierlijke hals, het glanzende hout en de precisie waarmee je haar, de viool, moest bespelen. De viool was een instrument uit een sprookje. En een instrument dat ving hoe verliefdheid eruitzag. 'En ze leefden nog lang en gelukkig', zo zag een viool eruit. Ik keek naar mama en bedacht me dat ze misschien hoopte dat we ooit samen zouden spelen, zij op de harp en ik op de viool.

We namen geen verkeerde afslag en mama bracht me bij de ingang van het schoolplein. 'Ik kom vanmiddag kijken,' zei ze. Dat had ze de avond ervoor met papa overlegd. 'Ik ben heel benieuwd, ik zal je een sms'je sturen als ik er ben, doe voorzichtig, blijf jezelf, geniet ervan, je kunt het, je zult het fantastisch doen, ik ben sowieso trots, wat je ook doet.' Ik gaf haar een kus en stapte uit de auto. Ik wilde niet alleen het schoolplein opwandelen, maar moest wel. Onder mijn arm had ik een grote tas met kleding erin die ik voor die dag nodig had.

Het podium zag er prachtig uit. De aula was donker gemaakt, alsof de avond in dit stukje van de school al begonnen was. We deden eerst een repetitie, zonder kledingwissels en zonder kostuums, om eerst het geluid en licht te controleren. Meneer Schooll kwam naar mij toe. '*Hello hellooo helloooooo, mister, Sir! Goooood to see you!* Fijn dat je er bent. Luister, kijk, ik heb van mijn vrouw een panty meegenomen, een panty met rode stippen, die mag je lenen, ze gebruikt hem zelf nooit, maar ik denk dat die prachtig onder de rok zal staan. Ik heb ook een rok bij me en jijzelf had de hakken en het jasje geregeld hè?' Ik keek hem aan. De hakken had ik inderdaad geregeld. Dat had me een zoekende blik van mijn moeder en vader opgeleverd. Na het avondeten, toen ik hielp met het inruimen van de vaatwasser, had ik het gevraagd. 'O mam, kan ik misschien wat hakken van je lenen?' Ik zag een kleine blik heen en weer gaan tussen mama en papa, geen gehaaste blik, geen paniekerige, nee, eerder alsof ze badminton aan het spelen waren. 'Ja hoor,' had mama gezegd, waarna ik tussen haar verzameling hakken twee zwarte exemplaren had gevonden met aan de voorkant gouden versiersels. 'Je moet wel even kijken of je ze past en of je erop kunt lopen.' Ik had de hakken aangedaan, ze pasten, en ik probeerde omhoog te komen. Mama hielp. Op de houten vloer klónken mijn hakken in ieder geval alsof ze echt waren. Alsof ik een echte dame was. Nu was het nog zaak om te leren lopen. Mama deed het voor. Ik vermoedde dat ze zo ook ooit had gelopen toen ze een poging deed om voor eeuwig in papa's hoofd te komen. Dat was haar gelukt en ze was het sierlijk lopen niet verleerd.

Ze hielp me overeind van de bank en begeleidde me bij de eerste paar stappen, met haar handen die mijn handen vasthielden om me in evenwicht te houden. Alsof ze me opnieuw leerde lopen. Maar dit keer mooier en bewuster dan als klein kind. 'Je moet het gewoon doen, dat is de kunst, niet nadenken over je balans, die balans zit in je lichaam. Ik vermoed dat als ik je loslaat, je vanzelf loopt. Doe maar, durf maar, wees een balletdanseres en loop van deze kant van de kamer naar de andere kant.' En ze liet me los.

Ik liep, de hakken tikten op de vloer, mijn lopen klonk als dat van een meisje. Als dat van een dame. Ik zette mijn ene voet voor de andere. Balans houden was geen probleem. 'Komt vast door het paardrijden, dat ik zo makkelijk balans kan houden,' zei ik, een beetje verontschuldigend. Ik wist niet waarom, maar ergens voelde het alsof ik dit niet zo makkelijk en goed had moeten kunnen. Alsof het niet hoorde. Maar toen ik een kleine pirouette uitvoerde en ik niet langer met mijn rug naar mijn mama stond maar haar in de ogen keek, toen wist ik dat het prima was om op hakken te lopen.

Een aantal keren had ik ze later nog aangedaan in mijn slaapkamer. Alleen als mijn broertje er niet was. Dan liep ik zachtjes op de hakken tussen onze bedden, een minicatwalk. 'Ja, ik heb de hakken geregeld, meneer Schooll,' zei ik terwijl ik de tas met kleding van hem overnam. 'Suuuuuper! *Great!* Topper!'

Na de repetities zaten we in de kleedkamer. Normaal werd die gebruikt voor de gymlessen, maar die gingen vandaag niet door – wij hadden de kleedruimte nodig. Ik knoopte mijn overhemd los. Hoewel de zenuwen inmiddels waren gezakt, misschien dankzij de goede repetitie, aarzelde ik toch bij het losmaken van de knoopjes. Waarom wist ik niet precies. Ondertussen wurmde ik mijn voeten uit mijn schoenen. Ik had geen zin om mijn veters helemaal los te maken. Nadat ik mijn overhemd en mijn T-shirt uit had getrokken, deed ik het damesbloesje aan en vervolgens het zwarte glitterjasje. Als ik rondjes draaide in dat jasje en er lichten op stonden gericht, zou het een bewegende sterrenhemel zijn. Of alsof de hele klas een sterretje aanstak in een donker klaslokaal. Ik had het jasje ooit op vakantie gekregen van mama en papa. Het hing bij de damesafdeling, maar ik vond het zo mooi dat ik het toch had gepast. Ik vond de kleren voor jongens maar saai en was een beetje jaloers op de ruime keuze die dames hadden. Toen ze me zag had de eigenaresse van de winkel in haar handen geklapt en dat applaus was voldoende geweest om het jasje te kopen. Hoewel het eigenlijk veel te warm was had ik er de hele vakantie in rondgelopen. Ik was er blij mee. Nu deed ik het aan om mevrouw Vlieger te spelen en het jasje gaf me energie.

Ik trok mijn broek uit en ging zitten om de panty aan te doen. Gelukkig was het een wat dikkere, en zwart, want mijn benen waren niet geschoren. Ik deed immers niet aan wielrennen. Vervolgens trok ik het rokje aan dat tot ruim twintig centimeter boven de knie kwam. Kort maar niet te kort. Sexy maar niet te sexy. Vervolgens liet ik mijn voeten glijden in de hakken van mijn moeder. Ik voelde me Assepoester op de trappen van een paleis. Mijn glazen muiltjes gingen nu aan.

'Jaaaaahhaaaaa!' riep Ryanne. Ryanne was een meisje uit de bovenbouw. Eentje die haar haren vaker liet verven dan dat de regenboog kleuren had en een lijf vol tatoeages had. Althans, ze zag eruit alsof ze dat zou kunnen hebben. Lange gekleurde nepnagels maakten haar extra bijzonder. Ze was de enige op school die er zo uitzag. Veel leerlingen vonden haar een tikje ordinair, waarschijnlijk omdat hun ouders dat ooit gezegd hadden, maar eigenlijk vond iedereen haar toch ook gewoon wel stoer.

'Jajajajajaja! Wat goed dit!' gilde ze door de kleedkamer. Ze maakte een dansje. Dat kon ze als geen ander. Ze was een danseres en een performer, dat zag je aan alles. Ze was het inspirerende type. Zo iemand waarvan je weet en ziet, ook al kende je haar nog niet: die gaat haar eigen pad, of je dat nou leuk vindt of niet. Ze gaat ervoor en niemand kan haar stoppen.

'Ik ga je make-up doen, lieverd!' riep ze. Daar had ik helemaal niet over nagedacht, maar eigenlijk leek het mij ook wel logisch dat ik opgemaakt zou worden. Ik ging zitten en ze kwam voor me staan met een enorm etui aan verfspullen. Klaar om te schilderen. Aan haar gezicht kon ik zien dat ze dit eerder had gedaan. Ze begon met mijn wenkbrauwen, kamde ze en tekende wat. Vervolgens mijn ogen. 'Even omhoogkijken', met een potlood trok ze er lijntjes onder.

'Oké, ogen openhouden en naar beneden kijken.' Ze pakte mascara en verlengde met kleine haaltjes mijn wimpers. 'Je hebt lange wimpers van jezelf, dit wordt echt heel mooi.' Ik moest lachen, kon niet zien wat ze aan het doen was, maar wist wel dat ik het leuk vond.

'Zooo, nog even wat blush en dan je lippen!' Waarna ze met een kwast twee klopjes op mijn wangen gaf en ze vervolgens met een licht roodroze lippenstift mijn lippen stiftte. Ik voelde me prachtig, mijn gezicht voelde als een feest.

Na de generale repetitie kwam meneer Schooll naar de kleedkamer om een laatste keer te zeggen wat hij ervan vond. Een kleine peptalk. Hij was enthousiast, zweepte ons op – iedereen had er zin in. We voelden ons als circusartiesten. Heerlijk. Op het einde wendde hij zich nog even tot mij. 'Je lijkt sprekend op haar in manier van doen en lopen, helemaal super! Je had zo een vrouw kunnen zijn! Te gek! Alleen: niet te veel make-up meer opdoen hoor, vanaf nu,' zei hij, meer tegen de dames om me heen dan tegen mij, 'want anders wordt hij te mooi. En zo knap is mevrouw Vlieger niet,' maakte meneer Schooll zijn verhaal af. Ik had mevrouw Vlieger nog steeds niet ontmoet, maar blijkbaar leek ik als twee druppels water op haar. En het voelde als een compliment.

De eerste uitvoering ging goed. De tweede ook. Voordat we aan de derde zouden beginnen hadden we even pauze. Ik zag mijn mobiel oplichten. Mama was er. Snel verliet ik de kleedkamer. Met mijn hakken, mijn rokje en mijn glitterjasje liep ik door het trappenhuis naar beneden, de kantine in. Ik moest door de kantine om mama te kunnen opvangen. Ik zag wat leerlingen kijken. Een jongen verkleed als dame, dat gebeurde niet elke dag. Maar omdat dit mijn optreedkostuum was, kon het. Daarnaast, en dat wist ik, was ik een mooi meisje. Ik was geslaagd als dame, en dat zorgde ervoor dat ik nog vrouwelijker en nog krachtiger mijn ene hak voor de andere plaatste. Geen hakken in het zand, maar hakken die me vooruitduwden, alsof ze íéts omhoog stonden, zodat ik een beetje naar voren viel en omdat ik niet wilde omvallen gedwongen was ferm vooruit te wandelen.

Ik zag mijn moeder de kantine binnenkomen, aan de andere kant van de zaal. Ik liep naar haar toe en zwaaide. Ze zag mij ook. Maar zwaaide niet terug. Heel even wankelde mijn hak. Een miniseconde. Uit balans. Ik zwaaide nog een keer, mijn moeder keek een beetje weg, alsof ze bang was dat iemand zou zien dat ik haar kende. Ik liep op haar af en ze ontweek mijn blik. Ze leek te zoeken, te zoeken naar een uitweg, een plek waar ze heen kon. Ik voelde me geen mooie dame meer, eerder een clown. Mijn make-up was niet meer prachtige gezichtsverf, maar eerder een clownsmasker. Maar ik bleef doorlopen, doorlopen naar mijn mama.

'Mam,' zei ik. Ze keek op, wierp een blik op de deuren van de aula en rommelde in haar tas, waarschijnlijk op zoek naar haar mobiel. De aula grensde aan de kantine en mama keek vermoedelijk hoe ze straks de zaal in kon komen. 'Mam,' zei ik nog een keer. Ze keek me nu echt aan. Heel even was ik bang, maar m'n hak wiebelde niet nog een keer.

'Jij bent het!' zei mijn mama. 'Ik had je helemaal niet herkend, ik dacht nog, wat een mooie dame, wat een mooi meisje komt daar aanlopen, maar ik zie nu pas dat jij het bent. Wat goed, lieverd! Wat goed je te zien, ik wilde je net gaan bellen waar je was.' Ze glimlachte, trots twinkelde in haar ogen. Opeens besefte ik dat ik bang was geweest, die paar seconden, die paar stappen die ik in haar richting liep, bang dat ik haar teleur zou stellen. Maar dat was ze niet. Gelukkig. Overduidelijk niet.

'Gaat het zo beginnen, ben ik nog op tijd?' vroeg ze.

'Jazeker, we gaan zo aan de derde uitvoering beginnen. Meneer Schooll, van wie het rokje en de panty zijn,' – en ik wees op mijn benen— 'of eigenlijk van zijn vrouw, die heeft speciaal voor jou een plekje gereserveerd helemaal vooraan in de zaal.'

We stonden daar even te kletsen, totdat mevrouw Wolkenvanger langsliep. Ze was geen docent, maar de persoon die altijd in de Olympus zat. De Olympus was een ruimte helemaal boven in het gebouw, waar je alleen via het oude gedeelte van de school kon komen, over drie krakende trappen. Daar kon je boeken lenen en in stilte studeren. Het was een bijzondere plek en voelde eerder als een huiskamer dan als een bibliotheek. De ruimte was bezaaid met van die glazen sneeuwbollen die je in souvenirwinkels kunt kopen. Als je flink schudde zweefden alle sneeuwvlokken, alle glitters erin rond. Mevrouw Wolkenvanger had er tientallen, zo niet honderden van. Ze stonden overal op de planken, in de kozijnen en op de tafels. Tussen al die bollen en boeken zat ze achter haar bureau. Vaak was ze aan het lezen, of anders hielp ze leerlingen bij hun huiswerk. Maar blijkbaar was mevrouw Wolkenvanger vanachter dat bureau vandaan gekomen. Ze kwam even naast ons staan, naast mama en mij. En wees op mijn benen.

'Ach kind, wat heb jij goede benen, doe mij ook zo'n setje, ik ben er helemaal jaloers op.' En ze liep verder, zonder een reactie van mijn kant af te wachten. Ik vond het een mooi compliment en sloeg het op in de bibliotheek die in mijn hoofd zat.

'Jammer dat papa je zo niet kan zien,' zei mama. 'Wordt het ergens opgenomen, zodat hij het later terug kan zien?'

'Volgens mij niet,' zei ik.

'Ah, dan is het al helemaal zonde.'

Toch was ik stiekem blij dat papa er niet was. Niet dat hij het erg had gevonden mij zo te zien, maar ik was er toch een beetje bang voor. Ik keek om me heen, zag de merkkleding, de blauwe truien van de jongens en de zwarte Eastpak-rugtassen die leerlingen op de banken hadden gegooid. Ik voelde dat ik er anders uitzag. Nu. Maar ook de andere dagen. Deze make-up, de glinsterende oorbellen, de ringen om mijn nagels. Ergens zaten ze ook in de andere dagen al in mij verstopt. En ik voelde het. Een spanning kwam in mijn lichaam omhoog. Weer die spanning die ik niet kon verklaren. Nu was het prettig, omdat ik het gevoel had dat ik even wat meer vrij was door in de schijnwerpers te stappen, door als mevrouw Vlieger het podium te bestijgen, als haar door de gangen van het schoolgebouw te lopen. Door iemand anders te spelen kon ik vrijer zijn dan buiten de schijnwerpers. Misschien speelde ik wel meer mezelf dan mevrouw Vlieger. De spanning was nu fijn, maar ik voelde ook dat hij zich de komende dagen tegen mij zou keren. Omdat ik na vandaag niet meer als mevrouw Vlieger door het schoolgebouw kon lopen en ik weer een jaar moest wachten totdat ik opnieuw op die manier het podium kon bestijgen.

En dat zou ik ook echt blijven doen, het podium bestijgen als mevrouw Vlieger. Alle zes jaren die ik op het VCL zat zou ik mevrouw Vlieger spelen.

Het applaus was nog hoorbaar toen we vanuit de coulissen het trapje richting de kleedkamer opklommen. Iedereen was blij. Ook ik. Ik had deze keer de eerste rij extra goed in de gaten gehouden. Had mijn mama moeten lachen? Had ze geklapt? Had ze ervan genoten? Voor zover haar gezicht de waarheid vertelde, was dat zeker het geval geweest. Ik was blij en tevreden, al voelde ik meteen dat ik het ook jammer vond dat het voorbij was. Ik wilde nog niet dat het zou stoppen. Maar het was al gestopt. Iedereen begon zich om te kleden, maar ik twijfelde nog. Wilde ik nu al stoppen mevrouw Vlieger te zijn?

12.

Eerder dat schooljaar, zo'n drie weken na mijn initiatie als brugpieper, was ik wat onrustig. Ik werd vaker lastiggevallen door wat oudere jongens die dingen zeiden die ik niet begreep. 'Homooo,' hoorde ik een keer. En 'Ha! Gayyy!' als ik voorbijliep. Ik wist eigenlijk niet wat dat inhield, behalve dat het niet iets positiefs was, of, niet als zodanig werd bedoeld. Er leek wat veranderd te zijn. Sinds ik op school was gekomen hadden anderen, vooral oudere scholieren, soms een beetje vreemd gedaan als ik langsliep. Zeker in de kantine. Maar het leek steeds heftiger te worden, zichtbaarder. Ik begreep niet zo goed wat de aanleiding was geweest, maar probeerde me er niks van aan te trekken. Toch was ik vandaag onrustiger. Op de gang had een groepje stoere jongens staan wachten. Jongens die naar rook roken. En van wie de rits van hun tassen kapot was. Ze hadden les in het lokaal naast dat van mij. Ze waren aan het lachen en maakten grappen tegen elkaar toen ik stond te wachten op de gang. Ik probeerde het te negeren, maar ergens drongen zich toch splinters in mijn gevoel. Ik stond naast Floris, een flamboyante jongen, die niet alleen kleurrijke kleding droeg maar ook kleurrijk líép. Over hem werd nog veel vaker gelachen en geroddeld. Niet alleen door de ouderejaars, ook door zijn leeftijdsgenoten. Ik had met

Floris te doen maar kon hem niet helpen. Floris deed alsof hij niks hoorde en samen hadden we onze rug naar de jongens toe gekeerd.

'Oeooeoeoee lalaaa,' klonk het vervolgens. Ik voelde me niet prettig. Ongemakkelijk. Wilde mezelf even wegtoveren. Gelukkig hadden we biologieles van meneer Rugh. Een zeer toepasselijke naam voor een biologieleraar. Zijn collega heette mevrouw Botman. De klas vermoedde dat ze eerst hun beroep hadden gekozen en daarna pas hun achternaam. Meneer Rugh was het type docent dat altijd te vroeg in het klaslokaal was en dat eigenlijk ook van de leerlingen verwachtte. Vandaag was dit onze redding, we konden eerder de klas in.

Meneer Rugh gaf les op zijn manier. Hij had langer haar dan de meeste meisjes op school. En dan heb ik het niet over z'n borsthaar dat boven zijn houthakkershemd uitkwam omdat hij altijd twee tot drie knoopjes openhield. Nee, de haren op zijn hoofd waren langer dan die van de meeste meisjes. In de gangen liet meneer Rugh zijn haren nog wel eens los wapperen, maar als hij lesgaf deed hij ze in een staart. Het stond hem niet verkeerd. Meneer Rugh was ook het type leraar dat het leuk vond om aan de klas te vertellen wat hij zoal deed. Zo brouwde hij zelf zijn bier en beloofde hij dat hij dat een keertje mee zou nemen. We wisten niet of we het zouden durven drinken.

Meneer Rugh nam zijn vak zeer serieus en vertelde overtuigend en meeslepend. Over de natuur, over de dieren, over het menselijk lichaam. Alle leerlingen, of ze biologie nou wel of niet leuk vonden, luisterden vol aandacht. Meestal.

In zijn lokaal waren in de muren glazen vitrinekasten gemaakt. Ze stonden vol glazen potten met sterk water erin. In sommige daarvan zaten ogen, in andere een rat, een slang en een ongeboren kip. Als je gevoelig was voor nachtmerries, moest je niet te lang voor de kasten gaan staan. Verder stonden er glazen bakken met dieren erin. Naast het schoolbord stond een bak met drie baardagamen erin, ze hadden iets prehistorisch. In twee andere bakken zaten slangen, kleine slangen. Meneer Rugh grapte er wel eens over dat ze ontsnapt waren en dat er daarom nu extra boeken en dozen op de deksels stonden.

Omdat meneer Rugh zijn vak zo serieus nam was het belangrijk dat zijn leerlingen goed in bedwang werden gehouden. Hij had een streepjessysteem. Als iemand de klas stoorde kwam er een streepje op het schoolbord. Verstoorde vervolgens iemand de les, dan kwam er een tweede streepje op het bord. Degene die het derde streepje op zijn geweten had, zou er met een rode kaart worden uitgestuurd. In plaats van strafregels schrijven moest je dan wit papier gaan voorzien van een kantlijn aan de zijkant (met een breedte van precies 3,5 centimeter) en een lijn aan de bovenkant (6 centimeter breed). Als de strepen ook maar een beetje scheef waren, moest alles opnieuw. Iedereen in de klas wilde dit voorkomen.

Tijdens deze les was er iets gebeurd waardoor meneer Rugh meteen twee strepen op het schoolbord had gezet. Dat was problematisch, want de kans dat er in de resterende veertig minuten nog iets zou gebeuren was groot. Ik was aan het klooien met mijn pennen en had mijn boek nog dicht toen meneer Rugh heel rustig aan zijn bureau ging zitten in het midden van zijn verhaal. Terwijl hij doorpraatte opende hij zijn bureaula en haalde er een rood briefje uit. Meneer Rugh had de eigenaardige gewoonte om een voorraad kant-en-klare rode briefjes in zijn la te hebben. Hij hoefde alleen nog maar de datum en de naam van de leerling die eruit moest op te schrijven, de rest stond er al op.

Hij haalde het rode briefje omhoog, schreef een naam op en onderbrak pas daarna zijn verhaal over de ontwikkelingen van planten.

‘Wobie, deze is voor jou,’ zei hij tegen mij. ‘Je boek is dicht, je bent met je etui bezig, je let niet op en bent onrustig. Ga je maar melden.’ ‘Ik schrijf alles mee in mijn schrift, ik heb hier letterlijk uw laatste zin staan.’ Zo werkte ik altijd als de docent verhalend te werk ging. Dan kon ik als ik ging leren met mijn schrift in de hand door de kamer lopen en doen alsof ik zelf aan een groot publiek lesgaf. Dat deed mijn vader ook altijd. Die liep bij het repeteren eindeloos heen en weer in de benedenkamer, met de deur dicht. Dan was hij aan het vertellen alsof hij op een podium stond. Dat was dé manier om alles uit z’n hoofd te kunnen leren en ik was erachter gekomen dat het voor mij en mijn lessen ook werkte. Alles repeteren alsof je moest optreden. Het optreden was de toets zelf. Maar dat deed er nu niet toe. Ik had niet de klas gestoord, maar de docent. ‘Maakt me niet uit, ik ben afgeleid door jouw houding, dus hier heb je de rode kaart,’ zei hij.

Het gekke was: hij zei het niet eens boos. Ik had gedacht dat het uitdelen van een rode kaart gepaard zou gaan met slaande deuren en een woedend gezicht. Maar meneer Rugh stuurde mij heel rustig weg, zonder gedoe. Ik vond dit een prettige manier om eruit te worden gestuurd.

Toen ik buiten stond baalde ik wel. Ik voelde me schuldig, alsof ik iets kapot had gemaakt, of iets heel vies had gedaan. Ik wist ook eigenlijk niet zo goed waar ik heen moest. Bij de rector, de conrector of de decaan was ik nog nooit geweest. Een beetje hulpeloos liep ik langzaam weg bij de klas. Ik zag wat meisjes aan het begin van de kantine, ze hadden duidelijk een tussenuur.

‘Mag ik wat vragen?’ Ik durfde het eigenlijk niet, maar de angst voor wat er zou gebeuren als ik me niet meldde bij de decaan, was groter.

Een meisje draaide zich om. ‘Wat is er?’ vroeg ze verrassend lief.

'Weet jij waar ik heen moet als ik zo'n kaart heb?' Ik liet mijn rode kaart zien alsof ik iets had gestolen.

'Hier de trap op en dan naar links de gang in, daar zitten de rector, de decaan en de conrector. Je zit in de brugklas, dus je moet mevrouw Arding hebben.'

Ik liep naar boven en klopte aan bij mevrouw Arding. Ik wachtte even en klopte toen nog eens. Ik hoorde niks, maar duwde toch voorzichtig de deurklink omlaag. De deur ging open. Ik duwde hem verder, hoorde geen 'even wachten', overigens evenmin 'kom verder', maar dat had ik ook niet verwacht. Dat hoorde niet bij de rode-kaartsituatie. Recht tegenover de deuropening stond aan het eind van de kamer een groot bureau. Grijs. Met een computer erop, wat boeken op een keurige stapel met daarnaast een agenda en een vulpen die al even recht lag als al het andere hier. Het was een kamer van hoeken en rechte lijnen. Zoals regels en wetten op papier zijn. Rechttoe rechtaan. Ik werd er een beetje kriegelig van, maar was te nerveus om er bewust mee bezig te zijn.

Achter het bureau zat een mevrouw. Haar haar Beatrixsterk in vorm gespoten. Ze had het bovenstuk van een mantelpakje aan. Een rood jasje. Iets te fel voor haar leeftijd, zouden sommige mensen misschien zeggen. Haar hoofd kwam langzaam omhoog, terwijl haar ogen nog gericht waren op dat wat voor haar op het bureau lag. Pas toen haar gezicht zich mijn kant op had gedraaid, rolden haar ogen ook richting mij. Op het puntje van haar neus balanceerde een bril. Gevaarlijk ver naar voren zat die. Ik vroeg me af of de bril een ontsnappingspoging deed, of hij van haar neus wilde springen maar twijfelde of hij het zou overleven. Maar ze keek me aan en haalde zelf de bril van haar neus. Er was geen ontkomen aan voor de bril. Voor mij overigens ook niet, ik was gevangen in haar blik. De bril zat gevangen in een koordje dat om haar nek hing. Ik bleef in de deuropening staan. Over mijn schouder hing mijn rugzak, te scheef, wist ik, voor deze kamer. Tussen duim en wijsvinger hing mijn rode kaart onwennig te wachten.

'Is rood jouw kleur?' vroeg ze.

Ik schrok. Was dit een strikvraag? Ik had een rode kaart, maar zij droeg een rood jasje. 'Niet echt, mevrouw,' zei ik.

Ze kwam me bekend voor, alsof ik haar eerder ergens was tegengekomen. Ik herkende iets van mezelf in haar, en dat terwijl ik totaal niet op haar leek. Ze was star, bewoog bijna niet, hield haar lippen stijf op elkaar, alsof ze het ijskoud had.

'Dan zullen we dit maar zien als iets waar je geen gewoonte van maakt, toch?' Ze wenkte me met een handgebaar en ik gaf haar de rode kaart. Ze wierp er een blik op en pakte toen haar vulpen.

'Bent u mevrouw Arding?' vroeg ik.

'Nee, dat ben ik niet. Mevrouw Arding is vandaag niet op school.' Ze keek niet op tijdens het zetten van haar handtekening. Ze had duidelijk een hele lange. Eentje die haar belangrijk maakte, of die haar het idee gaf dat ze belangrijk was.

'Meneer Rugh kennende zal je je straf bij hem moeten uitvoeren.' Ze gaf me de rode kaart terug en keek me aan. Indringender dan eerst. 'We zullen zien of rood niet je kleur is, maar laten we proberen dit te zien als een incident.' Ik mocht haar wel, ze zag me niet als een foute en stoute jongen, maar eerder als iemand die een beetje per ongeluk de klas uitgestuurd was. Ik liep haar kantoor weer uit, deed de deur achter me dicht en toen ik het hoekje om was merkte ik dat ik toen pas op de rode kaart durfde te kijken.

Getekend door en goedgekeurd door: mevrouw dr. Vlieger.

13.

Als laatste die dag hadden we geschiedenis. Ik vond dat een geweldig vak. Duiken in het verleden. Maar vooral: de docent, meneer Schaephock. Een man die geboren leek te zijn voor grijs haar. Het stond hem goed en gek genoeg bleef hij toch iets jongs houden. Ik had begrepen dat hij over een paar jaar met pensioen zou gaan. Hij gaf geen geschiedenislés, hij vertélde de geschiedenis. In al die jaren dat ik bij hem in de klas zat sloeg hij het boek geen seconde open. Hij snapte wat je moet doen als je kinderen iets wilt leren: hij liet zijn vak leven. Door woorden op zo'n manier achter elkaar te zetten dat hij als het ware een film liet afspelen in onze hoofden. De stoel achter zijn bureau stond op een verhoging, als een soort minipodium. Dankzij hem zagen we hoe ridders vochten, hoe de stoommachine werd uitgevonden en hoe Napoleon ten strijde trok. Als hij het had over de bestorming van de Bastille, het symbolische startpunt van de Franse Revolutie, dan sprong hij op, klom hij op tafel en schreeuwde: '*Liberté, égalité, fraternité!*' En daarna: '*Fête de la Fédération!*' Heel even waren we dan in Frankrijk, heel even voelden we hoe het was om in opstand te komen. Hij liet dat wat al geleefd had opnieuw leven.

Ik zat helemaal vooraan, pal tegen zijn bureau. Waar ik die

plek op de basisschool als stráf kreeg, had ik hem bij zijn vak zelf gekozen. Het was een geschenk om zo dicht bij hem te mogen zitten. Omdat hij hoger zat kon hij af en toe over zijn bureau heen kijken om te zien of ik nog druk mee pende. Ik schreef namelijk alles op wat hij zei. Letterlijk. Woord voor woord. Zo snel als hij sprak moest ik schrijven. Heel af en toe kwam ik met mijn hoofd omhoog en keek hem aan. Dan wist hij dat hij iets moest vertragen.

Het was inmiddels maart. Ik was net jarig geweest. In het weekend. Daarom had ik deze maandag een traktatie bij me. Hoewel ik wist dat het niet meer zo gevierd werd als op de basisschool, had ik toch een traktatie gekocht. De avond ervoor was ik naar de Albert Heijn gegaan om chocolaatjes te kopen. Ik had het idee gehad ze aan de klas uit te delen, maar toen ik mijn schooltas opende bij de geschiedenisles, zag ik dat ik het niet gedurfd had. Het einde van de dag was in zicht en alsof ik ze verborgen moest houden en moest verstoppen zaten de chocolaatjes nog in mijn rugzak. Blijkbaar hield iets me tegen om de traktatietraditie voort te zetten. Ik vond het jammer, maar kon er niks aan veranderen.

Toen de schoolbel klonk en ik de laatste paar regels van meneer Schaephock opschreef, pakte ik mijn tas en liep naar buiten. Daar kwam ik Pieter tegen. Pieter zat in dezelfde klas als ik, en we kenden elkaar nog van vroeger. Hij was gespierd, deed veel aan voetbal en zo nu en dan rugby. Hij zou bijna van school gaan, omdat zijn ouders hadden besloten te verhuizen. 'Nog een laatste maandje,' zei hij, 'nog een laatste maandje, misschien twee, en dan zijn we weg. We gaan naar Drenthe.' Ik keek hem een beetje vreemd aan. Drenthe. Dat kenden we allebei alleen van de lessen van de basisschool. 'Ik weet het, hunebedden,' zei hij, 'maar dat is niet de reden, we kunnen daar een groot huis kopen met veel groen en dat vinden mijn ouders fijn.' Ik keek hem aan. 'Ga je mee, naar mijn huis?'

stelde hij voor. 'Maken we samen ons huiswerk.' Onze huizen lagen dicht bij elkaar. In dezelfde buurt. 'Prima,' zei ik.

In zijn kamer gingen we aan het bureau zitten. Eerst werkten we. Wiskunde. Optellen. Aftrekken. Vermenigvuldigen. Cijfers, cijfers, cijfers. Ik keek hem aan. In mijn buik voelde ik de spanning komen die ik vaker had gevoeld maar niet kon verklaren. Ik wist niet of ik de spanning nou prettig vond of niet. Ik plaatste mijn voet tegen die van hem aan. Hij reageerde niet afstandelijk. Of hij reageerde niet. Dat was onduidelijk. Ik zuchtte een beetje, voorzichtig, alsof ik niet uit een rekensom kwam. Hij keek op en boog zich een beetje naar mij toe.

'Wat begrijp je niet?' Voelde ik dat nou goed, schoof hij zijn dijbeen tegen dat van mij aan? Ik keek op van mijn schrift, hij was dichtbij, zijn hoofd, misschien te dichtbij.

'Nou,' zei ik, en ik wees naar een willekeurige plek in mijn wiskundeboek, 'ik snap dit niet helemaal.' Hij kwam nu nog dichterbij en keek ingespannen in mijn schoolboek. Zijn schouder zat tegen mijn schouder aan. Ik duwde zachtjes tegen de zijne, geen wegduwduw, maar een blijfhierduw. Ik wist niet waarom ik dat deed. Waarom doe je dit? Waar ben je mee bezig? sprak ik mezelf in gedachten toe. Ik merkte dat de spanning in mijn lichaam het overnam, ik deed dingen vanzelf. Alsof ik een op afstand bestuurbaar autootje was geworden. Ik wilde de regie houden maar was die kwijt, al langer, realiseerde ik me.

Hij duwde zachtjes terug. De spanning zat nu overal in mijn lichaam. Het voelde alsof de bliksem was ingeslagen en ik zo snel mogelijk op zoek moest naar een bliksemafleider. Maar waar ik ook keek en wat ik ook bedacht, ik kon niks vinden.

'Ik kan je het wel uitleggen, heb alleen wel een beetje last van mijn borst,' zei hij, alsof dat het uitleggen lastiger maakte.

'O,' zei ik, 'waar dan?' En ik legde mijn hand op het midden van zijn borstkas. Hij begon te vertellen hoe de som werkte, terwijl ik met mijn hand zijn shirt inging, in een poging om al aaiend de pijn weg te nemen. Althans, dat was het excuus. Waarvoor het een excuus was, dat wist ik niet, maar dat we eigenlijk iets anders aan het doen waren, had ik wel door, en het voelde alsof we ons aan iemand moesten verexcuseren. Met mijn hand ging ik over zijn buik, totdat hij mijn hand pakte en die langzaam verder naar beneden over zijn broek bracht. Daar lieten we mijn hand rusten. Vervolgens bracht hij zijn hand op dezelfde plek bij mij, waarna hij mijn gulp lospeuterde. Ik deed hetzelfde bij hem.

'Pieter! Eten! Komen!' riep zijn moeder toen het bijna avond was en de zon verstoppertje ging spelen. Nadat we onze onderbroeken weer hadden aangedaan en onze broeken hadden dichtgeknoopt, waren we verder gegaan met ons huiswerk alsof er niks aan de hand was. Alsof er niks gebeurd was. Maar het voelde alsof we net zonder paraplu door de regen hadden gerend en nu thuis op de bank tv zaten te kijken in onze kletsnatte kleren terwijl we deden alsof we allebei droog waren. Hoe hard we ook ons best deden om te doen alsof het niet was gebeurd en hoe hard we onszelf ook voorhielden dat er niks was veranderd, dat was er wel. Zoals zaken soms veranderen wanneer je iets uitspreekt, wanneer je eerlijk naar jezelf bent, zo was er nu iets onomkeerbaars veranderd en dat wisten we allebei. En we baalden ervan.

We liepen in stilte de trappen af. In de tuin pakte ik mijn fiets. Pieter stak z'n hand op. We zeiden niks meer tegen elkaar. Ik keek hem nog één keer aan en wist dat er iets kapot was. Een vaas was gevallen en geen lijm kon haar helen.

Die avond zei ik dat ik onder de douche ging. Dat deed ik eigenlijk alleen in de ochtend, maar nu wilde ik heel graag douchen.

‘Waarom jong?’ vroeg mijn papa. Ergens wilde ik hem zeggen wat er gebeurd was, maar ik kon het niet. Ik wilde het niet. Ik had het gevoel dat ik iets heel erg stouts had gedaan, maar niet iets stouts in de zin van een koekje te veel eten of een zak snoepgoed bij de boodschappen gooien. Niet iets stouts in de zin van kattenkwaad. Nee. Dit was echt stout geweest, geen enkele strafregel kon het goedmaken, of ongedaan.

‘Ik zou gewoon heel graag willen douchen,’ zei ik, ‘we hadden vandaag gym, dus vandaar.’

‘Je hebt toch op de donderdagen gym?’ zei mijn vader. Er klonk geen wantrouwen, hij was gewoon zijn eigen geheugen aan het checken.

‘Nee, ja, dat klopt, maar we hadden een soort van extra gym, gewoon op het schoolplein, beetje druk spelen en, nou, ja, zweet en zo.’

‘Het is al goed jong, slaap lekker alvast, mama komt laat thuis vanavond en geeft je waarschijnlijk pas een kus als je al slaapt.’

Onder de douche probeerde ik mezelf schoon te schrobben. Ik voelde me schuldig tegenover Pieter. Ik wist niet waarom, we hadden het allebei gewild, maar ik had het gevoel dat we allebei iets hadden gedaan wat niet mocht. Ik voelde me vies en ranzig. Maar hoe hard ik ook boende, ik kreeg mezelf niet schoon. Die spanning zat weer in mijn buik. Ik begon het te haten, wist niet wat de bedoeling ervan was. Het water kletterde op mijn kop. Net zo hard en onstuimig als de gedachten in mijn hoofd. Een jongen, dacht ik. Gadver. Gadverdamme. Dat kon niet goed zijn. Het voelde alsof er iets niet klopte. Op tv had ik wel eens twee mannen – nee dat wilde ik niet. Klaar. Zo wilde ik niet zijn. Ik pakte voor de tweede keer de shampoofles om m’n haar te wassen. Ik probeerde er alles aan te doen om schoon te worden. Maar wat ik ook deed, hoe hard ik ook boende, die avond onder de douche, schoon zou ik niet worden.

14.

We stonden voor het schoolbord, de pauze was afgelopen en we waren met z'n allen eerder in de klas. We hadden een mentoruur en van de docent mochten we de eerste vijf minuten iets voor onszelf doen. Met een groepje stond ik nu wat te krijten. We schreven woorden op en maakten snelle tekeningen. Iedereen had zijn eigen stukje en zijn eigen krijtje. Er leek niks aan de hand te zijn.

Tot ik opzij keek. Pieter stond ineens naast me. Doordat sommige klasgenootjes na het schrijven van één woord, vaak hun naam, het schoolbord weer hadden gelaten voor wat het was, stonden wij nu naast elkaar. We hadden elkaar niet meer gesproken sinds het gebeurd was. Ik keek hem aan, hij keek terug. Onweer in zijn ogen. Ik ging verder waar ik gebleven was. Hij ook. Totdat we steeds dichter bij elkaar kwamen. Onze krijtjes schoven naar elkaar toe, onze tekeningen hadden meer ruimte nodig en dreigden de andere tekening als het ware aan te vallen, een veldslag leek in aantocht. We schoten allebei tegelijk uit en raakten elkaars vuisten.

'Kappen,' beet hij me toe.

'Kap zelf,' zei ik.

'We hadden het niet moeten doen,' snauwde hij.

‘Ik wou dat het nooit gebeurd was, viespeuk.’

‘Dat ben je zelf. Homo!’

‘Hoe noemde je mij? Dan ben jij dat ook hè, ho–’ Ik slikte het woord net op tijd in. Ik wilde het niet tegen hem roepen. Niet zo. Iets in mijn lichaam voelde dat het niet klopte. Maar als hij mij zo noemde, waarom zou ik het dan niet terug mogen zeggen?

‘Waag het niet mij zo te noemen!’ zei hij.

‘Hoezo niet? Het is toch gewoon zo. Jij bent het, als je denkt dat ik het ben,’ zei ik.

‘Als je het maar niet waagt mij zo te noemen, ik ben niet zoals jij.’ Ik zag de woede in zijn ogen, maar ook in mij begon het te razen. Ik voelde dat ik het tegen hem ging zeggen. Als hij me zo noemde, dan waren we het allebei. Wat we dus niet waren!

‘Als je me zo noemt geef ik je een klap, dan ram ik je in je buik,’ zei hij.

Dat was de druppel. Fysiek geweld. We hadden thuis geleerd dat je alleen verbaal mag vechten. Wie zijn vuisten gebruikt heeft het gevecht verloren, was thuis de regel. Ik haalde heel rustig adem. Ik zou het heel rustig, bijna lief tegen hem gaan zeggen, bedacht ik me. Ik rechtte mijn rug en keek hem aan.

‘Homo.’ Ik zei het zacht. Tot nu toe hadden de andere leerlingen niks gezien van onze ruzie en dat wilde ik graag zo houden. Maar aan Pieters lichaamstaal zag ik dat dat snel zou veranderen. Voordat ik het woord goed en wel had uitgesproken, vloog zijn vuist op mij af. Hij raakte me vol in mijn maag. Ik klapte naar voren, kreeg geen lucht en begon te hoesten. In Pieters ogen sprongen tranen. In die van mij ook.

De rest van het mentoruur hadden we het over druk en aanwezig zijn in de klas. Over hoe je rekening houdt met elkaar. De meester en de klasgenootjes dachten dat Pieter en ik ruzie hadden gekregen over het schoolbord.

Een paar avonden later was het schoolfeest. Pieter werd afgezet door zijn moeder, precies op het moment dat ik kwam aanfietsen. Onze ouders waren gebeld over ons akkefietje en we hadden ons er allebei met een smoes vanaf gemaakt. Ik keek Pieter aan en we maakten het goed. 'Zullen we het vergeten?' 'Dat lijkt me een goed idee.' We hielden elkaars handen even vast. Langer dan normaal, alsof iets in ons lichaam wel wílde dat het goed zou komen, maar dat we de laatste stap niet konden zetten. Toen we elkaar daarna loslieten wisten we dat het klaar was. Samen huiswerk maken was er niet meer bij en toen hij een maand later naar Drenthe vertrok hadden we elkaar niet meer gesproken.

Het was niet veel later dat mijn ouders besloten dat mijn broertje en ik niet langer op dezelfde kamer zouden slapen. Mijn broertje bleef in onze grote slaapkamer, ik ging naar de derde verdieping, voorheen het domein van mijn oudste broer. Hij was op reis geweest, gelukkig wel alweer terug, maar ook uit huis gegaan. Ik betrok zijn zolderachtige kamer, waar weinig licht binnenkwam en de komende jaren steeds minder licht zou komen. Het was de allerlaatste kamer van het huis, dat viel me pas op toen ik voor het eerst de trap naar mijn nieuwe domein nam. Het was de allerlaatste deur. Ik vond dat een veilig idee. Als er iemand zou inbreken of achter ons aan zat, dan was dit de beste plek om je te verstoppen.

Mijn ouders hingen rode gordijnen op voor de kleine ramen. Als ik ze opendeed kon ik de top van de grote boom voor ons huis zien. In de winter leek het alsof het wortels waren die omhoog kronkelden, vingers die naar iets wilden grijpen, dunne heksenvingers. Als het lente en zomer werd kon je feestelijk groen zien. Duizenden tinten groen versierden mijn uitzicht, ik kon eindeloos verdwalen in de bladeren.

Ik ging er steeds vaker zitten, daar op mijn slaapkamer. Ik wilde alleen zijn en probeerde de spanning die in mijn lichaam zat te verklaren. Maar dat lukte niet. Het was alsof ik op een hele hoge duikplank stond, maar als ik naar beneden keek zag ik geen water om in te springen. Ik kon wel op de duikplank gaan staan, maar niet naar beneden kijken. Ik wist niet waar ik in zou belanden als ik sprong. Dus sprong ik niet.

Zo druk als mijn hoofd was, zo druk was ook mijn kamer. Overal stonden spullen. Beeldjes, glitters en lichtjes. Een kamerkermis. Ik vond het er fijn, kon er mijn weg in vinden en erin verdwalen. Precies waar ik behoefte aan had. Als ik zittend op mijn bed keek naar het glitterjasje dat ik aan had gehad toen ik mevrouw Vlieger speelde, moest ik denken aan een moment dat een van mijn broers mij een tijdlang pesterig en zeurderig had toegezongen. '*You are my sister*,' zong hij dan, uit het gelijknamige nummer van Antony and the Johnsons. Hoewel ik niet begreep waarom hij me 'zusje' noemde, wist ik wel dat ik het heel erg onprettig vond. Het had me het gevoel gegeven dat er iets fout met mij was, dat er iets aan me niet klopte. Dat ik in veel opzichten op mijn broers leek, maar dat er iets groots en problematisch anders aan mij was. Het was een herinnering die ik niet wilde hebben, maar hij was vastgezet in mijn hoofd, gespannen als prikkeldraad, en telkens als ik er onbedoeld langsliep haalde ik mezelf opnieuw open.

Ik ging steeds meer tijd besteden aan buitenschoolse activiteiten. Om te zorgen dat mijn cijfers toch op niveau zouden blijven, mocht ik in een aparte kamer op de begane grond een klein werkbureau inrichten. Het was een kleine vierkante tafel, eigenlijk de oude schaaktafel, van een Alice in Wonderland-achtige omvang; de inmiddels opgeborgen schaakstukken waren groter dan een hand en het bord was groter dan de gemiddelde bijzettafel. Die tafel werd de plek waar ik mijn best deed om me te concentreren op huiswerk. Dat lukte maar half, mijn gedachten dwaalden vaak af. Ik had in het kastje in die kamer de oude tv geïnstalleerd, een tv zonder afstandsbediening. Je kon alleen van zender wisselen via de knopjes aan de zijkant. Ik kende dit soort toestellen enkel uit de geschiedenisboeken en had het gevoel dat ik een museumitem tot leven bracht als ik hem aanzette. Als de televisie lang aan had gestaan begon het wat branderig te ruiken. Waarschijnlijk was dat stof, maar ik vond het een leuker idee dat het kwam doordat het oude bakbeest zo hard moest werken.

Als ik in mijn studeerkamer zat keek ik stiekem naar een soap, GTST. Waarom wist ik niet precies, maar ik had van vriendinnen op school gehoord dat het leuk was. Op den duur zag ik dat in de serie een liefde ontstond tussen twee mannen. Als ik in de woonkamer zou hebben gezeten met de rest van het gezin, zou ik iets bedenken om door te kunnen zappen. Maar hier, alleen in de studeerkamer, bleef ik kijken.

15.

Toen het schooljaar voorbij was, werd het spannend wat er met mij zou gebeuren. Op de basisschool vonden sommige juffen en meesters dat ik op zoek moest naar een andere school, en het leek erop dat dat nu weer zou gebeuren. 'Zijn cijfers zijn oké, niet bijzonder goed, maar ook niet slecht, het zit hem er vooral in dat hij weinig doet. En wat hij doet is of buitenschools, of onrust stoken en grapjes maken in de klas, dat levert niet de sympathie van mijn collega's op,' aldus mijn mentor.

'Dat weet ik,' antwoordde mijn vader, 'maar we hebben precies hetzelfde gehad op de basisschool. Hij verveelt zich. Weet niet wat hij moet doen en gaat dan maar andere dingen zitten doen. En ja, hij moet zich meer op zijn werk gaan focussen, maar daar zullen wij thuis voor zorgen.'

Ik kreeg het voordeel van de twijfel.

In de zomervakantie gingen we met het gezin naar Frankrijk. Tussen het lezen, sporten en spelen door bezochten we vaak een of ander dorp in de buurt. Geregeld waren de levens van de mensen daar net zo versleten als de huizen en de straten. Ramen kraakten, stoeptegels lagen schots en scheef op straat als tanden in een slecht onderhouden gebit en mos en klimopplanten veroverden langzaam natuur terug op steen.

Al lang had niemand meer naar hen omgekeken, naar de mensen in het dorp. In sommige dorpjes waren meer huizen te koop dan dat er mensen woonden. Het had iets triests. Als ik er rondliep werd ik me altijd even bewust van het geluk dat ik had gehad met de plek van mijn wieg. Het had er zomaar anders uit kunnen zien. Heel anders.

In zo'n dorp gingen we altijd naar de plaatselijke kerk. Opvallend genoeg was die altijd goed onderhouden. Voor de Heilige Geest was het goed toeven daar, in die leeggelopen dorpen. Omdat we alleen in vakanties kerken bezochten – in Nederland deden we dat nooit – associeerde ik het met een vakantiegevoel. De geur van zonnebrandcrème, een geïrriteerde huid door de zwembroek die je al drie dagen aanhad en de kerk: dat was vakantie. Mama stak er altijd een kaarsje aan, voor iemand die was overleden of voor de terugreis. Voor de zekerheid, het hardnekkige geloof was bij mijn ouders nooit aanwezig geweest en bij ons als kinderen al helemaal niet. Behalve het geloof in Sinterklaas dan, papa geloofde daar zelfs nog steeds in, vertrouwde hij ons altijd toe.

In zo'n kerk maakte ik me altijd los van de rest van het gezin. Ik had steeds vaker de behoefte om alleen te zijn, ook nu we op vakantie waren. Of misschien juist nu we op vakantie waren. Ik kon mijn vriendinnen niet meer spreken en miste hen.

Ik liep over de tegels. Ze waren glad. Alsof ik me als kerkbezoeker op glad ijs begaf. En misschien was dat ook wel zo. De geur van wierook hing in de stilte. Voorbij het altaar was een koster bezig met het vervangen van de dienstkaarsen. Ik keek naar een van de schilderijen aan de muur. Een engel, naast nog een engel, naast nog een engel. Drie engelen, keurig op een rij. Krachtige vleugels die bijna niet op het doek pasten. Hun haren wapperden in de wind. Blijkbaar kon het ook waaien in de hemel. De engelen waren gespierd. Overdreven gespierd. Maar niet storend. Ze keken met z'n allen dezelfde kant op. Begeerte in de ogen. Ik vermoedde dat ze naar God keken. De drie mannelijke, gespierde engelen, hun vleugels klapperend in de lucht, hun toga's bijna van het lichaam gegleden. Het was een aparte gewaarwording. Hoewel Nietzsche zei dat God dood was – dat had ik mijn broer ooit aan tafel horen zeggen – zou je ook kunnen stellen dat God gay is, of op z'n minst biseksueel en in een constante staat van geilheid. Waarom ik dat dacht wist ik niet. Het was door mijn hoofd geschoten en ik vond het geen ernstige gedachte. Ik was niet opeens in vlammen opgegaan, bij wijze van straf. Misschien had God wel elke avond een gangbang met zijn engelen. Oké, dacht ik bij mezelf, dat ging misschien wat te ver, maar het zou me niets verbazen.

Ik bleef lang staan, behoorlijk lang. Vergat de tijd en bleef staren naar die engelen. Als ik heel erg lang mijn ogen openhield, zodat ze bijna gingen tranen, leek het haast alsof ze in beweging kwamen. Alsof de drie engelen tot leven waren gekomen, stiekem, alleen voor mij. Alsof ze me een plezier deden. Alsof hun toga's nog verder zouden afglijden. Die engelen die vol begeerte naar God keken, steunend op de zachte witte wolken.

Ik hoorde een van mijn broers roepen. Of eigenlijk, ik hoorde de galmende echo van zijn stem. Hij riep vanuit de ingang voorzichtig mijn naam. Het was tijd om te gaan. Ik zwaaide ze gedag, de engelen. Ze zwaaiden niet terug.

16.

In het tweede jaar van de middelbare school begonnen steeds meer zaken te veranderen. Ik zat vaker op mijn kamer. Meer afgezonderd van de rest van het gezin. De gordijnen deed ik niet elke dag open. Ik voelde me alleen, ook al was ik dat niet. Ik dacht veel aan de spanning in mijn lichaam die maar bleef groeien.

Tijdens scheikunde zat ik naast Jack. Jack was een rustige jongen, maar wel eentje die als knap werd beschouwd. Hij was licht gespierd, had een smal, puntig gezicht en felle blauwe ogen. We verveelden ons. Dat wisten we van elkaar, want in de zijkant van onze schriften waren we allebei tegelijk tekeningetjes aan het maken. Vanuit het niets legde Jack zijn pen neer, stopte met tekenen en liet zijn hand onder tafel verdwijnen. Ik had het eerst niet door, totdat ik opeens zijn hand rondom mijn knie voelde. Vijf vingers werden als spinnenpoten om mijn knieschijf geplaatst. Ik mocht niet schrikken, want dan zou de docent of een van de klasgenoten iets doorhebben, dus sperde ik in plaats daarvan mijn ogen wijd open. Jack moest lachen. En kneep vervolgens zachtjes. 'Een wedstrijdje,' zei Jack, 'in het zo stil mogelijk reageren. Kijken wie het beste tegen de kneepjes van de ander kan.' Dat had ik niet zien aankomen, een zachte knijpwedstrijd tijdens de scheikundeles. Maar ik stopte met tekenen en deed mee.

Langzaam kwam weer dat gevoel, die spanning. Ik wist niet of Jack het ook voelde. En hoewel ik ergens graag wilde stoppen met deze stiekeme handelingen, bleef het maar doorgaan. Een kleine kneep van Jack werd beantwoord met eentje van mij. Langzaam schoven onze handen steeds verder naar boven. De vingers klommen langzaam omhoog, als bergbeklimmers die door het verlaagde zuurstofgehalte extra rustig en voorzichtig moesten manoeuvreren. Van de knie gingen we allebei met onze kneepjes naar het bovenbeen en van daaruit steeds een paar centimeter hoger, totdat we zo ongeveer in elkaars lies knepen. Ik wist niet wat ik nou het spannendst vond: de angst dat we zouden worden betrapt in ons spel, of dat dit het been van Jack was. Op het eind kreeg het toch iets ongemakkelijks. En vervolgens stopte het.

Steeds meer zaken werden ongemakkelijk. Het was niet zo dat er van de een op de andere dag iets was veranderd, maar er was een grijzige mist neergedaald over de dagen. De mist kwam niet vanuit de omgeving maar vanuit mezelf. Ik begon het steeds lastiger te vinden om met jongens om te gaan. Steeds meer trok ik naar vriendinnen. In de pauze, huppelend van groepje naar groepje. Door alle verschillende vriendinnen zat ik niet vast op één eiland. Dat was aan de ene kant een voordeel, maar voelde aan de andere kant ook onvast. Ik had geen vast eiland.

De grijze mist bereidde zich ook uit naar de gymlessen. Ik vond het steeds ingewikkelder worden om naar gymlessen te gaan. Vooral vanwege het omkleden. De kleedkamers waren gescheiden, mannen bij de mannen, vrouwen bij de vrouwen. En ze waren wat aan de kleine kant, waardoor je altijd half tegen elkaar aan stond. Ik begon erg tegen gym op te zien. Eerst een paar uur van tevoren, later al dagen van tevoren. Ook thuis werd het anders. Ik leek meer op te vallen. Alsof ik iets aanhad dat aandacht trok, waar je automatisch naar keek of waar je je op straat voor omdraaide. Soms ging ik voor de spiegel staan om te kijken of er wat veranderd was. Maar hoe goed ik ook keek, ik zag niks.

17.

We zaten aan een kerstdiner. Niet dat het al kerst was, het zou nog even duren voordat de kerstbomen in huis verschenen, maar dat nam niet weg dat we aan een kerstdiner zaten. Zo voelde het althans. Met het hele gezin aan tafel. Inmiddels niet meer aan de pingpongwedstrijdtafel. In groep zeven waren mijn ouders een verbouwing gestart en nu aten we in de keuken beneden. Op tafel stonden kaarsen. Zoals altijd hingen er kerstlichtjes voor het raam. En de nieuwe open haard in de keuken brandde. We zaten te eten. Ik was wat stilletjes. Dat viel me pas op toen ik merkte dat er reactie van me verwacht werd.

'Weet je waar ik me op verheug, dat op een dag al jullie vriendinnetjes met jullie meekomen en hier aan tafel zitten,' begon mijn moeder. Daar schrok ik van, waarom wist ik niet. 'Dat lijkt me zo leuk. Of een vriendje, dat is natuurlijk ook goed, het lijkt me heerlijk om een schoonzoon te hebben, dus een van jullie moet dat doen hoor,' vervolgde ze. Hoewel het niet stil werd aan tafel, werd het in mij wel stil. Doodstil. Hoewel ik wist dat mama het tegen iedereen aan tafel zei en hoewel ik wist dat het lief bedoeld was, voelde het alsof ze zich tot mij had gericht. Een schoonzoon?

'Of jullie nou hetero of homo zijn, dat maakt ons allemaal

niks uit, als jullie maar gelukkig zijn.' Mijn moeder keek mijn vader aan. 'Ja,' zei mijn vader, 'ik heb hartstikke veel vrienden die homo zijn en heel veel vrienden die hetero zijn, iedereen is even gelukkig.'

Het werd nog stiller in mijn hoofd. Voor zover dat mogelijk was. En stiller in mijn buik. Was ik dat? Dat woord? Dat woord met die h? Nee, dat was ik niet. Ik was net als de rest. Ik was niet iets anders – ik probeerde de storm van vragen tot rust te laten komen. Ik voelde me onprettig. Daar aan tafel met mijn broers. En mijn ouders. Ik had het gevoel alsof ze naar me keken. Terwijl niemand dat deed. Dit soort situaties deden zich de laatste tijd steeds vaker voor. Dat mijn ouders lieten merken dat ze écht níks tegen homoseksualiteit hadden. Dat ze het alleen maar geweldig vonden. Het voelde voor mij benauwend omdat ik niet begreep wat ze ermee wilden zeggen. Hoezo moesten wij als kinderen weten dat ze alles prima vonden? Of wilden ze iets aan een van ons kwijt? Wilden ze iets aan míj kwijt? Maar ik... Maar ik... stop met denken. Stop met denken. Mijn hoofd bleef razen. Ik nam nog een hap van mijn bord, luisterde niet naar wat er gezegd werd. Voelde me lelijk. Waarom wist ik niet.

In mijn kamer bleef dat woord hangen. *Homo*. Ik probeerde het uit mijn hoofd te halen. Met mijn handen in mijn haar probeerde ik het eruit te trekken. Alsof het woord aan mijn haren zou blijven hangen. Zonder mama en papa een kusje te geven ging ik slapen. Waarom ik dat deed wist ik niet, maar dat het een van de zwaarste straffen was die ik als kind thuis kon opleggen, dat wist ik wel. In bed moest ik huilen. Was die spanning, was die spanning in mijn buik. Was dat. Nee dat kon het niet zijn. Ik ben gewoon ik. Net als alle anderen. Ik ben niet anders, zei ik tegen mezelf. Dat wist ik zeker. Ja, ik was misschien wat enthousiaster. Ja, ik stond misschien wat vaker op het podium en ik hield van dieren, van paardrijden, van vioolspelen, zei ik tegen mezelf terwijl ik mijn best deed in slaap te vallen, maar ik was niet écht anders. Al die hobby's koos ik zelf. Maar dat veranderde niks aan wie ik wás. Ik voelde de spanning, ik voelde de grijze mist. De grijze mist die om mij heen leek te hangen en die mijn klasgenootjes konden zien. Die mijn ouders en mijn broers konden zien. Maar die ikzelf op de een of andere manier niet kon zien. Dat maakte me nog onrustiger, het leek alsof die mist mij wilde wurgen. Langzaam om me heen kronkelde, mij gevangen had. Oké. Rustig nu. Dacht ik. Rustig nu. Slapen. Weg uit deze wereld.

18.

We gingen samen de hond uitlaten in het bos, een van mijn broers en ik. Hoewel het geregend had, was de lente al volop aanwezig. Her en der begonnen bloemen moedig aan hun strijd opwaarts. Geel, paars, rood. Langzaam werd het gras van extra kleurendruppels voorzien. Alsof iemand wild had staan schilderen en zijn verf rijkelijk had laten uitschieten, tot op het tapijt.

We kregen ruzie. Waarover ben ik vergeten. Maar al snel kwamen we in een verbaal vuurgevecht terecht. Ik zei lelijke dingen tegen hem, hij zei lelijke dingen tegen mij.

'Dikzak,' zei ik.

'Sukkel,' zei hij.

'Idioot.' Ik.

'Mongool.' Hij.

'Ga lekker vrienden zoeken, bolle.'

'Ach, jouw soort wordt in Rusland in kampen gestopt of in elkaar geslagen, dus zoek het lekker uit.' Die bleef haken. Heftiger en harder dan had gemoeten. Elkaar uitschelden is niet het mooiste wat je als broers doet, maar meestal vielen de woorden uiteindelijk van je af. Als je hoofdkussen dat je voor je gaat slapen even opklopt en daardoor weer aanvoelt als nieuw. Maar deze woorden niet. Deze haakten vast. 'Mijn soort,' dreunde het door mijn hoofd. 'In kampen – in elkaar geslagen.' Zou hij dat goed vinden, wat daar gebeurde? vroeg ik me af. Ik wilde het hem vragen, ik wilde horen dat hij het niet meende, dat hij, wat er ook zou gebeuren, wie ik ook zou zijn, van me zou houden. Maar ik kon het niet vragen, want dan zou het net lijken of ik écht van dat soort was. En dat was ik niet. Dat wist ik zeker. Of. Nee. Ja. Dat wist ik zeker.

Ik vond het altijd ongemakkelijk en pijnlijk als we met het gezin naar *Het Journaal* keken – de jaren dat het nieuws bij ons werd weggehouden, lagen alweer even achter ons – en we zagen hoe kleurrijke protesten in andere landen hardhandig werden neergeslagen. Mannen met ringen en make-up die met bebloede hoofden door de politie hardhandig werden afgevoerd. Als we dat zagen werd het op een andere manier stil in de kamer. Ik voelde de spanning in mijn lichaam weer opkomen en merkte dat de grijze mist mij weer begon te wurgen. Het voelde alsof iedereen naar mij wilde kijken maar niemand het lef had. Ik wilde dan weglopen of van zender veranderen, maar dat kon niet. Dan zou ik laten zien dat er iets was. En ik was niet zoals die mensen op de tv. Nee. Ik had het gevoel dat ik het gezin te schande zou maken als ik dat wel was. Terwijl, ik wist dat dat misschien niet zo zou zijn. Maar zo voelde het wel. Alsof ik de teleurstelling was, zoals elk gezin een teleurstelling heeft waarmee het vroeg of laat leert leven. Ik zou de teleurstelling zijn van mijn gezin.

'Mijn soort. Kampen. In elkaar slaan.' Het dreunde maar door en door. Bij elke stap die we op het bospad zetten hoorde ik niet onze voetstappen, maar die drie stukjes zin. Bij elke stap die we zetten had ik het gevoel dat ik naar achteren viel en wegzonk in een zompig moeras. Hij bedoelt het niet zo, probeerde ik in mijn hoofd tegen zijn opmerking in te brengen.

Door allebei tijdens de rest van de wandeling niks meer te

zeggen, zeiden we een soort van sorry. Of op z'n minst gunden we elkaar de tijd om na te denken over onze ruzie. Wie had wat gezegd, wat was de aanleiding geweest, waar had ik zaken overdreven en waar had ik fout gezeten? Ik wist dat ik zo dacht en dat ik me dan uiteindelijk schuldig ging voelen – en ik wist dat het voor mijn broer ook zo werkte. Alleen, ik kon zijn woorden niet vergeten. Op de een of andere manier had hij iets in mijn lichaam gekerfd. Zoals wanneer je verliefd bent en in een boomstam een liefdeslitteken maakt, zo had hij dat bij mij ook gedaan. Maar dit was geen fijn litteken.

Het bos lag er vrolijker bij dan mijn hoofd. Dikke regenwolken klonterden in mijn kop samen. Ik wilde het liefst een paraplu opzetten, of een doek pakken, of iets anders – als ik maar iets had om me te beschermen tegen de regen. Maar hoe goed ik ook zocht in mijn hoofd, iets om onder te schuilen vond ik niet.

19.

Ik had een heel leger aan vriendinnen. En dit jaar kwam daar een hele belangrijke bij. Lisanne. Liesje, zoals ze op school werd aangesproken. Drukker dan druk. Stouter dan stout. Huppeliger dan huppelend. Een menselijke discobal, een gigantisch feest in haar eentje. Tijdens de eerste les van het nieuwe jaar, de derde, liep ik haar tegen het lijf.

Ik fietste naar school. We zouden een lange mentorles hebben en direct erna de eerste wiskundeles. Zo'n eerste schooldag was belangrijk. Vooral naast wie je ging zitten in het klaslokaal. Dat bepaalde je sociale situatie voor de rest van het jaar. Zat je bij leuke mensen in de buurt, dan had je het goed voor elkaar en huppelde je zo het schooljaar door. Maar zat je op de verkeerde plek, of zelfs naast helemaal niemand, dan werd het een stuk ingewikkelder.

Ik fietste met een groep van vier vriendinnen. Dat deden we elke ochtend. Later zou een van hen een scooter krijgen en zouden we met z'n allen gaan 'hangen'. Dat hield in dat je de scooterrijder vasthield en je liet voortslepen. Totaal illegaal, maar het scheelde reistijd, waardoor iedereen langer in bed kon blijven liggen of zich kon optutten. Maar nu fietsten we nog gewoon. Onderweg naar school probeerde ik te bedenken naast wie ik zou kunnen zitten.

We hadden les van mevrouw Ritseflits, wiskundedocent en dit jaar onze mentor. Ze was lief en sportief: ze kon de hele klas eruit rennen. Ze genoot van haar werk en was typisch zo iemand die na haar pensioen zou blijven doorwerken – uit liefde voor het vak. In het lokaal waren er drie rijen met schoolbanken. De middelste en de rechterrij waren twee schoolbanken breed, de linkerrij drie. Moest ik alvast gaan zitten? Dan kon iemand naast mij komen zitten? Of moest ik wachten totdat iemand mij zou vragen? Hoeveel opties had ik eigenlijk? Er zou nog een vriendinnetje komen waar ik naast kon gaan zitten. Als ze nu binnen kwam lopen, zouden we nog redelijk achterin bij een ander vriendinnengroepje kunnen zitten. Dat zou ideaal zijn; een beetje achterin zitten was fijn en dan zaten we ook nog bij anderen in de buurt. Dan konden we makkelijker kletsen of samenwerken. Maar waar was ze? Inmiddels vulden de tafels achterin zich. Had ik dan – had ik dan verkeerd onthouden wie er in de klas zouden zitten? Zat ze misschien niet bij mij in de groep? 'Weet jij of Marie nog komt?' vroeg ik aan een van mijn klasgenoten. 'Nee joh, die zit in een andere mentorgroep.' Ik stond stil. Alle vriendinnen waar ik graag naast had willen zitten, zaten al naast iemand anders. En ik zag dat ook de laatste persoon inmiddels was binnengekomen en plaats had genomen. Moest ik dan alleen gaan zitten? Dat zou een ramp zijn. Dan zou ik het hele jaar als enige in de klas alleen aan een tafeltje zitten. En toen viel mijn oog op een meisje vooraan.

Ze zat helemaal vooraan bij het bureau van de docent, aan de linkerkant. Ik kende haar niet. De twee stoelen naast haar waren nog leeg. Hoewel vooraan zitten niet ideaal was, was dat beter dan helemaal alleen. Ik liep naar voren, ze zou het vast gezellig vinden als ik naast haar kwam zitten. Maar aan haar blik zag ik dat ze daar misschien anders over dacht. Ze keek op, een tikje verveeld, een blik waarmee ze aangaf dat ze hier niet hoorde en dat ze eigenlijk door niemand van de klas gestoord wilde worden. Ik ging zitten maar hield de stoel tussen ons in vrij. Dat is wat haar blik mij had opgedragen.

Even later begon mevrouw Ritseflits aan het wiskundegedeelte. Ik pakte mijn boek en mijn schrift en zag dat mijn buurvrouw geen leerboek bij zich had. Met zichtbare tegenzin haalde ze haar tas van de stoel die tussen ons in stond. Het was mij niet opgevallen dat de tas daar had gestaan, maar nu ze hem weghaalde zag ik dat als teken dat ik moest opschuiven. Ik ging naast haar zitten, legde mijn boek in het midden, dat zij vervolgens net wat dichter naar zich toe schoof.

'Wie ben jij eigenlijk?' vroeg ik haar. Ze had iets bijzonders. Ik wist niet of ze nou aardig was of niet, maar iets in haar trok me aan.

'Ik ben Liesje en ik hoor niet in deze klas te zitten, want ik hoor eigenlijk in de bovenbouw.' Ze keek me niet aan.

'Waarom ben je hier dan?'

Nu keek ze me wel aan. 'Ik ben blijven zitten, maar onterecht. Ik ken in deze klas dus niemand, en hoef ook niemand te leren kennen, mijn vriendinnen zitten in de bovenbouw.'

Ik keek haar aan. Ze had iets rebels in haar ogen. Een vuur dat ik herkende, maar mijn hoofd liet geen concrete herinnering zien. 'Ah,' zei ik, 'dat is vervelend.'

En we gingen verder met onze wiskundesom. Liesje liet een zucht horen, ze vond het saai, maar kwam er ook niet helemaal uit.

'Misschien kan Wobie het je uitleggen,' zei juf Ritseflits. Ze was naar ons tafeltje toe gelopen toen Liesje haar hand had opgestoken. In mijn enthousiasme stak ik van wal.

'Sssst! Je mag dan misschien wel weten hoe wiskunde werkt, maar ik ben nog steeds een jaar ouder dus je hoeft niet zo bijdehand te doen.'

Ik moest daar een beetje om lachen, maar paste me aan.

'Kijk, als je deze uitleg leest en ziet dat je x altijd kunt verplaatsen in de som...' We fluisterden alsof we aan het roddelen waren. Ik zag de boosheid bij Liesje wegstromen toen ze de som vervolgens zelf maakte. De eerste keer nog met een kleine fout, maar de tweede keer helemaal correct.

'Eigenlijk is het helemaal niet moeilijk,' zei ze, en leunde triomfantelijk achterover. 'Het is een makkie!' Ik moest lachen.

De bel ging, samen met Liesje liep ik naar de uitgang. Vlak voordat we het lokaal uitstapten draaide ze zich om. 'Kun je me anders wiskundebijles geven?' Ik keek haar met grote ogen aan. Ik realiseerde me dat ik in geen jaren meer bij anderen thuis was geweest. Ik had veel vriendinnen, bleef lang op school vanwege andere activiteiten, maar kwam allang niet meer bij iemand over de vloer.

'Eh, ja hoor, als je dat fijn vindt.'

'Mooi, laten we volgend weekend meteen afspreken, dan kan ik zorgen dat ik een beetje goed aan het jaar begin.' Ik kende mijn agenda niet, maar wist dat ik alles opzij zou zetten en zei dat ik kon.

20.

Toen ik mijn fiets pakte liepen mama en papa met me mee naar buiten. Het was zaterdag, een beetje aan het einde van de middag. Volgens mij was mijn vader naar het ziekenhuis geweest. Ik wist niet precies waarvoor.

'Jong?' zei papa. 'Voordat je weggaat moet papa je nog iets vertellen,' vulde mijn moeder aan. Ze stonden arm in arm, alsof ze één geheel aan het worden waren. Ze waren inmiddels al zo lang verliefd en zo lang bij elkaar dat het me niks had verbaasd als ze op een moment écht vergroeiden. Dit waren vast de eerste stapjes.

'Oké.' Ik haalde snel mijn fiets van het slot. Ik wilde heel graag naar Liesje toe. Ik wist niet waarom, maar ik verheugde me er al de hele dag op.

'We zijn bij het ziekenhuis geweest, je moeder en ik,' zei mijn vader. 'Je hoeft je geen zorgen te maken, maar het is wel goed dat je het alvast weet,' vulde mijn moeder opnieuw aan. Ik had het gevoel dat er iets niet klopte. Niet zoals wanneer je het gevoel hebt dat er een surpriseparty aankomt, maar eerder zoals je in een slechte horrorfilm het schrikmoment al mijlenver van tevoren ziet aankomen. Waar je vervolgens alsnog van schrikt.

'De dokters hebben de scan bekeken en ik heb een tumor,

een brughoektumor,' zei mijn vader. Hij zei het zo rustig dat ik bijna het gevoel kreeg alsof me gevraagd werd om vandaag eens de boodschappen te doen. Ik keek ze aan. Maar waarschijnlijk met een andere blik.

'We gaan alles uitzoeken,' zei mijn moeder, mijn moeder was dokter. Waar papa toverde met taal, toverde mama met medicijnen. Ze kon iedereen beter maken, dat idee hadden we als kinderen gehad. Ze noemde zichzelf een heks. Een goede heks. Dat had ik altijd een fijn idee gevonden. Hoewel ik nu ouder was, had ik nog steeds het gevoel dat ze een goede heks was, dat ze de wereld kon bestieren en aansturen.

'We gaan alles uitzoeken, misschien dat papa bestraald moet worden, misschien dat hij geopereerd wordt. We zijn er in ieder geval op tijd bij, dus je hoeft je geen zorgen te maken, maar we wilden wel graag dat je het weet. We zullen het ook aan je andere broers vertellen en we zullen de school inlichten.'

'Ik hou van je pap, ook met tumor,' – en ik gaf hem en mama een kus – 'maar ik moet nu echt naar Liesje toe, die zit op me te wachten.' Ik stapte op de fiets. In de ogen van mijn ouders zag ik dat ze blij waren. Er was geen reden tot paniek of drama, dat gevoel hadden ze willen overbrengen en dat was ze duidelijk gelukt. Ik reed over de stoep en draaide een paar keer om, mama en papa stonden samen op de stoep te zwaaien. Dat was een traditie bij ons thuis; elke keer dat iemand wegging werd hij uitgebreid uitgezwaaid. Het was begonnen toen papa ging optreden en inmiddels deden we het nog steeds. Als mijn oudste broer terugging naar zijn eigen huis, als iemand een weekend wegging, en zelfs als we met het hele gezin op vakantie gingen. Dan kwamen onze buren meneer en mevrouw Van Kroon naar buiten en hielden de traditie levend: met witte zakdoeken zwaaiden ze ons dan uit. En ook nu dus. Ik keek om, vanuit de verte leken mijn vader en moeder nu écht één geheel.

Onderweg naar Liesje dacht ik er nog eens over na. Ik moest een beetje huilen, maar ik had vooral het gevoel alsof iemand had besloten dat er meer sensatie in ons leven moest komen. Alsof iemand een boek schreef en er een ingewikkelde en moeilijke periode in verwerkte omdat dat goed was voor het verhaal, maar dat uiteindelijk alles goed zou komen. Ik zag mijn ouders als twee pilaren, twee pilaren die een veilig huis voor hun kinderen omhooghielden. In die pilaren konden geen barstjes komen. Toch leek het nu alsof die barsten er toch kwamen. Dat wilde ik niet. Ik concentreerde me op het fietsen en op Liesje. Ik had veel zin om haar te zien.

Ik parkeerde mijn fiets bij haar huis. Ze had gezegd dat ik via de tuin naar binnen kon wandelen, dat de deur daar altijd open was. 'Mijn ouders zullen daar vast aan het borrelen zijn,' had ze nog gezegd. Ik had direct geantwoord dat ik dat niet durfde. En dat ik gewoon bij de voordeur zou aanbellen. 'Maar die gebruiken we nooit,' had ze geantwoord. Dat geloofde ik niet.

Ik belde aan. Het duurde even voordat ik iets hoorde. Het was een deur met een kerstkrans. Eentje die er overduidelijk al heel lang hing. Toen ik voor de tweede keer aanbelde, hoorde ik achter de deur allerlei spullen opzijgeschoven worden. Er viel iets, nog iets. Toen klonk er een dreun tegen de muur, waarschijnlijk een groot meubelstuk dat definitief aan de kant werd gezet. Vervolgens klonk er een roestig geluid uit het slot. Misschien dat ze de deur inderdaad niet zo vaak gebruikten...

Voor me stond een lange jongen. Bijna een man. Hij was al achttien, zou ik later horen. Hij had een smal, knap en guitig gezicht en straalde iets van joligheid, van baldadigheid uit. Alsof het in zijn botten zat. Ik keek hem aan en wist even niet wat ik moest zeggen. Mijn mond viel een beetje open, in een poging iets te gaan zeggen.

‘Ennnn wie ben jij?’

‘Ah je bent er, doos, toch via de voordeur.’ Liesje kwam de trap aflopen. ‘Hij is een vriend van mij,’ zei ze tegen haar broer. Nu wist ik al helemaal niet meer wat ik moest zeggen. ‘Vriend’ – dat was snel gegaan. Het voelde alsof iets in mijn lichaam touwtje was gaan springen.

‘Je moet heel even zwaaien, dan kunnen we naar boven,’ zei Liesje. Ik ging de woonkamer binnen en werd betoverd. Hun huis was als een droom. Net zoals mijn ouders overal kleur en pracht en praal schots en scheef door elkaar hadden gezet. Ik had dat nog nooit bij anderen gezien. Andere huizen waren altijd leeg, alsof mensen constant paraat stonden voor een mogelijke verhuizing. Of alsof ze bang waren dat je als bezoeker dan misschien iets van iemands ziel kon zien. Zo leeg dat je zelf niet eens je glas water of kop thee ergens durfde neer te zetten. Zo was mijn ouderlijk huis allesbehalve, en het huis van Liesje evenmin. Overal hing en stond plezier. In de kroonluchters, in de Versailles-achtige gordijnen, in het tapijt, in de overal aanwezige kaarsen, de open haard die brandde, de stoelen in paars, roze, aubergine, beige en rood – uitnodigingen om vooral te gaan zitten en lang te blijven. Er waren maar een paar geschilderde muren zichtbaar, verder zag je langs de wand louter boekenkast.

‘Wie hebben we daar?’ De moeder van Liesje zat in de woonkamer aan een lange eettafel. In haar hand hield ze sierlijk een sigaret, haar elleboog leunde op tafel. Haar andere hand lag op tafel, bij haar glas witte wijn. Een soort moderne Audrey Hepburn. Maar dan blond. En zonder sigarettenhouder, maar met sigaret. En in plaats van Tiffany-oorbellen droeg ze brillen in haar opgestoken haar. Twee of drie brillen. Het stond haar goed. Haar lippen waren paars gestift.

‘Dit is een vriend van mij,’ zei Liesje. Aan haar houding merkte ik dat ze zo snel mogelijk naar boven wilde gaan.

'Ah,' zei de moeder van Liesje, 'wat goed, jij gaat onze Loezepoes slim maken, je mag met haar trouwen als je wilt hoor!'

'Mam, doe normaal!' riep Liesje.

Nadat we een tijdje op haar kamer wiskundesommen hadden zitten maken, besloot ik het erop te wagen en haar te vragen naar de naam van haar broer. Op de een of andere manier móést ik gewoon weten hoe hij heette. Ik kon me bijna niet concentreren op de sommen, hij zat de hele tijd in mijn hoofd. Misschien zou hij eruit verdwijnen als ik zijn naam wist.

Liesje keek me aan. Ik hoefde niks meer te zeggen. Het was alsof ze me ontmaskerde, zonder dat ze me een betrapt gevoel gaf. 'Knapperd, hè! Hier, deze som, kun je die uitleggen?' En ze ging verder alsof het de normaalste zaak van de wereld was. Ik was even stil. In de ogen van Liesje was ik niet anders, ik was gewoon.

'Je mag met haar trouwen hoor, kom maar snel weer langs,' riep haar moeder nog een keer toen we afscheid namen.

Op school waren we tijdens de les vrienden. Maar in de pauze ging ik naar de kantine, van eiland naar eiland, omdat ik overal en nergens bij hoorde, terwijl Liesje bij haar vriendinnen op het schoolplein zat. Op de apenrots, op de piramide, met een sigaret in haar handen.

'Ga je mee?' Ze hield haar hand als een dienblad kaarsrecht voor mijn neus. Ik wist wat dat betekende, ze deed het vaak, op die manier om een kauwgompje vragen. Ik had altijd kauwgom bij me. Dat was omdat ik overdag niet meer wilde eten. 's Ochtends ontbeet ik en 's avonds at ik ook. Maar 's middags at ik al een paar jaar vrijwel niks meer. Eerst legde ik de onaangeroerde boterhammen in mijn locker, maar omdat ik nooit een goed moment kon vinden om ze weg te gooien, bouwde ik al snel een voorraad beschimmelde boterhammen in boterhamzakjes op. Dus besloot ik om überhaupt geen brood meer te smeren en als mijn ouders dat doorhadden en me wel iets meegaven, dan gooide ik het direct weg. Behalve als mama er een kusje op had gegeven, dan kon ik het niet weggooien en at ik het met veel moeite op. Ik wist niet waarom ik niet wilde eten op school. In de spiegel kon ik zien dat ik dun was. Graatmager, zeiden mijn vriendinnen, broers en ouders altijd. Ik was niet ziek, ik wilde gewoon overdag niet eten, dat vond ik niet prettig. Maar wie amper eet gaat niet bepaald lekker uit zijn mond ruiken. Daarom had ik altijd kauwgom bij me. Toen Liesje dat ontdekte werd ik ook haar persoonlijke leverancier. Dat vond ik leuk, alsof ik haar elke dag een minicadeautje kon geven.

'Ga je mee?' vroeg ze nog een keer. Ze had een kort lontje als het aankwam op besluiteloosheid. Ze vond dat ik minder moest twijfelen, meer moest doen.

'Waarheen?' Ik legde een kauwgompje in haar hand.

'Naar buiten natuurlijk, ga je mee?'

Ik was verbaasd. Ergens had ik het idee dat ze niet met mij gezien wilde worden.

'Maar...' stamelde ik.

'Hup, niet zo aanstellen, gewoon met mij mee naar buiten lopen.'

'Ik durf niet zo goed,' zei ik toen we de laatste trap richting de uitgang afliepen.

Ze keek me aan. 'Weet je wat, dan lopen we arm in arm naar buiten, als een getrouwd stel.'

En dat is wat we deden. We waren bijna één geworden. Toen we bij haar vriendinnen aankwamen wist ik niet wat ik moest zeggen. In een reflex haalde ik mijn pakje kauwgom tevoorschijn en vroeg of iemand er eentje wilde. Alle vriendinnen wilden er eentje. Toen het rondje af was, en mijn pakje leeg, liet ik Liesje los.

'Ik zie je straks in de les,' fluisterde ik in haar oor. En liep weg.

‘Ik dacht dat je eigenlijk niet met mij buiten de klas gezien wilde worden,’ zei ik tegen Liesje. We zaten zoals altijd naast elkaar bij handvaardigheid en waren aan het knutselen. We moesten een openvouwboek maken. Iedereen in de klas maakte een verhaaltje over dieren, of een nieuw huis, of een mooie vakantie – die van ons ging over seks; een jongen en een meisje gingen samen kamperen en op het eind zouden we een rits maken die je een beetje open kon doen zodat het schaamhaar er bovenuit kwam. Zelf vonden we het hilarisch en voor de zekerheid hadden we ons idee niet aan de docent voorgelegd, uit angst dat het niet goedgekeurd zou worden.

‘Waarom dacht je dat?’ Liesje vond het duidelijk een rare gedachte.

‘Nou, zodra we het klaslokaal uitliepen, ging jij altijd naar jouw vriendinnen en liep ik ook weer verder, dus ik dacht: het is alleen iets voor in de klas.’

‘Nee joh,’ zei ze, ‘of misschien een beetje,’ – en ze lachte – ‘maar vooral omdat je zo druk bent, en wij samen al helemaal en we zitten vijf dagen per week op school samen, dan vind ik het soms ook wel lekker om even wat rust te hebben, dat jij even vrij bent en ik even vrij. Anders wordt het wel heel veel allemaal.’

Ik begreep het eigenlijk wel. We legden de laatste paar stukjes zwarte breidraden op de lijm op het papier. Het schaamhaar was af – en daarmee ook ons boek. ‘Kom, we laten het meteen zien.’ Liesje pakte het boek op voordat de lijm de tijd kreeg om te drogen.

De docent vouwde de eerste bladzijde open. *Het verhaal van De Tent* stond er te lezen. Niks bijzonders, tot zover. De volgende bladzijden sloeg de docent ook nog nietsvermoedend om, maar na pagina vier begon haar iets te dagen. Opeens doken de twee personages samen de tent in. Ze bladerde door, steeds sneller, totdat ze bij de laatste pagina met de open broek en het net opgeplakte schaamhaar kwam. De rits probeerde ze niet uit. Ze deed het boek dicht. Ze kon niet boos worden, dat wist ze zelf ook wel, want er stond niks verkeerds in, maar de manier waarop ze naar haar bureau bleef kijken, deed vermoeden dat ze een bepaalde seksuele vrijheid nooit echt had ervaren. Liesje gaf me een klein tikje in mijn zij, 'zo maken we de wereld nog eens wat vrijer,' zei ze. We kregen een zes. Waarom begrepen we niet, of eigenlijk wel, maar we deden van niet. Liesje keek hoe de docent het cijfer opschreef. 'U heeft het verkeerd om opgeschreven, het cijfer, maar wij doen niet moeilijk hoor, we zullen thuis het goede cijfer wel doorgeven!'

21.

Precies in de periode dat papa bestraald zou worden, ging ik met school naar Londen. Toen ik wegging zag hij er goed uit. Hij deed luchtig over de tumor, waardoor wij er thuis makkelijk mee om konden gaan. Boodschappen doen en bestraald worden, het viel in dezelfde categorie volgens mijn vader. Mij was verzekerd dat ik gewoon op reis kon.

John, George en ik sliepen bij hetzelfde gastgezin, waar we werden ontvangen door een vrouw met een grote moedervlek, of wrat. Het was een uitdaging daar niet naar te staren. Het huis was heel druk ingericht met allerlei soorten behang. John en George vonden dat een tikje te heftig, ik niet. Na het avondeten gingen we naar boven. Er waren twee slaapkamers. Eentje met twee bedden en eentje met één bed. John en George zouden bij elkaar slapen en ik in mijn eentje. Ergens vond ik dat fijn, ergens ook jammer. Ik legde mijn spullen in mijn kamer en deed mijn pyjama aan.

'Wobie,' riep John, 'kom je nog?' Ik wist niet waarom, maar was blij dat ze me uitnodigden. Op mijn blote voeten liep ik naar hun kamer. John stond in zijn onderbroek en had alleen nog een sportshirt aan. Ik wist niet zo goed waar ik moest kijken. George lag op bed, alleen z'n sokken waren uit, verder had hij zijn vest en zijn spijkerbroek nog aan. Zijn vest was open. Door zijn shirt kon je zien dat hij gespierd was, als een standbeeld van Michelangelo. Ik betrapte mezelf erop dat ik de contouren vast probeerde te stellen. Ik keek weg.

'We gaan boy talk doen,' zei John. Met mijn vriendinnen hadden we het over kleding, over wat er op school en daarbuiten gebeurde. Soms hadden ze het over jongens, dan hield ik mijn mond en luisterde ik. Maar welk soort gesprek we ook voerden, we hadden er nog nooit een naam aan gegeven.

'Boy talk?' vroeg ik voorzichtig.

'Ja, boy talk.' George gaf drie klopjes op zijn matras, als om aan te geven waar ik kon gaan zitten.

'Gewoon, welk meisje je het leukst vindt,' zei John.

'Wie vind jij leuk?' vroeg George aan John.

'Janine, sowieso Janine,' zei John. Ik kon me er wel in vinden. Janine kende ik al heel lang, sinds de basisschool en ze was een dierbare vriendin. Ze sprak prachtig Engels, was een rekenwonder en speelde piano.

'Ja, Janine,' zei John nog een keer, 'ze heeft ook echt grote tieten. Van die volle borsten. Terwijl ze nog sowieso drie jaar doorgroeien.' Hij bedoelde het niet verkeerd, maar het was alsof iemand vlak bij mijn hoofd een enorm hard alarm liet afgaan. Deze wending had ik niet zien aankomen. In mijn hoofd begonnen radertjes te draaien, maar niet in een goed geoliede machine. John noemde nog een paar namen, en nog een paar. George zei waar hij het wel mee eens was en waar niet.

'Ja, maar zij heeft alleen zulke grote borsten omdat ze zo dik is, tieten bestaan voor een groot deel uit vet, hè dus als zij zich zo vol vreet, dan krijgt ze ook megadikke borsten.'

Ik wist niet zo goed wat ik moest zeggen. Ook dit was een vriendin van mij. Opeens merkte ik dat bijna alle dames van onze leeftijd vriendinnen van me waren. En hoewel ik elke dag met ze sprak, elke dag mijn twijfels over van alles en nog wat met ze doornam, had ik op deze manier nog nooit naar ze gekeken. Nog geen seconde. Ja. Ze hadden borsten, maar het enige wat daar interessant aan was, was dat je er een leuk stofje omheen kon doen. Dat was bij mannen lastiger. En ja, ze waren handig voor het voeden van baby's. Maar ik had er nooit zo naar gekeken als John en George.

'Ben jij een borsten- of een billenman?' vroeg George mij.

Mijn hoofd leek een lege oceaan, ik kon geen land zien waar antwoorden op lagen, had bij dit soort zaken nooit stilgestaan. 'Nou, ik denk, ik denk dat ik van allebei hou?' zei ik voorzichtig.

Ze moesten lachen, het werd goedgekeurd.

Ze gingen verder met een reeks namen.

'En wie vind jij dan eigenlijk leuk?' vroeg George. Hij stond op van het bed en deed zijn vest uit. Ik vermoedde dat hij zich ging omkleden om straks te gaan slapen. Ergens wist ik dat het niet de bedoeling was te kijken, maar ik kon m'n ogen moeilijk van hem afhouden. Hij knoopte zijn broek los en liet hem zakken. Met een zwiepende beweging van eerst zijn ene en daarna zijn andere voet, alsof het schommels waren, wierp hij zijn spijkerbroek in de hoek. Hij had gespierde benen. Jaloersmakende, gespierde benen. Je zou hem zo kunnen inhuren voor de biologieles, dan kon de leraar op zijn lichaam aanwijzen waar welke spier zat. Ik voelde dat mijn ogen als magneten naar zijn lichaam werden getrokken. Hij scheen niks door te hebben. Voor de vorm, om niet op te vallen, begon ik aan mijn antwoord. Ik ratelde iets over dat ik het lastig in te schatten vond, maar dat ik alle genoemde meisjes erg leuk vond. Vaag genoeg om geen concreet antwoord te hoeven geven en hopelijk concreet genoeg zodat ze zelf het een en ander in hun hoofd konden invullen. George trok zijn shirt uit. Ik wist niet wat het was, maar ik kon niet anders dan kijken. Inderdaad Michelangelo, dacht ik. Zijn borstspieren waren omlijnd, kleine kussentjes waar een hoofd een warm welkom zou kunnen vinden. Zijn buik bestond uit blokjes waar je je vingers tussen te rusten zou kunnen leggen. Bij zijn navel begon een *way to heaven*, zo had ik dat een vriendin ooit horen noemen. Ook daar was zijn haar blond. Goudblonde haartjes als een ladder richting zijn kruis. Met zijn hand ging hij even kort zijn onderbroek in. Klokkenspel goed hangen, dat was duidelijk. Ik wist niet hoe ik mijn ogen van zijn lichaam moest halen, maar ik wist wel dat ik het niet wilde, dat ik niet wilde stoppen met kijken, dat ik m'n best deed om alle lijntjes te onthouden. Omdat het zo mooi was. In mijn buik voelde ik die spanning weer opkomen. Bewondering was het, bedacht ik me, bewondering. Voor. Voor? Voor wat?! Voor het zo goed onderhouden van je lichaam. Ja dat zou het vast zijn. Ik keek hem aan, scande in een seconde zijn ogen, hem was niks opgevallen. Ik liet een naam vallen. 'Zeta?' zei ik.

'Ja,' zei George, terwijl hij me aankeek, 'ja, dat is een mooie chick!'

In mijn eigen slaapkamer werd ik wakker. Ik moest naar de wc, maar durfde niet. Ik was bang dat ik John en George wakker zou maken. Het was zo gezellig geweest, die avond, hoewel ik het gevoel had dat ik me anders had voorgedaan. Ik wilde hun niet tot last zijn, ik wilde ze niet wakker maken. Ik probeerde eerst opnieuw in slaap te komen, bedacht een droom in mijn hoofd waarvan ik hoopte dat ik er ook mee in slaap zou vallen. Het werkte niet. Ik probeerde te tellen, kijken of dat zou afleiden. Werkte ook niet. Ik probeerde een gesprek in het Engels met mezelf te voeren – iets dat ik niet leuk vond om te doen, waardoor ik uit verveling alsnog in slaap hoopt te vallen. Maar wat ik ook deed, het werkte niet. Ik moest steeds nodiger plassen. Het leek te klotsen tegen de wanden van mijn blaas. Zoveel had ik toch niet gedronken? Ik baalde. Wat kon ik doen? Ronddraaien. Ronddraaien! Bedacht ik me.

Ronddraaien was iets dat we zelf bedacht hadden, mijn broertje en ik. Wanneer en hoe we het bedacht hadden, wisten we niet meer. Het leek wel alsof het altijd al bestaan had, dat ronddraaien, alsof we het altijd al deden. Iets genetisch, wat we vanaf onze geboorte meegekegen hadden. Maar we hadden het zelf bedacht. Als we gingen ronddraaien, gingen we allebei op ons eigen bed liggen. En dan gingen we ronddraaien. Met ons hoofd heen en weer rollend op ons kussen. We deden het voor het slapengaan, terwijl we zelfbedachte liedjes zongen en componeerden. We deden het in de ochtend als we wakker werden, als het nog te vroeg was om op te staan.

Heel voorzichtig begon ik ook nu met ronddraaien. Hopend dat ik de zon eerder kon laten opkomen. De zon kwam niet eerder, die nacht niet.

Ik baalde, inmiddels moest ik zo ontzettend nodig dat ik bang was in slaap te vallen. Ik kende dat, dan viel je in slaap, droomde je dat je bij een wc stond en plaste je je bed vol. Werd je wakker in een gele zee. Of wakker door de extreme lucht. Dat mocht niet gebeuren. Maar ik wist niet wat ik moest doen om én wakker te blijven én minder last te hebben van mijn blaas.

Uiteindelijk pakte ik mijn mp3-speler en deed de oortjes in. Mijn blaas voelde als een champagnefles die geschud was en waarvan de kurk elk moment de lucht in kon schieten, maar met twee handen werd de kurk op de fles gehouden. Ik zette de mp3-speler aan. Het eerste nummer speelde. Whitney Houston. *If I should stay, I would only be in your way // So I'll go, but I know // I'll think of you every step of the way*. Ik luisterde het nummer opnieuw en opnieuw en opnieuw, wetende dat ik het daarmee voor de rest van mijn leven voor mezelf zou verpesten omdat ik het voor eeuwig zou associëren met het feit dat ik te bang was om te gaan plassen. Ik werd misselijk. Van moeheid en van het nummer. Met mijn hoofd bleef ik ronddraaien. Totdat het echt niet meer ging. Als ik nog een paar seconden zou wachten – of – kon ik het al niet meer tegenhouden?

Ik bewoog voorzichtig mijn voeten uit bed. Probeerde te zien waar de vloer zou kunnen gaan kraken. En plaatste vervolgens heel voorzichtig mijn voet een stap vooruit. Het kraakte, de vloer. Ik dook direct terug in mijn bed. In foetushouding bleef ik daar liggen. Ik miste mama en papa. Wilde naar huis – maar wist dat ik hier nog drie dagen zou slapen. Ik ging weer ronddraaien, wenste dat mijn blaas als een lichtschakelaar uitgeschakeld zou worden. Ik stopte met ronddraaien, ademde heel diep in en uit en kwam opnieuw overeind. Een tweede poging, waarbij ik met mezelf afsprak dat wat er ook gebeurde, ik niet terug mijn bed in mocht voordat ik naar de wc was geweest. De eerste twintig minuten stond ik in mijn kamer. Door de kou en de stress voelde mijn blaas minder aanwezig. Toen opende ik de deur naar de gang en begon ik aan de tocht die nog veel langer zou duren. Het was een minigang, echt piepklein, in vier grote stappen was je bij de badkamerdeur. Maar ik durfde het niet. Beetje bij beetje ging ik vooruit. Millimeters. Alsof ik langs een levensgevaarlijk ravijn liep.

Uiteindelijk, het zal een halfuur geduurd hebben, kwam ik bij de wc aan. Toen ik ging zitten – thuis hadden we van jongs af aan geleerd zittend te plassen – moest ik huilen. Eerst dacht ik dat het kwam doordat ik niet durfde te plassen. Ik had daar al jaren last van, als ik bij vriendinnetjes ging slapen of op kamp ging; ik was altijd bang om anderen wakker te maken. Maar ik moest nu huilen door George. Of eigenlijk, door zijn lichaam. Dat ik daar zo naar had zitten kijken. Wat betekende dat? Betekende dat dat ik misschien dan toch? Nee. Dat wilde ik niet. IK WIL DIT NIET, schreeuwde ik in gedachten tegen mezelf. Ik wil ZELF kunnen bepalen hoe of wat. Laat me met rust. Bemoei je niet met mijn voorkeuren, wie je ook bent, laat iemand anders maar verliefd worden op, op – ik kon het niet eens denken. Ik huilde totdat ik beneden de vrouw met de moedervlek in de keuken hoorde rommelen. Via het badkamerraam zag ik dat het langzaam licht werd, zwart werd lichtblauw. Ik stond snel op, deed mijn onderbroek aan en ging terug naar mijn slaapkamer.

Ongeveer een uur later zaten we met z'n allen aan de ontbijttafel. Ik durfde George niet meer aan te kijken. Voelde me schuldig tegenover hem. Wilde het liefst dat hij mijn arm zou pakken, een knuffel zou geven, dat hij zou zien dat ik hem heel aardig vond. Maar hij had, logischerwijs, niks door. Ik wel. Ik wist dat er iets aan de hand was, vanbinnen. Er groeide iets in mijn buik. Geen mooie bloem of een sterke plant. Nee er groeide iets wat ik niet wilde. Iets verschrikkelijks. Iets wat ik eruit wilde halen. Maar dat lukte niet. Het groeien ging door. Wat groeide er – WAT GROEIT HIERBINNEN – schreeuwde ik in mezelf. Hoewel we met z'n vieren aan tafel zaten, voelde ik me alleen.

Ik besloot in de avond niks meer te drinken, zodat ik niet weer naar de wc zou moeten gaan. Stiekem hoopte ik dat we één van de dagen erna nog een keer een boy talk zouden hebben. Niet omdat ik nu wel goede antwoorden zou kunnen geven, maar omdat ik dan een reden had om bij John en George op de slaapkamer te zijn. En misschien dat een van de twee zich nog moest omkleden voor het slapengaan. Maar een nieuwe boy talk zou er niet komen.

Toen ik terugkwam uit Londen werd ik opgehaald door mama. Papa had ik aan de telefoon gehad nadat hij bestraald was geweest. Hij klonk wat vreemd, alsof er stukken vlees voor zijn mond hingen, waardoor zijn woorden niet goed verstaanbaar meer waren.

'Papa's gezicht is een beetje verlamd, lieverd,' zei mijn moeder, 'niks om je zorgen over te maken, het komt vast weer goed. En o ja, ze hebben schroeven in zijn hoofd gedraaid, dus hij heeft afdrukken, of nou ja, wondjes op zijn hoofd. Dan weet je dat vast. Schrik maar niet te veel, oké? Mama zal hem beter toveren.' Ik hield mama's hand vast totdat ze de auto startte en ging rijden.

Toen ik thuiskwam zag ik mijn vader liggen. Ik wilde niet huilen en sloeg het verdriet op voor als ik alleen was. Uitgesteld verdriet. Zijn hoofd was zichtbaar toegetakeld. Iemand had mijn vader pijn gedaan, en dat kon ik niet hebben. Niet mijn papa. Ik was boos op de dokters, dat ze dit mijn vader hadden aangedaan. Alsof hij een proefdier was geweest. Ik wist dat het een onredelijke gedachte was, maar ik vond het fijn om het iemand kwalijk te kunnen nemen.

'Dag jong,' zei mijn vader. Zonder bril had hij een molletjesgezicht, dat maakte hem lief, maar van het lieve gezicht was door alle zwellingen en wondjes nu weinig zichtbaar.

'Dag lieve papa,' perste ik uit mijn mond. Het kostte me moeite om te praten, het praten leek het tegenhouden van de tranen in de weg te staan.

'Geen zorgen jong. Papa komt erbovenop. Weet dat, papa komt erbovenop. Ik hou van je.'

'Ik ook van jou pap. Ik hou ook van jou.'

22.

Alleen een van mijn broers was boven. Mama was niet thuis en waar de anderen waren wist ik niet, maar volgens mij was ik hier alleen. Ik zat voor de huiscomputer. Tikte internet open. Google zei gedag. Ik twijfelde. Wist niet of ik iets fouts deed. Zo voelde het wel. Zweet drupte onder mijn oksels vandaan. Ik voelde me licht in mijn hoofd, alsof ik zuurstoftekort had. Ik tikte de eerste letter in. M. Twijfelde. Haalde hem weg. Tikte hem weer in. M. Ik dacht na. Volgens mij moest ik het gewoon doen. Ik deed het. Met een trillende vinger ging ik naar de volgende letter toe. O. En de volgende. D. En nog twee letters. EL. MODEL. Enter. Ik klikte op plaatjes. Eindeloos veel vrouwen verschenen. Blonde haren. Bruine haren. Ik scrolde erdoorheen. Het was alsof ik naar mijn vriendinnen keek. Ik ging terug naar de zoekbalk. Twijfelde opnieuw. En deed toen waarvoor ik bang was. Ik typte het tweede woord in en drukte op enter. Google begon te zoeken, zoeken naar MODEL MALE.

Ik bleef kijken. Zonder de muis aan te raken. Tientallen mannenogen keken mij aan. Ontblote bovenlijven. Gespierde borstkassen. Strakke kaaklijnen. Haren golvend als de zee. Of juist kortgeschoren. Ik keek. Voelde de spanning in mijn lichaam komen. Ik bleef kijken. Wat was hier nou zo boeiend aan? zei ik tegen mezelf. Kijk! Dit is toch niet boeiend. Kom op. Ik klikte op een van de plaatjes. De foto werd groter. Ik schrok ervan. Twee ogen keken mij betrapt aan. Dit. Dit? Dit is toch niet boeiend, zei ik tegen mezelf. Ik hoorde mijn eigen stem vol ongeloof tegen me praten. Ik schoot in paniek. Klikte het weg. Duwde het toetsenbord met een klap terug onder de tafel en smeet de stoel waarop ik zat opzij en liep de gang op. Ik wilde huilen. Ik wilde een van mijn vriendinnen bellen. Ik wilde zeggen dat ze me moesten helpen, dat er iets verschrikkelijks aan het gebeuren was, dat er iets in mijn lichaam... Maar ik durfde niet. Ik durfde niet te bellen, ik durfde niks te zeggen, ik durfde niet te praten. Als ik er iets over zou zeggen, zouden mijn gedachten de werkelijkheid ingaan. En dat mocht niet. Ik moest dit zelf oplossen, zelf zien te genezen. Ik moest wat stuk was heel proberen te maken. Ik wilde naar beneden lopen, maar realiseerde me dat iemand anders nu mijn zoekgeschiedenis zou kunnen zien. Ik liep terug en verwijderde eerst alleen de recente zoekgeschiedenis. Ik bleef zitten kijken naar het scherm. Wat nou als er ergens toch een spoor achter zou blijven, wat dan? Voor de zekerheid wiste ik alles. Alle dingen die ooit waren opgezocht. Alle automatische wachtwoorden. Het hele cachegeheugen.

Even later stond ik in de duinen. Samen met Hond Bril. Ik voelde me verdrietig en leeg, maakte me zorgen, zorgen om papa. Gelukkig ging hij langzaam vooruit. Af en toe kwam hij zelfs zijn bed al uit. Hij was lief en kwetsbaar. Nog steeds mijn vader, maar op een andere manier. Ik liep verder.

Bril gaf me een lik in mijn gezicht. Ik was gaan zitten op het helmgras. Dacht aan wat ik net had opgezocht op de huiscomputer. Had er spijt van. Nu zaten die mannenkoppen en die mannenlichamen in mijn hoofd. Ik probeerde ze eruit te krijgen. Ik tekende een hartje in het zand. Vroeger was ik verliefd geweest, maar wist ik niet hoe je hartjes tekende. Nu wist ik hoe je hartjes moest tekenen, maar niet meer wat verliefdheid was. Ik keek naar het hartje in het zand en sloeg het toen met drie vuistslagen weg. Het leek alsof een ziekte langzaam bezit van me nam. Maak me normaal. Maak me normaal. Ik wil niet anders zijn, ik wil niet gedwongen worden anders te zijn, riep ik bijna hardop, maar alleen het geluid van snikken kwam uit mijn mond. Hond Bril was komen aanrennen. Ze gaf mij een lik in mijn gezicht en kwam bij me liggen.

23.

'Weet je wat jij moet doen, Wobie, jij moet de Bond in!' zei Liesje.

De Bond was het leerlingenbestuur van de school. De nieuwe verkiezingen waren in aantocht. Liesje zat momenteel in de Bond.

'Echt wat voor jou,' voegde ze toe.

'Lies, ik ben daar totaal niet populair genoeg voor en daarnaast, dan moet de hele school op mij stemmen, wat nou als niemand dat doet?'

'Niet zo aanstellen, gewoon doen. Ik help je wel', en ze nam een hap van haar broodje. Dat broodje had ik voor haar gehaald. Ik deed dat de laatste tijd regelmatig. Van het oppasgeld dat ik verdiende kocht ik broodjes in de kantine. De kantinedames vond ik geweldig. Als ik in een tussenuur alleen was hing ik eindeloos bij ze rond. Vaak kreeg ik gratis een broodje of snack van ze mee. 'Tegen niemand zeggen, hè?' riepen ze dan. Door Liesje was ik überhaupt gebruik gaan maken van de kantine. 'Eet jij eigenlijk wel eens?' had ze een keer gevraagd. Om mij vervolgens de opdracht te geven om voor mezelf een broodje te halen. 'En als je dan toch bezig bent, haal er ook maar eentje voor mij.' Dat deed ik sindsdien heel vaak: een broodje voor mezelf en een broodje voor haar. Soms haalde ik ook snoep uit de automaat. Ook vandaag. Twee broodjes met roomkaas en komkommer en een zak winegums. Als we die aten werden we onhandelbaar, wist ik. Of er echt een verband was wist ik niet zeker, maar het werkte prima als selffulfilling prophecy.

'Ja, het lijkt me een goed idee als je meedoet,' zei Liesje nog een keer, met volle mond.

'Ik zal erover nadenken.'

'Is goed, lever na de pauze je sollicitatiebrief in, want dit is de laatste week dat het kan.'

Ik pakte m'n mp3-speler uit mijn tas. We hadden de eerste paar sommen gemaakt en werden allebei onrustig. 'Hier.' Ik gaf haar een van de twee oortjes. De muziek ging aan. Eerst deden we alsof we allebei keurig konden werken op de muziek. Maar dat was niet zo. Langzaam begonnen onze schouders heen en weer te bewegen. Er stond een rampzalig slecht nummer op, we moesten er allebei om lachen en konden niet anders dan er krankzinnig op dansen. *I look up at the sky // And I see the clouds // I looked down at the ground // And I see the rainbow down the drain // Fly away on Venga airways // Fly me high // Ibiza sky*. Het was muziek die klonk alsof je midden in een suikerrush zat, maar dan van het goedkope soort. Op de zeurende melodie wiegden we onze heupen heen en weer. Mevrouw Ritseflits zei er niks van, dus voelden wij ons geroepen onze act verder uit te vergroten. We bewogen steeds wilder. Naar elkaar, van elkaar. Het volgende nummer klonk. *I got chills they're multiplying // And I'm losing control // 'Cause the power you're supplying // It's electrifying*. We kwamen uit onze stoelen. Gingen staan en dansten alsof de hele klas de muziek kon horen. We dansten alsof de lente net was uitgebroken en we als jonge lammetjes voor het eerst naar buiten mochten. Het wiskundelokaal was een dansvloer en we waren allebei net heel erg dronken geworden. Liesje keek naar haar stoel, waarschijnlijk om te kijken of die naar achteren moest worden geschoven voor meer ruimte, maar het bracht mij op een ander idee.

'Kom, erop,' zei ik tegen haar. Ze keek me aan, sterretjes in haar ogen. We klommen op de stoelen en dansten. Juf Ritseflits kon ons nu écht niet meer negeren.

'Jullie twee, doe normaal, van die stoelen af!' zei ze. Niet heel boos, maar wel geïrriteerd.

'We komen zo naar beneden, na dit nummer,' zeiden we tegelijk.

'Is goed, dan mogen jullie je sommen op de gang afmaken,' zei ze. We dansten het nummer af, klommen van onze stoelen, pakten onze spullen en maakten de rest van de sommen op de gang.

'Nou, laat me je sollicitatiebrief maar zien.' De pauze was voorbij en we zaten bij natuurkunde. Vooraan, vlak bij de docent. Meneer Mats gaf ons les. Het was een oude man, een beetje een enge man, met een kale kop en gelige tanden. Hij rookte veel. Of beter gezegd, heel soms rookte hij niet. Als iemand een grapje maakte lachte hij zijn gele tanden bloot. Misschien dat die er niet heel gezellig uitzagen, lief was het wel. Hij was ook altijd bereid eindeloos te blijven uitleggen en zelfs voor leerlingen die er echt niks mee hadden kon hij natuurkunde boeiend maken. Ik vermoedde dat iedereen hem stiekem leuker vond dan ze zeiden of lieten merken.

'Nee, ik heb hem nog niet geschreven, maar woensdag hoef ik hem pas in te leveren, toch? En ik weet sowieso niet wat ik erin moet zetten,' zei ik tegen Liesje.

'Hier, geef me een stuk papier.' Ze hield haar hand op zoals wanneer ze om kauwgom vroeg. Ik scheurde een papiertje uit mijn schrift. Ze schreef van alles op en gaf het toen terug.

'Maak daar een mooi verhaal van en je zit geramd. Morgen

inleveren met de handtekening van je ouders en dan is vrijdag het sollicitatiegesprek.'

'Maar Lies, dit gaat me toch helemaal niet lukken. En een handtekening van mijn ouders, die ga ik nooit zo snel krijgen. Zij zijn niet bepaald fan van de Bond.'

'Vraag het nou maar eerst gewoon, dan kijken we later wel hoe we het oplossen als ze nee zeggen.'

'En wat is dat voor een sollicitatiegesprek dan?'

'Ja, dat is geheim, daar kan ik je niks over zeggen. Hoort bij de traditie.'

'Maar wat kan ik–'

BAM!

Met een keiharde klap schoten Liesje en ik enkele millimeters de lucht in. Om ons heen sprongen scherven door de lucht. We doken allebei weg. De klas moest lachen. Ik keek langzaam op en zag meneer Mats over ons bureau gebogen staan met een grote gebroken liniaal. Die had hij kennelijk kapotgeslagen op onze tafel.

'En nu opletten jullie!'

24.

'Zou je er alsjeblieft nog een keer over na kunnen denken, of er op z'n minst een nachtje over willen slapen, ik wil dit echt heel heel heel erg graag,' zei ik tegen mijn mama. Ze had met papa overlegd en ze vonden het allebei geen goed idee dat ik bij de Bond ging.

'Eerst je cijfers beter op orde. Daarnaast, ik heb altijd hele slechte verhalen gehoord over de Bond. Er wordt altijd enorm veel gezopen en gerookt. Dat wil ik niet hebben. Ik vind dit helemaal geen goed idee.' Ik was niet blij met de reactie van mijn moeder en mijn vader. Die avond had ik voorzichtig aan mijn ouders om toestemming gevraagd. Maar het was alsof ik keihard tegen een muur opliep. Dit ging niet werken.

'Je hebt je handen al vol aan de zaken die je nu doet, dus nee,' zei mijn vader. Nog een schepje erbovenop. Ik baalde. Maar wist dat ik het voor nu moest laten.

'Wat?! Hoezo mag je niet?!' vroeg Liesje toen ik haar de volgende dag sprak. Ik legde uit wat er gebeurd was en hoe ze over de Bond dachten.

'Oké, we doen het als volgt, je levert je sollicitatiebrief gewoon in, doet het gesprek en dan regelen we die handtekening wel later. Begin maar met rustig vertellen dat het allemaal meevalt en dat de Bond de afgelopen jaren enorm veranderd is, of zo.'

'Is dat zo dan?' vroeg ik.

'Nee, natuurlijk niet, maar het gaat er nu om dat je mee mag doen.'

Het sollicitatiegesprek die vrijdag ging anders dan ik verwacht had. Ik moest niet op de stoel gaan zitten, maar gaan staan en ik keek vanuit de lucht op zeven boze gezichten. Ik moest iets grappigs doen met een beker. Een mop vertellen. Een dansje doen. Toen ik vertelde wat mijn plannen waren, werd er gelachen en gezucht en gesteund. Dat was duidelijk ingestudeerd. Bij het toetreden tot de Bond hoorde een soort ontgroening. Dat had ik van tevoren niet geweten, maar ondervond ik nu direct.

Toen ik die avond thuiskwam vertelde ik dat ik toch had gesolliciteerd en dat ik het nummer van mevrouw Ardorante voor ze had. Zij begeleidde de boel als docent.

'Ze heeft gezegd dat jullie mochten bellen, dat er geen gekke dingen gebeuren en dat er tijdens het Bondskamp, ja, dat had ik inderdaad nog niet verteld, maar, luister nou heel even, dat is een soort van kennismakingskamp aan het einde van het schooljaar waarbij het oude Bondsbestuur een overdracht doet aan het nieuwe Bondsbestuur. Nee, heus niet, daar gebeuren geen rare dingen, de docent is er de hele tijd bij en we leren er vooral hoe we het leerlingenbestuur moeten uitvoeren.'

Mama en papa gingen erover nadenken, maar ik had zo'n vermoeden dat de kaarten niet goed lagen.

Toen ik net in bed lag werd ik geroepen.

'Wobie, kan je even beneden komen?'

Ik kwam uit bed, deed een kimono aan en liep naar de slaapkamer van mijn ouders.

'We hebben erover nagedacht,' zei mijn mama.

'Wil je echt heel graag?' vroeg mijn papa.

'Ja, echt heel erg graag, Liesje doet het nu en het lijkt me geweldig om het volgend jaar te doen.'

'We geven onze handtekening, op één voorwaarde, dat je schoolcijfers er niet onder lijden. Zodra we merken dat dat wel gebeurt, of als je gaat drinken, dan halen we je er direct uit.' Ik hoorde hun voorwaarden eigenlijk al niet meer, ik was zo blij dat mijn oren op slot waren gegaan. Welke eisen ze ook zouden stellen, ik zou ja zeggen. Ik was dolgelukkig.

Een paar maanden later was de campagne. Een hele week lang deden we keihard ons best om zoveel mogelijk stemmen te trekken. Waar in het grotemensenleven geld werd ingezet, gebruikten wij snoepgoed. Wie het meeste snoep kon uitdelen won geheid de verkiezingen. De schoolleiding was hier niet blij mee en voerde nieuwe regels in. Er mocht niks meer uitgedeeld worden en er kwam een limiet voor het aantal posters. Op de tv's werden nog wel campagnefilmpjes getoond. Mijn broer had mijn campagnevideo gemaakt. Hij was zo lief geweest om zijn camera mee te nemen naar zijn voetbaltraining. Hij trainde met veel jongens van onze school, het stoere en coole type. In de douches had hij de camera aangezet. Een twintigtal jongvolwassen mannen, net klaar van het sporten, danste in hun nakie terwijl ze mijn campagneslogan riepen. Ik was door het dolle heen en toen het vertoond werd in de aula was ik apetrots. De leerlingen vonden het hilarisch, bij de docenten maakte ik een minder goede beurt. Omdat iemand zich voortijdig had teruggetrokken, kwamen álle kandidaten in het bestuur. Ik was trots dat ik in de Bond zat en blij dat Liesje me had overgehaald. Ik had even geen last van grijze mist.

25.

Ik zat er weer. Achter de huiscomputer. Mijn gedachten en mijn gevoelens hadden mij ernaartoe geroepen. Ik móést erheen. Ik móést opnieuw zoeken. Om zeker te weten dat het goed ging. Ik wist namelijk dat ik de vrouwelijke modellen mooier vond. Ja dat wist ik zeker. Maar ik moest het checken. Gewoon voor de zekerheid. Ik zou alleen maar naar MODEL MALE zoeken, omdat ik dan kon zien wat ik niet wilde zien. Om zeker te weten dat het echt niet boeiend was. Ik ging alleen kijken om te zien wat ik niet wilde zien.

MODEL MALE. Google zocht. Google denkt vast dat ik het interessant vind, die mannelijke modellen, bedacht ik me. Mooi, dan is er nog iemand die dat systeem voor de gek kan houden, zei ik tegen mezelf. Ik keek. Scrolde. Die spanning weer in mijn lichaam. De ruimte vulde zich langzaam met een grijze wolk. De kleuren in de kamer werden weggezogen. Alles werd grijs, alsof ik in een oude film zat. Geen kleur. Nergens meer.

Moest ik verder gaan? Gewoon? Om zeker te weten dat ik dit niet wilde zien? Ik dacht van wel. Ik dacht dat het verstandig was om verder te gaan. Ik veranderde de zoektermen. Draaide eerst MODEL en MALE om. Dat leek me bij nader inzien correcter. En plaatste er toen HOT voor. HOT MALE MODEL. Ik drukte op enter. Google zocht. En Google vond. Ik keek. Scrolde langs de plaatjes. Engelen zonder vleugels. Mannelijke standbeelden van vlees en bloed. De spanning steeg, een kriebelend gevoel pompte zichzelf door mijn bloedvaten. Ik voelde mijn hart bonken, bijna mijn borstkas uit. Onder mijn shirt kon ik hem zien. Ik moest meer eten, bedacht ik me. En ik keek weer naar de modellen. Moest ik misschien, gewoon voor de zekerheid, een plaatje printen? Ik stond op, liep naar de gang en luisterde onder aan de trap naar het geluid van boven. Schrijversregen. Mooi. Dat zou wel even aanhouden. Ik zocht twee mannen uit, plakte ze in een Word-document en printte. De printer was langzaam, hij zat me te pesten. Dat wist ik zeker. Hij wilde dat ik betrapt werd. 'Niet vandaag, printertje,' zei ik, 'niet vandaag', en ik legde alvast mijn hand op de zijkant voor het geval hij het in zijn hoofd haalde om toch ingewikkeld te gaan doen. Toen de plaatjes klaar waren, kleiner dan ik gehoopt had, vouwde ik ze snel op. Opnieuw verwijderde ik de zoekgeschiedenis.

Een paar dagen later zat ik weer achter de pc. Ik had op mijn kamer zitten kijken naar de plaatjes. En nadat ik mijn tranen had gedroogd en de plaatjes verscheurd, zat ik nu toch weer achter die klotecomputer. Godverdomme! Godverdomme! Ik keek in de spiegel en gaf mezelf een klap met vlakke hand. Mijn wang werd rood. Kom op! Zorg dat het stopt! Hou jezelf onder controle!

Ik opende Google. Klikte op Afbeeldingen en voerde wat anders in. Ik typte de werkelijkheid in, om te zien hoe de werkelijkheid eruitzag. Ik typte GAY RUSSIA in. Ik zag mannen die gearresteerd werden door zwaarbewapende politieagenten. Ik zag bebloede gezichten. Mannen die huilden. Iemand die weggesleept werd terwijl hij een regenboogvlag vasthield. Ik zag een foto van een man die een klap vol in zijn gezicht kreeg. Ik keek. Schaamde me. Voor mijn broers. Voor mijn ouders. Ik typte HOMO in. Scrolde en zag toegetakelde gezichten.

De realiteit lachte me uit. Spuugde me in mijn gezicht. Geen mannelijke modellen in strakke onderbroeken. Vanaf dat moment onthield ik het steeds beter als iemand op tv, de paus, of iemand in de krant een verbod op verliefdheid afkondigde. Ik sloeg alles op en nam me voor om overal heen te gaan waar ik verboden was. Ik wist niet waarom. Maar zo voelde het.

Ik moest kokhalzen van de zenuwen. Ik rende weg van de computer, terug naar mijn kamer waar ik op bed ging liggen. In foetushouding. Terug naar de oorsprong, daar was het fout gegaan. En ik huilde.

26.

'Eindelijk,' zei een van mijn vriendinnen, 'eindelijk begin je er eens over.' Het was alsof ik eindeloos iets had uitgesteld waar mijn vriendinnen al heel lang op zaten te wachten. We zaten samen op het schoolplein. Het officiële schooljaar was voorbij, iedereen ging naar huis, maar ik bleef altijd wat langer hangen. Ik wilde niet thuis zijn. Sinds de spanning meer en meer in mijn lichaam voer en de grijze wolk steeds vaker om me heen hing, vond ik het thuis verstikkend. Ik had voortdurend het gevoel dat ik iets met me meedroeg dat thuis als een grote teleurstelling zou worden gezien. Thuis was ik bovendien alleen met mijn gedachten en werd ik voortdurend geconfronteerd met dingen die ik niet begreep, met gevoelens en behoeften die ik niet kon verklaren.

'Het is toch ook gewoon een knappe jongen, E,' zei ik. E, of eigenlijk Eveline, maar ik noemde haar E, had een vriendje, of: was bezig met een vriendje krijgen. Cees heette hij. Een jongen die je met gemak het stempel 'knap' kon geven.

'Zeker, hij is zeker knap', en ze keek me aan. Ik kon meer zeggen, als ik dat wilde, maar dat hoefde ik nu niet. Dit kleine beetje gaf me al wat meer lucht. Ik deed alsof ik gewoon objectief vaststelde dat het een knappe jongen was. Niets meer. Niets minder. Dat was niet vreemd, zei ik tegen mezelf, iedereen kan over iedereen zeggen of ie wel of niet knap is.

'Wat vind je zo knap aan hem?' vroeg E. Ik keek haar aan, in haar ogen zag ik dat ze het spel mee zou spelen, dat ze de regels die ik in mijn hoofd had bedacht niet zou overtreden.

'Ik vind, gewoon als je er objectief naar kijkt hè, nou, dan heeft hij mooie ogen, en hij draagt altijd van die Uggs, dat vind ik hem ook goed staan. En volgens mij is hij gespierd. Nee, ik kan wel begrijpen dat je het fijn zou vinden om in de ochtend naast hem wakker te worden. Hij is natuurlijk niks voor mij, maar ik begrijp wel wat jij knap aan hem vindt.'

Ze sloeg haar arm om me heen en legde haar hoofd op mijn schouder.

'Waar ga je heen op vakantie?' vroeg ze.

Ik had een manier gevonden om te kunnen praten over dat wat in mij groeide. Ik kon een sluier over de werkelijkheid leggen, waardoor die niet helemaal zichtbaar was maar ik er wel over kon praten. Het gaf me iets meer lucht, alsof ik niet meer door een rietje hoefde te ademen. Ik realiseerde me dat ik die manier van opnieuw leren ademen bij Liesje had geleerd en dat ik het nu langzaamaan ook met mijn andere vriendinnen kon gaan bespreken.

27.

Bondskamp was anders dan ik verwacht had. Ik leerde wat ik niet leuk vond. Ik leerde hoe mensen ook met elkaar om konden gaan. We werden met rauwe eieren besmeurd, moesten door water en deegpoeder rollen. We mochten niet douchen en stonken een uur in de wind. We sliepen – de paar uur die ons werden gegund – in een oude varkensstal waar we met z'n vijven drie matrassen moesten delen. De hele week zaten de harde deegstukken in mijn haar. 's Nachts werden we wakkergemaakt, geblinddoekt en weggebracht. We moesten *mumzelen* door het gras, een soort van tijgeren, maar dan terwijl je met je handen je enkels vasthield. Supersoakers gevuld met energydrink werden op ons leeggespoten, waardoor we helemaal plakkerig werden. We verloren elk besef van tijd, van dag en nacht, doordat we geen klokken mochten zien en we niet in spiegels mochten kijken. Het was vervreemdend. En alles onder de noemer van elkaar beter leren kennen.

Door het mumzelen kreeg ik schaafwonden aan de binnenkant van mijn knieën. We deden er verband op, maar de volgende ochtend bleek dat het vast was komen te zitten aan de wond. Terwijl het verband werd losgetrokken, beet ik zo hard als ik kon op mijn vinger, met tandenstempels als resultaat. Nu waren het grotere wonden en moest er zeker verband omheen. Dat gebeurde. Alleen. Toen we het verband aan het einde van de dag wilden vervangen, bleek het weer verkleefd met de wonden. Ik stampvoette. Wilde niet dat het er nog een keer af werd getrokken, maar het moest wel. Met een nat doekje probeerden we het eerst voorzichtig los te krijgen, maar dat lukte niet, dus zat er niks anders op dan opnieuw mijn vinger in mijn mond te stoppen en te wachten tot het verband eraf ging. Ik zag kleine stroompjes met wondvocht en bloed naar beneden druppelen. Een derde keer ging er verband op. Toen 's nachts bleek dat het weer was gaan vastkleven, wilde ik geen verband meer. Ik mocht douchen om de boel schoon te spoelen en verder was het afwachten hoe het zou herstellen. Gelukkig was het de laatste avond. Onze ontgroeners hadden ons verzekerd dat er niks ergs meer zou gebeuren, maar inmiddels durfden we dat niet meer te geloven. We waren zo bang geworden. Bang dat je tijdens het slapen weer onder luid kabaal naar buiten werd geroepen en dat je dat, hoe snel je ook was, altijd te langzaam deed. Angst is een gevaarlijk machtsmiddel. Dat leerden we in die dagen snel. En daarom dachten we dat we weer in de maling werden genomen. Maar dat was niet het geval. De overdracht was nu officieel. Tijdens het kamp hadden we in de middagen les gehad over hoe het leerlingenbestuur werkte en hadden we ook onze functieverdeling besproken. Ik zou secretaris worden, de rechterhand van de voorzitter.

Toen ik thuiskwam van het Bondskamp en we een aantal dagen later op vakantie gingen, wist ik niet goed hoe ik het verhaal van mijn knieën moest uitleggen. Als ik ging zitten moest ik heel traag in mijn stoel zakken. Omdat de huid rondom mijn knie strakker was gaan staan, barstten de twee wonden elke keer opnieuw open. Als ik opstond perste alles weer samen. Ik kon het niet verborgen houden voor mijn ouders. Woest was mijn moeder. Mijn vader geschokt. Ik weet niet wat mijn ouders gezegd of gedaan hebben, maar een jaar later was er van alles stopgezet en mocht ik niet mee op kamp – maar dat had weer een andere reden.

28.

De zomervakantie was bijna voorbij en ik wilde naar bed. Mama had ik net een kus gegeven, waarna ze had gevraagd of alles goed ging.

'Ja,' had ik geantwoord. En was naar boven vertrokken. Ik kwam de tweede trap op en zag papa in zijn schrijfkamer zitten. Schrijversregen klonk.

'Pap, ik ga naar bed.' Hij draaide zich om. 'Dat is goed, jong. Slaap lekker.' Hij kwam uit zijn schrijfstoel om me een kus te geven.

'Gaat alles goed?' vroeg ook hij. Ik keek hem aan. Het voelde alsof mama en papa mij op iets betrapt hadden, ik vreesde dat ze misschien iets hadden gezien op de computer. Ik hoopte dat ze van me zouden blijven houden, wie of wat ik ook was.

'Ik zou wel wat vaker een knuffel van je willen de komende tijd,' zei ik voorzichtig.

'Dat is goed jong, slaap lekker, ik hou van jou.'

29.

Het nieuwe schooljaar begon. De vierde. Een week van tevoren was ik vriendinnen gaan appen om te kijken met wie ik samen naar school kon fietsen. Dat durfde ik nog steeds niet alleen. En die angst was erger geworden. Gelukkig had ik net op tijd weer een groepje gevonden.

De school rook nieuw. Meestal rook het er verlaten na de vakantie, maar deze zomer was gebruikt om de kantine te verbouwen. Her en der was schilderwerk gedaan, alsof de muren en de vloeren waren gaan shoppen tijdens de vakantie. De muren wilden duidelijk ook eens iets anders. Het zou een bijzonder jaar worden, dat wist ik, want ik zat in het leerlingenbestuur.

We kregen dat jaar voor het eerst Natuurkunde, Leven en Techniek, NLT. Een soort handvaardigheid voor de bèta's. 'Joh, Wobie, kom je ook bij ons in het groepje?' vroeg Daniël. We hadden opdracht gekregen om een presentatie over drank te maken die we in november moesten houden voor een aantal onderbouwklassen. De docent maakte geen groepjes, dat mochten we zelf doen. Even was ik in paniek geschoten, ik wilde het schooljaar niet meteen beginnen met het gevoel dat je als laatste wordt gekozen tijdens gym. Dat gebeurde dit keer gelukkig niet. Daniël had meteen een groepje gevormd en mij onderdeel gemaakt van het team. Ik kende hem eigenlijk niet, hij mij blijkbaar wel. Ik was blij dat hij mij erbij betrok. In de afgelopen paar jaar deden wat verhalen over mij de ronde, dat ik op mannen zou vallen. Ik had er steeds meer last van en was tijdens de zomervakantie bang geweest dat mensen me erom zouden ontwijken. Daniël liet die nachtmerrie die eerste les verdwijnen. Hij leek een dromenvanger.

'Gezellig,' zei ik, en ik schoof mijn stoel tot bij hun tafeltjes. Ik ging zitten en legde mijn schrift en mijn map op tafel. Daniel gaf me een vriendschappelijke stomp. Ik keek hem aan en gaf er eentje terug op zijn schouder. Daniël lachte en gaf als reactie nog een stomp terug, dit keer op mijn been. Het was op deze manier niet erg een boksbal te zijn. Ik moest lachen.

Tijdens het bedenken van ideeën keek ik naar Daniël. Ik vroeg me af waarom ik hem eigenlijk niet kende. Hij had bruine haren met een slag erin. Zo krachtig en vol als die van een wild Fries paard. Het leek alsof er iets van de natuur in zijn haren was blijven zitten. Zijn ogen waren bruin. Donkerder dan zijn haren en er zat iets van een constante ondeugendheid in. Ogen met een belofte. Ik was benieuwd hoe zijn ogen naar de wereld keken, hoe hij de dingen zag en hoe dat zijn gedachten vormgaf. Hij had een lichtbruine huid. Alsof de zon elke dag voor hem scheen en hem bruin kleurde zonder dat hij zou verbranden. Het viel me op dat er zelfs wanneer hij serieus aan het nadenken was, een glimlach in zijn gezicht verborgen lag. Hij keek me aan, had gemerkt dat ik naar hem zat te kijken, en hij glimlachte. Ik glimlachte terug.

Toen de bel ging pakten we onze tassen in. 'Zal ik onze mappen even terug in de bak leggen?' vroeg ik aan ons groepje. Ik realiseerde me dat ik de afgelopen drie jaar alleen maar vriendinnen had gehad. Vriendinnen die er altijd voor me waren, me een warm nest boden, maar ik merkte hoe leuk ik het vond om nu ook een keer in een jongensgroepje te zitten.

‘Wat chill, ja is goed gozer,’ zei een van de jongens. Ik stapelde de mappen op om ze weg te brengen. Daniël gaf me een schouderklopje. ‘Bedankt baas.’ Het leek alsof er een fontein van vriendelijkheid binnen in hem zat, een fontein waar je geen muntje in hoefde te gooien om er iets voor terug te krijgen. Nee, de fontein deelde haar spetters sprankelend uit. Ik hoopte dat we vrienden konden worden. Ook buiten deze les.

Het rooster gaf langzaam vorm aan de dag en ik kwam erachter dat Daniël en ik bij heel veel vakken samen in de klas zaten. Scheikunde, natuurkunde, biologie. En in alle lessen deed hij even aardig, alsof we elkaar al lang kenden.

De pauze begon. Ik stond in de kantine en was met vriendinnen in gesprek. In mijn buik was er een kleine oorlog uitgebroken. Ik had mijn rooster gecheckt en we zouden die middag gym hebben. Ik probeerde smoesjes te bedenken om daar weg te kunnen blijven. Het voelde alsof ik een muis was die onderweg was naar een blokje kaas. Een blokje kaas op een houten plank met erachter een ijzeren pin. De paniek nam toe toen een van mijn vriendinnen vertelde dat we vanaf de bovenbouw geen gezamenlijke gymles meer zouden hebben. De appels bij de appels en de peren bij de peren, zeg maar. Ik trok wit weg. Gym vond ik sowieso al een enorme opgave, vooral het omkleden, maar dan lag altijd nog in het vooruitzicht dat ik in de gymzaal bij mijn vriendinnen kon gaan zitten. Nu moest ik me niet alleen omkleden met de jongens maar ook twee uur lang met hen alleen gymmen. Geen steunpilaren of afdakjes waar ik kon schuilen, nee, open in het veld als een opgejaagd hert. Bambi zonder moeder.

Toen ik de kleedkamer binnenkwam was er nog weinig plek over. Ik wist niet wat een betere tactiek was; lang wachten in de hoop dat iedereen alvast naar de zaal was gelopen, waardoor ik me makkelijk en relatief alleen kon omkleden. Of voordat de pauzebel ging alvast naar de kleedkamer gaan zodat ik verzekerd was van een plekje en al bijna omgekleed zou zijn wanneer de rest binnen zou komen. Het hield me al dagen bezig, maar een beslissing had ik niet kunnen maken. Uiteindelijk was het uitstellen van de beslissing de beslissing zelf geworden, waardoor ik dus laat de kleedkamer in kwam. Er was een klein stukje over waar ik onhandig mijn tas ophing. Alsof ik voor het eerst in een kleedkamer kwam. Ik merkte nu pas hoe heftig de negatieve energie van het gymmen in mijn lichaam was gekropen. De afgelopen drie jaar had ik dat opgebouwd, maar het was nu wel heel heftig. Overal klotste de spanning in mijn lichaam tegen de muren van mijn huid op.

Ik was bijna klaar met omkleden toen ik een gespierde arm een tas aan het haakje naast mij zag hangen. Ik keek op. Een grote glimlach. Dansende engelen. Het was Daniël.

'Hé Daniël,' zei ik. Het kwam eruit alsof ik net uit bed was gekomen en nog niemand had gesproken. Een schorre en droge stem.

'Wat gezellig, baasje, gymmen we ook nog eens samen.'

Waar de anderen sportief en sterk waren, druk met ballen gooien en haantjesgedrag, voelde ik me anders. Een herfstblad in de lente. Ik miste de meisjes met wie ik kon kletsen en bij wie ik me veilig voelde. Ik had niet verwacht dat mijn onzekerheid zich zo meester zou kunnen maken van mijn lichaam en houding.

Tijdens de klassikale sport deed ik mijn best om mee te komen met de rest. We speelden die eerste les een soort voetbal. Teams van vier tegen vier. Als er gescoord werd moest je naar de bank en zou iemand anders je plek innemen. Er werd snel gespeeld en de jongens op de bank joelden en juichten. Ze hadden het naar hun zin, ik vermoedde dat het voor hen voelde als een soort vakantie op school. Ik had niks met voetbal, als mijn broers het in de vakantie speelden bleef ik liever lezen. Maar dat kon nu niet. Ik rende heen en weer, in een poging om te laten zien dat ik het wel kon. Toen er een aantal keer gescoord was, mocht ik eindelijk naar de bank. Daar merkte ik hoe warm ik het had en dat ik begon te zweten. Ik deed er alles aan om mijn gymshirt niet mijn lichaam te laten raken. De gymshirts van het VCL waren blauw, vochtplekken zag je direct. Ik wapperde en bleef onnatuurlijk recht staan, terwijl de rest ontspannen tegen de muur leunde. Ik had het gevoel dat ik niet mocht zweten.

30.

Binnen het leerlingenbestuur waren Alice, de voorzitter, en ik bezig met de Praagreis. Al jaren was mevrouw Tuvar, docent economie en zijdelings betrokken bij het Sinterklaascabaret, de drijvende kracht achter de reis. Zelf was ze lang geleden gevlucht uit Praag. Ze had altijd vreemde schoenen aan, alsof ze uit een Harry Potter-film was komen lopen. Het was haar persoonlijkheid die de reis magie gaf, en daarmee was het de reis geworden waar leerlingen het meest naar uitkeken.

En elk jaar zat de Praagreis stampvol, terwijl die niet verplicht was. De verhalen over wat er tijdens die reis gebeurde, waren nog wilder dan sommige filmscenario's. En hing een mysterieuze sluier rondom de reis waardoor iedereen nieuwsgierig was. Alleen, sinds het aantreden van de nieuwe schooldirecteur was de reis van de jaarplanning gehaald. Mevrouw Tuvar was erg teleurgesteld geweest, het was haar laatste jaar op het VCL en ze was ooit gestart met de reis. Stiekem had ze gehoopt dat de reis haar cadeau voor de school kon zijn, iets wat ze kon nalaten.

Alice en ik kregen de opdracht uit te zoeken waarom. 'Ja, dat was mevrouw Vlieger, maar dat maakt voor de rest niet uit,' antwoordde de altijd ongemakkelijke meneer Willemse nadat we hem vroegen wie de reis uit zijn overdracht had weten te houden. Alice en ik keken elkaar aan. Dat maakte nou juist wel uit. Precies waar ik bang voor was, meneer Willemse was simpelweg te lief, te aardig, om door te hebben dat iemand anders meedeed aan het schaakspel.

Toen Alice en ik terugkwamen bij mevrouw Tuvar met onze nieuwe informatie over mevrouw Vlieger bleek dat we haar niets nieuws vertelden. 'Ik wist dat al jongens,' zei ze, 'maar ik wist niet zeker of ik jullie dat mocht vertellen.' Daarop legde ze de situatie verder uit: 'Mevrouw Vlieger vindt mij te losjes en de reis onzin. Ik vermoed dat ze het heeft gedaan om te pesten, maar dat kan ik niet hardmaken. Ik hoop dat jullie het voor elkaar krijgen de reis wel door te laten gaan.'

Plastic zakjes vlogen als herfstbladeren over het schoolplein, de pauze was net voorbij. Alleen ik zat nog buiten. Ik was blijven zitten toen mijn groepje wegging en had gezien dat Liesje aan kwam lopen. Zij had ook een tussenuur, wist ik. Zoals je op de basisschool het nummer van je moeder uit je hoofd leerde, zo leerde ik tegenwoordig de tussenuren van vriendinnen uit mijn hoofd. Liesje liep alsof ze altijd hoge hakken aanhad én een tikkeltje teut was. Als een paradijsvogel. Soms wilde ik verliefd op haar worden, maar het lukte nooit.

'Liesje,' zei ik, 'kan ik even met je praten?'

'Ben je in *trouble paradise*?' zei ze met een knipoog.

We gingen onder de brandtrap tegen de muur zitten. Ze had haar sjaal op de grond gelegd, zodat we allebei niet op de koude stenen hoefden te zitten.

'De billetjes, die willen ook wat,' riep ze tijdens het neerleggen van haar sjaal.

'Ik zit ergens mee,' zei ik. Ik was Liesje inmiddels gaan zien als een wandelend dagboek.

'Nou, als jij mij even helpt met een sigaret opsteken luister ik, lieverd!' Met mijn handen maakte ik een menselijke vissenkom. Een menselijk muurtje tegen de wind en Lies haar sigaret begon te gloeien.

'Het gaat over Daniël,' begon ik. Ik vertelde haar hoe aardig hij was geweest tijdens de eerste NLT-les, dat hij me erbij betrok en dat hij zich blijkbaar niks aantrok van alle verhalen die over mij de ronde deden. Ik vertelde haar dat ik het gevoel had dat we echt vrienden aan het worden waren. Dat ik daar heel blij mee was. Dat ik nu pas besefte dat ik eigenlijk geen mannelijke vrienden had. En dat ik het echt heel fijn vond dat hij dat wel leek te worden. En dat ik het fijn vond als we samen les hadden. Dat ik misschien wel eens hoopte dat we nog vaker en nog meer samen les zouden hebben en dat ik ervan baalde als een van onze sessies uitviel omdat er een docent ziek of afwezig was.

'Dat is goed toch?' vroeg ik aan haar. Ze keek me aan en perste haar mond een beetje samen. Ik herkende deze blik, die leek uit te drukken: 'Wat wil je eigenlijk zeggen?'

'Maar, soms, ik weet niet wat het is, zit er ook iets van een spanning in mijn lichaam als ik hem zie. Waarvan ik in de war raak, alsof mijn lichaam deze vriendschap wil verpesten. Denk je dat ik afstand moet houden, dat ik me meer moet afzonderen van hem?'

'Lieverd,' zei ze terwijl ze rook de lucht in blies, 'gewoon contact houden. Gewoon verder gaan, ik denk dat het heel goed is dat je een keer een mannelijke vriend krijgt. Kijk gewoon hoe het gaat. Daniël vindt je sowieso aardig, dat is duidelijk, dus waar zou je moeilijk over doen?'

Ik knikte.

'Alleen,' ging ze wat aarzelend verder, 'kijk, ik bedoel, dat weet je vast, maar Daniël valt natuurlijk wel op meisjes. Jíj óók, dat weet ik wel, ja, dat weet ik, maar je twijfelt soms een beetje. Hij niet. Hij twijfelt niet. Dat moet je wel weten, dus pas een beetje op.'

31.

Ryanne en ik zaten op het muurtje van de school bij de straat. Af en toe kwam er een auto voorbij, maar eigenlijk was het stil. Het leek alsof de buurt collectief met pensioen was. Niet alleen de mensen, maar alles. De auto's, de planten en de bomen, alles leek in een ruststand te verkeren. Ook het gesprek tussen Ryanne en mij was met pensioen. Tijdelijk dan. Ik had het met haar gehad over mijn twijfels, over de jongens op school, over Daniël. Ze was de zoveelste die ik het vertelde. Elke ochtend sprak ik met mezelf af dat ik het niet aan nóg een vriendin zou vertellen, maar als ik op school was, onrustig geworden van alles om me heen, en als ik hem weer had zien lopen, dan moest ik het er gewoon over hebben. Alsof een hand via mijn keel naar mijn buik ging en daar mijn gevoelens vastpakte en omhoogtrok. Misschien was ik zelf die hand wel, want ik wilde van dat gevoel af. Ik wilde van die spanning af. Als ik niks zei ging het borrelen in mijn buik. Alsof een fluitketel met onbeperkt water eindeloos stond te gieren. Ik móést praten, alleen dan kon ik ademen en mijn hoofd en buik rustig krijgen. Ik realiseerde me dat ik in hem misschien een antwoord, of een deel van een antwoord vond. Een antwoord waar ik nog niet aan toe was. Maar hij was er wel, en hoe. Als een bak glitters die over je wordt uitgestrooid, waardoor je eindeloos, dagen en maanden lang, overal die glitters tegen blijft komen. Hoe erg je ook je best doet, je komt er niet vanaf. Als ik naar huis fietste, merkte ik dat ik per ongeluk aan hem dacht. Ik wilde dat niet. Ik kneep in mijn stuur, zo hard als ik kon, mijn nagels in de rubberen handvatten, maar hoe hard ik ook kneep, hij bleef in mijn hoofd zitten. Hij kleefde aan alle verhalen en fantasieën. Zelfs als ik in slaap viel liet hij me niet met rust. En het erge was dat de dromen waarin hij voorkwam geen nachtmerries waren. Ik haatte mezelf erom. Als ik 's ochtends wakker werd keek ik mezelf teleurgesteld aan in de spiegel.

'Kun je niet één moment proberen normaal met iemand bevriend te raken?' beet ik mezelf in stilte toe. 'Krijg jezelf onder controle, stap uit die achtbaan.'

Ik hoopte hem niet te zien, die nieuwe schooldag, maar tegelijkertijd wilde ik niets liever.

Het was weer maandag. Maandag betekende gym, dus dan waren mijn vriendinnen altijd in een staat van paraatheid. Ryanne had gevraagd hoe het ging. Het ging simpelweg niet. Als ik ging gymmen leek het alsof alle kleur uit de zaal, uit de school, uit mijn hoofd verdween. Alles werd grijs. Alles werd stil. Ik hoorde de jongens lachen en praten, maar ik durfde zelf niet te bewegen. Ik had het gevoel dat alle jongens op een vreemde manier naar me keken, terwijl ze helemaal niet naar me keken. Ik voelde dat ik anders was, dat er iets niet klopte, dat er een verschil was tussen ons. Gym was een marteling. Steeds verder van tevoren keek ik ertegen op. Had ik maandag gym, dan kon ik vrijdagavond al niet meer slapen. Ik bedacht duizend smoezen om mijn hoofd rustig te krijgen. Ik ging er zelfs over dromen, dat waren wel nachtmerries, waardoor ik uiteindelijk niet één maar wel zes keer in de week gymles had.

'Lukt het je niet om rustig te worden tijdens de les?' vroeg ze.

'Nee, wat ik ook doe, alles in mijn lichaam lijkt in paniek,' zei ik. 'Sterker nog, een van de jongens vroeg dit keer of het wel goed met me ging. Ik heb volgens mij in drie verschillende talen gezegd dat het super ging, waarop hij mij een beetje vreemd aankeek.'

'Hmm, gekkie toch,' zei Ryanne, 'en Daniël?'

'Die was aardig, gaf me toen we de kleedkamer verlieten een boks op mijn arm en zei dat we elkaar zo bij scheikunde zouden zien.'

'Dat is fijn.'

'Ja,' zuchtte ik, 'heel fijn.'

Ons gesprek werd onderbroken. Vijf opgefokte types kwamen de straat in, onze kant op. Schreeuwend. Blikjes werden op de grond gesmeten. We bleven rustig zitten.

'Hebben jullie Dorian gezien, Dorian Peters?' schreeuwde een van hen.

Ik keek op. 'Nee, die hebben we niet gezien,' antwoordde ik.

'Klotekakkers! Wil je hem laten weten dat we hier op hem wachten!' schreeuwde hij.

Ryanne en ik keken elkaar aan. 'We kunnen ook wat voor jullie doorgeven hoor,' zeiden we. We kenden Dorian allebei. Dorian was het broertje van een vriendinnetje en ergens voelden we dat het verstandiger was om te proberen te achterhalen waar deze jongens voor kwamen en om hem of zijn zus te waarschuwen.

'Ja! Geef maar door dat we op hem wachten! Dat joch!' schreeuwden ze terug.

'Oké, maar waar komen jullie voor?' vroegen we.

'Haal hem anders maar, ja haal hem maar!' werd er geschreeuwd. Ze waren inmiddels zo dichtbij dat schreeuwen wel heel vreemd werd. We zaten nog steeds op het muurtje.

'Dat gaan we niet doen, we zullen doorgeven dat jullie hier geweest zijn, en dan zien we verder wel,' zeiden we. Langzaam lieten we ons van het muurtje glijden, alsof we een valse hond stoorden bij het eten en we nu voorzichtig weg wilden gaan. We werden uitgescholden. In verschillende bewoordingen waarvan het zonde is dat ze zijn uitgevonden. Sommige raakten harder dan andere, misschien omdat ik vond dat ze niet mochten dienen als scheldwoord. En omdat ze persoonlijk waren. Ryanne keek ze aan, ik zag dat ze er klaar mee was om beleefd te blijven doen. 'Doe even normaal, stelletje rotjochies!' Het orkest van scheldwoorden nam toe. We riepen terug dat ze lekker een paar andere mensen moesten gaan irriteren maar niet hier ruzie moesten gaan zoeken. Het gescheld ging door. We riepen terug dat ze moesten oprotten. En vervolgens draaiden we onszelf om zodat we terug konden lopen naar het schoolgebouw. Ze stapten op hun fietsen terwijl ze bleven schreeuwen. Toen we het zat waren riepen we uit volle borst: 'Stelletje sukkels!'

We liepen verder het schoolplein op toen we achter ons een fiets hoorden neerknallen. We hadden het als een alarm moeten zien. Drie seconden later viel ik op de grond. Een van de jongens was op mijn rug gesprongen en legde zijn arm om mijn keel. Met mijn handen greep ik zijn jas, met mijn vingers probeerde ik tussen mijn nek en zijn arm te komen. Ik wilde ruimte maken, een kiertje, zijn arm van mijn hals afhalen. Ik kreeg geen lucht. Op mijn rug regende het vuisten. Maar die voelde ik niet. Ik voelde alleen die arm, die als een boomstam op mijn nek drukte en mijn luchtwegen afsloot. Mijn luchttunnels stortten in. Ik wilde hem duidelijk maken dat hij mijn zuurstof ontnam, dit deed hij vast per ongeluk, maar hij liet niet los. Hij drukte alleen maar harder. Ik zag Ryanne omdraaien, net op tijd, want ook bij haar wilde iemand op de rug springen. Die kon ze ontwijken. Ik keek weer naar de grond en probeerde met alle kracht die ik in mij had mijn vingers tussen zijn en mijn lichaam te krijgen. Maar veel kracht had ik niet. Ik wist niet wat ik moest doen, totdat ik een enorm, keihard gekrijs hoorde. Een schreeuw alsof een gorilla werd aangevallen door jagers. De arm om mijn nek ontspande iets en vervolgens viel hij weg. Ik kwam omhoog en zag Ryanne keihard schreeuwen. Ze had het haar van de jongen vastgepakt en sleurde hem nu met alle kracht die ze had over het schoolplein.

'Snel!' riep ze naar mij. Ze liet los en we renden naar de ingang van de school. Achter ons zagen we dat de conciërges werden aangevallen. Vijf tegen twee. Hoewel het volwassenen waren wisten we niet of ze het wel zouden redden en we beseften dat er extra hulp nodig was. We vroegen aan meneer Van Beezen, de man die alles bij de ingang in de gaten hield, of hij direct kon bellen naar de docenten.

'Ik ben al bezig,' zei hij met schrik in zijn ogen, 'jullie moeten nu naar beneden komen, er is een gevecht ontstaan op het schoolplein en we hebben extra hulp nodig.' Gek genoeg hoorden we geen docenten de trap af komen. Op de verdieping waar de directeur zat, en de docenten die geen lesgaven, bleef het stil. We keken meneer Van Beezen aan en terwijl hij naar buiten ging, renden wij de trap op. Drie treden per stap.

Op de verdieping van de docenten was geen deur opengegaan. Alsof er niet gebeld was. We renden naar de kamer van de rector toe en zagen dat het lampje bij de deur brandde. Rood licht. Dat betekende dat we niet mochten storen. Dat ze in vergadering zaten.

'Schijt.' Ryanne gooide de deur open. In de kamer van meneer Willemse zaten een aantal docenten, twee decanen, de rector en de conrector. Ze waren onverstoorbaar verder gegaan met vergaderen. In het hoofd van Ryanne ontplofte iets.

'Jullie móéten NU naar beneden komen! Godverdomme! Er wordt gevochten!' schreeuwde ze de kamer in.

We waren bij de politie geweest om ons verhaal te doen en klaar om naar huis te gaan toen ik werd gebeld. Daniël. Hij had me nog nooit gebeld. Ik nam op.

'Wat is er gebeurd?'

Ik vertelde het verhaal met alle details erbij.

'Baasje, wat klote! Weet je wat, ik ga je leren trainen zodat je sterk kan worden. En tot die tijd heb je ons, hè. Als je je onveilig voelt moet je dat gewoon laten weten!'

'Wie belde je?' vroeg mama toen we in de auto zaten. Papa zat achter het stuur. 'O niemand,' zei ik, 'gewoon een vriend van school.'

Hoe meer ik aan mijn vriendinnen begon te vertellen, hoe minder ik tegen mijn ouders zei. Elke keer dat ik me bewust werd van mijn gevoel leek ik me schuldiger te voelen tegenover mijn ouders en mijn broers. Ik wilde niet het zwarte schaap zijn. Hoewel ik wist dat zwijgen niks zou opleveren en mama en papa regelmatig zeiden dat ze van me hielden, schoof ik steeds vaker weg uit de gemeenschappelijke ruimtes. Op mijn kamer ging ik vroeg naar bed, om zo niet met ze te hoeven praten.

De hekken rondom het schoolplein werden gesloten. Leerlingen stonden vanuit de kantine te kijken hoe het slot op het hek werd gezet en hoe klasgenoten op het schoolplein naar binnen werden gestuurd. Deze pauze geen ruimte om te roken of buiten te luchten. Op straat hadden een tiental, misschien wel meer dan een tiental, jongeren zich verzameld. Ze kwamen even verhaal halen, hadden ze de conciërges laten weten. Omdat hun vrienden in de cel zaten.

Een decaan was het schoolplein opgelopen. 'Zolang jullie daar blijven staan is het oké, maar zodra je het schoolplein opkomt heb je een probleem, want dit is eigen terrein.' De jongens aan de andere kant van het hek knikten grijnzend. Een van de docenten die tijdens de pauze de boel in de gaten moest houden, stuurde ons weg bij de ramen. Ik hoorde ze zeggen dat voor de zekerheid de politie al gebeld was.

Ik maakte me zorgen; Ryanne en mij was niets verteld over dat de andere jongens in de cel hadden gezeten. 'We denken dat het verstandiger is als je de school verlaat,' zei een docent tegen me. Ik begreep het niet helemaal en keek hem vreemd aan. 'Wij regelen de rest wel, maar het is handiger als je naar huis gaat. Ben je met een scooter?' vroeg hij. Ik heb geen scooter, zei ik, alleen een fiets. Terwijl ik het zei was ik bang dat ze mij in m'n eentje naar huis zouden laten fietsen. Ryanne, die me was komen zoeken, zag mijn blik verschieten. 'Ik heb wel een scooter, ik laat hem wel bij mij hangen en dan breng ik hem richting huis.' Maar hoewel ik veilig thuis werd gebracht en het gevaar daarmee weg leek te zijn, hield angst mij nog lang gezelschap. Een sieraad dat ik liever af had willen doen, maar niet van mijn vinger kreeg.

32.

Het was de avond voordat ik met Daniël en de andere jongens van het groepje de NLT-presentatie moest geven. Ik had de powerpoint in elkaar gezet en rondgestuurd. Naar Daniël stuurde ik een sms om te vragen of hij de cijfers had kunnen vinden die hoorden bij het aantal alcoholgerelateerde verkeersongelukken en wat hij van de powerpoint vond. Ik werd snel beloond met een berichtje terug. 'Yo, ik heb die kutgetallen niet meer man, maar het is een prima powerpoint!' kreeg ik terug. Mocht ik zo vrolijk worden van een berichtje? Ik vond van wel. Dat zouden vast alle vrienden hebben. Vriendschappen waren vrolijk, toch? Ik sms'te terug of hij zijn tekst voor morgen naar me op kon sturen zodat ik kon zorgen dat niemand iets dubbel zou vertellen. Hoewel we allemaal het vak volgden hadden we niet de tijd gehad of genomen om bij elkaar te komen en de presentatie te oefenen. Mijn mobiel ging. Alweer antwoord. 'Ok dikke.' Ik moest weer lachen. 'Je kunt veel van mij zeggen, maar dik ben ik niet ;),' stuurde ik terug. Vriendschap voelde geweldig. Glimlachend ging ik op mijn kussens liggen, Tijger gaf ik een aai over zijn kop.

Opnieuw klonk mijn mobiel. Ik hield de telefoon voor mijn gezicht. Wederom Daniël. 'Papzak.' Ik wilde dansen. Moest lachen. Langzaam kreeg ik die spanning in mijn lichaam, maar dit keer liet ik me ontvoeren. Ik liet me gewillig gevangennemen door de spanning. Kom maar op, dacht ik, ik weet wat je bent. Je bent het vriendschapsgevoel, zei ik tegen mezelf. Verzekerde ik mezelf.

Ik reageerde niet op zijn bericht. Dommelde langzaam een droom in. Opnieuw hoorde ik mijn telefoon en ik deed mijn ogen open. 'Vetje, hoeveel kantjes moet het zijn?' Ik werd op een prettige manier duizelig. 'Twee kantjes is goed!' stuurde ik terug. Ik wist niet of het klopte maar ik moest toch wat zeggen. Binnen een minuut lichtte mijn scherm op: 'Ik heb 4 kantjes. En allemaal onderzoeken helemaal uit mijn hoofdje geleerd xxxxx.'

Mijn ogen bleven kleven, plakken, nee, waren vastgelijmd op de 'xxxxx'. Het voelde als dansen op wolken waar engelen wachten op een kus van God. Het voelde alsof er duizend sterretjes tegelijk in mijn hoofd werden afgestoken.

Ik typte mijn antwoord: 'Oké, fijn! Super van je, ik zorg dat de powerpoint gereet staat, mail jij me dan nog even je tekst en dan is alles geregeld.' Ik twijfelde even, durfde het eigenlijk niet zo goed, maar de dwarrelende sneeuw in mijn hoofd ontnam niet alleen mijn zicht maar ook heel even mijn angst en ik tikte 'xxxxxx' als afsluiting erachteraan. Binnen een minuut had ik antwoord. 'Gereed met een D dikke, ik heb gemaild naar je Hotmailadres.' Hij was een vuurwerkshow op zichzelf. En een witte kerst. Ik klikte het licht in mijn kamer uit en nodigde Daniël uit in mijn slaap.

33.

Onze wielen knetterden over de straattegels. Er kwamen nog net geen vonken vanaf. We reden door rood licht. Snelden snoeihard over het kruispunt. Knalden met onze fietsbanden van de stoeptegels. De presentatie was goed gegaan. Dat cijfer hadden we binnen. De schooldag zat erop en ik ging niet naar huis maar fietste met Daniël. We babbelden. Ik had zijn roze markeerstift gejat en die zat nog in mijn tas. In de pauze was hij achter me aan gekomen. Zoals hij dat vaker deed. Ik jatte iets van hem of ik riep dat ik sterker of sneller was. Ik voelde me erg jongensachtig als ik dat deed. Was ergens trots op mezelf dat ik hem durfde uit te dagen. Hij reageerde er vrijwel altijd op. In zijn eentje of met twee andere jongens kwam hij dan achter me aan. Ik rende dan de trappen naar de bovenste verdiepingen op. Daar mocht je eigenlijk niet komen in de pauzes van de docenten, maar ze hielden mij nooit tegen als ze me zagen rennen en spelen. Misschien vonden ze het plezier ontwapenend.

Als ik met twee treden tegelijk de trap opging, dan deed Daniël dat met drie. Ik probeerde er dan vier, maar dat lukte nooit. Ik rende over de gangen van de bovenste etage. Soms waren de andere twee jongens zo slim geweest om via de andere kant naar boven te komen, dan werd ik ingesloten. Hoe je het ook wendde of keerde, uiteindelijk kreeg Daniël me wel te pakken. Hij werkte me dan naar de grond en klemde mijn hoofd tussen zijn benen. Als een puppy lag ik op mijn rug. Buiten adem. Mijn handen rondom zijn enkels om te voorkomen dat hij zijn benen te hard zou samenknijpen.

Op die momenten voelde het alsof ik weer even op de basisschool mocht zijn. Ik genoot ervan de gangen en de trappen van de middelbare school te zien als speeltuin. Elke week was het raak. Vaak na de NLT-lessen. Dan waren we al ontspoord in de klas, waren er stompen uitgedeeld en moest de verder opgewekte energie als uit een accu kunnen wegstromen. Ook na de presentatie was het raak geweest. Dit keer had ik dus zijn roze marker gejat. Eerst had hij hem terug kunnen pakken, nadat hij mijn hand had ondergekliederd. Maar toen hij even niet oplette had ik hem weer teruggepakt.

'Waar woon je eigenlijk?' vroeg Daniël.

'Aan de andere kant van waar we nu heen fietsen,' zei ik. Daniël moest lachen.

'Waarom fiets je dan mee, is dat niet superonhandig voor je?'

'Ja, maar ik vind het wel gezellig.'

'Hahaha! Dat is aardig.'

'Maar ik rijd wel tot aan die hoek, dan keer ik om.'

'Is goed.'

We stopten bij de plek die ik had aangewezen. 'Trouwens,' – en ik haalde mijn tas van mijn rug – 'deze kreeg je nog terug.' Daniël lachte opnieuw en stopte de roze stift in zijn tas.

Mijn rode gordijnen waren dicht. De witte kerst in mijn hoofd was weggesmolten. Weggespoeld. Was het wel normaal dat ik het zo leuk vond om te stoeien? Was dit wel hoe vriendschap voelde? Of was dit meer? En als het meer was, hoe kon ik dat dan stoppen, hoe kon ik dat tegenhouden? Ik plukte aan Tijger die ik in mijn armen had genomen. Ik vroeg me af of het niet vreemd was dat ik met hem meefietste. Of het niet abnormaal was dat ik precies wist wanneer we les hadden. Ik wist dat ik in de puberteit zat en wilde in alle vrijheid dingen kunnen uitproberen, zoals pubers dat deden. Met vriendinnen uitgaan, dansen en drinken, meisjes vinden, zoals iedereen dat deed. Maar ik voelde me niet vrij. Ik had nog steeds het gevoel dat er in mij iets groeide wat daar niet mocht groeien. Alles om me heen liet mij zien hoe het eigenlijk hoorde. Wat ik op internet zag, in de krant en op tv. Als je niet aan de norm voldeed, kwam je in de problemen. Alles was dan lastiger. En dat wilde ik niet. Ik wilde niet leven op de handrem. Door die onzichtbare wetten werd je gezien als afwijkend. Ik vond het niet erg om iets anders te doen dan wat de meesten misschien deden, maar ik wilde daar wel zelf de controle over hebben. En nu groeide er iets onbeheersbaars vanbinnen, waardoor anderen me zagen als anders. Alsof ik een lachspiegel aan het worden was. Ik dacht aan mama en papa, ik zonderde me steeds meer van ze af. In gedachten was ik bij ze, maar echt aanwezig in huis was ik niet. Ook was ik lastig tegenover docenten. Ik pakte mijn viool niet meer op. Voelde me langzaam anders worden, merkte dat ik iemand werd die ik niet wilde zijn. Nee, diep vanbinnen wás ik iemand die ik niet wilde zijn. Omdat het anders was, omdat mensen erover zouden praten, omdat ik in andere landen verboden was. Niemand had me gevraagd of ik dit wilde zijn. Niemand had bij me geïnformeerd wat ik ervan zou vinden. Niemand had verteld hoe ik ermee om moest gaan. Opeens was ik het gewoon. En hoe hard, hoe lang, hoe heftig ik het ook bleef ontkennen, ik kon het niet tegenhouden.

34.

'Als het echt niet meer gaat, moet je misschien wat tegen de docent zeggen,' zei Annah.

Ik zat weer met een vriendin op het schoolplein, het leek alsof ze allemaal onderdeel waren van een praatschema. Bij elke vriendin liet ik een stukje worsteling zien. Soms had ik er spijt van als ik iets blootgaf. Dan regende het vanbinnen. Ik was bang dat ze me anders zouden gaan bekijken, dat ze afstand zouden nemen, alsof ik bedorven en besmettelijk was. Maar dat deden ze nooit. Geen mondkapjes, geen zakdoeken voor het gezicht, geen plastic handschoentjes. Niets van dat alles, sterker nog, vaak schoven ze dichter naar me toe.

Annah had gezien dat het niet goed ging. 'Gym hè?' Ze had het al van een aantal anderen gehoord. Ze bevestigde wat ik al vermoedde; mijn vriendinnen hielden elkaar op de hoogte. Stiekem gaf me dat wel een veilig gevoel. Maar soms was het ook onhandig. Op feestjes wist ik mezelf steeds minder goed onder controle te houden, en ze maakten zich zorgen over telkens die fles bij het diner. 'Laat me nou maar, dan ben ik gewoon wat rustiger en kan ik ook wat makkelijker met die mannen omgaan,' zei ik dan. Maar als ik beloofde het enigszins onder controle te houden die avond, lieten ze het gaan. Hoewel we allemaal wisten dat de belofte een ijspegel in de zomer was.

'Ja, ik heb na de pauze gym, mijn lichaam is al dagen een aardbeving.' Ik keek haar aan.

'Misschien moet je met, van wie had je ook alweer les, meneer IJzinger? Misschien moet je met hem gaan praten?'

Ze had gelijk, maar met hem gaan praten was ook een eng vooruitzicht. Hoe moest ik dat doen zonder te zeggen wat er in mij aan de hand was?

'Hij begrijpt het sowieso, heus,' zei Annah.

We leunden tegen het muurtje en ik deed mijn ogen dicht, alsof ik mezelf van mijn zenuwen weg kon denken. Ik voelde de oorlog in mijn buik. De gymlessen waren een confrontatie met alles waar ik nog niet aan toe was.

'Joh, ik hoorde iets over dat je verliefd was op Daniël?' Ik schrok overeind. Ineens was Marc erbij komen staan, een jongen uit mijn jaar. De oorlog in mijn buik was in één keer beslecht. Maar niet in mijn voordeel. Rustig ademhalen, dacht ik, gewoon ontkennen.

'Sorry, wat zei je?'

Hij moest een beetje lachen. 'Ja, ik hoorde iets over dat je verliefd was op Daniël of zo, klopt dat?'

Weer moest hij een beetje lachen. Ik begreep niet wat er grappig aan was.

'Hoe kom je daarbij?'

'Ja, ik hoorde zoiets, iemand zei er wat over in de klas, maar heb ik dat niet goed gehoord?'

Ik moest lachen, gespeeld lachen – niet Oscarwaardig, maar geloofwaardig genoeg, hoopte ik. 'Nee joh, wat denk jij nou, ik vind hem alleen een aardige jongen, we zijn vrienden, niets meer, niets minder. Wel flauw dat als ik een keer bevriend raak met een jongen, dat mensen dan meteen denken dat er wat is.' Had ik een te lang antwoord gegeven voor zo'n korte vraag? Ik wist het niet, maar hoopte wel dat hij zou stoppen met doorvragen.

‘O, oké, nou, dan zie ik je zo bij gym.’

Ik keek Annah aan, die had zich gelukkig niet bemoeid met het gesprek en gedaan alsof er niks aan de hand was. Net als ik. Nu Marc weg was viel haar mond open.

‘Wie is dat überhaupt?’ vroeg ze.

‘Ja, geen idee, ik zit volgens mij soms bij hem in de klas, maar dit is wel echt heel erg klote.’

Meteen vroeg ik me af of ik het niet te vaak en te hard over Daniël had, dat mensen het misschien konden horen. Of had ik het misschien te veel vriendinnen verteld? In mijn hoofd begon ik al een lijstje te maken.

‘Geen zorgen, dit zijn gewoon van die verhalen, niks van aantrekken.’ Ik keek haar aan. Ze wist dat haar woorden niet als vliegen in een web zouden blijven hangen. Ik hing er zelf.

‘Nu kan ik het al helemaal niet meer.’ Ik doelde op de gymles.

‘Oké, weet je wat je doet, je gaat nu naar meneer IJzinger toe en zegt dat je niet kunt gymmen en dat je graag na de les met hem wil praten.’

Ik was nerveuzer dan een kind voor Sinterklaas, maar ik wist dat ik dit nu moest doen.

Met mijn kleren aan was ik naar de gymzaal gelopen, de kleedkamer had ik overgeslagen. Ik hoorde aapachtige geluiden, de mannen lachten en loeiden. In hun onderbroeken sprongen ze soms de banken op, of ze deelden klappen uit met een shirt. Ooit zou er een dag zijn waarop ik dat zelf ook durfde te doen. Ik liep naar meneer IJzinger.

‘Meneer,’ begon ik, het leek alsof mijn stem gestolen was, ik was bijna onverstaanbaar, terwijl ik alle energie in mijn lichaam had verzameld om hem aan te spreken. Hij draaide zich om en wist meteen dat er iets was.

‘Pak maar alvast wat ballen uit het hok,’ zei hij tegen een leerling die al eerder in de gymzaal was.

‘Kan ik u heel even spreken?’ Mijn vingers leken rietjes in de wind. Niet alleen mijn stem maar álles trilde. Ik dacht aan mama en wilde dat ze me naar huis toverde. In haar armen, mij zou verbergen voor de buitenwereld. Maar ik wist dat dat niet zou gebeuren. Ze wist niet wat er speelde, dit moest ik alleen doen.

‘Natuurlijk. Gaat het wel? Wat is er aan de hand?’ Ik had geoefend hoe ik het wilde zeggen, maar ik was mijn tekst direct kwijt.

‘Nou, kijk, er is een probleem, ik zit ergens heel erg mee en, deze gymlessen, ze maken mij op een hele nare manier, of, het ligt niet aan de lessen maar, ik voel me gewoon heel erg niet fijn tijdens de gymles, maar echt echt echt heel erg onprettig. En ik zou u willen vragen of ik vandaag niet hoef te gymmen, misschien dat ik u zo na de les kan uitleggen wat er is, want er komen nu steeds meer mensen binnen, maar, misschien dat we dan even kunnen praten.’ Ik wist dat ik niks concreets had gezegd, maar mijn gevoel lag in ieder geval wel al op tafel.

‘Natuurlijk. We praten na de les, ga lekker bij mij zitten vandaag, oké? En misschien dat je dan ook wat rustiger wordt?’ Ik was blij dat ik niet mee hoefde te doen.

Het bankje van de gymdocent was recht tegenover de muur waar wij als leerlingen altijd moesten gaan zitten. Daar had ik niet bij stilgestaan en meneer IJzinger volgens mij ook niet. Hij ging op de bank staan, ten teken dat hij wilde beginnen en iedereen moest gaan zitten. Ik zat ernaast. Toen iedereen zat keek ik zo’n twintig tot dertig jongenshoofden aan. Ik deed alsof er iets heel belangrijks op mijn mobiel verschenen was en ondertussen wreef ik over mijn scheenbeen, alsof ik alle jongens in de klas wilde laten denken ‘o wat naar, hij heeft een blessure’.

Het werd handbal en ik mocht de scores bijhouden en fungeren als scheidsrechter. Ik was blij dat ik een taak had. De gekleurde hesjes werden uitgedeeld en met een fluit stond ik op de gymlerarenbank. Als ik een beetje moest lopen, deed ik dat licht hinkend. Dat sloeg natuurlijk nergens op, want de hele dag had ik prima kunnen bewegen, maar het leek me toch verstandig om nog een extra signaal af te geven aan de rest.

'Wat is er aan de hand?' vroeg Oliver. Oliver was een van de knappe en stoere jongens uit onze klas. Hij had eerder al eens tijdens gym gevraagd of alles wel goed ging. Hoewel hij populair was, was hij eigenlijk altijd heel aardig tegen mij.

'Ja, heel raar, iets met een blessure, moeten even kijken hoe en wat,' antwoordde ik. Hij knikte en gooide de bal weer het veld in.

De gymzaal liep langzaam leeg, ik bleef op het bankje van de gymleraar zitten. Meneer IJzinger deed de deur dicht. De gymzaal was leeg en stil, alleen wij waren er nog. Ik voelde me opeens meer op mijn gemak. De afgelopen maanden had ik deze zaal als een nachtmerrie ervaren. Meneer IJzinger kwam naast mij zitten. Het was aan mij om nu iets te zeggen.

'Hoe vond je dit? Gaf je dat een beetje vertrouwen voor volgende keer?'

Ik keek hem aan, wist dat ik nu niet maar gewoon ja moest zeggen omdat ik het gesprek dan uit de weg kon gaan, want dan zat ik volgende week weer in de problemen.

'Het was fijn om op deze manier toch nog even aanwezig te zijn, maar ik blijf me overbewust van alles.' Ik was even stil.

'Je hoeft je geen zorgen te maken, wat we hier bespreken blijft tussen ons, je kunt gewoon eerlijk zeggen wat er aan de hand is.'

'Ik weet niet zo goed wat er aan de hand is, behalve dat ik het echt heel erg niet fijn vind om te gymmen, niet dat de jongens vervelend doen, maar ik word me gewoon bewust van dingen waar ik nog heel erg mee worstel en ik heb gewoon meer afstand nodig,' begon ik. Hij liet me doorratelen zodat ik mijn verhaal kon doen. Ik zei veel, zonder misschien te zeggen wat er écht was, maar dat maakte voor hem niet uit.

'Ik loop er al heel lang mee en het wordt alleen maar erger en soms moet ik bijna huilen als ik aan de les moet beginnen. Ik weet dat ik niet moet weglopen van zaken, en ik ben ermee bezig, alleen, het is gewoon te veel, te bedrukkend om hier te zijn.'

Ik zag dat hij me begreep. 'Laten we afspreken dat je kijkt hoe je je volgende week voelt. Als je het niet trekt geef je dat gewoon aan en dan hoef je niet te gymmen, maar zeg dat niet tegen te veel mensen.'

Ik wist dat hij online moest invoeren of ik in de les verschenen was en dat mijn ouders dan een melding kregen als ik afwezig was. 'Mijn ouders weten er niks van.'

'Geen zorgen. Ik zal invoeren dat je er gewoon bent, oké? En weet dat je altijd met mij kunt praten, of met de vertrouwenspersoon op school, we zijn er om je te helpen, en hoewel veel jongens misschien stoer doen, mogen ze je wel.'

Ik zou de komende drie jaar geen gymlessen meer volgen die binnen plaatsvonden. Soms wel de buitengymlessen. Thuis vertelde ik niks. Het voelde als een enorme opluchting. Alsof ik weer adem kon halen.

35.

Ik lag al in bed, de lichten in mijn kamer en in mijn hoofd waren uit. In de verte hoorde ik mijn slaapkamerdeur opengaan. Mama ging op de rand van mijn bed zitten. Ik wist niet meer zeker of ik haar wel of niet een slaaplekker-ikhouvanjou-kus had gegeven. Ik dacht van niet.

'Dag lieverd, slaap je al?' Ik draaide me op mijn rug zodat ik mama kon zien. Ik pakte haar hand, die kon ik zonder problemen vinden in het donker.

'Gaat alles wel goed met je, lieverd?' Ik zei niks. Knikte een beetje. Mama probeerde mij de laatste tijd vaak te bereiken, maar hoe hard ze ook haar best deed, ik wist dat het haar niet zou lukken. Ik vond dat ik deze strijd in mijn eentje moest voeren. Weer knikte ik een beetje. Misschien wilde ik haar wel wat zeggen, in de beslotenheid van de nacht, maar ik wist dat ik haar morgenochtend weer zou zien. En ik wilde geen definitieve dingen delen.

'Je weet dat we van je houden hè? Papa en ik maken ons een beetje zorgen om je. Je kunt ons altijd alles zeggen.' Ik knikte weer.

Toen mama weg was pakte ik het fotolijstje dat op mijn nachtkastje stond. Ik had het daar laatst neergezet, dichtbij, zodat ik er vaker naar kon kijken. Het was een roze lijstje met als omhulsel een boa, maar dan zonder veren maar met zachte, wollige roze haartjes. Wilde je de foto zien, dan moest je de haartjes wegblazen. Ik keek er de laatste tijd steeds vaker naar. De foto waarop mama mij als kind een kus gaf terwijl ik glunderend in mijn apenpak de camera inkeek. Ik vroeg me af of ze me ooit nog eens zo liefdevol zou kussen als ik alles vertelde. Ik blies nog eens. Op de foto werd zichtbaar wat ik in het dagelijks leven nooit had gezien. Sinds het moment dat deze foto was genomen, had mama meer leeftijdslittekens in haar gezicht gekregen. Hoewel ze haar prachtig stonden, maakten ze me toch verdrietig.

36.

Mijn vader en ik hadden ruzie gekregen. Het was vrijdag en mijn vriendinnen én de jongens – dat hadden mijn vriendinnen gezegd – gingen naar de Westwood. De Westwood was de nachtclub waar alle VCL'ers bijna elke vrijdag heen gingen. Het was een soort kruising tussen een bunker en een zwarte betonnen schuur, maar het waren de mensen die het leuk maakten. Daar gebeurden zaken waar het de rest van de week over zou gaan. Verhalen werden er geboren.

Vriendinnetjes hadden gevraagd of ik meeging en dat wilde ik dolgraag, maar mijn ouders vonden het geen goed idee. Vraag maar aan je moeder, had papa eerst gezegd. Vraag maar aan je vader, had mijn moeder gezegd. Ik liep weer naar beneden waar papa het avondeten aan het maken was.

'Van mama moet ik het aan jou vragen,' zei ik. Ik vond het stom en dom dat ik om toestemming moest vragen.

'Ik vind het geen goed idee,' begon mijn vader. Op de trap hoorde ik mama naar beneden komen.

'Waarom niet?' Domme vraag. Dat wist ik. Foute vraag.

'Is je kamer opgeruimd, hoe zijn je cijfers, heb je al vioolgespeeld?' kreeg ik van mijn vader te horen. Mama was inmiddels beneden.

'Ik ben ermee bezig en heb vandaag de hele dag gewerkt,'

zei ik. Niet een hele sterke comeback.

'Nou, als je kamer is opgeruimd en je huiswerk helemaal af is en je viool hebt gespeeld – dat heb je nog niet gedaan, minimaal een halfuur –, dan mag je misschien uit. Maar we gaan straks eerst eten.'

Ik liep boos weg en begon met vioolspelen. Mama zei altijd dat ik mooi speelde als ik boos was – ik vermoedde dat ik nu prachtig speelde. Ik schopte tegen de doos met bladmuziek. Op de achtergrond hoorde ik mama en papa de discussie voortzetten.

'Hè jezus, doe nou niet zo streng, dat kind moet ook een keer uit,' zei mijn moeder.

'Jij zegt net zelf tegen hem dat hij het aan mij moet vragen en je hebt vanmiddag zelf gezegd dat je het geen goed idee vond!' bracht mijn vader ertegen in.

Ik speelde verder, ondertussen hoorde ik mijn oudste broer thuiskomen. Blijkbaar zou hij komen eten. Hij stak even zijn blije hoofd om de hoek van de deur. Ik wilde boos kijken, maar dat lukte niet echt. Hij glimlachte en zwaaide en wiebelde met zijn hoofd heen en weer. Ik liet een lach ontsnappen. Vervolgens ging hij naar de keuken om mama en papa gedag te zeggen. Ik hoorde dat hij hen heel even verder liet gaan met de discussie en een goed moment zocht om ertussen te komen.

'Ja, klopt, maar hij heeft vandaag zijn huiswerk al gemaakt en is nu aan het vioolspelen, dus dan heeft hij morgen vast de tijd om zijn kamer op te ruimen.' Er was een diplomaat aan mijn oudste broer verloren gegaan.

Na het eten keek papa me aan. 'Je mag vanavond uit, mits je morgen je kamer opruimt.'

'Super!' Ik rende meteen naar boven om me om te kleden. Onderweg gaf ik mijn oudste broer een elleboogje. Ik was hem dankbaar.

'Hoe laat ben je thuis?' vroeg mama vanuit de woonkamer.

‘Als het afgelopen is,’ stelde ik voor.

‘Hoe laat is dat?’ vroeg ze.

‘Ik denk een uur of drie, uiterlijk?’ Ik wist dat dat niet waar was, maar kon moeilijk zeggen dat de lichten pas om vijf uur aan zouden gaan.

‘O nee, geen sprake van, dan doe ik geen oog dicht!’ Mijn moeder maakte zich altijd zorgen. Als we later thuiskwamen, doordat iemand ergens moest oppassen of als een van mijn oudere broers thuiskwam van het uitgaan, moest mama altijd wakker worden gemaakt. Ook belde ze vaak om te weten waar je uithing.

‘Je kan toch gewoon doorslapen?’ bracht ik ertegen in.

‘Nee, kom nou, drie uur, dat gaan we niet doen.’

Inmiddels was ook mijn vader de kamer binnengekomen. ‘Wat is er aan de hand?’

‘Hij wil om drie uur pas thuiskomen.’

‘O nee, geen sprake van. Halfeen, dan moet je thuis zijn.’

‘Halfeen?! Dan zijn we er nog niet eens, we gaan er pas om een uur heen?!’

‘Om een uur pas?! Nou, dat is dan mooi opgelost, dan hoef je helemaal niet te gaan, wat belachelijk!’

‘Mogen al jouw vriendinnen van hun ouders allemaal tot zo laat uit ja?’ vroeg mijn moeder.

‘Ja! Ja, echt waar, ze mogen soms zelfs zelf weten hoe laat ze thuiskomen, andere vriendinnetjes van mij gaan tot vijf uur uit.’

Mijn moeder tikte met een wijsvinger op haar voorhoofd. Mijn vader viel haar bij.

‘Dit kunnen jullie niet menen! Laat me nou een keer gaan, ik word helemaal gek, iedereen mag uit en van jullie mag ik niks!’ riep ik. De hormonen flitsten als paparazzifotografen door mijn lijf. Ik wilde de werkelijkheid naar mijn hand zetten, maar wist niet hoe.

'Nou, ik ga dan wel even bellen naar een van mijn vriendinnen of het überhaupt zin heeft om te komen, jullie worden bedankt.' En ik smeet de deur achter me dicht. Toen ik een vriendin aan de lijn kreeg wist ze al hoe laat het was. Het was elke keer gedoe, mijn eindtijd, als we uit wilden. Mijn vriendinnen kregen geen eindtijd of hielden zich er niet aan. Bij mij leverde het altijd strijd op.

'Je mag tot halftwee uit, maximaal twee uur,' zei hij toen ik weer beneden was. Mama, papa en mijn oudste broer zaten aan de keukentafel. Ik wist niet wat mijn oudste broer had gezegd, maar wel dat hij had geprobeerd de eindtijd zo ver mogelijk naar achteren te brengen. Twee uur. Met een kwartier speling was dat kwart over twee en met een beetje geknutsel kon ik het misschien wel oprekken naar halfdrie, als ik zei dat ik een vriendinnetje thuis moest brengen of zo.

'Oké,' zei ik. Zonder al te dankbaar te zijn, behalve tegenover mijn broer.

Ik stond voor de deur maar kreeg mijn fiets niet op slot. Ik had het al drie keer geprobeerd. Alles bewoog, het voelde alsof ik in een draaimolen was gestapt die vanuit het niets op de turbostand was gegaan, waardoor ik niet kon ontsnappen. Alsof de aarde echt rond was en ik daardoor omviel. Alle jongens waren er geweest en om dat allemaal aan te kunnen had het me handig geleken om wat extra shotjes naar binnen te gooien. Het had me wel losser gemaakt, dat was niet alleen mijzelf opgevallen. 'Ik heb je wel eens in een betere staat gezien,' grapte Daniël. Op de dansvloer was ik toegejuicht. Mijn vriendinnen hadden een aantal keer water gehaald, maar dat dronk ik niet op. De zesde keer kreeg ik eindelijk mijn fiets op slot, met een hoop kabaal omdat ik over de fietsen heen viel.

Binnen bleek Hond Bril voor de tochtdeur te zijn gaan staan. Ik hurkte bij haar neer en begon haar te aaien. Ik werd misselijk. Alles tolde. Ik moet even gaan zitten, bedacht ik me. Heel even zitten, nog een aai voor Hond Bril, maar even gaan zitten, dan kan ik straks in één keer naar boven lopen, mama wakker maken en snel naar bed gaan. Heel even zitten. Heel even maar.

Ik deed mijn ogen open, werd wakker, wist niet door wat, maar ik merkte dat ik op de grond lag. Shit, dacht ik, shit. Ik keek de gang in en zag Hond Bril kwispelen, maar niet naar mij. Ze keek het hoekje om, alsof iemand – shit, shit, shit! Er staat iemand om de hoek. Ik kwam zo stil en zo snel mogelijk overeind en liet mijn jas van mijn schouders glijden. Net op tijd. Vanachter de hoek zag ik mijn moeder verschijnen. Een slaperig maar bezorgd gezicht.

'Wat ben je aan het doen?' vroeg ze. Ik bedacht me dat ze niet alleen slaperig en bezorgd was maar ook boos.

'O niks, ik ben mijn jas aan het ophangen.'

'Je jas aan het ophangen? Maar ik heb al drie kwartier geleden de deur dicht horen gaan!' zei ze. Kut, dacht ik, klote, hoe lang heb ik op de grond gelegen?

'Jaaa, ja dat klopt, maar Bril was zo lief, dus ik heb haar eerst een tijdje zitten aaien en een glas water gedronken en nu wilde ik mijn jas ophangen om vervolgens naar boven te gaan om tegen jou te zeggen dat ik thuis was.'

'Wat praat je raar, heb je gedronken?' vroeg ze. Officieel mocht ik nog niet drinken. Die keren dat ik dat wel deed en mama daarachter kwam was ze altijd boos en teleurgesteld.

'Nee, niet echt, misschien een beetje, maar ik ga naar bed nu, goed?'

'Kijk me aan.' Ik voelde dat ze bloeddoorlopen ogen zag. Met haar neus rook ze een paar keer.

'Hè bah! Je ruikt helemaal naar drank!'

De volgende ochtend begon voor mij pas aan het begin van de middag, toen ik werd geroepen om Hond Bril uit te laten.

Dat was nou eenmaal mijn taak en met uitbrakken hadden mijn ouders weinig te maken. Ze waren niet blij. Meestal kon ik het aardig verbloemen als ik te veel had gedronken, maar dit keer was ik betrapt. Van opruimen kwam die dag weinig terecht.

37.

Ik probeerde Alice te bereiken maar kreeg haar niet te pakken. Ik moest haar spreken en zat op mijn kamer te wachten totdat ze online kwam.

'Wo! *What's up*???'

Ik belde haar op.

'Wat is er aan de hand?'

'Een probleem. Mijn ouders hebben mijn cijferlijst gezien en nu willen ze me uit de Bond halen!'

'Neeee! Dat meen je niet, doe normaal!'

'Ja, echt fucking klote, en het wordt nog erger want meneer Van Druistert, je weet wel, de Engels docent, die wilde dus mijn ouders spreken en zou vandaag bellen. Dus nu heb ik helemaal een probleem.'

'Neeee, dit meen je niet.'

'Ja, alleen, ik heb meneer Van Druistert expres het verkeerde nummer gegeven, dus hij belt nu al de hele ochtend naar de huistelefoon, maar die wordt bij ons thuis nooit opgenomen.'

'Ah, wat mooi ouwe!' Ze lachte even.

'Maar ja, ik weet dus niet hoe dit gaat aflopen.'

'Ja, maar je kunt de Bond echt niet uit hoor, we moeten zoveel doen nog en we hebben de Praagreis er bijna doorheen en ik vind het niet leuk zonder jou.'

‘Nee, *I know*, ik wilde ook met jou afspreken dat als ik wél de Bond uit moet, dat ik dan tegen mijn ouders zeg dat ik eruit ga, maar dat ik stiekem er gewoon in blijf.’

‘Ja, dat is een goeie, desnoods maken we een briefje na van de begeleidend docent of zo.’

‘O ja, goeie.’

‘Maar wat is er nu aan de hand dan, moet je niet met ze praten?’

‘Nee nee, als ik dat doe werkt dat averechts. Maar mijn oudste broer is met ze aan het praten. Hij kan dat goed en zit met ze in de keuken.’

Een paar uur later stuurde ik Alice een bericht: ‘De beslissing is uitgesteld tot na de proefwerkweek, als die goed gaat mag ik erin blijven!’ Een paar seconden later kreeg ik haar antwoord, inclusief een advies: ‘Oké, super! Gewoon alleen de goede cijfers vertellen! Haha! Xxx kus.’

38.

We moesten proefjes doen met een soort bonen. Er kwam een grote bak aan de voorkant van de klas te staan en iedereen kreeg een paar petrischaaltjes met die bonen erop. Het waren droge dingen, een beetje rond, en ze nodigden vooral uit om er kattenkwaad mee uit te halen. Ideaal om mee te gooien of ze in elkaars nek te laten glijden. Misschien dat onder streng toezicht alles goed zou zijn gegaan, maar mevrouw Botman had bedacht dat het een goed idee was geweest om koffie te gaan halen. Haar kennende zou ze ook nog blijven kletsen met een collega-docent. Buiten was het prettig koud. Een typische januaridag. Vanbinnen was ik warm. Ik keek naar Daniël, die zat bij mij aan het tafeltje. Ergens wilde ik hem bedanken voor het plezier dat hij me gaf.

'Oké,' riep Daniël toen mevrouw Botman weg was, 'muziek!' En hij liep naar de docentencomputer. Er werd hard en aanmoedigend gelachen. Aan de computer van de docent zitten was uiterst riskant en je moest erop vertrouwen dat niemand in de klas je zou verraden. We vroegen ons af wat Daniël aan zou zetten. Hij opende YouTube en al snel klonk er muziek uit de speakers. Hij draaide de volumeknop nog even extra aan, alsof hij er daarmee voor kon zorgen dat er als vanzelf discobollen, discolichten en discodames in de klas zouden verschijnen.

Daniël liep met een grote grijns terug naar ons tafeltje. Ik kende de muziek niet, het was 'Bagagedrager' van Gers Pardoel, zo bleek later – een liefdesliedje. En ik besefte dat vriendschap inderdaad anders voelde dan wat er in dit nummer beschreven werd. Wat mijn vriendinnen mij al duidelijk probeerden te maken kon ik steeds minder hard ontkennen. Ik had meerdere keren per jaar muziek- en toneeloptredens, had als Bondsbestuurder een medaille gekregen, maar er was niets wat me enthousiaster maakte of meer energie gaf dan Daniël. Ik keek naar Daniël. Hij keek terug. Als hij wist wat hij met een blik kon doen, had hij er vast meer gegeven.

Een paar seconden later hagelde het bonen. Overal hoorde je ze neerkomen. Ze knalden tegen de ramen, stuiterden over de tafels, vlogen over de vloer. Met handenvol tegelijk werden ze over je hoofd uitgestrooid en verdwenen ze in je haar en je kleren. De muziek dreunde door en de bonenhagel leek eindeloos. Totdat ik een keiharde dreun hoorde. De deur werd dichtgesmeten. Mevrouw Botman stond met een rood aanlopend gezicht de klas in te kijken. Vooral ons tafeltje had een probleem. We hadden alle vooroordelen weer eens bevestigd.

Na de les moesten wij blijven zitten. De muziek werd langzaam uitgezet, gek genoeg had mevrouw Botman die aan laten staan. Ik vermoedde dat ze hem stiekem wel leuk vond. Had ik haar heupen nou zien wiegen? Of gunde ik haar die losheid zo dat ik het me had ingebeeld? Ik besloot het niet te vragen, dat leek me onverstandig. Ze liet ons niet nablijven. We moesten alle mappen netjes in de mand doen en die naar beneden brengen, naar het opslaghok. En alle bonen die op de grond lagen, en weet ik veel waar nog meer, opruimen.

Het schoolplein was al leeg toen ik mijn fiets pakte om naar huis te gaan. Alleen de vlag met het schoollogo bracht beweging in het geheel. Voor de rest leek het alsof ik in een foto of op een poster was beland. Mijn fiets was omgevallen en met het stuur in de bak met aarde gevallen. Ik klopte de meeste modder eraf en fietste de hoek om. In de verte had ik al wat gelach gehoord, maar ik had het niet kunnen plaatsen. Toen ik de hoek om kwam zag ik aan de straatkant vier jongens met hun fietsen tussen hun benen praten. Ze maakten grappen. Ik vermoedde een gevalletje boy talk. Een van de jongens, de grootste van de vier, liet zijn fiets af en toe steigeren. Daardoor leek zijn fiets net een paard. Hoe meer ik dichterbij kwam, hoe meer het me opviel dat hij haast iets Herculeaans had. Het was geen jongen die het slecht zou doen op een poster. Voor een feest. Of zo. Ik wilde er voorbijfietsen, totdat ik de rug van een van de jongens herkende. Dat was Daniël en opeens wist ik wat dit voor groepje was. Dit waren jongens van zijn sportclub.

De jongens riepen me. Ik remde af. Nu zag ik dat er ook nog twee andere jongens van school waren.

'Kom even hier.' Ik reed met mijn fiets het gras over. Takjes tikten omhoog of knakten uit elkaar. Een takjesregen voor de insecten tussen het gras, bedacht ik me.

'Wat is er?' vroeg ik. Ik merkte dat ik me ongemakkelijk voelde. Ik wist mezelf geen houding te geven. Het voelde gymachtig aan, de situatie, en dat zorgde voor een benauwend gevoel. De Hercules-achtige jongen, Jim heette hij, wees op mijn stuur. 'Heb je er stront op zitten?' Hij begon hard te lachen. Op mijn rechterhandvat zat nog wat modder.

'Nee, nee, mijn fiets was in de plantenbak –' Ik hoorde de andere jongens ook lachen. Het had weinig zin om het uit te leggen. Het ging ze alleen om de grap.

'Ben je erop gaan zitten?' riep Jim toen. Nog harder gelach.

'In je kont, lekker,' zei een van de andere jongens, die kende ik ook niet, hij had bruine krullen. Ik schrompelde ineen, van het plezier en de blijdschap van eerder vandaag was in één klap niks meer over. Ik voelde me een totale mislukking.

‘Ah! Ah! Ah! Oeeeh!’ deed Daniël. Ik keek hem aan, ik schrok ervan. In mijn kop ontstond een kleine kortsluiting. Ergens had ik gehoopt dat hij er wat van zou zeggen, van de grapjes. Dat had hij niet gedaan, sterker nog, hij maakte het nog erger. In mijn ogen ontstond teleurstelling, of verdriet, of allebei, ik wist het niet. Daniël begreep mijn blik niet. Of zag hem überhaupt niet.

‘Lekker in je anus laten nemen door je stuur, goed hoor, zo lekker voorovergebogen!’ ging Jim nog een stap verder. Het gelach kreeg een extra impuls. Ik deed zelf maar een beetje mee met lachen, in de hoop er zo controle over te krijgen.

Toen ze klaar waren besloot ik te gaan. ‘Doei,’ zei ik. Heel veel meer kon ik er niet uitkrijgen. Ik voelde me lelijk en vies. De grappen deden me meer dan ik had gewild. Toen ik de straat verder uit fietste hoorde ik opnieuw kreungeluiden.

39.

Een week later zat ik achter mijn computer. Liesje stond paraat. Ik zou Daniël een berichtje sturen. De hele week had ik wakker gelegen van wat er gebeurd was. Ik was bang dat Daniël misschien iets over mijn twijfels had gehoord en het er met zijn sportmaatjes over had gehad. Uiteraard kon ik hem dat niet verbieden, maar de grapjes hadden mij pijn gedaan, me geraakt op plekken waar ik kwetsbaar was. Daniël haalde me uit balans en alles werd extreem. De vrolijkheid. Het stuiterballengedrag. Maar ook de onrust, de onzekerheid en de twijfel. Ik had het gevoel dat ik op een rodeostier zat en hoewel ik er dolgraag af wilde wist ik niet hoe. Ik liep eindeloos in de duinen, zat op mijn kamer, ging zonder kusjes te geven naar bed. Ik wilde loskomen van mijn gevoel. Zoals je van een lelijke broek of een hemd af wilt waarvan je denkt dat het ongeluk brengt. Je hangt het ergens in een kast aan een haakje, doet de deur dicht en bent ervan af. Maar mijn gevoel kon ik niet aan een haakje hangen. Het zat vastgegroeid aan mijn vlees en bloed.

Liesje vond al langer dat de situatie de verkeerde kant op ging.

'Je kunt het over bijna niks anders meer hebben, maar je ontkent nog steeds dat je misschien gewoon verliefd bent,' zei ze dan.

‘Maar ik wil niet verliefd zijn, ik heb hier niet voor gekozen. Ik wil dat alles net zo makkelijk gaat als bij iedereen. Wat er nu ook gebeurt, het is een fase, als ik straks groot en ouder ben, dan trouw ik met een vrouw en heb ik kinderen.’

‘Geloof je dat echt? Zie je echt een vrouw voor je bij het altaar?’

Ik werd dan stil. Voor het altaar zag ik niks en helemaal niemand naast me. Het gaf me een leeg gevoel.

‘Maar weet je wat, stuur hem een bericht, dat je het niet leuk vindt wat er gebeurd is.’

En dat deed ik. Achter de computer, terwijl Liesje thuis online was.

‘Hij heeft geantwoord,’ stuurde ik naar haar. ‘Ik stuur het door.’

Ja, goed dat je een berichtje stuurt. Ik had al gehoord dat je iets kut vond. Wat vervelend, natuurlijk niet de bedoeling. Wat ik nog tegen je wilde zeggen is dat ik met die gasten altijd dat soort grapjes maak. Was dus niets persoonlijks, echt niet. Ik hoop dat je het begrijpt? Was dus echt niet persoonlijk! Jij ook een fijn weekend. Daniël. Ik was er blij mee.

‘Ooo oké, gelukkig, zorgen om niks, zie je wel!’ stuurde Liesje.

‘Maar wat zal ik terugsturen?’ Ik tikte niet zélf mijn berichtjes, nee, ik overlegde alles eerst met mijn vriendinnen. Ik was een soort trekpop geworden. Zeiden ze zus of zo, dan deed ik zus of zo. Was er een feestje en kon ik met niemand meefietsen, dan bleef ik thuis. Mijn onzekerheid had de macht over me gegrepen en bepaalde mijn dagelijkse routines. ‘Naja, hier hoef je toch niks op terug te sturen gekkie!’ Ik wist niet of ik het met haar eens was, maar luisterde wel.

40.

De zon was zacht die dag. Met wat jongens van de NLT-groep waren we aan de achterkant van het schoolgebouw aan het spelen met de scooter van Oliver, een zwarte Puch waar hij graag aan sleutelde.

'Oliver, mag ik even rijden?' vroeg Daniël.

'Heb je een rijbewijs?' Oliver liet zijn Puch ronken door af en toe aan het gaspedaal te gaan hangen.

'Nee, dus ik kan het vast!' Er werd gelachen.

'Hier heb je de helm,' zei Oliver, 'die moet je wel ophouden.'

Daniël ging zitten. Het stond hem niet verkeerd, die scooter. Die helm overigens ook niet.

Hij liet de motor snuiven en snorken. Ook het gebrom stond hem goed. Hij had zijn vest uitgedaan en had nu alleen nog maar zijn T-shirt aan. Donkergroen. Ik keek naar een moderne Jan Cremer.

Hij liet zijn tanden zien, beet op zijn onderlip, haalde zijn voeten van de grond en gaf vol gas. Weg was ie.

Oliver moest lachen, maar ik kon zien dat hij vanbinnen ook even een schietgebedje deed – als die scooter maar heelhuids terugkwam...

En die kwam terug. Zonder kleerscheuren. Daniël stond

weer bij ons voor de stoep, de Puch grommend onder hem. 'Wie durft er achterop?'

Een van de jongens stak direct z'n hand op en sprong achterop. Toen ik naar ze keek schoten heel even foto's van de huiscomputer aan me voorbij. Ik schudde het van me af en juichte ze toe.

'Wie gaat deze tweede ronde mee?' vroeg Daniël. Dit keer stapte Oliver zelf op – hij kon er de humor wel van inzien. Ze waren de straat uit, we wachtten even en ze waren weer terug.

'Ga jij nu achterop?' vroeg Daniël me. Ik zag de plek achter hem op de scooter. Het zwarte zadel van de Puch was niet zo groot, wat betekende dat je letterlijk tegen elkaar aan zat. Bovendien was er geen ruggensteun of iets van een riem, dus je moest Daniël vasthouden. Of beter gezegd, je moest je armen rondom zijn middel doen om er niet vanaf te vallen. Ik wilde niets liever dan achterop bij hem springen. Hem vasthouden. En hem eindeloos laten rijden. Weg uit het hier en nu. Weg uit Den Haag, weg van de school, weg van alle onzekerheden. Gewoon samen doorrijden. De wind tegemoet. De zon die net zo lang op onze huid zou schijnen totdat we krenterige wangen kregen. We zouden geen hotels en bedden nodig hebben. Nee, we konden in het gezelschap van de maan en haar sterren, prima op het gras of het zand slapen. Zijn borstkas zou als kussen dienen. Ik keek nog een keer. Desnoods alleen het rondje, en dat we op het einde dan een ongeluk zouden krijgen. Hem zou niks overkomen, maar ik zou gewond zijn. Misschien mocht ik in zijn armen wel alles laten gaan en eindelijk vrijheid vinden in het eeuwige donker.

'Kom je?' vroeg Daniël.

Ik durfde niet.

'Nee joh, dat is niks voor mij,' riep ik. Meteen had ik spijt, ik hoopte dat hij het nog een keer zou vragen, of dat zijn vrienden me zouden dwingen om achterop te springen, als grapje. Dat ze zouden roepen 'doe niet zo laf', maar dat deden ze niet.

41.

Ze moest hard lachen, Eveline, E, toen ik het haar vroeg. ‘Doe normaal, dat lijkt me niet handig?’ Het verbaasde haar niet dat ik het bedacht had, maar wel dat ik van plan was het uit te voeren.

‘Het is gewoon dat ik dan een manier heb om te zeggen wat ik echt heel erg graag tegen hem wil zeggen,’ zei ik.

‘Oké, oké, oké. Ik vind het prima schat!’ zei ze.

‘En uiteindelijk is het ook maar een grapje hè, ik bedoel er niks mee, het is gewoon een grapje.’ Dat zei ik eigenlijk altijd. Elke keer als ik met vriendinnen ergens over sprak zei ik aan het eind dat het een grapje was. Alsof ik dan de waarheid in wat ik allemaal op tafel had gelegd zelf in twijfel trok, waardoor er een zweem van onduidelijkheid achterbleef waar ik me in kon verbergen.

‘Ik vind het prima, schat. Alleen, hoe zorg je ervoor dat het niet uitlekt?’

Ik keek haar aan. ‘Dat is de reden dat ik wil dat jij het schrijft, jouw handschrift, dat is een meisjeshandschrift, dan kan hij het nooit achterhalen.’ Ik vond het zelf wel een goed idee.

De Bond deelde op Valentijnsdag rozen en lolly’s uit die waren bedoeld voor leerlingen onderling. Meestal stuurden vooral vriendinnen iets naar elkaar, of jongens om elkaar te plagen. Een enkele keer zat er een échte Valentijn tussen. Ik had het rode briefje dat ingevuld moest worden al in mijn zak zitten en gaf het aan Eveline.

'Wat wil je sturen, een roos of een lolly?' We stonden in het midden van de kantine aan een van de witte statafels. Borreltafels zonder borrel.

'Een lolly,' zei ik.

'Oké, en wat wil je als tekst?'

'Vandaag is het Valentijnsdag, dus ik kan het nu een keer tegen je zeggen, maar stiekem vind ik je echt een hele leuke jongen. Liefs! En dan drie kusjes!'

Eveline oefende eerst op een wit stukje papier en schreef het vervolgens op het rode papier. Ik glunderde.

Het was vrijdag aan het eind van de dag. Geen pauzes meer, langzaam nam stilte de gangen en de klaslokalen over. Fleur had gevraagd of ik naar de aula wilde komen. Ik maakte me zorgen, want ik wist dat Daniël een van de weinigen was die op vrijdag een extra laat vak had en ik vreesde dat ze met hem in de aula hing. Ik was dol op Fleur. En Fleur ook op mij, dacht ik. En ze wist alles van me. Vaak genoeg hadden we het over jongens gehad en ook Daniël fladderde door onze gesprekken heen. Ze was goed bevriend met hem. Ze leken ergens ook wel een beetje op elkaar. Maar Fleur had een vriendje, dus al zou ze willen, gebeuren zou het niet.

Toen ik de trap afliep richting de kantine, hoorde ik de jongens. Toen ik het hoekje omging, zag ik ze ook. Fleur lachte en was omringd door een groep van vijf jongens. Ze leek hen als een zeemeermin betoverd te hebben. 'Lieverd, ik heb een vraagje over Valentijnsdag, jij bent vanuit de Bond verantwoordelijk voor de rozen en de lolly's toch?'

Ik knikte.

'Ah mooi, ik heb namelijk een vraagje. Of eigenlijk, Daniël heeft een vraagje.'

Iets ging hier fout.

Daniël kwam naar me toe. Bijna fluisterend begon hij zijn zin. 'Kan je nog iets voor me regelen? Ik wil graag nog een roos versturen.' De deadline was eigenlijk al verstreken.

'Ja hoor, dat kan, dan moet je dat wel nu doen, want vanmiddag gaan we alles in elkaar zetten en klaarmaken.'

'Ik loop wel direct met je mee.'

Toen we door de gang liepen wist ik niet zo goed wat ik moest zeggen. Hij lachte een beetje.

'Hier moet je je kaart ingooien,' zei ik toen we bij de brievenbus van de Bond waren aangekomen.

'O, ja, juist, heb jij zo'n kaartje voor me?'

Ik voelde aan mijn binnenzak. Daar zat er een. Ik haalde het eruit en kreeg een kleine hartaanval. In mijn hand had ik niet alleen een extra Valentijnskaartje, maar ook het kaartje waar Eveline mijn tekst op had geschreven, ter oefening. Ik keek hem aan, hij zag nog niks. Snel verfrommelde ik het witte papiertje tot een prop in mijn linkerhand.

'Hier. Hier heb je er een.' Ik gaf hem het rode Valentijnskaartje. Ik keek ernaar en vond het ergens wel Hollywoodachtig. Het kaartje dat ik hem gaf was mijn reservekaart voor het geval dat Eveline toch een schrijffout zou maken.

'Dank je. Heb je misschien ook een pen?'

'O ja hoor, die heb ik ook.' Het klonk sarcastischer dan ik bedoeld had, hij kon er per slot van rekening ook niks aan doen. In mijn hoofd dacht ik aan Fleur. Waar zou zij nu aan denken? Dacht ze überhaupt wel na, of kon het haar niks schelen?

'Hier.' Ik gaf hem de pen die ik had meegenomen voor Eveline. De pen waarmee ze de tekst op mijn Valentijnskaartje kon schrijven. Voor mijn Valentijn.

'Wat zal ik erop zetten?' vroeg Daniël.

Er vielen twee vazen in mijn hoofd kapot. Dát moest hij toch wel zelf kunnen bedenken? Het was inmiddels al pijnlijk genoeg en ik vond het bijna ongeloofwaardig dat hij niet kon zien dat ik me niet op m'n gemak voelde.

Hij boog zich voorover, met zijn ellebogen op tafel om netjes te kunnen schrijven. Dat kostte hem duidelijk meer moeite dan Eveline. Ik kon niet anders dan naar hem kijken. Het was een kwelling en een beloning. Als ik nu goed naar hem keek, hoopte ik, zou mijn hoofd hem vanavond laten terugkomen in mijn slaap. Ik vroeg me af hoe het kon dat je én mooie haren hebt, én mooie tanden, én lieve ogen, én een atletisch lichaam, en dat je óók nog zo slim was. Die oneerlijkheid was niet erg, maar ik vond het wel jammer dat ik niet ook hem kon betoveren. Zodat hij zou stoppen met schrijven, me aan zou kijken, langzaam op me af zou lopen en me in zijn armen zou nemen. Ik hoefde niet eens te zoenen. Nee. Ik wilde gewoon zijn armen om mijn lijf voelen. Waardoor ik zou weten dat het niet erg was, dat het niet erg was dat ik misschien op jongens viel. Ik wilde het vanuit hem voelen, zodat ik me veilig zou wanen. Als hij mij een knuffel gaf, zou het verdriet en de onzekerheid wegsmelten, dat wist ik zeker.

'Ik weet niet zo goed wat ik moet opschrijven,' zei hij nog een keer.

'Voor wie is het eigenlijk?' Misschien vroeg ik het wel omdat ik ergens van de pijnlijkheid genoot.

'Voor Fleur.'

'O. Leuk.' Ergens had ik het kunnen weten. 'Wat wil je tegen haar zeggen?'

'Gewoon, een geintje, fijne Valentijnsdag of zo.'

'Dan zet je dat erop toch?'

'Ja, goeie.'

En hij gooide zijn kaartje in de Bondsbrievenbus.

42.

Valentijnsdag was geweest. Ik had een roze hemd gedragen, een rode das met witte hartjes waar je op kon drukken en dan een zoengeluid hoorde, en op mijn wangen had ik kusjes gemaakt met rode lippenstift. Nog nooit had ik de liefde zo zichtbaar aangetrokken en nog nooit had ik haar vanbinnen zozeer verborgen gehouden. Toen we naar de les gingen waar Daniël ook in zat, durfde ik niet eens naar binnen. Eerst had ik bedacht dat ik de lolly zelf zou geven. Maar daar was ik snel van teruggekomen, ik had hem aan Alice toevertrouwd. Vervolgens dacht ik dat ik wel kon kijken hoe hij hem in ontvangst nam, maar toen we bij het lokaal aankwamen durfde ik niet naar binnen. Vanaf de gang hoorde ik gejoel. Hij had hem. Hij had mijn lolly gekregen. 'Geniet ervan lieve Daniël, fijne Valentijnsdag,' zei ik zachtjes tegen de muren van de gang.

Nog geen week later gingen er al verhalen dat de lolly van mij was geweest. Hoe dat kon begreep ik niet. Steeds luider klonk het gerucht dat ik op mannen viel, en hoewel ik dat niet leuk vond, kon ik dáár nog mee leven. Die geruchten waren er al sinds de brugklas. Maar het vervelendste vond ik dat Daniël er nu bij werd betrokken. Ik was doodsbang dat het onze vriendschap kapot zou maken. Twee weken geleden vroeg hij nog of ik meeging om buiten school te 'chillen', zoals hij dat noemde. Ik had dolgraag gewild, maar ik had les en durfde niet te spijbelen.

Nu zat ik op mijn kamer. Ik was zo blij geweest dat ik de lolly naar hem had kunnen opsturen, maar dat feestje ontplofte nu al in mijn gezicht. Thuis was zo ongeveer alles onbespreekbaar. Ik kon niks zeggen over Daniël, ik kon niks zeggen over de Bond. Als ik vertelde dat ik weer ergens ging optreden, dat ik een vioolconcert had, of dat ik met de Bond iets ging doen, dan kwam er altijd de vraag hoe het met mijn cijfers ging. Er was één ding dat wel goed ging. We hadden met de Bond elke donderdag, tijdens de grote pauze, afgesproken om te kijken hoe we de Praagreis toch door konden laten gaan. Na alle mogelijkheden bekeken te hebben, kwamen we erop uit dat we de reis buiten school om zouden organiseren. We verzamelden handtekeningen en zochten contact met de Ouderraad, waar Liesjes moeder in zat. En met hun steun, kon de school niet anders dan meewerken. We kregen nog een mail met allemaal randvoorwaarden maar het belangrijkste: de reis kon doorgaan!

'Ik weet dus niet zeker of ik mee mag,' stuurde ik Eveline.

'Doe normaal?! Je hebt die hele reis georganiseerd.'

'Ja, dat weet ik, maar dat krijg ik niet aan mijn ouders uitgelegd. En daarnaast, mijn moeder heeft de verhalen van vroeger gehoord over de reis, dat iedereen alleen maar dronken was, en je kent mijn moeder en drank...'

'O ja.'

'Ja, en papa zit op mijn cijfers te letten, ik moet oppassen dat ik niet uit de Bond word gezet – als ik maar even brutaal ben beginnen ze daar ook over. Dat vind ik zo vervelend.'

'Ja dat is het ook, maar wat ga je nu doen dan?'

'Ja ik weet het niet, eerlijk gezegd weet ik het echt niet. Het voelt gewoon alsof alles instort. Ik weet niet meer goed wie ik ben, wat ik leuk vind. Ik ben bang dat Daniël me eng en vies gaat vinden en me niet meer wil zien en ik weet niet hoe ik het aan mijn ouders kan vertellen. Over Daniël kan ik sowieso niks zeggen.'

'Uiteindelijk komt het vast goed, maar dit is nu wel echt klote.'

'Ja. Soms denk ik dat het me allemaal is aangepraat, dat ik dénk dat ik Daniël leuk vind omdat iedereen al vier jaar lang tegen me zegt dat ik homo ben.'

'Hmmhmm, ik begrijp wat je bedoelt, maar je voelt wel wat voor hem toch?'

'Ja, maar dat kan toch ook vriendschap zijn? Soms denk ik, ja, ik voel wat, maar dan denk ik een seconde later, nee, ik voel niks. Dat is gewoon zo verwarrend. Ik heb dagen waarop ik denk, hè hè, nu weet ik het zeker, en dan kan het de volgende dag, of het volgende uur of soms zelfs de volgende minuut alweer anders zijn, dan word ik gewoon alle kanten op gesleurd. En dan weet ik niet waar ik heen kan met mijn gedachten en mijn gevoelens.'

'Nee maar je kunt altijd naar ons hè, we staan altijd voor je klaar.'

'Ja maar jullie worden er vast zo langzamerhand ook wel gek van, van al dat gezeur en gezeik.'

'Nee hoor. Daarvoor zijn we er juist, om je met dit soort zaken te helpen.'

'Dat vind ik lief. Maar je vindt dus echt dat ik niks moet zeggen over die lolly?'

'Nee, schat, doe dat maar niet, het waait vast over.'

'Oké.'

'Wanneer ga je met je ouders bespreken of je mee naar Praag mag?'

'Morgen. Alleen, ik weet gewoon niet hoe ik het moet zeggen. Ik durf gewoon niet te zeggen waarom het belangrijk voor mij is. Ik durf het niet over Daniël te hebben. Soms zou ik wel willen dat ik alles gewoon uit kon zetten, dat ik alles gewoon kon stoppen. Dan was ik ervan af.'

'Nee joh, gekkie. Dit is gewoon even een lastig moment, dat komt uiteindelijk goed, en je mag me altijd bellen, oké.'

'Is goed. Dank je. Hou van je!'

'Ik ook van jou.'

De volgende dag vroeg ik mijn ouders opnieuw om toestemming voor de Praagreis. Maar hoe hard ik ook mijn best deed, het antwoord bleef nee. Al het gedoe bij elkaar maakte dat ik helemaal dichtsloeg. Daniël, die Praagreis, het Valentijnsgedoe, de grijze mist. Eigenlijk had ik er diep vanbinnen geen zin meer in. Als ik aan de toekomst dacht zag ik niks. Waar anderen misschien iets riepen over hoe ze ooit zouden gaan trouwen, en met wie, was dat voor mij volkomen blanco. Als ik me toch probeerde in te beelden met wie ik voor eeuwig zou worden verbonden, dan kon ik me elk detail, elke bloem, elke gast, elke kaars en elke zonnestraal voorstellen, maar de persoon die mijn hand zou moeten vasthouden bleef onzichtbaar.

In de avond legde ik een eerste brief op het bed van mijn ouders. Op het kussen van mijn moeder. Wat erin stond: dat wat ik niet rechtstreeks wilde zeggen, omdat het dan direct definitief zou zijn. En omdat ik dan de eerste primaire reactie op hun gezichten zou kunnen zien. Ik had er puzzelstukjes in verstopt over datgene wat ik eigenlijk tegen ze wilde zeggen. Ik hoopte dat ze de boodschap zouden ontvangen, door de letters en door het papier heen. Als papa het niet lukt, dan op zijn minst mama wel, hoopte ik. In bed deed ik alsof ik sliep als mama boven de was kwam doen en hoorde ik hoe ze de brief vonden. De eerste brief werd niet beantwoord. Maar ook later kreeg ik niet het antwoord waar ik op had gehoopt.

Uiteindelijk besloot ik eind februari in stiltestaking te gaan. Niet dat ik me bewust had voorgenomen om vanaf dat moment mijn mond te gaan houden, maar ik had het gevoel dat ik mijn ouders niks meer kon vertellen. En dat wat ik probéérde te vertellen, daarvan had ik het gevoel dat het niet was gehoord. Mijn woorden waren op.

43.

Ik zat op het schoolplein, mijn verjaardag lag achter me. Thuis was ik in totale stilte vervallen, de stiltestaking duurde voort, bijna een halve maand inmiddels. Ik zei alleen soms nog ja of nee als erom werd gevraagd. Ik was een soort mimespeler geworden en het verbaasde me hoe goed ik daarin was. Het maakte me wel heel verdrietig en als ik 's avonds voor de zoveelste keer naar bed ging zonder mama en papa een kusje te geven, voelde ik me schuldig. Maar ik moest het doen. Ik moest ze op een manier duidelijk proberen te maken dat ik mee wilde naar Praag, dat ik mee wilde met Daniël, dat ik even weg wilde zijn van thuis.

Fleur haalde me uit mijn gedachten. 'Heb jij ook een tussenuur?'

'Geen gym, hè. Dat levert wat extra tussenuren op.'

'Wat toevallig. Heb je het al gehoord?'

'Ehm, ik denk het niet?'

'Jawel, jij hebt dit sowieso al gehoord, gekkerd,' zei ze.

Ik keek haar aan met een totale ik-begrijp-deze-wiskunde-som-echt-niet-blik.

'Nou, Daniël heeft dus een lolly gekregen op Valentijnsdag en hij dacht dat die van mij was!' En vervolgens begon ze hard te lachen. Ik lachte mee.

'Wat grappig.'

'Ja hè?'

'Heel erg.'

'Ik vermoed dat jij hem hebt gestuurd, heb ik dat goed ingeschat?'

'Nou, ik ben stiekem op jou verliefd hoor Fleur,' begon ik. Ik was er klaar mee, ik wilde weer op meisjes vallen, zoals op de basisschool. Dit soort momenten had ik soms meerdere keren op een dag. Dan wist ik het opeens allemaal weer zeker – ik viel weer op meisjes, zo had ik dat even besloten en bepaald voor mezelf.

'Wat zeg jij nou allemaal, gekkerd?'

'Nou gewoon, dat ik heel stiekem jou heel leuk vind!'

'Jaja, het is goed met je!' Ze porde me in mijn maag. 'Daaaaaaniiëëëël,' zei ze plagerig.

'Dat is lullig. Je weet dat ik hem alleen heel erg aardig vind.' Terwijl ik dat zei voelde ik dat het ongeloofwaardig was, maar bovenal vond ik dat het Daniël geen eer aandeed, hij was meer dan alleen aardig. 'Oké, misschien iets meer dan aardig, maar toch.'

Fleur moest weer lachen. Ondertussen stak ze een sigaret op.

'Ik heb besloten om jou leuk te gaan vinden. Ik ken je al lang genoeg, ik kan je vertrouwen, altijd met je lachen, we hebben vaak een hoop lol samen, ja, ik heb besloten om jou leuk te gaan vinden. Moeten we alleen die vriend van je nog even opruimen, maar die woont nu toch al een tijdje in Spanje, dus dat scheelt.'

'Grapjes.' Fleur haalde haar lipgloss tevoorschijn. 'Wil jij ook wat?'

Ik knikte. 'Ik ben bloedserieus hoor.'

'Jajaja, het is al goed.'

'Ben je me nou gewoon aan het afwijzen?' Nu mocht ik even

lachen. Met mijn vingers probeerde ik het roze spul weer een beetje van mijn lippen te halen.

'Je bent verliefd op Daniël. Accepteer dat nou maar, dat scheelt een hoop gedoe en geworstel. En tegen je vriendinnen kun je gewoon eerlijk zijn.'

'Ik vind het gewoon veel leuker én gezelliger om jou leuk te vinden.'

'Doe normaal. Als je Daniël ziet verander je in zachte klei. Het is dat hij er geen misbruik van maakt, anders kon hij je alles laten doen.'

'Mag ik niet hetero zijn?' Ik wist niet waar het gesprek heen ging, maar vond het wel een legitieme vraag.

'Al zou je hetero zijn hé, ik zeg, al zou je, even daargelaten wat je er zelf van denkt, maar stel dat je hetero zou zijn, dan zou je verliefd worden op Liesje, of zo, maar echt niet op mij.' Ik begreep wel wat ze bedoelde, Liesje zou logisch zijn, maar dat vond ik toch anders.

'Hoezo mag ik niet meer bepalen wie ik leuk vind? Dat zou ik gewoon het fijnst vinden, dat we onze verliefdheid als een op afstand bestuurbaar autootje konden beheersen. Liesje is gewoon een van mijn beste vriendinnetjes aan wie ik alles toevertrouw, maar ik zal nooit verliefd op haar worden, denk ik. Dus Fleur, hoeveel kinderen wil je?' En ik ging met mijn hoofd op haar schouder liggen.

Ze stak haar tweede sigaret op. Of was het al haar derde?

'Een paar dagen geleden was je nog helemaal hoteldebotel op Daniël.'

'Ja, ik vind het wel een hele leuke jongen, maar ik ben niet verliefd, ik wil alleen graag contact met hem!'

'Nou, ik zie je anders helemaal stralen als je bij hem in de buurt komt hoor.'

Ik moest lachen. Daar had ze een punt.

44.

Het was nu meer dan een maand geleden dat ik de Valentijnslolly had gestuurd. Ik had er geen spijt van, maar het verhaal dat ik verliefd was op Daniël bleef rondgaan. Ik wist dat hij het inmiddels ook had gehoord en het zorgde voor een ongemakkelijke situatie in de lessen. Hij leek te doen alsof er niks aan de hand was, terwijl ik continu in de kramp schoot.

We zaten aan het avondeten, vroeg deze keer, want papa moest optreden en mama zou met hem meegaan.

'Hoe was het op school?' probeerde mijn moeder.

'Prima,' zei ik.

'Was het leuk, ja?'

'Ja.' Ik hoorde mijn vader zuchten.

'Wat is er toch?' vroeg mijn moeder. Ik vond het een stomme vraag. Natúúrlijk wist ze wat er was. Konden mama en papa dat niet zien dan? Ik was verliefd en in de war, ik wilde mee op Praagreis omdat ik daar de hele week vrijer kon zijn en ik werd gek van het feit dat mijn buitenschoolse activiteiten voortdurend onder druk stonden van mijn cijferlijst. Maar ik zei het niet. Ik zei helemaal geen woord. Het was hun taak als ouders om uit te zoeken wat er was. Ik wist dat ik ontzettend puberaal bezig was, maar ik kon mezelf niet uit deze mal wurmen.

'Niks.' Ik zag ook mijn broertje kijken, hij leek te willen zeggen dat ik beter gewoon kon gaan praten, maar ik ontweek zijn blik.

In mijn slaapkamer keek Tijger moedeloos toe, alsof ook hij het lastig vond dat ik geen woord meer zei. Ik gaf hem een aai over zijn bol. En ging op mama's bank zitten. Ik stuurde Eveline een bericht, de tekst die ik naar Daniël wilde sturen. Zoals ik het fietsen van tevoren afstemde met vriendinnen en zelfs mijn kleding vaak bij hun checkte, zo liet ik nu Eveline alles wat ik naar Daniël stuurde controleren. Ondertussen keek ik of hij online zou komen.

'Hij is online!'

'Doen doen doen doen!!!' stuurde ze terug

'Dus het is goed?'

'Jaaa perfect!!!'

'Daniël, ik wilde nog even wat tegen je zeggen. Ik hoorde namelijk dat er een aantal verhalen rondgingen, je weet volgens mij wel wat ik bedoel. Dat is waarom ik vorige week een beetje raar deed. Ik vind het namelijk gewoon heel erg jammer als dat soort dingen meteen gezegd en gedacht worden... Ik wilde even tegen je zeggen dat het niet waar is en dat ik alleen maar vrienden wilde zijn!!!'

Toen ik het had gestuurd, schakelde ik snel terug naar Eveline.

'Ik heb het gestuurd!!! Maar ben heel bang voor de reactie!!!' Ik hoorde mijn mobiel een kassa-achtig geluid maken, dat betekende dat ik antwoord had van Daniël.

'Ja hoorde ook die dingen en heb echt geen idee hoe die rare shit de wereld in is gekomen!'

'Hoi, maar je begrijpt dat het niet waar is?' antwoordde ik.

'Ja nu wel!'

Ik stuurde het direct door naar Eveline. Ik was weer een halve trekpop. Daniël stuurde nog een bericht. 'Maar dat gaat al heel lang rond hè! Maar dacht zelf ook al dat het niet klopte, want het is kk rare poep.' Aan de ene kant voelde het vervelend om te lezen dat hij het al heel lang wist, aan de andere kant gaf het alleen maar meer aan dat hij zich er niks van aantrok. Hij was normaal blijven doen en had me in de les elke keer in zijn groepje erbij getrokken. Alleen het stoeien was minder geworden, en het praten buiten school om. Maar dat kwam ook doordat ik het niet meer kon.

'Ja ik wist dat dit al een tijdje rondging, maar eerst had ik bedacht om het gewoon te laten zitten, maar nu leek het me wel zo handig om even aan jou te laten weten dat het niet zo was...' Het voelde vreemd, het gesprek. Ik was een millimeter verwijderd van de werkelijkheid, maar die ene millimeter was nou juist de cruciale. Ik wist alleen niet wat er zou gebeuren als ik die millimeter zou verwijderen; was het de laatste millimeter voor een ongeluk en zou ik keihard op een afwijzing knallen, of was het de laatste millimeter voor een warme knuffel en zou hij zeggen dat het allemaal niet uitmaakte en dat we sowieso vrienden zouden blijven? Ik durfde het risico niet te nemen.

'Ik zie je morgen op school! Doei!!!' stuurde ik.

'*Challas*,' antwoordde hij.

Ergens vond ik het jammer dat het gesprek voorbij was. Misschien had ik stiekem gehoopt dat hij zou bellen en dat we als twee vrienden de hele avond zouden kletsen.

Vlak voordat ik ging slapen schreef ik een brief voor mijn ouders. Nieuwe puzzelstukjes. In de hoop dat ze eindelijk zouden gaan puzzelen. Ik legde de brief op hun bed. Ik moest denken aan die fijne tijd dat ik nog mini was. Dat ik daar in dat bed tussen mama en papa in mocht genieten van een verjaardag. Ik zag de zilveren plastic plakoorbellen voor me. Dit keer legde ik de brief niet op het kussen van mijn moeder of op het kussen van mijn vader, maar ertussenin, op de plek waar ik als klein jochie gezeten had.

45.

'Je moet écht nú naar beneden gaan en sorry zeggen,' zei mijn oudste broer. Vlak ervoor had ik met mama en papa aan de keukentafel gezeten. Ze hadden me geroepen. Ik wilde niet komen, maar kon het ook niet weigeren. Aan de keukentafel was ik verschenen en gaan zitten toen mama vroeg: 'Waarom zeg je de hele tijd zo weinig?'

Ik had haar aangekeken en mijn schouders opgehaald. 'Doe ik niet,' had ik gezegd.

'Waarom ben je nou zo boos?' vroeg ze. Ik kon me die vraag niet voorstellen, keek even naar papa en keek weer terug. Ze hadden toch die brieven gezien, ze wisten toch van de Praagreis – hoe konden ze dat nou niet zien? Het was alsof je in een brandend huis stond maar zou zeggen dat je het niet warm had.

'Ik. Ben. Niet. Boos.'

Mijn ouders keken me aan.

'Praat met ons. We zijn er klaar mee, al maandenlang zeg je geen woord, wat is er aan de hand?'

'Niks.'

'Weet je het zeker?'

'Ja.' Het was even stil geweest, mama en papa hadden me alleen aangekeken, maar een magisch kunstje had ik niet voor ze in petto.

‘Mag ik naar boven?’ vroeg ik, zo emotieloos mogelijk,

‘Ja,’ zeiden mijn ouders. Terwijl ik de trap opliep moest ik weer huilen. Ik wilde zó graag op reis, ik wilde zó graag weg van huis, ik wilde zó graag bij Daniël zijn, vrienden met hem zijn, avonturen met hem beleven in een vreemde stad waar ik niks en niemand kende. Ik wilde zó graag af van die twijfels over wie ik was. Ik wilde gewoon mezelf zijn. Ik was aangekomen in mijn slaapkamer toen mijn oudste broer belde.

‘Als je nu niet naar beneden gaat, dan...’ – hij was even stil – ‘...het was bijna allemaal geregeld, maar je bent het nu in een heel hoog tempo aan het kwijtraken.’

‘Wat bedoel je?’ Mijn broers had ik niet in vertrouwen genomen over mijn stiltestaking en aan de stem van mijn broer kon ik horen dat ik iets doms had gedaan wat hij bijna niet meer recht kon zetten.

‘Mama en papa zouden vanavond met je komen eten, hier bij de strandtent, ze hadden een reservering gemaakt en we hebben het hier leuk aangekleed. Vervolgens zouden ze je vertellen dat je toch mee mocht naar de Praagreis. Maar ze hebben net afgebeld, dus ik heb ze meteen opgebeld om te vragen wat er aan de hand was en toen vertelden ze dat je echt niks wilde zeggen en dat ze dat gedrag niet willen belonen en dat ze op die manier geen zin hadden in het etentje, dus nu ben je je laatste kans aan het kwijtraken. Eten komen jullie niet meer, dat gaat niet meer lukken, maar ga nu naar beneden en zeg wat er is, dan moet je reis hopelijk nog lukken.’

Ik was dolblij en diep ongelukkig tegelijk. Ik vond het onmetelijk lief wat mijn oudste broer had geregeld en voelde mezelf een ongelofelijke eikel dat ik het nu uit mijn handen liet glippen. Alleen, ik zag ook niet voor me wat ik beneden moest gaan zeggen, want ik kon niks zeggen.

‘Naar beneden en zeg wat er aan de hand is, bied je excuses aan en hopelijk komt het goed.’

'Wat lief, dank je! Echt heel erg lief! Dank! Alleen, ik kan niet zeggen waarom ik niet praat, ik kan dat niet tegen ze zeggen'

'Waarom niet?'

Ik wist geen antwoord te geven.

'Verzin dan wat, maar zeg in ieder geval sorry,' zei mijn broer.

Het voelde raar om te moeten gaan praten tegen mijn ouders. Voordat ik ook maar een woord had gezegd, ging mijn stem al op slot. En nu moest ik opeens sorry zeggen. Er was zo'n lange stilte geweest dat ik wist dat het niet alleen voor mij onwennig zou zijn, maar ook voor mijn ouders.

'Mam. Pap,' begon ik. Shit, dacht ik, shit, waar is de stemolie. Mijn stem zit op slot. En wat ga ik tegen ze zeggen? 'Sorry.'

Ze keken me aan.

'Sorry dat ik zo stil ben. Maar. Ik ben gewoon bezig. Bezig met veel. En. Ik wil gewoon echt heel erg graag. Ja. Ik wil echt gewoon heel erg graag mee op reis. Het is voor mij. Ja. Voor mij meer dan een reis. Het is ook een kans. Zoals ik in die brieven. Toch. In die brieven heb geschreven. Ik. Er is gewoon een hele belangrijke vriend bij. Ik heb zoveel voor die reis gedaan. Ik ben minder eenzaam als ik mee kan. Denk ik. Ik weet niet hoe ik dat moet zeggen. Maar ik wil echt heel heel heel erg graag. Niets liever. De reis dan hè. Ja. Dus. Goed.'

Ik had tussen de woorden door meer gezegd dan alleen de woorden zelf. Ik hoopte dat ze het konden horen. Ook al hoopte ik ook dat ze het niet zouden begrijpen en niet zouden horen. Ik was er nog niet klaar voor.

'Je mag mee,' zeiden mijn ouders, 'mits...'

Ik hoorde niks meer. Alles was leeg en stil.

46.

Praag stalde haar stad uit als in een sprookje. De zon leek er niet onder te kunnen gaan, en als hij onderging voelde je zijn aanwezigheid in de duizenden kaarslichtachtige lichtjes van de huizen en de lantaarnpalen. De stad was een sprookje en in onze groep zat een prins.

Meneer Schaephock vertelde ons over de geschiedkundige geheimen van de stad; over de astronomische kerkklok waarvoor we precies op tijd verschenen om de apostelen uit de klok te kunnen zien komen. Hij vertelde ons hoe het kon dat de communisten er de macht hadden gegrepen en politici uit hun raam konden vallen. We liepen naar de plek waar Jan Palach zichzelf in brand had gestoken als statement tegen het stalinistische regime. En we liepen naar de Oude Joodse Begraafplaats, de oudste van Europa. Er waren zoveel joodse mensen begraven dat de grafstenen schots en scheef stonden, als een slecht onderhouden gebit. Overal waar je keek stonden grafstenen, alsof ze aan het dansen waren. Een dodendans. Hoewel ik niemand van hen kende werd ik direct verdrietig. Mevrouw Tuvar had haar handen laten glijden over een van de muren die de begraafplaats omsloten. De naam van een van haar familieleden stond erop.

We liepen door het concentratiekamp Theresienstadt,

waar joodse mensen werden vastgezet en gruwelijk behandeld. We waren er stil. Verdrietig stil. Volgens mij wilde iedereen elkaar een knuffel geven, maar het was een verdriet dat we uiteindelijk toch alleen verwerkten. We hoorden daar over homo's die werden vastgezet en roze driehoekjes moesten dragen. Dan was het duidelijk wat je was. Vies. Fout. Minderwaardig.

Hoewel ik dolblij was dat we eindelijk met z'n allen op reis waren, slingerde mijn hoofd alle kanten op. In het hotel had ik mijn matras op de grond gelegd – ik was bang dat mijn kamergenoot het vervelend zou vinden om samen in het tweepersoonsbed te moeten slapen. De helft van de tijd liep ik met een klein flesje rosé rond. Als ik 's ochtends wakker werd stond het flesje naast mijn kussen.

In de avonden gingen we naar toneel of de opera. Ondertussen gaven de jongens aan elkaar een fles wodka door. Het werd weer bewolkt in mijn hoofd. En rustiger. Na de opera liepen we langs het water, waarin de lichtjes weerkaatsten als sterren. Als je niet al verliefd was zou Praag wel zorgen dat je het werd. En ik was dat ook. Ik wist het.

We hadden die laatste dag een afscheidsdiner op een afgehuurde boot. Terwijl om ons heen de stad en haar levens aan ons voorbijtrokken, verdronken wij in onze eigen levens en verhalen. We speelden een drankspelletje.

'Nu mag jij iets kiezen, Daniël,' zei een van de jongens.

'Ja, wat zal ik eens vragen,' zei Daniël. Hij moest lachen. Ik vermoedde dat er iets vies of vunzigs zou komen.

Hij keek me aan, ik vroeg me af of hij twijfelde over wat hij ging zeggen.

'*Never have I ever*,' begon hij – weer was hij even stil, nu wist ik zeker dat hij twijfelde – 'gefantaseerd over seks met iemand van hetzelfde geslacht.'

Het donderde in mijn hoofd. Als je het wel had gedaan,

moest je drinken; had je het niet gedaan, dan mocht je je glas laten staan. Ik wist niet wat ik moest doen. Liegen wilde ik niet, maar zo openlijk iets laten weten ook niet. Daniël zat naast me, ontweek mijn blik niet, maar keek me ook niet aan. Er ontstond wat gelach aan de tafel, niemand durfde te drinken. Totdat Daniël zelf een slok van zijn drank nam. Ik voelde me een verrader als ik niet zou drinken, maar deed het pas toen ik merkte dat de jongens zich richtten op Daniël.

'Tuurlijk heb ik daar wel eens over nagedacht.' Daniël moest lachen. Uiteraard werd er op zijn verhaal gedronken, waardoor ik stiekem kon drinken. Volgens mij zag Daniël het. Helemaal niet erg.

'Gewoon dat je er even aan denkt, hoe dat zou zijn,' ging hij verder, 'dat hebben jullie toch ook wel eens gedaan?' vroeg hij. Dat kon niemand echt ontkennen. Hoewel ik er misschien op een andere manier over dacht, voelde ik me heel even niet eenzaam. Heel even niet anders. Heel even niet vreemd.

De laatste nacht was ik weer dronken, zoals vaker deze week. Vanaf de verdieping van mijn hotelkamer liep ik met mijn flesje rosé de gang op. Ik had mijn smoking nog aan, maar mijn strikje hing los en mijn manchetknopen waren uit. Ik ging de trap af naar de tweede verdieping. Eigenlijk met maar één reden. Ik wist dat Daniël daar zijn kamer had en wilde weten of ze misschien een feestje hadden. Terwijl ik de trap afliep probeerde ik ervoor te zorgen dat ik er niet vanaf zou vallen. Op de overloop hoorde ik iemand naar boven komen. Langzaam bracht ik mijn hoofd omhoog en keek ik in de ogen van dat wat ik zocht. Daniël.

'Hé,' zei hij.

'Hé hoi! Of haai! Nee, hoi hoi. Haha. Hoi!'

'Waar ga je heen?'

'O, gewoon even naar beneden.'

'Er is daar weinig te zien hoor.' Hij ging verder de trap op en ik liep naar beneden alsof ik nog een doel had. Ik wachtte een tijdje op de gang en liep toen weer naar boven. Daar was een kamerdeur open. Een vriendinnetje van mij keek me geschokt aan toen ze me zag en ging voor de deur staan zoals mensen alleen doen als ze zo onopvallend mogelijk iets willen verbergen maar dat zo opvallend en krampachtig doen dat je vrijwel direct weet hoe laat het is. Ik kon over haar heen kijken en achter het bed zag ik twee hoofden wegduiken. Of beeldde ik me dat in?

'Waar ga je heen?' vroeg ze. 'Er is hier niets. Er is hier niemand.' Zij kon ook niet weten dat ik Daniël net op de trap was tegengekomen. En ik wist met wie dit vriendinnetje de kamer deelde. Met Fleur.

Misschien had ik het wel niet willen zien. Op school maar nog veel meer tijdens de reis. Daniël en Fleur waren naar elkaar toe getrokken. Ze liepen soms met hun armen over elkaars schouders en zaten veel naast elkaar tijdens de diners. Af en toe zag ik hoe Daniël haar schouders masseerde en hoe zij dat dan weer bij hem deed. Elke aanraking voelde alsof iemand mijn keel langzaam dichtkneep. Maar nu kon ik er echt niet meer omheen. Ik zat in mijn kamer, naast die waar ik net twee hoofden achter het bed had zien duiken. Inmiddels was duidelijk geworden dat onze kamer gebruikt zou worden als locatie voor het kamerfeestje. Mijn krampachtige er-is-niks-te-zien-vriendin kwam binnen.

'Waar zijn Daniël en Fleur?' vroeg ik haar.

Ze stotterde. Nu wist ik het zeker.

Op de gang bleek dat de slaapkamerdeur van Fleur op slot was gegaan. En het licht was uit. Iets knapte er in mijn hoofd. Een vriendin van mij. Die alles wist. Met hem. In de slaapkamer naast me. Met een beetje pech kon ik ze seks hóren hebben. Terwijl ik zo hard gewerkt had om deze reis mogelijk te maken. Ik huilde. Sloeg op de deur. Had er direct spijt van. Deed het toch nog een keer. Als een kind dat schreeuwt in een lege kerk, zo galmde mijn gebonk door het trappenhuis van het hotel. Het was donker. In de gang en in mijn hoofd.

Op de weg terug naar huis reden we langs het Ossuarium van Sedlec. Een kapel gemaakt van de botten van bijna zeventigduizend personen. Overal waar je keek klemde de dood zich aan je vast. Rijen schedels waren opgestapeld. De kroonluchters waren van botten. Er hingen slingers van schedels. Een altaar was opgebouwd uit opgestapelde skeletten. De dood lachte je toe en zei je dat ze altijd zou overwinnen. Ik kocht een kaart als aandenken. Misschien kon ik mijn verliefdheid er achterlaten. Of mezelf. Maar toen ik tijdens de terugreis het lawaai van achteren uit de bus hoorde, wist ik dat mijn verliefdheid er nog steeds was. Ik wilde dat de deuren van de bus dichtgelijmd zouden worden, dat we eindeloos zouden blijven reizen, zodat ik bij hem kon zijn. Zijn uitgeblazen adem weer in kon blazen, als een airco. Ik deed mijn ogen dicht en genoot van zijn stem. Ik wist dat zo'n reis niet meer zou komen, dat ik niet meer zo lang onafgebroken bij hem zou zijn en ik besloot van elke komma, van elke grap die hij maakte, van elke lach die hij deelde, te genieten. En op te slaan. Voor later.

47.

Een week na de Praagreis kreeg ik een berichtje van Fleur. Ik wist meteen hoe laat het was. Ze had gezoend met Daniël, schreef ze, en vond dat ik er recht op had om dat niet via via te horen. Ze was bang dat ik boos was. Dat was ik niet. Misschien was ik ergens wel blij. Blij voor hem. Dat hij gelukkig was. Dat hij iemand had met wie hij plezier kon hebben. Iemand met wie hij een lichaamsavonturier kon worden. En misschien dat ik het ook Fleur toch gunde. Maar pijn het deed wel. Zeker de schooldagen, die voelden nu als een soort *bitch slap*. Als ze samen op de kantinebanken lagen te knuffelen, of bij elkaar op schoot zaten op het schoolplein... Om het draaglijk te maken fantaseerde ik dat ik over dertig jaar nog steeds met ze bevriend zou zijn, dat ik de peetoom van de kinderen zou worden. En dat Daniël en ik dan samen zouden vertellen dat ik vroeger verliefd op hem was geweest.

Met het gezin gingen we op vakantie. Terwijl ik in de zon zat dacht ik terug aan het gesprek dat ik kort daarvoor met Sylvia had gehad. 'Weet je lieverd, zoals het nu gaat kom je niet vooruit,' zei ze. We hadden het de hele tijd over Daniël gehad, maar toegeven dat ik echt verliefd was en op mannen viel, dat kon ik nog steeds niet. 'We zitten allemaal in de puberteit. Schoppen tegen zaken aan. Maar jij schopt tegen iets wat in jezelf zit. Pas als je jezelf accepteert kun je vooruit. Tot die tijd worden je wonden alleen maar dieper en dieper.'

Ik was er stil van geweest – en nu eigenlijk nog steeds. Mijn wonden waren niet geheeld. Sterker nog, nu ik zonder vriendinnen zat om mee te praten waren die wonden gaan etteren en ontstoken geraakt. Ik was omringd door mijn broers en ouders, maar praten kon ik niet. Het was alsof iemand mijn lippen had dichtgeplakt. Zoals Wojnarowicz, maar dan onzichtbaar. Mijn oudste broer moet het aan me hebben gezien.

Tijdens het avondeten had ik met Daniël in mijn hoofd gezeten. Gedacht aan Sylvia's woorden. En het aan mezelf toegegeven. Nee, ik val niet op mannen, althans, niet per se, maar ja, ik was wel verliefd. En ik was er verdrietig om. Ik wist dat Daniël mijn gevoel nooit zou kunnen beantwoorden. Ik had tijdens het avondeten niks gezegd, de salade op mijn bord bijna onaangeroerd teruggebracht naar de keuken. Toen ik weer de buitentrap wilde aflopen naar het zwembad, verscheen mijn oudste broer opeens op het balkon. Hij keek me aan. Maar niet zomaar. Hij keek me aan, écht aan. Alsof hij alles zag. En alsof hij dat allemaal al heel lang had gezien.

'Wat is er, Wobie?'

Ik keek hem aan. Er sprongen tranen in mijn ogen.

'Zeg het maar. Wat is er toch?'

Ik keek hem aan. Ik wilde tegen hem zeggen dat ik verliefd was. Verliefd op Daniël. Nee, ik wilde het niet zeggen, ik wilde het schreeuwen. Mijn hele lichaam schreeuwde. Maar ik kon het niet. Ik keek hem aan en ik kon het niet. Ik was te bang dat ik de blik in zijn ogen zou zien veranderen. Ik huilde. Hij wilde me een knuffel geven. Maar voordat hij mij in zijn armen veiligheid had kunnen geven, was ik al weg, de trap af.

48.

De vijfde. Ik had een nieuwe gymdocent. Daar begon het eerste probleem van het jaar. Terwijl de andere jongens sportief de trap richting kleedkamer op renden voelde het voor mij alsof elke stap er eentje richting mijn ondergang was. Ik had een paar dagen eerder met de gymdocent gesproken. Hoewel ik hem had uitgelegd dat ik vorig jaar niet gymde en dat er iets speelde, had hij gezegd dat het hem goed leek als ik gewoon mee zou doen. Om te zien hoe het was. Ik durfde er niet tegenin te gaan. Thuis was het zoeken geweest naar mijn gymkleding, die had ik wel op een hangertje kunnen opbergen.

Ik liep de trap op en hoopte dat ik uit zou glijden. Ik smeekte om een hartaanval. Onder aan de trap richting de kleedkamers hoorde ik de jongens al praten. Een van hen zag me staan. 'Hé, gym je weer mee!' Hoewel het aardig bedoeld was voelde het als een duw. Toen ik de kleedkamerdeur opendeed wist ik dat ik mezelf aan het vernietigen was. Twee uur lang gymmen. Grijze mist was zwart geworden. En het was nu overal. Het droop door mijn hoofd. Ik liet de deur los. Ik stond weer op de gang. Tegen de muur hield ik mezelf overeind. In mijn hoofd galmden echo's: 'Ik kan dit niet, ik kan dit niet, ik kan dit niet.'

Even later stond ik beneden, op zoek naar meneer IJzinger.

Hij zou me kunnen helpen, had ik bedacht, hij kon het uitleggen aan meneer Roest. Hij zag direct aan mijn gezicht dat er iets heel erg niet goed ging. Alles was weggetrokken. Niet alleen de kleur. In mijn blik zat niks meer. 'Ik heb u nodig voor meneer Roest,' zei ik. Hij begreep het.

Meneer Roest en meneer IJzinger zaten aan het bureau, ik stond. Ik merkte dat ik mijn gymkleren al aanhad. Blijkbaar was ik wel de kleedkamer ingegaan, maar had ik dat uit mijn geheugen gewist. Samen met meneer IJzinger had ik uitgelegd dat het niet ging. Meneer Roest leek nu dan toch bij te draaien.

'Ik begrijp je verhaal. Ik heb alleen één vraag, mag ik raden om wie het gaat?' zei hij.

Die vraag had ik niet verwacht. 'Dat mag.'

'Is het vanwege één jongen? Is het vanwege Daniël?' zei hij.

Ik keek hem aan. Hoewel ik het niet wilde, kon ik niets anders doen dan knikken.

49.

Met mijn balpen tekende ik een nieuwe jurk. Of hij voor een man of een vrouw was wist ik nog niet. Er stonden vooral tekeningen in mijn schrift. Vrouwen die kristallen droegen in hun jurk, vrouwen die vastgegoten waren in betonnen bedenksels, vrouwen die met puntige schouders elk plafond konden doorbreken dat er maar was. Het was een diepe wens om ooit modeontwerper te worden. Thuis had ik een boek van Alexander McQueen liggen. In zijn kleding zat worsteling, strijd, een gevecht. Soms letterlijk, met dieren die de kleding aanvielen of speren die door de stof heen kwamen. Ik kon er eindeloos naar kijken. McQueen had zelf het leven uitgezwaaid, door te zweven in een touw. Het maakte sommige verwijzingen in zijn werk nog donkerder. Ik keek er bijna elke ochtend in en anders wel elke avond.

Ondertussen zat ik met Liesje te praten. Zachtjes, want de les was al begonnen. Engels, geen tekenen. De docent hoorde ons en stopte met lesgeven. Hij keek naar ons. We waren vertraging. Hij maakte aanstalten om weer verder te gaan toen Truusje – meestal een vriendinnetje – riep. 'Gooi hem er maar niet uit hoor,' begon ze. 'Hij is droevig vanwege gisteren.' Ze liet een stilte vallen. Iedereen leek te wachten op wat ze nu zou gaan zeggen. 'Gisteren was de nationale uit-de-kast-kom-dag. Hij heeft zijn dag gemist en is daarom nu verdrietig.'

De klas viel stil. Van achteren zag ik een paar hoofden draaien. De jongens. Ik lachte het weg en de docent ging verder.

'Gaat het?' vroeg Eveline. Ze zat voor me en had zich snel even omgedraaid. Ik knikte. Na de les vroeg ook de docent of het wel ging. Wederom knikte ik.

50.

We zaten in het computerlokaal, voor natuurkunde moesten we een opdracht uitvoeren. We waren met zijn vieren, en een van hen was Daniël. Het was me niet eens echt opgevallen dat hij was opgestaan, maar zoals de zon je nek opeens onverwacht kan verwarmen, zo verscheen Daniël achter mij. Hij stond daar gewoon, achter mijn stoel, mee te kijken op mijn scherm. Ik durfde niet om te kijken, maar ik zag hem via de reflectie. Ik had het gevoel dat hij terugkeek. Hoe beter ik me concentreerde op het scherm, hoe duidelijker het werd dat hij mij aanstaarde. Ik schrok ervan. Maar ik bleef terugkijken. Hij keek niet weg. De seconden werden halve minuten, werden minuten en vervolgens kwam hij een stap dichterbij. Door de stoelleuning heen voelde ik in mijn rug zijn benen en onderlichaam. Hij stond tegen me aan, dat was duidelijk.

Ik ging verder met formules invoeren, maar voelde opeens zijn hand op mijn schouder. Hij had hem daar neergelegd, zijn hand. Niet om me even vast te pakken, nee, om hem te laten rusten. Ik voelde hem landen, alsof het een vliegtuig was dat na een lange vlucht terugkwam. Het leek alsof Daniël in één keer al mijn onrust en stress liet wegvloeien. Ik was bang voor het moment dat hij zijn hand weg zou halen. Ik keek hem aan. Kwam Medusa maar door het computerscherm heen om ons zo te vereeuwigen. Met een beetje Midasiaanse kracht, zodat onze standbeelden niet koud en grijs zouden zijn maar van glinsterend goud. Hij haalde zijn hand niet weg, maar liet die langzaam over mijn schouder glijden, verder naar voren, langs mijn nek verder naar beneden, over mijn sleutelbeen, totdat hij hem liet rusten op mijn borst. Zijn andere hand rustte op mijn rechterschouder. Ik wist niet waarom hij dit deed, maar ik voelde me gelukkig. Ik keek hem via het scherm aan. Zo voelde dat dus, bedacht ik me, écht betoverd worden. En Daniël had het aangedurfd me te betoveren. Tot elke micrometer in mijn lichaam. Een lichtpunt in de zwarte dagen.

51.

We vierden kerst op school. Liesje en ik waren aan het dansen. De tango en de Weense wals, vonden we zelf. Ik moest lachen. Keek haar aan, genoot van haar. Ze was levend en lopend geluk. We dansten als enigen. Het diner moest nog beginnen maar we waren al dronken. Samen hadden we meteen onze drankmuntjes buitgemaakt en vervolgens waren we langs de dinertafels gelopen om mensen gedag te zeggen, terwijl we zo nu en dan glazen pakten en eruit dronken. Soms sloegen we ze steil achterover. Door de drankjes kon ik de grijze mist van kleur voorzien.

Als de fotograaf langskwam poseerden we overdreven. Alsof we sterren waren. En zo voelden we ons ook. We hielden elkaar omhoog, *Dirty Dancing*-style. Bogen voorover als stijldansers. Leunden achterover met onze handen op ons hoofd, *Absolutely Fabulous*. Zo wild als wij dansten, zo rustig was de rest van de gasten.

Toen er zweetdruppeltjes op onze gezichten zichtbaar begonnen te worden, verlieten we de dansvloer en gingen naar buiten. Zij om te roken, ik om af te koelen.

'Waarom vertel je het niet gewoon vanavond?' zei ze.

'Daar ben ik echt, echt, echt niet aan toe, dat trek ik niet.'

'Je bent er anders wel goed voor gekleed.' Ze knikte goedkeurend in de richting van mijn pak maar vooral van mijn strik. Ik had een paarse strik omgedaan. Ongeveer een week geleden was het paarse vrijdag geweest. De docenten hadden paarse details in hun kleding verwerkt. Voor de leerlingen die niet wisten wat de boodschap was veranderde er niks. Maar voor leerlingen die de boodschap wel begrepen was het een collectieve knuffel geweest. Het voelde voor mij alsof al die docenten mij heel zachtjes toezongen en zeiden dat het goed was. Ik had bedacht dat ik met een paarse strik die onzichtbare communicatie door kon zetten.

'Doe het!' zei Liesje nog een keer.

'Ik kan het echt niet, ben er echt nog niet klaar voor.'

Toen we langs de tafels naar buiten liepen kwamen we Daniël tegen. Liesje zei hem gedag, ik durfde dat op de een of andere manier niet, maar deed het uiteindelijk toch. Vanuit mijn ooghoek zag ik vervolgens de fotograaf weer voorbijlopen. En opeens wist ik wat mijn grootste kerstcadeau zou zijn. Een foto met Daniël. Daar zou ik eeuwig van kunnen genieten. Dat we elkaar gekend hadden, vastgelegd in pixels. Ik kon mij geen mooier kerstgeschenk bedenken. En de fotograaf dacht er duidelijk hetzelfde over.

'Gaan jullie even op de foto samen?'

Ik knikte en stak mijn arm uit naar Daniël.

'Nee, ga maar met iemand anders,' antwoordde hij.

Ik had de klap in de verste verte niet zien aankomen. Ik keek hem aan, hopend dat zijn mondhoeken omhoog zouden gaan en dat hij zou zeggen dat het een grapje was. Maar nee. Hij wilde niet op de foto, althans, niet met mij. Hij liep weg.

Op dat moment knalde de alcohol de verkeerde kant op. Door zijn resolute afwijzing voelde ik me een beest, een walgelijk beest, een monster waarmee hij niet op de foto wilde. Hij wilde niet met mij geassocieerd worden. Ik wilde naar buiten toe, de tranen voelde ik al opkomen. Onderweg kreeg ik Daniël in het vizier, hij stond met een groepje jongens te praten. Achter me hoorde ik twee vriendinnen opstaan, ze hadden door dat het niet goed ging en besloten achter me aan te gaan.

'Als je een beetje respect voor me hebt, dan...' begon ik. Ik had er direct spijt van. Hij was al die tijd zo lief voor me geweest, hij had het vast niet zo bedoeld. Dat wist ik ook wel. Maar hij kon me met zo weinig zo veel pijn doen. En dat had hij gedaan, dus ik liet mijn laatste paar woorden eruit rollen: '...dan praten we een keer als ik nuchter ben.'

Al zijn vrienden stonden eromheen. Ik zag dat hij het niet leuk vond. En ik had spijt, eindeloos veel spijt, wilde sorry zeggen, maar dat was te laat. Ik moest weg. Terwijl ik naar buiten liep hoorde ik achter me vier paar hakken. Ze zouden die nacht bij me blijven.

52.

Een aantal maanden later ging ik mee op reis naar Londen. Ik had er weken van wakker gelegen. Het probleem was dat niemand van mijn vriendinnen mee zou gaan. De Londenreis was een mannenreis, vrijwel alle bètatypes gingen mee. Ook Daniël en de andere jongens. Op school ontliep ik de docenten die de reis organiseerden. Ze moesten mij zien voor mijn definitieve bevestiging en om te bepalen met wie ik in een gastgezin zou gaan slapen. En wanneer ik zou gaan betalen. Ik ontkwam er niet aan, ik kreeg les van een van de organiserende docenten.

'We gaan er nu van uit dat je meegaat,' zei hij. Al mijn vriendinnen vonden dat ik het moest doen. Maar ik wilde niet. Ik was zo bang dat de jongens mij niet leuk zouden vinden, of dat ik niet met een van de groepjes mee kon, waardoor ik de hele reis alleen zou zijn.

'Ik heb ook rondgevraagd bij alle jongens, of je bij hen op de kamer kan slapen.'

Ik keek de docent aan. Zoveel ging achter mijn rug om.

'Oké, en?' Wat nou als ze nee hadden gezegd?

'Iedereen vindt het heel erg leuk als je meegaat en iedereen vindt het gezellig om je op de kamer te hebben.'

Ergens wilde ik ze allemaal een bedankje sturen.

‘Echt iedereen: van de jongeren die – zeg maar – hard leren tot de leerlingen die het vaakst roepen, zoals Oliver en Daniël en, nou ja, je begrijpt, allemaal geen probleem.’

Ik was even blij, maar het schip kantelde snel weer ondersteboven. Misschien hadden ze wel alleen maar ja gezegd omdat de docent het had gevraagd. En duimde nu iedereen dat ik niet bij ze op de kamer kwam. Misschien hadden ze het er wel met elkaar over, of met het groepje waarmee ze dachten gezellig samen een kamer te kunnen delen.

‘Ik heb je bij een groepje geplaatst, de jongens van de natuurkunde,’ zei de docent. Dat waren de types die hard leerden. Ik bood in mijn hoofd alvast mijn excuses aan ze aan.

In de auto naar de boot naar Engeland vroeg ik mama en papa of ze om konden keren. Ik smeekte ze, maar ze waren ervan overtuigd dat het beter voor me zou zijn als ik wel ging.

53.

We zaten in het theater. Billy Elliot. Een kwetsbaar jongetje maar o zo sterk als hij danste. Ballet. Pirouetjes. Ondertussen werd er drank doorgegeven. Daniël keek me aan en gaf mij de fles. Het was cola met wodka, maar met weinig cola. 'Hier,' zei hij, 'maar doe wel voorzichtig.'

Het werd nog donkerder in de zaal. Stiller. Alsof er niet meer geademd mocht worden. Op het podium was nog maar één lichtspot aan. Billy zat op een houten krukje. Zo alleen, omringd door duister, maar wel in het volle licht. Gevangen in de ogen van de mensen die hem zagen, terwijl hij eenzaam en alleen was. Het licht scheen van boven. Hij zat met één been over het andere en pakte een envelop. De brief van zijn moeder. Een mama die niet meer mama kon zijn in het leven. Geen warme kussen, op schoot zitten of samen films kijken voor Billy. Hij pakte de brief en las hem voor.

Heel langzaam voelde ik mijn ogen warm worden. Warm van de tranen. Overvol. Ik huilde, dat wist ik. Ik huilde. Dacht aan mijn brief voor mijn mama. De jongens naast me moesten ook slikken. Iedereen was even alleen. Iedereen was even alleen met zijn mama in zijn hoofd. En iedereen wilde een knuffel en kus. Iedereen wilde weer even kind zijn, verstoppertje spelen en gevonden worden, tikkertje spelen en tikker zijn, iedereen wilde vooruitgeduwd worden op een schommel. Heel even was Daniël naar voren geschoven. De tranen bleven niet langer in mijn ogen zitten, maar gleden Maximaliaans over mijn wangen. Daniël hing iets naar voren en draaide toen, zo rustig en wijs als een uil, zijn hoofd naar mij toe. Ik keek niet terug, maar hij wist dat ik hem zag. Ik slikte. Hij zag hoe de tranen van mijn kin vielen. In mijn schoot. Hij bleef even kijken en schoof toen weer langzaam naar achteren.

'Moest je aan je mama denken?' vroeg Daniël in de Mexicaanse pub waar we na afloop naartoe gingen. Ik was met de jongens meegelopen, of eigenlijk hadden ze me eerder arm in arm meegesleept. Ze konden er wel om lachen. Wat mijn vriendinnen meestal deden, dat deden zij nu. Zij waren mijn krukken en ik had het nog nooit zo prettig gevonden om kreupel te zijn. Toen ik drankjes voor iedereen wilde bestellen, was Daniël opgestaan vanaf de grote tafel waaraan we zaten. De rest van de tent was leeg en zou dat zolang wij er zaten ook blijven. Hij was opgestaan en naast me komen zitten aan de bar. 'Moest je aan je mama denken?'

'Ja.' Ik keek hem aan.

'Omdat thuis niet alles makkelijk is geweest, ook met je papa?'

'Ja, onder andere.' Ik wilde heel graag praten, maar wist niet hoe. Ik hoopte dat hij de taal van mijn lichaam zou lezen.

'Wat nog meer?' vroeg hij, heel voorzichtig, alsof hij iemand wakker maakte maar die persoon niet wilde laten schrikken.

'Ik herkende me er ergens in, omdat ik soms dingen ook niet weet.'

Hij keek me aan. 'Dat is toch prima.' Langzaam, zonder me te laten schrikken, had hij me wakker gemaakt uit een nachtmerrie, had hij een hand uitgestoken naar een droom.

We liepen over straat. Of wat daarvoor doorging. We hadden eindeloos veel shotjes genomen en drankspellen gespeeld. Terwijl we dronken had de bareigenaar uit de verkleeddoos Mexicaanse hoeden gehaald die we als kronen op onze hoofden plaatsten. Verkleedpartijtje zonder verstoppertje. Ik was gelukkig. Met de sombrero's op onze hoofden liepen we door Londen. Ik had een tastbare herinnering gewild aan het moment, de dag, de reis. Want die was geweldig. Als een dikke knuffel na lang van huis te zijn geweest. We hadden geld geboden voor de hoeden, maar de bareigenaar had het weggewuifd. We mochten ze houden en liepen langs de straten, langs de auto's, langs de mensen die vreemd opkeken. Uiteindelijk kwamen we aan op Piccadilly Circus. Voelden ons heer en meester van de stad en gingen met z'n allen op de foto, onder de vleugels van de Griekse god Anteros, de god van de wederliefde. Alle pijlen mochten me doorboren.

54.

Hoewel de zomervakantie voorbij was scheen de zon nog een paar dagen flink door in september. Ik voelde me vreemd. Het laatste schooljaar was aangebroken. Ik hield een dagboek bij. Voor mijn ouders. Voor mijn broers. En het was een manier voor mezelf om rustig afstand te kunnen nemen. Van alles. Een manier om zelf weer controle te krijgen, definitieve controle. Ik wilde de regie weer in eigen handen nemen. Ik schreef over mijn laatste jaar, over hoe het voor mij op school was. Niet de lessen die ik leerde maar met wie ik sprak, hoe de jongens op mij reageerden. Ik wilde ze laten zien dat ik geen mislukking was geweest. Dat de jongens heel vaak om mij moesten lachen, dat ik ze op allerlei momenten tegenkwam en dat ze lief voor me waren. Dat ze met me durfden te dansen, dat ze me soms een knuffel of een plaagstootje gunden. Dat ik soms in een buik mocht stompen, wat ik dan heel zachtjes deed. Ik wilde dat ze dat zouden lezen, zodat ze zouden weten dat ik ervan genoten had, dat ze zich niet hoefden te schamen, dat ik niet de teleurstelling was die ik in mijn ogen voor hen was geworden. Want ik wist dat ik dat was. Ik was steeds beter geworden in het wissen van mijn sporen op de huiscomputer. En had verder gezocht, niet alleen naar de liefde, maar ook naar de haat, en gezien dat ik op veel plekken verboden was. Niet welkom. Dat hand-in-hand onmogelijk werd gemaakt. Op die haat wilde ik een antwoord geven.

55.

Voor het eerst ging ik weer mee gymmen, omdat het buiten was, waar de kleedkamers groter waren, en omdat we weer gemengd gym hadden. Het was een opgave, maar een horde die ik wilde nemen. En het lukte. Ik reed van het hockeyveld terug naar school. Alleen. Even helemaal alleen. En dat vond ik niet erg. Ik genoot van het groen dat lentevers voelde, ook al was het herfst.

Toen ik bijna op school was hoorde ik een fiets van achteren aan komen rijden. De fiets leek sneller en sneller te gaan. Ik draaide niet om, keek niet wie of wat het was. Reed rustig door. Langzaam zag ik vanuit mijn ooghoek een fietswiel in beeld komen. Ik werd ingehaald. Dacht ik. Maar ik werd niet ingehaald. De fiets was gestopt met versnellen.

'Hoe is het?' vroeg de fietser.

Ik keek. Hij was ook alleen naar school aan het fietsen. Het was Daniël.

'Goed, zeker, was een fijne gymles, hoe is het met jou?'

'Ook goed,' zei hij. We lieten onze fietsen de laatste heuvel afrollen. Gaven geen gas, maar remden ook niet.

'Twee jaar geleden kreeg ik op Valentijnsdag een lolly. Ik weet nog steeds niet van wie ik die gekregen heb, jij weet van wie die is,' zei hij. Van alles schoot door mijn hoofd. Ik keek opzij, hij keek niet terug, concentreerde zich op de weg, alsof het een hele normale vraag was geweest. Ik wist niet wat ik ermee moest. Het voelde niet als een klap, maar hoe dan wel? En waarom? Waarom nu, waarom het na al die tijd opnieuw vragen? Ik begreep het niet.

'Nee, ik weet dat niet,' zei ik. Hij keek me aan terwijl we het schoolplein op fietsten. Dit keer keek ik niet terug.

'Dat weet je wel.'

'Nee dat weet ik niet,' zei ik, volledig ongeloofwaardig. Het was er eerder strompelend uitgekomen dan sterk en krachtig.

We stonden met de fietsen tussen onze benen inmiddels stil op het schoolplein. Hij stond dicht naast me. Hij keek me aan. Ik keek hem aan. Hij was carnaval, kerst, circus en kermis ineen. Vuurwerk vlamde overal.

Voordat ik iets kon zeggen onderbrak hij me. Hij wilde niet nog een ontkenning horen. 'Jawel, je weet het wel.'

Ik bleef hem aankijken. Hij kon mijn antwoord zien, maar ik durfde het niet te zeggen. Het leek alsof hij wílde dat ik het deed. Dat hij me wilde helpen. Dat hij met zijn vraag en met zijn ogen wilde zeggen dat het allemaal niet uitmaakte. En hoe graag ik het ook wilde zeggen, tegen hem, alleen tegen hem, ik durfde het niet. Maar liegen kon ik ook niet.

'Ik kan het je niet zeggen,' zei ik zachtjes. En ik ontweek zijn blik en parkeerde mijn fiets.

56.

Er lag een wit tapijt over het schoolplein. De sneeuw was onaangeraakt, geen voetsporen te bekennen. Elke stap die erop gezet zou worden, moest nog worden gezet. De school was leeg. De vakantie was een paar uur begonnen, de kerstdagen lagen in het verschiet. Ik stond met Sylvia onder het afdakje van de school. De schooldag was voorbij, zij was aan het roken. We hadden het over Daniël, hij had me een week eerder een berichtje gestuurd. 'Zeg nou van wie die Valentijnslolly was.' Ik had er niet op geantwoord.

Sylvia keek langs me heen, een tel. Toen keek ze terug. Achter me hoorde ik een deur dichtvallen. Er was iemand naar buiten gekomen. Blijkbaar was er nog wel iemand op school.

'Als je het nu niet zegt, ga je het nooit meer zeggen,' zei ze. Ik keek achterom en zag Daniël, de sneeuw niet langer onaangeraakt. 'Ik durf het niet.' Achter Sylvia zag ik hoe Daniël naar zijn fiets liep. Hij zocht zijn fietssleutel. Om hem heen dwarrelden sneeuwvlokjes.

'Als je het nu niet zegt, ga je het nooit meer tegen hem zeggen,' zei ze nog een keer. Ze keek me aan. Ik moest dit alleen doen, wilde ze ermee zeggen. En wel nu.

'Daniël!' riep ik. Direct keek ik Sylvia geschokt aan. Ik had zijn naam geroepen, en daarmee mezelf gedwongen iets te zeggen. Misschien hét te zeggen. Ik wist dat ik mezelf daarmee een duw had gegeven, gedwongen had iets te doen waarvan ik niet wist hoe het moest. Een mechanisme in gang gezet dat ik niet meer kon stoppen. Als ik dat al wilde. Hij keek op. Stopte met zoeken naar zijn sleutel en wachtte. In alle rust. Ik liep de sneeuwdeken op. Langs de voetsporen van Daniël. *In* zijn voetsporen, even één. Sylvia keek niet meer. Liet ons alleen. 'Daniël,' zei ik. Hij bleef rustig wachten totdat ik helemaal bij hem was.

Ik stond voor hem. Had mijn handen in mijn zakken. Mijn schouders hingen wat. Ik was zo bang om het te zeggen, maar wilde het wel, vanbinnen voelde ik dat. Alleen tegen hem, tegen niemand anders, ik wilde het tegen hem zeggen.

'Die lolly van Valentijnsdag...' zei ik. Ik was even stil. Ik realiseerde me hoeveel stappen ik gezet had.

'Ja.' In zijn stem lag een onmetelijk geduld.

'Die was van mij.'

'Oké,' zei hij, alsof ik iets heel erg gewoons zei, 'en val je dan ook op mannen?'

'Dat weet ik nog niet,' zei ik. Het was de eerste keer dat ik dat tegen een jongen zei. En dan ook nog eens zo helder en duidelijk.

'Nou, dat hoeft toch ook niet,' zei hij. Ik keek hem aan. De zwarte mist gleed van me af. Vluchtte. Daniël gaf me weer adem en kleur.

Hij pakte zijn fiets en samen liepen we naar het einde van het schoolplein. We zeiden niks. Totdat hij opstapte. Voordat hij wegreed keek hij me nog één keer aan.

'Fijne kerst, lieve Wobie.'

Het was een witte kerst. Witter dan wit. Ik wist dat er nog een lange weg te gaan was, maar mijn schouders zouden niet langer hangen en in mijn boekje hield ik de dagen niet meer bij.

57.

Er hing een feeststemming op het schoolplein. Bloemen, champagne, kleurrijke jurken en pakken. We waren geslaagd. Allemaal. Ik knuffelde mijn ouders. Ze waren trots en blij. Ik proostte met mijn vriendinnen. Al een aantal weken was ik niet meer zo dramatisch dronken geworden. Er was veel veranderd. Alles leek te glitteren en te schitteren. Ik voelde me een discobol in een warm stomend bad.

Jim kwam op me af, nog steeds even Hercules-achtig als altijd. Hij gaf me een knuffel en een kus op mijn voorhoofd. Vervolgens boog hij zich naar mijn oor. 'Dit zeg ik alleen even tegen jou,' zei hij. Mijn vriendinnen luisterden onopvallend mee, 'maar je moet straks even die kant op kijken.' Hij wees naar de andere kant van het schoolplein, de plek waar de scooters stonden. 'Geloof mij, kijk daar, niet doorvertellen.' Ik keek hem aan, hij gaf nog een knuffel en ging vervolgens achter een champagnefles aan.

Ik keek. Bleef kijken. Vanaf de straatkant kwam iemand aanrennen. Het schoolplein op. Ik moest lachen, glunderde van oor tot oor. Langzaam begonnen ouders en andere leerlingen het te zien. Hij kwam aanrennen. Daniël kwam aanrennen. Zijn haren, zijn huid, zijn hele lichaam glimmend in de zon. Hij had geen kleren meer aan, alleen een sok om zijn kruis. Zoals Jezus aan het kruis ging, zo rende Daniël bijna huppelend het schoolplein op, langs een rij leraren en leerlingen, terwijl hij joelde. En wij joelden ook. 'Mooi hè!' riep Jim, terwijl hij even omkeek en een knipoog gaf. Daniël rende het schoolgebouw in.

DEEL 3

ARTHUR

58.

Meer dan de studie koos ik de stad. Tegen het advies van mijn ouders, die wilden dat ik eerst zou bedenken wat ik wilde studeren en dan pas de instelling en stad. Maar ik wilde naar de stad van de buitenbeentjes, de stad van de vrijheid, de stad van de onrust, daar waar je jezelf kwijt kon raken. De stad waar zoveel jonge meisjes en jonge jongens heen gingen die getwijfeld en geworsteld hadden.

Ik vond een studio tegenover Artis, op de Plantage Middenlaan. Als ik het pand uitliep kon ik door de hekken achter de donkergroene bladeren de flamingo's zien. Elke ochtend werd ik begroet met roze. Om het af te maken hing ik een douchegordijn op met flamingo's. Op de binnenplaats die ik vanuit mijn raam kon zien stond een soort kerk. Een laatste gedeelte van een kapel, die voorheen door de bewoners van dit complex werd gebruikt. Grappig, die combinatie van roze en religie. Aan de muur hingen posters van David Bowie en Prince. Als je je ogen snel langs de posters bewoog, leek het net alsof Bowie en Prince nog steeds aan het dansen waren. Via de poster konden ze eeuwig dansen. Ze hadden de werkelijkheid schaakmat gezet.

Naast en boven mij woonden tientallen andere studenten. Als ik de gordijnen dichthield en zachtjes op bed naar muziek luisterde voelde ik me thuis. Een beetje lezen. Wat theedrinken. Maar vooral eindeloos op bed liggen en naar muziek luisteren. Met naast me Tijger. Ik had getwijfeld of ik die wel in m'n studentenkamer kon neerzetten, maar dacht toen: waarom zou ik het meest knuffelbare uit mijn kindertijd niet meenemen? En daar stond hij vervolgens. Mijn Tijger, ondanks zijn gemaakte vorm toch vrijer dan de dieren in de dierentuin.

Ik had het naar m'n zin maar vond het op mezelf wonen ook lastig. Vooral het naar buiten gaan. De deur door, de gang op, richting de uitgang naar de straat. Alleen in je kamer zijn was niet zo bewust alleen. Maar als je naar buiten liep waren er geen broers die meeliepen naar de supermarkt. Of ouders om ergens mee naartoe te gaan. Ik wist niet wat het was, maar ik voelde een bepaald soort angst, zonder echt bang te zijn. Als ik de straat opging richting de Albert Heijn, vijf minuten verderop, kreeg ik het benauwd. Het was een kleine supermarkt. Het assortiment was beperkt en er hing een haastige sfeer. Altijd. Alsof iedereen iets veel belangrijkers te doen had dan boodschappen. Ik maakte van tevoren altijd een boodschappenlijstje, maar in de winkel durfde ik het er niet bij te pakken omdat ik het niemand anders zag doen. De volgende keer wel, zo beloofde ik mezelf. De belofte als goedkeuring voor uitgesteld gedrag, al kwam ik hem nooit na. En zo vergat ik altijd wel wat. Eenmaal thuis was ik kletsnat van de zenuwen. Op den duur werd boodschappen doen zo'n opgave dat ik het zoveel mogelijk probeerde uit te stellen. Lang in bed blijven liggen, want dan kreeg je minder snel honger en ging de dag sneller voorbij. Zoeken in de kastjes of er nog ergens een pak rijstwafels en een pot pindakaas was voor ontbijt, lunch en avondeten. Dit moest veranderen, dat wist ik ook wel. Maar het lukte pas toen mijn vriendinnen te hulp schoten.

Een van de vriendinnen, die samen met mij studeerde, had het al vroeg door. Ze was degene met wie ik ook voor de hoorcolleges altijd afsprak om samen naar binnen te gaan. Eenmaal in de collegezaal voerde ik het hoogste woord, zeker toen ik een beetje aan de groep gewend was, maar erheen gaan was nog best lastig. Toen ze eens vroeg wat ik zoal kookte kwam ze erachter dat ik moeite had met boodschappen doen. 'Bel me maar als je boodschappen gaat doen, of als je je huis uit moet, dan praten we,' had ze gezegd. En dat deed ik. Vaak. Vrijwel altijd. Haar bellen, waarbij er een gesprekloos gesprek ontstond, maar wat haar toch aanwezig liet zijn. Een manier om de eerste drempels van zelfstandigheid en alleen zijn weg te werken.

Mijn buren heb ik nooit leren kennen. Het was een komen en gaan van studenten die nooit lang bleven. Op mijn bovenbuurvrouw na. Ongeveer drie à vier keer per week kwam haar vriend langs en dan klonk boven een opera met vocale noten van zaligheid. De eerste keer was het midden in de nacht geweest, ik was wakker geworden. Eerst niet wetend waardoor, toen denkend dat mijn wekker afging en daarna viel het kwartje. Helemaal niet onaangenaam. Ik had rustig liggen wachten totdat de laatste zucht zou klinken en keerde toen terug naar dromenland. Zo ging dat een tijd door, totdat ik een ruzie hoorde waarna de vriend niet meer langskwam. Hoewel ik haar nooit gezien heb, de bovenbuurvrouw, was het toch de persoon met wie ik het meeste contact had gemaakt. Aan mijn gang zaten een stuk of dertig deuren naar mensenlevens, maar nooit ben ik bij iemand anders naar binnen gegaan of heb ik aangeklopt. Sterker nog, als ik naar buiten wilde, luisterde ik altijd eerst of ik iets op de gang hoorde. Zo ja, dan bleef ik net zo lang wachten totdat het stil werd en ging ik dan pas naar buiten. Snel over de gang, alsof ik aan een wedstrijd snelwandelen meedeed. Ik baalde van deze onzinnige angsten, maar er echt iets aan veranderen kon ik niet.

Ik had geen wasmachine in mijn studio, maar er stond er wel een in de gemeenschappelijke ruimte, net als een droger. De deurloze kamer straalde een angstige eenzaamheid uit voor een gemeenschappelijke kamer; de enige interactie hier was die tussen de muizen. Na de eerste paar weken elk weekend mijn was te hebben opgespaard en in een reiskoffer mee naar Den Haag te hebben versjouwd, kocht ik een pak waspoeder. Ik had nog een emmer staan, die mama had achtergelaten toen ik verhuisde. Dan kon ik zo nu en dan dweilen. Met de emmer, de doos met waspoeder en een heuvel van kleren zat ik op een krukje in de badkamer. In mijn handen de douchekop. Ik liet de emmer vollopen met water en gooide er ondertussen een aantal bekers wasmiddel in leeg. Het water werd wit. Toen de emmer bijna vol was gelopen pakte ik de T-shirts. Wat de wasmachine kon, kon ik ook. Het water was veel te heet. Langzaam verbrandde ik mijn armen. Ik deed ze er om en om in om mijn T-shirts onder te dompelen. Het water koelde iets af maar was nog steeds te warm. Uiteindelijk liet ik de emmer ongeveer een uur staan, spoelde vervolgens het nog steeds niet koude water weg en realiseerde me dat ik geen wasrek had om de boel te laten drogen. Over de verwarming dan maar en een paar over de stang van het douchegordijn, een set over de wasbak, een paar hangend aan de haakjes bestemd voor de handdoeken. Toen ze na eindeloos lang wachten droog waren bleken de T-shirts keihard te zijn geworden. Ik had te veel zeep gebruikt.

Maar dit waren avonturen van andere dagen, die deden er nu niet toe. Ik had nu andere problemen aan mijn hoofd, of eigenlijk, andere pleziertjes. Want vanavond zou het leuk worden. Heel leuk. Ik zette Prince op en zwiepte mee. *I just can't believe all the things people say // Controversy // Am I black or white? Am I straight or gay? // Controversy.* Ik spoot nog een keer parfum op. Achter de oren. Zo had ik dat ooit ergens gehoord of gelezen, parfum moet je achter de oren spuiten, want als iemand je gedag zegt, met drie kussen of een knuffel, trakteer je de neus van die persoon direct ook op een kus.

In mijn studio, de vierkante ruimte die zowel slaap- als woon- en werkkamer was, keek ik naar mijn kleren. Ik had ze allemaal op bed gegooid. 'Paisley Park' klonk door de kamer. Ik zette de muziek harder, iets te hard, in de hoop dat de buren het zouden horen, het ze zou raken en ze vervolgens zelf in de wereld van Prince zouden duiken. Ik maakte een handkusje naar de buren, een naar links, een naar rechts, een naar boven – bij wijze van excuus. En ging vervolgens verder met aankleden. Kleding was belangrijk voor mij. Je hebt je innerlijk, datgene wat je bent, hoe je je voelt, wat er in je omgaat, dat zit vanbinnen. Daarnaast heb je je uiterlijk. Het is de kunst om je innerlijk en je uiterlijk goed met elkaar te combineren. Geen laagje leugen over jezelf heen leggen, want met kleding kun je juist verhalen vertellen. Laten zien hoe je je voelt, wie je bent, hoe je de wereld over danst. Ik vind het jammer om te zien dat veel mensen grijze muizen zijn; volgens mij leggen te veel mensen met hun kledingkeuze een laagje leugen over zichzelf heen. Ik zou willen dat de wereld wat meer catwalkerig werd. De dagen zijn soms al grijs en grauw genoeg. Ik trok een kleurrijke boxershort aan, roze sokken, een zwart T-shirt voor onder mijn overhemd, een donkere skinny jeans met een smokingstreep in verschillende kleurtjes aan de zijkant en een paars, blauwig overhemd dat strak mijn lichaam omspande. Knoopjes in verschillende kleuren, alsof het de van kleur veranderende lichten van een discotheek waren. Op het overhemd zaten rode stippen, minipolkadots. Afgemaakt met zwarte puntige lakschoenen met een gekleurde rits. Het waren stevige schoenen, van die schoenen waardoor je je stoerder en zekerder gaat voelen.

Ik ging nog één keer m'n tanden poetsen. Voor de zekerheid. Toen ik weer van de badkamer afkwam was Prince inmiddels overgeschakeld naar een nieuw nummer. *Soft and wet* zong Prince nu. Seks, spanning en sensatie de wereld in slingerend. Hoewel ik weg moest om op tijd te komen bij de vriendin met wie ik had afgesproken, kon ik de muziek niet afzetten. Ik moest dansen, zoals alles in de ruimte moest dansen. In mijn hoofd nodigde ik de meubels uit op de dansvloer. Ze draaiden en dansten om me heen. Op mijn tenen draaide ik pirouetjes met ze. Nog een rondje, nog een rondje, nog een rondje. Vrolijk te laat komend.

Ik had nog geen fiets in Amsterdam waardoor ik veel met het ov deed, alleen, de drukte in sommige trams vond ik niet prettig, dus verkoos ik als het maar even kon de benenwagen. Amsterdam was een heerlijke stad om doorheen te lopen. Over de bruggen, langs de grachten, wandelend langs de prettige onrust in de cafés en restaurants waar mensen nieuwe herinneringen met elkaar aan het maken waren. Het zag er gelukkig en goed uit, de stad. Veel mensen waren al op weg naar het einde van de avond, voor mij moest die nog beginnen.

Ik belde aan bij een van mijn vriendinnen. Ze woonde aan de overkant van Carré. Rood licht aan de grachten van Amsterdam, maar dan net anders. De rode gloed van de letters weerspiegelde in de Amstel. Het leek een beetje op de zon die ondergaat aan zee. Rood licht, weerkaatsend en wegzakkend in het water. Een theateravondzon, stralend aan de grachten. Wat moest het een droom en een feest zijn om het toneel en het publiek van Carré te mogen bespelen. Mijn toneelvoorstelling zou vanavond elders plaats gaan vinden, zei ik tegen mezelf, terwijl ik stond te wachten totdat de zoemer van de deur zou gaan waardoor ik naar binnen kon. De muziek stond aan, te hard, want ik kon het buiten horen. De muziek overstemde de deurbel. Ik belde nog een keer aan en knikte twee voorbijgangers gedag. Het was een stel, arm in arm, voor de gezelligheid, maar ook om hun lichaamswarmte te delen. Het was koud buiten, de winter had er zin in vanavond, was er vroeg bij. Ze liepen langzaam, rustig. Aan de buik van de vrouw te zien was ze zwanger. Met haar vrije hand wreef ze er af en toe over, alsof ze contact kon maken met het nieuwe leven dat daar groeide en kon zeggen: 'Ja, ik weet het, het is koud.' Het was bijna kerst, een mooi moment om de wereld en het leven in te stappen. Je ziet de wereld dan direct op haar mooist. De wereld versierd met kleurenlichtjes in de huiskamers, met opgetuigde en verleidende kerstbomen. Met kerst beheersen glitter en versiering een paar dagen lang het dagelijks leven. Geen beter moment om aan het aardse bestaan te beginnen.

Nieuw leven zouden deze twee ouders brengen. En het nieuwe leven zou alles nog moeten leren. Álles. Daar op de stoep realiseerde ik me dat ik daar gisteren over na had zitten denken. Toen ik na het eten van een rijstwafel met pindakaas mijn mes aflikte. Terwijl ik dat deed zag ik in gedachten mijn vader me boos aankijken en mijn moeder zuchten. Je mes aflikken, dat mocht thuis niet. Ik vond het een raar idee, dat je als kind op de wereld komt en alles nog moet leren. Geen regels, geen gebruiken, geen schaamte en gewoontes. Je weet niet wat wel en niet hoort. Je bent vrij van elke remming die een samenleving je oplegt. Je wereldbeeld is van de zachtste klei die je je maar kunt bedenken, en het is aan je omgeving de taak om die klei langzaam vorm te geven. Te boetseren tot een beeld, kunstig en krachtig. Volgens mij is het de kunst om die klei die je als kind bent je hele leven te behouden. De klei niet te laten uitdrogen, maar juist nat te houden, zodat je altijd kunt blijven leren, iedereen je kan blijven vormen en je altijd kunt blijven veranderen. Hoewel de klei toch vaak opdroogt en hardheid erin sluipt, op den duur misschien zelfs barsten gaat vertonen, is het willen streven naar het zijn van zachte klei volgens mij geen slecht idee. Alles wat verhardt tot steen werkt uiteindelijk remmend, het kan dan niet meer bewegen. Juist de beweeglijkheid, het flexibele, het mee willen vormen, juist dat brengt vooruitgang. Oude opvattingen kunnen prachtig zijn, zolang ze anderen – en jezelf – niet remmen in hun vrijheid. Gek genoeg, bedacht ik me, terwijl ik de pindakaas van het mes afspoelde, zetten veel van die oude ideeën zich toch als stukken steen vast in de klei. Het zijn de eerste momenten waarop de vormbaarheid van iedere persoon, ieder kind, als het ware wordt vastgezet. Met de juiste vrijheid zouden de eigenschappen die al vanaf het begin in de klei zitten, de glitters, de steentjes en de veren, zonder remming van buitenaf tot een prachtig kunstwerk kunnen uitgroeien. Klei komt niet kleurloos ter wereld. Iedereen is een kunstenaar in spe. De maker van het meesterwerk dat je leven is. En daarvoor is vrijheid essentieel. Maar die echte vrijheid, die totale vrijheid van de omgeving, die is er eigenlijk nooit. Niet echt. Er is schijnvrijheid, of later ingehaalde onvrijheid, maar die echte vrijheid, het totale gebrek aan tekening in de klei van ieder kind, dat raakt vrijwel iedereen voor altijd kwijt.

Wachtend tot iemand de deur voor me open zou doen, liet ik mijn gedachten nog verder afdwalen. Naar de twee kleuren die misschien wel direct aangeven dat kindklei nooit vrij blijft van beïnvloeding van buitenaf. Roze en blauw. Ik hield van roze. Ik zou er in de rest van mijn leven in steeds sterkere mate mee vertrouwd en getrouwd raken, maar het is voor een jongen een kleur die je moet opeisen, je moet toe-eigenen, want zomaar aangedragen krijg je hem niet. Roze en blauw. Als het kind van het passerende stel geboren werd, enthousiast het eerste gejammer de wereld in slingerend, zou het waarschijnlijk vrijwel direct gebeuren: het zou worden ondergedompeld in een van de twee kleuren. Werd het een meisje, dan zou het worden omringd door roze kleding, roze speelgoed en roze spullen. Werd het een jongetje, dan waren er blauwe kleren, blauwe speeltjes en blauwe spullen.

Ik zag ze verder lopen, het stel, arm in arm. Het ritme van een verliefd paar dat zin in de toekomst had klonk in de steeg met het tikken van hun schoenen. Over niet zo heel lang zouden het geen vier voeten meer zijn die loopmuziek maakten, maar zes. Zes voeten die de wereld bewandelden, allemaal op zoek naar hun eigen pad, zoekend naar het ritme waarin ze het liefst wilden bewegen. Het kind leefde nog niet maar leefde al wel. In het hier en nu waren de aankomende ouders, de familie, de vrienden en de vriendinnen al bezig met de ongeborene. Zonder dat het kind het wist leefde het al in de hoofden van de anderen – in de verwachtingen van de omgeving waarin het terecht zou gaan komen.

Ze stonden op het punt de hoek om te slaan toen de zoemer klonk: de deur werd automatisch ontgrendeld. De avond kon nu echt gaan beginnen.

Binnen dronken we wat. Indrinken, zoals dat heet. Een nieuwe stap in de evolutie van de zuipcultuur; steeds verder van tevoren alcohol naar binnen gieten voordat het 'echte' drinken begint. Een interessante ontwikkeling, misschien ook wel overbodig, maar wel eentje die soms goed van pas kon komen. Als je zenuwachtig was, was dit natuurlijk de ideale voorbereiding. Met een klein groepje waarmee je het wel gezellig vond alvast de vloeibare gezelligheid haar werk in je lichaam te laten doen, waardoor alles waar je tegen opzag in één keer kon worden weggespoeld.

We luisterden muziek en moesten lachen. We namen de roddels en de verhalen van de afgelopen tijd door. Daar zou zo dadelijk namelijk geen ruimte meer voor zijn. Op de feestlocatie waar we heen gingen was de kans om elkaar kwijt te raken vrij groot en de kans om verstaanbaar met elkaar te kunnen praten heel klein.

59.

Op de fiets gingen we richting de Warmoesstraat. Daar was de club waar we zouden dansen die avond. Een club van een studentenvereniging in Amsterdam. Al fietsend, zij achterop bij mij, ik haar vervoerend op haar fiets, genoten we van de koude lucht. De lucht die onze door de drankjes wiebelende hoofden iets minder liet wiebelen. De fietstocht werd zwabberender afgelegd dan normaal, maar genoeg onder controle om ongelukken te voorkomen. Ik was nerveus. Ik kon niet duiden waarom, maar in mijn buik waaide het net als buiten. Misschien was ik nerveus omdat ik wist dat de plek waar we heen gingen een beetje een machoplek was. Mannen in jasje-dasje, de borrelzaal verdeeld in verschillende hoeken. Misschien was ik ook nerveus omdat ik er niet echt bij hoorde. Ik was geen lid, had daarom geen jasje en dasje en zou direct opvallen. 'Dat is er eentje van buiten,' was op mijn voorhoofd geschreven.

De dansruimte was enorm, wel zo'n tien meter hoog, zonder ramen. Aan de ene kant stond een groot podium, waar de muziek die avond vandaan zou komen. Recht daartegenover een grote bar. Een bar waar je volgens de interne regels niet met je rug naartoe mocht staan. In de muren zaten verschillende biertappunten waar groepjes van bepaalde disputen stonden: hun eigen borrelhoek. De hele zaal was van een donker dik hout. De paar pilaren die de balustrade iets hoger in de zaal ondersteunden, de vloer, de bar, de muur, het plafond; alles was donkerbruin. In de zaal hing een aparte lucht. Een natte houtlucht, vermengd met bier. Het was duidelijk dat de vloer door de liters bier die erop werden gemorst, nooit echt helemaal opdroogde. Het was een geur die je, als je hem eenmaal geroken had, altijd en overal in herinnering kon roepen. Lekker was het niet.

In de zaal stonden honderden jongeren, pratend, schreeuwend, roepend naar elkaar. Sommigen speelde drankspelletjes, anderen deden een biertje-atten-wedstrijd. Weer een ander werd op een borreltafel geplaatst en kreeg een trechter in zijn mond, van bovenaf werd er dan een grote ton met bier in de student gegoten. Onder groot gejuich stroomden te veel liters bier zijn lichaam in. En langs zijn mondhoeken over zijn kleding. Aan andere tafels stonden dames elkaar zaken in de oren te fluisteren, wijzend naar andere borrelgroepen. Soms glimlachend, soms treurig kijkend. Ik vermoedde dat de laatste bedpartners-tussenstanden werden doorgenomen. Het was een gigakabaal. Alsof twee handen van massief geluid zich bij binnenkomst om je oren sloten. Terwijl de muziek nog niet eens aanstond.

Emma zocht de hoek waar haar jaargenoten stonden en zei haar vriendinnen er gedag. Snel en formeel werden er handen geschud, waarbij het er vooral op aankwam dat je deed alsof je de naam van de ander verstond. Vervolgens gingen we drank halen. Bier. Wat ik eigenlijk niet lekker vond. Bier. In elke hand een. En drinken deden we, terwijl we daar met elkaar in een kring rond de borreltafel stonden. Een beetje doen alsof we een gesprek voerden. Ondertussen werden er kaarten uitgedeeld, zo konden we bussen, een drankspel. Ik was een paar keer de pineut, moest mijn drank achterover tikken, maar hoefde gelukkig niet 'de bus in'. Terwijl de kaarten opnieuw werden geschud werd Emma door iemand begroet. In mijn ooghoek zag ik een lange jongen, maar echt kijken deed ik niet. Terwijl ik me concentreerde op degene die de kaarten aan het schudden was, voelde ik heel even een hand op mijn schouder. Een grote hand, lange vingers die mijn schouder voorzichtig aanraakten. Niet aantíkten, nee, eerder alsof de hand zichzelf heel even te ruste legde op mijn schouder. Niet onprettig. Maar ik schrok er ook een beetje van. Ik draaide me om. Het was de jongen die Emma net gedag had gezegd. Inderdaad lang, blond, smal, blauwe ogen. Ze keken vrolijk, ook nog eens ondersteund door een grote glimlach. Emma wees naar me en gaf aan dat ik met haar mee was, gevolgd door een knipoog naar mij. Die knipoog moest iets zeggen van 'knappe jongen toch'. Ik kreeg er een zenuwachtige grijns van, van de knipoog maar ook van zijn verschijning. Het was inderdaad fijn om naar hem te kijken. Hij gaf me een hand, bewoog zijn hoofd naar mijn oor en zei zijn naam, 'Arthur', hoorde ik hem zeggen. Ik beantwoordde met mijn naam, in zijn oor. En we lieten elkaars hand weer los. Hij ging verder, zonder een gesprek te hebben gevoerd of beleefdheidsvragen af te hebben gewerkt. Hij ging door en verdween in de borrelende mensenmassa, al even vluchtig als hij aan onze tafel was verschenen.

Het was nog even wachten totdat de muziek zou beginnen, vertelde Emma mij, nog ongeveer een uurtje. 'Wil je anders het pand even zien?' vroeg ze. Ik voelde me zeer ongemakkelijk tussen al die stoere mannen. Al die mannen die ergens bij hoorden, die met hun das en jas ergens onderdeel van waren, die een plaats in een hiërarchie hadden gekregen en in de vereniging ook een identiteit ontvingen. Juist dat waar ik nog zo erg naar op zoek was, dat was hier in overvloed aanwezig en maakte mij in hogere mate bewust van mijn onzekerheid.

Twijfel sijpelde mijn lichaam in. Het liefst wilde ik weg, maar ik gaf mezelf de opdracht om op z'n minst te wachten totdat de muziek aan zou gaan en dan in ieder geval een halfuurtje te dansen. Daarna kon ik met goed fatsoen wel weg, ontsnappen, sprak ik tegen mezelf. 'Ja! Graag! Laat het vooral zien!' zei ik. Als we samen door het pand zouden lopen, konden we in ieder geval even uit deze ruimte.

Ze liet alles zien, de trappen, de gangen, de ruimtes waar we eigenlijk niet mochten komen. Het was enorm. Zonder begeleiding zou je er direct verdwalen. Overal hingen verwijzingen naar het rijke verleden van de vereniging. Schilderingen, leuzen, attributen. Het had iets betoverends. Een instituut dat al heel lang bestond en nog zeker veel langer zou blijven bestaan. Dat ademde het. 'Jij bent hier even maar ik heel lang,' leek het tegen je te willen zeggen. Ik werd wat rustiger doordat we uit de massale onrust waren. Om de rondleiding zo lang mogelijk te laten duren stelde ik eindeloos vragen. Wat betekent dit, wat houdt dat in, wat zie ik hier? Als een mitrailleur vuurde ik vragen op haar af. Ze kon vrijwel alles beantwoorden.

'Hier kunnen we maar even op.' Ze wees naar een dichte deur. 'Want als we er te lang staan zullen anderen ons zien, en volgens mij mogen we er nu nog niet komen, omdat er externen zijn.' We liepen de deur door en kwamen op de balustrade. Vanaf daar kon je vanuit de hoogte naar beneden de feestzaal inkijken. Een menselijk mierennest. Stoeiende mannen, lachende jongeren, kaartspellen die werden gespeeld. Iedereen was bezig, druk in de weer. Een spaghetti van sociale activiteiten. We liepen een rondje, terwijl Emma vertelde welke disputen er wel en niet leuk waren, wijzend naar bepaalde hoeken in de zaal. Elk dispuut had dus een eigen hoek met een eigen tap, die dan weer bediend werd door dispuutsgenoten die elkaar afwisselden in verschillende rondes.

‘O, kijk daar, dat wordt leuk.’ Emma wees naar een jongen en een meisje die stonden te zoenen. Het duurde even totdat men ook daar beneden doorhad dat er gezoend werd. Blijkbaar mocht dat niet, want vanuit het niets klonk er een kolossaal gejoel en werden ze overgoten met bier. Ondertussen kwam iemand anders aanlopen met een pakje.

‘Pakje koffiemelk,’ zei Emma zonder haar blik los te maken van het tafereel. ‘Ik ben benieuwd wat ie gaat doen.’ De jongen kreeg de koffiemelk aangereikt en wist duidelijk wat er van hem verwacht werd. Hij zette het aan zijn mond en onder juichsalvo’s en een bierregen van zijn dispuutsgenoten kieperde hij de inhoud naar binnen, de boel in één keer wegdrinkend. Ook het meisje kreeg een pak koffiemelk. Even werd het stiller, het lawaai veranderde van forte naar pianissimo. Voordat het meisje het pak aan haar mond kon zetten, pakte de jongen met wie ze zo-even had staan zoenen het pak uit haar handen. Pianissimo werd weer keihard forte. Zijn dispuutsgenoten waren nog uitzinniger. Alsof ze zojuist het wereldkampioenschap voetbal binnen hadden gehaald. Arm in arm stonden ze te juichen en joelen. ‘Wat goed, hij doet het,’ fluisterde Emma, niet per se tegen mij. En ook dit keer zette de jongen, terwijl hij een nog grotere bierdouche kreeg dan even daarvoor, het pak melk aan zijn mond en klokte het naar binnen. Af en toe tegengewerkt door het lichaam dat kokhalsde. Langs zijn mondhoeken ontstonden kleine beekjes koffiemelk, maar het morsen bleef beperkt. Na afloop zocht hij naar de hand van de dame met wie hij gezoend had. Terwijl hij hun hand in hand gesloten handen als een bokskampioen omhooghield, draaiden ze zich om. Het gejoel werd luider en luider, en in de mensenmassa ontstond vanuit het niets een leegte waar ze doorheen konden wandelen. De menigte spleet als een zee uiteen, en sloot zich weer nadat ze gepasseerd waren. Ze liepen samen richting de deur van de feestzaal, waarschijnlijk een avond tegemoet waarop hun handen op veel meer plekken zouden komen dan nu het geval was.

Het was een interessant tafereel, daar beneden, van bovenaf bekeken. Honderden mensen, in verschillende vaste groepen. Orde in de chaos door regels, gebruiken en tradities. Hiërarchie en verhoudingen die bepaalde constructies mogelijk maakten en ervoor zorgden dat groepjes op een bepaalde manier met elkaar stonden te praten. Groepjes die wisten hoe ze zich tot elkaar dienden te verhouden, door al die onzichtbare regels. Van bovenaf kon je zo zien wie waar de populairste was, welke groepjes het meest gewaardeerd werden en welke misschien wel aanwezig mochten zijn, maar die iedereen toch een beetje vermeed. Je kon zo zien welke jongens het stoerst waren, welke dames het meest begeerd. De mannen stonden aan borreltafels met alleen mannen, de vrouwen stonden aan borreltafels met alleen vrouwen. Soms liep iemand even van de ene naar de andere tafel, maar dat was eigenlijk niet de bedoeling. Hoewel iedereen vrij in de ruimte stond, zonder ergens in letterlijke zin aan vast te zitten, kon je hier vanaf de balustrade duidelijk zien dat alles vastzat, samenhing, verbonden was. Onzichtbare draadjes die tafels, mensen, locaties met elkaar verbonden. De bewegingsvrijheid leek heel groot, maar was dat niet.

'We moeten naar beneden.' Emma knikte in de richting van het podium. Op de verhoging in de zaal zette de dj zijn draaitafel aan. De eerste lichtjes begonnen al te knipperen. Terwijl we langs de balustrade terugliepen, luidde de muziek de dansavond optimistisch in.

In de zaal deinde iedereen mee op de dreunende en deunende muziek. De lichten waren uit. Alleen gekleurde discolampen lieten de ruimte zo nu en dan oplichten. De rookmachines bij het podium bliezen ladingen witte wolken de zaal in. Je kon erin verdwalen, verdwijnen, veilig dansen – of zoenen zonder koffiemelkconsequenties. De tafels die hadden gediend als borrel- en spelmeubilair, waren nu opeens plateaus waarop mensen gingen dansen. Boven de groep uitstijgend, swingende moves makend en tonend welke heupbewegingen je in huis had. De muziek maakte alles los van wat zonet in onzichtbare afspraken was vastgelegd. Een katalysator van de vrijheid. Dames en heren duizelden en dansten door elkaar heen. Handen in de lucht. Vingers in de lucht. Swingend naar de vloer en weer even sexy omhoogkomend. Het was goed dat er geen collectieve controle meer was, anders zouden er liters koffiemelk moeten worden uitgedeeld. De muziek kreeg ook vat op mijn heupen, extra aangemoedigd door de drank in mijn lijf. Langzaam voelde ik vuurwerk opkomen in mijn lichaam. Vloeiend vuurwerk in mijn bloedbaan en spieren. Al snel dansten we, Emma en ik, alsof niemand keek, alsof niemand ons kon zien.

Na een tijdje stond ook ik op een van de borreltafels. Een dienblad om dansmoves te showen. Hoewel ik niet vergeten was waar ik was kon ik het mezelf wel laten vergeten. Schaamte leek even ver weg, voor nu. En daardoor kon ik dansen, vrij dansen. Emma was ik inmiddels kwijtgeraakt, maar gek genoeg maakte ik me daar geen zorgen over. In plaats van in blinde paniek en onzekerheid te gaan zitten zweten en zoeken, was ik blijven dansen. Emma zou vanzelf verschijnen en tot die tijd was de muziek mijn nieuwe vriendin.

'Wobie! Wo!' hoorde ik opeens. Ik keek naar de dansvloer, dichter bij mij, en zag Emma daar staan. Ik stak m'n hand uit en hielp haar de tafel op. 'Wo!' zei ze nog een keer. 'Wo! Arthur wil met je praten!' schreeuwde ze zo hard mogelijk in mijn oor. 'Arthur, die jongen van eerder op de avond, die wil graag met je praten!' Opeens viel me op hoezeer hij in mijn hoofd was blijven rondzweven. Als een parfum dat je al de hele dag draagt en daardoor zelf niet ruikt, maar opeens weer ruikbaar wordt als iemand er iets over zegt. Zo realiseerde ik me dat hij vanaf dat schouderaanraakmoment in mijn hoofd was gebleven. Het was prettig, die aanwezigheid, een beetje alsof iemand zachtjes op mijn rug had staan krabben. Hoewel ik alleen had staan dansen, had ik dat misschien niet echt alleen gedaan, of op z'n minst gehoopt dat hij ergens vanuit een donkere hoek in de feestzaal had staan kijken. Ik had uitbundig gedanst, zag ik, nu ik de afgelopen uren in mijn hoofd terugspoelde. Ja, uitbundig maar gecontroleerd. Niks om je echt voor te schamen of om je zorgen over te maken. Maar nu werd ik opeens zenuwachtig, de drank en de dans vloeiden uit mijn lichaam en ik werd me bewust van mijn omgeving.

'Nee, niet zo flauw doen!' antwoordde ik haar, ervan uitgaand dat het een grapje was.

'Maar het is echt zo, hij zag je, hij wil met je praten, hij vond je er leuk uitzien en dacht dat je vast aardig was!' zei ze, zichzelf verstaanbaar makend met haar handen aan haar mond.

'Emma, ik vind het stiekem echt een knappe man, dus ik vind het geen leuk grapje, het raakt m'n gevoel, begrijp je? Kom, zullen we samen verder dansen?'

'Wobie, serieus. Ik meen het! Als je me niet gelooft, prima, maar hij staat in de rokersruimte, echt, hij staat daar op je te wachten, daar kun je makkelijker praten!'

'Als dit een grapje is vind ik dat echt niet leuk hè, ik word nu helemaal zenuwachtig.'

'Jawel, geen zorgen, hij staat er echt, ik beloof het, geen zorgen, kom ga mee!'

Ze pakte mijn hand vast en ik liet me meevoeren. De danszaal uit, door de grote zware houten klapdeuren, de gang op. Klein trappetje af en vervolgens nog verder het gebouw in, een gang door. Aan het einde van de gang zat de rokersruimte. Je kon er roken zonder zelf ook maar een sigaret op te hoeven steken. Gewoon een paar keer ademen en je had je verslaving gevoed. Alleen op de achtergrond hoorde je nog zachtjes de muziek, als een lokroep naar de dansvloer.

Die lokroep zou ik deze avond niet meer beantwoorden.

60.

Hij stond daar, kwetsbaarder dan ik hem had onthouden, in het midden van de rokersruimte. Om hem heen waren vooral veel mensen met zichzelf en elkaar in de weer, haastig trekjes nemend van hun rookwaar. Arthur was duidelijk niet in gesprek met de vriendin die bij hem stond, en zij net zomin met hem. Alles in de manier waarop ze daar samen stonden gaf aan dat ze aan het wachten waren. Op iets of iemand. In dit geval op mij. Ze stond alsof ze eigenlijk al onderweg was naar een volgende afspraak, voeten en benen in de starthouding, wachtend op het startschot. Ik was het startschot, want zodra ik de ruimte inliep, met Emma aan mijn zijde, kwam ze los van haar plek. Arthur lachte. Ik voelde dat mijn gezicht volledig automatisch in de meest enthousiaste plooi schoot die er maar bestaat. Zonder het te kunnen checken wist ik dat mijn ogen zouden twinkelen en dat ze geen geheimen voor hem zouden kunnen bewaren. Mijn blik zei alles, net zoals zijn blik geen woorden nodig had. Toch zouden we woorden moeten zoeken, want iedereen in deze ruimte was met elkaar aan het praten. En iets anders dan praten konden we niet.

Toen ik voor hem stond was ik Emma al kwijt. Zonder er ook maar iets van door te hebben had ook zij de situatie verlaten. Een typische handeling van dit soort vriendinnen. De jongens bij elkaar brengen die zich niet veilig genoeg voelen om zelf de connectie te leggen. We waren nerveus. Als iemand ons had geanalyseerd, had je dat kunnen zien. Een brugpieperachtige zenuw zat in mijn lichaam. Maar dan de positieve vorm ervan. Geen zorgen over de vraag of je wel de juiste merkkleding aanhebt of een te grote tas op je rug draagt, maar eerder de spanning van het gegeven dat je met vriendinnetjes en vriendjes een nieuw avontuur tegemoetgaat, samen een nieuwe school ontdekken, zoekend door de gangen, rennend om voor de bel op tijd in het lokaal te zijn. Arthur en ik waren blij. Vrolijk. Misschien wel een beetje gelukkig op dat ene moment, wetende dat het bijzonder kon worden.

Hij begon te praten, eerst wat over zijn studie, waarom hij lid was geworden van deze vereniging en wat haar gebruiken zoal waren. Ik liet het ijsbreken volledig aan hem over en ook het voorkomen van stilte tussen ons was in zijn handen. Gelukkig kon hij van het ene verhaal overhuppelen in het andere, als een moeder of vader die zijn kind naar bed brengt en een verhaaltje vertelt voor het slapengaan. We rookten allebei niet. Wat opvallend was, maar in deze rookruimte nog niemand opviel. We waren allebei aan het wachten totdat het gesprek zich zou bewegen in de richting waarvan we allebei van tevoren wilden dat het heen zou gaan. Geen van beiden durfde het direct aan te snijden.

'Hoe vind je het hier?' vroeg hij.

'Ja, leuk, maar wel heftig. Al die mannen, best macho, als je begrijpt wat ik bedoel.'

Hij moest lachen. 'Ja, dat klopt, dat is een beetje de cultuur hier, ik vind het ook best wel heftig hoor, niet per se mijn ding.'

We hadden het over de studie. Hij deed kunstgeschiedenis – daar had ik een voorliefde voor –, gecombineerd met cultuurwetenschappen. Ik bleef hem erover vragen, alles om hem maar te laten praten. Af en toe stelde hij een vraag terug en vertelde ik dat ik politicologie studeerde en net in Amsterdam was komen wonen, tegenover de dierentuin. Ondertussen schoven we langzaam naar elkaar toe. De afstand tussen ons beiden was klein, misschien net aan de te kleine kant als twee jongens gewoon met elkaar zouden praten. We hielden in de gaten dat we niet te dicht op elkaar zouden staan, daar in de ruimte met zoveel anderen. Toch was er voldoende nabijheid om de spanning een beetje op te voeren. Het was fijn, zo dichtbij te zijn, zonder ongemak, zonder dat er iets gezegd hoefde te worden om elkaar te begrijpen. Onze lichamen konden communiceren zonder woorden. Ik ontspande erdoor, terwijl de spanning in mijn lichaam verder steeg.

Hij vertelde verder, hoe hij in Amsterdam was komen wonen, met vrienden, hier vlakbij. Aan de grachten, met z'n vieren. Ze hadden het huis samen verbouwd, gezellig gemaakt en het was een echt studentenhuis geworden. Hij vertelde hoe hij ver buiten de Randstad geboren en opgegroeid was. We keken elkaar aan. Met die blik liet hij me weten wat ervoor nodig was om het gesprek in de gewenste richting te sturen. 'Hoe was dat?' vroeg ik. Hij was het die de volgende stap durfde te zetten. Die de situatie definitief maakte. Direct, alsof het gevaarlijk was om het er hier over te hebben, een geheim dat niet gehoord mocht worden, gingen we allebei, voordat er ook maar iets gezegd was, zachter praten. 'Dat was niet altijd makkelijk, als je begrijpt wat ik bedoel, mijn vader was strenggelovig en had bepaalde verwachtingen. Van mij, van het gezin, van mijn zusje. Hij wilde dat ik als zoon zus en zo zou worden. Ik kon daar niet aan voldoen. Hij was iemand die veel belang hechtte aan etiquette. Ik moest met boeken op mijn hoofd rechtop lopen. Zou rechten moeten gaan studeren. Hij had het allemaal uitgedacht. Dat ik hier lid werd, ja, dat vond hij goed. En belangrijk. Dat wel.' Ik luisterde, wilde zijn verhaal horen om te weten dat ik niet de enige was die worstelde; de zoektocht van een ander kan een lantaarn zijn die de jouwe bijlicht. 'Uiteindelijk ben ik vrouwelijke en mannelijke modellen op internet gaan opzoeken, heb een selectie gemaakt, ze stiekem uitgeprint en toen bekeken welke ik leuker vond. Toen wist ik het zeker, als je begrijpt wat ik bedoel.' Hij vertelde verder en verder, begon steeds meer zijpaden, wegen en routes uit te leggen. Dat wat niet gezegd kon worden werd steeds explicieter gezegd. Van mij was nog niks officieel, bij hem was dat het wel. Hij had het al gedurfd de waaier van verscheidenheid in de liefde uit te klappen en het licht te gunnen. Het gaf mij veiligheid en ruimte om het erover te hebben.

'Hoe is dat bij jou?' vroeg hij.

Het was de allereerste keer dat ik het er uitgebreider over ging hebben met een jongen. Ik zei dat ik nog niks aan iemand verteld had, maar dat mijn vriendinnen het wel wisten. Dat ik het eigenlijk nog niet zeker wist, terwijl ik het ergens toch ook wél zeker wist, maar dat ik het nog niet definitief durfde uit te spreken. Ik vertelde dat ik het ook niet zeker dúrfde te weten, omdat, ja, ik nog nooit op die manier gezoend had, wel met meisjes, maar ja, niet met... Ik vertelde steeds meer. Ratelde. Sprak alles uit wat er bij me naar boven kwam. Als een pan die te lang met een dicht deksel op het fornuis staat en waarbij het water naar buiten komt, het deksel wegduwend, zich niet langer verstoppend. Ik vertelde verder. Over de middelbare school, de twijfel. Dat ik het zo graag zeker wilde weten. Dat ik mezelf soms gek maakte. Dat ik net als hij op internet had zitten zoeken, afwegingen had gemaakt. Dat ik er eindeloos veel met vriendinnen over gesproken had. Ondertussen stonden we gevaarlijk dicht bij elkaar, maar hadden we onszelf wel meer in de richting van de deur weten te verplaatsen. Alsof we aan het slowen waren, heel langzaam, zonder dat iemand het zag, millimeter voor millimeter, en zonder elkaar aan te raken.

‘Uiteindelijk is het fijn om het wel te vertellen,’ zei hij. ‘Het lucht op. Het zal je ruimte geven. Maar doe het wel in je eigen tempo. Niets hoeft zeker te zijn, maar het is wel fijn als iemand je de zekerheid kan geven.’ Hij legde zijn hand, heel even maar, op mijn heup. Lang genoeg om mij te laten weten wat ik moest weten, kort genoeg om te zorgen dat het de anderen in de ruimte niet zou opvallen. We keken elkaar aan. Weer die glimlach. We deden alsof we proostten. Al waren de glazen bijna leeg, was de schuimkraag volledig vervlogen en zou het bier lauwwarm smaken, het was de ideale manier om onze vingers onopvallend tegen elkaar aan te laten komen. Schrikdraad aanraken, maar zonder angst voor de pijn, maar juist in blijde verwachting van de vonk. We tikten zachtjes, onze vingers, handen, tegen elkaar. Bleven daar even en maakten toen het proostgebaar af.

Steeds vaker kwamen er korte aanrakingen van zijn kant. Even een elleboog die een klein stootje gaf, even een hand die bij het maken van een grapje op mijn schouder landde, even een duwtje met zijn onderarm tegen de mijne, als hij een punt duidelijk wilde maken. En ondertussen waren we bijna de ruimte uit. We keken elkaar aan, nu zonder iets te zeggen. Logischerwijs was dit het moment, in films, in verhalen, op dansvloeren, waarop je elkaar een kus geeft, twee hoofden bij elkaar die het woordelijk praten vervangen door lichamelijk communiceren. Fragmenten die iedereen eindeloos vaak heeft gezien. Ook wij. Maar bij ons was het anders. Het kon niet. Dat wisten we allebei. Niet hier. Niet in deze ruimte. Dat zou te veel aandacht, misschien wel te veel onrust opleveren. Niet dat er klappen zouden worden uitgedeeld, dacht ik, maar het zou wel heel anders zijn. Je voelde dat het niet kon, een soort onzichtbare wet die door de lucht zweefde en die je als twee jongens direct registreerde. De sterkste regels en wetten zijn die wetten die niet actief door anderen hoeven te worden afgedwongen, maar juist diegene waar mensen zich automatisch in hun handelen en doen naar voegen. Dit was er zo eentje. Die wet schreef ons voor dat zoenen voor ons hier, op deze plek, niet de bedoeling was. Misschien móchten we wel zoenen, maar dan uit het zicht, onzichtbaar voor hen die zonder de last van die onzichtbare wetten hoefden te leven. Het enige wat we konden doen om de stilte toch te doorbreken was doorpraten. Alleen, dat stadium waren we inmiddels wel gepasseerd.

En weer was hij het die de volgende stap durfde te zetten. Als we samen zouden dansen, een wals of een tango, dan was de rolverdeling direct duidelijk geweest. Hij zou leiden, ik zou volgen. Ik vond het voor deze keer prettig om te volgen, om iemand anders, een jongen, te mogen gehoorzamen. Dienend te zijn. Aangestuurd te worden. 'Zullen we hier weggaan?' vroeg hij. En ja, we gingen weg. Ergens anders heen. Samen.

Hoe het kon, dat weet ik niet meer, maar automatisch zochten en grepen onze handen elkaar. Mijn hand veilig gevangen tussen zijn grote vingers. Het was warm daar, in zijn hand, prettig warm. Een veilig gevoel stroomde vanuit die hand mijn lichaam in. Hand in hand, nu definitief de rokersruimte uit, door de lange houten gang. Hand in hand langs drinkende, dansende en dolende jongeren. Hand in hand liepen we daar, rustig, onderweg naar de uitgang. Het voelde als een statement, het voelde als verzet. Een daad van verzet tegen de onzichtbare wetten die ons aanstuurden en deze handelingen verboden. We waren in overtreding tegen het onzichtbare, en dat voelde heerlijk. Zo ziet liefde er óók uit, dacht ik.

In de gang kwamen we langs een groep vriendinnetjes, nog steeds hand in hand. Niet alleen mijn vriendinnen stonden daar bij elkaar, ook een aantal van hem. Alsof ze nadat ze Arthur en mij aan elkaar in de rokersruimte hadden overgedragen, naar elkaar op zoek waren gegaan en nu een gemeenschappelijk vergadermoment hadden om de situatie te bespreken en de verschillende scenario's uit te tekenen. Vanuit mijn ooghoek kon ik zien dat het scenario dat zich nu voor hun ogen manifesteerde tot een overvloed van plezier leidde. Toen we voorbij ze waren keek ik nog even snel achterom – alsof ze aangestuurd werden door een afstandsbediening, veranderden ze allen gelijktijdig: hun gezichten veranderden in grote glimlachen en de duimen schoten uitbundig de lucht in, stuiterend op en neer. Emma deed zelfs een dansje en draaide een pirouette. De wereld voelde opeens tolerant en alles accepterend en het was alsof we samen een zwanenmeer mochten zijn.

Heel even lieten onze handen elkaar los. In de garderobe, we moesten allebei onze jas pakken. Daar werd Arthur aangesproken door een vriend en zijn vriendin. Die kwamen pas net binnen, gingen hun jas ophangen en leken verbaasd om te zien dat hij al wegging. Hij sprak met ze, terwijl ik in de hoek onrustig begon te worden. Ik was bang dat hij zich zou bedenken, toch niet naar buiten zou gaan met mij, overtuigd zou raken van het feit dat we terug moesten naar de dansvloer. Ik was bang dat het hier, terwijl het zo mooi en dichtbij leek, opeens toch uit mijn handen zou glippen. Als een glazen bol die, zo licht dat je hem bijna niet vast kunt houden, uit je handen glipt en in duizend glitters op de grond kapotvalt. Terwijl hij aan het praten was keek hij op, de ruimte doorzoekend. Hij zag me en ving me. Met een glimlach, van het verontschuldigende soort, liet hij me weten dat ik me geen zorgen hoefde te maken. Hij kon het gesprek niet afkappen maar liet me weten dat er niets was veranderd en we zo zouden gaan. De vriendin van de vriend keek om, waarschijnlijk onbewust aangestuurd door de korte glimlach die Arthur kort daarvoor de ruimte in had geslingerd. In tegenstelling tot haar vriend, die druk doorpraatte, grapjes makend over de liters drank die ze weg moesten tikken en de at-wedstrijd die bij hem thuis op een kotsfestijn was uitgelopen, had zij de situatie door. Ze keek terug naar Arthur, gaf hem een knipoog en liet haar arm rond die van haar vriend glijden. Een liefdeswurggreep. 'Kom, we gaan wat drinken!' zei ze tegen hem. Die had ze onder controle, dat was duidelijk, want direct staakte hij zijn verhaal, gaf Arthur een duw met z'n vuist en liep met z'n vriendin mee de drink- en dansavond tegemoet. Ik durfde opgelucht adem te halen.

We liepen door Amsterdam, nog steeds hand in hand. Het leek alsof iemand had besloten de straten schoon te vegen en ze alleen even te gunnen aan ons. Tijdens het wandelen kwamen we niemand tegen, geen geluiden, geen mens, geen dier, helemaal niets. We waren alleen in Amsterdam. Alleen in de stad. Amsterdam was deze avond voor ons. We maakten er gebruik van, liepen langer en langzamer dan nodig was langs de grachten, over de bruggen en onder het lieve licht van de lantarenpalen. Ik moest zachtjes lachen. Mijn hoofd was een discodansvloer waarop ik alle ruimte kreeg om te dansen.

Achter de ramen was niemand meer te zien, maar de rode lichten stonden wel aan en leken een theaterdecor voor de liefde te willen creëren. We liepen van de Oudezijds Voorburgwal over de brug naar de Oudezijds Achterburgwal. Daar ergens woonde hij, aan de grachten, omgeven door de beroemde rode lichtjes die Amsterdam daar 's avonds niet helemaal terecht onschuldig kleurden.

We liepen de trap van zijn huis op. Hij woonde op de eerste, tweede en derde verdieping van het pand. Toen we in het smalle gangetje op de eerste verdieping stonden, bleek dat we allebei tegelijk naar de wc moesten, het bier eruit plassen. Hij ging op de tweede etage, ik op de eerste. Op het toilet leek het alsof in mijn hoofd een lichtknop werd aangezet en ik me opeens realiseerde wat er gaande was. Ik was met iemand mee naar huis! Dat was nog nooit gebeurd! Ik was mee met iemand naar huis! En het was een jongen! Een jongen met wie ik mee was. Ik ging met m'n broek aan op de wc zitten, keek voor me uit, ademde mezelf tot rust en merkte dat ik dat eigenlijk al was. Vervolgens plaste ik snel en waste m'n handen. In de gang van het voor mij onbekende huis ging ik de enige andere deur door die er was. Het bleek de woon-, eet- en zitkamer ineen te zijn. Het was een L-vormige ruimte. Leunend tegen het aanrecht probeerde ik mezelf een houding te geven voor het moment dat Arthur zo naar beneden zou komen. Met mijn handen over elkaar wachtte ik. Het licht deed ik niet aan.

'Waar ben je?' hoorde ik hem zeggen.

Ik wachtte even met antwoorden, hoorde zijn voetstappen al op de trap. 'Hier!' zei ik. Zonder duidelijkheid te geven. Ik hoorde zijn voeten de laatste drie treden overslaan, vervolgens was het stil. Vanuit de gang zag ik zijn hoofd verschijnen, hij keek de kamer in, de hoek om, eerst naar rechts, toen naar links, en daar zag hij mij staan, in het donker. Een grote lach volgde. Bij mij gebeurde hetzelfde. Langzaam kwam hij in z'n geheel tevoorschijn en liep naar me toe. Elke stap die hij dichterbij kwam zorgde voor een nieuwe injectie van plezier die zo rechtstreeks mijn bloedbaan werd ingespoten. Engelen sprongen op en neer door mijn lichaam. In totale stilte kwam hij mijn kant op. Ook ik had niet de behoefte iets te zeggen. Dat was niet meer nodig. De stilte voelde heerlijk. En vulde de spanning. Langzaam haalde ik mijn armen voor mijn lichaam weg en kwam ik van het aanrecht overeind. Mijn nonchalante leunhouding was niet meer nodig. Ik vroeg me af wat er ging gebeuren, hoewel ik dat wist. Ik vroeg me af wat ik moest doen, hoewel ik wist dat het vanzelf zou gaan. Ik maakte me zorgen, terwijl ik me eigenlijk geen echte zorgen meer maakte. Ik had verwacht dat mijn hoofd zou ontploffen van stress, aan een stuk door vragen en twijfels zou rondschieten, maar nee. Mijn hoofd was nog nooit zo rustig geweest. Geen grijze mist, maar rust. Arthur kwam dichterbij, zijn voeten zo neerzettend dat hij leek te sluipen. Hij liep langzaam maar kwam nu toch wel heel dichtbij. Nog een paar stappen. Nog een paar stappen. Heel dichtbij. Echt heel dichtbij. En dan.

Hij stond voor me. Ik kon alleen maar glimlachen. Wat ik ook deed, mijn mondhoeken waren vastgezet in een absolute gelukstoestand. Hetzelfde gold voor hem. Onze ogen fonkelden. Zo dicht bij elkaar, niemand die ons kon zien en toch voelde het alsof we in vol ornaat voor het oog van de wereld verschenen. Twee glimlachende gezichten.

En toen ontspande zijn lach, kwam hij nog dichterbij, heel erg dichtbij. Ik voelde de luchtverplaatsing van zijn adem, kleine briesjes gingen langs mijn wangen, over mijn gezicht. Er was bijna geen afstand meer tussen ons. We zoenden. Zijn ogen waren dicht, mijn ogen waren dicht. Het was alsof er niks anders meer bestond. Alsof de wereld er niet meer was. Alsof de werkelijkheid er niet meer was. Alsof we zweefden in het oneindige. We zoenden. Niks kon me meer schelen. De schaamte was weg. De twijfel was weg. De worsteling was weg. Had ik hier zo lang tegen gevochten? Was dit wat sommigen wilden verbieden? Was dit wat zo walgelijk was dat mensen erom vermoord werden? De misdaad smaakte nog nooit zo zoet. Voor heel even, zonder buitenwereld, zonder anderen, zonder schaamte, alleen met hem en de zoen, voelde ik de totale vrijheid, vrijheid gevangen in onze omhelzing.

We zoenden. Lang. Af en toe stopten we, keken we elkaar aan, zeiden niks, moesten lachen, en gingen door. Soms legde ik mijn hoofd tegen dat van hem aan. Te ruste, terwijl hij kusjes gaf in mijn oor en mijn nek. We keken elkaar aan. Alles was schemerdonker. Maar nog nooit had de wereld er zo eindeloos kleurrijk uitgezien. 'Als je wilt kun je blijven slapen,' zei hij, 'er hoeft niks te gebeuren, het is alleen te laat om naar huis te gaan. Je kunt gewoon blijven slapen als je dat fijn vindt.' Ik wilde blijven, eindeloos blijven. Ik bleef slapen, zei ik tegen hem door te knikken. We liepen samen de trap op. Nog een verdieping hoger de hemel ingaand.

In zijn slaapkamer stond het licht aan, daar schrok ik van. Op de een of andere manier vond ik het nachtelijke duister fijner, alsof ik daarin kon verdwijnen, er meer verborgen in was. We gingen op bed liggen en kleedden ons voorzichtig uit. Hemd open, riemen los, shirt over het hoofd. Hij trok z'n broek uit, ik stopte.

'Wat is er?' vroeg hij.

'Het licht,' zei ik.

'Je hoeft je geen zorgen te maken.'

Maar dat deed ik wel. Ik hoefde niks te zeggen, Arthur sprong al het bed uit, bediende het lichtknopje en bracht de veiligheid weer terug in de kamer. Daar werden twee lichamen bijna een. Ik was blij dat z'n huisgenoten nog niet thuis waren gekomen. Onze kledingstukken vlogen van het bed af, ongecontroleerd, wetend dat het de volgende ochtend een klus zou worden om ze allemaal terug te vinden. We dolden over elkaar heen, hij boven, ik boven, hij boven. Stoeien, maar dan anders. We deden niet alles, maar wel veel meer dan ik ooit had gedacht. Alles was de eerste keer, maar het leek al eeuwig zo te zijn gegaan.

61.

Hij had een slaapkamer zonder gordijnen. Daar kwam ik de volgende ochtend achter. Het licht van buiten had vrij spel en greep gretig om zich heen. Het was een stralende dag. Ik zag geen klok hangen en mijn mobiel was leeg, maar buiten hoorde ik de Munttoren luiden. Ik telde mee, maar raakte de tel kwijt. Vond dat minder erg dan ik gedacht had. Arthur sliep nog, ik hoorde zijn diepe ademhaling. Ik vermoedde dat hij binnenkort verkouden zou worden, zo zwaar klonk het. Zoals de kerk de klokken laat luiden om de tijd voor de mensen aan te geven, zo was Arthurs adem de klok voor de tijd van het menselijke.

Ik wachtte tot hij wakker werd, terwijl de onrust zich weer meester maakte van mijn lichaam. Al liggend probeerde ik te kijken waar mijn kleren lagen, maar doordat ik mijn bril kwijt was, zag ik alleen wazige vlekken. Kleren die van hem en mij konden zijn. Met mijn hand voelde ik op het nachtkastje, heel voorzichtig, zonder lawaai te maken. Niks te vinden. Ik tastte langs de bedrand en vervolgens op de grond. Ook daar lag niks. Ik voelde nog een keer. Misschien onder het bed? Mijn vingers strekten zich zo ver mogelijk uit. Ik voelde iets, een klein dingetje. Zou dat het pootje van mijn bril zijn? Met m'n vingertoppen trok ik het onder het bed vandaan. Inderdaad. Mijn bril.

Arthur was inmiddels wakker geworden. Hij draaide zijn hoofd op het kussen om mij te kunnen zien. Ik glimlachte. Een beetje een stomme glimlach, merkte ik, maar hij was zo vriendelijk om toch blij terug te lachen.

'Lekker geslapen?' vroeg hij met een stem die als een diesel op gang leek te moeten komen.

'Zeker hoor, jij ook?'

'Ben je al lang wakker?'

'Valt wel mee.'

Hij kwam een beetje overeind, bewoog mijn kant op en kwam vervolgens boven mij hangen, om zich daarna te laten zakken op mijn borstkas. Ik wist totaal niet meer wat ik moest doen. In de nacht was alles vanzelf gegaan, maar nu voelde ik me opeens echt naakt. Kwetsbaarder dan eerst. Als een etalagepop bleef ik liggen, één hand liet ik kunstmatig over zijn schouder en rug glijden. Ik wilde weg. Niet dat ik echt weg wilde, maar ik moest de balans opmaken, overzien wat er allemaal was gebeurd en ik wilde de avond niet bevuilen met een onhandige ochtend.

Hij had het door, gaf me een kus en vroeg of ik wilde douchen. 'Nee, dank je.' Iets eten dan misschien? Hoefde ik ook niet. Alleen even opfrissen? Ook daar wilde ik nu geen tijd aan vuilmaken. Ik wilde in m'n kleren schieten en dan verder kijken. Misschien met kleren aan knuffelen, misschien ook niet. Zittend op de rand van het bed zocht ik mijn onderbroek. Ik moest eigenlijk opstaan om hem te vinden. Maar dat wilde ik niet. Zo zichtbaar door het licht van buiten, terwijl Arthur alles kon overzien vanuit het bed. Steeds meer nam de onzekerheid mijn lichaam in zijn greep. Ook dit had Arthur door. Alsof hij de stadia herkende, ze ooit zelf had meegemaakt. Maar hij was niet van het soort dat je in die situatie laat, nee, hij kwam zelf uit bed, prachtig in het bloot, zichtbaar in het licht. Zette een paar stappen en dook naar de grond.

‘Hier, Wobie!’ Hij droeg mijn onderbroek aan me over, begeleid door een knipoog. Ik realiseerde me dat ik heel wat knipogen van hem had gekregen. Als ik een spaarkaart had gehad, was die nu zeker weten vol. Terwijl ik me aankleedde, pakte Arthur een handdoekje dat hij losjes rond zijn heupen knoopte en keek vervolgens toe hoe ik mijn broek dichtritste en de knoopjes van mijn hemd vastmaakte. Hij wist dat er nu snel een einde zou komen aan ons avontuur.

We stonden boven aan de trap op de eerste verdieping. In de andere kamers hielden zijn huisgenoten zich stil, opvallend stil. Ik stond er wat onwennig. Het was duidelijk dat hij deze laatste trap niet ook mee zou afdalen. Ik vroeg me af, zonder het hardop te zeggen, of het de laatste keer zou zijn dat ik hier zou zijn. Ik keek naar de deur die me naar buiten zou leiden en wendde me toen weer tot Arthur, met het idee hem snel een knuffel te geven en er vervolgens vandoor te gaan.

‘Je weet hoe je thuis moet komen? Ik vond het gezellig, ik zal je een berichtje sturen, succes voor vandaag.’ Hij gaf me een knuffel en een kus. Ik vergat een kus terug te geven. We lieten elkaar los en ik begon de trap af te dalen. Moest ik nog wat roepen, nog wat zeggen? Misschien omkijken en zwaaien? Toen ik bij de deur was keek ik toch maar even omhoog. Daar stond hij. Arthur. Alleen met een handdoekje om zijn middel. Dun, licht gespierd. Moe van de avond en het vroege ontwaken. Hij zag er mooi uit. Bloot en alleen beschermd door de lichte handdoek. Vrij heilig eigenlijk. De Zoon van de Liefde. ‘Toedeloe!’ riep ik naar boven, alsof ik even boodschappen ging doen bij de supermarkt en zo terug zou zijn. Ik had er direct spijt van en had het zo geforceerd hard geroepen dat ik wist dat het via het trapgat alle slaapkamers van zijn huisgenoten moest hebben bereikt. Die waren nu vast wakker. Ik durfde niet nog eens naar boven te kijken en deed de deur open. Stapte naar buiten, terug de wereld in, de hemel-voor-een-avond uit.

De wereld buiten was anders. Ik keek de lucht in. Er lag een blauwe blos over de hemel. Ik zoog diepe ladingen zuurstof op. Alsof ik op die manier de energie die ik vannacht had verbruikt in één keer kon terughalen. Ik zag drie vogels vliegen, vrij, onderweg naar iets nieuws, iets ouds verlatend. Toen keek ik naar rechts en zag daar het kruis. Het kruis van de Basiliek van de Heilige Nicolaas. Een driebeukige kruiskerk, kwam ik later achter toen ik het opzocht. En de kerk waar het boek *De vierde man* van Gerard Reve zich afspeelde. Terwijl ik het kruis, fier en krachtig overeind in de zoete winterlucht, zag staan, wist ik het zeker. God zou verliefdheid nooit verbieden.

Alles was anders. Terwijl ik daar stond merkte ik dat. Alles was anders. Toen ik begon te lopen besefte ik dat. Ik was weer terug in de wereld, maar de wereld was veranderd. Ik was veranderd. Ik liep over de stoep, zag dat de wereld wakker was geworden. Ik hoorde de fietsbellen, ze leken een liefdesconcert te spelen. Ik zag de amsterdammertjes staan, schots en scheef, alsof ze nieuwe dansmoves uitprobeerden. Ik zag de mensen die in alle drukte onderweg naar hun werk waren. Ze leken stiekem een collectieve balletvoorstelling op te voeren. Ik zag het water in de grachten kabbelen en het zonlicht weerkaatsen, alsof ze hadden besloten voor één keer in een spiegel te veranderen om licht te laten weerschijnen. In mijn hoofd sneeuwde het, het sneeuwde verliefdheid, als in een sprookje. De zon speelde ondertussen de jarige, met een traktatie van stralen in overvloed.

Ik liep, nee huppelde, nee danste, nee swingde – nee, deed dat alles tegelijk en net even anders – richting Amsterdam Centraal Station. Daar zou ik de metro naar huis pakken. Ik zweefde boven de grond. Niet alleen m'n hak, niet alleen die paar millimeter. Nee. Ik zweefde gigagantisch hoog. Vliegen kon ik, hoger dan hoog, zonder mijn vleugels te verbranden. De onzichtbare wetten wuifde ik met mijn vleugels weg.

62.

Mijn buren moesten het wederom ontgelden, dit keer door Bowie. Of ik trakteerde ze juist weer op een groot cadeau, het is maar hoe je het bekijkt. Alles in de kamer leek verliefd. De fotolijstjes stonden arm in arm, de boeken in de kast schoven dichter tegen elkaar aan, alsof ze met z'n allen hun eigen verliefdheidsfeestje hielden. De kussens op het bed knuffelden elkaar. De dekens krulden in zichzelf. Zelfs de muren leken te willen kroelen en trokken krom. *Boys, Boys, it's a sweet thing // Boys, Boys, it's a sweet thing, sweet thing* klonk het zwijmelend. Zo zacht, zo zoet. Ik luisterde niet echt naar de tekst, vooral naar de tonen, het langzaam in slaap wiegende deuntje en de zachte stemmen. Ik ging langzaam op bed liggen, dacht aan Arthur, alleen aan Arthur, de eindeloze zoen, de eindeloze nacht, alles wat eindeloos voelde maar niet eindeloos bleek te zijn. Ik ging liggen. *I'm glad that you're older than me. Makes me feel important and free.* Ik droomde weg.

Toen ik wakker werd bleek Bowie ongestoord verder te hebben gezongen. Ik zag hem uit mijn boxen kruipen, zingen in de kamer. Dansend. Bewegend. Energie opwekkend. 'Starman' klonk.

There's a starman waiting in the sky
He'd like to come and meet us
But he thinks he'd blow our minds
There's a starman waiting in the sky
He's told us not to blow it
Cause he knows it's all worthwhile. He told me:
Let the children lose it
Let the children use it
Let all the children boogie

Ik sprong uit bed en bleef springen, ene been de lucht in, andere been de lucht in. De energie, de spanning, de sensatie, de seks van de avond nog steeds als een tovermiddel door mijn lichaam gierend. Het leek alsof ik de wereld zó met één vinger kon optillen. Alsof het een roze ballon was, gevuld met de lichtste lucht. Ik kon ermee spelen. De wereld was licht en kleurrijk. Geen Atlas, geen schrijvende papa die de fantasiewereld als zware last op zijn schouders moest dragen. Nee. Vandaag was de wereld licht. Gevaarlijk licht. Dat wel. Een kleine windstoot en de wereld werd zo opzij geblazen. Maar in mijn kamer geen wind, geen briesje, alleen de trillingen van Bowies stem.

Ik zocht m'n mobiel. Had een bericht van Emma. Die wilde weten wat er gebeurd was. Ook had ik een bericht van Liesje. En toen ik verder keek ook eentje van Annah, eentje van Eveline, eentje van Sylvia, eentje van Alice, eentje van Fleur. Ping. Ping. Ping. Ping. Mijn mobiel bleef oplichten en de berichtjes bleven binnenkomen. Het ging maar door. Het vriendinnenleger had de informatie van die avond gedeeld. Ze wisten dat er íéts was gebeurd, maar wát? Ik pakte m'n agenda erbij, schrapte al mijn studieplannen, statistieklessen en opdrachten, de tentamens en de stukken die ik moest lezen. Ik veegde mijn werktafel leeg, gumde mijn tafel schoon en haalde alle overbodige herinneringen uit mijn hoofd. Zo kon ik me concentreren op dat wat momenteel echt van belang was, zo kon ik ruimte geven aan dat waarmee ik volledig, bijna obsessief, bezig wilde zijn. Mijn nieuwe ervaring, de verliefdheid, de zekerheid die het had gegeven, de vrijheid en Arthur.

Ik begon met inplannen. Thee hier, lunch daar, avondeten dan. Ik moest alle vriendinnen spreken. Ze allemaal persoonlijk het verhaal vertellen. Het leek alsof ik een theatertour moest doen. Ik vond het heerlijk. Elke keer het verhaal, met elke beweging, elke handeling, elke kus opnieuw tot in detail vertellend. Het was daardoor alsof ik alles opnieuw beleefde. En ik zorgde er op die manier voor dat de herinnering in mijn brein werd gekerfd als met een mes in een boombast. Ik kon elk detail, elke stap, nauwkeurig herhalen. Kon analyseren waar ik het de volgende keer anders zou moeten doen en inzien waar ik toevallig de juiste leuke dingen had gezegd die hij grappig aan mij vond. Mijn vriendinnen luisterden eindeloos. In hun ogen zag ik dat ik eindelijk was aangekomen op de plek die zij altijd al hadden voorzien. In hun ogen glom trots en na afloop deelden ze staande ovaties. Al tijdens mijn verhalen klapten ze, lachten ze, proostten ze. En daarna kwam de knuffel, de blijdschap, de vrolijkheid. Alsof ze zelf verliefd waren geworden, alsof ze zelf aanwezig waren geweest, een van hun mooiste avonden hadden beleefd en nu ook verdronken in de verliefdheid. Mijn agenda voorspelde een heerlijke tijd. Maar ik realiseerde me dat ik wel een toneelafspraak had. Samen met een groep jongeren moest ik een voorstelling maken. Daar was ik al veel te laat voor, maar ik moest er wel heen.

De uren die ik door moest brengen bij het toneelgroepje voelden vreemd. Voor hen leek alles hetzelfde te zijn, terwijl ik vanbinnen alleen maar dacht: zien jullie niet iets – hallo – zien jullie niet iets? Álles is vannacht veranderd. De wereld is nieuw, frisser, opgeschoond, puurder en eerlijker. Maar zolang ik niks zei zag niemand iets. Tijdens de uren die we bezig waren werd ik langzaam onrustig. Zou hij mij een berichtje sturen? Hoe laat? Hoe moest ik erop reageren? Ik nam me voor om ook dat met mijn vriendinnen te bespreken. En dat deden we. Elke keer het wonderlijke avontuur herbelevend en dan samen een plan makend voor hoe ik de toekomst naar mijn hand kon zetten.

Ik kwam elke dag moe thuis van het verhalen vertellen. Had elke dag een raar soort zenuwen, wetende dat er elk moment een bericht van Arthur binnen kon komen. Mijn vriendinnen stonden op stand-by. Zodra ik een bericht kreeg appte ik ze; als ze niet snel genoeg reageerden belde ik. Ze gaven advies, zeiden welke woorden ik moest gebruiken en welke emoticons. Welke leestekens wel en welke niet. Het zorgde voor een raar soort vertraging in de berichten tussen Arthur en mij. Maar ik vond het soms ook heerlijk om het berichtje nog niet te hebben geopend. Omdat ik dan het idee had dat hij heel vaak naar zijn mobiel zou kijken om te checken of ik al had geantwoord. En elke keer zou ik dus voor een miniseconde, als een klein vonkje dat even aangaat, in zijn hoofd aanwezig zijn. Dat vond ik zo'n fijne gedachte.

63.

Uiteindelijk zagen we elkaar nog twee keer als date. Eerst gingen we koffiedrinken. In een café in Amsterdam, terwijl het buiten licht was en iedereen ons dus kon zien zitten. Ik was doodnerveus die dag. Tijdens de werkgroep kon ik alleen maar wiebelen, geen zinnig woord bracht ik uit. Toen de docent kwam vragen of het wel goed ging en of het wat rustiger kon, gaf een van mijn vriendinnen aan dat ik een date had. De docent keek een beetje verbaasd op, alsof het misschien wel een verklaring was, maar niet voor al mijn gedragingen. Ik vond het doodeng, met een jongen afspreken in een café waar iedereen ons kon zien. Maar we deden het wel. Vlak voor we het café verlieten had hij een Smintje in zijn mond gedaan. Dat leek me een teken voor een kus. Maar dat kon ik niet. Niet in het openbaar. We stonden bij het paleis op de Dam. Aan de achterkant. Onze wegen zouden daar scheiden en onze afspraak van vandaag kwam tot een einde. Ik keek hem aan. Fluisterde dat ik het spannend vond. Hij kwam dichterbij. Ik zag mensen langs ons lopen. Mensen die boodschappen gingen doen, mensen die toerist waren, mensen die hipper dan hip liepen te hangen. Zoveel mensen, zoveel mensen die ons konden zien. Ik keek hem aan. Hij moest de onrust nu kunnen zien, misschien zelfs aan mijn ademhaling kunnen horen. 'Ik durf niet...'

'Hoeft ook niet,' zei hij. En hij gaf een knuffel. Ik knuffelde terug. We maakten de omhelzing langer dan vrienden zouden doen, het was immers de vervanging voor de kus. Een knuffel viel minder op. Toch checkte ik vanuit mijn ooghoeken of iemand keek. Gelukkig niet. Hij keek me weer aan. 'Zie je snel, wel thuis, we houden contact,' zei hij.

Ik keek hoe hij wegliep. Langs het paleis. Voor mij was hij een prins.

Weer een tijd later zou ik bij Arthur thuis langsgaan. Ik had er geen rekening mee gehouden dat zijn huisgenoten thuis waren, en met een veel te dure fles rode wijn stond ik onhandig weer in zijn keuken. Ik merkte dat ik er niet rechtop kon staan. Het plafond bleek veel lager dan ik me herinnerde. Zijn huisgenoten waren aardig, maar het voelde vreemd. Het voelde vreemd om nog niks tegen mijn ouders gezegd te hebben, of tegen mijn broers. Dat mijn vriendinnen het allemaal al wisten was prima, zij hadden er recht op en wisten altijd alles als eerste. Maar deze jongens, deze huisgenoten die ik niet kende, wisten nu iets waarvan ik vond dat ze daar nog geen recht op hadden. Bovendien dachten ze vast dat ik al jaren openlijk was wie ik nu eindelijk aan het worden was. Het voelde een beetje als verraad. Tegenover mijn mama. Dat ze een dag of drie terug had gebeld. Dat ze vroeg hoe het ging. Dat ik weinig antwoord had gegeven. Dat ik niet vertelde wat ik beleefd had. Dat ik wel iets zei, maar niet alles. Dat ik zei dat alles prima ging, dat ik aan het studeren was, dat het rustig was in Amsterdam, en dat ik in het weekend vast en zeker even thuis zou komen. Het voelde vreemd – niet dat ik loog, maar ik vertelde ook zeker niet de hele waarheid. En omdat de waarheid zoiets groots in zich verborgen hield, loog ik dus eigenlijk wel. Of tenminste, zo voelde het.

We gingen film kijken. Op het bed van een van zijn huisgenoten. Er moest een laken overheen, z'n huisgenoot had net schurft gehad. Ik wist niet precies wat dat was. Hij vertelde dat het kleine beestjes waren, spinachtig, die gangetjes groeven onder je huid. En dat ze daar eitjes legden die na een paar dagen uitkwamen en dat die nieuwe lading beestjes dan ook gangetjes ging graven. Rillingen rolden over mijn rug. Zijn huisgenoten kwamen nog even binnen, met waxinelichtjes. Een paar rondom de tv, een aantal op de grond, een paar rondom het bed. 'Veel plezier hè!' zeiden ze. Ik voelde de rivier van zenuwen buiten haar oevers treden. We keken *Hercules*. Een Disney-film. Eigenlijk keek ik nooit films uit mijn kindertijd terug, omdat ik mijn herinnering niet opnieuw wilde maken. Maar als Arthur vroeg wat ik wilde kijken, zei ik steeds: 'Maakt mij echt niet uit, ik vind alles goed.' Ik dacht daarmee een erg prettige gast te zijn, iemand die alles prima vond, maar eigenlijk was ik dat niet. Ik onttrok me daarmee in zekere zin aan mijn verantwoordelijkheid, waardoor Arthur steeds over alles moest beslissen. *Hercules* dus. Zelf vond ik het wel komisch. Twee jonge mannen, omringd door kaarsjes, een beetje onhandig tegen elkaar aan liggend, kijkend naar de gespierde en heldhaftige Hercules. Een cliché, bedacht ik me. Maar ik vond het heerlijk, om eindelijk het cliché zelf te leven, het cliché zelf te worden, zelf te zijn.

Toen we een paar uur later weer boven aan de trap stonden waar ik een paar weken eerder ook had gestaan, wist ik dat het de laatste keer zou zijn.

'Nou, wie weet tot ooit,' zei ik, misschien wat te dramatisch, maar het was wel precies dat wat het gapende gat in mijn buik me liet zeggen. Ik keek hem aan.

'Nee, nee, nee! We gaan elkaar zien, laten we anders een keer uitgaan samen, dan laat ik je de wereld zien. Er valt zoveel te ontdekken. Misschien met wat vriendinnen erbij.'

Ik hoorde wat hij zei, dacht alleen: maak het nou niet nog

erger. Niks is erger dan gebroken beloftes, behalve als iemand je beloftes doet waarvan je op voorhand weet dat ze niks waard zijn, dat ze worden gedaan en gezegd om dat ene moment minder pijnlijk te maken. Het ramde blauwe plekken in mijn buik. We gaven elkaar een kus, een knuffel. Ik wilde het eigenlijk niet, uit angst dat ik moest huilen, maar ik kon het ook niet weigeren. Ik perste mijn ogen dicht, me op die manier extra concentrerend op de omhelzing, op zijn huid, op zijn warme dunne lichaam, omdat ik er nu nog één keer van kon genieten. Zijn haar tegen mijn wangen. Het waren veilige armen, lange grote armen. Hij droeg een T-shirt, ik een hemd met opgestroopte mouwen, zodat ik door zijn shirt zijn lichaam kon voelen. Zijn huid was een katalysator van sprookjes en avonturen geweest. Ik zou zijn landschap missen. Ik zou het missen om op ontdekkingstocht te mogen gaan. Ik voelde nog één keer, de knuffel een laatste maal verstevigend. En toen lieten we los. Hoewel we elkaar in de toekomst nog wel eens de hand zouden schudden als we tegelijk op een feestje waren en ik mezelf na de drank ook te gewillig naast hem liet dansen, was dit toch eigenlijk de laatste keer dat we elkaar écht aanraakten. We lieten elkaar los.

Even daarvoor hadden we in zijn woonkamer gezeten. We hadden de Disney-film helemaal afgekeken – een slecht teken, wist ik. Maar ik had hem niet durven zoenen of aanraken, dus lag het initiatief volledig bij hem. En dat had hij niet genomen. Ik voelde een enorme teleurstelling, in het moment maar vooral in mezelf, toen de film afgelopen was en we onze schoenen weer aandeden. We zouden beneden nog een drankje doen. Ik baalde van mezelf. Waarom had ik niks gedaan, waarom had ik niks gedurfd? Maar ik vond ook dat het niet mijn schuld was. Hij wist toch dat alles voor mij nieuw was? Dat ik nooit had gedatet? Dat ik niet wist hoe het werkte? Hij had me toch kunnen begeleiden, iets kunnen zeggen van: wie vind je knapper, Hercules of mij? Gewoon, íéts, om de stilte tussen ons te doorbreken, zodat we niet meer naar de film maar naar elkaar zouden kijken. Onze eigen film en script in elkaar zouden zetten. Maar er was niks gebeurd. Alsof twee acteurs hun tekst kwijt waren geraakt en zonder regieaanwijzingen maar gewoon in het decor bleven staan. De kaarsen, het bed, de gesloten gordijnen. Alles romantisch, maar de acteurs wisten niet hoe de liefdesscène gespeeld moest worden. Ik baalde, ritste m'n schoenen dicht en bedacht dat ik het misschien tijdens ons drankje goed kon maken, een tweede kans. Ik zei dat tegen mezelf om te voorkomen dat ik daar in de slaapkamer in tranen zou uitbarsten.

Maar aan de keukentafel was het alleen maar erger geworden. Hoe het kon gebeuren wist ik niet, maar we hadden het opeens over een andere jongen. Arthur gaf aan dat hij het ingewikkeld vond, dat hij ook een andere jongen had ontmoet en het daar heel erg leuk mee had. Omdat ik het voor mezelf minder pijnlijk en zielig wilde maken, had ik enthousiast gereageerd. Alsof ik een van z'n beste vriendinnen was die bij elke vorm van liefde applaudisseerde. En vervolgens deed ik het domste wat ik daar had kunnen doen: ik ging doorvragen. In een poging te laten blijken dat het me niet uitmaakte, dat ik het niet erg vond, dat ik het hem gunde – wat ik overigens ook echt deed. En het ergste was: Arthur gaf antwoord. Hoe meer ik vroeg, des te meer hij vertelde. Mijn maag draaide zich om, het was alsof iemand met stokken inbeukte op mijn ziel. De ene na de andere klap kreeg ik te incasseren. Mijn verdediging was zelfvernietigend: ik bleef doorvragen. Waar hij hem ontmoet had? Een keer tijdens het uitgaan, het was direct raak geweest. Wat hij zo leuk aan hem vond? Zijn lach, en z'n Brabantse accent, en o ja, zijn grapjes, de grapjes waar zijn huisgenoten ook zo om konden lachen. Kennen je huisgenoten hem? Ja, die kenden hem, die hadden hem ontmoet, ze vonden hem erg aardig. Of hij hem binnenkort zou zien? Hopelijk wel, hopelijk zouden ze gaan schaatsen bij het Rijks. Wat romantisch! Ja, dat vind ik ook.

Ik hield het niet. Wilde weg. Bleef hem aanmoedigen om verder te vertellen. Ging hem zelfs advies geven. Dat hij hem moest berichten, initiatief moest nemen, niet bang moest zijn, en dat er niks leukers is dan als iemand ergens vol voor gaat. Dat verliefdheid omarmd moet worden. Ik realiseerde me dat dit het advies was dat ik mezelf had gegeven – bij wijze van regieaanwijzing, tijdens het kijken naar de film – maar dat ik zelf niet had opgevolgd. Hij moest glimlachen als hij over die jongen sprak. Ik voelde de mislukking als een drab door mijn lichaam klodderen. Wat moest ik me schamen; hoe ging ik dit vertellen aan mijn vriendinnen? Ze waren zo blij geweest, hadden, wist ik, ondertussen al berichtjes gestuurd om te vragen wat de tussenstand was. Ik moest ze straks allemaal gaan vertellen hoe ik volledig had gefaald.

Ik wilde weg, maar wist niet hoe ik de keukentafel moest verlaten – en ik wilde hem nog wat zeggen. Hoewel het totaal ongepast was en de setting er niet meer naar was, moest ik het toch met hem delen. 'Ik ga het mijn ouders en mijn broers vertellen.' Hij stopte met praten en keek me aan. Nu mag ik wat zeggen, dacht ik, ik draai m'n riedel af, en dan ga ik weg, sprak ik mezelf toe. 'Ik ga het aan mijn ouders vertellen, tijdens kerstavond, dat ik iemand ontmoet heb, en dat dat een jongen is. Ik vind dat ik niet uit de kast hoef te komen, dat ik moet zeggen 'ik bén homo', want dat ben ik niet, ik bén Wobie, en Wobie valt misschien op mannen. Dat ga ik ze vertellen. Ik heb mijn broers ook nooit horen zeggen dat ze hetero zijn, ik heb ze wel horen zeggen dat ze een leuk meisje hebben ontmoet. Dus ik ga dat ook op die manier zeggen. Dan mogen ze er zelf conclusies aan verbinden.' Ik ademde even snel, om een nieuwe teug zuurstof en energie naar binnen te zuigen, terwijl ik vanbinnen vocht tegen de donkere drab van triestheid die door mijn lichaam begon te druipen. Ik zorgde dat het een korte pauze was, zo kort dat ik zeker wist dat hij niet al een reactie kon geven. Dat liet ik niet toe. Eerst wilde ik alles zeggen, dan had hij één moment om te reageren en dan kon ik daarna gaan. 'Ik ga het vertellen tijdens kerstavond. Dat vind ik een mooi moment. Ik ga het vertellen, omdat jij mij de zekerheid hebt gegeven, de vrijheid van verliefdheid hebt gegeven, en me hebt laten inzien dat ik helemaal niet anders ben. Dat ik niet raar of vreemd ben, dat ik onveranderd ben. Dat ik gelukkig kan zijn. En omdat je me hebt laten voelen hoe verliefdheid moet kunnen vliegen, en daarvoor moet ik thuis, op de plek waar ik veilig zou moeten zijn, mijn vleugels kunnen uitslaan om ook echt te kunnen vliegen.' Ik keek hem aan. Godzijdank. Het was eruit. Mijn woorden nu op een andere manier de werkelijkheid in geslingerd dan ik jaren geleden op de middelbare school deed. Een nieuwe waarheid uitgesproken die ik in de toekomst definitief zou maken. Het bleef even stil en toen antwoordde hij. Lief. Heel lief. Dat hij het dapper vond. Dat hij het goed vond. Dat hij blij was dat hij zo'n bijzondere rol in het proces had mogen vervullen. Toen hij dat allemaal had gezegd vond ik het mooi om te gaan. Ik moest huilen, wilde huilen, omdat de avond zo anders gelopen was dan ik gedroomd en gehoopt had. Ik wilde weg, maar kon niet, want precies op het moment dat ik de zin wilde uitspreken die het afscheid zou aankondigen, hoorden we beneden de deur opengaan. 'Mijn huisgenoten zijn thuis!' zei Arthur harder dan dat we hadden zitten praten. En vervolgens sprong hij op, ze verwelkomend.

Toen hij weer aan tafel kwam zitten, was mijn momentum weg. Dat voelde ik. En het werd definitief toen een van zijn huisgenoten zei: 'Hé Wobie, doe je nog een drankje mee?' waarop Arthur direct reageerde: 'Ja! Gezellig! Blijf nog even!'

Ik zat klem, vast in een val, ik was beland in een nachtmerrie waar ik niet uit kon. Ik kreeg een drankje en Arthur en zijn huisgenoten begonnen een gesprek. Over hun studentenvereniging. Rampzalig voor mij, want ik wist er niks van af. Thuis, voordat de date begon, had ik wel wat dingen opgezocht op mijn computer. Zitten kijken of ik bepaalde gebruiken, woorden en handelingen zou kunnen vinden waar ik rekening mee kon houden. Zodat Arthur me leuker zou vinden, dat hij door zou hebben dat ik, hoewel ik geen onderdeel van de vereniging was, toch eigenlijk heel erg op al die mensen daar leek en dus een prima persoon was. Dat ik me er staande zou kunnen houden. Stiekem hoopte ik al dat hij me mee zou nemen. Maar die hoop was vervlogen. Terwijl zijn huisgenoten en Arthur aan het praten waren, schakelde ik steeds verder uit. Als ze lachten lachte ik mee, maar ik hoorde niet meer wat ze zeiden. Ik wilde weg – maar hoe? Mijn vluchtpoging was mislukt en ik kon door de duizelingwekkende situatie niet zo snel een nieuwe bedenken.

'Ik denk dat ik maar eens ga,' zei ik. Gewoon vanuit het niets. Omdat ik geen beter alternatief had. Ik moest het er dan maar gewoon ingooien, in de situatie. Als een judokaduw tegen het gesprek aan. Zodat het gesprek dat ze zonder mij voerden zou omvallen en ik erlangs kon.

'Maar het regent buiten,' zei een van z'n huisgenoten. Het was zo'n jongen die zo knap was dat je er zelf onzeker van werd. Zonder dat je jezelf kon zien wist je meteen wat er bij jou niet goed zat. Dat jouw gezicht uit verhouding was, je haar een vreemd plukje had en je ogen minder diep waren. Het regent buiten, galmde door mijn regieloze hoofd. Klote. Daar had ik me niet op voorbereid.

'Hoe ben je hier?' vroeg Arthur.

'Ehm, lopend, voor een deel, en voor een deel met het ov, ik wandel wel naar de Nieuwmarkt en dan pak ik daar de metro.'

Een van de huisgenoten keek uit het raam. Het regende hard, echt hard. Het zou raar zijn om nu naar buiten te gaan.

'Het regent heel hard, blijf nog even, totdat het droog is,' zei de huisgenoot.

'Nee joh, ik vind het niet erg, die regen.'

Ze vroegen of ik een paraplu had – had ik niet. Dat maakte het nog onlogischer. Die conclusie hing als een collectieve gedachte in de ruimte. Ik zag alle ogen mij een beetje vreemd aanstaren. Ik keek Arthur aan. Begreep hij nou echt niet dat ik weg wilde?

'Doe nog een drankje, en ga dan, misschien dat de regen dan minder hard is, dat scheelt!' zei de te knappe huisgenoot.

Ik zat in de val. Ik deed nog een drankje. Het ging wéér over die jongen waar Arthur en ik het eerder over hadden gehad. Ik wist niet hoe ik dit zou overleven. Ik keek naar mijn drankje, liet hun woorden langs me heen glijden, probeerde ze niet te vangen met mijn oren en al helemaal niet te verwerken. Ik keek naar mijn drankje, dronk het in drie teugen op en zei dat ik zou gaan. Om te zorgen dat ik niet opnieuw klem zou komen te zitten, stond ik direct op om mijn aankondiging definitief te maken. De naar-buiten-kijkjongen keek naar buiten maar zei niks. Waarschijnlijk wist hij dat een opmerking of goedbedoeld advies nu geen zin zou hebben.

Dat was de reden waarom ik boven aan de trap wist dat het de laatste keer zou zijn dat ik daar stond. Dat was de reden dat ik nog één keer, met alles wat ik had, van de knuffel genoot. Omdat ik wist dat ik de omhelzing vanaf dan aan andere gelukkigen moest laten. Dat de omhelzing niet meer van mij zou zijn. Dat zijn lichaam aan de jongen met het Brabantse accent zou worden overgelaten. Zou hij net zo grondig op avontuur gaan? Zou hij Arthurs lichaam net zo koesteren als ik had gedaan? Zou hij net zo genieten van de kleine blonde haartjes die

Arthur bij zijn navel had, de gouden engelenhaartjes? Ik moest het loslaten. Ik keek hem aan. Genoot van zijn bier met wijn gemengde adem. En liep de trap af.

Het regende buiten. Daar was ik wie dan ook heel erg dankbaar voor. Ik rilde, zonder het koud te hebben. Dit keer geen dansende stenen, mensen die me als in een balletvoorstelling voorbij huppelden, geen hemels gevoel. Alles was grijs, nat en grauw. Het regende, hard, dikke druppels kletsten overal neer. Ik was zo dankbaar, zo dankbaar voor die regen. Zolang ik de schokkerige bewegingen in mijn lichaam onder controle hield zouden voorbijgangers denken dat ik al heel lang buiten was. De regen was mijn camouflage, niemand kon zien wat ik echt deed; huilen. Ik huilde, had de dammen achter mijn ogen eindelijk laten doorbreken. Mijn tranen kregen nu de vrijheid om te stromen. Ik sloeg de metro over, wandelde naar huis, schreeuwde en sloeg tegen de garagedeuren in de achtersteeg vlak bij mijn huis, kroop in bed en hoopte dat ik snel in slaap zou vallen.

64.

Het was bijna kerst. Nog een paar uur. En dan zou kerstavond beginnen. Dan zou alles moeten veranderen. Alles helder moeten worden. De warmste tranen zouden vanavond moeten vloeien. Roze glittertranen. Tranen van verliefdheid, geen tranen van teleurstelling, maar tranen die stuk voor stuk vrijheid zouden geven. Tranen die stuk voor stuk vrijheid druppelden.

Het huis leek erop voorbereid. Alsof het wist dat er iets stond te gebeuren. Buiten sneeuwde het zachtjes. Binnen klonken de geluiden van een gelukkig gezin. Mijn moeder was bezig in de keuken, een plek waar ze de rest van het jaar niet te vinden was. Maar op kerstavond maakte ze het gerecht waarmee ze haar vader voor heel even weer tot leven wekte. De koperen kookset had ze geërfd, een koperen kookset om in te flamberen. Inclusief het handgeschreven recept van onze opa. Ze was het aan het voorbereiden. Een van de dierbare tradities die vanavond in ere werden gehouden. Rustig en alleen was ze bezig, in haar gedachten bij haar eigen papa.

In de bench lag Hond Bril op een zacht kleed. Ze snurkte zoals altijd zonder te slapen. Haar modderpoten had ze overgehouden aan het vrolijke rondspringen, die middag, in de duinen. Samen met mij en mijn oudste broer. Ze had haar ogen halfdicht. Keek af en toe naar mijn moeder en wist dat het een avond zou worden waarop al haar baasjes heel dicht bij haar zouden zijn, want de eettafel, de keuken en de bench stonden allemaal in één ruimte. Hond Bril vond dit de fijnste avonden, zo leek het. Al haar baasjes om zich heen, druk gebabbel. Soms kreeg ze zelfs een bot. Haar eigen kerstmaal. Het zou een warme avond worden, letterlijk en figuurlijk.

Verderop in het huis was mijn vader aan het schrijven, zijn toverwerk aan het vervolmaken. Ook tijdens kerst was de lokroep van zijn schrijfkamer onweerstaanbaar. Als hij nu even zou tikken, had hij gezegd, dan kon hij straks extra genieten. En misschien zelfs een extra glas drinken, omdat hij z'n woordenaantal zou hebben gehaald.

Het huis leek klaar voor vanavond. Het kerstbomenbos was al een aantal weken in aanbouw geweest en stond er prachtig bij. Dertien bomen waren het dit jaar geworden. De zwarte, de roze, de witte, de zilveren, de gouden, de twee groene, de ene in de tuin en het kleintje binnen, de kleine knalblauwe, de gekleurde en dan ook nog de twee kleine roze en zwarte, de broertjes en zusjes van de grote kerstbomen; ze waren allemaal opgetuigd. En wedijverden om de vraag wie het mooiste was. De kerstballen en de kerstlichtjes versierden de wereld, en al het slechte verdween als je langs de kerstbomen liep. Zo zou elk bos er elke dag uit mogen zien.

Mijn broers zaten op hun eigen kamers. Ze luisterden muziek. Dachten waarschijnlijk wat na. Zochten hun kleren voor de komende dagen uit. Ook zij hadden er zin in.

Helemaal boven in het huis, op de kamer waar de gordijnen zoals altijd dicht zaten en de kerstlichtjes zoals altijd vrij spel hadden, daar zat ik. Op mijn hemelbed. Aan de muur hingen de schilderijen die ik laatst had gemaakt. Kleurrijke doeken. Met confetti erop. Ik zat daar. Te friemelen aan mijn roze sokken. Af en toe keek ik naar mijn mobiel. Ergens hoopte ik dat

Arthur mij zou berichten. Hij was per slot van rekening een van de weinigen die wist hoe belangrijk deze avond zou gaan worden. Maar een bericht zou er niet komen. Ik had Prince opgezet. Muziek die klonk alsof het altijd kerst was. Het moest mij energie geven. Kracht voor kerstavond. Hij zong extra heftig, extra schreeuwerig, extra sterk, alsof hij het wist. Ik zat stil. Wilde niet huilen, maar kon sommige zaken niet meer tegenhouden. Het voelde alsof vanavond alles anders zou zijn, wat ik graag wilde. Maar hoewel alles anders zou zijn, zou alles toch ook volledig hetzelfde moeten blijven. Ondanks alles, ondanks dat ik wist dat het goed zou zijn, dat niemand mij zou veroordelen, dat ik veilig Wobie mocht zijn – ondanks dat alles maakte ik me zorgen. Ik keek nog een keer naar het gedicht dat ik jaren geleden van mijn oudste broer had gekregen en las de laatste regel: 'Voor heel even, mag je bij ons nog veilig Wobie wezen.' Ik was bang, maar had ook behoefte aan wat ging komen. Omdat ik eindelijk het zoekgedeelte van de reis zou kunnen afsluiten.

De rest van het huis wist nog niks. Mama deed alvast de kaarsen in de keuken aan. Ze checkte of alle lichtjes in de bomen aanstonden. Ze controleerde of de fietsen voor de deur op slot stonden en sloot de buitendeur af. Ze vond het fijn, de kinderen, haar kinderen, onder één dak. Samen aan tafel. Dan was ze het gelukkigst, als ze ons dicht bij zich had. Als ze ons daar had waarvan ze wist dat ze ons kon beschermen tegen de buitenwereld.

Die middag waren mijn oudste broer en ik gaan wandelen met Hond Bril. Een wandeling waarvan alleen wij tweetjes op voorhand wisten dat die lang zou gaan duren. Tegen de rest van het gezin hadden we gezegd dat we alleen even de hond gingen uitlaten. Een paar dagen daarvoor had ik een bericht naar m'n oudste broer gestuurd. Ik durfde het hem niet rechtstreeks te vertellen, bang dat ik in zijn ogen een teleurstelling zou zien. Zo'n onheelbaar litteken wilde ik mezelf besparen. Ik had een appje gestuurd, vaag maar ook duidelijk genoeg. En gevraagd of we samen konden wandelen voordat het kerstavond was. Daarom was mijn oudste broer eerder naar ons ouderlijk huis gekomen. Hadden we Hond Bril laten stoppen met snurken en uit haar bench gehaald, haar halsband en riem gezocht, een tennisbal meegenomen, voor de zekerheid, en waren we gaan wandelen. Het was stil in de duinen. Stil zoals het is tijdens de kerst. Een nog stillere stilte dan op zondagen. Het waren van die dagen dat je, als je in de duinen de juiste route liep, jezelf het idee kon geven dat het gebied jouw eigendom was, omdat je niemand anders tegenkwam.

De takken, de bomen, de paden, ze zagen er minder vrolijk uit dan de huiskamers. De duinen waren niet versierd. We praatten eerst over van alles, over de studie, over het leven in Amsterdam. Over wat hij uitspookte. Over wat ik uitspookte. Allebei het onderwerp waarvoor we eigenlijk op pad waren vermijdend. Ik wist niet of ik het al moest aansnijden, wilde het misschien ook nog niet. Mijn broer moet mijn worsteling hebben gezien, zag ongetwijfeld dat ik zenuwachtig was. Ik was ook stiller dan normaal.

Toen we verder de duinen inliepen, wist ik dat het aan mij was om het onderwerp aan te snijden. Hij wist dat ik íéts zou gaan zeggen, en ook wat ik ongeveer zou gaan zeggen. Daar had ik hem via mijn whatsappje op voorbereid. Het zou raar zijn om er nu niet over te beginnen. En ik wilde voorkomen dat we het er pas op de terugweg over zouden hebben en dan te weinig tijd zouden hebben voor ons gesprek. Ik raapte al mijn moed bij elkaar, bedacht me dat, áls ik al een teleurstelling zou zijn, we niet meer samen in een huis woonden, dus ook niet elke dag de straf van zijn blik zou hoeven voelen. Ik bedacht me dat ik me kon verstoppen in Amsterdam, desnoods bij vriendinnen kon gaan wonen als het problemen zou opleveren. En daarbij, het was mijn oudste broer, hij die altijd vertrouwen in alles had gehad. Ik mocht van hem Wobie wezen, de échte Wobie. Hij zou vast onbegrensd van me blijven houden, hield ik mezelf voor. Ik kneep in mijn vuist. Het komt vast goed, heus, zei ik tegen mezelf. Schreeuwde ik ergens tegen mezelf. Ik voelde de leegte in mijn hoofd die door mijn zorgen ontstond. De zorgen en de angst vraten alle andere emoties en gevoelens op en daar wilde ik vanaf zijn.

'Ik wil het er niet te uitgebreid over hebben, laat me eerst wat zeggen,' begon ik zachtjes. Ik creëerde een doodse sfeer. Alsof er iets zeer ernstigs te gebeuren stond. Alsof er iemand dodelijk ziek was, of dat ik ging meedelen dat er iemand was overleden. Zo hing ik rouwgordijnen over de werkelijkheid. In één klap leken de onversierde dennenbomen in de duinen de treurwilgvarianten van kerstbomen. Was ik verkeerd begonnen? Had ik het verkeerde gezegd? Moest ik stoppen met praten, kon dat überhaupt nog? Ik ging maar gewoon zachtjes verder. Ik was van start gegaan en door deze woorden in deze combinatie en in deze volgorde uit te spreken wist ik dat er geen weg terug meer was, ik had mezelf een pad op gestuurd, waarbij omdraaien niet meer mogelijk was. Een omgekeerde doodlopende weg. 'Ik heb iemand ontmoet met wie ik het leuk heb gehad, een jongen, en...' Het bleef even stil. Hond Bril, die eerst rustig voor ons uit slenterde met de tennisbal in haar bek, keek om. Er kwam iets aan. Tussen de bomen, over de duinen, verplaatste zich in hoog tempo een donkere vlek. We hoorden het kraken van takken die braken onder de voeten van datgene wat aan kwam rennen. Het kwam in een rotvaart op ons af, maakte grote sprongen om zich sneller te verplaatsen. Alsof het iets moest vangen, achtervolgen, inhalen. Toen de donkere vlek dichterbij kwam, konden we zien wat, of eigenlijk, wie het was. Het was ons jongste broertje. 'Ik wil ook mee wandelen!' riep hij naar ons. Kerstvrolijk. We keken elkaar aan, mijn oudste broer en ik. Hij begreep me. We konden er nu niet verder over praten. Ik vond het rampzalig, want nu kon ik het én niet afstemmen, én ik wist niet wat hij ervan vond, omdat hij geen gelegenheid had gehad te reageren of iets te zeggen. Ik maakte me zorgen, voelde me stom. Had ik iets gezegd wat ik niet moest zeggen? Was ik in zijn ogen nu veranderd? Iemand anders geworden? Ik baalde van mezelf. Wilde mezelf wegtoveren, maar er was geen onzichtbare mantel of toverstaf waarmee ik *ploef* kon verdwijnen of uitgesproken woorden ongedaan kon maken. Ik had snel naar z'n ogen gekeken, maar had daar niks gezien. Geen glimlach, geen geschoktheid. Was dat een slecht teken? Onleesbare ogen. Dat kon toch nooit goed zijn? Zou ik niet meer Wobie voor hem zijn, zou hij niet meer samen in een team tikkertje willen spelen? Zou hij het niet gezellig meer vinden om samen pizza aan het strand te eten na werk? Was ik überhaupt zijn broertje nog wel? Of was ik opeens iemand anders geworden? Iets anders. Ik wilde het zeggen, hem vastpakken, in zijn ogen kijken en roepen: 'KIJK! ZIE! KIJK! IK BEN NIET VERANDERD! Écht niet! Ik ben alleen vrijer, vrolijker, verliefder dan eerst. Ik heb meer zekerheid gevonden. Dat kan toch niet erg zijn?! Kijk, zie, kijk, ik ben nog steeds precies hetzelfde. Niet anders, want het is niet anders!' Maar het kon niet. Ons broertje was er bijna en ik was er al helemaal niet aan toe om ook hem nu in het verhaal te betrekken. Toen ons broertje er bijna was fluisterde mijn oudste broer snel, heel zachtjes, waardoor zijn woorden bijna gestolen werden door de wind: 'We hebben het er zo nog wel even over.'

We liepen terug met z'n drietjes en ik baalde. Ik twijfelde aan vanavond. Aan al mijn vriendinnen had ik verteld dat ik het vanavond ging vertellen. Ik had dat ook gedaan als een soort van stok achter de deur, een ingebouwd duwtje in de rug, omdat ik wist dat ze later op de avond of de volgende ochtend allemaal zouden appen of bellen om te vragen hoe het gegaan was. Mijn verwachting bleek ook te kloppen, want de hele dag had ik een stroom van berichtjes binnengekregen. Ze dachten aan me. Wensten me succes en verzekerden me dat het allemaal goed zou komen. Ik baalde ervan. Ik wilde hen niet teleurstellen, niet afwijken van het plan dat ik nu al eindeloos had voorbereid, maar voelde de kracht en de zekerheid die nodig was voor de uitvoering wegzakken. We liepen verder. Mijn broers voorop, ik achter hen. Ik keek nergens specifiek naar, maar mijn blik was gericht op de grond. In mijn hoofd herhaalde ik de bijna onverstaanbare zin van daarvoor: 'We hebben het er zo nog wel even over.' Wat betekende dat? Wat kon ik daaruit afleiden? Wat viel er te bespreken? Het was niet per se een afkeuring, maar het was ook niet per se een goedkeuring. Het was eerder een uitgesteld oordeel. En dat baarde me zorgen. Ik bleef in het niets kijken, de grijze, doornatte sneeuw, de vochtige grond voor me. Zag de voeten van mijn broers. Ze liepen hetzelfde. Ik misschien ook. Tot zover waren er geen verschillen. Ik durfde niet omhoog te kijken. Alsof het bos, de duinen, de wereld er even niet voor mij waren. Ik keek in het niets naar de grond, totdat ik mijn oudste broer zag bewegen. Toen durfde ik op te kijken en zag dat hij met zijn blik de mijne probeerde te vangen. Hij gaf me een knipoog. Een knipoog. Een knipoog! Het galmde door mijn hoofd. Een knipoog; dat was positief, dat was goed, dat was een teken van vertrouwen. Ik ontchaoste en kwam naast ze lopen, Hond Bril gebroederlijk begeleidend naar ons kersthuis.

Thuis knuffelde ik Hond Bril extra hard. Tegen de regels in gaf ik haar een kus. Zolang als die regel bestond deed ik dat al. Ik was dol op de hond. Toen ik nog thuis woonde was het elke ochtend mijn taak geweest om met haar te wandelen. Hoewel ze misschien onze taal niet kon verstaan, had zij van iedereen mijn twijfels en worstelingen misschien wel het dichtst bij meegemaakt. Ik bedankte haar nu met een extra lange knuffel en kreeg een lik in mijn gezicht. Zachtjes fluisterde ik in haar oor: 'Jij weet het al.' En toen ging ik terug naar boven, naar mijn slaapkamer. Terug naar de veilige plek achter de gesloten gordijnen. De rode gordijnen die in de toneelwereld het publiek van de voorstelling afzonderden, maar die op mijn kamer mijn wereld en fantasie scheidden van de werkelijke wereld buiten.

In mijn kamer ging Prince opnieuw aan: 'Mountains'. Ik wachtte tot mijn oudste broer boven zou komen. Prince moest mij de energie geven voor dit moment. *Once upon a time in a land called Fantasy*, begon hij, begeleid door muziek waardoor je gedwongen werd om te dansen. Stilzitten was hetzelfde als jezelf martelen. In mijn hoofd betrad ik de dansvloer. De dansvloer was bezaaid met discolichten. Ik kreeg alle ruimte. Ik kreeg langzaamaan vertrouwen in de avond. Op de achtergrond hoorde ik mijn broer naar boven komen. Hij kwam vluchtig en snel mijn kamer in. Ik liet hem toe in mijn kamer, mijn veilige plek. Ik zat op de rand van mijn bed. Binnenin lieten de zenuwen en twijfels een woeste wind waaien.

'Wobie, ik dacht, ik kom nog even snel naar boven, hoe wil je het gaan vertellen?' vroeg hij.

Ik had erover nagedacht, wilde het afdoen als een zakelijke mededeling. Iets wat afgestreept, afgevinkt moest worden en waar ik het vervolgens niet over wilde hebben. Ook uit angst om te huilen of uit te moeten leggen hoe het allemaal precies zat met Arthur. Daarnaast was ik nog steeds ergens bang voor mijn broers, dat het afstand tussen ons zou creëren als ik te veel details gaf. De opmerkingen over kampen en Rusland kon ik niet van me afschudden, hoe graag ik ook wilde. En daarnaast, misschien dat papa het allemaal prima zou vinden, maar dat hij het toch op een bepaalde manier zwak zou vinden. Als ik ging praten over jongens, dat hij dan zou zeggen 'je hoeft ook weer niet alles te delen hoor jong', dat zou als een afkeuring voelen. Ik zou het ervaren alsof hij me walgelijk vond. Ik wilde er alles aan doen om die scenario's te voorkomen. Dus het moest een snelle, zakelijke mededeling zijn, zonder gedoe. En het moest direct duidelijk zijn dat ik het er niet met het hele gezin tijdens het kerstdiner over wilde hebben.

Mijn oudste broer keek me een beetje verbaasd aan toen ik zei wat ik van plan was. 'Waarom zou je het op die manier vertellen? Ik weet zeker dat iedereen het geweldig nieuws vindt en het superfijn voor je vindt. Dus waarom zou je het zo negatief en zwaar brengen. Je moet het juist als een feestje brengen, als iets wat gevierd mag worden, waar we met z'n allen trots op kunnen zijn!'

Ik keek hem aan. Terwijl ik me afvroeg of het inderdaad een feestje was, of het iets was waar ik trots op mocht zijn. Vrijheid en jezelf zijn. Durven rebelleren tegen onzichtbare wetten. Ja. Dat is een feestje. En als je het doet, moet je zelf de slingers ophangen.

'Je hebt gelijk,' zei ik. Zoals zo vaak, dacht ik. 'Ik zal het vrolijk vertellen, zeggen dat ik iemand leuk vind, een jongen, en dat ik daar heel blij mee ben en het daarom nu met iedereen wil delen.'

'Ja! Super! Ik ben trots op je, lieve Wobie.' Mijn oudste broer maakte aanstalten om weer naar beneden te gaan. Toen hij weg was herhaalde ik de vrolijke versie van wat ik te vertellen had een aantal keer. Ik had toen nog het idee dat ik mijn mededeling zonder problemen zou kunnen uitspreken. Ik was klaar om de eerlijkheid, de openheid, de helderheid die ik al zo lang met zekerheid had willen delen, ook daadwerkelijk te gaan delen. Zodat ik nooit meer om zaken heen hoefde te draaien. Zodat ik nooit meer weg hoefde te kijken als er bepaalde grapjes gemaakt werden. Zodat ik geen lieve vragen van mijn moeder hoefde te negeren. Zodat ik geen brieven met puzzelstukjes meer op de kussens van mijn ouders hoefde te leggen. Zodat ik niet meer hoefde te huilen als ik een Sinterklaasgedicht kreeg waar onderhuidse boodschappen in verstopt zaten. Zodat ik niet meer hoefde mee te lachen als mijn broers en mijn vader een knappe vrouw bespraken. Ik kon niet wachten om eindelijk helemaal ongeremd mezelf te kunnen zijn. Zonder dat er iets aan mij was veranderd, zou ik de onzichtbare remmen en muren die ik jarenlang had laten ontstaan in één avond kunnen laten verdwijnen. Kerstavond zou prachtig worden. De traditie van het flamberen van opa's gerecht, de traditie van het kerstbomenbos, de traditie van papa die nog aan het toveren was, Hond Bril die lag te snurken zonder te slapen, de traditie waarbij iedereen in kleurrijke pakken naar de eettafel komt – daar zou een traditie bij komen. *Love will conquer if you just believe*, zong Prince.

Ik zou nog één keer, een laatste avond, als laatste naar beneden komen. Wachtend op mijn kamer. Maar dit keer niet om te verstoppen. Dit keer om mezelf klaar te maken om eindelijk alles helder en licht te maken.

65.

In de keuken zat het gezin aan tafel. De kaarsen brandden aan. Allemaal. Een soort skyline. Zoveel kaarsen dat het bijna een rommeltje werd. Maar dan een vlammende gezelligheidsrommel. De tafel was gedekt met het kerstservies en de gekleurde, zelfgemaakte tafel was uitgeschoven. De kroonluchter in de keuken hoefde niet aan, het licht van de kerstbomen en de kaarsen volstond. Iedereen zat op zijn vaste plek. Mama zoals altijd aan het hoofd. Het voorgerecht hadden ze allemaal op. Ik kon bijna geen hap door m'n keel krijgen. Dat was opgevallen. 'Ben je ergens nerveus voor?' had mijn vader gevraagd. Ik had er niet echt op geantwoord. Ik zei weinig, maakte me op voor het belangrijkste wat ik die avond zou zeggen. Als het gezin bij elkaar was wist de hele buurt het. Een vuurwerk van gelach en gebabbel knalde door de dunne glazen ruiten aan de achterkant van het huis de tuin in. De aanliggende huizen zouden het praatvuurwerk zeker horen. Het voorgerecht werd afgeruimd, op het aanrecht werd de eerste lading borden van die avond opgestapeld. Nu concentreerde het gezin en het hele huis zich op de belangrijkste traditie van de avond: het maken van het gerecht van opa. Flamberen in de koperen kookset.

Ik was doodnerveus. Durfde niet te praten, kon niet eten. Af en toe liep ik naar de gang. Alsof ik iets ging pakken, maar eigenlijk gewoon om extra adem te halen. Een rustmomentje te pakken. Mijn buik voelde als een plek waar allerlei rivieren en beekjes samenkwamen. En vanuit mijn buik stroomden ze de rest van mijn lichaam in. In mijn hoofd was ik licht. Alsof een grote lamp er in het midden was neergezet en alles verlichtte. Niet per se onprettig, maar het gaf me een beetje het gevoel alsof ik high was. Dat gevoel werd versterkt doordat mijn vingers tintelden. Kleine tintelingen. Alles wat er gebeurde, elk detail, elke pan die verschoven werd, elke zin die werd uitgesproken, elke grap waar om werd gelachen; ik sloeg het allemaal op. Alsof ik na afloop een drievoudig verslag zou moeten uitschrijven. Ik voelde me een camera die alles in beeld moest zien te krijgen.

Tegen de tijd dat mama begon met het klaarzetten van het hoofdgerecht traden de rivieren van emoties buiten haar oevers. Buiten was het donker, zag ik via de ramen in de keuken. Wat wilde ik graag de straat op rennen, omarmd worden door het niet-licht, verdwijnen uit de werkelijkheid. Verstopt voor wat zou gaan komen. Behalve eten kon ik nu ook niet meer drinken. Ik keek m'n broers een voor een aan. Misschien was dit wel de laatste keer dat ik ze zo zag, of, dat ze mij zo zouden zien. Ik pakte nog een keer extra de hand van mijn moeder. Gaf er een kus op. Ik wilde zo graag dat de zenuwen weggingen, maar wat ik ook deed, hoe ik ook ging zitten, op welke manier ik me ook probeerde te concentreren op de avond of het gezinsgesprek dat plaatsvond; niets hielp. Alles in mijn lichaam stond in stressstand voor dat wat ik met mezelf had afgesproken. Dat wat ik mezelf, mijn vriendinnen en mijn oudste broer had beloofd. Kon ik het? Ja ik kon het. Ja ik kan het. Ja jij kan het! Ik moest het tegen mezelf roepen. Ik bleef de zinnen die ik wilde zeggen herhalen, zodat ik zeker wist dat ik het er zo meteen zou laten uitrollen. Opeens vreesde ik dat ik moest overgeven. Mijn maag leek in een draaimolen te zijn gestapt. Ik wilde spugen, mijn buik net zo leeg en licht maken als mijn hoofd. Zodat er niks meer in me zat. Ik liep naar de gang, nieuwe zuurstof halend. In de spiegel zag ik mezelf staan. Adem. Zei ik tegen de spiegel. Adem. In. Uit. In. Uit. In. Uit. Iiiiin. Uuuuuit. Iiiiiiiiiiiinnnn, uuuuuuiiiit. Langzame lange slome teugen. Diep naar binnen, groots naar buiten. Het werkte. Ik werd wat rustiger.

Ik bleef nog even op de gang staan. Voor de spiegel. Rustig ademend. De spiegel hing in een houten frame. Aan de zijkanten speelden engelen. Kleine vleugels, kleine bewegingen makend, vastgezet in het hout. Zou dit de laatste keer zijn dat ik zag hoe mijn ogen eruitzagen als ze een diep en geworsteld geheim verborgen? Was dit de laatste keer dat mijn schouders onbewust meer zouden hangen door de last van het grote geheim? Zou dit de laatste keer zijn dat ik mezelf zag zonder de waarheid te hebben uitgesproken? En hoe zou ik er over een paar uur dan uitzien? Zouden mijn ogen glinsteren, fonkelen en glitteren? Ik hoopte het. Zo erg. En terwijl ik het hoopte voelde ik weer een zwelling van zenuwen opkomen. Ik begon al bijna te kokhalzen. Ik had al bijna negen jaar kleine inhoudelijke voorbereidingen voor de waarheid getroffen. Door soms kleine grapjes te maken. Door een verborgen zin uit te spreken tijdens de vakanties. Of door dubbelzinnige opmerkingen te maken als we met elkaar tv-keken of ergens naartoe gingen. Dat was allemaal goed gegaan, dat wist ik, want elke keer dat ik dat had gedaan, had ik als een onderzoeker de reacties van mijn broers en mijn ouders op een petrischaaltje gelegd, het onder een microscoop geschoven en alles geanalyseerd. Elke afwijking, elke opgetrokken wenkbrauw, elke neus die omhoogging, elke lach die niet echt lachte – ik had er allemaal voor gewaakt maar ze nooit echt gevonden. Het was allemaal goed gegaan, maar nu voelde het anders. Vanavond zou dat wat ik ging zeggen niet meer de kleine stukjes van een rode loper zijn die ergens heen leidt, nee, ze zouden in één keer uitgenodigd zijn in het theater, daar zitten, en ik zou op het podium, in de volle schijnwerpers, mijn verhaal gaan doen. Niet langer verborgen, maar in het stralende midden. Het maakte me nerveus en angstig, daar in de coulissen.

Het flamberen begon. Mama gooide de eerste scheut drank in de ovalen pan die boven twee vuurtjes hing. In koor riepen wij 'meer, meer, meer!' – dat was onderdeel van de traditie. 'Je weet hoe opa het gewild had, die zou hebben gezegd dat er veel meer in moest,' riep iemand. Mama antwoordde dan altijd hetzelfde: 'Ik doe al meer dan in het recept staat', waarna wij wisten dat we moesten zeggen: 'Jaaa, maar opa zei altijd dat er minimaal drie keer zoveel drank in het gerecht moest dan volgens het recept, en dat het zelfs dan eigenlijk te weinig was.' Het gerecht maken, met alle frutsels en fratsels eromheen, met alle zinnen en grappen die uitgesproken dienden te worden, was eigenlijk belangrijker geworden dan het gerecht daadwerkelijk te eten. Iedereen deed volop mee. Door deze scène ieder jaar weer te laten herleven, lieten we ook onze opa zelf herleven. Hij was er op deze manier altijd bij. Mama zou op een bepaald punt onzichtbaar, maar zichtbaar genoeg, ontroerd worden, en dan zou papa grappend aan tafel roepen 'nog niet gaan huilen hè! Dat mag pas bij het toetje!', waarna iedereen weer hard zou lachen en mama zou roepen: 'Mag ik even!' Het was feestelijk. Momenten waarvan je wilt dat ze nooit weg zullen gaan. Die je met elkaar moet beschermen, en als dat niet meer in de vertrouwde samenstelling kan, moet creëren in nieuwe samenstellingen. Het zijn de momenten waarop je op dat moment zélf al weet dat je ze zult onthouden en zult koesteren. Zo bijzonder en belangrijk waren ze. Momenten waarop je op dat moment zélf al weet dat je ze, later, heel veel later, als ze er niet meer in deze samenstelling zijn, ontzettend zult missen.

Mama stak de saus in de pan aan en grote vlammen stegen op. Ze grepen om zich heen in het niets. Lucht vangend en lucht opslokkend. Vuur. Dat vond ik altijd magisch. Prachtig mooi. De vlammen waren druk. Bijna onzichtbaar ontstonden ze in de pan, zweefden boven het eten en kwamen dan in de lucht in volle glorie tot leven. De warmte greep om zich heen. De kaarsen op tafel moesten hun meerdere erkennen en doken beschaamd weg. Ons eigen kerstvuur, opa die via de vlammen gedag kwam zeggen. Door de vlammen heen keken mijn ouders elkaar aan. Hun mond hoefde niet te lachen, dat deden hun ogen al. We waren via het vuur, heel even, met z'n allen één.

De stukken kalkoen werden op de borden geschept. De aardappelpuree en de rode kool kwamen op tafel. Mama lepelde de niet meer brandende saus over de kalkoen heen. Iedereen riep altijd 'meer, meer, meer', waarop iemand anders dan zou zeggen: 'Ahhh, en ik dan, ik kan mijn saus bijna niet vinden.' Ook een scène die we elk jaar met veel plezier weer tot leven brachten. Ik wist dat het moment nu echt heel erg dichtbij was. Geen kwestie van jaren meer. Geen kwestie van maanden meer. Geen kwestie van uren meer. Nee, nog enkele minuten, misschien zelfs maar een paar seconden, en dan zou ik het woord moeten nemen, het diner moeten onderbreken en om stilte vragen. Ik keek nog een keer naar mijn broers. Naar mijn moeder. En toen wat langer naar mijn vader. Ik hoopte zo erg op een goede reactie, hoewel ik niet wist hoe die eruit zou zien.

Iedereen had z'n bord volgeschept. Het wachten was nu alleen op mama die de koperen schaal wegzette en weer aan het hoofd van de tafel plaats zou nemen. Iedereen babbelde druk door elkaar heen. Het spraakvuurwerk was weer volop in gang en ik wist niet hoe ik tussen al die vuurpijlen, al die rotjes, al die klappers moest komen. Mama ging zitten. Ik voelde de zenuwzwelling opkomen, hij zaaide uit naar de rest van mijn lichaam. In mijn hoofd raakte ik in paniek. Hoe moest ik het in godsnaam stil gaan leggen? Als mama nu een hap nam zou het te laat zijn, dan had ik het moment gemist, dan was het weg. Want als mama ging eten, was dat het startschot voor de rest van de tafel. Hoe kon ik dat voorkomen? Ik voelde het al vallen, de glazen bal die dit moment was. Ik voelde het wegglippen, merkte dat ik direct teleurgesteld in mezelf raakte. Kom op. Kom op! KOM OP! riep, schreeuwde, krijste ik tegen mezelf, in mijn hoofd bonkten duizenden poppetjes tegen de wanden van mijn brein. Je moet wat doen! schreeuwden zij via het bonken.

'Ehmm,' bracht ik vrijwel onverstaanbaar uit. Maar m'n redding was dat ik op dat moment opkeek naar m'n oudste broer. Hij was naar me aan het kijken, net als een van de bonkende poppetjes bang dat ik niks zou zeggen en het moment voorbij zou laten gaan. Het voelde raar. Alleen hij en ik wisten hoe belangrijk dit moment was. Ik keek hem aan, hij had mijn 'ehmm' opgevangen en wist wat er gedaan moest worden. Hij knikte rustig en zette toen de eerste stap, net op tijd, want papa wilde al voordat mama begonnen was zijn mes in de kalkoen zetten. 'Jongens, voordat we gaan eten, heel even wachten,' zei mijn oudste broer, 'Wobie wil wat zeggen.' Grappend vroeg mijn vader of het niet kon wachten tot na het eten, omdat de kalkoen anders koud dreigde te worden. Aan de blik die mijn broer hem daarop toewierp las hij af dat het beter was om zijn mes en vork nog heel eventjes te laten wachten naast zijn bord.

'Ja, ik wil jullie graag wat vertellen. Het is nu natuurlijk kerstavond en ik heb gewacht totdat er een mooi moment was waarop ik het kon vertellen en vond dit de juiste en bijzondere avond om het met jullie te delen. Geen zorgen, het is geen slecht nieuws, het is alleen maar iets leuks. Maar het nieuws is als volgt.' Ik was even stil, haalde diep adem, het enige geluid dat er was. Iedereen luisterde, ademloos, roerloos, zelfs Hond Bril was gestopt met snurken en keek mee vanuit haar bench. 'Het zit namelijk zo. Ik heb iemand ontmoet met wie ik het heel erg leuk heb gehad, in Amsterdam, echt heel erg leuk.' Ik was weer even stil. Voelde de tranen al opkomen. Wat ik ook deed, hoe sterk en krachtig ik de muur en dam ook bouwde, ik voelde dat de tranen in zo'n gigantische vaart aan kwamen rollen, dat ik ze hoe dan ook niet tegen zou kunnen houden. Ze zouden keihard door de dam breken en hun weg naar buiten banen. Ik haalde snel adem in de hoop dat ik de volgende zin er nog net uit kon krijgen voordat de dam in botsing zou komen met de rivier die in aantocht was. 'Ik heb iemand ontmoet en het is een jong–' de dam brak. Volledig. Ik moest huilen, dook met mijn gezicht in mijn handen. Mama greep meteen mijn schouder: 'Ach lieve jongen toch, ach lieverd, kom hier, wat goed en fijn, kom hier, kleine lieverd van me.' Ik moest huilen, maar wilde per se mijn zin afmaken. Ik haalde mijn handen weg voor mijn gezicht, pakte mijn moeders hand, rechtte mijn rug en deed een tweede poging: 'Ik heb iemand ontmoet en het is een jonge–', en een derde poging, 'ik heb iemand ontmoet en het is een jongen en dat wilde ik graag met jullie delen.'

Het was eruit. Eindelijk. Ik had het gezegd. Door mijn betraande ogen zag ik de tranen van mijn broers en mijn ouders. Ze glimlachten. Ze waren blij. Ze waren trots. Het waren lieve gezichten.

'Maar Wobie,' hoorde ik papa zeggen terwijl ik in de armen van mijn moeder mamaliefde vond, 'je zei dat je iets nieuws wilde vertellen, wat is het nieuwe dan en waarom moet je zo huilen?' Ik moest lachen. Ik hield van mijn papa. En van mijn mama. En van mijn broers. En van Hond Bril. En van deze avond. Ik huilde, ik voelde de tranen in kleine beekjes langs mijn wangen glijden. Maar het waren een ander soort tranen dan normaal, een ander soort tranen dan ik had verwacht.

Het waren de warmste tranen die je je maar kunt bedenken. Ze gloeiden. Als lava. Zachtroze lava. Elke traan die viel, die drupte, was een traan die vrijheid gaf. Het waren tranen die me schoonspoelden. De worsteling lieten wegdruppelen. Met elke traan die viel werd ik een stukje vrijer. Viel er een stukje verleden van mijn schouders af. Viel er een stukje geheim dat ik verborgen had gehouden van me vandaan. Het waren roze tranen. Het waren de mooiste tranen die ik ooit zou huilen. Ik was blij dat ze vielen, blij dat ze door de dam waren gebroken, blij dat ze nog heel lang bleven druppelen.

Het waren roze tranen. Roze glittertranen.

66.

Mama en ik stonden samen in de tuin. Binnen hoorden we de gezelligheid van ons gezin. In het donker was niks te zien, maar we zagen allebei zo ontzettend veel. We zagen eindeloos veel. We hoefden niks te zeggen, alleen arm in arm, schouder aan schouder daar staan, een knuffel die al de hele avond duurde. In die ene hakkelende zin van vanavond had ik zoveel gezegd wat ik nooit had uitgesproken. Het voelde fijn. Veilig. Vrij. Schoon. We stonden daar. Gewoon samen. Er was niks veranderd maar alles was anders. De wereld was een stukje eerlijker geworden. In mijn hoofd regende het confetti.

De tuindeur ging open. Mijn jongste broertje kwam even de tuin in. Mama liet me los. Ik was, merkte ik nu, bang geweest voor zijn reactie. Dat hij als puber mij het hardst zou veroordelen. Mij niet meer als z'n oudere stoere broer zou zien. Hij kwam op me af, en gaf me een enorme knuffel. 'Top Wobie, ik hou van je! Ben trots op je! Echt! Top!' En alles was goed. We zouden in de toekomst vast weer ruzie krijgen, maar nu, door deze knuffel, wist ik dat alles wat was gezegd of ooit zou worden gezegd, vluchtige woorden uit woede waren. Hij liet me los en ik liet me weer in de armen sluiten door mama.

We bleven maar staan. Buiten. Kerstavond. Meestal zou je het op dit tijdstip en moment van het jaar bibberend koud hebben gekregen. Maar niks kon ons doen afkoelen. We gloeiden. Van geluk. Ik wist dat mama blij was. Dat ze mij eindelijk écht helemaal bij zich had. Dat ze blij was dat er geen laagje leugen of verborgenheid over me heen lag. Ze was blij dat ze haar zoon eindelijk weer terug had, in z'n volledigheid...

In de verte klonken de kerkklokken van kerstavond. Mama en ik keken elkaar aan. We hadden onze eigen heilige mis gehad. De klokken klonken als groetjes van God. Ook Hij gaf zijn goedkeuring. Terwijl het luiden van de klokken voortduurde bleven wij daar staan. In het donker. Arm in arm. Nog even het moment uitstellend dat we weer naar binnen zouden gaan.

67.

Na het kerstdiner zat ik op mijn slaapkamer. Ik had de muziek zachtjes aangezet. Ik luisterde die avond een laatste keer naar Prince. *The Beautiful Ones*. Een bijna zomerslapend begin. Een melodie waarin je langzaam wegzakte. Alsof je hoofd vol werd gespoten met de zoetste en suikerigste suikerspinnen die er zijn. Met zijn uithalen dwong hij mij bijna om ondeugend te zijn. Ik dacht aan Arthur. Aan wat hij mij had gegeven. Misschien had hij me wel het mooiste kerstcadeau gegeven dat ik krijgen kon. Hij had me zekerheid gegeven. Daar waar ik zo naar verlangde. Hij gaf me zekerheid en daarmee: vrijheid. Door mijn verliefdheid aan te wakkeren, waardoor ik zeker wist waar ik vrolijk van werd, had hij mij vrijheid gegeven. Grote vleugels op mijn rug laten groeien, die me vanaf nu over de wereld konden laten zweven. Ik kon vanaf nu overal en altijd opstijgen. Niet alleen maar meer in mijn dromen, in de fantasiewerelden die ik gebouwd had, nee, ik kon overal opstijgen, vliegen en fladderen.

Toen ik wist dat de broers die thuis bleven slapen onderweg waren naar bed en de anderen naar hun eigen huis waren vertrokken, liep ik de trap af. Drie trappen naar beneden. Ik wist dat mama en papa nog aan de eettafel zouden zitten. Dat deden ze altijd. Als iedereen weg was dronken zij samen nog wat. Het laatste beetje champagne. Of alvast de rooibosthee voor het slapengaan. Omringd door afwas; ravages en resten van gezelligheid.

Ik wilde mama en papa even alleen hebben. Even voor mezelf. Ik had al genoeg gedeeld met het hele gezin, en wat ik nu wilde delen, zeggen en doen, was alleen voor ons drietjes. Voor niemand anders.

In mijn handen had ik een doosje. Ik hield het met twee handen vast, heel voorzichtig, daarmee de regel overtredend dat ik altijd met één hand de leuning moest vasthouden. Zeker ik moest dat thuis doen, want ik was altijd onhandig geweest. Maar nu ging ik tegen die regel in, zoals ik die avond tegen heel veel regels, zichtbaar en onzichtbaar, was ingegaan. En dat voelde goed en fijn. In mijn handen hield ik vast wat ik mijn ouders wilde geven. Het moest de avond, dit moment, deze herinnering afmaken. En wat er ook zou gebeuren, het mocht niet kapotvallen.

Ik liep naar mama toe en gaf haar het cadeautje. 'Omdat alles gezegd is. En alles vanaf nu gezegd mag worden. Omdat alles helder is,' zei ik toen ik het haar overhandigde. Ze pakte het uit. Langzaam kwam het tevoorschijn. Ze haalde het eruit, trok het naar boven. Het was een glazen traan. De Glazen Traan. Breekbaar, zoals het proces was dat zulke tranen liet komen. Maar ook een vorm waarin een beweging was gevangen. Een glazen traan, zodat de tranen niet meer konden druppelen. Omdat ze niet meer hóéfden te druppelen. Een glazen traan. Helder. Omdat alles gezegd was. En vanaf dat moment alles gezegd mocht worden. En midden in de traan was een balletdanseres te zien. Een balletdanseres, staand, kwetsbaar en daarmee krachtig, op haar tenen. Terwijl ze een buiging maakte. De glitters op haar jurk en op haar huid in vol ornaat delend. Een buiging naar het publiek. Waar ze zojuist alles aan heeft gegeven. Alles aan heeft laten zien. Alles tegen heeft gezegd.

Voor eeuwig in De Glazen Traan, beglitterd een buiging makend voor het publiek.

68.

Toen ik de volgende ochtend wakker werd deed ik de rode gordijnen van mijn slaapkamer open. Ze zouden nooit meer dicht hoeven.

In de voorkamer, met de lichtroze geverfde muren en de sierlijke spiegels, alsof ze in een volwassen speeltuin staan, daar waar mama's kleren over stoelen liggen, waar prachtige sieraden op een houten kaptafel liggen uitgestald, waar haar administratie op een lange, zeer donkere en massief houten eettafel ligt voor zo'n acht personen, en waar in de hoek een stoel staat waarin je kunt zitten alsof het altijd zondag is, met daarnaast een bijzettafelhoge boekenstapel, haar leeshoekje, daar, in die ruimte, overheerst door mama, daar hangt, in de kristallen kroonluchter, nog altijd en voor altijd niet verplaatsbaar, De Glazen Traan met de balletdanseres die een diepe buiging maakt voor het langslopende publiek.

Ik sta er vaak even stil als ik door de kamer loop, onderweg naar de deur die naar boven leidt. Dan kijk ik naar De Glazen Traan, naar de buigende balletdanseres met haar glitters en haar krachtige kwetsbaarheid. Ik maak een buiging terug, soms met een opkomende glazen traan, die ik niet langer tegenhoud, maar gewoon laat vallen. Alles helder. Niets meer verborgen houden, niets meer laten verdwijnen. Een Glazen Traan laten vallen, omdat alles helder mag zijn.

EPILOOG

Het begint allemaal bij de Moeder. De Mama. De Maker. Een ode aan de mama, er kunnen er niet genoeg van zijn. Mijn grootste angst is het verliezen van mijn mama. Dat ik op een ochtend wakker word zonder moeder. Alleen op de wereld. Geen veilige armen waarin je altijd vluchten kunt. En bang dat ze zich voor eeuwig verstopt voordat ik alle lieve dingen heb kunnen zeggen.

Laatst werd ik onrustig toen ik haar handen zag. Ze lagen op de keukentafel, een tafel die ze zelf had geschuurd en geschilderd: geel, goud, rood, roze en lichtgroen concurreerden met elkaar over elke vierkante centimeter van het houten blad. Het tafelblad was een kleurrijke stoeipartij, een minicircus van tinten. Ze kon dat goed, iets creëren. Niet dat het haar beroep was; nee, mama was arts. Daardoor kon ze ons altijd beter toveren als we ziek waren. Het versterkte het idee dat je moeder alles kan. Nu lagen haar handen te wachten. Ze zat aan het hoofd, zoals altijd. Ik zat rechts van haar. Ze keek over de tafel of alles ging zoals het hoorde te gaan. Hoewel we aan het ontbijt zaten brandden de kaarsen. Kaarsen branden overdag bijna net zo vrolijk als in de avond, dus kregen ze bij ons thuis altijd de vrijheid om te flikkeren.

Daar lag haar rechterhand. Trouwring om haar vinger,

nooit afgedaan. Bijna nooit afgedaan. Misschien een keer voor het slapengaan, maar voor de rest nooit noemenswaardig lang af geweest. Ik werd onrustig toen ik haar handen zag. Ze waren ouder, met meer rimpels. Als een schilderij dat al langer bestond en barstjes begon te krijgen. De schoonheid van het kunstwerk was er niet minder op geworden, maar je zag wel dat het oud was. Kwetsbaarder. Haar huid was losser. Ook bij mama had de tijd grip gekregen op haar lichaam. Haar handen lieten zien wat haar gezicht verborgen wist te houden; mama was ouder geworden. Ze leken op de handen van de oude buurvrouw, mevrouw Van Kroon. Maar zij had de oorlog meegemaakt, zij was echt oud. Mijn mama niet. Haar handen deden me denken aan de vele keren uit het verleden waarbij ik eigenlijk haar hand had moeten pakken, maar besloot die af te wijzen.

Het gebeurde op een van die vele zondagen dat we aan het ontbijt zaten. Even normaal als altijd, maar dit keer toch anders; mijn drie broers waren niet thuis. Papa, mama en ik zaten samen te ontbijten. Het gesprek ging over de actualiteit, over zaken die toen van belang leken. Totdat de stemhoogte van mijn moeder veranderde. Sommige stemhoogtes bepalen de ernst van het onderwerp, dit was er zo eentje.

'Vind je iemand leuk? Ben je verliefd?' vroeg ze, terwijl ze me aankeek. Ik ontweek haar blik. Bij gebrek aan een antwoord ging ze verder. 'Je weet dat wij alles oké vinden hè. Dat je verliefd mag zijn op wie je wilt. Is er iemand die je leuk vindt?'

'Mag ik de boter,' vroeg ik aan mijn vader.

'Weet je dat het voor ons best ingewikkeld is als een moeder van een vriendinnetje op een feestje naar ons toe komt en zegt dat ze hoorde dat je een jongen leuk vindt, maar wij daar niks van afweten?'

'Mag ik de jam,' zei ik, wijzend naar de aardbeienjam die

ook bij papa stond, hoewel ik geen jam op mijn croissant wilde smeren.

'We hebben toen gezegd dat wij officieel van niks weten, dus dat we dat vanzelf wel horen, op het moment dat je het erover wilt hebben of erover wilt praten. Maar je kan alles zeggen, als je dat wilt, hè lieverd.'

'Lekker croissantje, hoor.' Ik wist dat het haar pijn deed, het negeren van de vragen. Het weigeren van de uitgestoken hand. Ik wist dat het haar pijn deed, omdat het haar het gevoel gaf dat ik me niet veilig voelde. Dat ik niet vertellen kon waar ik mee worstelde. En zoals het haar pijn deed, deed het mij ook pijn.

Ik keek naar haar hand en pakte hem vast. Inmiddels was er zoveel meer gezegd en verteld. Alles was helder geworden. Mijn hand was sterker, misschien minder wijs, maar inmiddels wel sterker. Met mijn duim bewoog ik over de rug van haar hand en zag de huid schaatsen. Ik gaf haar een kus. 'Je bent lief, lieve mama'.

Toen ik mijn mama vertelde dat als ik zou gaan schrijven, in dit boek of in welk boek dan ook, ze er altijd in terug zou komen, zei ze: 'Dat vind ik knap, wat kun je over mij schrijven dan?' Ik zei dat er wel duizenden woorden, duizenden verhalen te schrijven waren over mijn mama. Toen verschenen er tranen in haar ogen en zei ze: 'Ik zou maar drie woorden over mezelf kunnen opschrijven: *Ik ben gek*.' Maar de manier waarop haar geest werkt, is meerdere malen een redding voor mij geweest.

Zo kreeg ik op mijn veertiende van mijn moeder een bank. Een bank die ik zelf jaren daarvoor op de basisschool ontworpen had en tijdens de handvaardigheidlessen in het klein had gemaakt. Het was een divan-achtige bank. Met een koraalvormige, houten rugleuning, een armsteun en vier goudzilveren poten. Je kon er languit op liggen. De poten had ik asymmetrisch onder het zitvlak geplaatst. Nadat ik er een aantal lessen aan had gewerkt, ging ik met het knutselwerk naar de juf. Die keek me aan, kneep haar ogen tot spleetjes en pakte het over.

'Dít,' zei ze, en draaide het bankje om en wees op de vier asymmetrische, goudzilver geverfde poten, 'dit kan natuurlijk niet, hè. Dan valt het bankje natuurlijk om. Je hebt je best gedaan, ik vind het idee leuk bedacht, maar het is niet uitvoerbaar, niet haalbaar. Dus grappig bedacht, maar hier kan ik geen voldoende voor geven.' Zonder op te kijken gaf ze hem terug, terwijl ze achter mijn naam met haar rode pen een cijfer opschreef. Een onvoldoende.

Geblinddoekt moest ik naar de woonkamer terwijl de rest van het gezin achter me aan liep. Een losse polonaise van nieuwsgierigheid. Mijn moeder haalde de doek voor mijn ogen weg, maar zien kon ik nog niet. Iets in de kamer lag verscholen onder doeken. Het was iets groots.

'Pak jij het aan die kant, dan pak ik het aan deze kant.' Mijn mama wees op de uiteinden van de dekens die over het ding heen lagen.

'Een, twee, drie!' En samen toverden we het cadeau tevoorschijn.

Het was de bank. Mijn bank. De onmogelijke bank. Precies nagemaakt, in het groot. Met de koraalvormige rugleuning, de zachte bekleding, de armsteun met touw eromheen gewikkeld. En, de vier goudzilverkleurige poten. In het midden van de bank stond de minibank, mijn knutselwerk dat ik jaren ervoor had gemaakt. Alsof de bank een kind had gekregen. Moeder en zoon. Samen bij elkaar. De zoon bij de moeder op schoot. Een onvoldoende werd meer dan voldoende. 'Nu is het geen knutselwerk meer, maar een kunstwerk,' zei mijn moeder met trotse ogen.

Mijn vader en broers waren ondertussen in een orkest van verrassingsgeluiden veranderd. Dat gebeurde vaker bij ons.

Als iemand een groot cadeau kreeg leek het altijd alsof het hele gezin jarig was. De 'oehs' en 'ahs' vlogen je om de oren. Moderne componisten of dj's hadden er vast een goede dansplaat van kunnen maken.

'Jongens,' zei mama tegen de andere gezinsleden, 'jongens, gaan jullie maar alvast taart eten. Kunnen jullie ons even alleen laten? Wij komen zo.' Er verscheen een kleine collectieve teleurstelling op de gezichten, maar toen papa zich realiseerde dat er nog genoeg taart was voor een tweede ronde, kwam hij in beweging en volgde de rest vanzelf.

Mama deed de woonkamerdeur dicht. Ik wist niet zo goed wat de bedoeling was, maar afwachten leek me in deze situatie het beste. Mama kwam naast me staan. De houten vloer kraakte zachtjes, alsof ook die bang was weggestuurd te worden naar de keuken als hij te veel zou opvallen. Mama had nog steeds de blije ogen van een kind, maar haar blik veranderde. 'Kijk,' fluisterde ze, 'ik heb je bank helemaal nagemaakt, maar ik heb er ook iets aan toegevoegd. Zodat het écht jouw bank is.'

Ze boog zich over de bank heen, richting die ene armleuning. Bij het uiteinde pakte ze het bruinleren vlak vast, en begon een beetje te wrikken. Eerst ging het moeizaam, maar langzamerhand kwam het begin van de leuning los. Het bruine leer en de in touw gewikkelde leuning werden langzaam van elkaar gescheiden.

'Maak je hem niet kapot?' vroeg ik nog. Mama keek niet op, alsof ze met haar voortgezette handeling het antwoord al gaf. Na nog wat gedraai kwam het beginstuk helemaal los en gebaarde ze richting de armleuning, zoals obers dat doen bij bijzondere gerechten. Eindelijk kon ik het zien; de armleuning was voor een deel hol vanbinnen.

'Om de geheimen die in je hoofd zitten ook naar de wereld van het hier en nu te kunnen verplaatsen,' zei mama terwijl we elkaar aankeken. ‘Ik ben de enige die het weet en ik beloof je dat ik er nooit in zal kijken.’

Toen onze gezichten waren opgedroogd en onze ogen minder rood, keerden we terug naar de keuken om ook ons deel van de tweede taartronde op te eisen. Mama nam weer plaats aan het hoofd. Ik op mijn stoel rechts van haar. Hetzelfde als kort daarvoor, maar toch volledig anders. Ik had er een geheime plek bij, een geheime plek waar ik kon opbergen wat ik niet of nóg niet wilde delen. Maar dat hoefde ik niet langer meer alleen maar in mijn hoofd te doen.

De armleuning heeft mijn grootste geheim verborgen gehouden. Daar op mijn kamer schreef ik een brief. Na eindeloos veel in m’n eentje met de hond te hebben gewandeld in de duinen, om maar weg te blijven van huis. Na eindeloos manieren te hebben bedacht om niet meer naar de ongemengde gymlessen te hoeven gaan, waar ik omringd werd met de stoerheid die ik niet op die manier had. Na eindeloos vaak te hebben gevraagd aan een of andere alleswetende of ík veranderd kon worden – of iemand mijn voorkeuren niet kon overnemen. Na eindeloos vaak te hebben gewenst om iets of iemand anders te zijn, om normaal te zijn, wilde ik af van die worsteling. Van die twijfel. Van de schaamte. Ik wilde af van het gevaar en vooral de angst om teleur te stellen. Om een blik te moeten vangen die innerlijke blauwe plekken veroorzaakte. Mijn zelfvertrouwen leek doorzeefd met duizend splinters. Maar het leek alsof niemand ze eruit kon halen. Alleen ik kon dat doen. Een voor een. En ik was op zoek gegaan. Elke dag. Ik was op zoek gegaan door die duizenden splinters, kijkend welke er al uit konden, welke nog moesten wachten, wat geheeld kon worden.

Maar ik wilde het in één keer oplossen. In één keer alles eruit halen. En ik dacht dat ik daarvoor de oplossing had. Vandaar dat ik de brief schreef. In mijn slaapkamer, achter de gesloten rode gordijnen, waar ik eindeloos ronddwaalde.

Onbereikbaar voor mijn ouders. Omdat ik hun hulp niet aannam. Ik wilde het zelf doen. In kleermakerszit ging ik op bed zitten. Voor me lag een stapel papieren die ik eerder die week al uit de printer had gehaald. Een pen in mijn hand. Een roze pen, bezaaid met glitters. Een pen die niet gemaakt was om te schrijven wat ik ging schrijven.

Ik weet niet of het precies in diezelfde periode was, maar het zal niet lang daarna zijn geweest dat iemand iets zei wat ik altijd ben blijven onthouden.

We keken bij ons thuis vaak naar *De Wereld Draait Door*. *DWDD* zat in het avond- en eetpatroon. Met iedereen die thuis was verzamelden we ons in de zitkamer. Soms werd er zelfs geroepen dat het begon, dan hoorde je in het trapgat een stem van ver, die doorgaans voor huishoudelijke mededelingen was bestemd. En dan kwam je. Daar zaten we dan, met z'n allen voor de buis. Ook deze avond was dat zo. Mijn moeder en vader zaten tegen elkaar aan op de grote giraffenbank. Twee van mijn broers zaten op de stoelen recht voor de tv, ik zat in de grote stoel links van de televisie. Het was een bijzondere en opvallende stoel. Een stoel bekleed met een stof van donkergrijze, donkerpaarse en donkerbruine strepen. Het was de stof die modeontwerper Hans Ubbink ooit had gebruikt voor een reeks kostuums en pakken, maar waarvan hij stof overhad. Dat had hij aan mijn mama gegeven. Omdat mama in haar vrije tijd een cursus meubelmaken volgde, had ze de stoel die ze toen maakte bekleed met de stof van Ubbink. Het was een stoel waar je heerlijk in kon verdwijnen. Eentje die je omarmt, die je knuffelt, zonder dat je een knuffel terug hoeft te geven.

DWDD begon. Op de kruk zat Matthijs van Nieuwkerk, naast hem Marc-Marie Huijbregts. Hij wilde het hebben over het nieuws van die dag. De details weet ik niet meer, maar het was voor hem een persoonlijk onderwerp. En dat bleek het voor mij ook te zijn.

Het ging over een scholier. Een scholier die een einde aan zijn leven had gemaakt. Verstrikt geraakt in vertwijfeling en het niet willen zijn wie hij was. Marc-Marie vertelde er kort over, gaf een paar antwoorden op de vragen van Matthijs en zei toen iets wat ik altijd heb onthouden.

'Laat ik één ding zeggen, ja, laat ik één ding zeggen, tegen al die jonge meisjes en al die jonge jongens die thuis zitten te twijfelen, die niet goed weten wie ze zijn, wat ze zijn of wie ze leuk vinden. Laat ik één ding zeggen, speciaal tegen hen. Het wordt beter! Het. Wordt. Beter. Houd moed! Het is misschien lastig en ingewikkeld nu, maar groei door. En je zult zien, later, als je groter wordt; het zal beter worden. Echt!'

Voor mijn gevoel zei hij het recht in de camera, zonder in de camera te kijken. Voor mijn gevoel zei hij het recht in mijn gezicht. Ik had het idee dat hij zo uit het beeldscherm was gestapt. Eerst met z'n ene voet over de zwarte rand, even bungelend, zoekend naar de vloer, om vervolgens ook z'n andere voet buiten het beeldscherm op de grond te plaatsen. Daar was hij, in de kamer. Hij liep over de houten vloer naar me toe en pakte mijn hoofd vast. Mijn hoofd in zijn handen, zodat ik niet anders kon dan hem recht in z'n gezicht aankijken terwijl hij sprak. En spreken deed hij. Hij zei wat hij te zeggen had.

Ik keek en luisterde roerloos naar de televisie. Wilde niet bewegen om zo te voorkomen dat de aandacht in de kamer op mij gevestigd zou worden. Hoewel niemand keek voelde ik de anderen kijken. Alsof er een collectieve gedachte in de kamer hing die niemand durfde te benoemen, waardoor iedereen krampachtig stil bleef zitten. Toch zag ik vanuit mijn ooghoek mama langzaam bewegen. Ik voelde haar kijken, echt kijken. Haar hoofd was weggedraaid van de televisie en ze keek mijn kant op. Na even aarzelen keek ik terug. Allebei hadden we zichtbaar onzichtbare tranen. Ik deed mijn best ze niet te laten vallen. Iets zeggen hoefde niet, mama begreep dat ik de boodschap van Marc-Marie had gehoord. En hij kreeg gelijk. Zijn woorden dreunden als de drammerige bonken van een basdrum. Het. Wordt. Beter.

Uiteindelijk heb ik de brief nooit gegeven. Wel talloze andere, met dat wat ik niet rechtstreeks wilde zeggen. Vaak op het hoofdkussen van mijn moeder, met puzzelstukjes erin verstopt over datgene wat ik eigenlijk voorzichtig wilde zeggen. Maar nooit heb ik die definitieve brief op bed gelegd. En daar ben ik dolgelukkig mee. Want het wérd beter. Het wérd mooi. Hoe ouder ik werd, hoe vrijer.

Het was avond. Ik stond op de Nieuwmarkt en keek hem aan. De huizen, de grachten, zelfs de sterren; ze hadden plaatsgemaakt. Het was winter, lente en zomer tegelijk. Hij had witte haren met donkere uitgroei en groene ogen. Als hij lachte, bracht hij zijn tong een klein stukje naar buiten. Alsof hij je stiekem een beetje plaagde. Het was voor mij een extra reden geweest hem die avond te plagen. We hadden samen op een boot gezeten, waren aan elkaar geïntroduceerd door vriendinnen. Hij was me meteen opgevallen. Onze lichamen leken naar elkaar te wuiven, al voordat we elkaar hadden gezien. Sterren dansten op een trampoline in mijn buik. Aan een van mijn vriendinnen had ik gevraagd of hij misschien op jongens viel. Nee, had ze gezegd, nee. Hij valt niet op jongens. Hier op de Nieuwmarkt, vanavond, zeiden zijn ogen wat anders.

Ik zou hem kunnen zoenen, bedacht ik me. We waren allebei stil. We zouden kunnen zoenen. Ergens deden we dat al, dat voelde ik in mijn buik. Nog één keer keek ik hem in zijn ogen. Ik bleef kijken en bewoog niet. In zijn ogen zag ik de zoektocht, de speurtocht. Er zat nog twijfel, door het groen zat nog een grijze mist. In zijn ogen zag ik dat hij nog niet ver genoeg was, en ik zoende hem niet. Zijn tijd moest nog komen. In zijn ogen zag ik dat in zijn hoofd nog geen confettiregen bestond. Zijn tijd moest nog komen.

DANKWOORD

You must always be yourself,
no matter what the price,
it's the highest form of morality

Candy Darling,
Persoonlijk Dagboek

De mensen die ik moet bedanken zijn de mensen die mij maakten. De mensen die stukjes van mij geheimhielden, stukjes van mij beschermden en stukjes van mij vooruithielpen. Dus dank aan al mijn vriendinnen. Alle namen van het vriendinnenleger opnoemen is geen doen; dan heb ik meteen een tweede boek. En een derde. Maar dank, allemaal. Gigagantisch bedankt. Allemaal, die van de basisschool tot aan de middelbare school tot aan de studie. Van de vriendinnen uit *The Circle*, tot aan de vriendinnen uit de *Make Up Club*, tot aan de dames uit de *Twelve Pack* tot aan de vriendinnen uit de *Liefste Liefjes*. En alle vriendinnen die niet in die groepjes zaten maar er wel altijd waren, een jaar erboven, of een jaar eronder. Ik zou jullie als een sieraad allemaal bij me willen dragen, maar daarvoor zijn er niet genoeg diamanten op de wereld. En heb ik te weinig vingers.

Dank dat ik jullie alles eindeloos lang mocht vertellen. Dat jullie bleven luisteren. Eindeloos hetzelfde advies bleven geven en zelfs als ik niet luisterde, toch die krukken weer werden. Dank dat jullie me hielpen mezelf veilig en in hele kleine stapjes te ontdekken. En dank aan LieveLous, opperhoofd van het vriendinnenleger. Dank voor de vrijheid die je me gaf en geeft. Dank voor de vleugels.

Dank aan mijn lieve FashionTwin – een zus die er eigenlijk stiekem altijd al was.

Dank aan de docenten op Wolters en op het VCL die in me geloofden, die hun lessen als een wondermiddel zagen en elke dag lieten zien hoe mooi het is om te kunnen en mogen leren. Jullie lieten zien waarom het zo leuk is om eindeloos te lezen en eindeloos te ontdekken – een geschenk voor ieder kind.

Dank aan Peter George – Peter George d'Angelino Tap – de man die dromen draagbaar maakt.

Dank aan lieve Heleen – die me leerde dat je ook kunt praten zonder woorden te gebruiken.

Dank aan lieve Mevrouw van Kroon en Meneer van Kroon. Die ons op de stoep ijsjes en koekjes gaven toen we leerden fietsen. We kregen er een Oma en Opa bij.

Dank aan mijn bestuursgenootjes van toen ik voorzitter was – van 2016, 2017, 2018 en 2019 – jullie hebben het unicornregime overleefd! Fysiek dan.

Dank aan alle lieve vriendinnen (zowel de dames als de heren) die ik leerde kennen in Amsterdam en in Hillywood.

Dank aan iedereen bij POSVIDEO – sorry dat ik jullie altijd van het werk houd (als ik weer eens wat moest regelen voor het boek tijdens werktijd), maar dat jullie me nooit de gang op stuurden.

Enorm en oneindig veel dank vervolgens aan de mensen die dit boek op papier mogelijk hebben gemaakt. Die zich door de woorden heen worstelden en zeiden 'dat moet eruit, dat ook, en dit wat er wél in mag moet de helft korter'. Dank aan Renée, dank aan Barend, dank aan alle lieve mensen van Het Spectrum. Zeer dankbaar ben ik; dat jullie zoveel energie, liefde en aandacht in dit boek staken. Daardoor durfde ik alles open te gooien. Dank aan Jelte Nieuwenhuis!

En natuurlijk dank aan de dame die de roze trein op gang liet komen, haar liet stomen en ervoor heeft gezorgd dat de roze trein niet zou stoppen met denderen. Zij die de trein uiteindelijk liet huppelen: Sladjana Labovic. Dank aan jou, lieve Sladjana. *We don't need another hero* zong Tina Turner ooit. Ze had gelijk, want we hebben jou al!

Dank aan lieve A – Anton – voor het maken van de cover; zonder een woord gelezen te hebben wist je het verhaal in één beeld te vangen. Je had het verhaal al gezien, levend. Maar nog meer dank voor het zijn van mijn peetoom. Toen ik nog te klein was voor kunst, nam je me er toch mee naartoe. Dank voor het laten zien hoe je óók kunt kijken naar de wereld.

Dank aan alle voorvechters – de minderheid die de meerderheid aan de hand moet nemen, richting een vrijere wereld. Dank aan al die voorvechters, uit het verleden, heden én uit de toekomst, die zorgen dat elke stap van de innerlijke reis lichter en lichter wordt.

Dank aan alle rebellen. Die, soms letterlijk, de eerste steen wierpen, waarna muren konden breken.

Dank aan het lieve nest: onze hond, mijn broers en mijn ouders.

Dank aan lieve Hond Bril, dat je dit baasje uitliet en me een lik gaf als we samen in de duinen zaten te wachten. Je hebt veel geheimen van het gezin bij je gedragen en niemand ooit verraden.

Dank lieve Storm, samen voor altijd De Kleintjes – helemaal niet erg.

Dank lieve Mau, voor je vaak lieve woorden en krachtige knuffels.

Dank lieve Sebastiaan. Je hebt dit boek al heel lang zien huppelen en zei: schrijf het. Creëer een woestijn aan tijd om te kunnen schrijven. Dat deed ik, en het werd een woestijn. Met roze zand, suikerspinsprookjeszoet. Dank voor de blik in je ogen, die me zei dat ik veilig mezelf mocht zijn.

Dank lieve Papa. Voor het zijn van een lieve vader, dat ik terugdenk aan het naar school wandelen als ik denk aan 'mijn vaders hand'. Steeds vaker ontdek ik puzzelstukjes van jou in mezelf – zo weet ik dat je eeuwig bij me zal blijven.

Dank aan lieve Mama. Die mij maakte – dus dit maakte. Dank voor het toveren. Dank voor je veiligheid. Dank voor het zijn van mijn mama. Sorry dat ik even weg was, maar ik blijf vanaf nu voor altijd thuis.

Dank aan de jongens,
Dank aan lieve T,
En dank aan lieve B,

Liefs

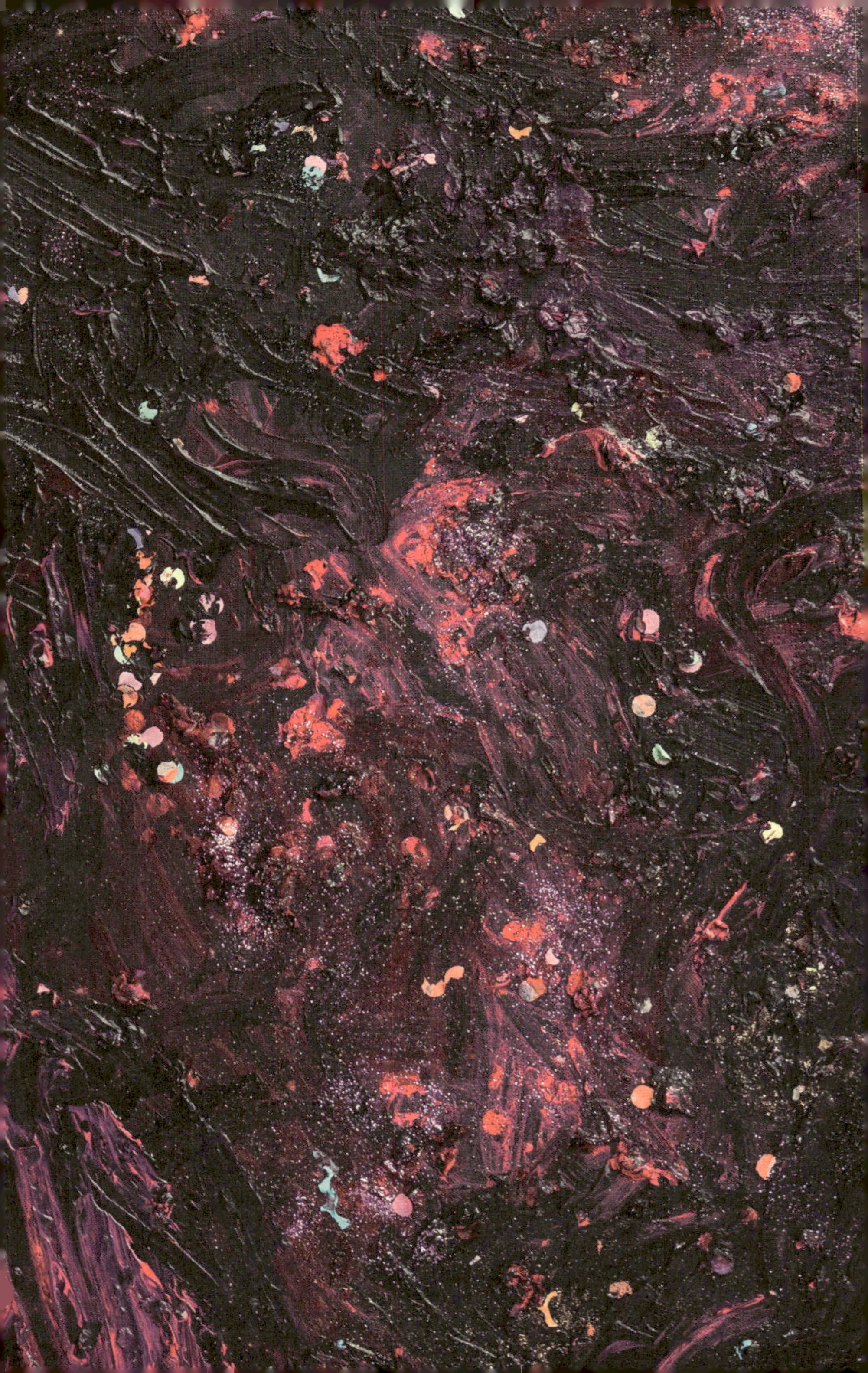